Multiple-Criteria Decision Making

Concepts, Techniques, and Extensions

MATHEMATICAL CONCEPTS AND METHODS IN SCIENCE AND ENGINEERING

Series Editor: **Angelo Miele**
Mechanical Engineering and Mathematical Sciences
Rice University

Recent volumes in this series:

A Continuation Order Plan is available for this series. A continuation order will bring delivery of each new volume immediately upon publication. Volumes are billed only upon actual shipment. For further information please contact the publisher.

Multiple-Criteria Decision Making

Concepts, Techniques, and Extensions

Po-Lung Yu

University of Kansas
Lawrence, Kansas

With the assistance of
Yoon-Ro Lee and
Antonie Stam

PLENUM PRESS • NEW YORK AND LONDON

Library of Congress Cataloging in Publication Data

Yu, Po-Lung, 1940–
  Multiple-criteria decision making.

  (Mathematical concepts and methods in science and engineering; 30)
  Bibliography: p.
  Includes index.
  1. Decision-making. I. Lee, Yoon-Ro. II. Stam, Antonie. III. Title. IV. Series.
T57.95.Y8   1985   658.4′03   85-16723
ISBN 978-1-4684-8397-0   ISBN 978-1-4684-8395-6 (eBook)
DOI 10.1007/978-1-4684-8395-6

©1985 Plenum Press, New York
Softcover reprint of the hardcover 1st edition 1985

A Division of Plenum Publishing Corporation
233 Spring Street, New York, N.Y. 10013

To Chao, Lily, and Lita

Preface

This book is an outgrowth of formal graduate courses in multiple-criteria decision making (MCDM) that the author has taught at the University of Rochester, University of Texas at Austin, and University of Kansas since 1972. The purpose is, on one hand, to offer the reader an integral and systematic view of various concepts and techniques in MCDM at an "introductory" level, and, on the other hand, to provide a basic conception of the human decision mechanism, which may improve our ability to apply the techniques we have learned and may broaden our mind for modeling human decision making.

The book is written with a goal in mind that the reader should be able to assimilate and benefit from most of the concepts in the book if he has the mathematical maturity equivalent to a course in operations research or optimization theory. Good training in linear and nonlinear programming is sufficient to digest, perhaps easily, most of the concepts in the book.

In order to achieve the above purposes and goals, we have tried to offer "adequate" motivation and intuitive insight for each concept or algorithm before formally specifying it. If the technical details are too involved we put them in an appendix or we drop them but provide the references for the interested readers. To help the reader, we also try to associate the new concepts with what has been learned. For instance, we use the ordering of the real-valued function to derive a representation of preference, and use the local analysis (continuity and derivatives) of the real-valued function to derive domination structures of preferences.

Deciding which concepts and techniques to include in this volume was an exercise in MCDM itself. On one hand, it was desirable to include all concepts and techniques now in existence. Unfortunately, that would have required a very large volume, and a beginning reader would become easily trapped in what has already become a very rich literature. Therefore, it was necessary to make a judicious selection of basic concepts that could be comprehended systematically, given a reasonable expenditure of time and effort. It was inevitable that certain concepts had to be omitted from this volume, especially concepts perceived to be beyond the introductory level. Nonlinear duality theory, fuzzy sets, integer programming, fractional programming, and network analysis with multicriteria are excluded for this reason.

We emphasize the integral and systematic descriptions of the concepts and techniques. A systematic overview of this book is given in Section 1.2. Roughly, the book offers five tracks of basic and interconnected concepts: (i) simple ordering, (ii) goal-setting and goal-seeking models, (iii) value function representations of preference, (iv) domination structures, and (v) behavior bases and habitual domains of decision making. Each track is a set of tools for us to solve nontrivial decision problems. The more tools we have, the more efficient and effective we are in resolving the problems. The reader is urged to learn all of them to avoid bias or becoming overenthusiastic with one particular method. We make shoes to comfort our feet, instead of cutting our feet to fit the shoes. Right?

Finally we note that problems of multiple-criteria decision making have existed since the existence of human beings. A complete historic record is technically impossible. Interested readers are referred to Stadler's survey and bibliography (see Bibliography). However, we shall note that over the last decade the rekindled interest and progress in the areas of engineering, management science, and economics are tremendous, as evidenced by the Bibliography. Just like operations research, optimal control, and economics, it is fair to say that the evolution of the first stage of MCDM has perhaps matured and fairly stabilized. Our book, except for Chapters 7 and 9, is based on this matured material. The second stage of the evolution of MCDM can come very soon when one begins to integrate the matured material with psychology (Chapter 9) and local analysis of mathematics (Chapter 7). There are many challenging problems waiting for the interested reader who wants to make contributions!

The following are some suggestions for the readers. For those whose interest is mainly in applications, we suggest that they go quickly over Chapters 1 and 2, then concentrate on Chapters 3-6. If they are familiar with linear programming, then they can continue on to Chapter 8 for the MC- and MC^2-simplex methods. Chapter 9 is important for applications. Skip all mathematics of Chapter 9 if necessary. For those with sophisticated mathematical training, we invite them to study Chapter 7 carefully. Hopefully, they can make a breakthrough in the area of local analysis of preferences and domination structures. The behavior bases and habitual domains of Chapter 9 are certainly waiting to be polished and expanded.

Many people have helped and encouraged me to complete this book. I am grateful to Professor G. Leitmann, who wisely advised me to have an experience of self-discipline by writing a book, and to Professor A. Miele, who arranged the contract for me to have a "no retreat" situation. Both of them have been very kind and generous in offering me the needed spiritual support and encouragement. Many results described in the book are based on the articles by the author and/or his friends. I am grateful to many of my colleagues, previous students, and friends, especially Drs. M. Zeleny, M. Freimer, J. Keilson, A. Charnes, K. Cogger, L. Seiford, Y. Kwon, C. Wrather, S. J. Chan, and C. L. Hwang; and I must gratefully salute all scholars listed in the Bibliography for their interest and contributions to MCDM. Their works have influenced my thinking and research. Without them, MCDM may not have reached its current state of art.

In preparing this book Mr. Y. R. Lee has sweated over the details in proofreading, and preparing the Bibliography and exercises, and Mr. A. Stam has greatly helped me since the revision of the first draft, including preparing the index. Their persistence, self-discipline, and hard work are memorable. Without their assistance, this book may not have been as complete as it is now. To honor their assistance I invited them to put their names with the author's.

With gratitude I want to acknowledge the constructive comments on the first draft kindly offered by Professors H. Benson of the University of Florida, G. Hazen of Northwestern University, and E. Takeda of Kobe University of Commerce, as well as the doctoral students enrolled in my MCDM seminar: I. S. Chien, K. Mellouli, A. Trabelsi, and F. R. Wondolowski, Jr. I also want to thank Mr. N. Pathipvanich for much miscellaneous assistance and to Mrs. T. Stam for her editing work, and Mrs. K. Wallace for her patient typing and correcting.

P. L. Yu
Lawrence, Kansas

Acknowledgments

The author would like to thank the following organizations for giving him permission to use parts of his earlier publications:

Academic Press, Inc., for
   YU, P. L. and ZELENY, M., The set of all nondominated solutions in linear cases and multicriteria simplex method, *Journal of Mathematical Analysis and Applications*, **49**, 430-468 (1975).
   SEIFORD, L. and YU, P. L., Potential solutions of linear systems: The multicriteria, multiple constraint levels program, *Journal of Mathematical Analysis and Applications*, **69**, 283-303 (1979).

Gower Publishing Company, for
   YU, P. L., and SEIFORD, L., Multistage decision problems with multicriteria, *Multicriteria Analysis: Practical Methods*, pp. 235-244, Edited by P. Nijkamp and J. Spronk, Gower Press, London (1981).

The Institute of Management Science, for
   YU, P. L., A class of solutions for group decision problems, *Management Science*, **19**, 936-946 (1973).
   FREIMER, M., and YU, P. L., Some new results on compromise solutions for group decision problems, *Management Science*, **22**, 688-693 (1976).

Intersystems Publications, for
   YU, P. L., Behavior bases and habitual domains of human decision/behavior—An integration of psychology, optimization theory and common wisdom, *International Journal of Systems, Measurement and Decisions*, **1**, 39-62 (1981).

Plenum Publishing Corporation, for
   YU, P. L., Cone convexity, cone extreme points and nondominated solutions in decision problems and multiobjectives, *Journal of Optimization Theory and Applications*, **14**, 319-376 (1974).
   YU, P. L., and LEITMANN, G., Nondominated decision and cone convexity in dynamic multicriteria decision problems, *Journal of Optimization Theory and Applications*, **14**, 573-584 (1974).
   WRATHER, C. and YU, P. L., Probability dominance in random outcomes, *Journal of Optimization Theory and Applications*, **36**, 315-334 (1982).
   YU, P. L., Second-order game problem: Decision dynamics in gaming phenomena, *Journal of Optimization Theory and Applications*, **27**, 147-166 (1979).

Contents

1

Introduction

1.1. The Needs and Basic Elements

Although most of the time decision making is almost routine and does not require sophisticated analysis, we may occasionally be confronted with important decision-making problems. Correct decisions become important for our own welfare, future happiness, and success. For instance, upon graduation from a university, we may be offered several kinds of jobs. Each job has a combination of elements including salary, advancement potential, working environment, living environment, and friendship possibilities with colleagues. This situation inevitably involves multiple criteria, and the decision could be very important to our success and happiness. A careful analysis before choosing a job is therefore important.

As another example, suppose that we are designing a photocopy machine A good design of the product could mean a business success, whereas a poor design may be fatal to corporate survival. Each design involves the cost of production, the speed of copying, the contrast of the copy, the cost of using the machine, the size and convenience of using the machine, etc. Theoretically, there is an infinite number of combinations of these attributes. One of the problems will be to determine a "best" combination of values of the attributes for the business' success. Again, the decision problem involves multiple criteria (or attributes).

Other examples that prevail in our daily lives might include the investment of our savings in security markets or real estate, allocation of resources to different projects, or the purchase of a house. Although this kind of decision problem does not occur every day, the impact of each important decision on the future is so strong that we must not ignore its careful analysis. Many techniques for useful analysis are available to help decision makers reach good decisions. This book is devoted to introducing the available techniques and concepts and their applications to the reader at an introductory level.

In the abstract, a multiple-criteria decision problem involves four important elements. These are as follows:

1. *The Set of Alternatives,* denoted by X, with its generic element denoted by x, from which we will choose our decision. Observe that the set may contain only a small number of choices, as in the above example of selecting jobs. It can also contain an infinite number of choices, as in the copy machine design example.

2. *The Set of Criteria,* denoted by $f = (f_1, \ldots, f_q)$, with which we are concerned for making a good decision. If we have only one criterion, the decision problem becomes a typical mathematical programming problem and no great difficulty will occur. Indeed, there are techniques that try to reduce multiple criteria into a reasonable single criterion. These will be discussed later.

3. *The Outcome of Each Choice,* $f(x) = (f_1(x), \ldots, f_q(x))$, measured in terms of the criteria, will also be important for consideration. The totality of each possible outcome will be denoted by $Y = \{f(x) | x \in X\}$, with y as its generic element. The potential outcome $f(x)$ of each decision can be a single point or deterministic. It can be represented by a random variable when uncertainty is involved.

In the job selection problem, $f(x)$ can be a set with some confidence levels. However, for convenience in analysis, $f(x)$ is often assumed to be a single point or deterministic. Unless otherwise specified, it will be so assumed in this book.

4. *The Preference Structures of the Decision Maker* will be another important element of a multiple-criteria decision problem. If the preferences over the possible outcomes Y are clearly and perfectly specified, then the decision problem can become easy, for if y^* is the best outcome in Y, then $x^* \in f^{-1}(y^*)$ will be the choice. Unfortunately, in real life this specification is not easy at all. This does not mean that we cannot make a decision without perfect specification of the preference of the outcome. After all, we do make decisions eventually.

Although in many important decision problems the above four elements can change and evolve with time and situation, to simplify our presentation we shall assume that they are steady and deterministic unless otherwise specified. The dynamic change and evolution of the four elements will be treated in the last two chapters of this book.

1.2. An Overview of the Book

Nontrivial decision making as part of human activities is a complex process. Each individual is unique and there is no simple theory or description that can fit the decision behavior of any person perfectly over a long period of time. However, there are three basic patterns of logic for good decision making. Upon these patterns, concepts and techniques for multicriteria decision making have been developed. We shall discuss each of them.

The first logic pattern is based on a simple ordering. A good decision should be such that there is no other alternative that can be better in some aspects and not worse in every aspect of consideration. This concept leads to the famous Pareto optimality, which we will explore in Chapter 3 after introducing necessary concepts of preferences such as binary relations in Chapter 2. Because of the special assumption on linearity, many beautiful results and concepts [such as the multiple-criteria (MC) simplex method, as well as multiple-criteria and multiple constraint level (MC^2) simplex methods] have been developed. This special topic is treated in Chapter 8 after other logic patterns have been explored.

The second logic pattern is based on human goal-setting and goal-seeking behavior. This leads to "satisficing" and compromise solutions which we will discuss in Chapter 4.

The last logic pattern is based on value maximization, where more is better. Thus, one tries to attach a value function to the possible decision outcomes. The best decision should be the one that offers the best value. In Chapter 5 we explore the conditions for different value functions to exist, and in Chapter 6 we describe practical methods for estimating and approximating value functions.

Underlying the above three basic patterns there is a common denominator—domination structures—which allows us to integrate the above concepts and enables us to identify more techniques to handle multiple-criteria problems. This idea will be explored in Chapter 7.

As a living system, each human being has a set of goals or equilibrium points to seek and maintain. Multicriteria decision problems are part of the problems that the living system must solve. To broaden our understanding of human decision making, to improve our ability to apply the techniques introduced, and to avoid being confined to a specific set of techniques it is very important for us to have a good grasp of human behavior and psychology. In Chapter 9 we introduce behavior bases and habitual domains to fill this need. The basic mechanisms of human decision/behavior are summarized in eight hypotheses. Applications to generate new alternatives, criteria, perception of decision outcomes, and preference are also discussed.

As concepts and techniques of multicriteria decision making have grown rapidly, inevitably we cannot cover all possible topics. In Chapter 10 we sketch the further topics, including interactive methods, preference over uncertain outcomes, multicriteria dynamic optimization problems, and second-order games. Further topics are chosen to expose the reader to the vast areas of research and applications. Certainly there are areas left unexplored which the reader can expand upon.

Let us use Figure 1.1 to illustrate the organization of the book's contents. We strongly suggest that the reader read Chapter 9 after Chapters 2–7. Chapter

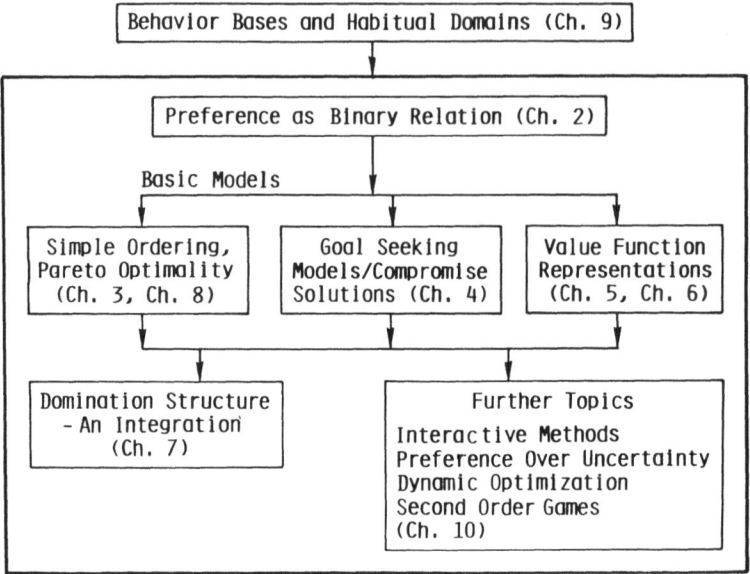

Figure 1.1

9 can expand your mind and horizon of thinking in multicriteria decision making.

1.3. Notation

The following notation will be used consistently throughout the book:

(i) Sets will be denoted by capital letters, such as X and Y, and their corresponding generic elements are denoted by lower-case letters, such as x and y.

(ii) The superscript is used to signify the elements of the set, such as x^k and y^k, for the elements of X and Y. The subscript signifies the *component* of the vector. For instance, if $x \in R^n$, it may be written as $(x_1, \ldots, x_n)^T$, where x_k is the kth component of x. Further, x_k^l is the kth component of x^l.

(iii) Given two sets, $Y \subset R^m$, $Z \subset R^m$, define

$$Y + Z = \{y + z \mid y \in Y, z \in Z\},$$

$$y + Z = \{y + z \mid z \in Z\},$$

$$Y \backslash Z = \{y \mid y \in Y, y \notin Z\}.$$

(iv) Given $x, y \in R^n$, define

$$x = y \qquad \text{iff } x_k = y_k \qquad \text{for all } k = 1, \ldots, n;$$

$$x \leqq y \qquad \text{iff } x_k \leqq y_k \qquad \text{for all } k = 1, \ldots, n;$$

$$x \leq y \qquad \text{iff } x \leqq y \quad \text{and} \quad x \neq y$$

(thus, there is at least one k such that $x_k < y_k$);

$$x < y \qquad \text{iff } x_k < y_k \qquad \text{for all } k = 1, \ldots, n.$$

(v) Given a set S, its closure, interior, and relative interior will be, respectively, denoted by Cl S, Int S and ri S.

(vi) Given x, y in R^n, $[x, y]$, $]x, y]$, $[x, y[$, and $]x, y[$ will denote the line segments connecting x and y, respectively, including x and y, excluding x but including y, including x but excluding y, and excluding both x and y.

2

Binary Relations

2.1. Preference as a Binary Relation

As mentioned in Section 1.1, if the preference over Y is clear and complete enough to identify a certain $y^* \in Y$ as the best choice, then $x^* \in f^{-1}(y^*)$ will be a final choice of the decision problem. If one can specify a *value function* $v(y): Y \to R^1$, so that $v(y^1) > v(y^2)$ implies that y^1 is prefered to y^2, then the decision problem reduces to max $v(f(x))$ over $x \in X$. Unfortunately, such a value function proves difficult to obtain in practice. Before we make strong assumptions to construct a "reasonable" value function (Chapter 5), it may be more important for us to understand what "preference" is and what its basic characteristics are. We shall study these in terms of binary relations that encompass real-valued functions as special cases.

Let us consider possible outcomes of the decision *a pair at a time.* For any pair, say y^1 and y^2, one and only one of the following can occur:

    i. we are convinced that y^1 is better than or preferred to y^2, denoted by $y^1 > y^2$;
    ii. we are convinced that y^1 is worse than or less preferred than y^2, denoted by $y^1 < y^2$; or
    (iii) Given two sets, $Y \subset R^m$, $Z \subset R^m$, define
        $y^1 \sim y^2$, thus, the preference relation between y^1 and y^2 is *indefinite* or *indifferent.*

Note that each of the above statements involves *a comparison or relation* between a pair of outcomes. The symbols ">", "<", and "~" are *operators* defining the comparisons and relations. Specifying whether ">", "<", or "~" is defined for each pair of Y, is equivalent to revealing preference information for each pair of Y. Any revealed preference information, accumulated or not, can then be represented by a subset of the Cartesian product $Y \times Y$ as follows:

Definition 2.1. By a *preference* we shall mean one or several of the following:

    i. A preference based on $>$ is a subset of $Y \times Y$, denoted by $\{>\}$, so that whenever $(y^1, y^2) \in \{>\}$, $y^1 > y^2$.

    ii. A preference based on $<$ is a subset of $Y \times Y$, denoted by $\{<\}$, so that whenever $(y^1, y^2) \in \{<\}$, $y^1 < y^2$.

    iii. A preference based on $\sim$ is a subset of $Y \times Y$, denoted by $\{\sim\}$, so that whenever $(y^1, y^2) \in \{\sim\}$, $y^1 \sim y^2$.

    iv. $\{\geq\} = \{>\} \cup \{\sim\}$.

    v. $\{\leq\} = \{<\} \cup \{\sim\}$.

Remark 2.1. (i) Note that $>$, $<$, and $\sim$ are operators, while $\{>\}$, $\{<\}$, and $\{\sim\}$ are sets of revealed preference information.

(ii) The sets $\{>\}$ and $\{<\}$ are *symmetric*. That is, $(y^1, y^2) \in \{>\}$ iff $(y^2, y^1) \in \{<\}$. This property is due to the need for logical consistency and to the fact that "better" and "worse" are antonyms.

(iii) Given a preference specified by $\{>\}$ or $\{<\}$, one can find $\{<\}$ or $\{>\}$, respectively, by (i) or (ii) of Definition 2.1 and also one can find $\{\sim\}$ by $\{\sim\} = Y \times Y \backslash (\{<\} \cup \{>\})$. Thus, one can reveal his/her preference by using $>$ or $<$ in the pairwise comparison. However, using only $\sim$ is not enough to specify the other types of preference. From (iv) and (v) of Definition 2.1, one needs $\{\geq\}$ and $\{\sim\}$ or $\{\leq\}$ and $\{\sim\}$ to specify $\{<\}$ and $\{>\}$.

(iv) In applications, one may want to ascertain as much information on a certain preference as possible. Due to the difficulty of obtaining or stating the preference precisely, it may be fruitful for us to specify the above five sets of preference first and then synthesize and simplify the presentation of the preference.

Example 2.1. Let $Y = \{y^1, y^2, \ldots, y^5\}$ and $y^1 > y^3$, $y^2 > y^4$, $y^3 > y^5$, $y^4 > y^1$, $y^2 > y^5$ be known. Then, the revealed preference specifies

$$\{>\} = \{(y^1, y^3), (y^2, y^4), (y^3, y^5), (y^4, y^1), (y^2, y^5)\},$$

$$\{<\} = \{(y^3, y^1), (y^4, y^2), (y^5, y^3), (y^1, y^4), (y^5, y^2)\},$$

$$\{\sim\} = \{(y^1, y^2), (y^1, y^5), (y^2, y^3), (y^3, y^4), (y^4, y^5)\}.$$

Using $\{y^j\}$ as the nodes and $\{>\}$ as the arcs, the above preferences can be represented by a network as in Figure 2.1. Note that each arc points in the "direction of preference" $>$; the reverse direction represents that of $<$.

Note also that one can connect those nodes in Figure 2.1 by an "undirected" arc for each pair of points in $\{\sim\}$. Then the resulting network becomes a complete graph in the sense that each pair of nodes is connected by an arc. This property is consistent with (iii) of Remark 2.1. In practice, the arcs

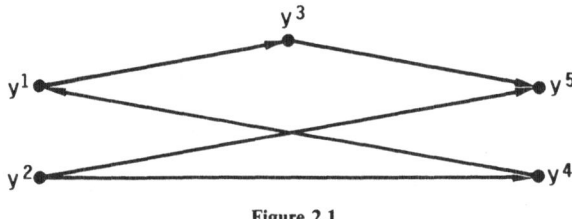

Figure 2.1

representing $\{\sim\}$ are not explicitly marked, in order to keep the graph simple yet informative.

Example 2.2. Consider the following preference over three candidates for a junior management position. Assume that each candidate is evaluated according to three criteria: ability, cooperation, and enthusiasm. Let the score of each criterion range from 0 to 9, the higher the better. Let y_i^j be the score on criterion i for candidate j. Since the score for each candidate is difficult to specify precisely, let the preference be given by $y^1 > y^2$ if and only if (iff) there is at least one criterion i so that $y_i^1 - y_i^2 \geq 2$, and $y_k^2 - y_k^1 < 2$ for the remaining criteria ($k \neq i$). Consider the scores given in Table 2.1. We obtain the following:

$$\{>\} = \{(y^1, y^2), (y^2, y^3), (y^3, y^1)\},$$
$$\{<\} = \{(y^2, y^1), (y^3, y^2), (y^1, y^3)\},$$
$$\{\sim\} = \varnothing.$$

Example 2.3. (A Lexicographic Ordering.) Let $y = (y_1, y_2, \ldots, y_q)$ be indexed so that the kth component is overwhelmingly more important than the $(k + 1)$th component for $k = 1, \ldots, q - 1$. A lexicographic ordering preference is defined as follows: the outcome $y^1 = (y_1^1, \ldots, y_q^1)$ is preferred to $y^2 = (y_1^2, \ldots, y_q^2)$ iff $y_1^1 > y_1^2$ or there is some $k \in \{2, \ldots, q\}$ so that $y_k^1 > y_k^2$ and $y_j^1 = y_j^2$ for $j = 1, \ldots, k - 1$. In locating the lexicographical maximum point over Y, one can first find the maximum points with respect to y_1 on Y. If the solution set, denoted by Y_1, contains only a single point, then stop; otherwise, find the maximum points with respect to y_2 on Y_1. If the solution

Table 2.1

Criteria	Candidate scores		
	y^1	y^2	y^3
Ability	7	8	9
Cooperation	8	9	7
Enthusiasm	9	7	8

set, denoted by Y_2, contains only a single point, then stop; otherwise find the maximum point with respect to y_3 on Y_2, etc. This process continues until a *unique* solution or no solution is found (no solution can be found when Y is an open set). Note that no two distinct points can be lexicographically "equal" in Y. We have

$$\{>\} = \{(y^1, y^2) | y^1 \text{ is lexicographically preferred to } y^2\};$$

$$\{\sim\} = \{(y, y) | y \in Y\}.$$

Example 2.4. (Pareto Preference.) For each component y_i, let greater values be more preferred, and assume that no other information on the preference is available or established. Then Pareto preference is defined by $y^1 > y^2$ iff $y^1 \geq y^2$, i.e., component-wise $y_i^1 \geq y_i^2$, $i = 1, \ldots, q$ and $y^1 \neq y^2$. Note that

$$\{>\} = \{(y^1, y^2) | y^1 \geq y^2\}$$

and

$$\{\sim\} = \{(y^1, y^2) | \text{neither } y^1 \geq y^2 \text{ nor } y^2 \geq y^1\}.$$

Similar to the lower and upper level sets (supports), one can define *better*, *worse*, or *indefinite* sets of a given preference as follows.

Definition 2.2. Given a preference and a point $y^0 \in Y$, we define the *better*, *worse*, or *indefinite* sets with respect to (w.r.t.) y^0 as

i. $\{y^0<\} = \{y \in Y | y^0 < y\}$ (the better set w.r.t. y^0);
ii. $\{y^0>\} = \{y \in Y | y^0 > y\}$ (the worse set w.r.t. y^0);
iii. $\{y^0\sim\} = \{y \in Y | y^0 \sim y\}$ (the indefinite or indifferent set w.r.t. y^0);
iv. $\{y^0\lesssim\} = \{y \in Y | y^0 \lesssim y\}$;
v. $\{y^0\gtrsim\} = \{y \in Y | y^0 \gtrsim y\}$;
vi. given a subset $Y^0 \subset Y$, define $\{Y^0<\} = \bigcup_{y^0 \in Y^0} \{y^0<\}$; other sets, such as $\{Y^0>\}$, $\{Y^0\lesssim\}$, etc., are similarly defined.

Remark 2.2. Note that

i. $\{y^0, \{y^0<\}\} = \{(y^0, y) | y \in \{y^0<\}\} \subset \{<\}$;
ii. $\{y^0, \{y^0>\}\} \subset \{>\}$;
iii. $\{y^0, \{y^0\sim\}\} \subset \{\sim\}$.

Remark 2.3. Given $\{<\}$ or $\{>\}$ one can define $\{y<\}$, $\{y>\}$, and $\{y\sim\}$ for each point of Y. (Refer to remark 2.1.) Conversely, if $\{y<\}$ or $\{y>\}$ is known at each point of Y, then $\{>\}$, $\{<\}$, and $\{\sim\}$ are also defined. However, in practical decisions $\{y<\}$, $\{y>\}$, or $\{y\sim\}$ are established or known only for some points in Y. These sets are elicited as needed at those points under consideration.

Example 2.5. (i) In Example 2.1, at y^2, $\{y^2>\} = \{y^4, y^5\}$, $\{y^2<\} = \varnothing$, and $\{y^2\sim\} = \{y^1, y^3\}$.
   (ii) In Example 2.2, at y^1, $\{y^1>\} = \{y^2\}$, $\{y^1<\} = \{y^3\}$, and $\{y^1\sim\} = \varnothing$.

The concept of the better, worse, and indifferent sets will become important in defining the concepts and conditions of optimality. (See Section 2.3.) Interactive and iterative techniques to solicit preference information and finally reach a "good" decision are to be discussed later.

2.2. Characteristics of Preferences

To study the characteristics of preference information, one may start with the general concept of binary relations on Y, which are defined to be subsets of $Y \times Y$. Denote this subset by R. Note that preferences defined by $\{>\}$, $\{<\}$, or $\{\sim\}$ are binary relations.

Definition 2.3. The binary relation R on Y is
  i. *reflexive* if $(y, y) \in R$ for every $y \in Y$; otherwise, it is *irreflexive*;
  ii. *symmetric* if $(y^1, y^2) \in R$ implies that $(y^2, y^1) \in R$ for every y^1, y^2 of Y; otherwise, it is *asymmetric*;
  iii. *transitive* if $(y^1, y^2) \in R$ and $(y^2, y^3) \in R$ implies that $(y^1, y^3) \in R$, for every y^1, y^2, $y^3 \in Y$; otherwise, it is *nontransitive*;
  iv. *complete* or *connected* if $(y^1, y^2) \in R$ or $(y^2, y^1) \in R$ for every $y^1, y^2 \in Y$ and $y^1 \neq y^2$.
  v. an *equivalence* if R is reflexive, symmetric, and transitive.

Example 2.6. Let Y be the students currently enrolled at a university.
  (i) Let R_1 be defined by "being a classmate in at least one class." Thus, $(y^1, y^2) \in R_1$ iff y^1 and y^2 are classmates in at least one class. Broadly speaking, one can be a classmate to himself or herself. Note that R_1 so defined is reflexive, symmetric, nontransitive (why?), and not complete.
  (ii) Let R_2 be defined by "being older than." Thus, $(y^1, y^2) \in R_2$ iff y^1 is older than y^2. Assume that no two students were born at the very same instance. We see that R_2 is irreflexive, asymmetric, transitive, and complete.
  (iii) Let R_3 be defined by "being of the same sex." Thus, $(y^1, y^2) \in R_3$ iff y^1 is of the same sex as y^2. Assume that each student is either male or female (not both as in the pathological case). We see that R_3 is reflexive, symmetric, and transitive, and therefore, is an *equivalence*. Note also that R_3 is not complete (why?).

Remark 2.4. (i) From Definition 2.1, regarding $\{>\}$, $\{<\}$, and $\{\sim\}$ as binary relations, in order to be consistent with logic and linguistic usage, we require and assume throughout this book that $\{>\}$ and $\{<\}$ are *both irreflexive and asymmetric* and that $\{\sim\}$ is *reflexive and symmetric.*

(ii) By definition, for every y^1, y^2 of Y, (y^1, y^2) belongs to exactly one of $\{>\}$, $\{<\}$, and $\{\sim\}$. Indeed, $\{>\}$, $\{<\}$, and $\{\sim\}$ form a *partition* of $Y \times Y$. (That is, they are mutually disjoint and collectively their union is equal to $Y \times Y$.) This observation immediately reveals that $\{\gtrsim\}$ and $\{\lesssim\}$ are connected or complete. To see this point, observe that $(y^1, y^2) \in \{\gtrsim\} \cup \{\lesssim\} = Y \times Y$. Thus, either $(y^1, y^2) \in \{\gtrsim\}$ or $(y^1, y^2) \in \{\lesssim\}$ or both.

Remark 2.5. To be consistent with logic and linguistic usage, we would like to establish that each of $\{>\}$, $\{<\}$, $\{\gtrsim\}$, $\{\lesssim\}$, and $\{\sim\}$ is transitive. Certainly, when this transitivity is available or established, the decision problem will become simpler. For instance, if the transitivity property is imposed on the preference $\{>\}$ stated in Example 2.1, then y^2 will become the unique best choice. Every other choice is worse than y^2. (Check it!) Unfortunately, such ideal properties and assumptions are not always valid or established. For instance, the preferences $\{>\}$ and $\{<\}$ stated in Example 2.2 are not transitive! (Why?) The reader may also construct an example [for instance, $y^1 = (1, 3)$, $y^2 = (2, 0)$, and $y^3 = (0, 1)$] to show that despite Pareto preference $\{>\}$ for Example 2.4 being transitive, its induced indefinite preference $\{\sim\}$ and $\{\gtrsim\}$ are not transitive. These examples demonstrate that although transitivity is nice to have for $\{>\}$, $\{<\}$, or $\{\sim\}$, in practice the transitivity may be lacking; and it is not valid to assume that the transitivity of $\{>\}$ or $\{<\}$ implies that of $\{\sim\}$. Special attention must be paid to each particular problem to ensure that such assumptions are valid.

As $\{\sim\}$ can be derived from $\{>\}$ or $\{<\}$, the following relationships are valid.

Theorem 2.1. Let $\{>\}$ and $\{\gtrsim\}$ be the preference on Y (as defined in Definition 2.1).

(i) If $\{>\}$ is transitive and complete, then $\{\gtrsim\}$ is transitive and complete.

(ii) $\{\gtrsim\}$ is transitive iff for every y^1, y^2, $y^3 \in Y$, $y^1 > y^3$ implies that $y^1 > y^2$ or $y^2 > y^3$.

Proof. *For* (i): That $\{\gtrsim\}$ is complete is clear because $\{>\} \subseteq \{\gtrsim\}$. To see that $\{\gtrsim\}$ is transitive, assume the contrary: that $y^1 \gtrsim y^2$ and $y^2 \gtrsim y^3$, but not $y^1 \gtrsim y^3$. Then $y^3 > y^1$. Since $\{>\}$ is complete, either $y^3 > y^2$ or $y^2 > y^3$ holds. Since $y^2 \gtrsim y^3$ is assumed, $y^2 > y^3$ must hold. Similarly, $y^1 > y^2$ must hold. The transitivity of $\{>\}$ will lead to $y^1 > y^3$, which is a contradiction!

For (ii): For the sufficiency, assume the contrary: that $y^1 \gtrsim y^2$ and $y^2 \gtrsim y^3$ but not $y^1 \gtrsim y^3$. Then $y^3 > y^1$ holds. Thus, $y^3 > y^2$ or $y^2 > y^1$ must hold. In either case, we have a contradiction.

For the necessity, assume the contrary: that $y^1 > y^3$ but neither $y^1 > y^2$ nor $y^2 > y^3$ holds. Then, $y^2 \succsim y^1$ and $y^3 \succsim y^2$ hold, which implies that $y^3 \succsim y^1$. Again, this is a contradiction. □

Remark 2.6. (i) The requirement of the completeness in (i) of Theorem 2.1 cannot be dropped. As an example, $\{>\}$ of the Pareto preference (Example 2.4) is transitive but not complete. The corresponding $\{\succsim\}$ is not transitive as indicated in Remark 2.5.

(ii) The assertion (ii) of Theorem 2.1 essentially says that $\{\succsim\}$ is transitive iff for every $y^1, y^3 \in Y$, $y^1 > y^3$ implies that $\{y^1>\}$ and $\{y^3<\}$ form a *covering* of Y. (That is, $Y \subset \{y^1>\} \cup \{y^3<\}$.) If $Y = R^q$, we see that $\{>\}$ of Pareto preference does not have this property, while that of lexicographical preference does. (Check it!)

The following terminology has been used extensively in the literature.

Definition 2.4. (i) A preference, $\{>\}$ or $\{<\}$, is a *partial order* if it is transitive. (Recall that they are assumed to be irreflexive and asymmetric in Remark 2.4.)

(ii) A preference $\{>\}$ or $\{<\}$ is a *weak order* if it is transitive and its induced preference $\{\succsim\}$ or $\{\precsim\}$ is also transitive.

(iii) A complete (or connected) weak order is called a *strict order*.

Weak ordering is a very strong property, as the following theorem indicates.

Theorem 2.2. Let $\{>\}$ be a partial order. Then it also is a weak order iff
  i. the induced preference $\{\sim\}$ is an equivalence (reflexive, symmetric, and transitive); and
  ii. if $y^1 > y^2$ and $y^2 \sim y^3$ or if $y^1 \sim y^2$ and $y^2 > y^3$, then $y^1 > y^3$.

Proof. For Sufficiency. Assume that $y^1 \succsim y^2$ and $y^2 \succsim y^3$. Then either $y^1 > y^2$ or $y^1 \sim y^2$ holds and either $y^2 > y^3$ or $y^2 \sim y^3$ holds. Using (i) and (ii), one obtains $y^1 > y^3$ or $y^1 \sim y^3$ for all four possible combinations. This implies that $y^1 \succsim y^3$. Thus, $\{\succsim\}$ is transitive.

For Necessity. *For* (i): It suffices to show that $\{\sim\}$ is transitive. Assume that $y^1 \sim y^2$, $y^2 \sim y^3$ and not $y^1 \sim y^3$. Then either $y^1 > y^3$ or $y^3 > y^1$ holds. In view of (ii) of Theorem 2.1, at least one of the following cases occurs: $y^1 > y^2$, $y^2 > y^3$, $y^3 > y^2$, or $y^2 > y^1$. This clearly contradicts the assumption that $y^1 \sim y^2$ and $y^2 \sim y^3$.

For (ii): We show that $y^1 > y^2$ and $y^2 \sim y^3$ imply that $y^1 > y^3$. The other half can be proven similarly. Since $y^1 > y^2$, (ii) of Theorem 2.1 implies that either $y^1 > y^3$ or $y^3 > y^2$. But $y^2 \sim y^3$ is assumed so only $y^1 > y^3$ can hold. □

Example 2.7. The preferences defined in Example 2.1 and 2.2 are not partial orders, so they are not weak orders. The Pareto preference in Example 2.4 is a partial order, but it is not a weak order. The preference represented by a value function (see Chapter 5) is a weak order. Lexicographical preference is a strict order (Example 2.3). More properties on orders and relations can be found in Fishburn (Ref. 139) and Exercises 2.9, 2.10, 2.11, and 2.12.

Suppose that Y is convex. Then the concept of quasi-convexity in real-valued functions can be extended to that of preferences as follows.

Definition 2.5. Let Y be a convex set.

(i) $\{>\}$ is *quasi-convex* iff $y^1 \succsim y^2$ implies that $y^1 \succsim (1 - \lambda)y^1 + \lambda y^2$ for any $\lambda \in]0, 1[$, the open interval from 0 to 1.

(ii) $\{>\}$ is *quasi-concave* iff $y^1 \precsim y^2$ implies that $y^1 \precsim (1 - \lambda)y^1 + \lambda y^2$ for any $\lambda \in]0, 1[$.

Theorem 2.3. Suppose that $\{>\}$ is a weak order (i.e., both $\{>\}$ and $\{\succsim\}$ are transitive) over a convex set Y. Then

i. $\{>\}$ is quasi-convex iff $\{y\succsim\}$ is a convex set for all $y \in Y$;

ii. $\{>\}$ is quasi-concave iff $\{y\precsim\}$ is a convex set for all $y \in Y$.

Proof. We shall prove only (i); (ii) can be proved similarly. (See Exercise 2.13.) For necessity, given three arbitrary points y^0, y^1, y^2, with y^1, y^2 contained in $\{y^0\succsim\}$. Since $\{\succsim\}$ is complete [Remark 2.4(ii)], without loss of generality assume $y^1 \succsim y^2$. By quasi-convexity, $y^1 \succsim (1 - \lambda)y^1 + \lambda y^2$ for all $\lambda \in]0, 1[$. Thus, by transitivity of $\{\succsim\}$, $(1 - \lambda)y^1 + \lambda y^2 \precsim y^1 \precsim y^0$ and $(1 - \lambda)y^1 + \lambda y^2 \in \{y^0\succsim\}$. Now to see the sufficiency, again assume $y^1 \succsim y^2$. Then $y^2 \in \{y^1 \succsim\}$ and $y^1 \in \{y^1\succsim\}$. As $\{y^1\succsim\}$ is convex, $(1 - \lambda)y^1 + \lambda y^2 \in \{y^1\succsim\}$ or $y^1 \succsim (1 - \lambda)y^1 + \lambda y^2$ for all $\lambda \in]0, 1[$. Thus $\{>\}$ is quasi-convex. ☐

Remark 2.7. Debreu (Ref. 105) refers to quasi-concave preference as "weak-convex" preference. One can extend the concept of quasi-concave preference to *strictly* quasi-concave preference (which Debreu refers to as convex preference) just as one can extend the concept of a quasi-concave function to a *strictly* quasi-concave function. [For instance see Mangasarian (Ref. 307) and Exercise 2.14.] Implications of quasi-concave preference on optimality will be further discussed in Chapter 7.

2.3. Optimality Condition

Given the set of outcomes Y and preference $\{>\}$, we want to know what constitutes the *optimal choice*. We shall use the better, worse, and indefinite sets (Definition 2.2) to clarify the idea.

Given a point $y^0 \in Y$, a *necessary condition* for y^0 to be optimal is that $\{y^0<\} = \varnothing$. Otherwise, there will be some other outcome better than y^0. In Example 2.1, $\{y^2<\} = \varnothing$. Thus, y^2 is a candidate for the optimal choice. In Example 2.2, $\{y^i<\} \neq \varnothing$, $i = 1, 2, 3$. So none of them can be a final optimal solution under the current preference. (This situation may be resolved when new criteria are added or perception of the outcomes is changed.)

Definition 2.6. Given a preference $\{>\}$ or $\{<\}$ defined on Y, the *nondominated set* and *dominated set* of Y with respect to $\{>\}$, denoted, respectively, by $N(\{>\}, Y)$ and $D(\{>\}, Y)$ or simply by N and D when no confusion can occur, are defined by

$$N(\{>\}, Y) = \{y^0 \in Y \,|\, \{y^0<\} = \varnothing\}, \tag{2.1}$$

$$D(\{>\}, Y) = \{y^0 \in Y \,|\, \{y^0<\} \neq \varnothing\}. \tag{2.2}$$

If $y^0 \in N = N(\{>\}, Y)$ or $y^0 \in D = D(\{>\}, Y)$, we call y^0 an *N-point* or a *D-point*, respectively.

Remark 2.8. (i) By (2.1) and (2.2), N and D are uniquely determined by $\{>\}$ and form a partition of Y.

(ii) The set $N(\{>\}, Y)$, depending on $\{>\}$ and Y, may be empty and $D = Y$. In Example 2.2, $N = \varnothing$ and Y contains only three points. Even for the lexicographical order, defined in Example 2.3, if $Y = \{(y^1, y^2) \,|\, 0 < y^1 < 1, 0 < y^2 < 1\}$, $N = \varnothing$ and $D = Y$.

(iii) It is also possible that $N = Y$ and $D = \varnothing$. That is, each $y \in Y$ is an *N*-point. It is readily verified that, in this case, $\{y>\} = \{y<\} = \varnothing$ and $\{y\sim\} = Y$ for each $y \in Y$. Thus, preference information $\{>\}$ is not adequate to discern the preference among any pair in Y. Further information on preference or conception is needed to reach a final decision.

(iv) Intuitively, the set N should contain all of the good solutions, and all the *D*-points can be eliminated from further analysis. Unfortunately, it is possible that some *D*-points may not be contained by $\{N>\}$, which is the set of outcomes worse than some point in N. They may be contained only by $\{D>\}$, the set of outcomes worse than some *D*-point. Their elimination from further consideration may not be fully justified. As an example, let $Y = \{(1, 1)\} \cup \{(y_1, y_2) \,|\, 0 < y_1 < 1, 0 < y_2 < 3;$ or $0 < y_1 < 3, 0 < y_2 < 1\}$. In Pareto preference ordering, $N = \{(1, 1)\}$ and $\{N>\}$ is much smaller than Y. Note that it is possible that $(0.9999, 2.9999)$, which is a *D*-point, may prove to be preferred to $(1, 1)$ when further preference information is available or established. If all *D*-points are eliminated, $(1, 1)$ will be the only remaining alternative, which may be a bad choice when further preference information is available or established. This leads to the following concept.

Definition 2.7. Given Y and $\{>\}$, Y is *nondominance bounded* (or *N-bounded*) with respect to $\{>\}$, if each point $y \in Y$ is either an N-point or there is an N-point y^0 so that $y^0 > y$.

Remark 2.9. In Example 2.2, Y is not N-bounded with respect to $\{>\}$. Note that Y is nondominance bounded iff $D = \{N>\}$ or $Y = N \cup \{N>\}$. When Y is N-bounded, all D-points may be eliminated from further consideration if further information on the preference is consistent with the current preference ordering.

Remark 2.10. In Example 2.2, we may decompose Y into $\{y^1, y^2\}$ and $\{y^3\}$. Since $y^1 > y^2$ and $y^3 > y^1$, if one selects the better one of $\{y^1, y^2\}$ and then compares the better one with the remaining one, one would end up with the choice of y^3. Similarly, one would end up with y^1 if Y is decomposed into $\{y^2, y^3\}$ and $\{y^1\}$, and with y^2 if Y is decomposed into $\{y^3, y^1\}$ and $\{y^2\}$. These inconsistent results from a seemingly consistent logic elimination sequence is due to the nontransitivity of $\{>\}$. Indeed, the reader can show that when Y is nondominance bounded or $\{>\}$ has the transitivity property, the inconsistent results will not occur. (See Exercise 2.2.)

2.4. Further Comments

Recall that, given $\{>\}$, we can define $\{y>\}$, $\{y<\}$, and $\{y\sim\}$. The latter may be regarded as point-to-set maps from $y \in Y$ to subsets of Y. The lower and upper semicontinuity of these *point-to-set maps* can be defined. The topological properties of these maps and their resultant solutions can be studied. For details see Debreu (Ref. 105), Hazen and Morin (Ref. 198), and Tanino and Sawaragi (Ref. 446).

More properties on preference and optimality will be described in Chapter 3–7 and 9. The reader also can find an interesting summary on optimality by White (Ref. 481).

Exercises

2.1. Let $Y = \{y^1, y^2, \ldots, y^6\}$ and $y^1 > y^4$, $y^4 > y^6$, $y^6 > y^2$, $y^3 > y^6$, $y^5 > y^1$, and $y^3 > y^5$ be known.
   a. Find the sets of revealed preference information $\{<\}$, $\{>\}$, and $\{\sim\}$.
   b. Using $\{y^j\}$ as the nodes and $\{>\}$ as the arcs, draw a graph (as shown in Figure 2.1) to represent the preferences.
   c. Find $\{y^6>\}$, $\{y^6<\}$, and $\{y^6\sim\}$.
   d. If the transitivity property is added to the preference, find the unique best choice.

2.2. Consider the following preference structure involving three alternatives. Each alternative is evaluated according to three criteria.

Criteria	Alternative (j)		
(i)	y^1	y^2	y^3
1	7	3	5
2	6	8	9
3	4	5	2

The preference is given by $y^j > y^s$ iff there is at least one criterion i so that $y^j_i - y^s_i \geq 3$ and $y^s_k - y^j_k \leq 2$ for the remaining criteria ($k \neq i$).
a. Specify $\{>\}$, $\{<\}$, and $\{\sim\}$.
b. Is the preference structure a partial order? Explain.
c. Suppose we decompose $Y = \{y^1, y^2, y^3\}$ into $\{y^1, y^2\}$ and $\{y^3\}$. If one selects the better one of $\{y^1, y^2\}$ and compares it with the remaining one, one would end up with the choice of y^1. Will the same result hold if Y is decomposed into $\{y^3, y^1\}$ and $\{y^2\}$?
d. (Refer to Remark 2.10.) Show that if Y is nondominance bounded or $\{>\}$ is transitive then the inconsistent results will not occur.

2.3. Let $y^1 = (0, 5)$, $y^2 = (2, 7)$, $y^3 = (4, 5)$, $y^4 = (4, 2)$, $y^5 = (2, 0)$, and $y^6 = (0, 0)$ be the extreme points of the polyhedral outcome space Y.
a. Let $y^0 = (2, 3)$. Sketch the region of the better, worse, and indefinite set for Pareto preference with respect to y^0.
b. Let x, y, and z be interior points in Y: $x = (1, 3)$, $y = (3, 2)$, and $z = (2, 4)$. Show that the indefinite preference $\{\sim\}$ is not transitive with respect to Pareto preference over $\{x, y, z\}$.
c. Specify the nondominated set of Y with respect to Pareto preference.

2.4. Explain graphically why (i) Pareto preference is not a weak order and (ii) lexicographical preference is a weak order. For instance consider $y^1 = (2, 4)$, $y^2 = (3, 1)$, and $y^3 = (1, 2)$.

2.5. The transitivity assumption may be criticized on the grounds that it does not correspond to manifest behavior when people are presented with a sequence of paired comparisons. Identify the reasons for such intransitivities. [For instance, Linda (woman) loves John (man) romantically and John loves Debbi (another woman) romantically. Most likely Linda will not love Debbi romantically. Right? Why?]

2.6. The XYZ company has been producing two kinds of well-known electronic products, type A and type B. Type A is a sophisticated product which requires high-quality workmanship and type B is acceptable for lower quality. The profits are $40 and $20 per unit, respectively, for types A and B. In the production, each unit of type A requires twice as much time as a unit of type B, and if all products were type B, the company production time allows making 500 units per day. The material consumptions for A and B are identical. The supply of material is sufficient for only 400 units per day (both A and B combined). Type A requires a special type of transistor and only 200 per day are available.

(a) Suppose that the company's problem is to determine the best possible combination of type A and type B to produce in order to maximize profits. Formulate a linear programming model for this problem.

(b) Suppose the XYZ company also wants to maximize the total production (i.e., the sum of two products) in addition to maximizing profits. Assume that the production manager ranks the importance of criteria as follows:

the most important criterion: maximizing profit

the second important criterion: maximizing total production

Solve the problem using the lexicographical method.

(Hint: Define f_1 and f_2 and maximize f_1 over X first. If this maximal solution is unique, it will be used for the decision. Otherwise we maximize f_2 over those points which maximize f_1 over X.)

2.7. Mr. Wilson, a college graduate, is offered three different jobs A, B, and C. He feels that salary, location (including degree of urbanization), and commuting travel time are important criteria for selecting a job. Mr. Wilson's rating according to the three criteria is as follows:

	Job		
Criteria	A	B	C
Salary	High	Medium	Low
Location	Medium	High	Low
Commuting travel time	Low	Medium	High

(a) Suppose Mr. Wilson's preference is given by B > A, C > B, and A > C. Specify $\{<\}$, $\{>\}$, and $\{\sim\}$.

(b) Suppose Mr. Wilson feels that salary is the most important, location is the next, and commuting travel time is the last. Assume that he quantifies his rating of the three criteria as follows:

	Job		
Criteria	A	B	C
Salary	$42,000	$39,000	$32,000
Location[a]	7	10	6
Commuting travel time[a]	3	5	10

[a] 10 points rating scale, where more is better.

Assume that preference will be based on salary unless the difference between two salaries is less than 4,000, in which case preference will be based on location unless the difference between two locations' rating is less than 2, in which case preference will be based on commuting travel time. Which job will be Mr. Wilson's choice according to his preference?

2.8. Consider two bundles of goods, A and B. If at some prices and income level the individual can afford both A and B, but chooses A, we say that it is revealed that A has been "preferred" to B. In economics, the principle of rationality states that under any different price-income arrangement, B can never be revealed preferred to A. Why would it be irrational to reveal that B is preferred to A in some other price-income configuration? Can our perception and/or preference change with time and situation? Criticize the above principle of rationality.

2.9. Show that $\{>\}$ is transitive (a partial order) if, for all $y^1, y^2, y^3, y^4 \in Y$:
(i) $y^1 > y^2$ and $y^3 > y^4$ imply that either $y^1 > y^4$ or $y^3 > y^2$; or (ii) $y^1 > y^2$ and $y^2 > y^3$ imply that either $y^1 > y^4$ or $y^4 > y^3$. [$\{>\}$ with property (i) is known as an *interval order* and $\{>\}$ with properties (i) and (ii) as a *semiorder*.]

2.10. Let $\{\gtrsim\}$ be a weak order over Y. Then Theorem 2.2 states that $\{\sim\}$ is an equivalence. Let $\tilde{Y}$ be the set of equivalence classes of Y under $\sim$. (Note that $\{y\sim\}$ is an element of $\tilde{Y}$.) Define ">'" over $\tilde{Y}$ by $\tilde{y}^1 >' \tilde{y}^2$ (note that $\tilde{y}^1$ and $\tilde{v}^2$ are subsets of Y) iff there is $y^1 \in \tilde{y}^1$, $y^2 \in \tilde{y}^2$, and $y^1 > y^2$. Show that $\{>'\}$ on $\tilde{Y}$ is a strict order.

2.11. Show that if $\{>\}$ is a strict ordering over Y, then $\{y\sim\} = \{y\}$. (That is, there are no two outcomes which are indifferent to each other.)

2.12. A preference $\{>\}$, in addition to irreflexiveness and asymmetry (as always assumed), may satisfy other properties. The following are some known properties:
(i) For every $y^1, y^2, y^3, y^4 \in Y$, if $y^1 > y^2$ and $y^3 > y^4$, then $y^1 > y^3$ or $y^3 > y^2$ (known as *interval ordering*).
(ii) For every $y^1, y^2, y^3, y^4 \in Y$, if $y^1 > y^2$ and $y^2 > y^3$, then $y^1 > y^4$ or $y^4 > y^3$.
(iii) For every $y^1, y^2, y^3 \in Y$, if $y^1 > y^2$ and $y^2 \sim y^3$, then $y^1 > y^3$.
(iv) For every $y^1, y^2, y^3 \in Y$, if $y^1 \sim y^2$ and $y^2 > y^3$, then $y^1 > y^3$.
Show that $\{>\}$ is a weak order if it satisfies (i) and (iii), (i) and (iv), (ii) and (iii), *or* (ii) and (iv). [Indeed, (iii) holds iff (iv) does, and (iii) and (iv) individually imply the transitivity of $\{\sim\}$.]

2.13. Prove Theorem 2.3(ii).

2.14. Define a strictly quasi-concave preference following the concept of a strictly quasi-concave function. What properties can you derive for a strictly quasi-concave preference?

Suggested Reading

The following references are particularly pertinent to this chapter: 105, 139, 198, 307, 446, 481.

3

Pareto Optimal or Efficient Solutions

3.1. Introduction

In this chapter we shall concentrate on Pareto preference and its induced nondominated solutions, both on Y and on X.

As indicated in Example 2.4, Pareto preference is based on the concept "more is better" for each criterion f_i, $i = 1, \ldots, q$; and that no other information about the tradeoff of $\{f_i\}$ is established or available. Thus, in the outcome space $Y = \{f(x) | x \in X\}$, $y^1 > y^2$ iff $y^1 \geq y^2$. Recall that $\{>\}$ is transitive but $\{\sim\}$ is not; consequently, $\{>\}$ is not a weak order.

The following notation for specific convex cones in R^q will be used throughout the book (note that Λ is used for convex cones because of its shape):

$$\Lambda^< = \{d \in R^q | d < 0\},$$

$$\Lambda^\leq = \{d \in R^q | d \leq 0\},$$

$$\Lambda^\leqq = \{d \in R^q | d \leqq 0\}.$$

(Recall that "$<$", "$\leq$", and "$\leqq$" are different. See Section 1.2.) Similarly, $\Lambda^>$, $\Lambda^\geq$, and $\Lambda^\geqq$ are defined. Note that $\Lambda^\leq = \Lambda^\leqq \setminus \{0\}$ and $\Lambda^> = \text{Int } \Lambda^\geq = \text{Int } \Lambda^\geqq$, where Int $\Lambda^\geq$ and Int $\Lambda^\geqq$ denote the interior of $\Lambda^\geq$ and $\Lambda^\geqq$, respectively.

With the above notation, $y^1 > y^2$ iff $y^2 \in y^1 + \Lambda^\leq$ or $y^2 - y^1 \in \Lambda^\leq$, and for each $y \in Y$,

$$\{y>\} = Y \cap (y + \Lambda^\leqq)$$

and

$$\{y<\} = Y \cap (y + \Lambda^\geqq).$$

21

Note that the above expressions hold for each point of Y and are independent of y. The nonpositive cone $\Lambda^{\leq}$ is usually called the *dominated cone*, and the nonnegative cone $\Lambda^{\geq}$, the *preferred cone*. They indicate, respectively, the direction of the dominated and preferred points from a point y under consideration. Observe that $\Lambda^{\leq}$ or $\Lambda^{\geq}$ is only $(1/2)^q$ of R^q and that $(1/2)^q$ reduces rapidly as q gets larger. The remaining sections of this chapter will deal with the properties of N-points of the Pareto preference and the methods to locate them.

3.2. General Properties of Pareto Optimal Solutions

An outcome y is *Pareto optimal* iff it is an N-point with respect to Pareto preference. A Pareto optimal solution is also called an *efficient, noninferior, nondominated*, or *admissible* solution in the literature.

Some examples of sets of nondominated solutions (N-points) are shown in Figure 3.1. In Figure 3.1, the heavily traced boundary corresponds to N-points. Figure 3.2 shows the N-points of a nonconvex set.

Unless otherwise stated, Pareto preference will be assumed throughout this chapter, and an N-point is defined with respect to Pareto preference. The following can be easily established.

Theorem 3.1. The following statements are equivalent:
  i. $y^0 \in Y$ is an N-point;
 ii. $\{y^0 <\} = \varnothing$;
iii. there is no $y \in Y$ such that $y > y^0$;
 iv. for every $y \in Y$, if $y \geq y^0$, then $y = y^0$.

Depending on Y, N-points may not exist! For instance, if Y is open, then N is empty. The same example also shows that Y is not necessarily N-bounded. (See Definition 2.7.) To emphasize that N is dependent on Y, the set of N-points will be denoted by $N[Y]$.

Theorem 3.2. $N[Y] = N[Y + \Lambda^{\leq}]$.

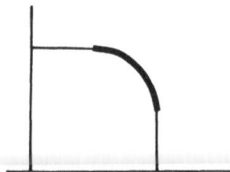

Figure 3.1. N-points of a convex set.

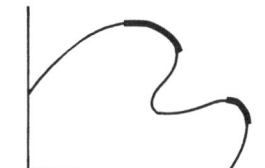

Figure 3.2. *N*-points of a nonconvex set.

Proof. Assume that $y^0 \in N[Y]$ but $y^0 \notin N[Y + \Lambda^{\leqq}]$. Then there is a $y \in Y$ and a $d \in \Lambda^{\leqq}$ such that $y + d \geq y^0$, or $y \geq y^0$ which implies $y^0 \notin N[Y]$, a contradiction! Thus, $N[Y] \subset N[Y + \Lambda^{\leqq}]$. On the other hand, assume that $y^0 \in N[Y + \Lambda^{\leqq}]$ but $y^0 \notin N[Y]$. Then there is a $y \in Y$, $y \geq y^0$. By continuity, there is a $d \in \Lambda^{\leqq}$ such that $y + d \geq y^0$. [For instance, select $d = \frac{1}{2}(y - y^0)$.] Thus, $y^0 \notin N[Y + \Lambda^{\leqq}]$. Again, we have a contradiction! Thus, $N[Y + \Lambda^{\leqq}] = N[Y]$. $\qquad\square$

To explore existence and N-boundedness problems, we first introduce the following definition.

Definition 3.1. Given a convex cone Λ with its closure denoted by Cl Λ, the outcome set Y is Λ-*compact* if, for every $y \in Y$, $Y \cap (y - \text{Cl } \Lambda)$ is a compact set.

Remark 3.1. Clearly, if Y is compact, then Y is Λ-compact for any Λ. However, that Y is Λ-compact for some Λ does not imply that Y is compact. For instance, let $Y = \Lambda^{\leqq}$. Then Y is $\Lambda^{\leqq}$-compact, but not compact.

Theorem 3.3. If Y is nonempty and $\Lambda^{\leqq}$-compact, then
  i. N is not empty, and
  ii. Y is N-bounded (thus $D = \{N>\}$).

Proof. *For* (*i*): Let $y' \in Y$ and y' be a D-point (otherwise, we have no problem). Select $\lambda \in \Lambda^{>}$ and let y^0 maximize $\lambda \cdot y$ over $Y \cap (y' - \Lambda^{\leqq})$. Such y^0 exists because $Y \cap (y' - \Lambda^{\leqq})$ is compact. It remains to show that y^0 is an N-point. Assume the contrary: Let $y^1 \in Y$ and $y^1 \geq y^0$. It is verified that $y^1 \in Y \cap (y' - \Lambda^{\leqq})$ and $\lambda \cdot y^1 > \lambda \cdot y^0$ (because $\lambda > 0$ and $y^1 = y^0 + d$ with $d \geq 0$). This leads to a contradiction.

For (*ii*): This follows the same argument as for (i). $\qquad\square$

As a consequence of Remark 3.1, we have the following corollary.

Corollary 3.1. If Y is compact and not empty, then Y is N-bounded and N is not empty.

3.3. Conditions for Pareto Optimality in the Outcome Space

In this section, necessary and/or sufficient conditions for a point y to be an N-point will be explored. In Section 3.3.1, a necessary and sufficient condition for general Y will be derived. In Section 3.3.2, conditions for the cases in which Y satisfies $\Lambda^{\leqq}$-convexity will be explored. Section 3.3.3 is devoted to a discussion of boundedness of tradeoff and proper efficient sets.

3.3.1. Conditions for a General Y

Theorem 3.4. $y^0 \in Y$ is an N-point iff for any $i \in \{1, 2, \ldots, q\}$, y^0 uniquely maximizes y_i for all $y \in Y_i(y^0) = \{y \in Y | y_k \geqq y_k^0, \ k \neq i, \ k = 1, \ldots, q\}$. [That is, $y_i^0 > y_i$ for all $y \in Y_i(y^0), y \neq y^0$).]

Proof. *For Sufficiency.* If y^0 uniquely maximizes y_i over $Y_i(y^0)$ for some $i \in \{1, \ldots, q\}$, then there is no $y \in Y$ such that $y \geqq y^0$. Thus, y^0 is an N-point.
For Necessity. If y^0 does not uniquely maximize y_i over $Y_i(y^0)$, then there is a $y \in Y_i(y^0)$, $y \neq y^0$ with $y_i \geqq y_i^0$. Thus, $y \geqq y^0$. As $y \neq y^0$, $y \geqq y^0$. This contradicts the statement that y^0 is an N-point.   □

Theorem 3.5. (i) If $y^0 \in Y$ maximizes $\lambda \cdot y$, for some $\lambda \in \Lambda^>$, over Y, then y^0 is an N-point.
(ii) If $y^0 \in Y$ *uniquely* maximizes $\lambda \cdot y$, for some $\lambda \in \Lambda^{\geqq}$, over Y, then y^0 is an N-point.

Proof. If y^0 is a D-point, then there is a $y \in Y$ with $y = y^0 + h$ and $h \in \Lambda^{\geqq}$. As $y = y^0 + h$, $\lambda \cdot y > \lambda \cdot y^0$ if $\lambda \in \Lambda^>$ and $\lambda \cdot y \geqq \lambda \cdot y^0$ if $\lambda \in \Lambda^{\geqq}$. Thus, y^0 cannot maximize $\lambda \cdot y$ with $\lambda \in \Lambda^>$ over Y [which proves (i)], and neither can y^0 uniquely maximize $\lambda \cdot y$ with $\lambda \in \Lambda^{\geqq}$ over Y [which proves (ii)].   □

Remark 3.2. Theorems 3.4 and 3.5 are valid for any set Y, clearly including nonconvex and discrete sets and sets of any shape. Theorem 3.5 states sufficient conditions, and Theorem 3.4 gives a necessary and sufficient condition. Theorem 3.5 states that if y^0 maximizes a linear weighted function $\lambda \cdot y$ with λ in a proper region, then y^0 is an N-point. Theorem 3.4 states that an N-point must *uniquely* maximize one axis y_i over $Y_i(y^0)$, which is the set of outcomes satisfying $y_k \geqq y_k^0$, $k \neq i$, $k = 1, \ldots, q$. The selection of i is arbitrary. Thus, in search of N-points, the maximization criterion and constraints are *interchangeable*. This is also related to a satisficing solution concept as follows.

Theorem 3.6. A necessary and sufficient condition for $y^0 \in Y$ to be an N-point is that for any $i \in \{1, 2, \ldots, q\}$, there are $q - 1$ constants $r(i) =$

$\{r_k | k \neq i, \ k = 1, \ldots, q\}$ so that y^0 *uniquely* maximizes y_i over $Y(r(i)) = \{y \in Y | y_k \geqq r_k, \ k \neq i, \ k = 1, \ldots, q\}$.

Proof. The necessity follows directly from Theorem 3.4 by setting $r_k = y^0_k$, $k \neq i, \ k = 1, \ldots, q$. To see the sufficiency, assume that y^0 is a D-point. Then there is a $y \in y^0 + \Lambda^{\geqq}$. Thus, any $Y(r(i))$ that contains y^0 will also contain y and y^0 cannot uniquely maximize y_i over $Y(r(i))$. This leads to a contradiction. $\square$

Remark 3.3. Each constant $r_k, \ k \neq i, \ i = 1, \ldots, q$, can be regarded as a satisficing level for criterion k. Theorem 3.6 essentially says that to be Pareto optimal, it is necessary and sufficient for the outcome y^0 to *uniquely maximize* some criterion, while maintaining some satisficing levels for the remaining criteria. The choice of i is arbitrary. Any criterion can be either the objective for maximization or a constraint at some satisficing level. Theorem 3.6 thus converts locating Pareto optimal solutions into solving mathematical programming problems or optimal control problems.

3.3.2. Conditions when Y Is $\Lambda^{\leqq}$-Convex

The following concept plays an important role in studying Pareto optimality.

Definition 3.2. The set Y is $\Lambda^{\leqq}$-*convex* iff $Y + \Lambda^{\leqq}$ is a convex set.

Example 3.1. Given $\Lambda^{\leqq}$, as shown in Figure 3.3a, Y_1 in Figure 3.3b is $\Lambda^{\leqq}$-convex, but Y_2 in Figure 3.3c is not $\Lambda^{\leqq}$-convex.

Example 3.2. The set $Y = \{(y_1, y_2) | 0 \leqq y_1 \leqq 1, \ 0 \leqq y_2 \leqq (1 - y_1)^2\}$ is not $\Lambda^{\leqq}$-convex. However, $\{(1, 1)\} \cup Y$ is $\Lambda^{\leqq}$-convex. (See Figure 3.4 and check it.)

Note that $\Lambda^{\leqq}$ is a convex cone. Indeed, the concept of $\Lambda^{\leqq}$-convexity is a special case of cone convexity of Yu (Ref. 495) which we will discuss in

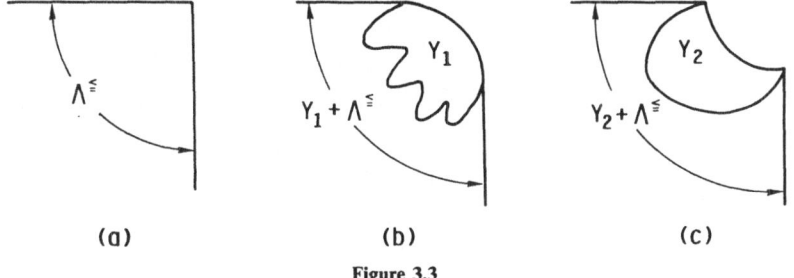

(a)   (b)   (c)

Figure 3.3

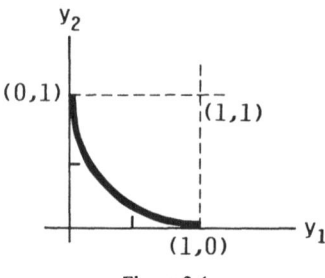

Figure 3.4

Chapter 7. As a special case of Theorem 7.13, of Chapter 7, we show the following.

Theorem 3.7. If each $f_i(x)$, $i = 1, \ldots, q$, is concave on a convex set X, then $Y = \{f(x) | x \in X\}$, where $f = (f_1, \ldots, f_q)$, is $\Lambda^\leqq$-convex.

Proof. Let $y^k = f(x^k) + h^k$ for $k = 1, 2$; $x^k \in X$ and $h^k \in \Lambda^\leqq$. For any $\lambda \in [0, 1]$, $\lambda y^1 + (1 - \lambda)y^2 = \lambda f(x^1) + (1 - \lambda)f(x^2) + \lambda h^1 + (1 - \lambda)h^2 \leqq f(\lambda x^1 + (1 - \lambda)x^2) + \lambda h^1 + (1 - \lambda)h^2 \in Y + \Lambda^\leqq$.

(The above inequality follows from the concavity of f. The last conclusion follows from the fact that $\lambda h^1 + (1 - \lambda)h^2 \in \Lambda^\leqq$ because $\Lambda^\leqq$ is convex.) Thus, $Y + \Lambda^\leqq$ is a convex set. $\qquad\square$

As a special case of Theorem 7.14 of Chapter 7, we have the following theorem.

Theorem 3.8. If Y is $\Lambda^\leqq$-convex, then a necessary condition for $y^0 \in Y$ to be an N-point is that y^0 maximizes $\lambda \cdot y$ over Y for some $\lambda \in \Lambda^\geqq$.

Proof. By Theorem 3.2, if y^0 is an N-point of Y, y^0 is also an N-point of $Y + \Lambda^\leqq$. This also implies that $0 = y^0 - y^0$ is an N-point of $(Y - y^0) + \Lambda^\leqq$. Thus, $(Y - y^0) + \Lambda^\leqq \cap \Lambda^\geqq = \varnothing$. Since both $(Y - y^0) + \Lambda^\leqq$ and $\Lambda^\geqq$ are convex sets, by the separation theorem of convex sets (for instance, see Ref. 438), there is $\lambda \neq 0$ so that

$$\lambda \cdot y \geqq 0 \quad \text{for all } y \in \Lambda^\geqq, \tag{3.1}$$

and

$$\lambda \cdot y \leqq 0 \quad \text{for all } y \in (Y - y^0) + \Lambda^\leqq. \tag{3.2}$$

However, (3.1) implies that $\lambda \in \Lambda^\geqq$; and (3.2) implies that $\lambda(y - y^0) \leqq 0$ for all $y \in Y$, or y^0 maximizes $\lambda \cdot y$ over Y, which we wanted to show. $\qquad\square$

Example 3.3. Let $Y = \{(y_1, y_2) | 0 \leqq y_1 \leqq 1, \; 0 \leqq y_2 \leqq (1 - y_1)^2\}$ as in Example 3.2. Recall that Y is not $\Lambda^\leqq$-convex. $N = \{(y_1, y_2) | y_2 = (1 - y_1)^2,$

$0 \leq y_1 \leq 1\}$. Except for points $(0, 1)$ and $(1, 0)$ of N, none of the N-points can be located by maximizing $\lambda \cdot y$ for some $\lambda \in \Lambda^=$ over Y. However, $Y \cup \{(1, 1)\}$ is $\Lambda^{\leq}$-convex and $N[Y \cup \{(1, 1)\}] = \{(1, 1)\}$, which can be easily located by maximizing $\lambda \cdot y$ for some $\lambda \in \Lambda^=$ over $Y \cup \{(1, 1)\}$.

Definition 3.3. Given $\lambda \in R^q$ and $\Lambda \subset R^q$, define $Y^0(\lambda) = \{y^0 \in Y | y^0$ maximizes $\lambda \cdot y$ over $Y\}$ and $Y^0(\Lambda) = \bigcup \{Y^0(\lambda) | \lambda \in \Lambda\}$.

By invoking Theorems 3.5 and 3.8, we have the following theorem.

Theorem 3.9. Given $Y \subset R^q$,
i. $Y^0(\Lambda^>) \subset N$;
ii. if Y is $\Lambda^{\leq}$-convex, then $N \subset Y^0(\Lambda^=)$, and $Y^0(\Lambda^>) \subset N \subset Y^0(\Lambda^=)$.
$$(3.3)$$

Remark 3.4. Theorem 3.9 says that if Y is $\Lambda^{\leq}$-convex, then to locate all Pareto optimal solutions, N, one can approximate by $Y^0(\Lambda^>)$, the *inner approximation*, and by $Y^0(\Lambda^=)$, the *outer approximation*. The "inclusion" of (3.3) can be sharpened as follows. [For its proof, see Hartley (Ref. 195) or Exercise 3.10.]

Theorem 3.10. If Y is compact and $\Lambda^{\leq}$-convex *or* $Y + \Lambda^{\leq}$ is convex and closed, then
$$Y^0(\Lambda^>) \subset N \subset \text{Cl } Y^0(\Lambda^>), \qquad (3.4)$$

where $\text{Cl } Y^0(\Lambda^>)$ denotes the closure of $Y^0(\Lambda^>)$.

Remark 3.5. Theorems 3.8–3.10 have important implications for applications. Suppose that only partial preference information is available. Under what conditions can one use maximization of the linearly weighted function $\lambda \cdot y$ to locate the "maximal preference" point? The "linear weighted method" has prevailed in literature and in practice. Here we shall supply a result to justify the linear weighted method without using the more traditional "preference separability or independence" assumptions. (See Chapters 5, 6 for more details.)

Definition 3.4. A value function $v: Y \to R^1$ is *increasing in a convex cone* Λ if $v(y + h) > v(y)$ whenever $\{y, y + h\} \subset Y$ and $h \in \Lambda$, $h \neq 0$.

Theorem 3.11. (i) If y^0 is a maximum point over Y of some value function that is increasing in $\Lambda^=$, then y^0 must be an N-point in Pareto preference.
(ii) If y^0 is a maximum point over Y of some value function that is increasing in $\Lambda^{\geq}$, and Y is $\Lambda^{\leq}$-convex, then there is a $\lambda \in \Lambda^=$ such that y^0 also maximizes $\lambda \cdot y$ over Y.

Proof. (i) can be obtained by contradiction, while (ii) follows immediately from Theorem 3.8.   □

Example 3.4. Consider an outcome space Y (not a convex set) and $Y + \Lambda^{\leqq}$ as shown in Figure 3.5.

The shaded boundary of Y represents the set of all nondominated points (N-points, Pareto optimal points). Every extreme or boundary point of this cone-convex set has a supporting function. Consider an extreme point y^0. Line L represents a supporting function. We see that there exists a λ such that $\lambda \cdot y$ has a maximum at y^0 over $Y + \Lambda^{\leqq}$. In other words, every other point in Y is inferior to y^0 since y^0 maximizes $\lambda \cdot y$ over Y (i.e., $\lambda \cdot y^0 \geqq \lambda \cdot y$).

Remark 3.6. To maximize a preference that reveals only that "more is better for each criterion" is equivalent, in the abstract, to maximizing a value function which is increasing in $\Lambda^{\geqq}$. Theorem 3.11 shows that, in search of an optimal point under this circumstance, one can start with maximizing $\lambda \cdot y$ (a linearly weighted function) over Y with $\lambda \in \Lambda^{\geqq}$ whenever Y is $\Lambda^{\leqq}$-convex. Note that no other conditions, such as preference separability (to be discussed in Chapter 5), are imposed. However, the search for optimality may take a sequence of iterations (by varying λ).

3.3.3. Boundedness of Tradeoff and Proper Efficiency

For illustration, let us first consider a two-criteria case. Here $q = 2$. If $y^0 = (y_1^0, y_2^0) \sim y^1 = (y_1^1, y_2^1)$, we may think that $y_1^0 - y_1^1 = \Delta y_1$ has been *traded for* $y_2^1 - y_2^0 = \Delta y_2$ to maintain "equal preference." The *rate of tradeoff* is $\Delta y_2 / \Delta y_1$ for each unit of y_1. The rate may vary with y^0 and y^1. This concept of exchange or tradeoff between y^0 and y^1 plays an important role in human thinking and

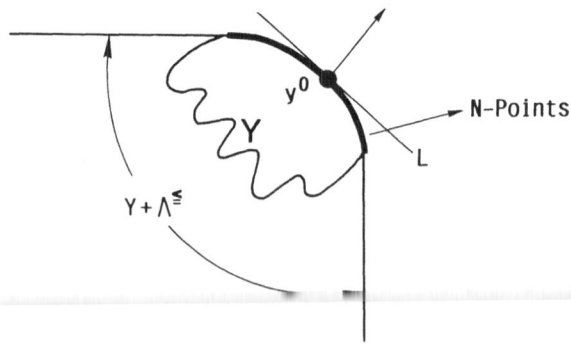

Figure 3.5

ranking processes and in economic literature. Our focus on this situation is to study the tradeoff among N-points. Is it possible to have an infinite rate of tradeoff among N-points? The following example answers this question in the affirmative.

Example 3.5. Let Y be defined by (see Figure 3.6)

$$0 < y_2 < 2,$$

and

$$0 \leq y_1 \leq 1 + (y_2 - 1)^2 \quad \text{if } 0 < y_2 \leq 1,$$

$$0 \leq y_1 \leq 1 - (y_2 - 1)^2 \quad \text{if } 1 \leq y_2 < 2.$$

Note that N is the northeastern boundary of Y or $N = \{(y_1, y_2)|0 < y_2 < 2,$ $y_1 = 1 + (y_2 - 1)^2$ if $0 < y_2 \leq 1$ and $y_1 = 1 - (y_2 - 1)^2$ if $1 \leq y_2 < 2\}$. Along N,

$$\frac{dy_1}{dy_2} = \begin{cases} 2(y_2 - 1) & \text{if } 0 < y_2 \leq 1, \\ -2(y_2 - 1) & \text{if } 1 \leq y_2 < 2. \end{cases}$$

At point $(1, 1)$, $dy_1/dy_2 = 0$ and dy_2/dy_1 is undefined $(-\infty)$. The tradeoff ratio between y_2 and y_1 is arbitrarily large when y_1 is sufficiently close to 1.

Recall that an N-point is also called an efficient point. An efficient point that allows unbounded tradeoff [such as $(1, 1)$ in Example 3.5] is usually called an *improper efficient point*. For simplicity, we shall define an *improper N-point*, according to Geoffrion (Ref. 163), as follows:

Definition 3.5. An N-point y^0 is *improper* iff for any arbitrary constant $M > 0$ (in R^1), there is $y \in Y$ and an i such that $y_i - y_i^0 > M(y_j^0 - y_j)$ for all $j \neq i$. An N-point y^0 is *proper* iff it is not improper; i.e., there is a constant $M > 0$ so that for every $y \in Y$ which has an i such that $y_i > y_i^0$, there is a j with $y_i - y_i^0 < M(y_j^0 - y_j)$.

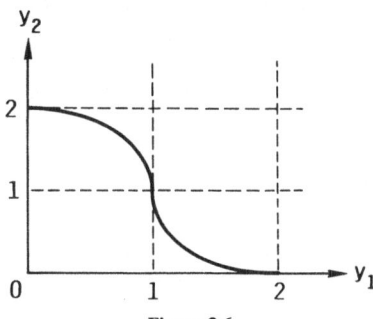

Figure 3.6

Note that in Example 3.5, except $(1, 1)$, all of the other N-points are proper. (Check it!)

Now suppose that N can be specified by an *isovalued surface* of a value function V as $N = \{y \mid V(y) = v^0\}$. Suppose that $y^0 \in N$ and N is smooth at y^0 (i.e., all partial derivatives of V are continuous and nonzero at y^0). Then, according to the implicit function theorem and differentiation of an implicit function (see Ref. 334, Chapter 9, for instance), any variable y_i can be expressed as a function of the other variables and the instantaneous tradeoff ratio among any y_i and y_j over N at y^0 (while other variables are held constant) is given by

$$\frac{\partial y_i}{\partial y_j} = -\frac{\dfrac{\partial V}{\partial y_j}(y^0)}{\dfrac{\partial V}{\partial y_i}(y^0)}. \tag{3.5}$$

Suppose that $V(y) = \sum_i \lambda_i y_i$, a linear weighted function with each $\lambda_i > 0$. Then, using (3.5) one obtains

$$\frac{\partial y_i}{\partial y_j} = -\frac{\lambda_j}{\lambda_i}, \tag{3.6}$$

which holds for any y_i and y_j at any point y with respect to any isovalued surface (hyperplane) of $V(y) = v^0$.

Assume that y^0 is an N-point which maximizes $\lambda \cdot y$, $\lambda \in \Lambda^>$, over Y. Then Y is contained by the half-space $\{y \in R^q \mid \lambda \cdot y \le \lambda \cdot y^0\}$. Since the tradeoff ratio on the plane defined by $\lambda \cdot y = \lambda \cdot y^0$ is bounded [because of (3.6)], one expects that y^0 must be a proper N-point. This is confirmed by the following theorem.

Theorem 3.12. If y^0 maximizes $\lambda \cdot y$, $\lambda > 0$, over Y, then y^0 is a proper N-point.

Proof. By theorem 3.5(i), we see that y^0 is an N-point. Assume the contrary, i.e., that y^0 is improper. Let $M = (q - 1)\max_{(i,j)}\{\lambda_i/\lambda_j\}$. Then there is a $y \in Y$ with some $y_i > y_i^0$ and $y_i - y_i^0 > M(y_j^0 - y_j) > (q - 1)(\lambda_j/\lambda_i)(y_j^0 - y_j)$ for all $j \ne i$. Multiplying the above inequalities by $\lambda_i/(q - 1)$ and summing over $j \ne i$, we have

$$\lambda_i(y_i - y_i^0) > \sum_{j \ne i} \lambda_j(y_j^0 - y_j)$$

or

$$\sum \lambda_k y_k = \lambda \cdot y > \sum \lambda_k y_k^0 = \lambda \cdot y^0,$$

which leads to a contradiction.   □

The following theorem further strengthens the relationship between proper N-points and maximization of $\lambda \cdot y$, $\lambda > 0$, when Y is $\Lambda^{\leqq}$-convex.

Theorem 3.13. Assume that Y is $\Lambda^{\leqq}$-convex. Then y^0 is a proper N-point iff y^0 maximizes $\lambda \cdot y$ over Y for some $\lambda > 0$.

Proof. The sufficiency is given by Theorem 3.12. It suffices to show the necessity. Assume that y^0 is a proper N-point in Y. By Definition 3.5, y^0 is also a proper N-point in $Y + \Lambda^{\leqq}$ (see Exercise 3.11). By assumption $Y + \Lambda^{\leqq}$ is a convex set. Thus, there is $M > 0$ such that for each $y \in Y + \Lambda^{\leqq}$ with $y_i > y_i^0$ there is $j \neq i$ such that

$$y_i - y_i^0 \leqq M(y_j^0 - y_j),$$

or the following system has no solution in $y + \Lambda^{\leqq}$:

$$y_i > y_i^0,$$

$$y_i + My_j > y_i^0 + My_j^0, \qquad j \neq i.$$

Using the Generalized Gordon Theorem (see Section 3.6), there are nonnegative λ_i^i, λ_j^i, $j = 1, 2, \ldots, q$, $j \neq i$, not all zero, so that, for all $y \in Y + \Lambda^{\leqq}$, the following holds:

$$\sum_k \lambda_k^i y_i + \sum_{j \neq i} \lambda_j^i My_j \leqq \sum_k \lambda_k^i y_i^0 + \sum_{j \neq i} \lambda_j^i My_j^0. \tag{3.7}$$

Note that

$$\sum_k \lambda_k^i > 0. \tag{3.8}$$

Since the choice of i is arbitrary, (3.7) is valid for all $i = 1, \ldots, q$. Summing over i, one obtains

$$\sum_i \left(\sum_k \lambda_k^i \right) y_i + \sum_i \sum_{j \neq i} \lambda_j^i My_j \leqq \sum_i \sum_k \lambda_k^i y^0 + \sum_i \sum_{j \neq i} \lambda_j^i My_j^0$$

or

$$\sum_i \left(\sum_k \lambda_k^i + M \sum_{k \neq i} \lambda_i^k \right) y_i \leqq \sum_i \left(\sum_k \lambda_k^i + M \sum_{k \neq i} \lambda_i^k \right) y_i^0.$$

In view of (3.8), each $\lambda_i^0 = \sum_k \lambda_k^i + M \sum_{k \neq i} \lambda_i^k > 0$. Let $\lambda^0 = (\lambda_1^0, \ldots, \lambda_q^0)$. We see that y^0 maximizes $\lambda^0 \cdot y$ and $\lambda^0 > 0$. $\qquad \square$

Remark 3.7. As many scholars have made contributions to proper efficiency [for instance, see Benson and Morin (Ref. 43), Borwein (Ref. 58), Hartley (Ref. 195), Henig (Ref. 205)], there are a number of definitions. Here for simplicity the definition is primarily adapted from that of Geoffrion (Ref. 163). Some further extension and discussion will be given in Chapter 7. One can observe that at improper N-points, tradeoff ratios can be made arbitrarily large. An improper N-point can then hardly be the final solution. Indeed, it will be shown (Chapter 7) that an improper N-point is a limit point of proper N-points when one varies the dominated cone.

3.4. Conditions for Pareto Optimality in the Decision Space

Definition 3.6. A point x^0 in decision space X is an N-point if and only if $f(x^0)$ is an N-point in the criteria space $Y = f[X]$. The set of all N-points in X will be denoted by N_X, or N when no confusion will occur.

Using the results of Section 3.3 and mathematical programming or optimal control theory, one can derive a number of results for the conditions of N-points in the decision space. In Section 3.4.1, we will summarize the results in terms of single criterion maximization. Section 3.4.2 will be devoted to problems with suitable differentiability. Section 3.4.3 gives a decomposition method while Section 3.4.4 gives an illustrative example.

3.4.1. Conditions in Terms of Single Criterion Maximization

Using Theorems 3.4–3.6, we obtain conditions for N-points in general cases as follows.

Theorem 3.14. (i) A necessary condition for $x^0 \in X$ to be an N-point is that for any $i \in \{1, 2, \ldots, q\}$, $f_i(x^0)$ uniquely maximizes $f_i(x)$ for all $x \in X_i(x^0) = \{x \in X | f_k(x) \geq f_k(x^0), k \neq i, k = 1, \ldots, q\}$. A sufficient condition for x^0 to be an N-point is that x^0 indeed is the unique maximum point of the above problem.

(ii) x^0 is an N-point if x^0 maximizes $\lambda \cdot f(x)$ over X for some $\lambda \in \Lambda^>$ or uniquely maximizes $\lambda \cdot f(x)$ over X for some $\lambda \in \Lambda^{\geq}$.

(iii) A necessary condition for x^0 to be an N-point is that for any $i \in \{1, 2, \ldots, q\}$, there are $q - 1$ constants $r(i) = \{r_k | k \neq i, k = 1, \ldots, q\}$, so that $f_i(x^0)$ uniquely maximizes $f_i(x)$ over

$$X(r(i)) = \{x \in X | f_k(x) \geq r_k, k \neq i, k = 1, \ldots, q\}. \tag{3.9}$$

A sufficient condition for x^0 to be an N-point is that x^0 indeed is the unique maximum point of the above problem.

Proof. (i) is from Theorem 3.4; (ii), from Theorem 3.5; and (iii), from Theorem 3.6. In the proof, one has to observe that $y_i = f_i(x)$ and that the maximization of y_i may not be unique. Given that it is unique, the corresponding solution in X may not be unique. □

Using Theorem 3.7 and 3.8, we have the following theorem.

Theorem 3.15. If X is a convex set and each $f_i(x)$, $i = 1, \ldots, q$ is concave or $f[X]$ is $\Lambda^\leq$-convex, then for $x^0 \in X$ to be an N-point it is necessary that x^0 maximizes $\lambda \cdot f(x)$ over X for some $\lambda \in \Lambda^\geq$.

Remark 3.8. Observe that Theorems 3.14 and 3.15 state conditions for N-points in terms of maximization of a single criterion with or without extra constraints. While Theorem 3.14 is true for all general cases, Theorem 3.15 requires cone-convexity. To find whether a particular point x^0 is an N-point or not, one can apply either of the two theorems. To find the entire set of N-points, one must use appropriate mathematical programming techniques, and vary the parameters $r(i)$ of Theorem 3.14(iii) or λ of Theorem 3.15 in their appropriate ranges. That is, $r(i)$ must vary from a lower bound to an upper bound of $f_j(x)$, $x \in X$, $j \neq i$, $j = 1, \ldots, q$; while λ must vary over $\Lambda^\geq$.

Example 3.6. Consider the following multicriteria problem with two objectives:

$$\text{Max } f_1(x_1, x_2) = 4x_1 - x_2,$$

$$\text{Max } f_2(x_1, x_2) = -2x_1 + 5x_2,$$

subject to

$$2x_1 + 3x_2 \leq 12,$$

$$x_2 \leq 3,$$

$$3x_1 - x_2 \geq 0,$$

$$x_1, x_2 \geq 0.$$

The set of points satisfying the above inequalities is X. We can convert the above problem to a mathematical programming problem with one objective using Theorem 3.14(iii). Let us assume that f_1 has been chosen for maximization. Then the problem can be set up in the following way:

$$\text{Max } f_1(x_1, x_2) = 4x_1 - x_2,$$

$$\text{s.t. } x \in X,$$

$$f_2(x_1, x_2) = -2x_1 + 5x_2 \geq r_2,$$

where r_2 is a satisficing level for f_2. By minimizing and maximizing f_2 over X, we find $-12 \leq f_2(x) \leq 13$.

Solving the above linear programs with r_2 varying from -12 to 13 we can find all N-points. The following are some representative N-points in X and Y corresponding to some values of r_2:

r_2	(x_1, x_2)	(f_1, f_2)
-12	$(6, 0)$	$(24, -12)$ A
-7	$(5.0625, 0.625)$	$(19.625, -7)$ B
-2	$(4.125, 1.25)$	$(15.25, -2)$ C
3	$(3.1875, 1.875)$	$(10.875, 3)$ D
8	$(2.25, 2.5)$	$(6.5, 8)$ E
13	$(1, 3)$	$(1, 13)$ F

Figures 3.7 and 3.8 illustrate X, Y, and the corresponding N-points. Note that as f is linear, f maps polyhedron X to another polyhedron Y and that the extreme points of Y correspond to those of X. As Y is convex, all N-points can also be located using Theorem 3.15. The reader can find such (λ_1, λ_2) for each N-point using Figure 3.8 [i.e., what (λ_1, λ_2) would make $A, B, \ldots,$ or F a maximum point of $\lambda_1 f_1 + \lambda_2 f_2$ over Y? Consider G for instance. All λ satisfying $\lambda \cdot (y - G) \leq 0, y \in Y$, can make G the maximum point of $\lambda \cdot f$].

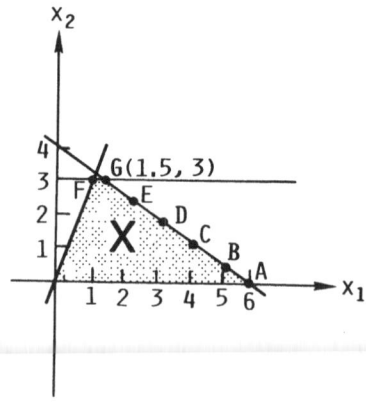

Figure 3.7. Decision space.

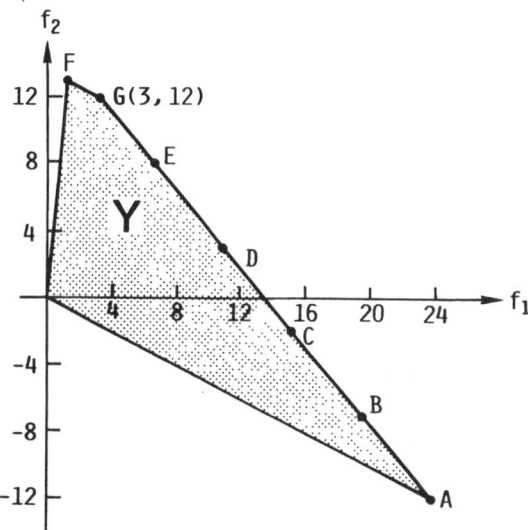

Figure 3.8. Outcome space.

3.4.2. Conditions in Terms of Differentiability

For simplicity, "a function is differentiable over X" is used to mean "the function is differentiable over an open set containing X."

Throughout this section it will be assumed that $X = \{x \in R^n | g(x) \leqq 0\}$ where $g(x) = (g_1(x), g_2(x), \ldots, g_m(x))$ and each $g_j \colon R^n \to R^1$ is differentiable over X. Also, it will be assumed that each criterion f_i is differentiable over X. Then one can readily apply the known results in mathematical programming and Theorems 3.14 and 3.15 to obtain necessary and/or sufficient conditions for N-points in the decision space. For instance, if (iii) of Theorem 3.14 is of interest, we can define

$$L = \mu_i f_i(x) - \sum_{k \neq i} \mu_k [r_k - f_k(x)] - \sum_{j=1}^{m} \lambda_j g_j(x)$$

$$= \sum_{k=1}^{q} \mu_k f_k(x) - \sum_{j=1}^{m} \lambda_j g_j(x) - \sum_{k \neq i} \mu_k r_k, \qquad (3.10)$$

where r_k, $k \neq i$, $k = 1, \ldots, q$ are parameters with values selected from $[\underline{r}_k, \bar{r}_k]$ where $\underline{r}_k$ and $\bar{r}_k$ are the greatest lower bound (g.l.b.) and the least upper bound (l.u.b.), respectively, of $\{f_k(x) | x \in X\}$. Let $\underline{r}(i)$ and $\bar{r}(i)$ be the vectors of $\{\underline{r}_k | k = 1, \ldots, q, k \neq i\}$ and $\{\bar{r}_k | k = 1, \ldots, q, k \neq i\}$, respectively.

Theorem 3.16. Suppose that $f(x)$ and $g(x)$ are differentiable over X. Then,

(i) a necessary condition for $x^0 \in X$ to be an N-point is that there exists $r(i) \in R^{q-1}$, $\underline{r}(i) \leq r(i) \leq \bar{r}(i)$, $\mu_k \geq 0$, $k = 1, \ldots, q$, and $\lambda_j \geq 0$, $j = 1, \ldots, m$, where not all μ_k and λ_j are zeros, such that, with respect to (3.10), the following conditions are satisfied:

$$\nabla_x L(x^0) = \upsilon \tag{3.11}$$

[$\nabla_x L(x^0)$ is the gradient of $L(x)$ w.r.t. x at x^0],

$$\mu_k(r_k - f_k(x^0)) = 0, \qquad k = 1, \ldots, q, \ k \neq i, \tag{3.12}$$

$$r_k - f_k(x^0) \leq 0, \qquad k = 1, \ldots, q, \ k \neq i, \tag{3.13}$$

$$\lambda_j \cdot g_j(x^0) = 0, \tag{3.14}$$

$$g_j(x^0) \leq 0, \qquad j = 1, \ldots, m; \tag{3.15}$$

(ii) if x^0 satisfies the necessary condition of (i), and $X(r(i))$ as defined in (3.9) is a convex set and $f_i(x)$ is strictly concave over $X(r(i))$ or if x^0 uniquely maximizes f_i over $X(r(i))$, then x^0 is an N-point.

Proof. (i) is a direct application of Fritz John's theorem (see Section 3.7 or Ref. 307 for an example) and Theorem 3.14(iii). Conditions in (ii) are imposed to assure that x^0 is the unique maximum point and thus is an N-point [(iii) of Theorem 3.14]. $\qquad\square$

Now let us apply Theorem 3.15 to obtain another set of conditions for x^0 to be an N-point. Toward this end, define

$$X^0(\lambda) = \{x^0 \in X | \lambda \cdot f(x^0) \geq \lambda \cdot f(x), \ x \in X\}, \tag{3.16}$$

$$X^0(\Lambda^{\geq}) = \bigcup \{X^0(\lambda) | \lambda \in \Lambda^{\geq}\}, \tag{3.17}$$

$$X^0(\Lambda^{>}) = \bigcup \{X^0(\lambda) | \lambda \in \Lambda^{>}\}. \tag{3.18}$$

Note that $X^0(\lambda)$ is the set of maximum points of $\lambda \cdot f(x)$ over X. Theorem 3.15 can be rewritten as follows.

Theorem 3.17. If X is convex and each $f_i(x)$, $i = 1, \ldots, q$, is concave *or* if $f[X]$ is $\Lambda^{\leq}$-convex, then $X^0(\Lambda^{>}) \subset N_X \subset X^0(\Lambda^{\geq})$.

In view of this theorem, it is appropriate to call $X^0(\Lambda^{>})$ and $X^0(\Lambda^{\geq})$ the *inner* and *outer approximate sets* of N_X. Since finding $X^0(\lambda)$ is a mathematical programming problem, Theorem 3.17 transforms the problem of finding N-points into a family of mathematical programming problems.

Recall that $X = \{x \in R^n | g(x) \leq 0\}$, where $g = (g_1, \ldots, g_m)$. Suppose that $f(x)$ and $g(x)$ are differentiable over X. By Fritz John's theorem, $x^0 \in X^0(\lambda)$, $\lambda \neq 0$, only if there are $\mu_0 \in R^1$ and $\mu \in R^m$ such that

$$\mu_0 \lambda \cdot \nabla f(x^0) - \mu \cdot \nabla g(x^0) = 0, \tag{3.19}$$

$$\mu \cdot g(x^0) = 0, \tag{3.20}$$

$$g(x^0) \leq 0, \tag{3.21}$$

$$\mu_0 \geq 0, \quad \mu \geq 0, \quad (\mu_0, \mu) \neq (0, 0). \tag{3.22}$$

In the above, $\nabla f = (\nabla f_1, \ldots, \nabla f_q)$. ∇g is defined similarly: Let $I(x^0) = \{i | g_i(x^0) = 0\}$, and let $\mu_{I(x^0)}$ and $g_{I(x^0)}(x^0)$ be the vectors derived from μ and $g(x^0)$, respectively, by deleting all components of μ and $g(x^0)$ which are not in $I(x^0)$. Define

$$F^=(x^0) = \{\lambda \cdot \nabla f(x^0) | \lambda \in \Lambda^=\}, \tag{3.23}$$

$$F^>(x^0) = \{\lambda \cdot \nabla f(x^0) | \lambda \in \Lambda^>\}, \tag{3.24}$$

$$G(x^0) = \{\mu_{I(x^0)} \cdot \nabla g_{I(x^0)}(x^0) | \mu_{I(x^0)} \geq 0\}. \tag{3.25}$$

It is understood that $G(x^0) = \{0\}$ if $I(x^0) = \emptyset$.

Note that $\mu \cdot g(x^0) = 0$ implies that $\mu_i = 0$ if $g_i(x^0) < 0$. By (3.19)–(3.22), two possible cases need to be considered.

Case 1: $\mu_0 = 0$. Then $\mu \neq 0$, $\mu_{I(x^0)} \geq 0$. Thus $x^0 \in X^0(\Lambda^=)$ or $x^0 \in X^0(\Lambda^>)$ only if

$$0 \in \{\mu_{I(x^0)} \cdot \nabla g_{I(x^0)}(x^0) | \mu_{I(x^0)} \geq 0\}. \tag{3.26}$$

Case 2: $\mu_0 > 0$. Without loss of generality, we can set $\mu_0 = 1$. [Divide (3.19) by μ_0, if necessary.] Then, $x^0 \in X^0(\Lambda^=)$ only if

$$F^=(x^0) \cap G(x^0) \neq \emptyset \tag{3.27}$$

and $x^0 \in X^0(\Lambda^>)$ only if

$$F^>(x^0) \cap G(x^0) \neq \emptyset. \tag{3.28}$$

The above results can be summarized as follows.

Theorem 3.18. Suppose $f[X]$ is $\Lambda^{\leq}$-convex and $f(x)$ and $g(x)$ are differentiable over X. Then
   i. $x^0 \in X^0(\Lambda^=)$ only if $x^0 \in X$ and (3.26) or (3.27) holds.
   ii. $x^0 \in X^0(\Lambda^>)$ only if $x^0 \in X$ and (3.26) or (3.28) holds.
   iii. x^0 is an N-point only if $x^0 \in X$ and (3.26) or (3.27) holds.

Observe that (3.19)–(3.22) can be a sufficient condition for $x^0 \in X^0(\lambda)$ when proper conditions are met.

Theorem 3.19. Suppose that over R^n or an open convex set containing X: (a) $g(x)$ is quasi-convex and differentiable, (b) each $f_i(x)$ is concave and differentiable, and (c) the Kuhn–Tucker constraint qualification is satisfied. Then

    i. $x^0 \in X^0(\Lambda^=)$ iff $x^0 \in X$ and $F^=(x^0) \cap G(x^0) \neq \varnothing$;

    ii. $x^0 \in X^0(\Lambda^>)$ iff $x^0 \in X$ and $F^>(x^0) \cap G(x^0) \neq \varnothing$;

    iii. given $x^0 \in X$, $F^=(x^0) \cap G(x^0) \neq \varnothing$ is a necessary condition for x^0 to be an N-point, and $F^>(x^0) \cap G(x^0) \neq \varnothing$ is a sufficient condition for x^0 to be an N-point.

Proof. Assertions (i) and (ii) come from the Kuhn–Tucker theorem. Under the assumptions, a necessary and sufficient condition for $x^0 \in X^0(\lambda)$ is that there is $\mu \in R^m$, $\mu \geqq 0$ such that (3.19)–(3.22) hold with $\mu_0 = 1$. Assertion (iii) is a restatement of Theorem 3.17. $\qquad\square$

Remark 3.9. (i) Note that Theorem 3.18 requires that $f[X]$ be $\Lambda^\leqq$-convex, while Theorem 3.19 requires conditions to ensure not only that $f[X]$ is $\Lambda^\leqq$-convex but also that $x^0 \in X^0(\lambda)$.

(ii) $F^=(x)$, $F^>(x)$, and $G(x)$, as defined by (3.23)–(3.25), are uniquely determined, for each $x \in X$. When f and g are linear in x, $F^=(x)$, $F^>(x)$, and $G(x)$ become constant convex cones, independent of x. When f and g are quadratic in x, $F^=(x)$, $F^>(x)$, and $G(x)$ are convex cones which vary linearly with x. These observations make it easier to locate the set of all N-points by using Theorems 3.18 and 3.19, as will be illustrated later.

(iii) Constraint qualifications other than Kuhn–Tucker (see Ref. 307) can be used to ensure the sufficiency conditions.

3.4.3. Decomposition Theorems of $X^0(\Lambda^=)$ and $X^0(\Lambda^>)$

Throughout this subsection, the assumptions of Section 3.4.2 will be used. Although Theorems 3.18 and 3.19 offer methods for locating $X^0(\Lambda^=)$ and $X^0(\Lambda^>)$, we still need some decomposition theorem on $X^0(\Lambda^=)$ and $X^0(\Lambda^>)$ to facilitate the procedure of locating them. Let $M = \{1, 2, \ldots, m\}$ and $\mathcal{M} = \{I | I \subset M\}$. For $I \in \mathcal{M}$, define

$$X_I = \{x \in R^n | g_I(x) \leqq 0\}, \tag{3.29}$$

where $g_I(x)$ is derived from $g(x)$ by deleting all components of $g(x)$ except those in I. Let N_I be *the set of all N-points in X_I*, and let $X_I^0(\Lambda^=)$ and $X_I^0(\Lambda^>)$

be the *outer* and *inner* approximate sets for N_I, respectively, as defined by (3.16)–(3.18) replacing X by X_I.

Example 3.7. To illustrate the main idea of decomposition theorems, let us consider the decision space X shown in Figure 3.9. To find N-points, we first try to find whether there are any N-points in the interior of X. We then check the boundary points with $g_i = 0$, $i = 1, 2, 3$. If there are no N-points among the boundary points with $g_i = 0$, $i = 1, 2, 3$, we can then check the possibility of N-points on the intersection points of $g_1 = 0$ and $g_2 = 0$, or $g_1 = 0$ and $g_3 = 0$, or $g_2 = 0$ and $g_3 = 0$, or $g_i = 0$ for all i.

Theorem 3.20. The following results hold:
i. $X^0(\Lambda^=) = \bigcup_{I \in \mathcal{M}} [X_I^0(\Lambda^=) \cap X]$;
ii. $X^0(\Lambda^>) = \bigcup_{I \in \mathcal{M}} [X_I^0(\Lambda^>) \cap X]$.

Proof. *For* (i): Because $X_M = X$ and $X^0(\Lambda^=) \subset X$, the fact that $X^0(\Lambda^=) \subset \bigcup_{I \in \mathcal{M}} [X_I^0(\Lambda^=) \cap X]$ is clear. Now suppose that $x^0 \in X_I^0(\Lambda^=) \cap X$ for some $I \in \mathcal{M}$. Then, since $x^0 \in X_I^0(\Lambda^=)$, x^0 maximizes $\lambda \cdot f(x)$ for some $\lambda \in \Lambda^=$ over $X_I \supset X$. Thus, $\lambda \cdot f(x^0) \geqq \lambda \cdot f(x)$ for all $x \in X$. Since $x^0 \in X$, $x^0 \in X^0(\Lambda^=)$. Thus, $X^0(\Lambda^=) \supset \bigcup_{I \in \mathcal{M}} [X_I^0(\Lambda^=) \cap X]$.

For (ii): The proof is similar to that for (i) and will be omitted.   □

Let us denote the number of elements in $I \in \mathcal{M}$ by $[I]$, and let $\mathcal{I}^k = \{I \in \mathcal{M} | [I] = k\}$, $k = 0, 1, \ldots, m$, with the understanding that $\mathcal{I}^0 = \{\varnothing\}$. For each $I \in \mathcal{M}$, define $\tilde{X}_I = \{x \in R^n | g_I(x) = 0\}$, with the understanding that $\tilde{X}_\varnothing = R^n$.

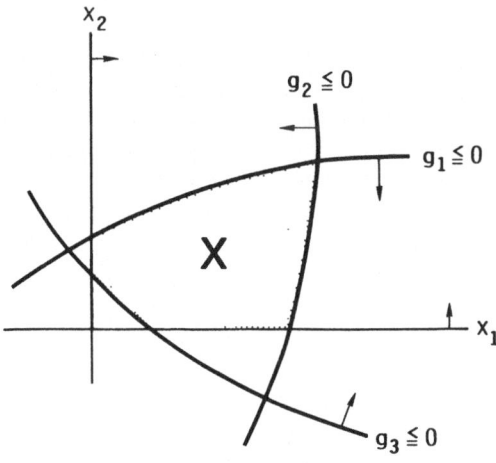

Figure 3.9

Theorem 3.21. If the assumptions of Theorem 3.19 are satisfied over R^n (instead of X), then

i. $X^0(\Lambda^=) = \bigcup_{k=0}^m \bigcup_{I \in \mathcal{I}^k} [X_I^0(\Lambda^=) \cap \tilde{X}_I \cap X]$;

ii. $X^0(\Lambda^>) = \bigcup_{k=0}^m \bigcup_{I \in \mathcal{I}^k} [X_I^0(\Lambda^>) \cap \tilde{X}_I \cap X]$;

iii. $X^0(\Lambda^>) \subset N_X \subset X^0(\Lambda^=)$.

Proof. *For* (i): It is clear from Theorem 3.20 that the sets on the right-hand side are contained by $X^0(\Lambda^=)$. In order to see that $X^0(\Lambda^=)$ is contained by the union of the sets in the right-hand side, let $x^0 \in X^0(\Lambda^=)$. By (i) of Theorem 3.19, $F^=(x^0) \cap G(x^0) \neq \varnothing$, where $F^=(x^0)$ and $G(x^0)$ are defined in (3.23) and (3.25), respectively. Recall that $I(x^0) = \{i | g_i(x^0) = 0\}$. Note that $F^=(x^0)$ is not dependent on $I(x^0)$. By applying Theorem 3.19 to the set $X_{I(x^0)}$, we see that $x^0 \in X_{I(x^0)}^0(\Lambda^=) \cap \tilde{X}_{I(x^0)}$. Since $x^0 \in X$, x^0 is contained by the union of the sets on the right-hand side with index $I(x^0)$.

The proof for (ii) is similar to that for (i) and will be omitted. Note that (iii) follows directly from Theorem 3.19. We rewrite it for the sake of completeness. $\qquad\square$

Remark 3.10. (i) The set $X_I^0(\Lambda^=) \cap \tilde{X}_I \cap X$ could be located by first finding those points of $X_I^0(\Lambda^=)$ on $\tilde{X}_I$, that is, $X_I^0(\Lambda^=) \cap \tilde{X}_I$, and then discarding those points of $X_I^0(\Lambda^=) \cap \tilde{X}_I$ which violate the constraints $g_i(x) \leq 0$, $i \in I$. Thus, Theorem 3.21 could be used to systematically locate $X_I^0(\Lambda^=)$, $X_I^0(\Lambda^>)$ and N_X.

(ii) Another application of Theorem 3.21 is to produce, for all $x^0 \in N_X$, *the set of optimal weights for* x^0. $\Lambda^*(x^0) = \{\lambda \in \Lambda^= | x^0 \in X^0(\lambda)\}$. Thus, if $\lambda \in \Lambda^*(x^0)$, then x^0 maximizes $\lambda \cdot f(x)$ over X. The set $\Lambda^*(x^0)$ is very important in the final deliberation of decision making. In the next subsection, an example is constructed to illustrate the procedures to generate $X^0(\Lambda^=)$, $X^0(\Lambda^>)$, N_X, and $\Lambda^*(x^0)$ for each $x^0 \in N_X$.

(iii) When both $f(x)$ and $g(x)$ are linear, one can first search for the set of all extreme N-points (i.e., extreme points which are N-points) and then use Theorem 3.21 to generate the entire set of N-points as will be discussed in Section 8.3.3. Observe that, when the number of constraints gets larger, the computational method directly using Theorem 3.21 may become very time consuming, unless the problem has a special structure such as $f(x)$ or $g(x)$ being linear in X.

3.4.4. An Example

Consider a multiple-criteria problem with the following objective functions:

$$f_1(x) = x_1 + x_2 + x_4,$$

$$f_2(x) = 2x_1 + x_3 - 2x_4,$$

and constraints

$$g_1(x) = x_1^2 + x_2^2 + x_3^2 \leqq 1,$$

$$g_2(x) = x_1 + x_4 \leqq 1,$$

$$g_3(x) = x_2 + x_3 - x_4 \leqq 1.$$

We want to find N_X, the set of all N-points. Note that the assumptions of Theorem 3.19 are satisfied. We shall use theorem 3.21 to find all N-points. Since

$$\nabla f_1(x) = (1, 1, 0, 1),$$

$$\nabla f_2(x) = (2, 0, 1, -2),$$

we have

$$F^>(x) = F^> = \{\lambda_1(1, 1, 0, 1) + \lambda_2(2, 0, 1, -2)|\lambda_1 > 0, \lambda_2 > 0\}$$

$$= \{(\lambda_1 + 2\lambda_2, \lambda_1, \lambda_2, \lambda_1 - 2\lambda_2)|\lambda_1, \lambda_2 > 0\}, \tag{3.30}$$

$$F^=(x) = F^= = \{(\lambda_1 + 2\lambda_2, \lambda_1, \lambda_2, \lambda_1 - 2\lambda_2)|(\lambda_1, \lambda_2) \geqq (0, 0)\}. \tag{3.31}$$

To emphasize the decomposition index, $G_I(x)$ will be used to denote $G(x)$ of (3.25), for all $x \in X_I$. Since

$$\nabla g_1(x) = (2x_1, 2x_2, 2x_3, 0), \qquad \nabla g_2(x) = (1, 0, 0, 1),$$

$$\nabla g_3(x) = (0, 1, 1, -1),$$

we have

$$G_{\{1\}}(x) = \{\mu(x_1, x_2, x_3, 0)|\mu \geqq 0\}, \tag{3.32}$$

$$G_{\{2\}}(x) = \{\mu(1, 0, 0, 1)|\mu \geqq 0\}, \tag{3.33}$$

$$G_{\{3\}}(x) = \{\mu(0, 1, 1, -1)|\mu \geqq 0\}, \tag{3.34}$$

$$G_{\{1,2\}}(x) = \{\mu_1 x_1 + \mu_2, \mu_1 x_2, \mu_1 x_3, \mu_2)|\mu_1, \mu_2 \geqq 0\}, \tag{3.35}$$

$$G_{\{1,3\}}(x) = \{(\mu_1 x_1, \mu_1 x_2 + \mu_3, \mu_1 x_3 + \mu_3, -\mu_3)|\mu_1, \mu_3 \geqq 0\}, \tag{3.36}$$

$$G_{\{2,3\}}(x) = \{(\mu_2, \mu_3, \mu_3, \mu_2 - \mu_3)|\mu_2, \mu_3 \geqq 0\}, \tag{3.37}$$

$$G_{\{1,2,3\}}(x) = \{(\mu_1 x_1 + \mu_2, \mu_1 x_2 + \mu_3, \mu_1 x_3 + \mu_3, \mu_2 - \mu_3)|\mu_1, \mu_2, \mu_3 \geqq 0\}. \tag{3.38}$$

We are now ready to find $X^0(\Lambda^=)$ and $X^0(\Lambda^>)$. Without confusion, we shall use X_I^0 and X_I' to represent $X_I^0(\Lambda^=)$ and $X_I^0(\Lambda^>)$, respectively,

Step (1). To find $X_\varnothing^0 \cap X$ and $X_\varnothing' \cap X$. In view of (3.30) and (3.31), we know that $0 \notin F^>$ and $0 \notin F^=$. Thus,

$$X_\varnothing^0 = \varnothing, \; X_\varnothing' = \varnothing, \text{ and } X_\varnothing^0 \cap X = X_\varnothing' \cap X = \varnothing.$$

Step (2). For all I such that $[I] = 1$, there are three cases.
Case 1: $I = \{1\}$. We first find the set

$$X_I^> = \{x | F^> \cap G_I(x) \neq \varnothing\}.$$

Note that $x \in X_I^0(\Lambda^>)$ iff $x \in X_I^> \cap X_I$. In view of (3.30) and (3.32) for each $x \in X_I^>$, the following equalities (obtained by componentwise comparison) must be satisfied for some $\lambda_1, \lambda_2 > 0$ and $\mu \geqq 0$:

$$\mu x_1 = \lambda_1 + 2\lambda_2 \Rightarrow x_1 = (\lambda_1 + 2\lambda_2)/\mu, \mu > 0,$$

$$\mu x_2 = \lambda_1 \Rightarrow x_2 = \lambda_1/\mu, \mu > 0,$$

$$\mu x_3 = \lambda_2 \Rightarrow x_3 = \lambda_2/\mu, \mu > 0,$$

$$0 = \lambda_1 - 2\lambda_2 \Rightarrow \lambda_1 = 2\lambda_2.$$

Thus,

$$X_I^> = \{(4\lambda/\mu, 2\lambda/\mu, \lambda/\mu, x_4) | \lambda, \mu > 0\} = \{4\bar{\lambda}, 2\bar{\lambda}, \bar{\lambda}, x_4) | \bar{\lambda} > 0\}$$

and

$$X_I' \cap X \cap \tilde{X}_I = X_I^> \cap X \cap \tilde{X}_I = \left\{ (4\bar{\lambda}, 2\bar{\lambda}, \bar{\lambda}, x_4) \left| \begin{array}{c} \bar{\lambda} > 0 \\ 16\bar{\lambda}^2 + 4\bar{\lambda}^2 + \bar{\lambda}^2 = 1 \\ 4\bar{\lambda} + x_4 \leqq 1 \\ 3\bar{\lambda} - x_4 \leqq 1 \end{array} \right. \right\}$$

$$= \{(4/\sqrt{21}, 2/\sqrt{21}, 1/\sqrt{21}, x_4) | 3/\sqrt{21} - 1 \leqq x_4 \leqq 1 - 4/\sqrt{21}\}.$$

Similarly, one finds that

$$X_I^= = \{x | F^= \cap G_I(x) \neq \varnothing\} = X_I^> = \{(4\lambda, 2\lambda, \lambda, x_4) | \lambda > 0\}$$

and

$$X_I^0 \cap X \cap \tilde{X}_I = \{(4/\sqrt{21}, 2/\sqrt{21}, 1/\sqrt{21}, x_4) | 3/\sqrt{21} - 1 \leqq x_4 \leqq 1 - 4/\sqrt{21}\}.$$

Note that, for all points in $X'_I \cap X \cap \tilde{X}_I$ and $X^0_I \cap X \cap \tilde{X}_I$,

$$\Lambda^*(x^0) = \{(\lambda_1, \lambda_2)|\lambda_1 = 2\lambda_2, (\lambda_1, \lambda_2) > (0, 0)\}.$$

Case 2: $I = \{2\}$. Then, in view of (3.30) and (3.33) for each $x \in X^>_I$, the following equalities (again obtained by componentwise comparison) hold for some $\lambda_1, \lambda_2 > 0$ and $\mu \geqq 0$:

$$\mu = \lambda_1 + 2\lambda_2, \qquad 0 = \lambda_1, \qquad 0 = \lambda_2, \qquad \mu = \lambda_1 - 2\lambda_2.$$

It is seen that $X^>_I = \varnothing$. Similarly, $X^=_I = \varnothing$. Thus

$$X'_I \cap X \cap \tilde{X}_I = X^0_I \cap X \cap \tilde{X}_I = \varnothing.$$

Case 3: $I = \{3\}$. Then, in view of (3.30) and (3.34) for each $x \in X^>_I$, the following equalities hold for some $\lambda_1, \lambda_2 > 0$ and $\mu \geqq 0$:

$$0 = \lambda_1 + 2\lambda_2, \qquad \mu = \lambda_1, \qquad \mu = \lambda_2, \qquad -\mu = \lambda_1 - 2\lambda_2.$$

Obviously, $X^>_I = \varnothing$. Similarly, $X^=_I = \varnothing$. Thus,

$$X'_I \cap X \cap \tilde{X}_I = X^0_I \cap X \cap \tilde{X}_I = \varnothing.$$

Step (3). For all I such that $[I] = 2$, there are three cases.

Case 1: $I = \{1, 2\}$. In view of (3.30) and (3.35) for each $x \in X^>_I$, the following equalities (again obtained by componentwise comparison) must hold for some $\lambda_1, \lambda_2 > 0$ and $\mu_1, \mu_2 \geqq 0$:

$$\mu_1 x_1 + \mu_2 = \lambda_1 + 2\lambda_2 \Rightarrow x_1 = (\lambda_1 + 2\lambda_2 - \mu_2)/\mu_1 = 4\lambda_2/\mu_1,$$

$$\mu_1 x_2 = \lambda_1 \Rightarrow x_2 = \lambda_1/\mu_1,$$

$$\mu_1 x_3 = \lambda_2 \Rightarrow x_3 = \lambda_2/\mu_1,$$

$$\mu_2 = \lambda_1 - 2\lambda_2, \qquad \mu_2 \geqq 0 \Rightarrow \lambda_1 \geqq 2\lambda_2.$$

Note that μ_1 cannot be zero. Thus by setting $\bar{\lambda}_1 = \lambda_1/\mu_1$ and $\bar{\lambda}_2 = \lambda_2/\mu_1$, we see that

$$X^>_I = \left\{ (4\bar{\lambda}_2, \bar{\lambda}_1, \bar{\lambda}_2, x_4) \left| \begin{array}{l} \bar{\lambda}_1, \bar{\lambda}_2 > 0 \\ \bar{\lambda}_1 \geqq 2\bar{\lambda}_2 \end{array} \right. \right\}$$

and

$$X_I' \cap X \cap \tilde{X}_I = X_I^> \cap X \cap \tilde{X}_I$$

$$= \left\{ (4\lambda_2, \lambda_1, \lambda_2, x_4) \;\middle|\; \begin{matrix} 16\lambda_2^2 + \lambda_1^2 + \lambda_2^2 = 1 \\ 4\lambda_2 + x_4 = 1 \\ \lambda_1 + \lambda_2 - x_4 \leqq 1 \\ \lambda_1 \geqq 2\lambda_2 \\ \lambda_1, \lambda_2 > 0 \end{matrix} \right\}$$

$$= \left\{ (4\lambda_2, \lambda_1, \lambda_2, 1 - 4\lambda_2) \;\middle|\; \begin{matrix} 17\lambda_2^2 + \lambda_1^2 = 1 \\ \lambda_1 + 5\lambda_2 \leqq 2 \\ \lambda_1 \geqq 2\lambda_2 \\ \lambda_1, \lambda_2 > 0 \end{matrix} \right\}$$

$$= \left\{ (4\lambda_2, \lambda_1, \lambda_2, 1 - 4\lambda_2) \;\middle|\; \begin{matrix} 17\lambda_2^2 + \lambda_1^2 = 1 \\ 2\lambda_2 \leqq \lambda_1 \leqq 2 - 5\lambda_2 \\ \lambda_1, \lambda_2 > 0 \end{matrix} \right\}.$$

Similarly,

$$X_I^> = \left\{ (4\lambda_2, \lambda_1, \lambda_2, x_4) \;\middle|\; \begin{matrix} \lambda_1 \geqq 2\lambda_2 \\ (\lambda_1, \lambda_2) \geqq (0, 0) \end{matrix} \right\}$$

and

$$X_I^0 \cap X \cap \tilde{X}_I = X_I^\geqq \cap X \cap \tilde{X}_I$$

$$= \left\{ (4\lambda_2, \lambda_1, \lambda_2, 1 - 4\lambda_2) \;\middle|\; \begin{matrix} 17\lambda_2^2 + \lambda_1^2 = 1 \\ 2\lambda_2 \leqq \lambda_1 \leqq 2 - 5\lambda_2 \\ (\lambda_1, \lambda_2) \geqq (0, 0) \end{matrix} \right\}.$$

Case 2: $I = \{1, 3\}$. In view of (3.30) and (3.36) for each $x \in X_I^>$, the following equalities must hold for some $\lambda_1, \lambda_2 > 0$ and $\mu_1, \mu_3 \geqq 0$:

$$\mu_1 x_1 = \lambda_1 + 2\lambda_2 \Rightarrow x_1 = \lambda_1/\mu_1 + 2\lambda_2/\mu_1,$$

$$\mu_1 x_2 + \mu_3 = \lambda_1 \Rightarrow x_2 = \lambda_1/\mu_1 - \mu_3/\mu_1 = 2\lambda_1/\mu_1 - 2\lambda_2/\mu_1,$$

$$\mu_1 x_3 + \mu_3 = \lambda_2 \Rightarrow x_3 = \lambda_1/\mu_1 - \lambda_2/\mu_1,$$

$$-\mu_3 = \lambda_1 - 2\lambda_2 \leqq 0 \Rightarrow \lambda_1 \leqq 2\lambda_2.$$

Note that $\mu_1 > 0$. By putting $\bar{\lambda}_1 = \lambda_1/\mu_1$ and $\bar{\lambda}_2 = \lambda_2/\mu_1$, we have

$$X_I^> = \left\{ (\bar{\lambda}_1 + 2\bar{\lambda}_2, 2\bar{\lambda}_1 - 2\bar{\lambda}_2, \bar{\lambda}_1 - \bar{\lambda}_2, x_4) \,\middle|\, \begin{array}{l} \bar{\lambda}_1, \bar{\lambda}_2 > 0 \\ \bar{\lambda}_1 \leq 2\bar{\lambda}_2 \end{array} \right\}.$$

Thus,

$$X_I' \cap X \cap \tilde{X}_I = X_I^> \cap X \cap \tilde{X}_I$$

$$= \left\{ (\bar{\lambda}_1 + 2\bar{\lambda}_2, 2\bar{\lambda}_1 - 2\bar{\lambda}_2, \bar{\lambda}_1 - \bar{\lambda}_2, x_4) \,\middle|\, \begin{array}{l} (\bar{\lambda}_1 + 2\bar{\lambda}_2)^2 + (2\bar{\lambda}_1 - 2\bar{\lambda}_2)^2 + (\bar{\lambda}_1 - \bar{\lambda}_2)^2 = 1 \\ \bar{\lambda}_1 + 2\bar{\lambda}_2 + x_4 \leq 1 \\ 2\bar{\lambda}_1 - 2\bar{\lambda}_2 + \bar{\lambda}_1 - \bar{\lambda}_2 - x_4 = 1 \\ \bar{\lambda}_1 \leq 2\bar{\lambda}_2, (\bar{\lambda}_1, \bar{\lambda}_2) > (0, 0) \end{array} \right\}$$

$$= \left\{ (\lambda_1 + 2\lambda_2, 2\lambda_1 - 2\lambda_2, \lambda_1 - \lambda_2, 3\lambda_1 - 3\lambda_2 - 1) \,\middle|\, \begin{array}{l} 6\lambda_1^2 - 6\lambda_1\lambda_2 + 9\lambda_2^2 = 1 \\ 4\lambda_1 - \lambda_2 \leq 2 \\ \lambda_1 \leq 2\lambda_2 \\ (\lambda_1, \lambda_2) > (0, 0) \end{array} \right\}.$$

Similarly,

$$X_I^\geqq = \left\{ (\lambda_1 + 2\lambda_2, 2\lambda_1 - 2\lambda_2, \lambda_1 - \lambda_2, x_4) \,\middle|\, \begin{array}{l} (\lambda_1, \lambda_2) \geq 0 \\ \lambda_1 \leq 2\lambda_2 \end{array} \right\}$$

and

$$X_I^0 \cap X \cap \tilde{X}_I = X_I^\geqq \cap X \cap \tilde{X}_I$$

$$= \left\{ (\lambda_1 + 2\lambda_2, 2\lambda_1 - 2\lambda_2, \lambda_1 - \lambda_2, 3\lambda_1 - 3\lambda_2 - 1) \,\middle|\, \begin{array}{l} 6\lambda_1^2 - 6\lambda_1\lambda_2 + 9\lambda_2^2 = 1 \\ 4\lambda_1 - \lambda_2 \leq 2 \\ \lambda_1 \leq 2\lambda_2 \\ (\lambda_1, \lambda_2) \geq (0, 0) \end{array} \right\}.$$

Case 3: $I = \{2, 3\}$. In view of (3.30) and (3.37) for each $x \in X_I^>$, the following equalities must hold for some $\lambda_1, \lambda_2 > 0$ and $\mu_2, \mu_3 \geq 0$:

$$\mu_2 = \lambda_1 + 2\lambda_2, \qquad \mu_3 = \lambda_1, \qquad \mu_3 = \lambda_2, \qquad \mu_2 - \mu_3 = \lambda_1 - 2\lambda_2.$$

It is seen that there are no $(\lambda_1, \lambda_2) > (0, 0)$, $(\mu_2, \mu_3) \geq (0, 0)$ which would satisfy the above system of equations. Thus, $X_I^> = \varnothing$ and

$$X_I' \cap X \cap \tilde{X}_I = X_I^> \cap X \cap \tilde{X}_I = \varnothing.$$

Similarly, $X_I^{\geqq} = \varnothing$ and

$$X_I^0 \cap X \cap \tilde{X}_I = \varnothing.$$

Step (4). For $I = \{1, 2, 3\} = M$. In view of (3.30) and (3.38) for each $x \in X_M^>$, the following equalities must hold for some $(\lambda_1, \lambda_2) > (0, 0)$ and $(\mu_1, \mu_2, \mu_3) \geqq (0, 0, 0)$:

$$\mu_1 x_1 + \mu_2 = \lambda_1 + 2\lambda_2 \Rightarrow x_1 = \lambda_1/\mu_1 + 2\lambda_2/\mu_1 - \mu_2/\mu_1 = 4\lambda_2/\mu_1 - \mu_3/\mu_1,$$

$$\mu_1 x_2 + \mu_3 = \lambda_1 \Rightarrow x_2 = \lambda_1/\mu_1 - \mu_3/\mu_1,$$

$$\mu_1 x_3 + \mu_3 = \lambda_2 \Rightarrow x_3 = \lambda_2/\mu_1 - \mu_3/\mu_1,$$

$$\mu_2 - \mu_3 = \lambda_1 - 2\lambda_2 \Rightarrow \mu_2 = \lambda_1 - 2\lambda_2 + \mu_3 \geqq 0.$$

Note that μ_1 cannot be zero. Thus, by putting $\bar{\lambda}_1 = \lambda_1/\mu_1$, $\bar{\lambda}_2 = \lambda_2/\mu_1$, $\bar{\mu} = \mu_3/\mu_1$, we have

$$X_M^> = \left\{ (4\bar{\lambda}_2 - \bar{\mu}, \bar{\lambda}_1 - \bar{\mu}, \bar{\lambda}_2 - \bar{\mu}, x_4) \;\middle|\; \begin{array}{c} (\bar{\lambda}_1, \bar{\lambda}_2) > (0, 0) \\ \bar{\mu} \geqq 0 \\ \bar{\lambda}_1 - 2\bar{\lambda}_2 + \bar{\mu} \geqq 0 \end{array} \right\}$$

and

$$X_M' \cap X \cap \tilde{X}_M = X_M^> \cap X \cap \tilde{X}_M$$

$$= \left\{ (4\lambda_2 - \mu, \lambda_1 - \mu, \lambda_2 - \mu, x_4) \;\middle|\; \begin{array}{c} (4\lambda_2 - \mu)^2 + (\lambda_1 - \mu)^2 + (\lambda_2 - \mu)^2 = 1 \\ 4\lambda_2 - \mu + x_4 = 1 \\ \lambda_1 - \mu + \lambda_2 - \mu - x_4 = 1 \\ \lambda_1 - 2\lambda_2 + \mu \geqq 0 \\ \lambda_1, \lambda_2 > 0, \mu \geqq 0 \end{array} \right\}$$

$$= \left\{ (4\lambda_2 - \mu, \lambda_1 - \mu, \lambda_2 - \mu, 1 - 4\lambda_2 + \mu) \;\middle|\; \begin{array}{c} (4\lambda_2 - \mu)^2 + (\lambda_1 - \mu)^2 + (\lambda_2 - \mu)^2 = 1 \\ \lambda_1 + 5\lambda_2 - 3\mu = 2 \\ \lambda_1 - 2\lambda_2 + \mu \geqq 0 \\ \lambda_1, \lambda_2 > 0, \mu \geqq 0 \end{array} \right\}$$

Similarly,

$$
X_M^\geqq = \left\{ (4\bar\lambda_2 - \bar\mu, \bar\lambda_1 - \bar\mu, \bar\lambda_2 - \bar\mu, x_4) \,\middle|\, \begin{array}{c} (\bar\lambda_1, \bar\lambda_2) \geqq (0,0) \\ \bar\mu \geqq 0 \\ \bar\lambda_1 - 2\bar\lambda_2 + \bar\mu \geqq 0 \end{array} \right\}
$$

and

$$
X_M^0 \cap X \cap \tilde X_M
$$

$$
= \left\{ (4\lambda_2 - \mu, \lambda_1 - \mu, \lambda_2 - \mu, 1 - 4\lambda_2 + \mu) \,\middle|\, \begin{array}{c} (4\lambda_2 - \mu)^2 + (\lambda_1 - \mu)^2 + (\lambda_2 - \mu)^2 = 1 \\ \lambda_1 + 5\lambda_2 - 3\mu = 2 \\ \lambda_1 - 2\lambda_2 + \mu \geqq 0 \\ (\lambda_1, \lambda_2) \geqq (0,0), \mu \geqq 0 \end{array} \right\}
$$

Step (5). To find $X^0(\Lambda^>)$, $X^0(\Lambda^=)$, and N_X. Set $I_1 = \{1\}$, $I_2 = \{1, 2\}$, $I_3 = \{1, 3\}$, $I_4 = \{1, 2, 3\}$. In view of Theorem 3.21 and Steps (1)–(4), we obtain

$$
X^0(\Lambda^>) = \bigcup_{K=1}^{4} (X'_{I_K} \cap X \cap \tilde X_{I_K})
$$

$$
= \{ (4/\sqrt{21}, 2/\sqrt{21}, 1/\sqrt{21}, x_4) | 3/\sqrt{21} - 1 \leqq x_4 \leqq 1 - 4/\sqrt{21} \}
$$

$$
\cup \left\{ (4\lambda_2, \lambda_1, \lambda_2, 1 - 4\lambda_2) \,\middle|\, \begin{array}{c} \lambda_1^2 + 17\lambda_2^2 = 1 \\ 2\lambda_2 \leqq \lambda_1 \leqq 2 - 5\lambda_2 \\ (\lambda_1, \lambda_2) > (0,0) \end{array} \right\}
$$

$$
\cup \left\{ (\lambda_1 + 2\lambda_2, 2\lambda_1 - 2\lambda_2, \lambda_1 - \lambda_2, 3\lambda_1 - 3\lambda_2 - 1) \,\middle|\, \begin{array}{c} 6\lambda_1^2 - 6\lambda_1\lambda_2 + 9\lambda_2^2 = 1 \\ 4\lambda_1 - \lambda_2 \leqq 2 \\ \lambda_1 \leqq 2\lambda_2 \\ (\lambda_1, \lambda_2) > (0,0) \end{array} \right\}
$$

$$
\cup \left\{ (4\lambda_2 - \mu, \lambda_1 - \mu, \lambda_2 - \mu, 1 - 4\lambda_2 + \mu) \,\middle|\, \begin{array}{c} (4\lambda_2 - \mu)^2 + (\lambda_1 - \mu)^2 + (\lambda_2 - \mu)^2 = 1 \\ \lambda_1 + 5\lambda_2 - 3\mu = 2 \\ \lambda_1 - 2\lambda_2 + \mu \geqq 0 \\ \lambda_1, \lambda_2 > 0, \mu \geqq 0 \end{array} \right\}
$$

and

$$X^0(\Lambda^=) = \bigcup_{K=1}^{4} (X^0_{I_K} \cap X \cap \tilde{X}_{I_K})$$

$$= \{(4/\sqrt{21}, 2/\sqrt{21}, 1/\sqrt{21}, x_4) | 3/\sqrt{21} - 1 \leqq x_4 \leqq 1 - 4/\sqrt{21}\}$$

$$\cup \left\{ (4\lambda_2, \lambda_1, \lambda_2, 1 - 4\lambda_2) \left| \begin{array}{l} \lambda_1^2 + 17\lambda_2^2 = 1 \\ 2\lambda_2 \leqq \lambda_1 \leqq 2 - 5\lambda_2 \\ (\lambda_1, \lambda_2) \geqq (0, 0) \end{array} \right. \right\}$$

$$\cup \left\{ (\lambda_1 + 2\lambda_2, 2\lambda_1 - 2\lambda_2, \lambda_1 - \lambda_2, 3\lambda_1 - 3\lambda_2 - 1) \left| \begin{array}{l} 6\lambda_1^2 - 6\lambda_1\lambda_2 + 9\lambda_2^2 = 1 \\ 4\lambda_1 - \lambda_2 \leqq 2; \lambda_1 \leqq 2\lambda_2 \\ (\lambda_1, \lambda_2) \geqq (0, 0) \end{array} \right. \right\}$$

$$\cup \left\{ (4\lambda_2 - \mu, \lambda_1 - \mu, \lambda_2 - \mu, 1 - 4\lambda_2 + \mu) \left| \begin{array}{l} (4\lambda_2 - \mu)^2 + (\lambda_1 - \mu)^2 + (\lambda_2 - \mu)^2 = 1 \\ \lambda_1 + 5\lambda_2 - 3\mu = 2 \\ \lambda_1 - 2\lambda_2 + \mu \geqq 0 \\ (\lambda_1, \lambda_2) \geqq (0, 0), \mu \geqq 0 \end{array} \right. \right\}$$

Observe that

   i. $X'_{I_1} \cap X \cap \tilde{X}_{I_1} = X^0_{I_1} \cap X \cap \tilde{X}_{I_1}$,

   ii. $(X^0_{I_2} \cap X \cap \tilde{X}_{I_2}) \backslash (X'_{I_2} \cap X \cap \tilde{X}_{I_2})$
      $= \{(0, 1, 0, 1)\}$,   by $(\lambda_1, \lambda_2) = (1, 0)$,

   iii. $(X^0_{I_3} \cap X \cap \tilde{X}_{I_3}) \backslash (X'_{I_3} \cap X \cap \tilde{X}_{I_3})$
      $= \{(2/3, -2/3, -1/3, -2)\}$,   by $(\lambda_1, \lambda_2) = (0, 1/3)$,

   iv. $X^0_{I_4} \cap X \cap \tilde{X}_{I_4} = X'_{I_4} \cap X \cap \tilde{X}_{I_4}$,
      because neither λ_1 nor λ_2 can be zero; thus,

   $$X^0(\Lambda^=) \backslash X^0(\Lambda^>) \subset \{(0, 1, 0, 1), (2/3, -2/3, -1/3, -2)\}.$$

   Since $(0, 1, 0, 1)$ and $(2/3, -2/3, -1/3, -2)$ are unique points in $X^0(\lambda_1, \lambda_2 = 0)$ and $X^0(\lambda_1 = 0, \lambda_2)$, respectively, by Theorem 3.14(ii) we know that both of them are N-points. Thus, we get $X^0(\Lambda^<) \subset N_X = X^0(\Lambda^=)$. Observe that $(0, 1, 0, 1)$ is the maximal point of $f_1(x)$ over X, while $(2/3, -2/3, -1/3, -2)$ is the maximal point of $f_2(x)$ over X. Note that, for each $x^0 \in N_X$, we have no difficulty in identifying $\Lambda^*(x^0)$ (see Remark 3.10), because throughout our process we have either expressed $\Lambda^*(x^0)$ explicitly or expressed x^0 directly or indirectly in terms of λ_1 and λ_2. In a decision process it may be useful to display (using a computer if possible) at least some selected points N_X and the corresponding $\Lambda^*(x^0)$ to facilitate information processing. We shall discuss this later.

3.5. Further Comments

Pareto was a famous Italian engineer. His work (Ref. 341) has inspired much research. For a review of the earlier work, the reader is referred to Stadler (Ref. 425). In Chapter 8 we shall further discuss the properties of Pareto solutions and the methods for locating them when both f and g are linear. Multicriteria (MC), and multicriteria-multiconstraint level (MC^2) simplex methods will be introduced for this purpose. In Chapter 7 we shall describe a natural extension of Pareto solutions by domination structures. Many of the results described in this chapter were treated as special cases of a more general setting in Ref. 495. Finally, one notes that the "functional efficiency" of Charnes and Cooper (Ref. 77) is a Pareto solution concept after the criteria have been restructured.

3.6. Appendix: Generalized Gordon Theorem [p. 65 of Mangasarian (Ref. 307)]

Let $f: \Gamma \to R^q, \Gamma \subset R^n$ be convex. Then either (i) $f(y) < 0$ has a solution in Γ or (ii) there is $\lambda \geq 0, \lambda \in R^q$ such that $\lambda \cdot f(y) \geq 0$ for all $y \in \Gamma$, but never both.

3.7. Appendix: Optimality Conditions

Let $X = \{x \in R^n | g(x) \leq 0\}$, where $g = (g_1, \ldots, g_m): R^n \to R^m$. We want to state some necessary and sufficient conditions for a scalar-valued function $f: R^n \to R^1$ to have a maximum point at $x^0 \in X$. For more general statements see Ref. 307.

Theorem 3.22. (Fritz John's Necessary Condition.) Let

$$L(x, \mu) = \mu_0 f(x) - \sum_{i=1}^{m} \mu_i g_i(x). \tag{3.39}$$

Assume that both f and g are differentiable at $x^0 \in X$. Then a necessary condition for $f(x^0) \geq f(x)$ for all $x \in X$ is that there exist $\mu^0 = (\mu_0^0, \mu_1^0, \ldots, \mu_m^0) \geq 0$ ($\neq 0$) such that

$$\nabla_x L(x^0, \mu^0) = 0$$

[where $\nabla_x L(x^0, \mu^0)$ is the gradient of $L(x, \mu^0)$ w.r.t. x at x^0],

$$\mu_j g_j(x^0) = 0, \qquad j = 1, \ldots, m,$$

$$g_j(x^0) \leq 0, \qquad j = 1, \ldots, m.$$

Definition 3.7. (The Kuhn–Tucker Constraint Qualification.) The Kuhn–Tucker constraint qualification is satisfied at $x^0 \in X$ if g is differentiable at x^0 and for every $h \in R^n$ such that $\nabla g_I(x^0) \cdot h \leq 0$, $I = \{i | g_i(x^0) = 0\}$ (g_I is derived from g by deleting all g_j with $j \notin I$), there is $\{x(t) | 0 \leq t \leq 1\} \subset X$ with $x(0) = x^0$, and $x(t)$ being differentiable at $t = 0$ with $dx(0)/dt = \alpha h$ for some $\alpha > 0$ ($\alpha \in R^1$).

Theorem 3.23. (Kuhn–Tucker's Necessary Condition.) In Theorem 3A.1 if, in addition the Kuhn–Tucker constraint qualification is satisfied at x^0, then $\mu_0^0 > 0$ and without loss of generality one can set $\mu_0^0 = 1$.

Definition 3.24. Let $f : R^n \to R^1$ be a scalar-valued function. We say that
  i. f is a *quasiconvex* function iff $\{x | f(x) \leq a\}$ is a convex set for all $a \in R^1$.
  ii. f is a *quasiconcave* function iff $\{x | f(x) \geq a\}$ is a convex set for all $a \in R^1$.

Theorem 3A.3. (Sufficient Condition.) Assume that f is a concave function and that each g_j, $j = 1, \ldots, m$, is a quasiconvex function in R^n. Suppose that f and each g_j, $j = 1, \ldots, m$, are differentiable at $x^0 \in X$ and that there exist $(\mu_1, \ldots, \mu_m) \geq 0$ such that

$$\nabla f(x^0) - \sum_i \mu_i \nabla g_i(x^0) = 0,$$

$$\mu_j g_j(x^0) = 0, \qquad j = 1, \ldots, m,$$

then $f(x^0) \geq f(x)$ for all $x \in X$.

Exercises

3.1. Consider the following five alternatives evaluated with respect to three criteria (more is better):

Alternative	f_1	f_2	f_3
A	350	400	250
B	500	300	100
C	250	200	200
D	200	800	600
E	200	900	750

Which of the five alternatives are nondominated?

3.2. Consider the following problem:

$$\text{Maximize} \quad f_1(x_1, x_2) = 4x_1 - 2x_2,$$

$$\text{maximize} \quad f_2(x_1, x_2) = -x_1 + 5x_2,$$

$$\text{subject to} \quad 4x_1 + 3x_2 \leq 48,$$

$$-3x_1 + 2x_2 \leq 12,$$

$$x_1 \leq 10,$$

$$x_2 \leq 8,$$

$$x_1, x_2 \geq 0.$$

a. Sketch the set of feasible solutions in the decision space (X) and identify all extreme points.
b. Sketch the outcome space (Y). Identify the nondominated points in X and Y.
c. Assume that f_1 has been arbitrarily chosen as a reference criterion for maximization. Set the satisficing level for f_2 as $r_2 = -10, 10, 30$ and find the corresponding nondominated points.
d. What difficulties will be involved in finding the set of all nondominated solutions using the approach taken in part (c)?

3.3. Consider the following investment problem. Suppose an investor has $12,000 to invest in the stock market. He particularly prefers two stocks. One is Omni Electronics, a fast-growing computer manufacturing company, and the other is Blue-Sky Airline. He considers two criteria, safety and expected return, for his investments. He wishes to maximize the expected annual return for his investment while maximizing safety (or equivalently minimizing the risk which is assumed to be expressed by the variance of a portfolio). Omni's stock is priced at $150 per share, with an annual expected return of $20. Blue-Sky Airline's is $100 per share, and the estimated return is $12. The investor wants to invest a minimum of $3000 in Omni Electronics and a maximum of $5000 in Blue-Sky Airline. The variance of a portfolio return is given by $0.08x_1^2 + 0.16x_2^2 + 0.1x_1x_2$, where x_1 and x_2 represent the number of shares of stock invested in Omni Electronics and Blue-Sky Airline, respectively.

a. Construct a two-criteria model for the investor who tries to maximize the expected return and maximize the safety (or the negative of the variance of his portfolio).

b. Sketch the set of feasible solutions in the decision space and identify all extreme points. Show that the criteria space Y has a nice $\Lambda^{\leq}$-convexity. Sketch Y to verify this.

c. Suppose the investor's tradeoff ratio between expected return and safety is given by $w_2/w_1 = 1/3$, i.e., he is willing to sacrifice $1/3$ units of expected return in order to increase safety by one unit. Since the investor's desired tradeoff between expected return and safety is shown as above this reduces to the additive weight method.

   i. Formulate this as a single objective optimization problem and solve it.

   ii. The optimal solution to the weighted problem in (i) is a nondominated solution to the original two-criteria problem. Why is this true?

d. Suppose the investor's desirable tradeoff ratio is given by the interval $1 < w_2/w_1 < 3$, instead of a constant ratio. Although the investor does not specify the constant ratio w_2/w_1, the bounds are very useful information for the investor to make a final decision. Find all nondominated solutions which satisfy the above bounds.

3.4. Let X be the subset of R^2 bounded by

$$g_1(x) = 3x_1 + x_2 - 12 \leq 0,$$

$$g_2(x) = 2x_1 + x_2 - 9 \leq 0,$$

$$g_3(x) = x_1 + 2x_2 - 12 \leq 0,$$

and

$$x_1 \geq 0, \qquad x_2 \geq 0.$$

These are resource constraints for producing x_1 and x_2 units of Products I and II, respectively. Two objective functions are under consideration:

$$y_1 = f_1(x) = x_1 + x_2,$$

$$y_2 = f_2(x) = 10x_1 - x_1^2 + 4x_2 - x_2^2,$$

representing gross output and net profit, respectively.

a. Specify the decision space X.

b. Specify the outcome space Y. What cone convexity does Y enjoy?

c. Identify the set of all nondominated solutions.

3.5. Consider the following two-criteria problem:

$$\text{maximize} \quad f_1(x_1, x_2) = 6x_1 - 4x_2,$$

$$\text{maximize} \quad f_2(x_1, x_2) = -x_1 + 2x_2,$$

$$\text{subject to} \quad g_1(x_1, x_2) = -x_1 + x_2 \leq 2,$$

$$g_2(x_1, x_2) = 2x_1 - x_2 \leq 10,$$

$$g_3(x_1, x_2) = x_1 + x_2 \leq 8,$$

$$x_1, x_2 \geq 0.$$

    a. Apply different weights to the objective functions to generate the set of all nondominated solutions.

    b. Suppose f_1 is to be maximized while maintaining some satisficing level for the remaining criterion f_2. Let the satisficing level r_2 vary from -2 to 7. Generate the set of all nondominated solutions which satisfy the above bounds.

3.6. Prove Theorem 3.9.

3.7. Consider the following problem:
Two criteria (more is better)

$$f_1(x_1, x_2) = 2x_1 + x_2,$$

$$f_2(x_1, x_2) = -x_1^2 - 2x_2 + x_1 x_2,$$

and X is defined by

$$x_1 - x_2 \leq 10,$$

$$x_1 + 2x_2 \leq 25,$$

$$x_1, x_2 \geq 0.$$

    i. Find X and Y graphically. (To find Y you can maximize f_2 when f_1 is fixed at various values.)

    ii. Does Y have $\Lambda^{\leq}$-convexity? Justify your answer without referring to the graphs.

    iii. Identify the N-points both on X and Y.

3.8. Consider the following problem:
Criteria (more is better):

$$f_1(x_1, x_2) = 2x_1 + x_2,$$

$$f_2(x_1, x_2) = x_1 - x_1^3 - x_1 x_2 - x_2^3$$

and X is as defined in Exercise 3.7.

    i. Can you depict Y? Is Y $\Lambda^{\leq}$-convex? Justify your answer.

    ii. Find the set of all N-points.

3.9. Let $\{f_1(x), \ldots, f_q(x)\}$ be q criteria and each $f_i(x)$, $i = 1, \ldots, q$, be concave over a convex set X. Assume that lexicographical ordering (see Example 2.3) is used to describe the preference. Show that if $x^* \in X$ is the solution for the lexicographical ordering, then there is a $\lambda \geq 0$ such that x^* also maximizes $\lambda \cdot f(x)$ over X.

3.10. Prove Theorem 3.10. (See Ref. 195 if needed.)

3.11. Show that if y^0 is a proper N-point in Y, then y^0 is also a proper N-point in $Y + \Lambda^{\leq}$. (Note that if y satisfies the inequalities of proper N-points then $y + h$, $h \in \Lambda^{\leq}$, also satisfies the same inequalities.)

Suggested Reading

The following references are particularly pertinent to this chapter: 43, 58, 77, 163, 195, 205, 307, 334, 341, 425, 438, 494, 495.

4

Goal Setting and Compromise Solutions

4.1. Introduction

As a living entity, each human being has, consciously or subconsciously, a set of goals or equilibrium states to achieve and maintain. These goals include (i) survival and security of the self: physiological health, safety, and freedom from danger; (ii) perpetuation of the species: sex, giving birth to the next generation, family love, and welfare; (iii) feelings of self-importance: self-respect and self-esteem, accumulation of wealth and power, dominance, recognition, prestige, achievement, etc.; (iv) social approval: esteem and respect from others, affiliation, conformity with a desired group, giving and accepting sympathy and protectiveness; (v) sensual gratification: sexual, visual, auditory, smell, taste, tactile; (vi) cognitive consistency and curiosity: consistency in thought and opinion, exploring and acquiring knowledge, truth, beauty, and religion; (vii) self-actualization: the ability to accept and depend on the self, to rely on one's own standard, to cease identifying with others.

Observe that some goals, such as the accumulation of wealth, reputation, and achievement, are self-suggested, adjustable, and can be characterized by "more is better." Other goal settings, such as body temperature and other biochemical states of the body, are fairly fixed, without much room for self-adjustment or change. Up too much or down too much from the ideal setting is not desirable. The deviation can be disastrous. Once a perceived state (or value) has deviated from its targeted or ideal state (or value), a charge (force or motive) will be produced to prompt an action to reduce or eliminate the deviation. This behavior of taking actions, including adjustment of the ideal values, to move the perceived states to the targeted ideal states will be called *goal-seeking behavior.*

This goal-seeking behavior, which has been well documented in psychological literature (for instance, see Ref. 297), has an important and pervasive impact on human decision making. In this chapter, we shall focus on two concepts that define human goal-seeking behavior. The first one is related to satisficing models, which are treated in Section 4.2. The other is related to compromise solutions such as goal programming, which are treated in Section 4.3. All of these are static models. In Chapter 9 the dynamic version of goal-seeking behaviors will be explored.

4.2. Satisficing Solutions

In Section 4.2.1, goal setting will be discussed, and in Section 4.2.2 the related preference ordering and optimality will be discussed. Note that the concept described here is more general than that suggested by Simon (Ref. 413). The related mathematical programming methods and interaction and iteration methods will be explored in Section 4.2.3.

4.2.1. Goal Setting

Definition 4.1. Goal setting for satisficing solutions is defined as the procedure of identifying a satisficing set S such that, whenever the decision outcome is an element of S, the decision maker will be happy and satisfied and is assumed to have reached the optimal solution.

Recall that we have the criteria $f = (f_1, \ldots, f_q)$ and the feasible set is $X = \{x \in R^n | g(x) \leq 0\}$, where $g = (g_1, \ldots, g_m)$. As mentioned in Section 4.1, there are two kinds of goal functions. In the first kind, goal values are *adjustable* and "*more is better*" (or "less is better"). For this kind of goal function, say $f_i(x)$, one may specify two critical values a_i and b_i (a_i for *above* and b_i for *below*), $b_i \leq a_i$, such that whenever $f_i(x^0) < b_i$ (i.e., x^0 yields a value *below* the lower critical value for f_i), x^0 is unacceptable, and whenever $f_i(x^0) \geq a_i$ (i.e., x^0 yields a value *above* the upper critical value for f_i), x^0 is acceptable with respect to f_i (although some other criteria may turn x^0 down). Note that since f_i is an adjustable criterion, its corresponding critical values $\{b_i, a_i\}$ may be subject to change as time and events change. For criteria of this kind we may add

$$f_i(x) \geq b_i \tag{4.1}$$

to the constraints, so defining a new feasible set X; and

$$f_i(x) \geq a_i \tag{4.2}$$

will be used to define the *satisficing set S*.

Observe that b_i and a_i may be interpreted as "the minimum limit" and "the aspiration level" for f_i, respectively. Also observe that whenever (4.2) is satisfied, (4.1) is satisfied. In satisficing solutions, (4.2) is important for modeling; in compromise solutions (4.1) is also important in the formulation. Note that when $a_i = b_i$, the two inequalities (4.1) and (4.2) become the same.

If the monotonicity is reversed, f_i exhibits "less is better." Then (4.1) and (4.2) can be replaced by (recall that $b_i \leqq a_i$)

$$f_i(x) \leqq b_i, \tag{4.3}$$

$$f_i(x) \leqq a_i, \tag{4.4}$$

where (4.3) defines the satisficing set S and (4.4) becomes a new constraint for X.

Note that in this case, b_i becomes the aspiration level and a_i becomes the maximum limit for f_i. Also note that by using $-f_i$ (instead of f_i), and $-b_i$ and $-a_i$ (instead of b_i, a_i), (4.3) and (4.4) reduce to (4.1) and (4.2).

The second kind of goal functions are those of which the target goal values are fairly fixed and not subject to much change; too much or too little is not acceptable. For this kind of goal function, say $f_j(x)$, one may again identify two values $\{b_j, a_j\}$ with $a_j \geqq b_j$ such that x is acceptable if and only if the following inequalities hold:

$$b_j \leqq f_j(x) \leqq a_j. \tag{4.5}$$

Note that whenever $a_j = b_j$, (4.5) reduces to an equality. Observe that b_j and a_j are two critical values of f_j so that whenever $f_j(x)$ is *below* b_j or *above* a_j, x is unacceptable.

In contrast to (4.5), there may be a criterion, say f_k, for which one may specify two parameters a_k, b_k, $a_k \geqq b_k$ such that x is acceptable iff

$$f_k(x) \leqq b_k \tag{4.6}$$

or

$$f_k(x) \geqq a_k. \tag{4.7}$$

For instance, $f_k(x)$ could be a position measurement from a potentially disastrous location (say, a nuclear power plant), for which one may specify that any acceptable site of a factory must satisfy

$$|f_k(x)| \geqq a_k,$$

where a_k is the minimum distance from the undesirable place. Using $b_k = -a_k$, the above inequality reduces to (4.6) and (4.7).

For future reference, let us summarize the above discussion in the following.

Remark 4.1. If the decision maker considers each criterion individually, one at a time, he can reach a satisficing set S which satisfies some or all of the inequalities of the types (4.1)–(4.7). Note that S so defined is a "rectangle" or the union of a number of "rectangles" [see (4.6) and (4.7)]. Also note that the satisficing set so defined does not reflect any consideration of tradeoffs among the criteria. When such consideration is important, one can define S by the union of

$$S_k = \{f \,|\, G_k(f) \geq 0\}, \qquad k = 1, \ldots, r, \tag{4.8}$$

where f is a point in S_k and G_k is a vector function which reflects the tradeoff over f (see Chapters 5 and 6 for further discussion). Note that when the union contains a single set (i.e., $r = 1$), $S = S_1$ and S is defined by a system of inequalities.

Example 4.1. Let us consider a problem of selecting an athlete for a basketball team. Assume quickness, f_1, and accuracy of shooting, f_2, of the player are essential. Let both f_1 and f_2 be indexed from 0 to 10, where the higher the index, the better the player. Assume that a player, x, will be selected with satisfaction if $f_1(x) \geq 9$ or $f_2(x) \geq 9$, or $f_1(x) + f_2(x) \geq 15$. Now set $G_1(f) = f_1(x) - 9$, $G_2(f) = f_2(x) - 9$, and $G_3(f) = f_1(x) + f_2(x) - 15$. We see that each $S_i = \{f \,|\, G_i(f) \geq 0\}$, $i = 1, 2, 3$, specifies a satisficing set and $S = S_1 \cup S_2 \cup S_3$ is not convex.

4.2.2. Preference Ordering and Optimality in Satisficing Solutions

Once the satisficing set S is identified, one can use the notation of Chapter 2 to define its corresponding preference ordering and optimality. Since an outcome is satisfied or optimal iff it is contained in S, we have the following theorem.

Theorem 4.1. Given the satisficing set S, the preference of satisficing solutions is given by $(y^1, y^2) \in \{>\}$ iff $y^1 \in S$ and $y^2 \in Y \backslash S$, where $Y \backslash S = \{y \,|\, y \in Y, y \notin S\}$ and

$$\{y^1 <\} = \begin{cases} \varnothing & \text{if } y^1 \in S, \\ S & \text{if } y^1 \in Y \backslash S, \end{cases}$$

$$\{y^1 >\} = \begin{cases} Y \backslash S & \text{if } y^1 \in S, \\ \varnothing & \text{if } y^1 \in Y \backslash S. \end{cases}$$

Remark 4.2. Recall that $Y = f[X]$ is the set of all possible outcomes. Suppose that $Y \cap S \neq \varnothing$. Then the nondominated set is $N = Y \cap S$ and the dominated set $D = Y \backslash S$. Indeed, each point in N is an optimal solution; and, when N is located, our decision process will be completed, at least temporarily, until the sets $X, f,$ and/or S are changed.

Example 4.2. Consider an example with two criteria f_1 and f_2. Figure 4.1a shows the situation where $Y \cap S = \varnothing$, while Figure 4.1b shows $Y \cap S \neq \varnothing$. In Figure 4.1b, $Y \cap S$ represents the nondominated set. Note that the better set with respect to y^1 is empty if y^1 is in S and is S if y^1 is in $Y \backslash S$.

Remark 4.3. Suppose that $Y \cap S = \varnothing$. Then a satisficing solution is not obtainable. In this case, $N = Y$ and $D = \varnothing$. The set of all nondominated solutions does not yield much information for the final solution. There are many ways to overcome or reduce the difficulty. We shall discuss four of them here:

(i) Establish or solicit more information on the preference. The concepts of compromise solutions (to be discussed in Section 4.3) and the tradeoff information among the criteria usually can help one establish or obtain more information on preference than those assumed by satisficing solutions.

(ii) Enlarge X or create a new feasible set X. Creating innovative alternatives has the effect of changing Y. The new Y may have a nonempty intersection with S, thus solving the problem. Many difficult decision problems are solved in this way.

(iii) Adjust the satisficing levels or modify S. Recall that the goals or targets may, in most cases, be adjustable. When Y itself and $Y \cap S = \varnothing$ are identified or revealed, the decision maker may be willing to change his or her satisficing levels, or the constraints of S. When S is changed, it may have a nonempty intersection with Y, thus solving the problem.

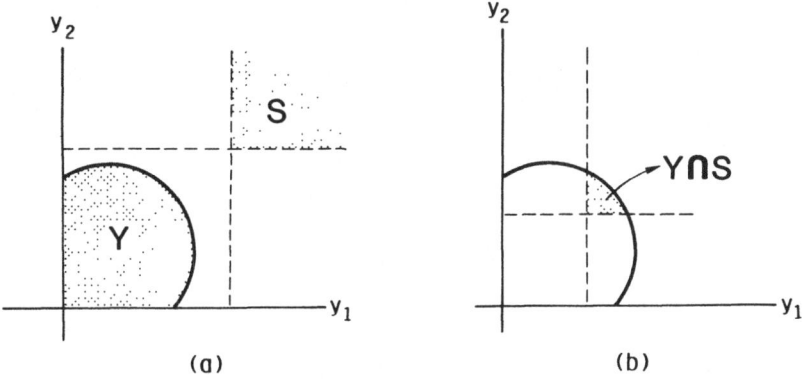

(a)   (b)

Figure 4.1

(iv) Reframe the criteria f. When the criteria, their form and measurement are reframed, the perception of the decision outcomes and of the satisficing set can be changed. In the new frame, one may be able to find a satisficing solution. Many difficult problems can be solved when the criteria are properly reframed.

Further discussion of the above four methods to solve difficult decision problems will be provided in Chapter 9.

4.2.3. Mathematical Programs and Interactive Methods

Once S, the satisficing set, has been determined, finding a satisficing solution x^0, such that $f(x^0) \in S$, is a mathematical programming problem. Recall from Section 4.2.1 that when each criterion is considered individually the satisficing set S will be defined by inequalities of the types of (4.1)-(4.7); and when the criteria are *jointly* considered, then S may be defined by a form such as (4.8). As (4.8) is the most general form, we shall assume that S is defined by the union of S_k, $k = 1, \ldots, r$, with each S_k defined as in (4.8).

Since $S = \bigcup_{k=1}^r S_k$, $Y \cap S \neq \emptyset$ iff there is an S_k such that $Y \cap S_k \neq \emptyset$. As we need only one point of $Y \cap S$ when it is nonempty, we could verify individually if $S_k \cap Y \neq \emptyset, k = 1, \ldots, r$, and find one point from the nonempty intersections.

Note that to verify whether or not $S_k \cap Y$ is empty and to find a point in $S_k \cap Y$, if it is nonempty, we can use the following mathematical program. Rewrite each set in (4.8) as

$$S_k = \{f(x) | G_{ki}(f(x)) \geq 0, j = 1, \ldots, J_k\}, \tag{4.9}$$

where G_{kj}, $j = 1, \ldots, J_k$, are components of G_k, and J_k is the number of components of G_k. Recall that all of the goal constraints (4.1)-(4.7), after properly rearranging the signs and terms, can be written as (4.9).

Program 4.1.

$$V_k = \min \sum_{j=1}^{J_k} d_j, \tag{4.10}$$

$$\text{s.t. } G_{kj}(f(x)) + d_j \geq 0, \qquad j = 1, \ldots, J_k \tag{4.11}$$

$$x \in X, \qquad d_j \geq 0 \tag{4.12}$$

$$j = 1, \ldots, J_k$$

It is readily verified that $S_k \cap Y \neq \emptyset$ iff $V_k = 0$ in (4.10). See Exercise 4.11. We thus have the following theorem.

Theorem 4.2. Let $S = \bigcup_{k=1}^{r} S_k$. Then a satisficing solution exists iff there is at least one $k \in \{1, \ldots, r\}$ such that Program 4.1 yields $V_k = 0$.

Remark 4.4. The objective function in (4.10) can be replaced by any strictly increasing function of d_j, $j = 1, \ldots, J_k$. In particular, one may use $\sum_{j=1}^{J_k} d_j^p$, $p \geq 1$. Then the resulting V_k measures the minimum l_p distance (see Section 4.3 for a further discussion) between Y and S_k. From a computational point of view the form (4.10), in which $p = 1$, has the advantage of simplicity. Especially when G_{kj}, f, and g are all linear, Program 4.1 can be reduced to a linear program (i.e., a linear goal program, which will be discussed in Section 4.3.4).

Remark 4.5. In view of (4.9), $G_{kj}(f(x))$ may be regarded as a newly defined criterion or goal function so that the nonnegative *orthant* $\Lambda^{\geqq}$ with respect to the G_{kj}'s is the satisficing set. With respect to these newly defined goal functions, goal setting becomes very simple. Program 4.1 can then be used to verify the existence of a satisficing solution by finding it when it exists.

Remark 4.6. In a degenerate case, the satisficing levels may be reduced to a point and (4.9) becomes

$$S_k = \{f(x) | G_{kj}(f(x)) = 0, j = 1, \ldots, J_k\}. \tag{4.13}$$

In this case, Program 4.1 can be replaced by the following.

Program 4.2.

$$V_2 = \min \sum_{j=1}^{J_k} |G_{kj}(f(x))|,$$

$$\text{s.t. } x \in X.$$

Then the goal, 0, is obtained iff $V_2 = 0$. We thus have the following theorem.

Theorem 4.3. If S_k is defined as in (4.13), then $S_k \cap Y \neq \emptyset$ iff Program 4.2 yields $V_2 = 0$.

Remark 4.7. Comparing Program 4.1 with Program 4.2, we note that Program 4.2 has a simpler form of the objective function and may in general be easier to solve computationally than Program 4.1. However, Program 4.2 is not valid for a general satisficing set defined as in (4.9).

Remark 4.8. Observe that when one satisficing solution is found the decision problem is solved, at least temporarily. Otherwise the decision maker can activate either *positive problem solving* or a *negative problem avoidance* to restructure the problem. The former will enable careful restudy and restructuring of the problem so as to find a solution, perhaps a new one, which lies in the satisficing set. The latter will try to reduce the aspiration levels or play down the importance of making a good decision, thus "lowering" the satisficing set to have a nonempty intersection with Y. While the psychological attitude in problem solving and in problem avoidance may be different (see Chapter 9 for further discussion), the final consequence is the same. That is, eventually, the newly structured problem enables the decision maker to have $S \cap Y \neq \emptyset$. Here we will not discuss the restructuring of a problem to obtain a satisficing solution. Instead we will examine helpful information to aid the decision maker in restructuring his satisficing set S and feasible set Y. The following provides some helpful information.

(i) Depending on the formation of S, if Program 4.1 is used to identify a satisficing solution, one can produce x^k, $k = 1, \ldots, r$, which solves Program 4.1 with S_k as the satisficing set. One can then compute $f(x^k)$, $G_k(f(x^k))$, the distance from $f(x^k)$ to S_k, and tradeoffs among the $G_{kj}(f(x))$, $j = 1, \ldots, J_k$, at x^k. All of these can be helpful for the decision maker to reframe S_k. If Program 4.2 is used, 0 is the target for $G_k(f(x))$ to attain. The solution x^k will thus give a minimum distance from $G_k(f(x))$ to 0. Again, information on $f(x^k)$, $G_k(f(x^k))$ and the minimum distance from $G_k(f(x^k))$ to 0, $k = 1, \ldots, r$, and the tradeoff among $G_{kj}(f(x^k))$, $j = 1, \ldots, J_k$, at x^k can prove valuable. This information can be used by the decision maker to realize what he can attain and how far away those attainable points are from his satisficing set.

(ii) Suppose that it has been revealed or established that "more is better" for each criterion. Then the revealed preference $\{>\}$ contains at least the Pareto preference. One can then generate: (A) all or some representatives of the N-points, the corresponding $f(x)$, and optimal weights $\Lambda^*(x)$ for the N-points; (B) the value $f_k^* = \max \{f_k(x) | x \in X\}$, $k = 1, \ldots, q$, which gives the best value of $f_k(x)$ over X. This information can help the decision maker to restructure his S. Relaxation of the target goal with reference to the ideal point $(f_1^*, \ldots, f_q^*)$ sequentially and iteratively with the decision maker, until a satisficing solution is obtained, is certainly an art. It is especially useful when X and f are fairly fixed and not subject to change.

(iii) If possible (for instance, in bicriteria cases), displaying Y and S, even if only partially, can help the decision maker conceptualize where Y and S are, to make it easier to restructure the problem.

We summarize the concept of satisficing solutions and the procedure of using it to obtain a final satisficing solution in Figure 4.2.

Observe that Box (1) is clear. Box (2) is described in Sections 4.2.1 and 4.2.3. Boxes (5), (7), and (9) are clear for a conclusion of decision analysis. Note that related information includes those points in $S \cap Y$ and the corresponding points in X. For boxes (6) and (8), one can refer to Remark 4.8 and Remark 4.3 and to Chapter 9 for further discussion.

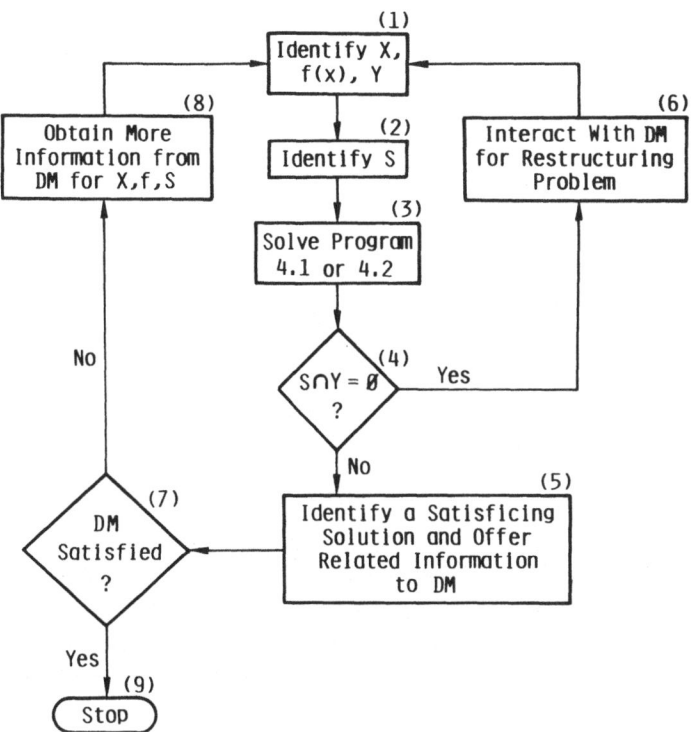

Figure 4.2

One must keep in mind that with X, $f(x)$, and S, one can generate as much information as one wishes, just as one can generate as many statistics from sample values as one wants. However, relevant information (e.g., useful statistics) which can positively affect the problem solving may not be too plentiful. Irrelevant information can become a burden for decision analysis and decision making.

Remark 4.9. Everyone is subject to suggestions, including self-suggestion, to change his perception of decision outcomes and satisficing sets. As each individual is unique, there is no universal way that is most effective for every individual for changing the satisficing set and obtaining a final solution. Changing or relaxing the aspiration levels of the criteria one at a time, two at a time, or all simultaneously, will depend on the individual. A good decision aid should be able to supply relevant information to facilitate proper changes of the satisficing set in order to get a good final solution.

Example 4.3. For illustrative purposes we will consider a very simple production example. We shall take for X the subset of R^2 bounded by

$$g_1(x) = 3x_1 + x_2 - 12 \leqq 0,$$

$$g_2(x) = 2x_1 + x_2 - 9 \leqq 0,$$

$$g_3(x) = x_1 + 2x_2 - 12 \leqq 0,$$

and

$$x_1 \geqq 0, \qquad x_2 \geqq 0.$$

These are resource constraints in the amounts produced, x_1 and x_2. We shall consider two objective functions

$$y_1 = f_1(x) = x_1 + x_2,$$

$$y_2 = f_2(x) = 10x_1 - x_1^2 + 4x_2 - x_2^2,$$

representing gross output and net profit, respectively. The decision space X is shown in Figure 4.3. The outcome space Y can be constructed by mapping all points of X into Y as shown in Figure 4.4. Note that the curves which

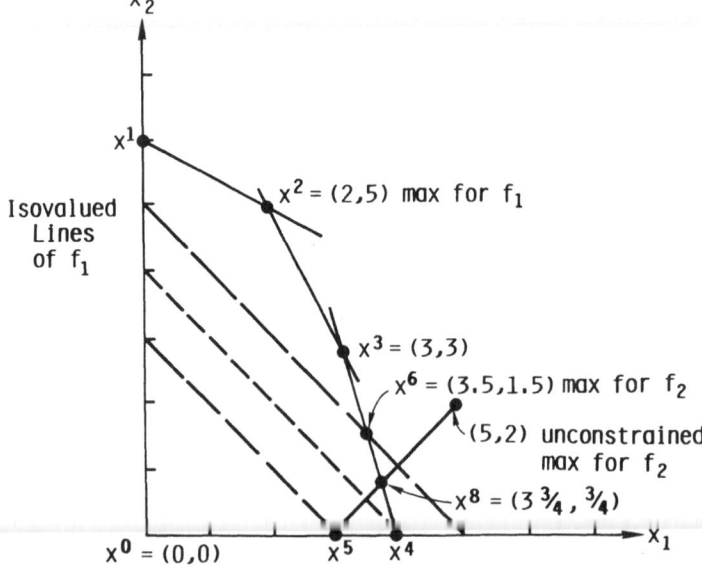

Figure 4.3. Decision space (X).

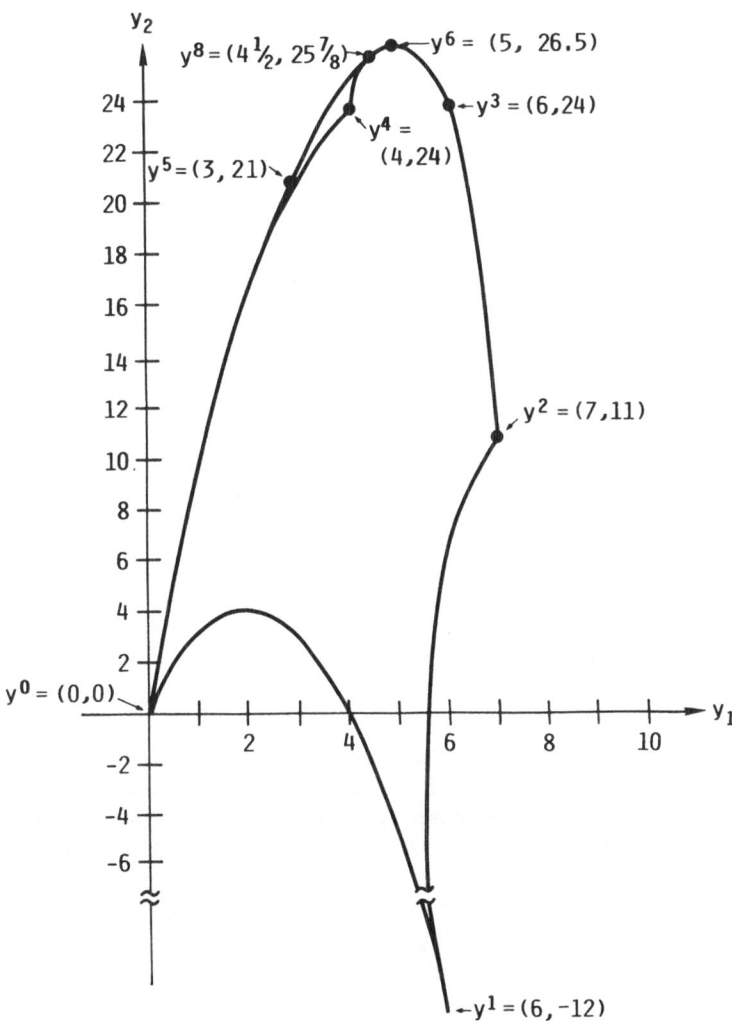

Figure 4.4. Outcome space (Y).

bound Y correspond to certain lines in X. For instance, the curve $[y^1, y^2]$ is the image of the line $[x^1, x^2]$ under f. Note that the upper curve $[y^8, y^5]$, the image of the line $[x^8, x^5]$, is obtained by maximizing f_2 while fixing f_1 at certain constants.

Assume that the decision maker defines his satisficing set by $S = \{(y_1, y_2)|y_1 \geqq 10, y_2 \geqq 30\}$. Then using Program 4.1, we solve the problem of

$$V = \text{minimize } d_1 + d_2,$$

s.t.

$$x_1 + x_2 + d_1 \geqq 10,$$

$$10x_1 - x_1^2 + 4x_2 - x_2^2 + d_2 \geqq 30,$$

$$3x_1 + x_2 \leqq 12,$$

$$2x_1 + x_2 \leqq 9,$$

$$x_1 + 2x_2 \leqq 12,$$

$$x_1 \geqq 0, \qquad x_2 \geqq 0.$$

From Figure 4.4, we know that $S \cap Y = \varnothing$ and $V > 0$. To find a satisficing solution we must restructure X, f, and/or S. If X and f are fairly fixed, we may offer the following information, which may cause a change in S (see Figure 4.4):

    i. that $f_1^* = 7$ and $f_2^* = 26.5$ (this implies that any y with $y_1 > 7$ or $y_2 > 26.5$ is unobtainable; thus the goals of $y_1 \geqq 10$ and $y_2 \geqq 30$ must come down);

    ii. that with respect to Pareto preference $N = $ curve $[y^6, y^3] \cup$ curve $[y^3, y^2]$, any good solution will be in N; A graphical display of Y (such as Figure 4.4) certainly will help the decision maker to conceptualize what he can and cannot attain.

The restructuring of S and Y will continue until a satisficing solution is found. Certainly during the interaction process, information of (i) and (ii) above will change with S and Y. Just as each individual is unique, so is the process, even though Figure 4.2 is a valid description of the process.

Observe that when there are three or more criteria a graphical representation of Y is almost impossible. The process according to Figure 4.2 will require several interactions before termination.

4.3. Compromise Solutions

In this section, mathematical formulation of goal-seeking behavior in terms of a distance function will be described. Because it is simple to understand and compute, the concept has much general appeal to many scholars. We shall start with the most simple form and then gradually extend the concept to more complex cases. In Section 4.3.1, the basic concept and preference structure of compromise solutions are introduced. Section 4.3.2 is devoted to the general properties of compromise solutions, Section 4.3.3 to the properties and impact of the parameters, and Section 4.3.4 to computational aspects including goal programming and *maximin* programming. Section 4.3.5 is devoted to a discussion on dynamic adjustment of ideal points for a final optimal solution.

4.3.1. Basic Concepts

Let the satisficing set S of Section 4.2 be a set of only one point y^*. That is, y^* is a unique target. Typically, when each criterion f_i, $i = 1, \ldots, q$, is characterized by "more is better," one can set $y^* = (y_1^*, \ldots, y_q^*)$, where $y_i^* = \sup \{f_i(x) | x \in X\}$. In this case, y^* is called an *ideal (or utopia) point* because usually y^* is not attainable. Note that, individually, the y_i^* may be attainable. But to find a point y^* which can simultaneously maximize each f_i, $i = 1, \ldots, q$, is usually very difficult.

Example 4.4. Consider the following two-criteria problem:

$$\max y_1 = f_1(x) = 6x_1 + 4x_2,$$

$$\max y_2 = f_2(x) = x_1,$$

$$\text{s.t. } g_1(x) = x_1 + x_2 \le 100,$$

$$g_2(x) = 2x_1 + x_2 \le 150,$$

$$x_1, x_2 \ge 0.$$

By mapping X into the outcome space, we obtain Y as shown in Figure 4.5. The point $y^* = (500, 75)$ indicates the ideal point. Note that this ideal solution

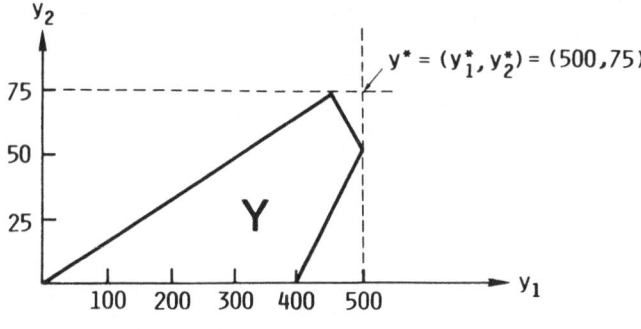

Figure 4.5

is not obtainable since it is not in Y. To find the ideal point, we solve the following two linear programs.

For y_1^*:

$$\max y_1 = f_1(x) = 6x_1 + 4x_2,$$

$$\text{s.t.} \quad x_1 + x_2 \leq 100,$$

$$2x_1 + x_2 \leq 150,$$

$$x_1, x_2 \geq 0.$$

The solution is $x_1^* = 50$ and $x_2^* = 50$. Thus, $y_1^* = f_1(x^*) = 500$.
For y_2^*:

$$\max y_2 = f_2(x) = x_1,$$

$$\text{s.t.} \quad x_1 + x_2 \leq 100,$$

$$2x_1 + x_2 \leq 150,$$

$$x_1, x_2 \geq 0.$$

The solution is $x_1^* = 75$, $x_2^* = 0$ with $y_2^* = f_2(x^*) = 75$.

In group decision problems, if each criterion represents a player's payoff, then y^*, if obtainable, would make each player happy because it simultaneously maximizes each player's payoff. Even if he is the dictator, he cannot do better than y^* for himself. As y^* is usually not attainable, to dissolve the group conflict, a compromise is needed if no other alternative is available. This offers a natural explanation of why the solution to be introduced is called a *compromise solution*. (See Ref. 493.) The reader can extend this explanation easily to multiple-criteria problems.

Now, given $y \in Y$, the *regret* of using y instead of obtaining the *ideal* point y^* may be approximated by the distance between y and y^*. Thus, we define the (group) regret of using y by

$$r(y) = \|y - y^*\|, \tag{4.14}$$

where $\|y - y^*\|$ is the distance from y to y^* according to some specified norm. Typically, the l_p-norm will be used in our discussion because of its ease in understanding, unless otherwise specified. To make this more specific, define

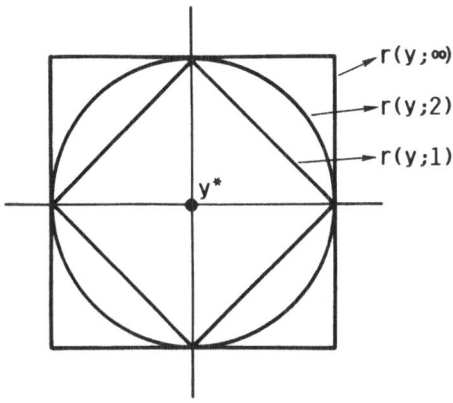

Figure 4.6

for $p \geq 1$

$$r(y; p) = \|y - y^*\|_p = \left[\sum_i |y_i - y_i^*|^p \right]^{1/p} \tag{4.15}$$

and

$$r(y; \infty) = \max \{|y_i - y_i^*|, i = 1, \ldots, q\}. \tag{4.16}$$

Then $r(y; p)$ is a measurement of regret from y to y^* according to the l_p-norm. Note that the isovalued curves of $r(y; p)$ centered at y^* have some special forms as in Figure 4.6 for the case $q = 2$. They change shape from a "square diamond" for $p = 1$, to a circle for $p = 2$, and to a square for $p = \infty$.

Definition 4.2. The compromise solution with respect to the l_p-norm is $y^p \in Y$, which minimizes $r(y; p)$ over Y; *or* is $x^p \in X$, which minimizes $r(f(x); p)$ over X.

Example 4.5. Given Y as in Figure 4.7, one can find y^* with $y_i^* = \max \{f_i(x)|x \in X\}$ as depicted. Using simple isovalued curves of Figure 4.6, we also depict in Figure 4.7, y^∞, which minimizes $r(y; \infty)$, y^2, which minimizes $r(y; 2)$, and y^1, which minimizes $r(y; 1)$. Mathematical programming for finding compromise solutions will be described and illustrated in Section 4.3.4.

Remark 4.10. In group decision problems, $r(y; p)$ may be interpreted as group regret and the compromise solution y^p is the one which minimizes the group regret in order to maintain a "cooperative group spirit." As the parameter

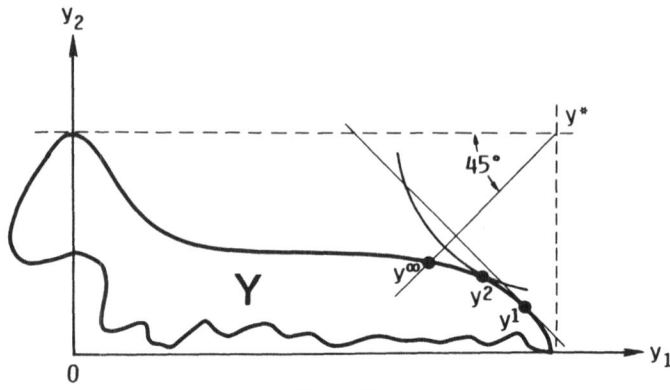

Figure 4.7

p varies, the solution y^p can change. We shall explore the impact of p on the solutions in Section 4.3.2.

Note that $r(y; p)$ treats each $|y_i^* - y_i|$ as having the same importance in forming the group regret. In multiple-criteria problems, if the criteria have different degrees of importance, then a weight vector $w = (w_1, w_2, \ldots, w_q)$, $w \geq 0$ may be assigned to signal the different degrees of importance. In this case, we define

$$r(y; p, w) = \|y - y^*\|_{p,w}$$

$$= \left[\sum_i w_i^p |y_i - y_i^*|^p \right]^{1/p}$$

$$= \left[\sum_i |w_i y_i - w_i y_i^*|^p \right]^{1/p} \tag{4.17}$$

The concept of compromise solutions can then naturally be extended to include the regret function of (4.17).

Definition 4.3. The compromise solution with respect to $r(y; p, w)$ of (4.17) is $y^{pw} \in Y$, which minimizes $r(y; p, w)$ over Y; or is $x^{pw} \in X$, which minimizes $r(f(x); p, w)$ over X.

Remark 4.11. Observe that the weight vector w as in (4.17) has the effect of changing the scale of each criterion. Once the scale is adjusted [i.e., by $w_i y_i = w_i f_i(x)$ for all $i = 1, \ldots, q$], the regret function is reduced to that of equal weight. Thus, in studying the properties of compromise solutions, without loss of generality, one may focus on the equal weight case. We shall so assume from now on, unless specified otherwise.

Remark 4.12. Observe that the compromise solution is *not scale independent*. Scale independence, an important criterion in group decision problems, can prevent players from artificially changing the scale to obtain a better arbitration for themselves. Note that when the scale of $f_i(x)$ or y_i is changed and the weight of importance of each criterion is changed, so is the compromise solution.

Definition 4.4. Given $r(y; p)$, define the *preference using $r(y; p)$* by $y^1 > y^2$ iff $r(y^1; p) < r(y^2; p)$.

Theorem 4.4. (i) The preference using $r(y; p)$ is a complete weak order and, for any y^1 and y^2, $y^1 \sim y^2$ if and only if $r(y^1; p) = r(y^2; p)$.

(ii) $y^0 \in Y$ is a compromise solution with respect to $r(y; p)$ iff $y^0 \in N(\{>\}, Y)$, where $\{>\}$ is the preference using $r(y; p)$ [refer to Section 2.3 for $N(\{>\}, Y)$, the set of all N-points w.r.t. $\{>\}$].

Proof. *For (i):* This follows directly from the fact that the numerical ordering of $r(y; p)$ is a complete weak order.

For (ii): This follows directly from Definition 2.6. □

Remark 4.13. Theorem 4.4 reveals that the concept of compromise solutions has implicitly assumed a very strong preference assumption. There are no ambiguities in preference comparison. For any two points y^1 and y^2, either y^1 is better than or worse than or equivalent to y^2. Exactly one of the three cases must happen. There is no such thing as "indefinite" in the preference of compromise solutions. Before we finally use it, precaution is needed to verify that the assumption is fulfilled; otherwise, a misleading solution may result.

4.3.2. General Properties of Compromise Solutions

Many solution concepts have been proposed in game theory and multicriteria problems. To understand each concept more thoroughly, one needs to study the properties of each concept. In the previous section, we stated that the preference induced by compromise solutions is a very strong "weak order" and that the solution is not independent of the "scaling" of the criteria. In this section we shall study those properties reported in Ref. 493. They are related to those imposed by game theorists (for instance, see Ref. 301).

For simplicity, throughout this section and the next we shall assume the following.

Assumption 4.1.
i. Y is a nonempty compact set.

    ii. The single satisficing point y^* is the ideal or utopia point. [Thus, $y_i^* = \sup\{f_i(x)|x \in X\}$.]

   iii. The preference revealed for each criterion is characterized by "more is better."

Remark 4.14. (i) The assumption that Y is nonempty is innocent; otherwise we have a no-choice problem. That Y is compact can make our discussion much simpler. The reader can relax the compactness to obtain properties similar to those which are to be discussed. Note that the compactness of Y implies the existence of the ideal point y^* because $\max\{y_i|y \in Y\}$ exists.

(ii) Assumptions (ii) and (iii) are used to simplify the presentation of the properties to be described. Most properties, with proper modification, hold even when the assumptions are changed. We shall leave the verification of this to the reader.

Under Assumption 4.1, the compromise solution y^p enjoys the following properties.

Property 4.1. (Feasibility.) The compromise solutions y^p and $x^p \in f^{-1}(y^p)$ are obtainable or feasible.

Many solution concepts in game theory, such as the core, stable set, etc., may not exist, even though they are well defined (see Ref. 301 for details). Note that y^p exists because Y is compact and $r(y; p)$ is continuous on Y.

Property 4.2. (Least Group Regret.) If $r(y; p)$ represents the group regret of using y instead of reaching y^*, then y^p, by definition, minimizes the group regret.

Remark 4.15. Observe that in statistics, the least-squares method is very similar to finding the y^2-compromise solution, while the robust method is very similar to finding the y^1-compromise solution. (See Exercise 4.6 for further details.)

Property 4.3. (No Dictatorship.) Since each criterion is used to form $r(y; p)$ to obtain y^p, there is no dictatorship in the process. That is, there is no sole j (dictator) such that y^p is completely determined by $f_j(x)$.

Note that in rare cases each f_i may be an increasing function of f_j for some j; then the utopia point is $y^* = y^p$ (check it). In these cases, y^* simultaneously maximizes each criterion. It is hard to argue that any one of them is a real dictator.

Property 4.4. (Pareto Optimality.) For $1 \leq p < \infty$, y^p is an N-point (or efficient point) with respect to Pareto preference. (See also Section 3.1.) If y^∞ is unique, then y^∞ is also an N-point.

Note that the property must hold; otherwise, y^p does not give the minimum for $1 \leq p < \infty$. Also, when y^∞ is unique, y^∞ must be an N-point; otherwise, it will lead to a contradiction (check it).

Observe that y^∞ may not always be an N-point. To see this point, let $Y = \{(y_1, y_2)|0 \leq y_1 \leq 2, \ 0 \leq y_2 \leq 2, \ \min\{y_1, y_2\} \leq 1\}$ (see Figure 4.8). Note that $Y^\infty = \{(y_1, y_2) \in Y|y_1 \geq 1, y_2 \geq 1\}$ is the set of all y^∞-points. However, except $(1, 2)$ and $(2, 1)$ none of the points in Y are N-points.

Definition 4.5. A set Y is said to be *strictly convex* if it is convex and contains no line segments in its boundary.

Property 4.5. (Uniqueness.) For $1 < p < \infty$, y^p is unique if Y is $\Lambda^\leqq$-convex. If Y is strictly convex, then y^1 and y^∞ are also unique.

In order to see the first part, observe that for $1 < p < \infty$, y^p minimizes $r(y; p)$ over Y iff y^p minimizes $r(y; p)$ over $Y + \Lambda^\leqq$ (check it). Let $A_p = \{y \in R^q|r(y; p) \leq r(y^p; p)\}$. For $1 < p < \infty$, A_p is a strictly convex set. Note that $Y + \Lambda^\leqq$ is convex, and $(Y + \Lambda^\leqq)$ and A_p can have only boundary points in common. If $A_p \cap (Y + \Lambda^\leqq)$ contained two or more points, then both A_p and $Y + \Lambda^\leqq$ would contain line segments in their boundaries. This is not possible because A_p is strictly convex. The remaining part of the property for $p = 1$ or ∞ can be proved similarly. We shall leave it to the reader.

Note that uniqueness is important, not only for mathematical reasons, but also for avoiding ambiguity in the final solution.

By "Y is closed with respect to cyclical rotation," we mean that if $(y_1, y_2, \ldots, y_q) \in Y$, then all vectors from cyclical rotation of y, that is, $(y_2, y_3, \ldots, y_q, y_1)$, $(y_3, y_4, \ldots, y_q, y_1, y_2), \ldots$ also belong to Y.

Property 4.6. (Symmetry.) If Y is convex and closed with respect to cyclical rotation, then for $1 < p \leq \infty$, $y_k^p = y_j^p$ for all $k, j = 1, \ldots, q$. When $p = 1$, then there is at least one y^1 with $y_k^1 = y_j^1$ for all $k, j = 1, \ldots, q$.

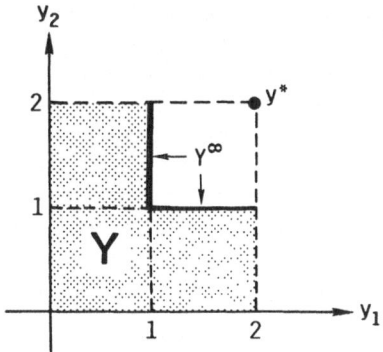

Figure 4.8

Note that this property essentially says that, if the stated assumptions are satisfied, then compromise solutions can ensure an equal "utility" for each criterion. Thus, an "equity principle" has been built into the compromise solution.

In order to see Property 4.6, first observe that, under the assumption of closure to cyclical rotation, y_j^*, $j = 1, \ldots, q$, are identical. For $1 < p < \infty$, if y_j^p, $j = 1, \ldots, q$, are not identical, then any vector obtained by rotating y^p will also minimize $r(y; p)$. This contradicts the uniqueness of Property 4.5. Now for $p = \infty$, if y_j^∞, $j = 1, \ldots, q$, are not identical, then $\bar{y} = (c, \ldots, c)$ with $c = (1/q) \sum_j y_j^\infty$ is a point of Y (by convexity) and, furthermore, $r(\bar{y}; \infty) < r(y^\infty, \infty)$, which leads to the contradiction that y^∞ minimizes $r(y; \infty)$ over Y. Finally, for $p = 1$, if y_j^1, $j = 1, \ldots, q$, are not identical let $\bar{y}^1 = (d, \ldots, d)$ with $d = (1/q) \sum_j y_j^1$. Then $r(\bar{y}^1; 1) = q(y_j^* - d) = qy_j^* - \sum_j y_j^1 = \sum_j (y_j^* - y_j^1) = r(y^1; 1)$. Thus, $\bar{y}^1$ is also an l_1-compromise solution, as we want to establish.

Property 4.7. (Independence of Irrelevant Alternatives.) Let $Y^0 \subset Y$ be such that $\sup\{y_i | y \in Y^0\} = y_i^* = \sup\{y_i | y \in Y\}$, $i = 1, \ldots, q$. If $y^p \in Y^0$, $1 \leq p \leq \infty$, then y^p is also the compromise solution with respect to $r(y; p)$ over Y^0.

Note that $Y \setminus Y^0$ is the set of irrelevant alternatives. Indeed, the property says that as long as the utopia point is not changed, any subset of Y not containing y^p can be discarded without changing the compromise solution.

In order to see that the property holds, observe that as long as the utopia point is not changed, $r(y; p)$ is not changed. If $y^p \in Y^0 \subset Y$ minimizes $r(y; p)$ over Y, y^p must also minimize $r(y; p)$ over Y^0. Thus, y^p is also the compromise solution over Y^0.

4.3.3. Properties Related to p

As $r(y; p)$ is a function of y and p, the compromise solution y^p depends not only on Y but also on p. Indeed, in this section it will be shown that, under suitable conditions, y^p is a continuous function of p and y^p is bounded and monotonic. In two-criteria problems, the parameter p has a special meaning in interpreting compromise solutions y^p. (See Property 4.11.) These properties were reported in Ref. 149 by Freimer and Yu.

Property 4.8. (Continuity.) If Y is compact and $\Lambda^{\leq}$-convex, then the compromise solution y^p is a continuous function of p for $1 < p < \infty$. In addition, if y^1 is unique, then y^p is continuous at $p = 1$; if y^∞ is unique then y^p is continuous at $p = \infty$. (Recall that if Y is strictly convex, then y^1 and y^∞ are unique—Property 4.5.)

Before attempting to prove this property, let us establish two basic properties of l_p norms.

Lemma 4.1. The norms $\|y\|_p$, $1 \leq p \leq \infty$, on a finite-dimensional Euclidean space R^q are an equicontinuous family of functions [i.e., given $\varepsilon > 0$, there is a neighborhood of zero $N(\varepsilon)$ such that for any $y^0 \in Y$, $|\|y\|_p - \|y^0\|_p| < \varepsilon$ for all p as long as $y \in y^0 + N(\varepsilon)$].

Proof. Define $N(\varepsilon) = \{y|\|y\|_1 < \varepsilon\}$. Then $y \in y^0 + N(\varepsilon)$ iff $\|y - y^0\|_1 < \varepsilon$. For any $p \geq 1$, the triangular inequality implies that $|\|y\|_p - \|y^0\|_p| < \|y - y^0\|_p$, while Jensen's inequality (Ref. 31, p. 18) states that $\|y - y^0\|_p \leq \|y - y^0\|_1$. Putting these inequalities together, we have $|\|y\|_p - \|y^0\|_p| \leq \|y - y^0\|_1 < \varepsilon$ whenever $y \in y^0 + N(\varepsilon)$, which verifies the equicontinuity. □

Lemma 4.2. Fix $s \geq 1$. Then as $p \to s$, $\|y\|_p \to \|y\|_s$. Furthermore, the convergence is uniform over every compact subset Y of R^q.

Proof. Since $\|y\|_p$ is a differentiable function of p it is certainly continuous if $1 \leq p < \infty$. That $\|y\|_p \to \|y\|_\infty$ as $p \to \infty$ is a standard result (see Ref. 31, p. 16). The proof of uniformity is the standard 3ε proof in real analysis. With y^0 as in Lemma 4.1, $|\|y^0\|_p - \|y^0\|_s| < \varepsilon$ if p is close enough to s (by continuity in p). But, if $y \in y^0 + N(\varepsilon)$, then $|\|y\|_p - \|y^0\|_p| < \varepsilon$ and $|\|y\|_s - \|y^0\|_s| < \varepsilon$. The last three inequalities imply that $|\|y\|_p - \|y\|_s| < 3\varepsilon$. By compactness of Y, a finite number of neighborhoods cover Y, so that if p is close enough to s for all of these neighborhoods, then $\|y\|_p$ will be close to $\|y\|_s$ throughout Y. □

We are now ready to prove Property 4.8. Fix $s \geq 1$. Since $r(y; p) = \|y^* - y\|_p$ and Y is a compact set, Lemma 4.2 shows that as $p \to s$, $r(y; p) \to r(y; s)$ uniformly over Y. Also y^s minimizes $r(y; s)$ over Y, so that

$$r(y^s; s) \leq r(y^p; s) \qquad \text{for all } p,$$

$$\leq r(y^p; p) + \varepsilon \qquad \text{if } p \text{ is close enough to } s.$$

Similarly, y^p minimizes $r(y; p)$ over Y, so that $r(y^p; p) \leq r(y^s; p) \leq r(y^s; s) + \varepsilon$ if p is close enough to s. Combining the inequalities, we have $r(y^s; s) \leq r(y^p; s) \leq r(y^s; s) + 2\varepsilon$ if p is close enough to s. From this we conclude that any limit point of the set of points $\{y^p\}$, as $p \to s$ must yield the same value as $r(y^s; s)$. But under the assumptions (see also Property 4.5), y^s is the unique minimizing point of $r(y; s)$, hence it is the unique limit point of the set, i.e., $y^p \to y^s$ as $p \to s$. □

Remark 4.16. Note that Property 4.5 asserts that a compromise solution y^p is unique when p is fixed and some conditions are fulfilled. Under a similar condition, Properties 4.8 and 4.4 assert that y^p is a continuous function of p and the set of all y^p-solutions, $p \geq 1$, forms a "one-dimensional" curve in the set of all N-points, which usually has $q - 1$ dimensions in q dimensions of Y. One recalls that compromise solutions induce strong preference assumptions, much stronger than Pareto preference; their solution sets are thus much smaller than that of Pareto solutions.

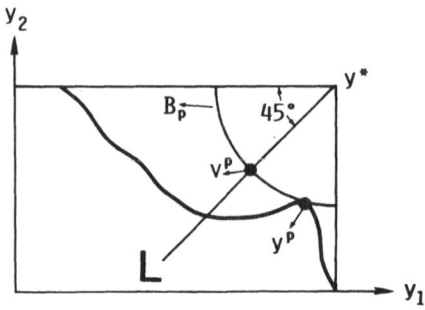

Figure 4.9

In order to describe monotonicity and bounds of compromise solutions, let L be the line of equal regrets. Thus L has the equation $y_1^* - y_1 = y_2^* - y_2 = \cdots = y_q^* - y_q$. Let B_p be the boundary of A_p defined in Property 4.5, i.e., $B_p = \{y \in R^q | r(y; p) = r(y^p; p)\}$. Let v^p be the point of intersection of B_p with the positive half of L (see Figure 4.9). This point may not be feasible, but it is equivalent to y^p with respect to $r(y; p)$. Furthermore, since $v^p \in L$, we have $y_i^* - v_i^p = d^p$, $i = 1, \ldots, q$, for some $d^p \geq 0$. Note that d^p is a function of p.

Property 4.9. (Monotonicity in General.) The function d^p is monotone nondecreasing for $1 \leq p \leq \infty$. (Thus the points v^p are arranged monotonically along L.)

Proof. Since*

$$[r(y^p; p)]^p = \sum_{i=1}^{q} [y_i^* - y_i^p]^p = \sum_{i=1}^{q} [y_i^* - v_i^p]^p = q[d^p]^p,$$

$$\left\{ \sum_{i=1}^{q} \frac{1}{q} \left[\frac{y_i^* - y_i^p}{d^p} \right]^p \right\}^{1/p} = 1.$$

By the inequality for means of order t (see Ref. 31, p. 17), if $s < p$, then

$$\left\{ \sum_{i=1}^{q} \frac{1}{q} \left[\frac{y_i^* - y_i^p}{d^p} \right]^s \right\}^{1/s} \leq 1$$

with equality if and only if all of the $y_i^* - y_i^p$ are equal, i.e., $y^p = v^p$. In any case,

$$\sum_{i=1}^{q} [y_i^* - y_i^p]^s \geq q[d^p]^s.$$

*Note that the superscript index on the right-hand bracket or parenthesis is an index of power.

But by definition of y^s and d^s

$$q[d^s]^s = [r(y^s; s)]^s$$

$$\leq \sum_{i=1}^{q} (y_i^* - y_i^p)^s \leq q[d^p]^s,$$

so $d^s \leq d^p$ whenever $s < p$ as desired. $\qquad\qquad\qquad\qquad \Box$

Property 4.10. (Bounds.) The following bounds hold:

i. $\sum_{i=1}^{q} v_i^\infty \leq \sum_{i=1}^{q} y_i^s \leq \sum_{i=1}^{q} y_i^1, \qquad 1 \leq s \leq \infty.$

ii. If y^∞ lies on the line L of equal regrets, then

$$\sum_{i=1}^{q} y_i^\infty \leq \sum_{i=1}^{q} y_i^s \leq \sum_{i=1}^{q} y_i^1, \qquad 1 \leq s \leq \infty.$$

Note that the property states that the sum of individual utility (which may be interpreted as the group's utility) is bounded from the top using parameter $p = 1$ and is bounded from the bottom using parameter $p = \infty$ under a mild assumption. Thus, if the sum of the utility is emphasized, parameter $p = 1$ should be used for the compromise solution. Note that because $\|y^* - y\|_\infty = \max_i \{y_i^* - y_i\}$, maximum individual regret is emphasized when $p = \infty$, but it results in the lowest sum of individual utility.

Proof of Property 4.10. Observe that, by Property 4.9,

$$\sum_{i=1}^{q} v_i^p \leq \sum_{i=1}^{q} v_i^s \qquad \text{for } 1 \leq s \leq p \leq \infty. \tag{4.18}$$

But the hyperplane whose equation is

$$\sum_{i=1}^{q} y_i - \sum_{i=1}^{q} v_i^s = 0$$

is a supporting hyperplane to the convex set A_s at its boundary point v^s. The points y^* and y^s are both on the same side of this hyperplane, which must be the positive side, hence

$$\sum_{i=1}^{q} y_i^s - \sum_{i=1}^{q} v_i^s \geq 0. \tag{4.19}$$

In view of (4.18) and (4.19), we have the left inequality in (i) by setting $p = \infty$. If $y^\infty = v^\infty$ then the left inequality in (ii) is also proved. The right inequalities follow from the fact that y^1 also maximizes $\sum_{i=1}^q y_i$ over Y. $\square$

Property 4.11. (Monotonicity in Two Criteria.) If $q = 2$ and $1 \leqq s \leqq p \leqq \infty$, then

(i) $\displaystyle\sum_{i=1}^q y_i^p \leqq \sum_{i=1}^q y_i^s$;

(ii) $\displaystyle\max_i \{y_i^* - y_i^p\} \leqq \max_i \{y_i^* - y_i^s\}$

(iii) In addition, if Y is compact and $\Lambda^{\leqq}$−convex, then y_i^p is a monotone function of p. If y_1^p is monotonically increasing, then y_2^p is monotonically decreasing, and vice versa.

Note that (i) implies that the sum of the utilities of the compromise solution is maximized when the parameter $p = 1$ is used, and as p gets larger, the sum of the utilities of the compromise solution will get smaller. On the other hand, (ii) implies that the "maximum individual regret" of the compromise solution is minimized when $p = \infty$ is used, and as p gets smaller the maximum individual regret of the compromise solution will get larger. *Thus, p plays the role of the balancing factor between the "group utility sum" and the maximum of the individual regrets.* If we want to emphasize the utility sum we should select a small p; otherwise, we should select large p in order to increase the weight given to the individual regrets.

Indeed, it can be shown (see Ref. 148) that the "simple majority rule" is a compromise solution with $p = 1$, thus, consistent with our intuition, the simple majority rule most emphasizes the sum of the individual utilities and least emphasizes the individual regret of the choice.

Proof. *For* (i): Refer to Figure 4.10. In the quadrant of nonnegative regrets, the curves B_p and B_s intersect at two points. These two points determine a line whose equation can be written as $y_1 + y_2 = c$, because of the symmetry about the line L of equal regrets. It follows from Property 4.9 that when the curves B_p and B_s lie below the line then B_p is below B_s. Since y^p lies on B_p and lies on or below B_s, it must fall in this region. Similarly, when B_p and B_s lie above the line, then B_s lies below B_p. It is in this region that y^s must fall. Thus,

$$\sum_{i=1}^q y_i^p \leqq c \leqq \sum_{i=1}^q y_i^s.$$

This proves (i).

For (ii): The proof is similar to (i). However, this time we shall use the fact that there is a constant d such that the curve of the equation is

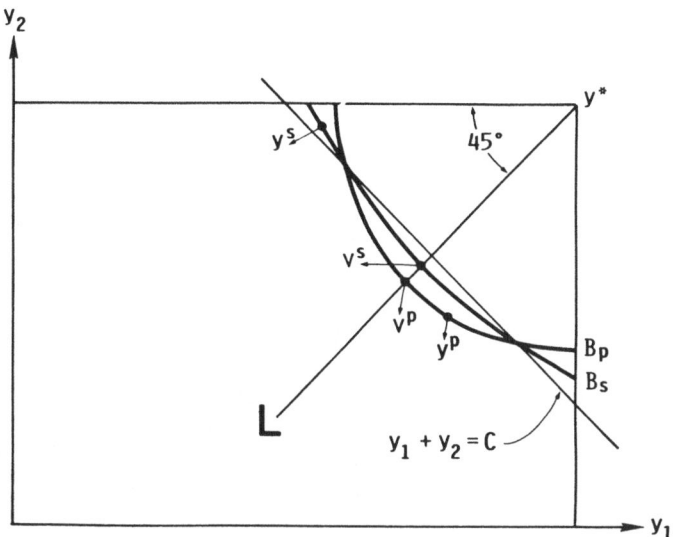

Figure 4.10

$\max_{i=1,2} \{y_i^* - y_i\} = d$ which passes through the two intersection points of B_p and B_s (see Figure 4.11). One can then easily show that y^p lies in the region of $\max_i \{y_i^* - y_i\} \leq d$ and y^s lies in the region of $\max_i \{y_i^* - y_i\} \geq d$. Thus, $\max_i \{y_i^* - y_i^p\} \leq d \leq \max_i \{y_i^* - y_i\}$ as desired.

For (*iii*): (Refer to Figure 4.12, where the converse case is illustrated.) In view of Property 4.8, the points y^p vary continuously along the Pareto optimal boundary of Y. Since $y_1^p + y_2^p$ is largest for $p = 1$, smallest for $p = \infty$, and is a monotonically nonincreasing function, the point y^p must move

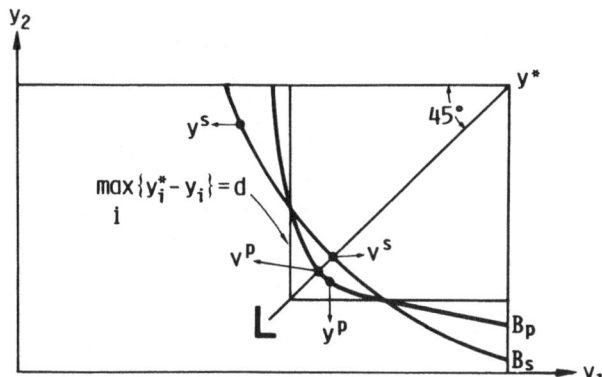

Figure 4.11

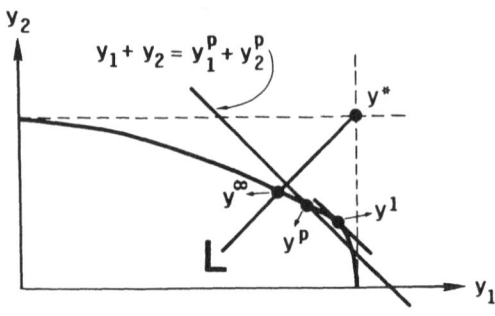

Figure 4.12

monotonically along the boundary segment from y^1 to y^∞. As we have drawn the picture, this means that y^p_1 decreases and y^p_2 increases with p. □

The following example shows that Property 4.11 may not be valid for $q > 2$ (i.e., when there are more than two criteria).

Example 4.6. (See Figure 4.13.) With $q = 3$, let Y be the convex set with vertices at the points $A = (44, 49, 54)$, $B = (43, 54, 49)$, $C = (54, 0, 0)$, and the origin. The set of N-points in Pareto preference is the triangle with vertices at A, B, C, so that any such points can be expressed as a linear combination, $y = (1 - \beta - \delta)A + \beta B + \delta C$, where the coefficients are nonnegative and sum to unity. Since the utopia point is $Y^* = (54, 54, 54)$, $r(y; p) = [(10 + \beta - 10\delta)^p + (5 - 5\beta + 49\delta)^p + (5\beta + 54\delta)^p]^{1/p}$. We can obtain y^p by minimizing this expression subject to the nonnegativity of β, δ, and $1 - \beta - \delta$. We find that for $p = 1$, y^1 coincides with A. As p increases, y^p first moves along the line segment AB toward B, then moves back toward A, and finally moves into the interior of the triangle. (Shown in Figure 4.13 are y^p for $p = 1$,

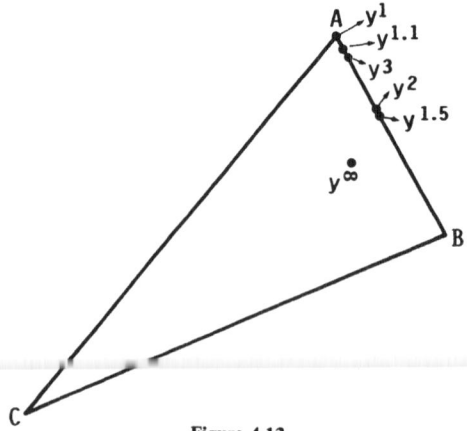

Figure 4.13

1.1, 1.5, 2, 3, and ∞.) Thus, there can be no monotonicity as a function p in the form of Property 4.11.

4.3.4. Computing Compromise Solutions

To find a compromise solution, one needs to know *the target point*, either the ideal point or not, and the parameter p for the regret function $r(f(x); p)$. When the target point is unknown, one may start with the ideal point as an approximation of the target. Hopefully, by an interactive process, one can gradually locate the target point and the compromise solution. When the ideal point is the target point, the computations of the compromise solution are not very complicated, at least theoretically. This will be discussed in Section 4.3.4.1. For general target points the computations can be slightly more complex. We shall discuss this in Section 4.3.4.2.

4.3.4.1. The Ideal Point as the Target Point

To find a compromise solution when the ideal point is the target point, we have to solve $q + 1$ mathematical programming problems. The first q problems are to find the utopia or ideal point, $y^* = (y_1^*, \ldots, y_q^*)$, where $y_i^* = \max \{f_i(x) \,|\, x \in X\}$. (See Example 4.4 for a linear case.) The last one is to find the compromise solution y^p. Suppose that X contains only countably many points. We will have $q + 1$ integer programming problems. Otherwise, if X is a region, we will have $q + 1$ nonlinear programming problems.

Suppose X and $f_i(x)$, $i = 1, \ldots, q$, have some special structure. More efficient computational techniques are available. For instance, if X is a convex set and each $f_i(x)$ is concave, then we first have q concave programming and then a convex programming problem [because $r(f(x); p)$ is convex under the assumptions (check it!)]. If X is a polyhedron defined by a system of linear inequalities and each $f_i(x)$ is linear, then the ideal points y^* can be found by q simple linear programming problems. Furthermore, the compromise solutions of y^1 and y^∞ can be found by a linear programming problem (the other compromise solution y^p, $1 < p < \infty$ can be found by convex programming). That y^1 can be found by linear programming is obvious. That y^∞ can be found by linear programming follows directly from the following well-known result.

Lemma 4.3. x^0 solves
Problem A: $\min_x \max_i \{y_i^* - f_i(x) \,|\, i = 1, \ldots, q, x \in X\}$ if and only if x^0 and $v^0 = \max_i \{y_i^* - f_i(x^0)\}$ solve
Problem B: $\min \{v \,|\, v \geq y_i^* - f_i(x), i = 1, \ldots, q, x \in X\}$.

Proof. *For Necessity*: Assume there is $x^1 \neq x^0$, $x^1 \in X$, and $v^1 = \max_i \{y_i^* - f_i(x^1)\} < v^0$. Then clearly x^0 cannot solve Problem A.

For Sufficiency: Assume that there is $x^1 \neq x^0$, $x^1 \in X$, so that in Problem A, $v^1 = \max_i \{y_i^* - f_i(x)\} < v^0$. Then (x^1, v^1) is a feasible solution of Problem B, and (x^0, v^0) cannot solve Problem B. $\square$

Example 4.7. Consider again the multicriteria decision problem discussed in Example 4.4:

$$\max y_1 = f_1(x) = 6x_1 + 4x_2,$$

$$\max y_2 = f_2(x) = x_1,$$

$$\text{s.t.} \quad g_1(x) = \quad x_1 + x_2 \leq 100,$$

$$g_2(x) = 2x_1 + x_2 \leq 150,$$

$$x_1, x_2 \geq 0.$$

The ideal point y^* is $(500, 75)$ as discussed in Example 4.4.

Now we illustrate how to find the y^1, y^2, and y^∞ compromise solutions using the above example.

(i) For the y^1 compromise solution, we solve

$$\min \{[500 - (6x_1 + 4x_2)] + [75 - x_1]\},$$

$$\text{s.t.} \quad x_1 + x_2 \leq 100,$$

$$2x_1 + x_2 \leq 150,$$

$$x_1, x_2 \geq 0.$$

We get $x_1^* = 50$, $x_2^* = 50$ and compromise solution $y^1 = (500, 50)$.

(ii) For the y^2 compromise solution, we solve

$$\min \{[500 - (6x_1 + 4x_2)]^2 + (75 - x_1)^2\},$$

$$\text{s.t.} \quad x_1 + x_2 \leq 100,$$

$$2x_1 + x_2 \leq 150,$$

$$x_1, x_2 \geq 0.$$

The solutions are $x_1^* = 55$, $x_2^* = 40$, and compromise solution $y^2 = (490, 55)$

(iii) For the y^∞ compromise solution, we solve

$$\min \max [500 - (6x_1 + 4x_2), 75 - x_1],$$

$$\text{s.t.} \quad x_1 + x_2 \leq 100,$$

$$2x_1 + x_2 \leq 150,$$

$$x_1, x_2 \geq 0.$$

The above problem, according to Lemma 4.3, can be simplified as follows:

$$\min v,$$

$$\text{s.t.} \quad v \geq 500 - (6x_1 + 4x_2),$$

$$v \geq 75 - x_1,$$

$$x_1 + x_2 \leq 100,$$

$$2x_1 + x_2 \leq 150,$$

$$x_1, x_2 \geq 0.$$

Note that this is a linear program. Solving the linear program, we get

$$x_1^* = 58.33, \quad x_2^* = 33.33, \quad y^\infty = (483.33, 58.33).$$

The following table is the summary of compromise solutions when $p = 1$, 2, and ∞:

	Compromise Solutions	
	(x_1, x_2)	(y_1, y_2)
$p = 1$	$(50, 50)$	$(500, 50) = y^1$
$p = 2$	$(55, 40)$	$(490, 55) = y^2$
$p = \infty$	$(58.33, 33.33)$	$(483.33, 58.33) = y^\infty$

The graphical presentation of y^1, y^2, and y^∞ compromise solutions is shown in Figure 4.14. Note that in Figure 4.14 the scales of y_1 and y_2 are different and y^∞ thus does not lie on the "45°-line" from y^*; compare with Example 4.5. Observe that according to Properties 4.8 and 4.11, as a function of p, y^p moves continuously and monotonically from y^1 to y^∞.

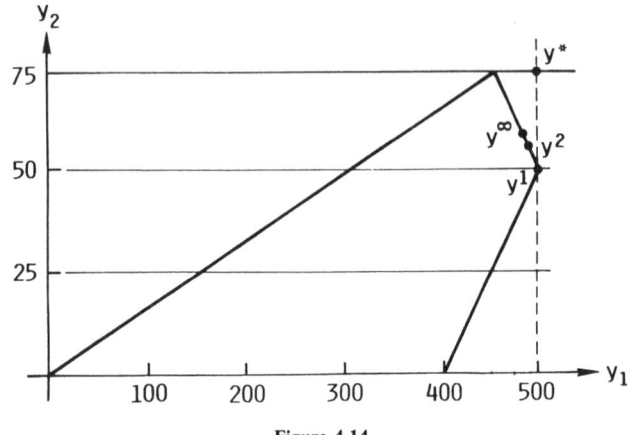

Figure 4.14

4.3.4.2. General Target Points and Goal Programming

Suppose that the target point for compromise solutions is known but is not the ideal point. Then not each f_i may be the type of "more is better." For instance, if the target for f_i is 10 and $f_i[X] = [8, 20]$, then $f_i = 15$ is attainable but not as good as $f_i = 10$. Thus the preference is not monotone over f. However, moving as closely to the target as possible is still the same. Note that the resulting compromise solution for the general target point may not be Pareto optimal over Y. Indeed, Pareto optimality does not make sense here as preference is no longer monotone over f. To regain the monotonicity, one needs to redefine the criteria. For instance, $f_i^- = \| f_i - y_i^* \|$, where y_i^* is the target of f_i, for smaller is better, and $\bar{f}_i = M - \| \bar{f}_i - y_i^* \|$, with M sufficiently large, for larger is better.

The computation for the compromise solution with general target point can be slightly more complicated. This is due to the possibility that $y_i^* \geqq y_i$ for all $y \in Y$ and $i = 1, \ldots, q$ may no longer hold. The following method of changing variables can be of help.

Lemma 4.4. Let

$$d_i^+ = \begin{cases} y_i - y_i^* & \text{if } y_i > y_i^*, \\ 0 & \text{otherwise}; \end{cases}$$

$$d_i^- = \begin{cases} y_i^* - y_i & \text{if } y_i < y_i^*, \\ 0 & \text{otherwise}. \end{cases}$$

Then

    i. $y_i^* - y_i = d_i^- - d_i^+$,
    ii. $|y_i^* - y_i| = d_i^- + d_i^+$,
    iii. $d_i^+, d_i^- \geqq 0$.

Note that d_i^+ is the value of y_i exceeding y_i^* (like a surplus variable) and d_i^- is the value of y_i below y_i^* (like a slack variable). The proof of the lemma is straightforward. (See Exercise 4.12.)

Lemma 4.5. The definition of d_i^+ and d_i^- in Lemma 4.4 is satisfied if and only if d_i^+ and d_i^- are nonnegative and satisfy

$$y_i^* - y_i = d_i^- - d_i^+, \tag{4.20}$$

$$d_i^+ \cdot d_i^- = 0. \tag{4.21}$$

Proof. The necessity is clear. To see the sufficiency, let us consider two possible cases.

Case 1: $y_i^* \geq y_i$. The nonnegativity and (4.21) imply that only one of d_i^+ and d_i^- can be positive and the other must be zero. Then by (4.20) we must have $d_i^- = y_i^* - y_i \geq 0$ and $d_i^+ = 0$; otherwise, we will have a contradiction.

Case 2: $y_i^* < y_i$. Similar arguments will lead to $d_i^+ = y_i - y_i^* > 0$ and $d_i^- = 0$ as we want to show. □

Now given a target point y^* the compromise solution with l_p-distance can be found by solving the following.

Program 4.3.

$$\min \sum_i |y_i^* - f_i(x)|^p = \min [r(f(x); p)]^p, \tag{4.22}$$

$$\text{s.t.} \quad g(x) \leq 0. \tag{4.23}$$

Note that since $[r(f(x); p)]^p$ is a strictly increasing function of $r(f(x); p)$, x^0 minimizes $[r(f(x); p)]^p$ if and only if it minimizes $r(f(x); p)$. The form of (4.22) makes it easier to find the compromise solution.

We now can apply Lemmas 4.4 and 4.5 to remove the sign of the absolute values in (4.22) and get the following program.

Program 4.4.

$$\min \sum_{i=1}^{q} (d_i^- + d_i^+)^p, \tag{4.24}$$

$$\text{s.t.} \quad y_i^* - f_i(x) = d_i^- - d_i^+, \tag{4.25}$$

$$d_i^+ \cdot d_i^- = 0, \tag{4.26}$$

$$d_i^+, d_i^- \geq 0, \tag{4.27}$$

$$g(x) \leq 0. \tag{4.28}$$

where $i = 1, 2, \ldots, q$ in (4.25)-(4.27).

Note that (4.24) follows from (ii) of Lemma 4.4, while (4.25)–(4.27) follow from Lemma 4.5.

A careful study reveals that (4.26) is a redundant constraint because the minimization of (4.24), (4.25), and (4.27) will ensure that only one of d_i^- and d_i^+ can be positive. In order to see this point, for any fixed x satisfying (4.28), let $y_i^* - f_i(x) > 0$ and $y_i^* - f_i(x) = d_i^- - d_i^+$. Assume both d_i^- and d_i^+ are positive. Then $d_i^- > d_i^+$. Now set $d_i^{-\prime} = d_i^- - d_i^+$ and $d_i^{+\prime} = 0$. Then $y_i^* - f_i(x) = d_i^{-\prime} - d_i^{+\prime}$ and $(d_i^{-\prime} + d_i^{+\prime})^p < (d_i^- + d_i^+)^p$. Thus, d_i^- and d_i^+ cannot minimize (4.24) if both are positive because the objective function in (4.24) is separable in i. We thus obtain that Program 4.3, Program 4.4, and Program below are equivalent.

Program 4.5. This is identical to Program 4.4 except that we delete constraint (4.26).

We summarize the above into the following theorem.

Theorem 4.5. Given a target point y^*, x^0 is the compromise solution with respect to the l_p-distance if and only if x^0 solves Program 4.5.

Remark 4.17. (i) Suppose that all $f_i(x)$, $i = 1, \ldots, q$, and $g(x)$ are linear. Then Program 4.5 for l_1-compromise solutions reduces to a linear program typically known as (linear) *goal programming*. By adding weights to or imposing lexicographical ordering on the criteria one can generalize the concept discussed here to a variety of goal programming formats. One notes that goal programming is a special class in the domain of compromise solutions. The major advantages of goal programming and l_1-compromise solutions are that they are easily understood and that they can easily be computed by linear programs. In applications, one should be aware of its endowed properties as discussed in Section 4.3.3 to avoid misuse or misleading conclusions.

(ii) When all $f_i(x)$, $i = 1, \ldots, q$, and $g(x)$ are linear, Program 4.5 for l_2-compromise solutions becomes a quadratic program. The program can be solved without major difficulty.

(iii) When all $f_i(x)$, $i = 1, \ldots, q$, and $g(x)$ are linear, Program 4.5 for l_∞-compromise solutions becomes a linear program by applying Lemma 4.3. (See Example 4.8.) This greatly simplifies the computations. Again, one should understand the properties endowed by the l_∞-compromise solution as discussed in Section 4.3.3 to avoid misuse.

Example 4.8. Consider the following problem which we discussed in Examples 4.4 and 4.7:

$$\max y_1 = f_1(x) = 6x_1 + 4x_2,$$

$$\max y_2 = f_2(x) = x_1,$$

$$\text{s.t.} \quad g_1(x) = \ x_1 + x_2 \leqq 100,$$

$$g_2(x) = 2x_1 + x_2 \leq 150,$$

$$x_1, x_2 \geq 0.$$

Assume that $y^* = (400, 80)$ is the target. Note that y^* is not the ideal point. We shall illustrate how to find compromise solutions using the goal programming approach of Program 4.5.

(i) *For the y^1-compromise solution.* Note that in this example $f_1(x)$ and $f_2(x)$ are linear and $g_1(x)$ and $g_2(x)$ are also linear. Thus, program 4.5 for l_1-compromise solutions reduces to a linear programming problem:

$$\min d_1^- + d_1^+ + d_2^- + d_2^+,$$

$$\text{s.t.} \quad 400 - (6x_1 + 4x_2) = d_1^- - d_1^+,$$

$$80 - x_1 = d_2^- - d_2^+,$$

$$d_1^+, d_1^-, d_2^+, d_2^- \geq 0,$$

$$x_1 + x_2 \leq 100,$$

$$2x_1 + x_2 \leq 150,$$

$$x_1, x_2 \geq 0.$$

Solving the linear program, we get

$$d_1^- = 0, \qquad d_1^+ = 0, \qquad d_2^- = 13.333, \qquad d_2^+ = 0,$$

$$x_1 = 66.667, \qquad x_2 = 0,$$

and therefore, the y^1 compromise solution is

$$y^1 = (400, 66.667).$$

(ii) *For the y^2-compromise solution.* Program 4.5 for the l_2-compromise solution becomes the following quadratic programming problem:

$$\min (d_1^- + d_1^+)^2 + (d_2^- + d_2^+)^2,$$

$$\text{s.t.} \quad 400 - (6x_1 + 4x_2) = d_1^- - d_1^+,$$

$$80 - x_1 = d_2^- - d_2^+,$$

$$d_1^+, d_1^-, d_2^+, d_2^- \geq 0,$$

$$x_1 + x_2 \leqq 100,$$

$$2x_1 + x_2 \leqq 150,$$

$$x_1, x_2 \geqq 0.$$

Solving the above nonlinear programming problem, we get

$$x_1 = 67, \qquad x_2 = 0.$$

Therefore, the y^2 compromise solution with the target point $y^* = (400, 80)$ is $[402, 67]$. Note that $d_1^- = 0$, $d_1^+ = 2$, $d_2^- = 13$, and $d_2^+ = 0$.

(*iii*) *For the y^∞-compromise solution.* Since $f_1(x)$, $f_2(x)$, $g_1(x)$, and $g_2(x)$ are linear, Program 4.5 for the l_∞-compromise solution becomes a linear program:

$$\min \max [d_1^- + d_1^+, d_2^- + d_2^+],$$

$$\text{s.t.} \quad 400 - (6x_1 + 4x_2) = d_1^- - d_1^+,$$

$$80 - x_1 = d_2^- - d_2^+,$$

$$d_1^+, d_1^-, d_2^+, d_2^- \geqq 0,$$

$$x \in X.$$

The above problem can be simplified as follows (using Lemma 4.3):

$$\min v$$

$$\text{s.t.} \quad v \geqq d_1^- + d_1^+,$$

$$v \geqq d_2^- + d_2^+,$$

$$400 - (6x_1 + 4x_2) = d_1^- - d_1^+,$$

$$80 - x_1 = d_2^- - d_2^+,$$

$$d_1^+, d_1^-, d_2^+, d_2^- \geqq 0,$$

$$x_1 + x_2 \leqq 100,$$

$$2x_1 + x_2 \leqq 150,$$

$$x_1, x_2 \geqq 0.$$

Solving the above linear program, we get $x_1 = 68.571$ and $x_2 = 0$. Thus, the y^∞ solution $= [411.426, 68.571]$. Note that $d_1^- = 0$, $d_1^+ = 11.429$, $d_2^- = 11.429$, $d_2^+ = 0$, and $v = 11.429$.

4.3.5. Interactive Methods

For nontrivial decision problems, an optimal decision usually cannot be reached by applying the compromise solution only once. The following interactive method, according to Figure 4.15, may be helpful.

Box 1. Identifying X, f, and y^* is an art that requires careful observation of and conversation with the decision maker. (See Chapter 9 for further discussion.) The target point y^*, weight vector w and p for l_p-distance may be more difficult to specify precisely. However, one can use the ideal point as the first step of approximation for y^*, select some representative weights for w, and let $p = 1, 2, \infty$ to begin.

Box 2. One can locate compromise solutions according to Program 4.5 for the specified values of y^*, w, and p.

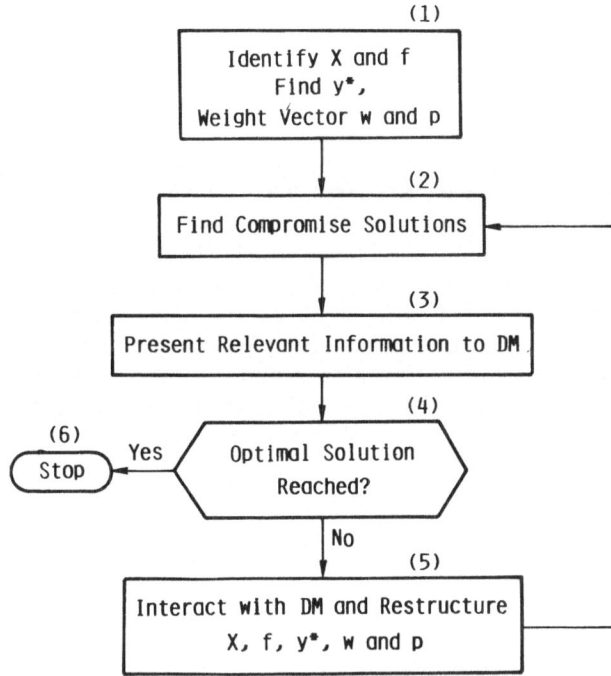

Figure 4.15

Box 3. All relevant information obtained in boxes 1 and 2 can be presented to the decision maker. These include X, f, Y, ideal points y_i^*, $i = 1, \ldots, q$, the optimal vector value which maximizes the ith criterion, the compromise solutions y^1, y^2, y^∞ with their weights and norms.

Boxes 4 and 6. If an optimal solution is reached in box 3 and the decision maker is satisfied, the process is terminated at box 6; otherwise, we go to box 5 to obtain more information.

Box 5. Through conversation, we may obtain new information on X, f, y^*, the weight vector w, and norm parameter p. Note that each of these five elements may change with time. To help the decision maker locate or change the target point, one may use the "one-at-a-time method." That is, only one value of f_i or y_i, $i = 1, \ldots, q$, is to be changed and the rest remain unchanged. One may ask the decision maker: "Since no satisfactory solution is obtained with the current target point y^*, would it be possible to decrease (or increase) the value of y_i^*? And, if so, by how much?" This kind of suggestive question may help the decision maker think hard and carefully of possible changes in the target points. The other method is called the "pairwise tradeoff method." We first select two criteria, say f_i and f_j, and then ask: "To maintain the same degree of satisfaction for the target point, everything else being equal, how many units f_j must be increased in order to compensate for a one-unit decrease in f_i?" Again, this kind of suggestive question can help the decision maker to think hard and carefully of the possible changes in the target points. Finally, we recall that the target point may be regarded as the satisficing set containing a single satisficing solution. Thus, by locating the satisficing set, we may locate the target point.

Remark 4.18. Comparing Section 4.2 with Section 4.3, we know that satisficing solutions are more general and flexible in applications, while compromise solutions are more specific and rigid. The former is loose while the latter makes sense only when strong assumptions are satisfied. However, with flexible interpretation and artful applications in the interaction with the decision maker, the two methods can complement each other. After all, both concepts stem from the goal-seeking assumption and try to minimize the distance from the criteria space to a set of satisficing solutions or a taget point. In a broader perspective, they are the same.

Example 4.9. We shall use the previously discussed example (see Example 4.7) to illustrate the interactive methods.

Step 1. Identify $X, f, y^*, w, and p$. The decision space, X, is given by

$$g_1(x) = x_1 + x_2 \leq 100,$$

$$g_2(x) = 2x_1 + x_2 \leq 150,$$

$$x_1, x_2 \geq 0,$$

and the objective functions f_1 and f_2 are

$$y_1 = f_1(x) = 6x_1 + 4x_2,$$

$$y_2 = f_2(x) = x_1.$$

Through conversations with the decision maker, assume that the ideal point will be used as the approximation for the target point. The ideal point (y_1^*, y_2^*) is (500, 75). We shall assume that each criterion carries the same weight (i.e., $w_1 = w_2$). For the purpose of finding the compromise solutions, we shall use $p = 1, 2,$ and ∞ for l_p-distance measure.

    Step 2. Find Compromise Solutions. The computation of compromise solutions for $p = 1, 2,$ and ∞ was illustrated in Example 4.7. The compromise solutions are $y^1 = (500, 50)$, $y^2 = (490, 55)$, and $y^\infty = (483.33, 58.33)$.

    Step 3. Present Relevant Information to DM. All relevant information obtained in steps 1 and 2 will be presented to the decision maker. This includes $X, f, Y,$ ideal points and the compromise solutions $y^1, y^2,$ and y^∞ with their weights (w) and norms (p). Certainly a graphic display of this information, such as Figure 4.14, will greatly help the decision maker to conceptualize what he can and cannot attain.

    Step 4. Optimal solution reached? Suppose the decision maker is not satisfied with the information (including compromise solutions) presented to him. Assume that he is not satisfied with the target point (y^*) and the weight vector (w). He prefers to have the target point a little bit closer to the set Y. He also feels that more weight should be given to the first criterion (f_1) rather than having equal weights.

    Step 5. Through conversations with the decision maker new relevant information on the target point (y^*) and the weight vector (w) will be obtained. Assume that the information on $X, f,$ and p remains the same and that the new y^* and w are as follows:

$$y^* = (450, 75) \quad \text{and} \quad w = (\tfrac{2}{3}, \tfrac{1}{3}).$$

With this new information, compromise solutions $y^1, y^2,$ and y^∞ can be recalculated. New solutions will be presented to the decision maker. If the decision maker is satisfied with the new solutions, the procedure will be terminated. If he is not satisfied with the solutions, then again more information from the decision maker on $X, f, y^*, w,$ and p will be needed. We go to box 5 and the process continues.

4.4. Further Comments

    Using human goal-seeking behavior, we have described satisficing and compromise solutions. The art of specifying the satisficing set or the target point is not easy. However, one can always start with the ideal point and then interact with the decision maker. Note that l_1-compromise solutions with general target points are known solution concepts in goal programming which have enjoyed a large volume of literature [for instance, see Charnes and Cooper (Ref. 77), and Lee (Ref. 281) and those quoted therein].

We have only discussed the l_p-distance. In theory, the distance can be defined by other kinds of norms. The reader may be interested in Gearhart (Ref. 157) for such an extension. Also in a broader sense, penalty functions, instead of distance functions, can be used to derive a solution close to the goal. In this respect, the reader may be interested in the works of White (Ref. 482), and Pascoletti and Serafini (Ref. 343). For the restructuring of ideal points the reader may also be interested in the work of Zeleny (Ref. 515). Finally we should point out that there is a rich literature in social science which also uses the compromise solution concept. For this the reader may be interested in Ref. 103 by Davis, DeGroot, and Hinich and those quoted therein. For further references, see also Dinkelbach (Ref. 110).

Exercises

4.1. Discuss the similarities and differences between the compromise solutions approach and the satisficing solutions approach.

4.2. Consider the following linear multiobjective problem:

$$\text{maximize } y_1 = f_1(x_1, x_2) = 2x_1 + 3x_2,$$

$$\text{maximize } y_2 = f_2(x_1, x_2) = 2x_1 + x_2,$$

$$\text{subject to } \quad x_1 + x_2 \leq 10,$$

$$x_1 \leq 6,$$

$$x_2 \leq 6,$$

$$x_1, x_2 \leq 0.$$

a. Find the point in X which will maximize f_1 and f_2, respectively.
b. Find the ideal solution $y^* = (y_1^*, y_2^*)$ which will provide the maxima of the objective functions.
c. Draw the outcome space Y.
d. Assuming that each criterion carries the same weight, find the compromise solutions for $p = 1, 2,$ and ∞.
e. Identify the set of all compromise solutions with $p \geq 1$.

4.3. Refer to Example 4.1. Sketch the satisficing set $S = S_1 \cup S_2 \cup S_3$. (Note that in this example, $S_1 \cup S_2 \cup S_3$ is not convex.)

4.4. Let the outcome space Y be

$$Y = \left\{ (y_1, y_2) \,\middle|\, \begin{array}{l} y_1 + 2y_2 \leq 10 \\ 3y_1 + 2y_2 \leq 15 \end{array}, y_1, y_2 \geq 0 \right\}$$

a. Sketch the outcome space Y and find the ideal point y^*.
b. Identify y^1, y^2, and y^∞ in the graph without calculating the exact values.
c. Find the compromise solutions y^1, y^2, and y^∞ mathematically.

4.5. Consider the following problem:

$$\text{maximize } f_1 = x_1 + x_2,$$

$$\text{maximize } f_2 = 10x_1 - x_1^2 + 4x_2 - x_2^2,$$

$$\text{subject to } 3x_1 + x_2 \leq 12,$$

$$2x_1 + x_2 \leq 9,$$

$$x_1 + 2x_2 \leq 12,$$

$$x_1, x_2 \geq 0.$$

a. Find compromise solutions with $p = 1$, 2, and ∞ assuming equal weights to the objective functions.
b. Sketch the outcome space Y and identify compromise solutions obtained in (a). Identify the set of all compromise solutions with $p \geq 1$.
c. Now let the target be $(y_1^*, y_2^*) = (15, 15)$. Use Program 4.5 to find y^1, y^2, and y^∞ compromise solutions. Identify these solution in the graph of (b).

4.6. Verify that the least-squares method and the robust method are y^2- and y^1-compromise solutions, respectively. (Hint: the observed sample values form "the target point".)

4.7. The compromise solution is based on the minimization of "badness" of any compromise relative to the ideal point. Thus, the compromise solution with respect to p is a particular arbitration form of conflict resolution among the available alternatives. Discuss some special interpretations of the compromise solutions with $p = 1, 2$, and ∞ in group decision making or conflict resolution.

$$y_1 \geq 5 \quad \text{and} \quad y_2 \geq 3.$$

4.8. Refer to Exercise 4.2. Suppose that the satisficing levels for each objective function are given in the following way:

a. Sketch the satisficing region in the decision space (X) and the outcome space (Y).
b. Determine whether $Y \cap S = \varnothing$.
c. If $Y \cap S \neq \varnothing$ in (b), then find the satisficing solutions using Program 4.1 discussed in Section 4.2.3.

4.9. The XYZ Company makes TV sets. They make black and white TV sets with a profit of $25 per set, and they make color TV sets with a profit of $55 per set. The time (in hours) required in each of the three departments to make one of each set is summarized below:

	Time Required (hrs)		
TV set	Department 1	Department 2	Department 3
Black and white	0.4	0.5	0
Color	0.5	1.0	1.5

The number of man-hours available per day in each of the three departments is 16, 22, and 30, respectively.
a. Find the number of each type of TV sets that should be made to maximize the profit.
b. Assume that the company has been experiencing a significant decrease in productivity due to low morale among employees. The production manager blames this low productivity on the company's "maximizing profit" policy. The president of the XYZ Company with the advice of the production manager decides to set a minimal satisfaction level for profit and production as an experimental attempt to improve the organizational climate to increase productivity. The minimal satisfaction is set in the following way:

The minimal satisfaction level for profit is $750.

The minimal satisfaction level for production (i.e., the sum of black and white and color TV sets to be produced) is 25 sets.

i. Define the satisficing set and sketch the satisficing set in the decision space.
ii. Find at least two satisficing solutions using Program 4.1 discussed in Section 4.2.3.

4.10. Gembicki (Ref. 159) proposed the *goal attainment method* as a variation of the goal programming method. The method requires that the decision maker give a goal vector b and weight vector w relating the relative under- or overattainment of the desired goals. The mathematical formulation of the problem is

$$\text{minimize } z$$

$$\text{s.t. } g_j(x) \leq 0, \qquad j = 1, 2, \ldots, m,$$

$$f_i(x) \geq b_i + w_i z, \qquad i = 1, 2, \ldots, k.$$

Show that the goal attainment method is a weighted y^∞ compromise solution with weights given by

$$\left(\frac{1}{|w_1|}, \frac{1}{|w_2|}, \frac{1}{|w_3|}, \ldots, \frac{1}{|w_k|} \right).$$

4.11. Verify that, with respect to Program 4.1 [(4.10)–(4.12)], $S_k \cap Y \neq \emptyset$ iff $V_k = 0$.

4.12. Prove Lemma 4.4.

Suggested Reading

The following references are particularly pertinent to this chapter: 31, 77, 103, 110, 148, 149, 157, 159, 281, 297, 301, 343, 413, 482, 493, 515.

5

Value Function

Numerical systems, as a great invention of human beings, have a prevailing impact on our culture and thinking. It is natural and important for us to ask: is it possible to express our preference over the outcomes in terms of numbers so that the larger the number the stronger the preference? And if it is, then how should we achieve this?

In the previous chapter we used the distance function $r(y; p)$ from the ideal or target point to express our preference over Y. It is a model to approximate human goal-seeking behavior. If we know our goal or the ideal points, the distance function can always be constructed. In a broad sense it is a usage of numerical systems to express our preference. However, the basic idea is to minimize the distance from the outcome to the ideal or target point.

In contrast to the concept of minimizing the distance from the ideal point or the satisficing concept as discussed in Chapter 4, there is a school of thought that each outcome has "utility" to the decision maker and the decision maker tends to or should choose the one which maximizes his/her "utility." The following are some immediate questions: Are there any real-valued functions $v(y)$ defined on Y such that $y^1 > y^2$ iff $v(y^1) > v(y^2)$? Under what conditions can such functions exist? These questions will be discussed in this chapter. To avoid confusion the above function $v(y)$ is called a *value function* instead of utility function which is reserved for the discussion when uncertainty in the outcomes is involved. Many methods for constructing value functions from revealed preference will be described in the next chapter.

To facilitate our presentation and understanding we shall start with what can be said about preference if a value function exists (Section 5.1). We then discuss what would be the minimum requirement for a value function to exist (Section 5.2). As the additive and monotonic value functions play an important role in applications, we shall devote Section 5.3 to the discussion of the conditions for additive and monotonic value functions to exist. To avoid distraction from presenting the main concepts, we will drop the complicated mathematical proofs of the theorems. However, references will be given so that the interested readers can refer to them.

5.1. Revealed Preference from a Value Function

For ease of presentation, the following assumption is needed. Recall that
$Y \subset R^q$.

Assumption 5.1. (i) There exists a *value function*: $v: Y \to R^1$ so that $y^1 > y^2$
iff $v(y^1) > v(y^2)$.
(ii) Y is convex and v is continuous on Y.

Given v, Assumption 5.1(i) gives its induced preference. The corresponding sets $\{>\}$, $\{\sim\}$, and $\{<\}$ can be defined as in Chapter 2. Unless otherwise
specified, in this section $\{>\}$ and $\{\sim\}$ will be used to denote the preference
relation induced by v. We want to study some basic properties of these
preference relations.
The following can easily be established.

Property 5.1. If Assumption 5.1(i) is satisfied, the induced $\{>\}$ is a weak
order. (Thus, $\{\sim\}$ is an equivalence relation.) (See Exercise 5.1.)

Let $\{\tilde{Y}\}$ be the collection of all *isovalued curves* of v in Y, which is the
set of equivalence classes of Y under $\sim$.
Define $\hat{a} \in \{\tilde{Y}\}$, by

$$\hat{a} = \{y | v(y) = a\}. \tag{5.1}$$

Note that $\hat{a}$ is an isovalued curve of v in Y with $v(y) = a$ for every $y \in \hat{a}$.
One can define $\{>'\}$ on $\{\tilde{Y}\}$ by $\hat{a} >' \hat{b}$ iff $a > b$ or $v(y^1) > v(y^2)$ for any
$y^1 \in \hat{a}$ and $y^2 \in \hat{b}$. Note that $\{>'\}$ is a *strict order* on $\{\tilde{Y}\}$. (That is, it is a weak
order and if $\hat{a} \neq \hat{b}$ then either $\hat{a} >' \hat{b}$ or $\hat{b} >' \hat{a}$.)
Let $A \subset Y$; we say A is *dense* in Y iff $Cl\ A = Y$. Note that the set of
rational numbers is dense in R^1, because there is a rational number between
every two distinct real numbers. In terms of the natural order of real numbers,
if $a < b$, $a, b \in R^1$, then there is a rational number r such that $a < r < b$. This
concept of "denseness" in terms of $<$ can be generalized as follows.

Definition 5.1. Let $>$ be a binary relation on Y. Then $A \subseteq Y$ is $>$-*dense*
in Y iff whenever $y^1 > y^2$ and y^1 and y^2 are in Y but not in A, there is a z in
A such that $y^1 > z$ and $z > y^2$ hold.

As discussed above, the set of rational number is $>$-dense in the set of
real numbers. The set of all odd numbers and the set of all even numbers is

$>$-dense in the set of all integer numbers. Similarly, if $Y = \{y^0, y^1, y^2, y^3, y^4\}$ and $y^0 > y^1 > y^2 > y^3 > y^4$, then $\{y^0, y^2, y^4\}$ and $\{y^1, y^3\}$ are $>$-dense in Y.

Property 5.2. If Assumption 5.1(i) is satisfied then there is a countable subset $\hat{A}$ of $\{\tilde{Y}\}$ which is $>'$-dense in $\{\tilde{Y}\}$.

A proof of the above property can be found in Fishburn (Ref. 139). To illustrate the main concept we shall prove it with the additional Assumption 5.1(ii). Since Y is convex and v is continuous, $V = v[Y]$ is an interval. If V degenerates to a point, the conclusion is clear. Otherwise let B be the set of rational numbers in V and define $\hat{B} = \{\hat{b} | b \in B\}$. Then $\hat{B}$ is countable because B is countable, and $\hat{B}$ is $>'$-dense in $\{\tilde{Y}\}$ because B is $>$-dense in V.

Remark 5.1. Property 5.2 states that given a value function v, there is a *countable* subset of isovalued curves which is $>'$-dense in the set of all isovalued curves $\{\tilde{Y}\}$. This countable $>'$-dense subset in $\{\tilde{Y}\}$ is very essential for a value function to exist as will be discussed in the next section.

The next property follows directly from the continuity of v on Y.

Property 5.3. If Assumption 5.1 holds, then for every $y \in Y$, $\{y>\}$ (the set inferior to y) and $\{y<\}$ (the set superior to y) are open sets in the relative usual topology for Y in R^q.

Remark 5.2. In addition to the above three important properties, given the value function v is known one can study the relative strength of preference in the following sense:

Given y^0, y^1, y^2 in Y, if $v(y^1) - v(y^0) > v(y^2) - v(y^0)$ then moving from y^0 to y^1 is *more preferred* than moving from y^0 to y^2. In general one can define an order $\gtrsim$ as follows: $(y^1 - y^0) \gtrsim (y^3 - y^2)$ iff $v(y^1) - v(y^0) > v(y^3) - v(y^2)$. Note that $\gtrsim$ is defined on $Y \times Y$. With respect to $\gtrsim$ again the above Properties 5.1–5.3 hold [because $w: Y \times Y \to R^1$ with $w(y^1, y^2) = v(y^1) - v(y^2)$ is a value function].

Remark 5.3. When v has some special structures such as differentiability or concavity further properties on the preference can be constructed. For instance, if v is differentiable then ∇v will give, locally, the direction of maximum increase in v or value of the preference. When $\nabla v \neq 0$, locally, $\{h | \nabla v \cdot h < 0\}$ and $\{h | \nabla v \cdot h > 0\}$ will give, respectively, the directions of decreasing and increasing value of v. These kinds of properties usually are not assumed when we study the existence of a value function. They may be assumed and studied when one tries to construct a value function with specific properties.

5.2. Conditions for Value Functions to Exist

In this section, the reverse statements of Properties 5.1–5.3 will be shown to be needed for the existence of value functions. Because the derivation and proofs are very much involved we shall only motivate the concepts and skip the proofs. The interested reader may refer to Fishburn (Ref. 139) for proofs.

Definition 5.2. By "v is a value function on Y for $\{>\}$" we shall mean that $v: Y \to R^1$, and for every $y^1, y^2 \in Y$, $y^1 > y^2$ iff $v(y^1) > v(y^2)$.

Recall that if $\{>\}$ is a weak order then $\{\sim\}$ is an equivalence relation. Then we can define $\{\tilde{Y}\}$ to be the set of equivalence classes of Y under $\sim$ (similar to the set of all isovalued curves). (See Exercise 2.10 for further discussion.) The following important theorem which reverses Properties 5.1–5.2 is adapted from Theorem 3.1 of Fishburn (Ref. 139).

Theorem 5.1. There is a value function v on Y for $\{>\}$ if and only if (i) $\{>\}$ on Y is a weak order and (ii) there is a countable subset of $\{\tilde{Y}\}$ that is $>'$-order dense in $\{\tilde{Y}\}$.

Remark 5.4. Weak order is a strong assumption as indicated in Theorem 2.2. Pareto preference as discussed in Chapter 2 and Chapter 3 and its generalization to constant cone domination structures (Chapter 7) are in general not a weak order, unless Y is degenerated into a finite number of points and/or with special structure. [For instance if $Y \subset R^2$ and Y is the straight line connecting $(0, 0)$ and $(1, 1)$ then Pareto preference is a weak order on Y (check it).] Thus, in general, Pareto preference cannot be represented by a value function.

Remark 5.5. The condition of a countable subset of isovalued curves which is $>'$-dense in $\{\tilde{Y}\}$ is also important. For instance, the lexicographical order $\{>_L\}$ in R^2 does not contain a countable subset which is $>'_L$-dense in $\{\tilde{Y}\}$, and therefore there is no value function on R^2 for $\{>_L\}$. In order to see this point, observe that $\{\tilde{Y}\} = \{\{y\} | y \in R^2\}$. That is, the indifferent set to each point $y \in Y$ induced by $>_L$ is the set of the single point y. Denote $y = (y_1, y_2)$. For each fixed y_1 it takes a countable subset of R^1 for y_2 to obtain an $>'_L$-dense subset on $\{y_1\} \times R^1$. But there is an uncountable number of such y_1 and it follows that no countable subset of R^2 is $>'_L$-dense in R^2.

To further appreciate that there is no value function on R^2 for $>_L$, let us assume to the contrary that there is $v: R^2 \to R^1$ such that $v(y^1) > v(y^2)$ iff $y^1 >_L y^2$ for every $y^1, y^2 \in Y$. Let $y = (y_1, y_2)$ and fix y_1. Then v maps $\{y_1\} \times R^1$ into a nondegenerate interval $I(y_1)$ of R^1 so as to preserve the $>_L$-order of $\{y_1\} \times R^1$. For different y_1, the intervals of $I(y_1)$ should not overlap because $(y_1^1, y_2^2) >_L (y_1^2, y_2^2)$ and $v(y_1^1, y_2^1) > v(y_1^2, y_2^2)$ whenever $y_1^1 > y_1^2$. Since there are uncountably many y_1 in R^1, there is an uncountable number of nonoverlapping intervals $I(y_1)$ covering R^1 as the image of v. Since each interval $I(y_1)$ which is not degenerated into a point must contain at least one rational number, this would imply that there are uncountably many rational numbers in R^1, which clearly contradicts the fact that the set of rational numbers is countable.

Theorem 5.1, elegant as it is, is not easy to apply in practice because the countable dense subset property of indifference curves is difficult to verify. The following sufficiency theorem [Theorem 3.3 of Fishburn (Ref. 139)] offers some remedy.

Theorem 5.2. Suppose that Y is a rectangular subset of R^q and that the following hold throughout Y:
   i. $\{>\}$ on Y is a weak order;
   ii. $y^1 \geq y^2$ (note, $y^1 \neq y^2$) implies that $y^1 > y^2$;
   iii. if $y^1 > y^2$ and $y^2 > y^3$ then there is $\alpha, \beta, 0 < \alpha < 1, 0 < \beta < 1$, so that $\alpha y^1 + (1 - \alpha)y^3 > y^2$ and $y^2 > \beta y^1 + (1 - \beta)y^3$.
Then there exists a value function v on Y for $\{>\}$.

Remark 5.6. Conditions (i)-(iii) are used to construct countable dense subsets of indifferent curves in $\{\check{Y}\}$. Indeed, the hypotheses of Theorem 5.2 imply that if $y^1 \leq y^2 \leq y^3, y^j \in Y, j = 1, 2, 3$, then there is one exact $\alpha, 0 < \alpha < 1$, such that $y^2 \sim \alpha y^1 + (1 - \alpha)y^3$. The reader who is interested in the proof of Theorem 5.2 is referred to Fishburn (Ref. 139).

In the remainder of this section we shall describe another elegant result based on topology structure. To help the reader we shall first briefly review some relevant concepts in topology, using Definitions 5.3–5.5.

Definition 5.3. A topology $\mathcal{T}$ for a set Y is a set of subsets of Y such that
   i. The empty set $\varnothing$ and Y are in $\mathcal{T}$.
   ii. The union of arbitrarily many sets of $\mathcal{T}$ is in $\mathcal{T}$.
   iii. The intersection of any finite number of sets of $\mathcal{T}$ is in $\mathcal{T}$. If $\mathcal{T}$ is a topology for Y, the pair $(Y, \mathcal{T})$ is a topological space.
By definition the subsets of Y in $\mathcal{T}$ are called *open sets*.

Let $\mathcal{U}$ be the set of open intervals of R^1 along with their arbitrary union and finite intersection. Note that $\mathcal{U}$ is the usual topology of R^1.

Definition 5.4. Given that $(Y, \mathcal{T})$ is a topological space, then a real-valued function v on Y is continuous in the topology $\mathcal{T}$ iff $U \in \mathcal{U}$ implies that $\{y | y \in Y, v(y) \in U\} \in \mathcal{T}$.

Definition 5.5. (i) A topological space $(Y, \mathcal{T})$ is *connected* iff Y cannot be partitioned into two nonempty open sets (in $\mathcal{T}$).
   (ii) The *closure*, Cl A, of $A \subset Y$ is the set of all $y \in Y$ for which every open set that contains y has a nonempty intersection with A.

(iii) $(Y, \mathcal{T})$ is *separable* iff Y includes a countable subset whose closure is Y.

Note that $(R^1, \mathcal{U})$ is connected and separable because the rational numbers are countable and dense in R^1. Also note that $(Y, \mathcal{T})$ is separable iff Y contains a countable dense subset. We are ready for the following famous result due to Debreu (Ref. 104), which reverses the statements of Properties 5.1–5.3.

Theorem 5.3. Suppose (i) $\{>\}$ on Y is a weak order, (ii) $(Y, \mathcal{T})$ is a connected and separable topological space, and (iii) $\{y<\} \in \mathcal{T}$ and $\{y>\} \in \mathcal{T}$ for every $y \in Y$. Then there is a value function v on Y that is continuous in the topology $\mathcal{T}$ for $\{>\}$.

Remark 5.7. For a proof of Theorem 5.3 the reader can refer to Debreu (Ref. 104) or Fishburn (Ref. 139). Note that (i) is identical to (i) of Theorem 5.1, while (ii) and (iii) are used to construct countable dense subsets as needed in (ii) of Theorem 5.1. The additional condition (iii), a reverse statement of Property 5.3, also ensures that the value function v is continuous.

5.3. Additive and Monotonic Value Functions and Preference Separability

In Section 5.3.1 we shall study the preference separability revealed by monotonic and additive value functions. Its converse, which describes the separability condition for a value function to be monotonic or additive will be discussed in Section 5.3.2. While our emphasis is on Section 5.3.2, Section 5.3.1 nevertheless gives the necessary motivation. Because preference separability plays an important role in constructing additive or monotonic value functions, further results on preference separability are discussed in Section 5.3.3.

Throughout this section it will be assumed that $Y = \prod_{i=1}^{q} Y_i$ (i.e., Y is the Cartesian product of $Y_1, \ldots, Y_q$), each $Y_i \subset R^1$, and the following notation will be used.

Let $Q = \{1, 2, \ldots, q\}$ be the index set of the criteria. Given $I \subset Q$, its complement will be denoted by $\bar{I} = Q \backslash I$. Let $\{I_1, I_2, \ldots, I_m\}$, each $I_k \neq \varnothing$, be a partition of Q (i.e., $I_i \cap I_k = \varnothing$ if $i \neq k$ and $\bigcup_{k=1}^{m} I_k = Q$). For $k = 1, \ldots, m$ let

$$z_k = y_{I_k} \text{ be the vector with } \{y_i | i \in I_k\} \text{ as its components} \qquad (5.2)$$

and

$$Y_{I_k} = \prod_{i \in I_k} Y_i. \qquad (5.3)$$

Note that $y_{I_k} \in Y_{I_k}$. Without confusion, we can write

$$y = (y_{I_1}, \ldots, y_{I_m}) = (z_1, \ldots, z_m). \tag{5.4}$$

Definition 5.6. By "$\{I_1, \ldots, I_m\}$ and $(z_1, \ldots, z_m)$ form a partition of Q and y, respectively" we shall mean the situation that (5.2) and (5.4) hold.

5.3.1. Additive and Monotonic Value Functions and Implied Preference Separability

Throughout this subsection a value function $v(y)$ is assumed to be given. Such $v(y)$ will induce a preference structure $\{>\}$ as discussed in Section 5.1. We shall study the important concept of *preference separability* when $v(y)$ has a special structure of additivity or monotonicity. First let us introduce the following definition:

Definition 5.7. Given $\{>\}$ and $I \subset Q$, $I \neq \varnothing$. Let $z \in Y_I$ and $w \in Y_{\bar{I}}$. We say that z and/or I is *preference-separable* or $>$-*separable* iff $(z^0, w^0) > (z^1, w^0)$ for any $z^0, z^1 \in Y_I$ and some $w^0 \in Y_{\bar{I}}$ implies that $(z^0, w) > (z^1, w)$ for all $w \in Y_{\bar{I}}$.

Note that the Pareto preference, the lexicographic preference, and the preference of a compromise solution are all $>$-separable for each subset of Q (see Exercises 5.12 and 5.13). The preference induced by the satisficing solution of arbitrary satisficing sets may not be $>$-separable for arbitrary subsets of Q.

Remark 5.8. (i) If needed, one can make $\varnothing$ and Q $>$-separable in an obvious way.

(ii) If I_1 and I_2 are $>$-separable, so is $I_1 \cap I_2$. (See Exercise 5.4.) However, that I is $>$-separable does not imply that $\bar{I}$ is $>$-separable. (See Remark 5.12 for an example.)

(iii) Note that $z \in Y_I$ is preference separable iff, when $w \in Y_{\bar{I}}$ is fixed at some $w^0 \in Y_{\bar{I}}$ and $(z^0, w^0) > (z^1, w^0)$ for any z^0, z^1, one can conclude that for all other $w \in Y_{\bar{I}}$, $(z^0, w) > (z^1, w)$ holds. Thus, whenever w is fixed, z^0 is preferred to z^1 no matter where w is fixed. In studying preference structure, separability becomes an important concept, because if z is $>$-separable, we may separate it from the remaining variables in constructing the overall value function or in finding the maximum value point. The reader may want to compare $>$-separability with the separability in dynamic programming. (See Exercise 5.5.)

Remark 5.9. Preference separability is used by Gorman (Ref. 170). Keeney and Raiffa (Ref. 254) use preference independence with respect to the complement to mean the same.

Definition 5.8. A value function $v(y)$ is *additive* iff there is $v_i(y_i)\colon Y_i \to R^1$, $i = 1, \ldots, q$ such that

$$v(y) = \sum_{i=1}^{q} v_i(y_i). \tag{5.5}$$

Now given any $I \subset Q$, $I \neq \varnothing$, if $v(y)$ is additive as in (5.5), we can write

$$v(y) = v_I(y_I) + v_{\bar{I}}(y_{\bar{I}}), \tag{5.6}$$

where

$$v_I(y_I) = \sum_{i \in I} v_i(y_i)$$

and $v_{\bar{I}}(y_{\bar{I}})$ is similarly defined. From (5.6), we see immediately that for any y_I^0, y_I^1 of Y_I, if $v_I(y_I^0) > v_I(y_I^1)$ then

$$v_I(y_I^0) + v_{\bar{I}}(y_{\bar{I}}) > v_I(y_I^1) + v_{\bar{I}}(y_{\bar{I}}).$$

Thus,

$$(y_I^0, y_{\bar{I}}) > (y_I^1, y_{\bar{I}}) \qquad \text{for any } y_{\bar{I}} \in Y_{\bar{I}}.$$

We have the following theorem.

Theorem 5.4. If $v(y)$ is additive then the induced preference $\{>\}$ enjoys $>$-separability for any subset of Q.

Remark 5.10. In the next section, it will be shown that the converse of Theorem 5.4 holds when other suitable conditions are added.

Definition 5.9. Let $\{I_1, \ldots, I_m\}$ and $(z_1, \ldots, z_m) = z$ be a partition of Q and y, respectively, and $v(z) = v(v_1(z_1), \ldots, v_m(z_m))$. We say that v is strictly increasing in v_i, $i \in \{1, \ldots, m\}$, iff v is strictly increasing in v_i while the other v_k, $k = 1, \ldots, m$, $k \neq i$, are fixed.

Now suppose that the value function can be expressed as $v(z)$ in Definition 5.9. To simplify the notation and to emphasize z_k, whenever possible and without confusion, we will write $v(z) = v(v_k(z_k), \bar{v}_k(\bar{z}_k))$, where $\bar{v}_k(\bar{z}_k)$ denotes the remaining functions of the remaining variables other than v_k and z_k. Note that if for any z_k^0, z_k^1 of Y_{I_k}, $v_k(z_k^0) > v_k(z_k^1)$ then the monotonicity implies that

$$v(v_k(z_k^0), \bar{v}_k(\bar{z}_k)) > v(v_k(z_k^1), \bar{v}_k(\bar{z}_k))$$

for any $\bar{v}_k(\bar{z}_k)$. This implies that $(z_k^0, \bar{z}_k) > (z_k^1, \bar{z}_k)$ for any fixed $\bar{z}_k$. Thus we have the following theorem.

Theorem 5.5. If the value function is defined as in Definition 5.9 and is strictly increasing in v_i, $i \in \{1, \ldots, m\}$, then z_i and I_i are $>$-separable.

Remark 5.11. The converse of Theorem 5.5 holds when suitable assumptions are added as to be discussed in the next subsection.

Remark 5.12. Given $\{>\}$ and $I \subset Q$, $I \neq \varnothing$. That I is $>$-separable does not imply that $\bar{I}$ is $>$-separable even if $\{>\}$ has a value function representation. As an example, let $\{>\}$ be represented by $v(y) = y_1 \exp(y_2)$; $y_1, y_2 \in R^1$. As $\exp(y_2) > 0$ we see that y_1 and $I = \{1\}$ are $>$-separable. But as y_1 can be negative, y_2 and $I = \{2\}$ are not $>$-separable. Further discussion on preference separability will be given in Section 5.3.3.

5.3.2. Conditions for Additive and Monotonic Value Functions

The material discussed in this section is due to Gorman (Ref. 170) and Debreu (Ref. 106). As the details of the derivations can be found in the above references, we shall be content with the description of the main results.

Definition 5.10. Given $I \subset Q$, $I \neq \varnothing$ we say that I is *essential* if there is some $y_{\bar{I}} \in Y_{\bar{I}}$ so that not all elements of Y_I are indifferent, and we say that I is *strictly essential* if for each $y_{\bar{I}} \in Y_{\bar{I}}$, not all elements of Y_I are indifferent.

Remark 5.13. If I is essential, then Y_I must contain at least two points. Also that I is strictly essential implies that I is essential. Note that if I is inessential then I can be neglected without affecting the value function construction or optimal selection of choices. This observation makes it innocent to assume that each i of Q is essential.

Assumption 5.2. (i) Each $(Y_i, \mathcal{T}_i)$, $i = 1, \ldots, q$, is topologically separable and connected. Thus, $(Y, \mathcal{T})$, with $Y = \prod_{i=1}^{q} Y_i$, $\mathcal{T} = \prod_{i=1}^{q} \mathcal{T}_i$ is topologically separable and connected.
(ii) $\{>\}$ on Y is a weak order and for each $y \in Y$, $\{y>\} \in \mathcal{T}$ and $\{y<\} \in \mathcal{T}$.

Remark 5.14. According to Theorem 5.3, Assumption 5.2 ensures the existence of a continuous value function v for representing $\{>\}$. The following theorem, attributed to Debreu (Ref. 106), further specifies the form of v.

Theorem 5.6. Assume that Assumption 5.2 holds. Then (i) the value function $v(y)$ can be written as

$$v(y) = F(v_1(y_1), \ldots, v_q(y_q)), \tag{5.7}$$

where F is continuous and strictly increasing in its components v_i, $i = 1, \ldots, q$, which are continuous, *iff* each $\{i\}$, $i = 1, \ldots, q$, is $>$-separable;

(ii) If there are at least three components of Q that are essential then $v(y)$ can be written as

$$v(y) = \sum_{i=1}^{q} v_i(y_i), \tag{5.8}$$

where each v_i is continuous, *iff* each $I \subset Q$ is $>$-separable.

Remark 5.15. Theorem 5.6 gives a partial converse of Theorems 5.4 and 5.5. Together, the three theorems show the importance of preference separability in determining the additive and monotonic forms of value functions in representing $\{>\}$.

Remark 5.16. Two value functions $v(y)$ and $u(y)$ are "equivalent" in preference representation iff, for any y^1, $y^2 \in Y$, $v(y^1) > v(y^2)$ iff $u(y^1) > u(y^2)$. Thus, if u is a strictly increasing function of v, then u and v are equivalent in preference representation. In particular, $u(y)$ and $v(y)$ are equivalent if

$$u(y) = a + bv(y) \tag{5.9}$$

with $a, b \in R^1$ and $b > 0$. Note that (5.9) can be used to normalize a value function so that $u(y^0) = 0$, where y^0 is a *reference point* [by taking $a = -bv(y^0)$]. Without confusion we shall use 0 to indicate the reference point for both y^0 and y_I^0 in Y and Y_I, $I \subset Q$, respectively. Again if we emphasize $y_I \in Y_I$, the value function will be written as

$$v(y) = v(y_I, y_{\bar{I}}). \tag{5.10}$$

Remark 5.17. The additive value function of (5.8) may be normalized at a reference point 0 so that $v(0) = 0$, $v_i(0) = 0$, $i = 1, \ldots, q$. Thus, $v(y_i, 0) = v_i(y_i)$. [Note that the notation (5.10) is used here.] The $v_i(y_i)$, $i = 1, \ldots, q$, are known as *subvalue functions*. Similarly, due to preference separability and strict increasingness, one can normalize (5.7) so that $v(0) = 0$, $v_i(0) = 0$, $i = 1, \ldots, q$, and

$$v_i(y_i) = v(y_i, 0) = F(0, \ldots, 0, v_i(y_i), 0, \ldots, 0). \tag{5.11}$$

Example 5.1. Let $Y = \{(y_1, y_2) | y_1 \geq 1, y_2 \geq 1\}$, $u(y) = y_1 e^{y_2}$ and $v(y) = \ln y_1 + y_2 - 1$. Then $v(y) = \ln u(y) - 1$ and v is strictly increasing in u. Thus, u and v are equivalent in preference representation. However, by setting $v_1(y_1) = \ln y_1$ and $v_2(y_2) = y_2 - 1$, we see that at the reference point $y^0 = (y_1^0, y_2^0) = (1, 1)$, $v_i(y_i^0) = 0$ and $v_i(y_i) = v(y_i, 0)$, $i = 1, 2$. [Note that 0 in $v(y_i, 0)$ is the reference point.]

Theorem 5.6(i) and (ii) have been generalized by Gorman (Lemmas 1 and 2 of ref. 170) in the following Theorems 5.7 and 5.8, respectively.

Theorem 5.7. Let $\{I_0, I_1, \ldots, I_m\}$ and $(z_0, z_1, \ldots, z_m)$ be a partition of Q and y, respectively. Assumption 5.2 implies that we can write

$$v(y) = F(z_0, v_1(z_1), \ldots, v_m(z_m)), \qquad (5.12)$$

where $F(z_0, \cdot)$ is strictly increasing in its components v_i, $i = 1, \ldots, m$, iff each I_i, $i = 1, \ldots, m$, is $\succ$-separable. If so, we can take, without loss of generality,

$$v_i(z_i) = v(z_i, 0) = F(0, \ldots, 0, z_i, 0, \ldots, 0), \qquad (5.13)$$

$$v_i(0) = v(0) = 0, \qquad i = 1, \ldots, m, \qquad (5.14)$$

in which case F is continuous.

Note that the zeros in (5.13) and (5.14) are the corresponding reference points.

Remark 5.18. Under the assumption of Theorem 5.6(i), we see that $I_0 = \varnothing$ and so z_0 is not existent. Clearly Theorem 5.7 reduces to Theorem 5.6(i). Also, observe that Theorem 5.7 gives, partially, the converse statement of Theorem 5.5.

Theorem 5.8. Let $\mathscr{I}^* = \{I_1, \ldots, I_m\}$ and $(z_1, \ldots, z_m)$ be a partition of Q and y, respectively, and $m \geqq 3$. Assume that for each $i \in Q$, $\{i\}$ is strictly essential and Assumption 5.2 holds. We can write

$$v(y) = \sum_{i=1}^{m} v_i(z_i) \qquad (5.15)$$

iff the union of any subsets of $\mathscr{I}^*$ (i.e., $\bigcup_{k \in S} I_k$, $S \subset M = \{1, \ldots, m\}$) is $\succ$-separable.

Note that when $\mathscr{I}^* = \{\{i\} | i \in Q\}$, Theorem 5.8 reduces to (ii) of Theorem 5.6.

From Theorems 5.6–5.8, we see that additive and monotonic forms of value functions are closely related to the structure of $\succ$-separability. For a value function to be additive, as has often been assumed in applications, $\succ$-separability is needed for every subset of Q. To verify this is not a simple task because there are $2^q - 1$ subsets of Q. Fortunately, Gorman's work (Ref. 170) has greatly reduced such work. We shall devote Section 5.3.3 to studying the structure of $\succ$-separability.

5.3.3. Structures of Preference Separability and Value Functions

Definition 5.11. Let $I_1, I_2 \subset Q$. We say that I_1 and I_2 *overlap* iff none of the following: $I_1 \cap I_2$, $I_1 \backslash I_2$ and $I_2 \backslash I_1$ is empty. (That is, I_1 and I_2 intersect and neither contains the other.)

The following is due to Gorman (Ref. 170, Theorem 1).

Theorem 5.9. Assume that
  i. $I_1, I_2 \subset Q$ overlap;
 ii. I_1, I_2 are $>$-separable;
iii. $I_1 \backslash I_2$ or $I_2 \backslash I_1$ is strictly essential and each $\{i\} \subset Q$ is essential (refer to Definition 5.10);
 iv. Assumption 5.2 is satisfied.
Then $I_1 \cup I_2$, $I_1 \cap I_2$, $I_1 \backslash I_2$, $I_2 \backslash I_1$, and $(I_1 \backslash I_2) \cup (I_2 \backslash I_1)$ are all $>$-separable and strictly essential.

Example 5.2. Let $I_1 = \{1, 2\}$, $I_2 = \{2, 3, 4\}$. If (i)-(iv) of Theorem 5.9 are satisfied, then $\{1, 2, 3, 4\}$, $\{1\}$, $\{2\}$, $\{3, 4\}$, and $\{1, 3, 4\}$ are all $>$-separable and strictly essential.

Theorem 5.9 is very powerful in studying the structure of $>$-separability.

Definition 5.12. (i) Let $\mathscr{I}$ be a collection of subsets of Q. We say that $\mathscr{I}$ is *complete* if (a) $\varnothing$, $Q \in \mathscr{I}$ and (b) if $I_1, I_2 \in \mathscr{I}$ overlap then $I_1 \cup I_2$, $I_1 \cap I_2$, $I_1 \backslash I_2$, $I_2 \backslash I_1$, and $(I_1 \backslash I_2) \cup (I_2 \backslash I_1)$ all belong to $\mathscr{I}$.

(ii) Given $\mathscr{I}$ (a collection of subsets of Q), the *completion* $\mathscr{C}(\mathscr{I})$ of $\mathscr{I}$ is defined to be the intersection of all the complete collections containing $\mathscr{I}$. [Thus, $\mathscr{C}(\mathscr{I})$ contains $\varnothing$, Q, and those sets that can be *progressively* generated by (b) in (i).]

(iii) Given $I \in \mathscr{I}$, I is a *top-element* of $\mathscr{I}$ if $I \neq Q$ and I is not contained by any element of $\mathscr{I}$ other than Q.

Example 5.3. Let $\mathscr{I} = \{\{1, 2\}, \{2, 3\}, \{4, 5, 6\}, \{6, 7\}\}$ and $Q = \{1, 2, \ldots, 9\}$. Then $\mathscr{C}(\mathscr{I}) = \{\varnothing, Q, \{1\}, \{2\}, \{3\}, \{1, 3\}, \{2, 3\}, \{1, 2\}, \{1, 2, 3\}, \{6\}, \{7\}, \{4, 5\}, \{6, 7\}, \{4, 5, 6\}, \{4, 5, 7\}, \{4, 5, 6, 7\}\}$, and $\{1, 2, 3\}$ and $\{4, 5, 6, 7\}$ are the two top elements of $\mathscr{C}(\mathscr{I})$. Observe that $\{2, 3\}$ and $\{1, 2\}$ of $\mathscr{C}(\mathscr{I})$ can also be obtained, respectively, by $\{1, 3\}$ with $\{1, 2\}$, and $\{1, 3\}$ with $\{2, 3\}$. Note that $\{1, 2, 3\}$, $\{4, 5, 6, 7\}$, and $\{8, 9\}$ form a partition of Q (no overlapping), and that $\{8, 9\}$ is not in $\mathscr{C}(\mathscr{I})$.

Example 5.4. Let $\mathscr{I}_1 = \{\{1, 2\}, \{2, 3\}, \{3, 4\}\}$, $\mathscr{I}_2 = \{\{1, 2\}, \{1, 3\}, \{1, 4\}\}$, and $Q = \{1, 2, 3, 4\}$. Then $\mathscr{C}(\mathscr{I}_1) = \mathscr{C}(\mathscr{I}_2) = \mathscr{P}(Q)$ (the collection of all subsets of Q). (Check it.) Note that $\{1, 2, 3\}$, $\{2, 3, 4\}$, $\{1, 3, 4\}$, and $\{1, 2, 4\}$ are the four top elements and some of them overlap. See Exercise 5.6 for verification.

Definition 5.13. Let $\mathcal{I}$ be a collection of subsets of Q. (i) $\mathcal{I}$ is *connected* if for any A, B of $\mathcal{I}$, there is a sequence $\{I_1, \ldots, I_r\}$ of $\mathcal{I}$ such that $I_1 = A$, $I_r = B$, and I_{k-1} overlaps with I_k, $k = 2, \ldots, r$.

(ii) $\mathcal{I}$ is $>$-separable if each element of $\mathcal{I}$ is $>$-separable.

The following is due to Gorman (Theorem 3 of Ref. 170), which generalizes Theorem 5.9.

Theorem 5.10. Assume that
  i. $\mathcal{I}$ is connected and $>$-separable;
  ii. there is at least one overlapping pair of elements A, B of $\mathcal{I}$ such that $A \backslash B$ or $B \backslash A$ is strictly essential;
  iii. each $\{i\} \subset Q$ is essential; and
  iv. Assumption 5.2 is satisfied.
Then $\mathscr{C}(\mathcal{I})$ is $>$-separable.

Example 5.5. The collections $\mathcal{I}_1$ and $\mathcal{I}_2$ in Example 5.4 are connected. Assume that Assumption 5.2 is satisfied. If $\mathcal{I}_1$ (or $\mathcal{I}_2$) is $>$-separable, each $\{i\} \subset Q$ is essential, and at least one $\{k\}$, $k = 1, \ldots, 4$ is strictly essential, then $\mathscr{C}(\mathcal{I}_1)$ [or $\mathscr{C}(\mathcal{I}_2)] = \mathscr{P}(Q)$ is $>$-separable. According to Theorem 5.6, the value function can be represented in an additive form as (5.8). The result of this example can indeed be generalized as follows.

Theorem 5.11. Let $\mathcal{I} = \{I_1, \ldots, I_r\}$ be a connected collection of pairs of elements of Q such that $\bigcup_{k=1}^{r} I_k = Q$. Assume that $q \geq 3$ and
  i. $\mathcal{I}$ is $>$-separable,
  ii. at least one $\{k\} = I_i \backslash I_j$, $k \in Q$, is strictly essential, $I_i, I_j \in \mathcal{I}$
  iii. each $\{k\}$, $k \in Q$, is essential, and
  iv. Assumption 5.2 is satisfied.
Then each subset of Q is $>$-separable and the preference can be represented by an additive value function as (5.8).

Proof. In view of Theorem 5.10 and Theorem 5.6 it suffices to show $\mathscr{C}(\mathcal{I}) = \mathscr{P}(Q)$ (the collection of all subsets of Q). We show this by induction on q. When $q = 3$, the conclusion is clear. (See Example 5.4 for a derivation.) Now assume that the conclusion is valid for $q = p \geq 3$, we shall show that it is also valid for $q = p + 1$. Select p elements of Q which is the union of some connected subset of $\mathcal{I}$. Denote the remaining element by $p + 1$ (renumber the index if needed). By connectedness, there is I_i, I_j of $\mathcal{I}$ so that $\{p + 1\} = I_i \backslash I_j$. Thus $\{p + 1\} \in \mathscr{C}(\mathcal{I})$.

It remains to show that for any $I \neq \phi$ of $Q \backslash \{p + 1\}$, $I \cup \{p + 1\} \in \mathscr{C}(\mathcal{I})$. Let $i \in I$ and select $\{I_k | k = 1, \ldots, r\}$ of $\mathcal{I}$ with I_k overlaps with I_{k+1}, $k = 1, \ldots, r - 1$, and i is only in I_1 and $p + 1$, only in I_r. Let us consider two possible cases.

Case (i): $I = \{i\}$. If $r = 1$, then $I_r = \{i, p + 1\} \in \mathcal{I}$ and the conclusion is clear. If $r > 1$, define $U = \bigcup_{k=1}^{r-1} I_k$ and $W = \bigcup_{k=2}^{r} I_k$. Then U and W overlap and are elements of $\mathcal{C}(\mathcal{I})$, and $\{i, p + 1\} = (U \backslash W) \cup (W \backslash U) \in \mathcal{C}(\mathcal{I})$.

Case (ii): I contains more than one point. If $r = 1$, then I and I_r overlap, and $I \cup \{p + 1\} = I \cup I_r \in \mathcal{C}(\mathcal{I})$. If $r > 1$, define $U = I \cup (\bigcup_{k=1}^{r-1} I_k)$ and $W = (\bigcup_{k=1}^{r} I_k) \backslash I$. Then U and W overlap and are elements of $\mathcal{C}(\mathcal{I})$; furthermore, $(U \backslash W) \cup (W \backslash U) = I \cup \{p + 1\} \in \mathcal{C}(\mathcal{I})$. □

Remark 5.19. Theorem 5.11 is important because for $q \geqq 3$, instead of verifying $>$-separability for $2^q - 1$ subsets, we need only to verify $(q - 1)$ pairs of elements of Q. For instance, in Example 5.4 when $q = 4$, instead of verifying $2^4 - 1 = 15$ subsets of Q, we need only to verify three pairs of elements of Q (such as $\mathcal{I}_1$ and $\mathcal{I}_2$) for $>$-separability.

In applications, we may start with Assumption 5.2 and locate a $>$-separable collection $\mathcal{I}$. Then we locate $\mathcal{C}(\mathcal{I})$. Gorman (Section 3, Ref. 170) demonstrates that there are two possible cases that can occur: (i) the top elements, denoted by $\{T_1, \ldots, T_m\}$, of $\mathcal{C}(\mathcal{I})$ do not overlap ($\mathcal{I}$ of Example 5.3 is an example); and (ii) some of the top elements of $\mathcal{C}(\mathcal{I})$ overlap ($\mathcal{I}_1$ and $\mathcal{I}_2$ of Example 5.4 are two examples).

Case (i): Top elements do not overlap. Let $T_0 = Q \backslash (\bigcup_{i=1}^{m} T_i)$. (Note that T_0 can be empty.) Then $\{T_0, T_1, \ldots, T_m\}$ forms a partition of Q and when the assumptions of Theorems 5.9–5.10 hold, T_i, $i = 1, \ldots, m$, are $>$-separable, and Theorem 5.7 will be readily applicable to express $v(y)$ in the form of (5.12).

Case (ii): Some top elements overlap. It can be shown (Ref. 170) that if $m \geqq 3$, $Q = \bigcup_{i=1}^{m} T_i$ and $\mathcal{I}^* = \{\bar{T}_1, \bar{T}_2, \ldots, \bar{T}_m\}$ form a partition of Q (recall $\bar{T}_i = Q \backslash T_i$). Furthermore, every union of subsets of $\mathcal{I}^*$ (i.e., $\bigcup_{k \in S} \bar{T}_k$, S is a subset of $M = \{1, 2, \ldots, m\}$) is an element of $\mathcal{C}(\mathcal{I})$. When the assumptions of Theorems 5.9–5.10 hold, each such union is $>$-separable. Then Theorem 5.8 is readily applicable to express $v(y)$ in the additive form of (5.15).

We shall summarize the above discussion into the following theorem.

Theorem 5.12. Assume that Assumption 5.2 holds and that $\mathcal{C}(\mathcal{I})$ is $>$-separable for some $>$-separable collection $\mathcal{I}$ of subsets of Q. There are two possible cases in terms of the top elements, $\{T_1, \ldots, T_m\}$ of $\mathcal{C}(\mathcal{I})$.

Case (i). $\{T_1, \ldots, T_m\}$ do not mutually overlap. Then $\{T_0, T_1, \ldots, T_m\}$, where $T_0 = Q \backslash (\bigcup_{i=1}^{m} T_i)$, forms a partition of Q and $v(y)$ can be written as (5.12) and Theorem 5.7 applies.

Case (ii). Some of $\{T_1, \ldots, T_m\}$ overlap. Then $\{\bar{T}_1, \ldots, \bar{T}_m\}$ forms a partition of Q, and $v(y)$ can be written as (5.15) and Theorem 5.8 applies when each $\{i\}$, $i \in Q$, is strictly essential.

Example 5.6. Given $\mathcal{I}$ of Example 5.3, assume that the assumptions of Theorem 5.12 hold. Then the value function can be written as

$$v(y) = F(y_8, y_9, v_1(y_1, y_2, y_3), v_2(y_4, y_5, y_6, y_7)), \qquad (5.16)$$

where F is continuous and strictly increasing in v_1 and v_2; furthermore, F, v_1, v_2 can be normalized so that (5.13) and (5.14) hold.

Example 5.7. Consider $\mathscr{I}_1$ and $\mathscr{I}_2$ of Example 5.4. As $\{1, 2, 3\}$, $\{2, 3, 4\}$, $\{1, 3, 4\}$, and $\{1, 2, 4\}$ are the four top elements and are overlapping, their complements are $\{4\}$, $\{1\}$, $\{2\}$, and $\{3\}$, respectively. Together they form a partition of Q and the union of any of their subsets is an element of $\mathscr{C}(\mathscr{I}_i)$, $i = 1, 2$. When the assumptions of Theorem 5.12 hold, the value function can be written as

$$v(y) = \sum_{i=1}^{4} v_i(y_i).$$

Remark 5.20. Theorem 5.12 offers a powerful decomposition theorem of the separability and function forms. It can be applied to further decompose the function form. As an example, consider Examples 5.3 and 5.6 together. Note that $T_0 = \{8, 9\}$, $T_1 = \{1, 2, 3\}$, and $T_2 = \{4, 5, 6, 7\}$. Let $\mathscr{C}_i(\mathscr{I}) = \{I \subset T_i$ and $I \in \mathscr{C}(\mathscr{I})\}$. Then $\mathscr{C}_1(\mathscr{I}) = \{\{1\}, \{2\}, \{3\}, \{1, 2\}, \{2, 3\}, \{1, 3\}, \{1, 2, 3\}, \varnothing\}$ and $\mathscr{C}_2(\mathscr{I}) = \{\{6\}, \{7\}, \{4, 5\}, \{6, 7\}, \{4, 5, 6\}, \{4, 5, 7\}, \{4, 5, 6, 7\}, \varnothing\}$. With respect to T_1, $\{1, 2\}$, $\{2, 3\}$, and $\{1, 3\}$ are the top elements of $\mathscr{C}_1(\mathscr{I})$. They are overlapping. Thus, their respective complements, $\{3\}$, $\{1\}$, and $\{2\}$ form a partition for T_1. Applying Theorem 5.12 with respect to T_1 we can replace $v_1(y_1, y_2, y_3)$ of (5.16) by

$$v_1(y_1, y_2, y_3) = \sum_{j=1}^{3} v_{1j}(y_j). \tag{5.17}$$

With respect to T_2, $\{6, 7\}$, $\{4, 5, 6\}$, and $\{4, 5, 7\}$ are the three top elements. They are overlapping. Thus, their respective complements: $\{4, 5\}$, $\{7\}$, and $\{6\}$ form a partition of T_2. According to Theorem 5.12 (replacing Q by T_2), we can write

$$v_2(y_4, y_5, y_6, y_7) = v_{21}(y_4, y_5) + v_{22}(y_7) + v_{23}(y_6). \tag{5.18}$$

Now let $T_{21} = \{4, 5\}$. Then $\mathscr{C}_{21}(\mathscr{I}) = \{I \subset T_{21}, I \in \mathscr{C}(\mathscr{I})\} = \{\varnothing, \{4, 5\}\}$. No further information can be obtained.

Combining (5.16)–(5.18), the preference of Example 5.3, when the appropriate assumptions of Theorem 5.12 hold, can be written as

$$v(y_1, \ldots, y_9) = F\left(y_8, y_9, \sum_{j=1}^{3} v_{1j}(y_j), v_{21}(y_4, y_5) + v_{22}(y_7) + v_{23}(y_6)\right). \tag{5.19}$$

Graphically the structure of $\mathscr{C}(\mathscr{I})$ may be represented by a nested graph as in Figure 5.1. Note that in Figure 5.1 the partition is of the type in case (ii) iff "overlap" is denoted at the corresponding branching point. The graph of Figure 5.1 can help us construct $v(y)$ as shown in (5.19).

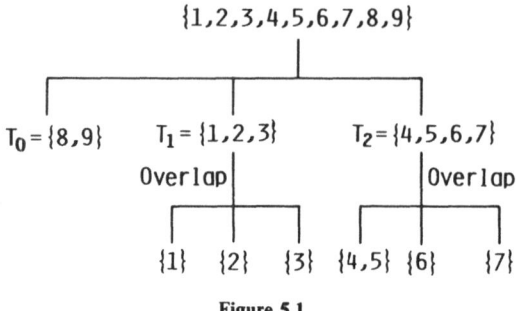

Figure 5.1

5.4. Further Comments

In this chapter we have described the conditions under which a value function for a preference can exist and the conditions under which the value function can be written in additive and monotonic form. Preference separability plays an important role in determining the form of a value function. We have drawn heavily from Refs. 139, 104, 106, and 170. Our description emphasizes motivating the concepts rather than the mathematical details. For the mathematical derivations we encourage the reader to read the above references and those quoted therein. Also, the reader may be interested in Refs. 254 and 268 for further motivating discussion.

Exercises

5.1. Suppose that the value function $v: Y \to R^1$ exists such that $y^1 > y^2$ iff $v(y^1) > v(y^2)$. Show that the induced preference $\{>\}$ is a weak order and $\{\sim\}$ is an equivalence relation.

5.2. Comment on this statement in the text: "In general, Pareto preference cannot be represented by a value function." Show under what conditions we can use a value function to represent a Pareto preference.

5.3. Show that if u is strictly increasing in v and $v(y)$ is a value function representing $\{>\}$ over Y, then $u(v(y))$ is also a value function representing $\{>\}$ over Y. [Thus $u(v(y))$ and $v(y)$ are equivalent in representing $\{>\}$ (see Remark 5.16).]

5.4. Let $Q = \{1, 2, \dots, q\}$ be the index set of the criteria. Let $I_1 \subset Q$ and $I_2 \subset Q$. Prove that if I_1 and I_2 are $>$-separable, then $I_1 \cap I_2$ is also $>$-separable.

5.5. Compare $>$-separability discussed in Section 5.3 with the separability in dynamic programming [see Nemhauser (Ref. 322)].

5.6. Let $\mathscr{I}_1 = \{\{1, 2\}, \{2, 3\}, \{3, 4\}\}$, $\mathscr{I}_2 = \{\{1, 2\}, \{1, 3\}, \{1, 4\}\}$, and $Q = \{1, 2, 3, 4\}$. Show that $\mathscr{C}(\mathscr{I}_1) = \mathscr{C}(\mathscr{I}_2) = \mathscr{P}(Q)$ and that $\{1, 2, 3\}, \{2, 3, 4\}, \{1, 3, 4\}$, and $\{1, 2, 4\}$ are the top elements of $\mathscr{C}(\mathscr{I}_i)$, $i = 1, 2$.

5.7. Let $Q = \{1, 2, \dots, 7\}$ be the index set of criteria. Let $I_1 = \{1, 2, 3\}$, $I_2 = \{3, 4, 5\}$. Assume that I_1, I_2 are $>$-separable and $I_1 \backslash I_2$ or $I_2 \backslash I_1$ is strictly essential and each $\{i\} \subset Q$ is essential and that Assumption 5.2 is satisfied. Find all subsets of the index set that are $>$-separable and strictly essential. What kind of value function can you describe for the preference?

5.8. Let $Q = \{1, 2, \ldots, 9\}$ be the index set of the criteria and $\mathscr{I} = \{\{1, 2, 3\}, \{2, 3, 4\}, \{5, 6, 7\}, \{7, 8\}\}$.

   a. Find the completion of $\mathscr{I}$, $\mathscr{C}(\mathscr{I})$.

   b. Find the top elements of $\mathscr{C}(\mathscr{I})$ and determine whether the top elements $\{T_1, T_2, \ldots, T_m\}$ overlap or not.

   c. Suppose that Assumption (5.2) holds. Write a general form of $v(y)$ using Theorem 5.12 and Remark 5.20.

5.9. Consider the two-criteria decision problem. In the following table, five different value functions v_1–v_5 for four alternatives are listed. If we assume each criterion exhibits "more is better," which of these five value functions are consistent with that assumption?

| Alternatives | Criteria | | Value functions | | | | |
	f_1	f_2	v_1	v_2	v_3	v_4	v_5
A	1	1	10	5	2	20	3
B	2	3	30	10	2	60	6
C	3	1	20	10	4	60	3
D	1	4	30	10	4	30	3

5.10. Summarize the assumptions that are needed for $\{>\}$ to have an additive value function representation. Give a practical example which demonstrates the assumptions you list.

5.11. Summarize the assumptions that are needed for $\{>\}$ to have a monotonic value function representation like (5.12) of Theorem 5.7. Give a practical example which demonstrates the assumptions you list.

5.12. Show that the lexicographical preference and the Pareto preference are $>$-separable for each nonempty subset of Q. Why can they not have an additive value function representation?

5.13. Show that the preference induced by a compromise solution is $>$-separable for each nonempty subset of Q. Show that the preference induced by a compromise solution indeed has an additive value function representation.

Suggested Reading

The following references are particularly pertinent to this chapter: 104, 106, 139, 170, 254, 268, 292, 322.

6

Some Basic Techniques for Constructing Value Functions

Once we are convinced that the existence conditions for the value function are satisfied, or are willing to take the risk to simplify the problem so that we can focus on a value function, we may begin to construct a value function to represent the revealed preference information. One must realize that such an attempt is tantamount to the acceptance of the assumptions described in the previous sections. If one is not sure that the assumptions hold, then at best one can regard the value function to be derived as *an approximation* of the preference. Thus, admittedly, errors and biases may exist in the preference representation.

Observe that a value function, once constructed, tends to provide a focus of consideration for the decision makers and analysts. In the extreme, it may *hypnotize* or trap them, making them unable to see the larger scope or other more correct ways of presenting the revealed preference. This mistake certainly should be avoided.

In this chapter we shall explore some basic techniques for constructing value functions. In Section 6.1 methods for constructing indifference curves, tangent planes, gradients, and the value function itself will be explored. In Section 6.2 some specially effective methods for constructing additive value functions, when assumed to exist, are described. In Section 6.3 we explore methods for constructing value functions for possibly conflicting information on the revealed preference. Clearly, conflicting information suggests that the existence conditions for value functions may be violated. However, one may want to construct one function in order to have a focus of consideration at the risk of misrepresentation. The goal is to make the representation as consistent with the revealed information as possible.

For convenience throughout this chapter we shall again assume that $Y = \prod_{i=1}^{q} Y_i$ is a connected "rectangle," where each $Y_i = [a_i, b_i]$ is a connected interval. It should be noted that constructing value functions has prevailed in the literature of applied mathematics including calculus, (partial) differential equations, algebra, statistics, optimal control, and differential games. Here we shall only sketch some concepts important for our applications.

6.1. Constructing General Value Functions

Indifference (isovalued) curves (surfaces), tangent planes, normal vectors/gradients, and the value function itself are some of the main concepts to be described in this subsection.

6.1.1. Constructing Indifference Curves (Surfaces)

Let us start with two-dimensional problems. That is, $q = 2$ and $y = (y_1, y_2)$. Refer to Figure 6.1. We can first select either y_1 or y_2 as an arbitrarily chosen reference criterion. For convenience, select y_1. The following procedure allows us to construct an indifference curve $\{y^0 \sim\}$ passing through an arbitrary point $y^0 \in Y$.

Step 0. Let $k = 0$.

Step 1. With y^k as a reference point, ask the decision maker how much he is willing to sacrifice y_2 in order to receive one more unit of y_1 (or how much he must be compensated in y_2 in order to sacrifice one unit of y_1). Let the answer be Δy^k. Then by assumption $(y_1^k + 1, y_2^k - \Delta y^k) \sim y^k$ [or $(y_1^k - 1, y_2^k + \Delta y^k) \sim y^k$]. Note that Δy^k is *the (marginal) rate of substitution* of y_2 for each unit of y_1 at y^k.

Step 2. Let $y^{k+1} = (y_1^k + 1, y_2^k - \Delta y^k)$ [or $(y_1^k - 1, y_2^k + \Delta y^k)$].

Step 3. If we have enough number $\{y^k\}$, we draw a curve passing through them. Then the curve is, assumingly, a representation of the indifference curve $\{y^0 \sim\}$. Otherwise, we go back to Step 1 to find more points for $\{y^k\}$.

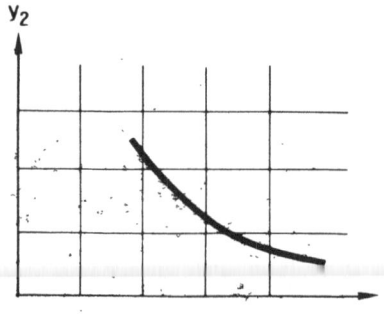

Figure 6.1

Remark 6.1. The "unit" used in Step 1 can be flexible. If a "fine" unit is used, more localized information can be obtained. It may be more accurate; but it may take a large amount of units to get a general picture of the preference. As most decision makers can be fairly impatient or easily get overloaded, in order to cooperate in eliciting the preference information, an analyst may not want to use too fine a unit in step 1.

Remark 6.2. Some suggestive questions such as "is $\Delta y^k = 2$ too high or too low?" can be helpful. The answer can help us with adjusting Δy^k in order to reach some indifferent value.

Remark 6.3. In step 3, some observations on $\{\Delta y^k\}$ may be helpful. For instance, as y_1 is increased, is Δy^k decreasing (or increasing) in k? If it is decreasing (or increasing), then the decreasing (or increasing) rate of substitution may indicate "concavity" (or "convexity") of the value function. The information can be very useful in drawing in the curve over $\{y^k\}$.

Remark 6.4. Once an indifference curve $\{y^0\sim\}$ is constructed, a prudent decision maker or analyst will try to check whether the preference consistency conditions (as described in the previous chapter) are satisfied. One way to check them is to select a point $y' \in \{y^0\sim\}$ and construct $\{y'\sim\}$. By comparing $\{y^0\sim\}$ with $\{y'\sim\}$ (perhaps other $\{y''\sim\}$), one may roughly see if the conditions are satisfied. Also one needs to verify that the indifference curves so constructed are "stable" over the time interval. One can construct the indifference curves at different times (say the next day) and compare them to see if the indifference curves over the time interval are consistent and stable. If they are not consistent and stable, the indifference curves may not be reliable or the assumptions for such curves to exist may not hold. Take precautions!

Remark 6.5. The indifference curve $\{y^0\sim\}$ can be constructed for a number of points in Y with different levels of preference. The totality of them will form an approximation of the preference. They may form a basis to further construct the value function as follows.

Observe that as the unit of y_1 (in Step 1) gets sufficiently small, the marginal rate of substitution Δy^k will approach the negative of $(dy_2/dy_1)(y^k)$. Note that $\Delta y^k \geqq 0$, if y_1 and y_2 are both characterized by "more is better."

Now suppose that dy_2/dy_1 is sufficiently smooth, as indicated by Δy^k; then we may write $dy_2/dy_1 = g(y_1, y_2)$. The differential equation can then be solved for every initial point y^0 in Y. The resulting paths will be the isovalued curves. With appropriate assumptions the normal vector of the proper direction to the isovalued curves can represent the gradient of the value function. Then the value function can be obtained by using the line integral of the gradient along the line from a preference point to any particular point in Y. We shall further discuss this concept in Section 6.1.3.

The above construction of indifference curves for $q = 2$ can be extended to any $q > 2$.

The following, called *Method* 1, is a way to elicit indifference (isovalued) surface or marginal rates of substitution for $q \geqq 2$.

Method 1: Elicitation of Indifference Surfaces

Step 0. Select a point $y^0 = (y_1^0, \ldots, y_q^0) \in Y$. Let $k = 0$.

Step 1. With y^k as a reference point ask the decision maker how much he is willing to *decrease* (or increase) y_p, $p \in \{2, 3, \ldots, q\}$, in order to *increase* (or decrease) y_1 by one unit while all the other components are unchanged. (Here y_1 is chosen arbitrarily for convenience. One can choose any y_i, $i = 1, \ldots, q$, as the main reference measure for comparison. If necessary, renumber so that $y_i = y_1$.) Let the rate of substitution be Δy_p^k, and

$$\tilde{y}_p^k = (1, 0, \ldots, 0, -\Delta y_p^k, 0, \ldots, 0). \tag{6.1}$$

Then, by assumption

$$y^k \sim y^k + \tilde{y}_p^k \qquad (\text{or } y^k \sim y^k - \tilde{y}_p^k), \qquad p \in \{2, 3, \ldots, q\}. \tag{6.2}$$

Note that $\Delta y_p^k > 0$ means that y_1 and y_p can substitute each other, and $\Delta y_p^k < 0$ means y_1 and y_p must both be increased or decreased (perhaps not in the same proportion) to maintain the same level of preference.

Step 2. Let $y^{k+p} = y^k + \tilde{y}_p^k$ (or $y^k - \tilde{y}_p^k$).

Step 3. If there are enough $\{y^k\}$, we draw in a surface passing through them. (This task is not easy when $q = 3$, and is impossible when $q > 3$. Later we shall mention a differential method to overcome this difficulty.) Then the surface is presumably an approximation of the indifference surface $\{y^0 \sim\}$. If the number of $\{y^k\}$ is not large enough, we go back to Step 1 to find more points for $\{y^k\}$.

Note that Remarks 6.1–6.5 are applicable to Method 1. (Recheck them!) We shall not repeat them here.

6.1.2. Constructing the Tangent Planes and the Gradients of Value Functions

Recall that Δy_p^k is the marginal substitution rate of y_p for each unit of y_1 at a particular point y^k. When each $\Delta y_p^k \neq 0$ the vectors $\tilde{y}_p^k$, $p = 2, \ldots, q$, of (6.1) are linearly independent (check it) and thus jointly generate a $(q - 1)$-dimensional hyperplane $H(y^k)$ [precisely, $H(y^k) = y^k + L(y^k)$, where $L(y^k)$ is the linear subspace generated by $\{\tilde{y}_p^k\}$] which can be used as an approximation of the tangent plane of the value function at y^k when it exists. This is especially true when the unit of y_1 is small. The normal vectors of the hyperplane $H(y^k)$ are given by

$$n^{\pm}(y^k) = \pm(1, 1/\Delta y_2^k, 1/\Delta y_3^k, \ldots, 1/\Delta y_q^k). \tag{6.3}$$

This is true because $n^{\pm}(y^k)$ is normal to each $\tilde{y}_p^k$ [because $\tilde{y}_p^k \cdot n^{\pm}(y^k) = 0$], $p = 2, \ldots, q$, of (6.1), and is consequently normal to the hyperplane.

By selecting the $+$ or $-$ sign properly, the normal vector points to the side, at least locally, of the more preferred outcomes. Such a selected normal vector, denoted by $n(y^k)$ is, then, an approximation of the direction of *the gradient* of the value function at y^k when it exists. Note that with the "more is better" assumption on preference, the sign will be positive, i.e., $n(y^k) = +(1, 1/\Delta y_2^k, 1/\Delta y_3^k, \ldots, 1/\Delta y_q^k)$. (See Exercise 6.8.)

We summarize the above discussion in the following theorem.

Theorem 6.1. Suppose that the value function $v(y)$ is smooth (say, differentiable and having nonzero first-order continuous derivatives) at y^k. Then as the unit of y_1 gets smaller, $\tilde{y}_p^k$, obtained by Method 1, $p = 2, \ldots, q$, jointly generate a hyperplane $H(y^k)$ which approximates the tangent plane of $v(y)$ at y^k, and the normal vector $n(y^k)$ of $H(y^k)$, with properly selected sign, approximates the direction of the gradient of $v(y)$ at y^k.

Remark 6.6. The approximated gradient we derived using Method 1 is not necessarily to be elicited for each point of Y, just as is the case with the "gradient search method" in mathematical programming, where the gradient is not necessarily to be measured at each point. With suitable assumptions, the gradient search method can be adapted to an interactive and iterative method to obtain the "optimal" solution for the decision maker. This will be discussed in Chapter 10.

6.1.3. Constructing the Value Function

In the previous subsection, we obtained a normal vector approximating the direction of the gradient of the value function. In most applications, this may be adequate for locating an "optimal" solution. If one is interested in the exact form of the value function, one needs to refine the procedure and utilize the result of the line integral. This will be discussed in this subsection.

Using Method 1, we can obtain Δy_p^k, $p = 2, \ldots, q$, for each y^k. As the unit of y_1 gets smaller (say, approaching 0 if necessary), then we may interpret Δy_p^k as an approximation of $-\partial y_p/\partial y_1$ at y^k. To emphasize this relation we write

$$\frac{\partial y_p}{\partial y_1}(y) = -g_p(y), \qquad p = 2, \ldots, q, \tag{6.4}$$

where $g_p(y^k)$ is approximated by Δy_p^k.

Assume that each $g_p(y)$, $p \geq 2$, has continuous derivatives and is nonzero throughout Y. As discussed in Section 6.1.2, the vectors

$$n^{\pm}(y) = \pm(1, 1/g_2(y), 1/g_3(y), \ldots, 1/g_q(y)) \tag{6.5}$$

will be normal to the indifference surface at y.

Select the direction which points into the side of increasing preference and denote it by $n(y)$. That is,

$$n(y) = \begin{cases} n^+(y) & \text{if } y + \alpha n^+(y) > y \\ & \quad \text{for all } \alpha \in (0, a) \text{ for some } a > 0, \\ n^-(y) & \text{otherwise.} \end{cases} \tag{6.6}$$

Note that $n(y)$ is assumed to have continuous first derivatives, and that $n(y) = (n_1(y), \ldots, n_q(y))$ is a vector function with $n_1(y) = +1$ or -1 [because of (6.5)].

Now to be sure that $n(y)$ is the gradient of a value function $v(y)$, we need to verify some conditions on the line integral. Let us first assume that $v(y)$ has continuous second derivatives and denote

$$D_i v(y) = \partial v / \partial y_i. \tag{6.7}$$

Thus

$$\nabla v(y) = (D_1 v(y), \ldots, D_q v(y)). \tag{6.8}$$

Since v has continuous second derivatives (can be relaxed a little bit), we have

$$D_i D_j v(y) = D_j D_i v(y) \tag{6.9}$$

for all $i, j \in Q$.

Indeed, this suggests a necessary and sufficient condition for a vector function, such as $n(y)$, to be the gradient of a value function. We state the result as follows.

Theorem 6.2. (i) Let $n(y) = (n_1(y), \ldots, n_q(y))$ be continuously differentiable over Y. Then $n = \nabla v$ for some value function v if and only if

$$D_i n_j(y) = D_j n_i(y) \tag{6.10}$$

for all $i, j \in Q$.

(ii) If (6.10) holds for all $i, j \in Q$, then

$$v(y) = \int_S n(z(t)) \, dz(t) + v(y^0), \tag{6.11}$$

where $S = \{z(t) | 0 \le t \le t(y)\}$ is a piecewise smooth path connecting a reference point y^0 and y.

Remark 6.7. The above theorem is known in calculus. For instance see Theorem 10.9 in Apostol (Ref. 7). Note that (6.11) is a line integral. By assumption, the integral is independent of the path. Also, $v(y^0)$ is an arbitrary constant. For simplicity, we can set $v(y^0) = 0$. As Y is assumed convex, one easy path for the line integral of (6.11) is $S = \{t(y - y^0)|0 \leqq t \leqq 1\}$. These observations yield the following corollary.

Corollary 6.1. If the assumptions of Theorem 6.2 hold, then

$$n(y) = \nabla v(y) \quad \text{with} \quad v(y) = \int_0^1 n(t(y - y^0)) \cdot (y - y^0) \, dt. \quad (6.12)$$

Remark 6.8. By our construction $n_1(y) = \pm 1$ for all $y \in Y$. The assumptions of theorem 6.2 imply that $D_1 n_j(y) = D_j n_1(y) = 0$ for $j = 2, \ldots, q$. Thus, this implicitly assumes that y_1 is $>$-separable. While the selection of y_1 from $\{y_1, \ldots, y_q\}$ is arbitrary, we need to realize that this preference separability is implicitly assumed.

Example 6.1. Assume that $Y = R^3$ and $n(y) = (1, y_2 y_3^2, y_2^2 y_3)$ is obtained. Note that (6.10) is satisfied. Thus, we can construct $v(y)$, using 0 and $v(0) = 0$. Note that the line connecting 0 and $y^0 = (y_1^0, y_2^0, y_3^0)$ is given by $S = \{(y_1^0 t, y_2^0 t, y_3^0 t)|0 \leqq t \leqq 1\}$. Thus, by Corollary 6.1, we can write, for any $y^0 \in Y$,

$$v(y^0) = \int_0^1 (1, (y_2^0 t)(y_3^0 t)^2, (y_2^0 t)^2 (y_3^0 t)) \cdot (y_1^0, y_2^0, y_3^0) \, dt$$

$$= \int_0^1 (y_1^0 + (y_2^0 y_3^0)^2 t^3 + (y_2^0 y_3^0)^2 t^3) \, dt$$

$$= y_1^0 + \tfrac{1}{2}(y_2^0 y_3^0)^2.$$

Note that the second equation is obtained by the inner product of the two vectors. We obtain consequently $v(y) = y_1 + \tfrac{1}{2} y_2^2 y_3^2$. The reader can readily verify that $\nabla v = n$ as we wish.

Remark 6.9. Condition (6.10), which is obtained from (6.9), is crucial in our construction of the value function. From (6.5), to be sure that (6.10) is satisfied, we need to verify if $D_i(1/g_j(y)) = D_j(1/g_i(y))$ or $D_i g_j(y)/g_j^2(y) = D_j g_i(y)/g_i^2(y)$ holds for all $i, j \in \{2, 3, \ldots, q\}$. This will become another consistency test to see if a value function of continuous second derivatives "really" exists or not.

6.2. Constructing Additive Value Functions

When an additive value function is assumed, the elicitation of a representation function becomes fairly easy. Two methods will be discussed here. The first uses the indifference concept to obtain the value function, the other uses the concept of midvalue points to construct individual value functions and then aggregates them with "weights" for the overall value function.

6.2.1. A First Method for Constructing Additive Value Functions

Let us start with $q = 2$, $y = (y_1, y_2)$. Refer to Figure 6.2. Recall that we want to construct

$$v(y) = \sum_{i=1}^{q} v_i(y_i). \tag{6.13}$$

Step 1. Select a reference point $y^0 = (y_1^0, y_2^0)$ and assign $v_i(y_i^0) = 0$, $i = 1, 2$.

Step 2. Select y_1^1 so that $(y_1^1, y_2^0) > (y_1^0, y_2^0)$ and set $v_1(y_1^1) = 1$.

Step 3. Select y_2^1 so that $(y_1^0, y_2^1) \sim (y_1^1, y_2^0)$ and set $v_2(y_2^1) = 1$.

Step 4. Given $r = 1, 2, 3, \ldots$. Select y_1^{r+1} so that $(y_1^{r+1}, y_2^0) \sim (y_1^r, y_2^1)$, and y_2^{r+1} so that $(y_1^0, y_2^{r+1}) \sim (y_1^1, y_2^r)$; and set $v_i(y_i^{r+1}) = r + 1$, $i = 1, 2$.

Step 5. If we have enough points $\{y_i^r\}$, $i = 1, 2$, $r = 1, 2, \ldots$, we draw the value function $v_i(y_i)$ (as Figure 6.3). Otherwise, we use step 4 to generate more points of $\{y_i^r\}$ and $v_i(y_i^r)$.

Step 6. Verify consistency conditions and make necessary adjustment or interpretation. Note that in order to satisfy (6.13) the construction (using steps 1–6) of $\{y_i^r\}$, $i = 1, 2$, $r = 1, 2, 3, \ldots$, must satisfy

$$v_i(y_i^r) = v_1(y_1^a) + v_2(y_2^b) \tag{6.14}$$

for $i = 1, 2$, and $r = a + b$, where $a, b = 0, 1, 2, \ldots$. This condition offers a "check" to see if the consistency conditions are satisfied or if it is necessary to redo or adjust the values of $\{y_i^r\}$, $i = 1, 2$. As r gets larger, condition (6.14) becomes more difficult to satisfy. Note that Step 6 may be performed in

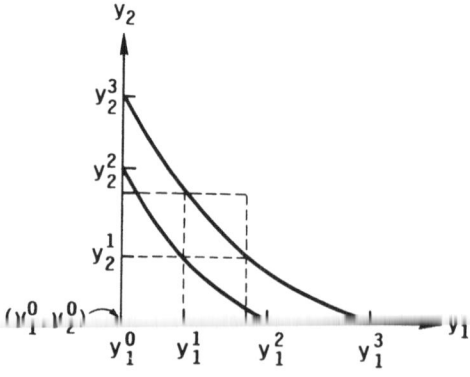

Figure 6.2

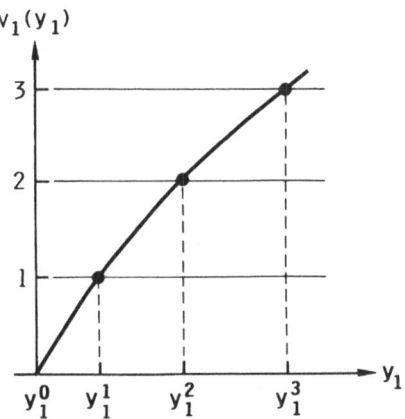

Figure 6.3

combination with Steps 4 and 5. That is, on the one hand we generate $\{y_i^r\}$, on the other we verify the consistency condition.

Step 7. Use $v_i(y_i^r) = r$ to draw $v_i(y_i)$, $i = 1, 2$. See Figure 6.3.

The above method can readily be extended to the dimensions $q \geq 3$. Recall that when y_i, or y_t and y_k are emphasized we will write

$$y = (y_i, y_{\bar{\imath}}) = (y_i, y_k, y_{\overline{ik}}).\tag{6.15}$$

We state the method as follows.

Step 1: Initialization

1.1. Find y^0 and set $v_k(y_k^0) = 0$, $k = 1, \ldots, q$.

1.2. Select y_1^1 so that $(y_1^1, y_{\bar{1}}^0) > y^0$. [Note, $(y_1^1, y_{\bar{1}}^0) = (y_1^1, y_2^0, \ldots, y_q^0)$.] Set $v_1(y_1^1) = 1$.

1.3. For $k = 2, \ldots, q$, select y_k^1 so that $(y_k^1, y_{\bar{k}}^0) \sim (y_1^1, y_{\bar{1}}^0)$ and set $v_k(y_k^1) = 1$.

Step 2: Iteration

2.1. Given $r = 1, 2, \ldots$, for each $k \in Q$, select a $j \neq k$ and y_k^{r+1} so that $(y_k^{r+1}, y_{\bar{k}}^0) \sim (y_k^r, y_j^1, y_{\overline{kj}}^0)$. Set $v_k(y_k^{r+1}) = r + 1$.

2.2. If we have generated enough points $\{y_k^r\}$, $k = 1, \ldots, q$, we draw the value function $v_k(y_k)$ for each $k = 1, \ldots, q$. Otherwise, we use 2.1 to generate more points of $\{y_k^r\}$ and $v_k(y_k^r)$.

Step 3: Consistency Verification and Adjustment. In order to satisfy (6.13), the elicited $\{y_k^r\}$, $k = 1, \ldots, q$, $r = 1, 2, \ldots$, must satisfy

$$v_k(y_k^r) = \sum_{i=1}^{q} v_i(y_i^{r_i})\tag{6.16}$$

as long as

$$r = \sum_{i=1}^{q} r_i$$

for all $k = 1, \ldots, q$ and $r = 1, 2, \ldots$. That is,

$$(y_k^r, y_k^0) \sim (y_1^{r_1}, y_2^{r_2}, \ldots, y_q^{r_q}) \tag{6.17}$$

holds for all k and all $\{r_i\}$ whenever $\sum_{i=1}^{q} r_i = r$.

Clearly, as r gets large, condition (6.16) or (6.17) becomes very difficult to satisfy. When inconsistency occurs, one needs to double check the consistency assumptions to see if it is useful or desirable to use an additive value function to express the preference. If it is still considered desirable, readjustment of $\{y_k^r\}$ is needed. Caution for bias and error in using the value function is needed!

Note that Step 3 can be imbedded into Step 2 so that on the one hand we generate $\{y_k^r\}$, and on the other we verify the consistency.

6.2.2. A Second Method for Constructing Additive Value Functions

In this method we shall first construct $v_k(y_k)$, $k \in Q$, individually. Then we aggregate them into $v(y)$ with proper weights. Assume that more is better for each y_k. The formula we are looking for is

$$v(y) = \sum_{k=1}^{q} w_k v_k(y_k). \tag{6.18}$$

Recall that $Y_k = [a_k, b_k]$. Rescaling if necessary, we can assume that $v_k(a_k) = 0$ and $v_k(b_k) = 1$. The $\{w_k\}$ which need to be determined will rank the relative scales in their proper order.

The following method, called the Midvalue Method [Keeney and Raiffa (Ref. 254)], can be used to assess $v_k(y_k)$ individually.

Step 1. Identify $[a_k, b_k]$. Set $v_k(a_k) = 0$ and $v_k(b_k) = 1$. Denote $y_k^0 = a_k$, $y_k^1 = b_k$.

Step 2. Find $y_k^{0.5}$ so that $v_k(y_k^{0.5}) = 0.5$.

Note that $v_k(y_k^{0.5}) - v_k(y_k^0) = v_k(y_k^1) - v_k(y_k^{0.5}) = 0.5$. Thus a typical question to address is "where is y_k^* such that you feel as good moving from y_k^0 to y_k^* as moving from y_k^* to y_k^1?" Let such $y_k^* = y^{0.5}$.

Again starting with some initial suggestive value of y_k^* and readjusting it with interactive information may be helpful in reaching the "true" value of $y^{0.5}$. As an example, let y_k be the monetary reward for work. Assume that $a_k = \$500$ and $b_k = \$1,000$. We set $y_k^0 = 500$ and $y_k^1 = 1,000$. We then ask the decision maker, "Would you be as happy to increase the reward from \$500 to $y_k^* = \$800$ as to increase from $y_k^* = \$800$ to \$1,000?" If the answer is "yes," we set $y_k^{0.5} = 800$. If \$800 is too low for y_k^*, we can change it to \$850; if \$800 is too high for y_k^* we change it to \$750, and repeat the question. Eventually we may get close to the true value for y_k^*.

Step 3. For any known $y_k^\alpha, y_k^\beta, 0 \le \alpha < \beta \le 1$, find y_k^γ so that $v_k(y_k^\gamma) = \gamma = \frac{1}{2}(\alpha + \beta)$. Note that $v_k(y_k^\gamma) - v_k(y_k^\alpha) = v_k(y_k^\beta) - v_k(y_k^\gamma) = \frac{1}{2}(\beta - \alpha)$. Thus a typical question to address is "where is y_k^* which would make you feel as good moving from y_k^α to y_k^* as moving from y_k^* to y_k^β?" The answer to this question is y_k^γ. Again, as in step 2, some suggestion and interaction can help the decision maker approximate the true value y_k^*.

Step 4. If we find enough points $\{y_k^\alpha\}$ we can draw a curve for $v_k(y_k)$. Otherwise, we repeat step 3 to generate more midvalue points.

Step 5: Consistency Test. For any three points y_k^α, y_k^β, and y_k^γ, with $\gamma = \frac{1}{2}(\alpha + \beta)$, generated by the above process, we must have $v_k(y_k^\gamma) - v_k(y_k^\alpha) = v_k(y_k^\beta) - v_k(y_k^\gamma) = \frac{1}{2}(\beta - \alpha)$. Thus, moving from y_k^α to y_k^γ should be equally preferred as moving from y_k^γ to y_k^β. This supplies a powerful check for consistency for all generated points $\{y_k^\alpha\}$. If inconsistency occurs, we need to redo or adjust $\{y_k^\alpha\}$ as to make it "look" consistent and take the risk of mispresentation of preference, or we need to abort the process and find a better form of preference presentation.

Note that step 5 can be imbedded into steps 3 and 4. Thus, on the one hand we generate $\{y_k^\alpha\}$ and on the other we verify the consistency condition.

Now assume that we have successfully generated the individual value functions $\{v_k\}$ in the above process for all $k \in Q$. We want to aggregate them in $v(y)$ as (6.18) indicates, that is, we need to find proper weights $\{w_k\}$ for $\{v_k\}$.

Recall that for each $v_k(a_k) = v_k(y_k^0) = 0$ and $v_k(b_k) = v_k(y_k^1) = 1$. Define $y^0 = (y_1^0, \ldots, y_q^0)$ and $y^1 = (y_1^1, \ldots, y_q^1)$. Then $(y_k^1, y_k^0) = (y_1^0, \ldots, y_{k-1}^0, y_k^1, y_{k+1}^0, \ldots, y_q^0)$ and

$$v((y_k^1, y_k^0)) = w_k v_k(y_k^1) = w_k. \tag{6.19}$$

Thus if we know the value at $\{(y_k^1, y_k^0)\}$, we know w_k. Unfortunately, this may not be easy to accomplish. We shall further discuss this concept in the next subsection.

Instead, if we could identify $q - 1$ pairs of indifference points (use the method discussed in Section 6.1.1, for instance), then (6.18) would supply $q - 1$ linear equations for q unknowns (i.e., $\{w_k\}$). If one normalizes $\{w_k\}$ by

$$\sum_{k=1}^{q} w_k = 1, \tag{6.20}$$

then $\{w_k\}$ can usually be uniquely determined. Thus, determining $\{w_k\}$ is usually not a very difficult task. However, one should not forget the consistency check. As every $q - 1$ pairs of indifferent points can determine $\{w_k\}$ uniquely, the $\{w_k\}$ depend on the choice of the $q - 1$ pairs of indifferent points. When an inconsistency occurs, we need to check if the consistency conditions are satisfied. If not, are we willing to take the risk of mispresentation? How do we redo or adjust the value function and avoid bias or errors in interpreting the value function obtained? Should we find a better form to represent the preference?

In a consistency test, one can verify the value function with the information contained in $\{>\}$. For instance, if we know $(y_k^1, y_k^0) > (y_j^1, y_j^0)$, using (6.19) do we have $w_k > w_j$? If we know $y^2 > y^3$, do we have $v(y^2) > v(y^3)$, etc.

Example 6.2. Let $Y_1 = [0, 1]$, $Y_2 = Y_3 = [0, 2]$. Suppose that we have obtained

$$v_1(y_1) = \tfrac{3}{2}y_1 - \tfrac{1}{2}y_1^2, \tag{6.21}$$

$$v_2(y_2) = \tfrac{3}{4}y_2 - \tfrac{1}{8}y_2^2, \tag{6.22}$$

$$v_3(y_3) = y_3 - \tfrac{1}{4}y_3^2, \tag{6.23}$$

and

$$(0, 1, 1) \sim (1, 0, 1), \tag{6.24}$$

$$(1, 1, 1) \sim (0, 2, 2). \tag{6.25}$$

Then substituting (6.24) into (6.21)-(6.23), (6.18) and using $v((0, 1, 1)) = v((1, 0, 1))$, we obtain

$$\tfrac{5}{8}w_2 + \tfrac{3}{4}w_3 = w_1 + \tfrac{3}{4}w_3,$$

or

$$w_1 = \tfrac{5}{8}w_2. \tag{6.26}$$

Similarly, substituting (6.25) into (6.21)-(6.23) and (6.18), and using $v((1, 1, 1)) = v((0, 2, 2))$, we obtain

$$w_1 + \tfrac{5}{8}w_2 + \tfrac{3}{4}w_3 = w_2 + w_3. \tag{6.27}$$

Using (6.26), (6.27) can be simplified as

$$w_2 = w_3, \tag{6.28}$$

Now (6.20), (6.26), and (6.28) uniquely determine $(w_1, w_2, w_3) = (5/21, 8/21, 8/21)$. Thus $v(y) = (5/21)v_1(y_1) + (8/21)v_2(y_2) + (8/21)v_3(y_3)$.

6.3. Approximation Method

As indicated in the previous sections, to obtain a "consistent" value function is not an easy job. Let $\{>\}^0$ and $\{\sim\}^0$ be the sets of revealed preference. Both sets can be used to verify the consistency. When the sets get sufficiently large, a value function consistent with these may practically not exist.

In this section, we shall start with the understanding that a value function totally consistent with $\{>\}^0$ and $\{\sim\}^0$ may not exist; however, we want to find one which, in some sense, is the best approximation. One can, just as in statistics, regard $\{>\}^0$ and $\{\sim\}^0$ as some *observed preference* from a *true preference* which contains randomness, errors, and/or noises (due to perhaps environmental inputs and/or the change of psychological states). See Chapter 9 for details. With this observed preference we want to find the "true" preference. Of course we admit the possibility of making mistakes and errors. In Section 6.3.1 we shall focus on a general concept. Section 6.3.2 concentrates on linear models. Section 6.3.3 describes the eigenvector approximation for the weights in additive value functions. In Section 6.3.4, the least-distance approximation will be discussed.

6.3.1. A General Concept

Suppose that a value function $v(y)$ exists. However, due to external information inputs and/or changes in the internal psychological states (see Chapter 9 for further details), the observed preference may not reflect $v(y)$ precisely. To incorporate this situation, we can write

$$u(y, \varepsilon) = v(y) + \varepsilon. \tag{6.29}$$

Note that $u(y, \varepsilon)$ is the "observed" value function, $v(y)$ is the "true" value function, and ε represents the aggregation of randomness, bias, and error. The explicit functions $u(y, \varepsilon)$ and $v(y)$ are not completely known. However, they are presumably revealed by the preference $\{>\}^0$ and $\{\sim\}^0$. Our task is to find an approximation function $\hat{v}(y)$ for $v(y)$ such that

$$\hat{v}(y^1) > \hat{v}(y^2) \qquad \text{for all } (y^1, y^2) \in \{>\}^0, \tag{6.30}$$

$$\hat{v}(y^1) = \hat{v}(y^2) \qquad \text{for all } (y^1, y^2) \in \{\sim\}^0. \tag{6.31}$$

If the above (6.30) and (6.31) cannot be attained, we shall find the approximation function that makes it the "least" inconsistent to (6.30) and (6.31). The "least inconsistency" criterion can be defined in a number of ways. We shall discuss them as we introduce the individual methods.

Now suppose that through the observations on $\{>\}^0$ and $\{\sim\}^0$, we predetermine a functional form for $v(y)$, say

$$v(y) = h(\alpha_1, \ldots, \alpha_m ; y_1, \ldots, y_q)$$

$$\doteq h(\alpha, y), \tag{6.32}$$

where $\alpha = (\alpha_1, \ldots, \alpha_m)$ is unknown and is to be estimated. Then we can write

$$u(y, \varepsilon) = h(\alpha, y) + \varepsilon. \tag{6.33}$$

Our goal is then to estimate α by $\hat{\alpha}$ so as to obtain

$$\hat{v}(y) = h(\hat{\alpha}, y), \tag{6.34}$$

so that $\hat{v}(y)$ [or $h(\hat{\alpha}, y)$] is closest to $v(y)$ [or $h(\alpha, y)$].

Observe that our model and conception of estimation are very similar to traditional statistics. However, the "sample" information $\{>\}^0$ and $\{\sim\}^0$ are just *orderings* and does not offer *numerical* comparisons, which makes our analysis somehow different from traditional statistics. Unless proper assumptions are further added, statistical methods may not be directly applicable.

6.3.2. Approximation for Additive Value Functions

In Section 6.2.2 we discussed two methods for assessing an additive value function based on the *pairwise* comparison information of $\{\sim\}^0$ and $\{>\}^0$. In this section we shall discuss two other methods based on *holistic* assessment. The first one is to assess the weights for individual value functions assuming that they have been obtained successfully as discussed in Section 6.2.2. The other is based on orthogonal designs of experiment discussed in traditional statistics.

6.3.2.1. First Method

Assume that $v_i(y_i)$, $i \in Q$, have been successfully assessed. In Section 6.2.2 we wanted to find w_i, $i \in Q$, so that (6.18) holds. Since we are willing to broaden our mind to accept that errors, biases, and noise may exist, using (6.33) and (6.18) we write

$$u(y, \varepsilon) = \sum_{i=1}^{q} \alpha_i v_i(y_i) + \varepsilon. \tag{6.35}$$

Assume that $E\varepsilon = 0$. (Here $E\varepsilon$ means the expected value of ε.) Then

$$Eu(y, \varepsilon) = \sum_{i=1}^{q} \alpha_i v_i(y_i). \tag{6.36}$$

Note that (6.36) is very similar to (6.18) [$Eu(y, \varepsilon)$ for $v(y)$ and α_i for w_i]. Let us also normalize $\{\alpha_i\}$ as to make $\sum_{i=1}^{q} \alpha_i = 1$.

Recall that for each k, the following notation is used:

$$y_k^0 = \{y_i^0 | i \neq k, i = 1, \ldots, q\}$$

and

$$(y_k^1, y_k^0) = (y_1^0, \ldots, y_{k-1}^0, y_k^1, y_{k+1}^0, \ldots, y_q^0),$$

$$(y_k^0, y_k^1) = (y_1^1, \ldots, y_{k-1}^1, y_k^0, y_{k+1}^1, \ldots, y_q^1).$$

Recall that for each k, $v_k(y_k^0) = 0$ and $v_k(y_k^1) = 1$. Similar to (6.19), using (6.36) we obtain

$$Eu((y_k^1, y_k^0), \varepsilon) = \alpha_k, \tag{6.37}$$

$$Eu((y_k^0, y_k^1), \varepsilon) = \sum_{i \neq k} \alpha_i = 1 - \alpha_k. \tag{6.38}$$

Using (6.37) and (6.38) we can have the following holistic estimation of $\{\alpha_k\}$.

Ask the decision maker, "if $u(y^1) = 1$ and $u(y^0) = 0$, on the average how much value would you assign to (y_k^1, y_k^0) [or (y_k^0, y_k^1)]?" The answer to this question will be $\hat{\alpha}_k$ (or $1 - \hat{\alpha}_k$; thus $\hat{\alpha}_k$ is obtained too).

Again, to be effective some suggestive questions (such as "Is 0.25 too high or too low?") and interactive adjustments can be efficient in narrowing down the value. Again one has to run a *consistency test* against the revealed information $\{\sim\}^0$ and $\{>\}^0$ to see if adjustment or abortion of the method is needed. Also, one has to run a *stability test* over time. If $\{\hat{\alpha}_{kt} | t = 1, 2, \ldots, n\}$ are obtained,

$$\bar{\alpha}_k = \frac{1}{n} \sum_{t=1}^{n} \hat{\alpha}_{kt} \tag{6.39}$$

may be used to estimate α_k. Of course, with proper assumptions, all statistical knowledge can be used to describe the properties of $\bar{\alpha}_k$. We shall not stop to do so.

We summarize the procedure of assessing additive value functions as follows.

Step 1. Assess $v_i(y_i)$, $i = 1, \ldots, q$, according to the method discussed in Section 6.2.2.

Step 2. Assess the weights according to the method discussed in this subsection using (6.35)–(6.39).

6.3.2.2. Second Method—Orthogonal Designs

In this section we shall describe a method similar to orthogonal designs of experiment in traditional statistics to elicit value functions. The method is simple and elegant, but valid only when a set of assumptions is met, and the reader should be cautious in interpreting it.

Assumption 6.1.

(i) $\quad Y = \prod_{i=1}^{q} Y_i \quad$ with each $Y_i = \{1, 2, \ldots, r\}$,

(ii) $\quad u(y, \varepsilon) = \sum_{i=1}^{q} v_i(y_i) + \varepsilon,$ $\hfill (6.40)$

with $E\varepsilon = 0$ and for each i

$$\sum_{k=1}^{r} v_i(k) = \sum_{y_i \in Y_i} v_i(y_i) = 0. \hfill (6.41)$$

Remark 6.10 (i) Assumption 6.1(i) means that each criterion has the same finite number of possible outcomes. This can occur when the decision maker qualitatively designates the outcomes, for instance 1, 2, and 3, respectively, "bad," "average," and "good" for criteria such as "working environment" and "promotion potential." Although the method may be extended to include the cases in which the number of outcome levels of each criterion may be different and in which the outcomes are not discrete but can be represented by a finite number of discrete points, we shall leave the extension to the readers.

(ii) Assumption 6.1(ii) is important for the orthogonal design. The assumption implies that $Eu(y, \varepsilon) = \sum_{i=1}^{q} v_i(y_i)$. Equation (6.41) is important. The "0" assumption of (6.41) may be replaced by any constant without changing the substance of our method.

We shall first start with a simple example and then summarize the method.

Example 6.3. Consider a job selection problem in which salary, job interest, working environment and promotion opportunity are the four criteria to be evaluated. The criteria are respectively designated by $Q = \{1, \ldots, 4\}$ and for each criterion $R = \{1, 2, 3\}$ is used to represent {bad, average, good} respectively. Let us also assume that Assumption 6.1 is satisfied. Table 6.1 gives an orthogonal design for evaluating $v_i(y_i)$.

Table 6.1

Combinations {k} (0)	Criteria				Assessed value {a_k} (5)
	1 (1)	2 (2)	3 (3)	4 (4)	
1	1	1	1	1	−1
2	1	2	2	3	0
3	1	3	3	2	0.4
4	2	1	2	2	−0.5
5	2	2	3	1	0.4
6	2	3	1	3	0.5
7	3	1	3	3	0.2
8	3	2	1	2	0.4
9	3	3	2	1	0.8

We explain Table 6.1 as follows:

(i) Column 0 gives the designated number of combinations of designed outcome levels for each criterion. Columns 1-4 designate the corresponding criteria. Thus, for $k = 1$, row 1 means a combination in which the outcome level of each criterion is "1"; for $k = 2$, row 2 means a combination in which the outcomes of criteria 1, 2, 3 and 4 are at level 1, 2, 2 and 3 respectively. A similar interpretation is valid for other k.

(ii) Since each criterion has three levels of outcome, there are $81 = (3)^4$ possible combinations of the outcomes. In Table 6.1, there are only nine combinations that are sufficient for our method to assess $v_i(y_i)$.

Define

$$C(i, j) = \text{the collection of all combinations that have the } i\text{th} \\ \text{criterion at the } j\text{th level.} \qquad (6.42)$$

For instance $C(2, 3) = \{3, 6, 9\}$ and $C(4, 2) = \{3, 4, 8\}$. Observe that each $C(i, j)$, $i \in \{1, \ldots, 4\}$ (criteria) and $j \in \{1, 2, 3\}$ (levels), contains all combinations of the jth level of the ith criterion (ith column of Table 6.1) and enjoys the property that for all criteria (column) other than the ith, each level is contained exactly once in $C(i, j)$. Using (6.41), we see that effects of all criteria other than the ith are neutralized. "Orthogonal designs" gains its name from this mutual neutralization of the effect of all other criteria. Thus, $v_i(j)$ can be estimated by

$$v_i'(j) = \tfrac{1}{3} \sum_{k \in C(i,j)} a_k, \qquad (6.43)$$

where a_k is the assessed value for combination k.

Table 6.2

Criterion i:	1			2			3			4		
Level j:	1	2	3	1	2	3	1	2	3	1	2	3
1	-1	-0.5	0.2	-1	0	0.4	-1	0	0.4	-1	0.4	0
2	0	0.4	0.4	-0.5	0.4	0.5	0.5	-0.5	0.4	0.4	-0.5	0.5
3	0.4	0.5	0.8	0.2	0.4	0.8	0.4	0.8	0.2	0.8	0.4	0.2
4 Σ	-0.6	0.4	1.4	-1.3	0.8	1.7	-0.1	0.3	1.0	0.2	0.3	0.7
5 $v_i'(j)$	$\dfrac{-6}{30}$	$\dfrac{4}{30}$	$\dfrac{14}{30}$	$\dfrac{-13}{30}$	$\dfrac{8}{30}$	$\dfrac{17}{30}$	$\dfrac{-1}{30}$	$\dfrac{3}{30}$	$\dfrac{10}{30}$	$\dfrac{2}{30}$	$\dfrac{3}{30}$	$\dfrac{7}{30}$
6 $\hat{v}_i(j)$	$\dfrac{-10}{32}$	0	$\dfrac{10}{32}$	$\dfrac{-17}{32}$	$\dfrac{4}{32}$	$\dfrac{13}{32}$	$\dfrac{-5}{32}$	$\dfrac{-1}{32}$	$\dfrac{6}{32}$	$\dfrac{-2}{32}$	$\dfrac{-1}{32}$	$\dfrac{3}{32}$

(iii) To obtain a_k, the assessed value for combination k, one can start with an understanding with the decision maker that the worst combination $(1, 1, 1, 1)$ has value -1 [instead of 0 because of (6.41)], and the best combination $(3, 3, 3, 3)$ has value 1. Then we use interactive and iterative methods as discussed in the previous sections to narrow down the value for combination k (the kth row).

To effectively use (6.43), Table 6.1 can be rearranged as Table 6.2 to compute $v_i(j)$.

Let us explain Table 6.2 and the computation of $\hat{v}_i(j)$, the estimates for $v_i(j)$, as follows:

(i) The heading of criterion i and level j is self-explanatory. Rows 1-3 for each column (i, j) are those a_k of Table 6.1 with $k \in C(i, j)$. For instance, for column $(4, 2)$, since $C(4, 2) = \{3, 4, 8\}$, the corresponding figures in rows 1-3 are a_3, a_4, and a_8, respectively.

(ii) Row 4 is the sum of rows 1-3. Row 5, $v_i'(j)$, is obtained by dividing row 4 by 3, as (6.43) demonstrates.

(iii) Observe that $\sum_{j=1}^{3} v_i'(j) = 12/30$ for all $i \in \{1, \ldots, 4\}$. It is a constant for all i because $\sum_{j=1}^{3} \sum_{k \in C(i,j)} a_k$ is constant (it is a sum of all a_k, with different permutations).

(iv) Observe that

$$\sum_{j=1}^{3} v_i'(j) \neq 0, \qquad \sum_{i=1}^{4} v_i'(1) \neq -1, \qquad \sum_{i=1}^{4} v_i'(3) \neq 1.$$

These are inconsistent with (6.41) (perhaps due to ε and other perception errors) and with the understanding that the values of the worst and the best combinations are -1 and 1, respectively. These inconsistencies can be partially remedied by a positive linear transformation:

$$\hat{v}_i(j) = b(v_i'(j) - c) \tag{6.44}$$

for all $i \in \{1, 2, 3, 4\}$, so as to make

$$\sum_{j=1}^{3} \hat{v}_i(j) = 0 \tag{6.45}$$

and either

$$\sum_{i=1}^{4} \hat{v}_i(3) = 1 \tag{6.46}$$

or

$$\sum_{i=1}^{4} \hat{v}_i(1) = -1. \tag{6.47}$$

Selecting $c = \frac{1}{3} \sum_{j=1}^{3} v_i'(j)$ will ensure that (6.45) is satisfied and selecting

$$b = \frac{1}{\sum_{i=1}^{4} v_i'(3) - 4c} \qquad \left[\text{or } b = \frac{1}{-\sum_{i=1}^{4} v_i'(1) + 4c} \right]$$

will satisfy (6.46) [or (6.47)]. Row (6) is obtained by satisfying (6.45) and (6.46),

$$\left[\text{i.e., } c = \frac{1}{3} \sum_{j=1}^{3} v_i'(j) = \frac{4}{30} \quad \text{and} \quad b = \frac{1}{\sum_{i=1}^{4} v_i'(3) - 4c} = \frac{30}{32} \right].$$

Refer to Example 6.3 as we summarize the second method for assessing additive value functions.

Step 1. Verify if Assumption 6.1 is reasonably satisfied. If not, the method may not be suitable for the problem. Restructure the problem or abort the method.

Step 2. Construct an "orthogonal design" as in columns 0–4 of Table 6.1. Table 6.3 offers an "orthogonal design" of five criteria with four levels for each criterion. The readers may find "designs of experiments" in statistics useful for constructing an "orthogonal design." For instance see Addelman (Ref. 2).

Table 6.3. A Five-Criterion, Four-Level Orthogonal Design

Combination {k}	Criteria				
	1	2	3	4	5
1	1	1	1	1	1
2	1	2	2	3	4
3	1	3	3	4	2
4	1	4	4	2	3
5	2	1	2	2	2
6	2	2	3	4	3
7	2	3	4	3	1
8	2	4	1	1	4
9	3	1	3	3	3
10	3	2	4	1	2
11	3	3	1	2	4
12	3	4	2	4	1
13	4	1	4	4	4
14	4	2	1	2	1
15	4	3	2	1	3
16	4	4	3	3	2

Step 3. Assess the value of each combination (row) in the orthogonal design assuming that the best and the worst combinations have values 1 and −1, respectively (1 and −1 can be changed, for instance, to 100 and −100 if the decision maker is more comfortable using them). In assessing the value of each combination, interactive and iterative suggestions as discussed in the previous section may be useful in effectively narrowing down the value for the combination.

Step 4. Compute $v_i'(j)$ as described in (ii) (or Table 6.2) of Example 6.3 using (6.43). Observe that, in general, if there are r levels of outcomes then (6.43) is replaced by

$$v_i'(j) = \frac{1}{r} \sum_{k \in C(i,j)} a_k, \tag{6.48}$$

where $C(i,j)$ is the collection of all combinations that have level j in the ith criterion in the orthogonal design.

Step 5. Modify $v_i'(j)$ so that $\sum_{j=1}^r v_i'(j) = 0$ and either $\sum_{i=1}^q v_i'(r) = 1$ or $\sum_{i=1}^q v_i'(1) = -1$ are satisfied using equations similar to (6.44)-(6.47) [refer to (iv) of Example 6.3]. The modification is obvious. We shall leave it to the reader.

Step 6. Perform consistency tests to determine whether or not the derived value function can represent the revealed preference. Make adjustments or repeat the process if necessary.

6.3.3. Eigenweight Vectors for Additive Value Functions

Two kinds of eigenweight vectors will be presented in this section. One is due to Saaty (Ref. 389) (Section 6.3.3.1); the other is due to Cogger and Yu (Ref. 91) (Section 6.3.3.2).

6.3.3.1. Saaty's Eigenweight Vector

Suppose that the value function has the form

$$v(y) = \sum_{i=1}^q w_i y_i. \tag{6.49}$$

If $w_i = 0$, the corresponding outcome y_i can be deleted from consideration. Thus, in this section we shall assume that $w_i > 0$, $i \in \{1, \ldots, q\}$.

Define the weight ratio by

$$w_{ij} = w_i / w_j. \tag{6.50}$$

Note that, for any $i, j, k \in \{1, \ldots, q\}$,

$$w_{ij} = w_{ji}^{-1}, \tag{6.51}$$

$$w_{ij} = w_{ik}w_{kj}. \tag{6.52}$$

Define the matrix of weight ratios as

$$W = [w_{ij}]_{q \times q}. \tag{6.53}$$

Definition 6.1. A matrix $W = [w_{ij}]_{q \times q}$ is called *consistent* if its components satisfy (6.51) and (6.52) for any $i, j, k \in \{1, \ldots, q\}$.

Saaty (Ref. 389) observed:

(i) Since each row of W is a multiple of the first, the rank of W is one, and thus there is only one nonzero eigenvalue which is q. This is due to the fact that $w_{ii} = 1$ and that the sum of all eigenvalues is equal to the trace of W (i.e., $\sum_{i=1}^{q} w_{ii}$), which is q in this case.

(ii) By using (i), one obtains $(W - qI)\, w = 0$, where I is an identity matrix, or $Ww = qw$, and therefore w must be the eigenvector of W corresponding to the maximum eigenvalue q. Indeed one can check that each column of W is an eigenvector of W. Note that normalizing by

$$\sum_{i=1}^{q} w_i = 1 \tag{6.54}$$

and

$$w_i > 0, \qquad i = 1, \ldots, q,$$

the eigenvector corresponding to q is uniquely determined.

Note that the above observation is valid for any matrix which is consistent. We summarize the above observation into the following theorem.

Theorem 6.3. Let $W_{q \times q}$ be any consistent matrix. Then

i. The maximum eigenvalue for W is q and all the other eigenvalues are 0;

ii. The eigenvector corresponding to the maximum eigenvalue, which is unique after normalization by (6.54), is the weight vector $w = (w_1, \ldots, w_q)$ which can generate W by (6.50);

iii. Each column of W is an eigenvector corresponding to the maximum eigenvalue q.

As a living system, human perception and judgment are subject to change when the information inputs or psychological states of the decision maker change. A fixed weight vector is difficult to find. Saaty (Ref. 389) proposed the following to overcome this difficulty.

Step 1. Estimate or elicit the weight ratio w_{ij} by a_{ij} and let $A = [a_{ij}]_{q \times q}$ be the matrix with components $\{a_{ij}\}$. Note that as each $w_i > 0$, we expect and shall assume that all $a_{ij} > 0$. Furthermore, as $w_{ij} = w_{ji}^{-1}$, Saaty suggested that in practice, only $a_{ij}, j > i$ [a total of $q(q-1)/2$ terms; instead of q^2], need to be assessed. The remaining $a_{ij}, i > j$, can be obtained by $a_{ij} = a_{ji}^{-1}$. Throughout this section we shall assume this for A.

Step 2. Since A is found as an approximate for W, when the consistency conditions (6.51) and (6.52) are almost satisfied for A, one would expect that the normalized eigenvector corresponding to the maximum eigenvalue of A, denoted by $\lambda_{\max}$, will be close to w. Thus, when the consistency condition is almost satisfied for A, one can estimate w by the normalized eigenvector corresponding to $\lambda_{\max}$.

Theorem 6.4. (i) The maximum eigenvalue, $\lambda_{\max}$, of A is a positive real constant.

(ii) Let $\hat{w}$ be the normalized eigenvector corresponding to $\lambda_{\max}$ of A. Then $\hat{w}_i > 0$ for all $i = 1, \ldots, q$.

Proof. As $a_{ij} > 0$ for all $i, j \in \{1, \ldots, q\}$. The conclusions (i) and (ii) follow immediately from the Perron and Frobenius theorem. (See Section 6.10.) $\qquad\square$

Theorem 6.5. [Saaty (Ref. 389).] $\lambda_{\max} \geqq q$, and the equality holds if and only if the consistency conditions are satisfied.

Proof. Let $\hat{w}$ be the eigenvector corresponding to $\lambda_{\max}$. Then

$$(A - \lambda_{\max} I)\hat{w} = 0. \tag{6.55}$$

The ith equation in (6.55) is

$$\sum_{j=1}^{q} a_{ij}\hat{w}_j - \lambda_{\max}\hat{w}_i = 0.$$

Thus

$$\lambda_{\max} = \sum_{j=1}^{q} a_{ij}\hat{w}_j / \hat{w}_i. \tag{6.56}$$

Summing (6.56) over $i \in \{1, \ldots, q\}$ (note, $a_{ii} = 1$) we have

$$q\lambda_{\max} = q + \sum_{i=1}^{q} \sum_{\substack{j=1 \\ j \neq i}}^{q} a_{ij}\hat{w}_j / \hat{w}_i. \tag{6.57}$$

Since $a_{ij} = a_{ji}^{-1}$, $a_{ji}\hat{w}_i/\hat{w}_j = (a_{ij}\hat{w}_j/\hat{w}_i)^{-1}$ and

$$\lambda_{max} = 1 + \frac{1}{q} \sum_{i=1}^{q} \sum_{j=i+1}^{q} [a_{ij}\hat{w}_j/\hat{w}_i + (a_{ij}\hat{w}_j/\hat{w}_i)^{-1}]. \tag{6.58}$$

As $x + x^{-1} = 2 + (x-1)^2/x$, with $x = a_{ij}\hat{w}_j/\hat{w}_i$, (6.58) can be rewritten as

$$\lambda_{max} = q + \sum_{i=1}^{q} \sum_{j=i+1}^{q} (\hat{w}_j a_{ij} - \hat{w}_i)^2/\hat{w}_i\hat{w}_j a_{ij} q. \tag{6.59}$$

[Note, in the above transition there are $q(q-1)/2$ terms in the summation. Thus "2" is repeated in $q(q-1)/2$ summation terms.]

Now from (6.59) we see immediately that $\lambda_{max} \geqq q$, and equality holds if and only if $\hat{w}_j a_{ij} = \hat{w}_i$ or $a_{ij} = \hat{w}_i/\hat{w}_j$ for all $i, j \in \{1, \ldots, q\}$. Using (ii) of Theorem 6.3, we see that $a_{ij} = \hat{w}_i/\hat{w}_j$ for all $(i,j) \in \{1, \ldots, q\}$ if and only if A satisfies the consistency conditions.   □

Remark 6.11. Saaty (Ref. 389) shows that the sum of the eigenvalues other than λ_{max} is equal to

$$\lambda_{max} - q = \sum_{i=1}^{q} \sum_{j=i+1}^{q} (\hat{w}_j a_{ij} - \hat{w}_i)^2/\hat{w}_i\hat{w}_j a_{ij} q,$$

which is the summation part of (6.59). Thus, when the consistency condition is satisfied, $\lambda_{max} = q$ and the sum of all other eigenvalues is 0.

The following preference-preserving result is due to Saaty.

Theorem 6.6. [Saaty (Ref. 389).] If $a_{ij} \geqq a_{kj}$ for all $j \in \{1, \ldots, q\}$ then $\hat{w}_i \geqq \hat{w}_k$.

Proof. The ith equation in (6.55) is

$$\sum_{j=1}^{q} a_{ij}\hat{w}_j - \lambda_{max}\hat{w}_i = 0$$

or

$$\hat{w}_i = \frac{1}{\lambda_{max}} \sum_{j=1}^{q} a_{ij}\hat{w}_j.$$

The conclusion follows immediately from the above equation.   □

Example 6.4. Let us consider an example of Saaty (Ref. 389),

$$A = \begin{bmatrix} 1 & 9 & 7 \\ 1/9 & 1 & 1/5 \\ 1/7 & 5 & 1 \end{bmatrix}.$$

To find λ_{max}, we solve $\det[A - \lambda I] = 0$, or

$$\det \begin{bmatrix} 1 - \lambda & 9 & 7 \\ 1/9 & 1 - \lambda & 1/5 \\ 1/7 & 5 & 1 - \lambda \end{bmatrix}.$$

$= (1 - \lambda)^3 - 3(1 - \lambda) + 9/35 + 35/9 = 0$. The maximum solution of the above is $\lambda_{max} \doteq 3.21$ (note, $\lambda_{max} > 3 = q$). Now (6.55) becomes

$$\begin{bmatrix} -2.21 & 9 & 7 \\ 1/9 & -2.21 & 1/5 \\ 1/7 & 5 & -2.21 \end{bmatrix} \begin{bmatrix} \hat{w}_1 \\ \hat{w}_2 \\ \hat{w}_3 \end{bmatrix} = \begin{bmatrix} 0 \\ 0 \\ 0 \end{bmatrix}. \tag{6.60}$$

Note that normalization implies

$$\hat{w}_1 + \hat{w}_2 + \hat{w}_3 = 1. \tag{6.61}$$

(6.60) and (6.61) offer Saaty's eigenweight vector as $\hat{w}^T = (0.77, 0.05, 0.17)$.

6.3.3.2. Cogger and Yu's Eigenweight Vector

Note that Saaty only needs $\{a_{ij}, j > i\}$ to construct the matrix A. The parts of A with a_{ij}, $i > j$ are derived using $a_{ij} = a_{ji}^{-1}$. The raw data are $\{a_{ij}, j > i\}$. The added a_{ij}, $i > j$, are included, perhaps, just for convenience of analysis. Other kinds of matrices can be constructed with the raw data $\{a_{ij}, j > i\}$. In this section, we shall be interested in the following upper triangular matrix:

$$T = [t_{ij}]_{q \times q}, \tag{6.62}$$

$$t_{ij} = \begin{cases} a_{ij} & \text{if } j \geqq i, \\ 0 & \text{otherwise.} \end{cases} \tag{6.63}$$

The upper triangular matrix T enjoys a number of nice properties, including producing an interesting eigenweight vector which is different from that of Saaty.

Define the upper triangular matrix

$$U = [u_{ij}]_{q \times q}, \tag{6.64}$$

with

$$u_{ij} = \begin{cases} w_{ij} & \text{if } i \le j, \\ 0 & \text{otherwise.} \end{cases} \tag{6.65}$$

Let D be the diagonal matrix

$$D = [d_{ij}]_{q \times q}, \tag{6.66}$$

with

$$d_{ij} = \begin{cases} q - i + 1 & \text{if } i = j, \\ 0 & \text{otherwise.} \end{cases} \tag{6.67}$$

Note that D^{-1} is diagonal with component $\tilde{d}_{ii} = 1/(q - i + 1)$. From (6.64)–(6.67), we see that

$$Uw = Dw.$$

Thus

$$(D^{-1}U - I)w = 0, \tag{6.68}$$

and the weight vector w must be the normalized eigenvector of $D^{-1}U$ corresponding to the unit eigenvalue. Indeed we have the following theorem.

Theorem 6.7.
   i. The eigenvalues of $D^{-1}U$ are $1, 1/2, 1/3, \ldots, 1/q$.
   ii. After normalization by (6.54) the eigenvector of $D^{-1}U$ corresponding to the unit eigenvalue has all positive components and is equal to w.

   Proof. As $D^{-1}U$ is upper triangular, $|D^{-1}U - \lambda I| = (1 - \lambda)(\frac{1}{2} - \lambda)(\frac{1}{3} - \lambda) \cdots (1/q - \lambda)$. This expression makes (i) clear. To prove (ii), we observe that (6.68) holds for the unit eigenvalue. Now put (6.68) and (6.54) together and rearrange; we have the following:

$$\begin{bmatrix} (1 - q) & w_{1,2} & \cdots & w_{1,q-1} & w_{1,q} \\ 0 & 2 - q & \cdots & w_{2,q-1} & w_{2,q} \\ \vdots & \vdots & \ddots & & \\ 0 & 0 & & -1 & w_{q-1,q} \\ 1 & 1 & \cdots & 1 & 1 \end{bmatrix} \cdot \begin{bmatrix} \bar{w}_1 \\ \bar{w}_2 \\ \vdots \\ \bar{w}_q \end{bmatrix} = \begin{bmatrix} 0 \\ 0 \\ \vdots \\ 0 \\ 1 \end{bmatrix}.$$

Inducing from bottom to top, starting at the second equation from the bottom, we obtain

$$\bar{w}_{q-1} = w_{q-1,q}\bar{w}_q,$$
$$\bar{w}_{q-2} = \tfrac{1}{2}(w_{q-2,q-1}\bar{w}_{q-1} + w_{q-2,q}\bar{w}_q),$$
$$\vdots$$
$$\bar{w}_1 = \frac{1}{q-1}(w_{1,2}\bar{w}_2 + w_{1,3}\bar{w}_3 + \cdots + w_{1,q}\bar{w}_q).$$

By induction, it is easily seen that if $\bar{w}_q > 0$ then all $\bar{w}_k > 0$, $k = 1, \ldots, q-1$, and if $\bar{w}_q < 0$ then all $\bar{w}_k < 0$, $k = 1, \ldots, q-1$. However, in order to satisfy the last equation [which is (6.54)], we must have all $\bar{w}_k > 0$, $k = 1, \ldots, q$. That the eigenvector $(\bar{w}_1, \ldots, \bar{w}_q)$ is indeed w follows from (6.68). $\square$

As w and U are usually unknown a priori, we shall use T, as defined in (6.62) and (6.63), to substitute for U, and similarly to Saaty's approach, we use the normalized eigenvector corresponding to the maximum eigenvalue of T (which is always one) to estimate w. Because of the special structure of T, is fairly easy to find the eigenvector, as will be shown shortly.

Theorem 6.8. (i) The eigenvalues of $D^{-1}T$ are identical to those of $D^{-1}U$. (That is, $1, 1/2, 1/3, \ldots, 1/q$.)

(ii) The maximum eigenvalue of $D^{-1}T$ is one and the corresponding eigenvector after normalization is unique with all of its components positive.

Proof. The proof follows the same steps as that for Theorem 6.7. $\square$

Theorem 6.9. The normalized eigenvector $\tilde{w}$ corresponding to the maximum eigenvalue (unity) of $D^{-1}T$ can be expressed as

$$\tilde{w} = (A^*)^{-1}e, \tag{6.69}$$

where $e = (0, 0, \ldots, 0, 1)^T$ and

$$A^* = \begin{bmatrix} (1-q) & a_{1,2} & \cdots & a_{1,q-1} & a_{1,q} \\ 0 & (2-q) & \cdots & a_{2,q-1} & a_{2,q} \\ \vdots & \vdots & \ddots & & \\ 0 & 0 & & -1 & a_{q-1,q} \\ 1 & 1 & \cdots & 1 & 1 \end{bmatrix}. \tag{6.70}$$

Proof. Since the maximum eigenvalue of $D^{-1}T$ is one, $(D^{-1}T - I)\tilde{w} = 0$, or

$$(T - D)\tilde{w} = 0. \tag{6.71}$$

The first $(q - 1)$ rows of $T - D$ are those of A^* of (6.70), while the last row is the null vector. Since $\sum_i \tilde{w}_i = 1$, substitution of a row of unit elements yields

$$A^* \tilde{w} = e. \tag{6.72}$$

In view of (6.69), the proof is complete provided A^* is nonsingular. Partition

$$A^* = \begin{bmatrix} A_{11}^* & A_{12}^* \\ A_{21}^* & A_{22}^* \end{bmatrix},$$

where A_{11}^* is $(q - 1) \times (q - 1)$, A_{12}^* is $(q - 1) \times 1$, A_{21}^* is $1 \times (q - 1)$, and $A_{22}^* = 1$. It follows from Rao (Ref. 365, p. 32) that

$$|A^*| = |A_{11}^*| \cdot |A_{22}^* - A_{21}^*(A_{11}^*)^{-1}A_{12}^*|. \tag{6.73}$$

As A_{11}^* is triangular, $|A_{11}^*| = (-1)^{q-1}(q - 1)! \neq 0$.
Let $\tilde{w}^T = (\tilde{w}_1^T, \tilde{w}_q^T)$, where $\tilde{w}_1$ is $(q - 1) \times 1$. Rewrite (6.72) as

$$A_{11}^* \tilde{w}_1 + A_{12}^* \tilde{w}_q = 0, \tag{6.74}$$

$$A_{21}^* \tilde{w}_1 + A_{22}^* \tilde{w}_q = 1. \tag{6.75}$$

From (6.74), one obtains

$$\tilde{w}_1 = -(A_{11}^*)^{-1} A_{12}^* \tilde{w}_q. \tag{6.76}$$

Substitution into (6.75) yields

$$[-A_{21}^*(A_{11}^*)^{-1}A_{12}^* + A_{22}^*]\tilde{w}_q = 1.$$

As $\tilde{w}_q > 0$ (Theorem 6.9), $1/\tilde{w}_q > 0$ and

$$(\tilde{w}_q)^{-1} = A_{22}^* - A_{21}^*(A_{11}^*)^{-1}A_{12}^* > 0. \tag{6.77}$$

In view of (6.73) and (6.76) and (6.77), and that $|A_{11}^*| \neq 0$, we conclude that A^* is nonsingular. $\square$

Remark 6.12. Theorems 6.8 and 6.9 make the job of finding $\tilde{w}$ very easy. Unlike Saaty's eigenweight vector (which involves solving a nonlinear equation for λ_{max}), $\tilde{w}$ can be solved easily because of the special structure of (6.70). Note that starting at the second equation from the bottom of (6.70) and inducing from bottom to top, we obtain

$$\tilde{w}_{q-1} = a_{q-1,q}\tilde{w}_q,$$
$$\tilde{w}_{q-2} = \tfrac{1}{2}(a_{q-2,q-1}\tilde{w}_{q-1} + a_{q-2,q}\tilde{w}_q),$$
$$\vdots$$
$$\tilde{w}_1 = \frac{1}{q-1}(a_{1,2}\tilde{w}_2 + a_{1,3}\tilde{w}_3 + \cdots + a_{1,q}\tilde{w}_q).$$

The above allows us to write $\tilde{w}_k$, $k = 1, \ldots, q - 1$ in terms of $\tilde{w}_q$. The last equation (normalization) allows us to solve $\tilde{w}_q$ and $\tilde{w}_k$, $k = 1, \ldots, q - 1$, easily. The other nice features which are not enjoyed by Saaty's method will be discussed in the next section.

Example 6.5. Consider the matrix A given in Example 6.4. As $q = 3$, we write

$$A^* = \begin{bmatrix} -2 & 9 & 7 \\ 0 & -1 & 1/5 \\ 1 & 1 & 1 \end{bmatrix}.$$

Using (6.70), we obtain (from bottom to top as mentioned in Remark 6.12)

$$\tilde{w}_2 = \tfrac{1}{5}\tilde{w}_3,$$

$$\tilde{w}_1 = \tfrac{1}{2}(9\tilde{w}_2 + 7\tilde{w}_3) = \tfrac{22}{5}\tilde{w}_3,$$

$$\tilde{w}_1 + \tilde{w}_2 + \tilde{w}_3 = \tfrac{28}{5}\tilde{w}_3 = 1.$$

Thus $\tilde{w}_3 = \tfrac{5}{28}$, $\tilde{w}_2 = \tfrac{1}{28}$, and $\tilde{w}_1 = \tfrac{22}{28}$. One also finds (using the simplex method)

$$(A^*)^{-1} = \begin{bmatrix} -6/56 & -10/56 & 44/56 \\ 1/56 & -45/56 & 2/56 \\ 5/56 & 55/56 & 10/56 \end{bmatrix}.$$

According to Theorem 6.9, the last column of $(A^*)^{-1}$ is $\tilde{w}$. That is,

$$\tilde{w} = (44/56, 2/56, 10/56)^T$$

$$\doteq (0.7857, 0.0357, 0.1786)^T.$$

The above $\tilde{w}$ is slightly different from $\hat{w}$ of Saaty's eigenweight vector.

From the above two subsections, one can see that more eigenweight vectors can be generated than the above two. However, one should pay attention to their meaning and implications, in addition to the computational aspects. We shall further explore these ideas in the next subsection.

6.3.4. Least-Distance Approximation Methods

In this section least-distance approximation methods will be discussed for two kinds of raw data. One is related to $\{a_{ij}\}$, the weight ratios discussed in Section 6.3.3; the other is related to $\{>\}^0$ and $\{\sim\}^0$.

6.3.4.1. Least-Distance Approximations in Weight Ratios

Recall that we obtained estimates a_{ij} for the weight ratios w_{ij}. Assume

$$Ea_{ij} = w_{ij}, \tag{6.78}$$

which holds if either

$$a_{ij} = w_{ij} + \varepsilon_{ij}, \tag{6.79}$$

with

$$E\varepsilon_{ij} = 0,$$

or

$$a_{ij} = w_{ij}\varepsilon_{ij}, \tag{6.80}$$

$$Ec_{ij} - 1.$$

Then

$$E(w_j a_{ij} - w_i) = 0, \tag{6.81}$$

$$E(a_{ij} - w_{ij}) = 0, \tag{6.82}$$

$$E\left(\sum_{j=i+1}^{q} (w_j a_{ij} - w_i)\right) = 0. \tag{6.83}$$

These observations offer three types of least-distance approximation models.

Model 1: $$\min S^1(w) = \sum_{i=1}^{q} \sum_{j=1}^{q} (w_j a_{ij} - w_i)^2, \tag{6.84}$$

$$\text{s.t.} \quad \sum_{i=1}^{q} w_i = 1.$$

Model 2: $$\min S^2(w) = \sum_{i=1}^{q} \sum_{j=1}^{q} \left(a_{ij} - \frac{w_i}{w_j} \right)^2, \qquad (6.85)$$

s.t. $\sum_{i=1}^{q} w_i = 1.$

Model 3: $$S^3(w) = \sum_{i=1}^{q-1} \left[\sum_{j=i+1}^{q} (w_j a_{ij} - w_i)/\sigma_i \right]^2, \qquad (6.86)$$

s.t. $\sum_{i=1}^{q} w_i = 1, \qquad w_i > 0, \qquad i = 1, \ldots, q,$

where σ_i, $i = 1, \ldots, q$ are some positive constants.

Models 1 and 2 are discussed in Chu, Kalaba, and Spingarn (Ref. 87), while Model 3 is given in Cogger and Yu (Ref. 91).

Define g_{ij}^k for Model k, $k = 1, 2$, respectively, as

$$g_{ij}^1(w) = w_j a_{ij} - w_i, \qquad (6.87)$$

$$g_{ij}^2(w) = a_{ij} - w_i/w_j, \qquad (6.88)$$

and for Model 3

$$g_i^3(w) = \sum_{j=i+1}^{q} \frac{1}{\sigma_i} (w_j a_{ij} - w_i), \qquad (6.89)$$

where $\sigma_i > 0$.

Using (6.78), we see that

$$Eg_{ij}^k(w) = 0 \qquad \text{for } k = 1, 2$$

and

$$Eg_i^3(w) = 0.$$

Thus, if we assume that for each $k = 1, 2$, $\{g_{ij}^k\}$ and $\{g_i^3\}$ are i.i.d. (independently and identically distributed), then all the above models reduce to a typical constrained least-squares method. The residual sum of squares, after the solutions $\hat{w}$ to the models are found, may be used to estimate $\text{Var}(g_{ij}^k)$ or $\text{Var}(g_i^3)$. Note that the solution $\hat{w}$ minimizes the l_2-distance of the corresponding point $\{g_{ij}^k\}$ or $\{g_i^3\}$ to point 0. When the consistency condition (Definition 6.1) holds, $g_{ij}^k(\hat{w}) = 0$, and $g_i^3(\hat{w}) = 0$ for all $k = 1, 2; i, j = 1, \ldots, q$. The extension to the general l_p-distance, $p \geq 1$, is obvious.

Remark 6.13. The assumption that $g_{ij}^k(w)$, $k = 1, 2$ [refer to (6.87) and (6.88)] for model k are i.i.d. is less than desirable. Observe that there are $q \times q$ variables for g_{ij}^k. They are not necessarily independent. From the consistency condition, one expects that, at least roughly, $a_{ik}a_{kj} = a_{ij}$. Thus, the $\{a_{ij}\}$ may be correlated and so may $\{g_{ij}^k\}$. More damagingly, in the construction of A, it is assumed that $a_{ji} = a_{ij}^{-1}$ for $j > i$. This clearly shows the interrelationship between g_{ij}^k and g_{ji}^k. These observations make one wonder whether Models 1 and 2 should be used at all because of lack of independence. Finally, one observes that Model 1, after taking the necessary condition for optimality, is reduced to a system of linear equations; while Model 2, a nonlinear model in terms of $\{w_i\}$, is much more time consuming to solve.

Remark 6.14. In Model 3, $g_i^3(w)$, $i = 1, \ldots, q - 1$, as defined in (6.89), are assumed to be i.i.d. There are only $q - 1$ terms (instead of the q^2 terms of Models 1 and 2). Similar to what is done in familiar orthogonal transformations, the variables $\{a_{ij}\}$ are transformed into $\{g_i^3\}$. Note that $\sum_{j=i+1}^{q} (w_j a_{ij} - w_i)$ can be interpreted as the *aggregate discrepancy* due to attribute i, and σ_i can be the standard deviation of such discrepancy. The assumption that $\{g_i^3\}$ are independent is conveniently reasonable. The independence implies that when a decision maker focuses upon a particular "base criterion" (or attribute), say i, the aggregate discrepancy, g_i^3, is not going to be influenced in a systematic manner by whatever the discrepancy was when another "base criterion" was being considered. This appears to be reasonable. Consider, for example, a problem of assessing the relative importance of "learning" in high school over three topics: Art (A), Mathematics (M), and Social Science (S). Then independence of aggregate discrepancies implies that in comparing M and S to A, the total discrepancy, even if known, would not cause us to alter our opinion about the comparison of M and S and their corresponding aggregate discrepancy. The independence assumption is thus not too much out of line under this circumstance.

Eigenweight vectors discussed in Section 6.3.3 are closely related to least-distance approximation methods, especially the eigenweight vector of Cogger and Yu discussed in Section 6.3.3.2. Indeed, in the remaining part of this section we shall show that the eigenweight vector of Cogger and Yu is the unique solution to the problems of a class of models represented by Model 3.

From Theorem 6.9, equation (6.69) can be rewritten as

$$A^* \tilde{w} = e$$

or

$$(i - q)\tilde{w}_i + \sum_{j=i+1}^{q} \tilde{w}_j a_{ij} = 0, \qquad i = 1, \ldots, q - 1,$$

or

$$\sum_{j=i+1}^{q} (\tilde{w}_j a_{ij} - \tilde{w}_i) = 0 \tag{6.90}$$

and

$$\sum_{i=1}^{q} \tilde{w}_i = 1, \qquad w_i > 0, \qquad i = 1, \ldots, q. \tag{6.91}$$

Theorem 6.9 demonstrates that the unique solution to (6.90) and (6.91) exists and can easily be found. However, the unique solution to (6.90) and (6.91) is also the unique solution to Model 3. In order to see this point, observe that $S^3(w) \geqq 0$, and feasibility and equality hold if and only if (6.90) and (6.91) hold. Thus $\tilde{w}$ is the new eigenweight vector if and only if it solves the problem of Model 3. All the comments concerning Model 3 are thus applicable to the new eigenweight vector.

Note that any distance function that is strictly increasing in $|g_i^3| = |\sum_{j=i+1}^{q} (w_j a_{ij} - w_i)/\sigma_i|$ can replace the implied l_2-distance in g_i^3 of Model 3 without changing the conclusion that the eigenweight vector is still the unique solution to the corresponding approximation problem. This indicates the robust feature of the Cogger and Yu eigenweight vector.

We summarize the above into the following theorem.

Theorem 6.10. (i) The eigenweight vector $\tilde{w}$ of Section 6.3.3.2 is the unique solution to the problem of Model 3.

(ii) Any distance function that is strictly increasing in $|g_i^3|$ can replace the implied l_2-distance in g_i^3 of Model 3 without changing the conclusion that $\tilde{w}$ is still the unique solution to the corresponding approximation problem.

Remark 6.15. According to Theorems 6.9 and 6.10, solution to the problem of Model 3 can easily be computed. Theorem 6.10 shows an intimate relationship between the eigenweight vector of Cogger and Yu and the least-distance approximation models. Such an intimate relationship is not very clear for Saaty's eigenweight vector. However, one can show that if the consistency condition is *almost* satisfied for A then Saaty's eigenweight vector approximates to the solution to the following problem:

$$\min \sum_{i=1}^{q} \sum_{j=i+1}^{q} [a_{ij} w_j / w_i + (a_{ij} w_j / w_i)^{-1}],$$

$$\text{s.t.} \quad \sum_{i=1}^{q} w_i = 1, \qquad w_i > 0, \qquad i = 1, \ldots, q.$$

Observe that the objective function is equivalent to the residual terms of $\lambda_{\max}$ in (6.58). A derivation of the above result and further discussion can be found in Cogger and Yu (Ref. 91). (See Exercise 6.10.)

6.3.4.2. Least-Distance Approximation Using Pairwise Preference Information

Assume that $\{>\}^0$ and $\{\sim\}^0$ are revealed and that

$$u(y, \varepsilon) = \sum_{i=1}^{q} w_i y_i + \varepsilon,$$

where ε is a random variable with $E\varepsilon = 0$. Thus

$$Eu(y, \varepsilon) \equiv v(w, y) = \sum_{i=1}^{q} w_i y_i. \tag{6.92}$$

We want to find $\hat{w}_i$ for (6.92) such that $v(\hat{w}, y)$ is most consistent with the revealed preference $\{>\}^0$ and $\{\sim\}^0$.

Note that if $(y^j, y^k) \in \{>\}^0$, then $d = y^j - y^k$ is a good "direction" in which to move, because $y^j > y^k$. We expect, barring the error term ε,

$$v(w, y^j - y^k) > 0$$

or

$$\sum_{i=1}^{q} (y_i^j - y_i^k) w_i > 0. \tag{6.93}$$

Similarly, if $(y^s, y^t) \in \{\sim\}^0$, expect

$$\sum_{i=1}^{q} (y_i^s - y_i^t) w_i = 0. \tag{6.94}$$

Our goal is to find $\{w_i\}$ such that (6.93) and (6.94) are most satisfied.

This problem can handily be converted into a mathematical programming problem as follows.

Program 6.1.

$$\min \sum_{\{>\}^0} (x_{jk})^p + \sum_{\{\sim\}^0} |z_{st}|^p, \tag{6.95}$$

$$\text{s.t.} \sum_{i=1}^{q} (y_i^j - y_i^k) w_i + x_{jk} \geq \delta, \tag{6.96}$$

for all $(y^j, y^k) \in \{>\}^0$,

$$\sum_{i=1}^{q} (y_i^s - y_i^t)w_i + z_{st} = 0, \qquad (6.97)$$

for all $(y^s, y^t) \in \{\sim\}^0$,

$$\sum_{i=1}^{q} w_i = 1, \qquad (6.98)$$

$$w_i \geqq 0, \qquad x_{jk} \geqq 0, \qquad (6.99)$$

z_{st} unrestricted (can be negative), where δ is an arbitrarily small positive constant. Note that on the right-hand side we have $\delta > 0$ rather than zero, in order to avoid the situation where $\sum_{i=1}^{q} (y_i^j - y_i^k)w_i = 0$ would hold, which would be in contradiction with (6.93).

Observe that x_{jk} and z_{st} are uniquely associated with the constraints related to (6.93) and (6.94) for each $(y^j, y^k) \in \{>\}^0$ and each $(y^s, y^t) \in \{\sim\}^0$. In (6.95) the summations are over each pair in $\{>\}^0$ and $\{\sim\}^0$, respectively.

Also observe that the objective function in (6.95) implies that we want to minimize the l_p-distance from the perfect fit [i.e., (6.93) and (6.94) are all satisfied] and that each revealed preference in $\{>\}^0$ and $\{\sim\}^0$ is equally credible or important in assessing the weight $\{w_i\}$. The impact of the l_p-distance on the solution is discussed within the context of compromise solutions (Chapter 4). Clearly, if there is evidence that the credibility or importance of the pairs of revealed preference is different, we can replace (6.95) by

$$\min \sum_{\{>\}^0} \lambda_{jk}(x_{jk})^p + \sum_{\{\sim\}^0} \lambda_{st}|z_{st}|^p. \qquad (6.100)$$

Recall that changing the weights $\{\lambda_{jk}\}$ and $\{\lambda_{st}\}$ has an effect similar to changing the scales of $\{x_{jk}\}$ and $\{z_{st}\}$. (See Chapter 4.)

Finally, observe that Program 6.1 is a convex programming problem. Constraint (6.98) is needed to avoid the trivial solution (i.e., all $w_i = 0$). When $p = 1$ (i.e., l_1-distance) is chosen the mathematical programming problem becomes a simple linear programming problem, which can easily be solved either by the primal or dual program.

Theorem 6.11. The optimal solution to Program 6.1 always exists.

Proof. Given $w_i \geqq 0$ satisfying (6.98),

$$x_{jk}(w) = \max\left\{0, \delta - \sum_{i=1}^{q} (y_i^j - y_i^k)w_i\right\} \qquad \text{for all } (y^j, y^k) \in \{>\}^0$$

and

$$z_{st}(w) = -\sum_{i=1}^{q} (y_i^s - y_i^t) w_i \qquad \text{for all } (y^s, y^t) \in \{\sim\}^0$$

uniquely minimize the objective function (6.95) and satisfy the constraints (6.96) and (6.97). Note that $x_{jk}(w)$ and $z_{st}(w)$ are continuous in w. Rewrite (6.95) as

$$\min_{\{w\}} r(w) = \sum_{\{>\}^0} [x_{jk}(w)]^p + \sum_{\{\sim\}^0} |z_{st}(w)|^p.$$

Note that the objective function $r(w)$ is continuous in w. As $w \geq 0$ and (6.98) defines a compact set, we know $r(w)$ must have a minimum point. This completes our proof.   □

Example 6.6. Let $q = 3$ and

$$y^1 = (3, 5, 3),$$

$$y^2 = (1, 7, 5),$$

$$y^3 = (5, 5, 3),$$

$$y^4 = (3, 1, 5),$$

$$y^5 = (7, 1, 1),$$

$$\{>\}^0 = \{(y^2, y^1), (y^3, y^1), (y^1, y^5), (y^5, y^2), (y^3, y^4), (y^3, y^5)\},$$

$$\{\sim\}^0 = \{(y^4, y^5)\},$$

Note that transitivity does not hold in $\{>\}^0$. For instance, $y^2 > y^1$, $y^1 > y^5$, and $y^5 > y^2$. To find $\{\hat{w}_i\}$ using Program 6.1, we obtain

$$\min x_{21}^p + x_{31}^p + x_{15}^p + x_{52}^p + x_{34}^p + x_{35}^p + |z_{45}|^p,$$

$$\text{s.t.} \quad (-2, 2, 2) \cdot w + x_{21} \geq 0, \qquad \text{because } y^2 - y^1 = (-2, 2, 2),$$

$$(2, 0, 0) \cdot w + x_{31} \geq 0,$$

$$(-4, 4, 2) \cdot w + x_{15} \geq 0,$$

$$(6, -6, -4) \cdot w + x_{52} \geq 0,$$

$$(2, 4, -2) \cdot w + x_{34} \geqq 0,$$

$$(-2, 4, 2) \cdot w + x_{35} \geqq 0,$$

$$(-4, 0, 4) \cdot w + z_{45} = 0,$$

$$w_1 + w_2 + w_3 = 1,$$

all $x_{jk} \geqq 0$, z_{45} unrestricted.

The above program can be solved easily when p is specified. When $p = 1$, the program can be converted into a linear programming problem. We shall not stop to do so. (See Exercise 6.11.)

Srinivasan and Shocker (Ref. 422) derived a similar program for solving the same problem of finding $\hat{w}$. Their derivation, although not as straightforward as the above, is interesting. We shall sketch it briefly.

Given $\{w_i\}$, define for each $(y^j, y^k) \in \{>\}^0$ the "badness" and "goodness" measures, respectively, by

$$B_{jk}(w) = \max \{0, (y^k - y^j) \cdot w\}, \tag{6.101}$$

$$G_{jk}(w) = \max \{0, (y^j - y^k) \cdot w\}. \tag{6.102}$$

Note, by definition

$$G_{jk}(w) - B_{jk}(w) = (y^j - y^k) \cdot w. \tag{6.103}$$

Observe that since $y^j > y^k$ we want to have $(y^j - y^k) \cdot w > 0$. Thus, the goodness of fit is given by $(y^j - y^k) \cdot w$ when it is positive; otherwise the goodness of fit is zero. Conversely if $(y^j - y^k) \cdot w$ is negative, $-(y^j - y^k) \cdot w = (y^k - y^j) \cdot w$ will be the badness of fit; otherwise, the badness is zero.

The goal is then to minimize the total badness of fit so that the total goodness must be over the badness by 1. That is

Program 6.2.

$$\min \sum_{\{>\}^0} B_{jk}(w) \tag{6.104}$$

$$\text{s.t.} \quad \sum_{\{>\}^0} [G_{jk}(w) - B_{jk}(w)] = 1 \tag{6.105}$$

$$w_i \geqq 0$$

In view of (6.101)-(6.103), Program 6.2 can be reduced to a linear program. (Review Section 4.3.4.2.) Indeed, if we set $\{\sim\}^0 = \varnothing$, Program 6.2 reduces to $p = 1$ (l_1-distance) of Program 6.1 with (6.98) being replaced by (6.105), which is $\sum_{\{>\}^0} (y^j - y^k) \cdot w = 1$. (See Exercise 6.12.) There is no convincing reason why constraint (6.105) would be superior to (6.98). Both can be intuitively justified. We shall leave it to the reader's creative imagination. (See Exercise 6.13.) Finally we remark that precise statistical inference is very difficult to obtain using the methods discussed in this subsection.

6.3.4.3. Least-Distance Approximation for the Ideal Point Using Revealed Preference

As mentioned in the previous section, the distance from the ideal point can be regarded as a value function, where the smaller the distance, the better. The distance function can be specified as

$$h(y, p; w, y^*) = \sum_{i=1}^{q} w_i^p |y_i - y_i^*|^p, \tag{6.106}$$

where $p \geq 1$ and $w_i \geq 0$, $i = 1, \ldots, q$. Note that $[h(y, p; w, y^*)]^{1/p}$ is a typical weighted l_p-distance of y from y^* (the ideal point) (see Chapter 4). As $h(y, p; w, y^*)$ is a strictly increasing function of the l_p-distance, we may and will use $h(y, p; w, y^*)$ for the preference representation for the ease of mathematical analysis. Now suppose that

$$u(y, \varepsilon) = h(y, p; w, y^*) + \varepsilon \qquad \text{with } E\varepsilon = 0.$$

Then

$$Eu(y, \varepsilon) = h(y, p; w, y^*). \tag{6.107}$$

We want to find $\hat{w}$ and $\hat{y}^*$, if y^* is unknown, so that $h(y, p; \hat{w}, \hat{y}^*)$ is most consistent with the revealed preference $\{>\}^0$ and $\{\sim\}^0$.

Note that if $(y^j, y^k) \in \{>\}^0$, we expect that

$$h(y^j, p; w, y^*) < h(y^k, p; w, y^*)$$

or

$$\sum_{i=1}^{q} w_i^p [|y_i^j - y_i^*|^p - |y_i^k - y_i^*|^p] < 0. \tag{6.108}$$

Similarly, if $(y^s, y^t) \in \{\sim\}^0$, we expect

$$h(y^s, p; w, y^*) = h(y^t, p; w, y^*)$$

or

$$\sum_{i=1}^{q} w_i^p [|y_i^s - y_i^*|^p - |y_i^t - y_i^*|^p] = 0. \tag{6.109}$$

Observe that y^j, y^k, y^s, y^t, etc. are assumed to be known. If y^* is predetermined, then (6.108) and (6.109) become a simple linear inequality and equality in terms of w_i^p.

To find $\hat{w}$ and $\hat{y}^*$ for $h(y, p; w, y^*)$ from $\{>\}^0$ and $\{\sim\}^0$ can be done, similar to the previous subsection, as follows.

Program 6.3.

$$\min H(w, y^*, x, z) = \sum_{\{>\}^0} x_{jk}^r + \sum_{\{\sim\}^0} |z_{st}|^r, \tag{6.110}$$

where x and z stand for $\{x_{jk}\}$ and $\{z_{st}\}$, respectively,

$$\text{s.t.} \left[\sum_{i=1}^{q} w_i^p [|y_i^j - y_i^*|^p - |y_i^k - y_i^*|^p] \right] - x_{jk} \leq -\delta, \tag{6.111}$$

for each $(y^j, y^t) \in \{>\}^0$,

$$\sum_{i=1}^{q} w_i^p [|y_i^s - y_i^*|^p - |y_i^t - y_i^*|^p] + z_{st} = 0, \tag{6.112}$$

for each $(y^s, y^x) \in \{\sim\}^0$,

$$\sum_{i=1}^{q} w_i^p = 1, \tag{6.113}$$

$$|y_i^*| \leq M, \qquad i = 1, \ldots, q, \tag{6.114}$$

$$\text{each } w_i \geq 0, \qquad \text{each } x_{jk} \geq 0, \tag{6.115}$$

$$z_{st} \text{ unrestricted.}$$

In (6.114), M is a sufficiently large constant, and in (6.11) δ is any arbitrarily small positive constant.

Observe that x_{jk} and z_{st} are uniquely associated with the constraints related to (6.108) and (6.109) for each $(y^j, y^k) \in \{>\}^0$ and each $(y^s, y^t) \in \{\sim\}^0$. In (6.110) the summations are over each pair in $\{>\}^0$ and $\{\sim\}^0$, respectively.

Note that the objective function of (6.110) implies that we want to minimize the l_r-distance, $r \geq 1$, from the perfect fit [i.e., (6.108) and (6.109) are all satisfied] and that each revealed preference in $\{>\}^0$ and $\{\sim\}^0$ is equally credible and important in assessing $h(y, p; w, y^*)$. The impact of the l_r-distance on the solution is discussed in Chapter 4. Clearly, if there is evidence that the credibility or importance of the pairs of revealed preference is different, we can replace (6.110) by

$$\min \sum_{\{>\}^0} \lambda_{jk} x_{jk}^r + \sum_{\{\sim\}^0} \lambda_{st} |z_{st}|^r. \tag{6.116}$$

Recall that changing the weight $\{\lambda_{jk}\}$ and $\{\lambda_{st}\}$ has an effect similar to changing the scales of $\{x_{jk}\}$ and $\{z_{st}\}$. (See Chapter 4.)

The following can be proved in a way similar to that of Theorem 6.11. (See Exercise 6.14.)

Theorem 6.12. The optimal solution to Program 6.3 always exists.

Remark 6.16. (i) Constraint (6.113) is needed to avoid the trivial solution (i.e., all $\hat{w}_i = 0$). Constraint (6.114) is used to prevent y^* from becoming arbitrarily large. When the solution to Program 6.3 happens to be $y_i^* = M$, one may want to increase M to determine the sensitivity of the choice of y_i^*. If $y_i^* = M$ occurs no matter how large M is (this is almost impossible to occur), then attribute i is clearly of the type "larger is better." Constraint (6.114) is for convenience of mathematical programming (see Exercise 6.15).

(ii) If y^* is predetermined, and $r = 1$ [i.e., the l_1-distance for (6.110) is used], Program 6.3 can be converted into a linear programming problem in finding $\{\hat{w}_i^p\}$. (See Exercise 6.16.)

(iii) If y^* is unknown, but $r = 1$ for (6.110) and $p = 2$ for (6.111) and (6.112), then Program 6.3 can also be converted into a linear programming problem. In order to see this, let us rewrite (6.111) into

$$\sum_{i=1}^{q} w_i^p [(y_i^j - y_i^*)^2 - (y_i^k - y_i^*)^2] - x_{jk} \leq -\delta$$

or

$$\sum_{i=1}^{q} w_i^p [(y_i^j)^2 - (y_i^k)^2] - 2 \sum_{i=1}^{q} w_i^p y_i^* (y_i^j - y_i^k) - x_{jk} \leq -\delta$$

or

$$\sum_{i=1}^{q} w_i^p [(y_i^j)^2 - (y_i^k)^2] - 2 \sum_{i=1}^{q} u_i (y_i^j - y_i^k) - x_{jk} \leq -\delta, \tag{6.117}$$

where

$$u_i = w_i^p y_i^*. \tag{6.118}$$

Similarly (6.112) can be written as

$$\sum_{i=1}^{q} w_i^p[(y_i^s)^2 - (y_i^t)^2] - 2 \sum_{i=1}^{q} u_i(y_i^s - y_i^t) + z_{st} = 0. \tag{6.119}$$

Observe that in (6.117) and (6.119), y_i^j, y_i^k, y_i^s, y_i^t are known. Thus, if we treat $\{x_{jk}\}$, $\{z_{st}\}$, $\{w_i^p\}$, and $\{u_i\}$ as variables, (6.117) and (6.119) become linear constraints. Also, note that the objective function (6.110) or (6.116) will not be changed by (6.118).

For convenience define the following.

Program 6.4. This is a modified version of Program 6.3 with $r = 1$ in (6.110), $p = 2$, and (6.117), (6.119) replacing (6.111) and (6.112).

Then the above discussion implies that Program 6.4 can be solved by a linear programming problem. Let $(w^0, (y^*)^0, x^0, z^0)$ be the solution to Program 6.4. Then the corresponding solution to Program 6.3 can be recovered using (6.118).

Example 6.7. Let $\{y^j\}$, $\{>\}^0$, and $\{\sim\}^0$ be as defined in Example 6.6. Instead of the linear value function, we want to find the ideal point y^* and weights $\{w_i\}$ using Program 6.3. Let us assume, for simplicity, $r = 1$ and $p = 2$, so that we can use Program 6.4. Observe that w_i here replaces $w_i^p = w_i^2$ in the previous program.

We first compute the coefficients for constraints (6.117) and (6.119) as follows:

	$y_i^j - y_i^k$			$(y_i^j)^2 - (y_i^k)^2$		
	$i = 1$	2	3	$i = 1$	2	3
(y^2, y^1)	−2	2	2	−8	24	16
(y^3, y^1)	2	0	0	16	0	0
(y^1, y^5)	−4	4	2	−40	24	8
(y^5, y^2)	6	−6	−4	48	−48	−24
(y^3, y^4)	2	4	−2	16	24	−16
(y^3, y^5)	−2	4	2	−24	24	8
(y^4, y^5)	−4	0	4	−40	0	24

The mathematical program using $\delta = 0.01$ can be written as:

$$\min x_{21} + x_{31} + x_{15} + x_{52} + x_{34} + x_{35} + |z_{45}|$$

$$\text{s.t.} \quad -8w_1 + 24w_2 + 16w_3 - 2(-2u_1 + 2u_2 + 2u_3) - x_{21} \leq -0.01,$$

$$16w_1 \qquad\qquad - 2(2u_1) \qquad\qquad - x_{31} \leq -0.01,$$

$$-40w_1 + 24w_2 + 8w_3 - 2(-4u_1 + 4u_2 + 2u_3) - x_{15} \leq -0.01,$$

$$48w_1 - 48w_2 - 24w_3 - 2(6u_1 - 6u_2 - 4u_3) - x_{52} \leq -0.01,$$

$$16w_1 + 24w_2 - 16w_3 - 2(2u_1 + 4u_2 - 2u_3) - x_{34} \leq -0.01,$$

$$-24w_1 + 24w_2 + 8w_3 - 2(-2u_1 + 4u_2 + 2u_3) - x_{35} \leq -0.01,$$

$$-40w_1 \qquad + 24w_3 - 2(-4u_1 + 4u_3) + z_{45} = 0,$$

$$w_1 + w_2 + w_3 \qquad\qquad = 1,$$

$$|u_i|_{i=1,2,3} \leq 10, \qquad (6.120)$$

$$w_i \geq 0, \qquad x_{jk} \geq 0, \qquad z_{45} \text{ unrestricted.}$$

The above can be solved by linear programming and we shall leave it to the reader. (See Exercise 6.17.) Note that (6.120) follows from (6.114) and (6.118). Because $w_i \leq 1$ and intuitively $|y_i^*| \leq \max \{|y_i^j|, i = 1, 2, 3, j = 1, \ldots, 5\} = M$ we can use $|u_i| \leq M$ for constraint (6.114). Here as each $|y_i^j| < 10$, we use "10" for M, which is a reasonable choice.

Remark 6.17. Let us compare the program above with the program derived by Srinivasan and Shocker (Ref. 421) for solving the same problem of finding y^* and $\hat{w}$. They focused on the case of $r = 1$, $p = 2$ and $\{\sim\}^0 = \varnothing$ and derived a linear program similar to Program 6.4. Their basic argument in the formulation is just like that sketched in the previous section. Let us sketch it briefly as follows.

Given $\{w_i\}$ and $\{y^*\}$, define for each $(y^j, y^k) \in \{>\}^0$ the "badness" and "goodness" measures by

$$B_{jk}(w, y^*) = \max \left\{ 0, \sum_i w_i^2 [(y_i^j - y_i^*)^2 - (y_i^k - y_i^*)^2] \right\}, \qquad (6.121)$$

$$G_{jk}(w, y^*) = \max \left\{ 0, \sum_i w_i^2 [(y_i^k - y_i^*)^2 - (y_i^j - y_i^*)^2] \right\}. \qquad (6.122)$$

Note, by definition

$$G_{jk}(w, y^*) - B_{jk}(w, y^*) = \sum_i w_i^2 [(y_i^k - y_i^*)^2 - (y_i^j - y_i^*)^2]. \qquad (6.123)$$

The goal is then to minimize the total badness of fit subject to the condition in which the total goodness must exceed the badness by a positive constant, say 1. That is, we have the following.

Program 6.5.

$$\min_{\{>\}^0} \sum B_{jk}(w, y^*), \qquad (6.124)$$

$$\text{s.t.} \sum_{\{>\}^0} [G_{jk}(w, y^*) - B_{jk}(w, y^*)] = 1, \qquad (6.125)$$

$$w_i \geqq 0.$$

Using Remark 6.16(iii), (6.121)-(6.124), Program 6.5 can be converted into a linear program similar to Program 6.4. (See Exercise 6.18.) The main difference between Program 6.4 and Program 6.5 is that Program 6.4 imposes constraints (6.113) and (6.114) while Program 6.5 imposes the constraints in (6.125). There is no convincing evidence for any one to be superior to the other. Both can be intuitively justified. We shall leave it to the reader's creative judgment.

6.4. Further Comments

We have introduced a variety of methods for constructing value functions. The first one (Section 6.1) is a direct application of calculus. Tangent planes, normal vectors, and line integrals play a central role. Our discussion is parallel to calculus of differentiation and integration. One observes that one of the most important jobs in optimal control problems or differential games (see Ref. 287 of Leitmann and Ref. 228 of Isaacs, for instance) is to construct suitable value functions for the problems or games. To avoid a lengthy digression we shall skip these topics. Interested readers can read the above two references.

The second class of methods (Section 6.2) focuses on additive value functions. Two interactive methods for direct assessment are described. While the methods are straightforward, their implementation is a sophisticated art. For further discussion of the art we refer to Ref. 254, and Ref. 250 of Keeney.

The third class of methods (Section 6.3) involves applications of statistics and/or mathematical programs. We have discussed the general concepts, orthogonal design, eigenvector approximation, and two mathematical programs for finding value functions and/or ideal points. Note that orthogonal designs involve holistic evaluation of abstract combinations of attribute levels, instead of revealed information on $\{>\}$ and $\{\sim\}$. The shortcoming is that the decision maker may find it difficult to comprehend cognitively the possible attribute combinations necessary to offer a reliable assessment of values. The reader is referred to Ref. 22 of Barron and Person for further discussion of holistic methods. Certainly the methods for using statistical approximation, eigenweight vectors and mathematical programs are valid only when suitable assumptions hold. There are many more such methods. The interested reader is referred to Ref. 223 of Hwang and Masud and Ref. 222 of Hwang and Yoon for other methods.

Finally, let us mention that as with tools each method has its unique strengths and weaknesses. Each method needs a special design for successful applications. A real master should be familiar with each tool for applications, rather than stick to a particular one and rigidly defend its validity. Besides, one should be aware of the fact that the credibility and posture of the elicitor of value functions play an important role in the process. Whether or not a method is accepted may be due to the credibility or posture (a Ph.D or a Professor) of the elicitor (Halo Effect as to be described in Chapter 9) rather than to the validity of the method. This casts a moral duty on the elicitor. He must make sure that the client (or decision maker) understands the assumptions and weaknesses of the methods used to avoid mispresentation.

6.5. Appendix: Perron–Frobenius Theorem

Theorem 6.13. (For a proof see Ref. 391 of Saaty.) Let $A \geqq 0$ (i.e., each component is nonnegative) be irreducible. Then
   i. A has a real positive simple (i.e., not multiple) eigenvalue λ_{max} which is not exceeded in modulus by any other eigenvalue of A.
   ii. The eigenvector of A corresponding to λ_{max} has positive components, and is essentially (within multiplication by a constant) unique.

Exercises

6.1. If a value function exists, then an indifference curve (or surface) of the value function can be considered a boundary between points preferred and points not preferred. Show that, in the two-dimensional space,
   a. indifference curves never intersect, and
   b. indifference curves can never be positively sloping if we assume that more is always preferred to less for each criterion.

6.2. Mr. Smith, a prospective buyer, is considering purchasing a new house. He considers four attributes (criteria) for each house: location, price, interior design, and neighborhood. The orthogonal design approach will be applied to assess his preference. The criteria (i) and preference levels (j) are numbered in the following way:

Criterion (i)	Preference level (j)
1 Location	0 Bad
2 Price	1 Average
3 Interior design	2 Good
4 Neighborhood	

The following table summarizes an orthogonal design for nine combinations of possible outcomes with associated values assigned by Mr. Smith.

	Criterion (i)				Associated
Combination (k)	1	2	3	4	value $\{a_k\}$
1	0	0	0	0	-1.0
2	0	1	1	2	-0.2
3	0	2	2	1	0.2
4	1	0	1	1	0.3
5	1	1	2	0	0.5
6	1	2	0	2	0.4
7	2	0	2	2	0.6
8	2	1	0	1	0.5
9	2	2	1	0	0.8

a. Find $v_i(j)$ and $\hat{v}_i(j)$ for criteria $i = 1, 2, 3, 4$ and preference levels $j = 0, 1, 2$.

b. Verify

i. $\sum_{j=0}^{2} \hat{v}_i(j) = 0$;

ii. either $\sum_{i=1}^{4} v_i(2) = 1$ or $\sum_{i=1}^{4} \hat{v}_i(0) = -1$.

c. Use this problem as an example to criticize the method of orthogonal design to elicit value functions. What are its strengths and weaknesses?

6.3. Table 6.3 in Section 6.3.2 shows five criteria and four levels of orthogonal design. Assume the four levels $\{1, 2, 3, 4\}$ represent $\{$bad, fair, good, excellent$\}$. Assume that the combinations have the following values:

Combination (k)	Associated value (a_k)
1	−1.0
2	0.2
3	0
4	0.4
5	−0.2
6	0.5
7	0.2
8	0.6
9	0.6
10	0.4
11	0.5
12	0.4
13	0.6
14	−0.4
15	0.6
16	0.6

a. Find $v_i'(j)$ and $\hat{v}_i(j)$ for $i = 1, 2, 3, 4, 5$, $j = 1, 2, 3, 4$.
b. Verify

   i. $\sum_{j=1}^{4} \hat{v}_i(j) = 0$;

   ii. either $\sum_{i=1}^{5} \hat{v}_i(4) = 1$ or $\sum_{i=1}^{5} \hat{v}_i(1) = -1$.

6.4. Consider the following matrix of weight ratios (See Section 6.3.3.1):

$$A = \begin{bmatrix} 1 & 1/4 & 1/8 \\ 4 & 1 & 1/2 \\ 8 & 2 & 1 \end{bmatrix}.$$

a. Determine $\lambda_{\max}$ of A.
b. Find Saaty's eigenweight vector.
c. Find Cogger and Yu's eigenweight vector.
d. Is the matrix A consistent? Explain.
e. Which eigenweight vector should be used? Justify your answer. Can you find a new eigenweight vector for the problem?

6.5. Miles per gallon (M.P.G.) is an index of the overall "energy efficiency" achieved by a motor vehicle. M.P.G. is determined by many factors. Four important attributes have been identified. These are (1) engine displacement, (2) curb weight, (3) PBPS (power brakes and power steering), and (4) transmission type. Suppose that an additive value function is to be used and one subject is selected to assess the "importance" weights of the attributes. By applying Saaty's procedure the following matrix of weight ratios is obtained:

	Displacement	Weight	PBPS	Transmission type
Displacement	1	3	5	6
Weight	1/3	1	3	4
PBPS	1/5	1/3	1	2
Transmission type	1/6	1/4	1/2	1

a. Find the maximum eigenvalue, λ_{max} of the above matrix.
b. Find Saaty's (normalized) eigenweight vector.
c. Find Cogger and Yu's eigenweight vector.
d. Is the matrix A consistent? Justify your answer.

6.6. Suppose that the value function is given by $v(y) = \sum_{i=1}^{3} w_i v_i(y_i)$, where $v_i(y_i)$, $i = 1, 2, 3$, are as follows:

$$v_1(y_1) = -\tfrac{1}{4} y_1^2 - 2y_1,$$

$$v_2(y_2) = -\tfrac{1}{2} y_2^2 + y_2,$$

$$v_3(y_3) = -y_3^2 + y_3.$$

Suppose that $Y_1 = [0, 4]$, $Y_2 = [0, 2]$, $Y_3 = [0, 2]$ and it is revealed that $(4, 2, 1) \sim (2, 1, 2)$ and $(0, 2, 1) \sim (1, 1, 2)$. Using $\sum_{k=1}^{q} w_k = 1$, find the weights w_i, $i = 1, 2, 3$ for the value function $v(y)$.

6.7. A prosperous investing firm, Morris & Kay, decided to purchase microcomputers from Computer Park Co. The Sales manager of Computer Park Co. provided the characteristic information $\{y^1, y^2, y^3, y^4\}$ of four different models according to five attributes: price (x_1), memory capacity (x_2), display (x_3), graphics (x_4), and mass storage devices (x_5). The characteristic values of the five attributes for each model are summarized in the following matrix.

			Attributes		
Models	Price (x_1)	Memory capacity (x_2)	Display (x_3)	Graphics (x_4)	Mass storage devices (x_5)
y^1	1,395	64	10	8	6
y^2	899	64	8	8	4
y^3	495	64	8	8	5
y^4	299	16	6	6	4

[Values of display (x_3), graphics (x_4), and mass storage devices (x_5) are based on 10-point scales (i.e., excellent = 10, very poor = 1).] Based on the above information, Morris & Kay revealed that

$$\{>\}^0 = \{\{1, 2\}, \{1, 3\}, \{4, 1\}, \{3, 4\}\}$$

and

$$\{\sim\}^0 = \{2, 3\}.$$

    a. Use Program 6.1 to formulate a mathematical program for finding an estimated value function for the above-revealed preference.

    b. Assuming $p = 1$, find a set of weights $\{\hat{w}_i\}$, $i = 1, 2, 3, 4$.

    c. Assume that $\{\sim\}^0 = \emptyset$. Show that Program 6.2 reduces to $p = 1$ of Program 6.1 with $\sum_{i=1}^{q} w_i = 1$ being replaced by $\sum_{\{>\}^0} [G_{jk}(w) - B_{jk}(w)] = 1$.

    d. Assume that the preference is to be represented by the distance from some ideal point (y^*). Use Program 6.3 to construct a mathematical program for finding the ideal point and the appropriate weights.

    e. Using Program 6.4 with $r = 1$ and $p = 2$, convert the above problem into a linear programming problem and find a set of weights $\{w_i\}$.

6.8. Suppose that each y_i, $i \in Q$, is characterized by more is better. Show that the vector $n(y^k) = n^+(y^k)$ of (6.3) points to, at least locally, the side of the more preferred outcomes.

6.9. Suppose that $W = [w_{ij}]_{q \times q}$, as defined by (6.50), is consistent. Show that each column of W is an eigenvector of W.

6.10. Show that if the consistency condition is almost satisfied for A (see Section 6.3.4.1), then Saaty's eigenweight vector approximates the solution of the following problem:

$$\min \sum_{i=1}^{q} \sum_{j=i+1}^{q} [a_{ij}w_j/w_i + (a_{ij}w_j/w_i)^{-1}]$$

$$\text{s.t.} \sum_{i=1}^{q} w_i = 1, \qquad w_i > 0, \qquad i = 1, \ldots, q.$$

(See Ref. 91 for a derivation, if necessary.)

6.11. Refer to Example 6.6. If $p = 1$, convert the mathematical program into a linear program and find the approximate value function for the revealed preference.

6.12. Convert Program 6.2 into a linear program and compare it with Program 6.1 from a computational point of view. (Review Section 4.3.4.2 if necessary.)

6.13. Programs 6.1 and 6.2 have been derived using the intuitive argument in the text. Can you offer any statistical interpretation using appropriate assumptions? From a viewpoint of application, which one is easier to implement? Describe how you would implement the two methods.

6.14. Prove Theorem 6.12.

6.15. Refer to Remark 6.16. Show under what circumstance $y_i^* = M$ occurs no matter how large M is. How would you take care of this problem?

6.16. Refer to Remark 6.16(ii). Convert Program 6.3 into a linear program when y^* is predetermined and $r = 1$.

6.17. Solve the problem described in Example 6.7. What are your estimated ideal point and weights?

6.18. Convert Program 6.5 into a linear program and compare it with Program 6.4.

6.19. Can you offer any statistical interpretation, using appropriate assumptions, of Programs 6.3 and 6.4, respectively? Describe how you would implement each of them.

6.20. Compare Program 6.1 with Program 6.2. Identify similarities and differences.

6.21. Compare Program 6.2 with Program 6.4. Identify similarities and differences.

6.22. Mr. Smith is thinking about using $v(y_1, y_2) = w_1 v_1(y_1) + w_2 v_2(y_2)$ to express his preference over y_1 (money) and y_2 (leisure) time he can have for the coming week. Assume that he can earn \$10 per hour and he can work as long as he wants at the same rate. Design a plan to interactively elicit the value function representation for his preference.

6.23. Criticize the method you designed in Problem 6.22. What are the difficulties? Can you design a better method? Instead of an additive value function, how would you elicit the preference of Mr. Smith?

Suggested Reading

The following references are particularly pertinent to this chapter: 2, 7, 22, 87, 91, 222, 223, 228, 250, 254, 287, 365, 389, 391, 421, 422.

7

Domination Structures and Nondominated Solutions

7.1. Introduction

In Chapter 3 we discussed that "Pareto preference" is based on the assumption that "more is better," with no other preference information assumed. This is the simplest kind of preference. Recall that Pareto preference is not a weak order because the induced indifference relation, $\{\sim\}$, is not transitive. On the other hand, from Chapters 4-6, we know that a value function or distance function associated with a compromise solution must assume that the corresponding preference $\{>\}$ is a weak order and the induced indifference curves must contain a countable dense subset with respect to $\{>\}$. The assumptions for $\{>\}$ to have a value function representation certainly are very restrictive, as discussed in Chapter 5. The gap between the assumption of Pareto preference and that of the preference having a value function representation is very large.

In order to see the gap in a more concrete way, recall that for Pareto preference, given any $y \in Y$, the "inferior" set and the "superior" set to y are given by $\{y>\} = (y + \Lambda^{\leq}) \cap Y$ and $\{y<\} = (y + \Lambda^{\geq}) \cap Y$, respectively. The dominated cone $\Lambda^{\leq}$ is the negative of the preferred cone $\Lambda^{\geq}$; and they are constant, independent of y. Note that $\Lambda^{\leq}$ and $\Lambda^{\geq}$ are only $(\frac{1}{2})^q$ of R^q. As q gets large, $\Lambda^{\leq}$ and $\Lambda^{\geq}$ become relatively small with respect to R^q. Now, for simplicity, let $v(y)$ be a differentiable concave value function defined on $R^q = Y$. Assume that the gradient $\nabla v(y) \neq 0$ in Y. Then for any $y^0 \in Y$, we have

$$\{y^0>\} \supset [y^0 + D(y^0)] \cap Y, \qquad (7.1)$$

where

$$D(y^0) = \{d \mid d \cdot \nabla v(y^0) < 0\}. \qquad (7.2)$$

163

Thus for each y^0, the inferior set to y^0 contains a "dominated cone" $D(y^0)$ which is a "half-space" of R^q, no matter how large q is. As q gets larger, $\Lambda^{\leq}$ gets smaller relative to $D(y^0)$, $(\frac{1}{2})^q$ comparing with $\frac{1}{2}$. The gap between $(\frac{1}{2})^q$ and half-space for a dominated cone is a representation of the gap between Pareto preference and preferences having a concave value function representation.

Between Pareto preference and preferences having a concave value function representation, there are infinitely many possible revealed preferences which have a dominated cone much larger than $(\frac{1}{2})^q$ but much smaller than one-half of R^q. A worker may reveal that he would be happy to work on Sunday if he gets paid at least $50 an hour; and a decision maker may reveal that if he can save at least $2,000 he would accept a two-day extension for job completion. These are just some examples. See Remark 7.19 for further discussion.

In this chapter, we shall use "domination structures" to describe revealed preferences that are between Pareto preference and preferences with a value function presentation. Indeed, "domination structures" is a common denominator for many revealed preferences. In Section 7.2 we shall describe the general concepts of global and local domination structures. In Section 7.3 we shall describe the mathematical properties of nondominated points (N-points) of given "constant" dominated cones. In Section 7.4 we shall describe mathematical properties of local and global N-points with domination structures. In Section 7.5 we shall discuss how to approximate N-points of some regular domination structures by N-points of constant dominated cone structures. Interactive methods for using information from domination structures to solve complicated decision problems are then discussed in this section.

7.2. Domination Structures

Given two points y^0 and y^1, if $y^0 > y^1$ we may think of this occurring because of $d = y^1 - y^0$. The point y^1 is inferior to y^0 because $y^1 = y^0 + d$. The vector d is a bad one to associate with. Note that d can also represent a "dominated direction" for y^0.

As Y may not be known precisely, domination structures will be defined on an open set $Y^0 \supset Y$. Sometimes, $Y^0 = R^q$. The set Y^0 indicates those "outcomes," obtainable or not, that we might be interested in.

Definition 7.1. Given $y^0 \in Y^0 \subset R^q$ and $d \in R^q$, $d \neq 0$,
  i. d is a *global dominated direction* for y^0, if $y^0 > y^0 + \alpha d$ whenever $\alpha > 0$ and $y^0 + \alpha d \in Y^0$;
  ii. d is a *local dominated direction* for y^0, if there is $\alpha_0 > 0$, no matter how small, such that $y^0 > y^0 + \alpha d$, whenever $0 < \alpha < \alpha_0$ and $y^0 + \alpha d \in Y^0$.

Note that d being a global dominated direction implies that d is a local dominated direction. But the converse is not necessarily true.

Example 7.1. (i) In Pareto preference, any $d \in \Lambda^{\leq}$ is a global dominated direction for any $y \in Y^0$.

(ii) Assume that $v(y)$ is differentiable and concave over a convex set Y^0. Then any d such that $d \cdot \nabla v(y) < 0$ is a global dominated direction for $y \in Y^0$ for the preference induced by $v(y)$.

(iii) Assume that y^0 is a disaster point (i.e., a nuclear power plant site or waste disposal site) and that the preference is such that the farther away from y^0 the better. Then for any two points y^1 and y^2 if $\|y^1 - y^0\| > \|y^2 - y^0\|$ then $y^1 > y^2$. It is readily checked that $d = y^2 - y^1$ is a *local*, but not a global, dominated direction for y^1. Check it. Indeed, the current preference is strict quasiconvex. (See Definition 2.5.)

(iv) In lexicographical ordering preference (Example 2.3), if $d = (d_1, \ldots, d_q)$ with the first nonzero component of d negative then d is a global dominated direction for any $y \in Y^0$.

Definition 7.2. Given $y \in Y^0$
i. the *global dominated cone* (or simply the dominated cone) of y, denoted by $D(y)$, is the collection of all global dominated directions for y;
ii. the *local dominated cone* of y, denoted by $\mathrm{LD}(y)$, is the collection of all local dominated directions for y.

Remark 7.1. (i) By definition, if $d \neq 0$ is a dominated direction, global or local, so is αd for any $\alpha > 0$. Thus, referring to $D(y)$ and $\mathrm{LD}(y)$ as dominated cone and local dominated cone makes sense. (See Section 7.3.1 for further discussion.)

(ii) $D(y)$ and $\mathrm{LD}(y)$ may not be convex. In Example 7.1, all corresponding $D(y)$ and $\mathrm{LD}(y)$ in (i)-(iv) are convex (note, the empty set $[D(y)$ of (iii)] is convex by definition). Consider a reward system for performance. Two criteria, namely, performance and reward, are under consideration. It is desirable to have reward as an increasing function of performance. Given a combination $y = (y_1, y_2)$, any $d = (d_1, d_2)$ such that $d_1 \cdot d_2 < 0$ (i.e., d_1 and d_2 run in the opposite way) is undesirable. Thus, $D(y) = \{d \mid d_1 \cdot d_2 < 0\}$. Note that $D(y) = R^2 \backslash (\Lambda^{\leq} \cup \Lambda^{\geq})$ is not convex.

(iii) Recall that if d is a global dominated direction then d is a local dominated direction. Thus $D(y) \subset \mathrm{LD}(y)$.

Remark 7.2. From $\{y>\}$ we can always construct $D(y)$ and $\mathrm{LD}(y)$. The converse is not always true. For instance, consider the preference $\{>\}$ defined on $Y^0 = R^2$ by $y^1 > y^2$ iff there is $i \in \{1, 2\}$ such that $y_i^1 - y_i^2 \geq 2$ and $y_k^2 - y_k^1 < 1$, $k \neq i$. (Refer to Example 2.2.) Then $D(y) = \mathrm{LD}(y) = \varnothing$. Thus we cannot recover $\{y>\}$ from $D(y)$ or $\mathrm{LD}(y)$. This example indicates that while $D(y)$

and $LD(y)$ may be a good tool to approximate $\{y>\}$ there are occasions in which $D(y)$ and $LD(y)$ cannot offer much help. The example also suggests that in applications we shall be aware of the "local" property (like continuity and differentiability of a function) of dominated cones. Although we can make $\{y>\} \cup \{y\}$ convex to obtain a new $D(y)$ and $LD(y)$, such convexization may not always be valid as the example illustrates.

Similar to dominated directions and the dominated cone, but in the opposite way, we have the following.

Definition 7.3. Given $y^0 \in Y^0 \subset R^q$ and $d \in R^q$, $d \neq 0$,
  i. d is a *global preferred direction* for y^0, if $y^0 < y^0 + \alpha d$ whenever $\alpha > 0$ and $y^0 + \alpha d \in Y^0$.
  ii. d is a *local preferred direction* for y^0, if there is $\alpha_0 > 0$, no matter how small, such that $y^0 < y^0 + \alpha d$, whenever $0 < \alpha < \alpha_0$ and $y^0 + \alpha d \in Y^0$.

Definition 7.4. Given $y \in Y^0$,
  i. the *global preferred cone* (or simply the preferred cone) of y, denoted by $P(y)$, is the collection of all global preferred directions for y;
  ii. the *local preferred cone*, denoted by $LP(y)$, is the collection of all local preferred directions for y.

Example 7.2. Consider a value function $v = y_1 y_2$ defined on $y_1 > 0$ and $y_2 > 0$. One can verify that $LP(y) = \{d \mid d \cdot (y_2, y_1) > 0\}$ but $P(y) = \Lambda^{\geq} \subset LP(y)$. (See Exercise 7.10.)

The reader may find it instructive to find $P(y)$ and $LP(y)$ for the preferences (i)-(iv) of Example 7.1.

Remark 7.3. Although $D(y) = -P(y)$ for the Pareto preference and $Cl\, LD(y) = -Cl\, LP(y)$ for the preference induced by differentiable concave value functions, it is not always true that $D(y) = -P(y)$ and $Cl\, LD(y) = -Cl\, LP(y)$. The preference discussed in the example for Remark 7.1(ii) and the preference induced by the l_∞-compromise solution when y lies at an equal distance line (i.e., $y_i^* - y_i = y_k^* - y_k$ for all $i, k = 1, \ldots, q$) (refer to Figure 4.5 of Chapter 4) are just some examples.

Remark 7.4. All comments in Remarks 7.1 and 7.2 are valid for $P(y)$ and $LP(y)$ [replace $D(y)$ and $LD(y)$ by $P(y)$ and $LP(y)$, respectively]. We shall not repeat them.

Note that $D(y)$ and $LD(y)$ approximate $\{y>\}$, and that $P(y)$ and $LP(y)$ approximate $\{y<\}$. One can also define indifference (or indefinite) cones as follows.

Definition 7.5. Given $y^0 \in Y^0 \subset R^q$ and $d \in R^q$, $d \neq 0$:
  i. d is a *global indifferent direction* for y^0, if $y^0 \sim y^0 + \alpha d$ whenever $\alpha > 0$

and $y^0 + \alpha d \in Y^0$; the collection of all global indifferent directions for y^0 is called the *global indifferent cone* for y^0 and will be denoted by $I(y^0)$;

ii. d is a *local indifferent direction* for y^0, if there is $\alpha_0 > 0$, no matter how small, such that $y^0 \sim y^0 + \alpha d$ whenever $0 < \alpha < \alpha_0$ and $y^0 + \alpha d \in Y^0$; the collection of all local indifferent directions for y^0 is called the *local indifferent cone* for y^0 and will be denoted by $\mathrm{LI}(y^0)$.

In analyzing local properties, the concept of "tangent cone" becomes handy.

Definition 7.6. (i) A nonzero vector $d \in R^q$ is a *tangent direction* of a set $S \subset R^q$ at a point $y^0 \in R^q$, if there is a sequence $\{y^k\} \subset S$ such that $\{y^k\}$ converges to y^0 in the direction d. That is $y^k \to y^0$ and $(y^k - y^0)/|y^k - y^0| \to d/|d|$.

(ii) The *tangent cone* of S at y^0, denoted by $T(y^0, S)$ is the collection of all tangent directions of S at y^0 and the 0 vector.

Definition 7.7.

   i. $T(y^0, <)$ is the tangent cone of $\{y^0 <\}$ at y^0;

   ii. $T(y^0, >)$ is the tangent cone of $\{y^0 >\}$ at y^0;

   iii. $T(y^0, \sim)$ is the tangent cone of $\{y^0 \sim\}$ at y^0.

Remark 7.5. (i) Tangent cones are closed (see Exercise 7.14) but not necessarily convex (see Example 7.2).

(ii) By definition, $\mathrm{LD}(y^0) \subset T(y^0, >)$, $\mathrm{LP}(y^0) \subset T(y^0, <)$ and $\mathrm{LI}(y^0) \subset T(y^0, \sim)$. If $\mathrm{LD}(y^0)$ is convex and $\mathrm{Int}\, T(y^0, >) \neq 0$, $\mathrm{Cl}\, \mathrm{LD}(y^0) = T(y^0, >)$ and $\mathrm{Int}\, T(y^0, >) \subset \mathrm{LD}(y^0)$ (see Exercise 7.14). A similar relationship between $\mathrm{LP}(y^0)$ and $T(y^0, <)$, and between $\mathrm{LI}(y^0)$ and $T(y^0, \sim)$ holds. The following example illustrates the interrelationships among the cones so far defined.

Example 7.3. Assume that the preference is represented by the isovalued curves of Figure 7.1. The outer curve has a higher value than the inner curve. We notice the following.

(i) $P(y^0) = \mathrm{LP}(y^0) = \mathscr{C}(d^1, d^2) \setminus \mathscr{H}(d^2) \cup \{0\}$, where $\mathscr{C}(d^1, d^2)$ is the convex cone generated by d^1 and d^2 while $\mathscr{H}(d^2)$ is the half-line of d^2. $T(y^0, <) = \mathrm{Cl}\, \mathrm{LP}(y^0)$.

(ii) $\mathrm{LI}(y^0) = \mathscr{H}(d^2)$, $I(y^0) = \varnothing$, and $T(y^0, \sim) = \mathscr{H}(d^2) \cup \mathscr{H}(d^1)$, which is not convex.

(iii) $D(y^0) = \varnothing$, $\mathrm{LD}(y^0) = R^2 \setminus \mathscr{C}(d^1, d^2)$ and $T(y^0, >) = \mathrm{Cl}\, \mathrm{LD}(y^0)$. Note that both $\mathrm{LD}(y^0)$ and $T(y^0, >)$ are not convex.

(iv) $\mathrm{LP}(y^0) \cup \mathrm{LD}(y^0) \cup \mathrm{LI}(y^0) \cup \{0\} = R^2$. $P(y^0) \cup D(y^0) \cup I(y^0) = P(y^0) \neq R^2$. $T(y^0, >) \cup T(y^0, <) \cup T(y^0, \sim) = R^2$. It may be instructive for the reader to explore under what conditions the equalities in (iv) hold. (See Exercise 7.15.)

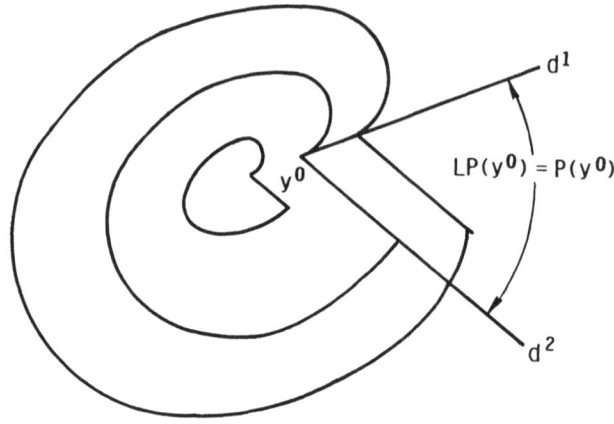

Figure 7.1

Definition 7.8. By a *domination structure* we mean a collection of $\mathscr{D} = \{D(y), \text{LD}(y), T(y, >); P(y), \text{LP}(y), T(y, <); I(y), \text{LI}(y), T(y, \sim)\}$ over an open set $Y^0 \supset Y$.

Remark 7.6. In Ref. 495, a domination structure is defined to be a collection of $\{D(y)\}$ defined over Y^0. Here we have expanded the concept to contain all possible relevant information at each point of Y^0. This generalization can cover more possible cases. However, in many analyses, such as those to be discussed in the next subsection, we may, for convenience, further assume that $D(y) = \text{LD}(y)$, $P(y) = \text{LP}(y)$, $D(y) = -P(y)$, etc. Furthermore, in applications, to estimate the entire set of domination structures would be practically inhibitive. Some simplifying assumptions are certainly needed. Note that $\mathscr{D}$ may be regarded as an approximation for a preference $\{>\}$, $\{<\}$, and $\{\sim\}$. We shall discuss later how to use $\mathscr{D}$ to locate N-points. It is an interesting research problem to explore under what conditions the following hold: $D(y) = -P(y)$, $\text{LD}(y) = -\text{LP}(y)$, $\text{Cl} \text{LD}(y) = -\text{Cl} \text{LP}(y)$.

7.3. Constant Dominated Cone Structures

In this section we shall focus on a special kind of domination structure which is induced by

$$\{y>\} = (y + \Lambda) \cap Y^0, \tag{7.3}$$

where Λ is a convex cone, not containing 0, in R^q. Note that (7.3) implies that for each $y \in Y^0$,

$$D(y) = \mathrm{LD}(y) = \Lambda, \tag{7.4}$$

$$P(y) = \mathrm{LP}(y) = -\Lambda. \tag{7.5}$$

Thus y^0 is an N-point iff $(y^0 - \Lambda) \cap Y = \varnothing$ or if there is no other point $y \in Y$ such that $y^0 \in y + \Lambda$. Note that $T(y, >) = \mathrm{Cl}\,\Lambda$ and $T(y, <) = -\mathrm{Cl}\,\Lambda$.

For convenience, we shall call the above domination structures *constant dominated cone structures*. Note that the preferences of Pareto optimality and lexicographical order have constant domination structures. Constant domination structures play an important role in general domination structures, as the latter may be approximated by the former. Note that Pareto preference is a constant dominated cone structure with $\Lambda = \Lambda^{\leq}$. Many results described in this section will be a generalization of Chapter 3. To make the presentation smooth we shall first describe some relevant concepts concerning cones in Section 7.3.1. A general characterization of N-points will be described in Sections 7.3.2 and 7.3.3. Characterization of N-points when Y is Λ-convex will be described in Section 7.3.4. Discussion of N-points in the decision space X will be given in Section 7.3.5. The concept of a proper-efficient point with respect to Λ will be described in Section 7.3.6.

7.3.1. Cones and their Polars

A set Λ is a cone if $\alpha\Lambda = \Lambda$ for any $\alpha > 0$ (i.e., $d \in \Lambda$ implies that $\alpha d \in \Lambda$). Note that a dominated cone does not contain $\{0\}$. For convenience, we shall use the following notation:

$$\Lambda' = \Lambda \cup \{0\},$$

$$'\Lambda = \Lambda \backslash \{0\}.$$

Thus, $\Lambda^{\leq} = (\Lambda^{\leq})'$ and $\Lambda^{\leq} = {}'(\Lambda^{\leq})$.

A *convex cone* is a cone that is also a convex set. It can be shown that Λ is a convex cone iff for any $\alpha > 0$, $\beta > 0$, and d^1, d^2 of Λ, $\alpha d^1 + \beta d^2 \in \Lambda$.

A *polyhedral cone* is a cone that is also a polyhedron. Thus, if Λ is a polyhedral cone then it can be represented by $\Lambda = \{d \mid Ad \leq 0\}$, where A is a matrix of proper dimension. It can also be represented by (see Ref. 438)

$$\Lambda = \left\{ \sum_{i=1}^{m} a_i v^i \,\middle|\, a_i \geq 0, \, a_i \in R^1 \right\} \tag{7.6}$$

for some $V = \{v^i \mid i = 1, \ldots, m\}$ which is called a *generator* of Λ. For simplicity,

(7.6) can be written as $\Lambda = \mathscr{C}[V]$, that is, Λ is the convex cone generated by V. Note that the generator of Λ may not be unique.

Example 7.4. $\Lambda = \{(d_1, d_2) | d_1 + 2d_2 \leqq 0, \ 2d_1 + d_2 \leqq 0\}$ is a polyhedral cone which can also be written as $\Lambda = \{a_1(-2, 1) + a_2(1, -2) | a_1 \geqq 0, a_2 \geqq 0\}$ or $\Lambda = \{a_1(-2, 1) + a_2(1, -2) + a_3(-1, -1) | a_1 \geqq 0, a_2 \geqq 0, a_3 \geqq 0\}$. Note that both $V^1 = \{(-2, 1), (1, -2)\}$ and $V^2 = \{(-2, 1), (1, -2), (-1, -1)\}$ are generators for Λ. Note that the generators are not unique.

To obtain a generator for Λ may not be very easy when Λ has a dimension higher than 3. However, the interested reader can refer to Tamura (Ref. 443) for a constructive derivation.

A cone Λ is *pointed* if $\Lambda' \cap (-\Lambda)' = \{0\}$. Thus a pointed cone contains no nontrivial subspace. Conversely a cone that contains no nontrivial subspace is pointed.

A cone Λ is *acute* if its closure is contained by an open half-space, H, and the origin. That is, $\text{Cl } \Lambda \subset H \cup \{0\}$. Alternatively, Λ is acute iff $\text{Cl } \Lambda$ is pointed.

The constant dominated cones of Pareto preference and lexicographical ordering (see Example 7.1) are pointed. Furthermore, the former is acute, and the latter is not acute.

The following decomposition theorem is useful (see Ref. 438, p. 60 for a proof).

Theorem 7.1. Let L be the maximum linear subspace contained by a convex cone $\Lambda' \subset R^q$. Let $L^\perp$ be the orthogonal space of L and $\Lambda^\perp = \Lambda \cap L^\perp$. Then $\Lambda = L + \Lambda^\perp$. (Note that $\Lambda' = \Lambda \cup \{0\}$, and $\Lambda^\perp$ is the projection of λ into $L^\perp$.)

Example 7.5. Let Λ be defined as in Figure 7.2. Then $\Lambda^\perp = L^\perp \cap \Lambda$ as depicted. Note that $L^\perp$ is the linear space spanned by $\Lambda^\perp$.

Let $S \subset R^q$. Then the *polar cone* of S, denoted by S^*, is defined by

$$S^* = \{d \in R^q | d \cdot y \leqq 0 \text{ for all } y \in S\}. \tag{7.7}$$

The following was proved in Ref. 438.

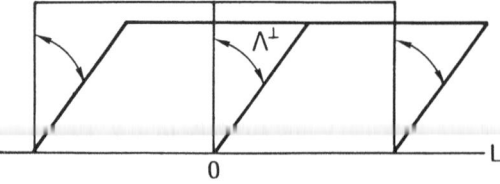

Figure 7.2

Lemma 7.1

i. For any set S, S^* is a closed convex cone, and $S^* = (\text{Cl } S)^*$.
ii. If $S_1 \subset S_2$ then $S_1^* \supset S_2^*$.
iii. Let Λ be a convex cone. Then $(\Lambda^*)^* = \text{Cl } \Lambda$ and Λ is closed iff $(\Lambda^*)^* = \Lambda$.

Theorem 7.2. (i) Let $\Lambda = \mathscr{C}[v^1, \dots, v^m]$ be a polyhedral cone generated by $\{v^1, \dots, v^m\}$ as defined in (7.6). Then $\Lambda^* = \{d \mid d \cdot v^i \leq 0, \ i = 1, \dots, m\}$, which is also a polyhedral cone.

(ii) Let Λ be a convex cone. Then, Λ^* is a polyhedral cone iff $\text{Cl } \Lambda$ is a *polyhedral* cone.

Proof. (i) Suppose that $d \in \Lambda^*$. Then, $d \cdot v^i \leq 0$ for all $i = 1, \dots, m$. Thus,

$$\Lambda^* \subset \{d \mid d \cdot v^i \leq 0 \qquad \text{for } i = 1, \dots, m\}.$$

On the other hand, if $d \cdot v^i \leq 0$ for $i = 1, \dots, m$, then

$$d \cdot \sum_{i=1}^{m} a_i v^i = \sum_{i=1}^{m} a_i(d \cdot v^i) \leq 0$$

since all $a_i \geq 0$. Thus, $d \in \Lambda^*$ and

$$\Lambda^* \supset \{d \mid d \cdot v^i \leq 0, \ i = 1, \dots, m\}.$$

The sufficiency of (ii) follows from (i) and $\Lambda^* = (\text{Cl } \Lambda)^*$. For the necessity of (ii), observe that $(\Lambda^*)^* = \text{Cl } \Lambda$, because of Lemma 7.1 and that Λ is a convex cone. In view of (i), we see that $\Lambda = (\Lambda^*)^*$ is a polyhedral cone. $\qquad \square$

The following result, which plays an important role later, was derived in Ref. 495. To avoid distraction, a constructive proof is given in Section 7.7.

Theorem 7.3. Let Λ be a cone (not necessarily convex) in R^q. Then
i. $\text{Int } \Lambda^* \neq \varnothing$ iff Λ is acute;
ii. when Λ is acute, $\text{Int } \Lambda^* = \{y \mid y \cdot x < 0 \text{ for all nonzero } x \in \text{Cl } \Lambda\}$.

7.3.2. General Properties of N-Points

For ease of analysis, let Λ be a cone containing 0. Thus, $'\Lambda = \Lambda \backslash \{0\}$ can be a dominated cone and $-'\Lambda$, a preferred cone. To emphasize that the set of N-points is dependent on Y and $'\Lambda$, we shall use $N[Y|\Lambda]$ to denote the set. Note that when we say Λ is a dominated cone we mean $'\Lambda$ is the collection of all dominated directions. Thus, if $\Lambda = \{0\}$ then $'\Lambda = \varnothing$ (no direction is dominated); and if $\Lambda = R^q$ then $'\Lambda = R^q\backslash\{0\}$ (each nonzero vector represents a dominated direction).

The following shows the relation of N-sets in terms of Λ.

Lemma 7.2

i. If $'\Lambda \neq \emptyset$ then $N[Y|\Lambda] \subset \partial Y$ (the boundary of Y), which is $\emptyset$, if Y is open.

ii. $N[Y|\Lambda] = \begin{cases} Y & \text{if } \Lambda = \{0\}, \\ \emptyset & \text{if } \Lambda = R^q; \end{cases}$

iii. $N[Y|\Lambda_2] \subset N[Y|\Lambda_1]$ if $\Lambda_1 \subset \Lambda_2$;

iv. $N[Y + \Lambda|\Lambda] \subset N[Y|\Lambda]$;

v. $N[Y|\Lambda] = N[Y + \Lambda|\Lambda]$ if Λ is pointed.

Proof. (i)–(ii) The statements are clear (check them).

(iii) Suppose that $y \in N[Y|\Lambda_2]$. If $y \notin N[Y|\Lambda_1]$, then there is $y^1 \in Y$, $y^1 \neq y$, such that $y \in y^1 + \Lambda_1 \subset y^1 + \Lambda_2$. Thus, $y \notin N[Y|\Lambda_2]$. This leads to a contradiction.

(iv) Suppose that $y \in N[Y + \Lambda|\Lambda]$. It suffices to show that $y \in Y$. Suppose that $y \notin Y$. Then, there are $y^1 \in Y$ and $h \neq 0$, $h \in \Lambda$ such that $y = y^1 + h$. Since $0 \in \Lambda$, $Y \subset Y + \Lambda$. We see that $y \notin N[Y + \Lambda|\Lambda]$. This leads to a contradiction.

(v) Let $y \in N[Y|\Lambda]$. Since $0 \in \Lambda$, $y \in Y + \Lambda$. Suppose that $y \notin N[Y + \Lambda|\Lambda]$. There are $y^1 \in Y + \Lambda$ and $h^1 \neq 0$, $h^1 \in \Lambda$ such that $y = y^1 + h^1$. Since $y^1 \in Y + \Lambda$, we could write $y^1 = y^0 + h^0$, $y^0 \in Y$ and $h^0 \in \Lambda$. Thus, $y = y^0 + (h^0 + h^1)$. Since Λ is pointed, it contains no subspace and $h^0 + h^1 \neq 0$. It is seen that $y \notin N[Y|\Lambda]$. This leads to a contradiction. ☐

Remark 7.7. Note that Lemma 7.2(iii) says that the larger Λ is, the smaller the set of N-points. This is intuitively clear and appealing. Note that the larger Λ is, the smaller the indifferent (or indefinite) cone because $I(y) = \text{LI}(y) = R^q\backslash[D(y) \cup P(y)] = R^q\backslash[\Lambda \cup (-\Lambda)]$. That is, as Λ increases, the set of dominated and preferred directions gets larger and the set of indefinite directions gets smaller. Thus, the resulting set of N-points gets smaller when Λ gets larger.

Remark 7.8. (a) Immediately from (iii), we see that $N[Y|\text{Cl }\Lambda] \subset N[Y|\Lambda]$. The converse inclusion is not generally true. As an example, let

$$Y = \{(x, y)|0 \leq x \leq 1, 0 \leq y \leq 1\}, \qquad \Lambda = \{(x, y)|x < 0\} \cup \{(0, 0)\}.$$

It is seen that $N[Y|\Lambda] = \{(x, y)|x = 1, 0 \leq y \leq 1\}$, but $N[Y|\text{Cl }\Lambda] = \emptyset$.

(b) The assumption in (v) of Lemma 7.2 cannot be relaxed. In order to see that Λ cannot contain any subspace, let us consider the following example. In R^2, let

$$Y = \{(x, y)|x = y, 0 \leq x \leq 1\}, \qquad \Lambda = \{(x, y)|x \leq 0\}.$$

We see that $N[Y|\Lambda] = \{(1, 1)\}$, $N[Y + \Lambda|\Lambda] = \emptyset$.

Recall that if L is the maximum linear subspace contained by Λ, then, by Theorem 7.1 we can write $\Lambda = L + \Lambda^\perp$, where $\Lambda^\perp = \Lambda \cap L^\perp$ and $L^\perp$ is the orthogonal space of L. Note that, if $L = \{0\}$, then $\Lambda = \Lambda^\perp$. Also, note that $\Lambda^\perp$ is uniquely determined for Λ. The following theorem takes care of the characterization of the N-points when Λ contains a subspace.

Theorem 7.4. A necessary and sufficient condition for $y_0 \in N[Y|\Lambda]$ is that

i. $Y \cap (y_0 + L) = \{y_0\}$,

ii. $y_0^\perp \in N[Y^\perp|\Lambda^\perp]$,

where L is the maximum linear space contained by Λ, and $y_0^\perp$, $Y^\perp$, $\Lambda^\perp$ are the projections of y_0, Y, and Λ into $L^\perp$, respectively.

Proof. *Necessity.* We shall show that, if (i) or (ii) does not hold, then $y_0 \notin N[Y|\Lambda]$.

Suppose that (i) does not hold; clearly, $y_0 \notin N[Y|\Lambda]$.

Now, suppose that (ii) does not hold. Then, there are $y^\perp \in Y^\perp$ and $h^\perp \neq 0$, $h^\perp \in \Lambda^\perp$ such that

$$y_0^\perp = y^\perp + h^\perp. \tag{7.8}$$

Let $y \in Y$ be a point such that its projection point into $L^\perp$ is $y^\perp$. Thus, $y = y^\perp + y^L$, with $y^L \in L$. Set $y_0 = y_0^\perp + y_0^L$, with $y_0^L \in L$. By (7.8) we have

$$y_0 = y^\perp + h^\perp + y_0^L = (y - y^L) + h^\perp + y_0^L = y + (y_0^L - y^L) + h^\perp.$$

Note that, because $h^\perp \neq 0$ and $y_0^L - y^L \in L$, we have $y_0^L - y^L + h^\perp \neq 0$. Thus, $y_0 \neq y$. Also,

$$y_0^L - y^L + h^\perp \in L + h^\perp \subset L + \Lambda^\perp = \Lambda.$$

We see that $y_0 \in y + \Lambda$ and $y_0 \neq y$. Thus, $y_0 \notin N[Y|\Lambda]$.

Sufficiency: Suppose that $y_0 \notin N[Y|\Lambda]$. We shall see that (i) or (ii) cannot hold. By the assumption, there are $y \in Y$ and $h \neq 0$, $h \in \Lambda$ such that

$$y_0 = y + h. \tag{7.9}$$

Write

$$y_0 = y_0^\perp + y_0^L, \qquad y = y^\perp + y^L, \qquad h = h^\perp + h^L,$$

where

$$y_0^L, y^L, h^L \in L, \qquad y_0^\perp, y^\perp, h^\perp \in L^\perp.$$

From (7.9), we get

$$y_0^\perp = y^\perp + h^\perp. \tag{7.10}$$

Observe that, for $h \neq 0$, $h^\perp$ and h^L cannot both be zero. Let us consider two possible cases.

Case 1: $h^\perp \neq 0$. Then, (ii) cannot hold, because of (7.10).

Case 2: $h^\perp = 0$. Then, $h^L = h \neq 0$ and, thus $y_0 = y + h^L$ or $y = y_0 - h^L$. Thus, (i) cannot hold, because $y \in y_0 + L$.   □

Corollary 7.1. Suppose that $\Lambda^\perp \neq \{0\}$, i.e., Λ is not a linear subspace. Then, $y_0 \in N[Y|\Lambda]$ implies that y_0 is a boundary point of $Y + \Lambda$.

Proof. By (ii) of Theorem 7.4, we have

$$y_0^\perp \in N[Y^\perp|\Lambda^\perp].$$

Note that $\Lambda^\perp$ contains no nontrivial subspace. Thus, by Lemma 7.2(v),

$$y_0^\perp \in N[Y^\perp + \Lambda^\perp|\Lambda^\perp].$$

By Lemma 7.2(i), we see that $y_0^\perp$ must be a boundary point (with respect to the topology induced by $L^\perp$) of $Y^\perp + \Lambda^\perp$, which implies that y_0 is a boundary point of $Y + \Lambda$. (Otherwise, we would have a contradiction.)   □

Remark 7.9. The assumption that $\Lambda^\perp \neq \{0\}$ cannot be eliminated. As an example, in R^2 let

$$Y = \{(x, y)|y = 1\}, \qquad \Lambda = \{(x, y)|x = 0\}.$$

Note that $\Lambda^\perp = \{0\}$ and $Y = N[Y|\Lambda]$. But when $R^2 = Y + \Lambda$, each point of Y is an interior point of $Y + \Lambda$.

Corollary 7.2. Suppose that $\Lambda^\perp \neq \{0\}$ and $Y + \Lambda = R^q$. Then, $N[Y|\Lambda] = \varnothing$.

Proof. It follows directly from Corollary 7.1.   □

Remark 7.10. In the example stated in the previous remark, $Y + \Lambda = R^2$. But $\Lambda^\perp = \{0\}$, $N[Y|\Lambda] \neq \varnothing$. The present corollary is useful in checking whether $N[Y|\Lambda] = \varnothing$. As an example, in R^2 let

$$Y = \{(x, y)|x = y\}, \qquad \Lambda = \{(x, y)|y \geq 0\}.$$

Note that $\Lambda^\perp \neq \{0\}$ and $Y + \Lambda = R^2$. Thus,

$$N[Y|\Lambda] = \varnothing.$$

Remark 7.11. If $\Lambda^{\perp} = \{0\}$, then Λ is a linear subspace. For any $d \in {}'\Lambda$, both d and $-d$ are dominated and preferred directions. This is a pathological case, totally contrary to logical consistency. We shall deal, later, only with $\Lambda^{\perp} \neq \{0\}$. Note that if Λ is pointed then $\Lambda^{\perp} \neq \{0\}$.

Lemma 7.3. $y^0 \in N[Y|\Lambda]$ if
 i. y^0 maximizes $\lambda \cdot y$ over Y for some $\lambda \in \text{Int } \Lambda^*$; or
 ii. y^0 *uniquely* maximizes $\lambda \cdot y$ over Y for some $\lambda \in \Lambda^* \backslash \{0\}$; or
 iii. y^0 maximizes $\lambda \cdot y$ over Y for some $\lambda \in \Lambda^* \backslash \{0\}$ and Λ is open.

Proof. Assume that $y^0 \notin N[Y|\Lambda]$. Then there is a $y \in Y$ such that $y = y^0 - d \in Y$ for some $d \in \Lambda$. Thus,

$$\lambda \cdot y - \lambda \cdot y^0 = -\lambda \cdot d \begin{cases} >0 & \text{if } \lambda \in \text{Int } \Lambda^* \\ & \text{or } \lambda \in \Lambda^* \backslash \{0\} \text{ and } \Lambda \text{ is open,} \\ \geqq 0 & \text{if } \lambda \in \Lambda^* \backslash \{0\}, \end{cases}$$

which would contradict (i), (ii), or (iii). This completes the proof. $\square$

7.3.3. A Characterization of N-Points

In this section we shall discuss necessary and sufficient conditions for N-points with polyhedral dominated cones. No assumption on Y is needed. To extend the result to general dominated cones, one can focus on a polyhedral cone contained in the dominated cone. Then Lemma 7.2(iii) and the result will offer necessary conditions for N-points.

The following assumption, which specifies the class of problems, will be assumed throughout this subsection.

Assumption 7.1. Λ is a polyhedral acute cone with $\Lambda^* = \mathscr{C}[h^1, \ldots, h^r]$ (i.e., Λ^* is the convex cone generated by $\{h^1, \ldots, h^r\}$).

Let $H = H_{r \times q}$ be a matrix with h^k being the kth row of H, $k = 1, \ldots, r$. Define $z = Hy$ and $Z = \{z = Hy | y \in Y\}$. Note that since Λ is acute, dim $\Lambda^* = q$ and dim $\{h^1, \ldots, h^r\} = q$ (Theorem 7.3). Thus, for any $d \in {}'\Lambda$, $Hd \leq 0$ (i.e., not all $d \cdot h^k = 0$, $k = 1, \ldots, r$). We first show the following.

Theorem 7.5. $y^0 \in N[Y|\Lambda]$ iff $z^0 = Hy^0 \in N[Z|\Lambda^{\leq}]$. (Note, $\Lambda^{\leq}$ is in R^r.)

Proof. *For Necessity.* Suppose that $z^0 \notin N[Z|\Lambda^{\leq}]$. Then there is a $z \in Z$ such that $z \geq z^0$. Thus, there is a $y \in Y$ such that $Hy = z \geq z^0 = Hy^0$ or $H(y^0 - y) \leq 0$. That is, $y^0 - y \in {}'\Lambda$ because $\{h^1, \ldots, h^r\}$ is a generator of Λ^*. Thus, $y^0 \in y + {}'\Lambda$ and $y^0 \notin N[Y|\Lambda]$.

For Sufficiency. Suppose that $y^0 \notin N[Y|\Lambda]$. Then there is $y \in Y$ such that $y^0 - y \in {}'\Lambda$. Thus, $H(y^0 - y) \le 0$ or $z^0 = Hy^0 \le Hy$, consequently $z^0 \notin N[Z|\Lambda^{\le}]$. $\qquad\square$

Remark 7.12. Theorem 7.5 states that by $z = Hy$ we can study the characteristics of N-points for an *acute* polyhedral dominated cone by the N-points of a Pareto preference in the Z-space. Theorems 3.4–3.6 are readily applicable for necessary and sufficient conditions for N-points which are stated in Theorems 7.6–7.8. (See Exercise 7.16.) One notes that Theorems 7.6–7.8 are valid even when Λ contains a subspace (i.e., Λ is not acute). For a direct proof see Ref. 495.

Corresponding to Theorem 3.4, we have the following.

Theorem 7.6. $y^0 \in N[Y|\Lambda]$ iff for any $i \in \{1, 2, \ldots, r\}$, y^0 uniquely maximizes $h^i \cdot y$ for all $y \in Y_i(y^0) = \{y \in Y | h^k \cdot y \ge h^k \cdot y^0, k \ne i, k = 1, \ldots, r\}$ [that is, $h^i \cdot y^0 > h^i \cdot y$ for all $y \ne y^0$ and $y \in Y_i(y^0)$].

Example 7.6. In Figure 7.3, y^1 uniquely maximizes $h^1 \cdot y$ for all y such that $h^2 \cdot y \ge h^2 \cdot y^1$; y^1 also uniquely maximizes $h^2 \cdot y$ for all y such that $h^1 \cdot y \ge h^1 \cdot y^1$. Clearly $y^1 \in N[Y|\Lambda]$. On the other hand y^2 does not uniquely maximize $h^1 \cdot y$ for all y such that $h^2 \cdot y \ge h^2 \cdot y^2$; neither does y^2 uniquely maximize $h^2 \cdot y$ for all y such that $h^1 \cdot y \ge h^1 \cdot y^2$. Thus, $y^2 \notin N[Y|\Lambda]$.

Corresponding to Theorem 3.5 we have the following.

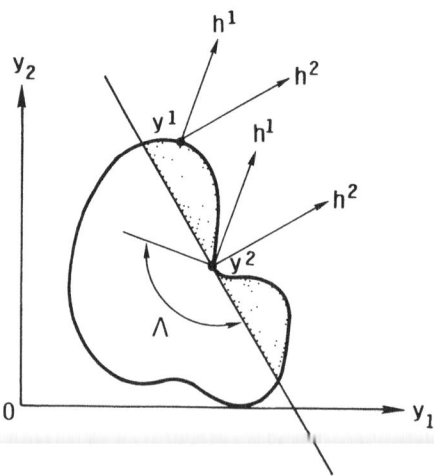

Figure 7.3

Theorem 7.7. (i) If $y^0 \in Y$ maximizes $\lambda H y$ for some $\lambda \in \Lambda^> \subset R^r$ [or y^0 maximizes $h \cdot y$ for some $h \in \text{Int } \Lambda^*$ (because $\lambda H \in \text{Int } \Lambda^*$)] over Y, then $y^0 \in N[Y|\Lambda]$.

(ii) If $y^0 \in Y$ *uniquely* maximizes $\lambda H y$ for some $\lambda \in \Lambda^=$ (or y^0 uniquely maximizes $h \cdot y$, $h \in '\Lambda^*$) over Y, then $y^0 \in N[Y|\Lambda]$.

Corresponding to Theorem 3.6, we have the following.

Theorem 7.8. A necessary and sufficient condition for $y^0 \in N[Y|\Lambda]$ is that for any $i \in \{1, 2, \ldots, r\}$, there are $r - 1$ constants $c(i) = \{c_k | k \neq i, k = 1, \ldots, r\}$ such that y^0 *uniquely* maximizes $h^i \cdot y$ over

$$Y(c(i)) = \{y \in Y | y_k \geq c_k, k \neq i, k = 1, \ldots, r\}.$$

Example 7.7. In Figure 7.3, y^1 uniquely maximizes $h^1 \cdot y$ for all y such that $h^2 \cdot y \geq c_2 = h^2 \cdot y^1$; and y^1 uniquely maximizes $h^2 \cdot y$ for all y such that $h^1 \cdot y \geq c_1 = h^1 \cdot y^1$. There are no such c_1 and c_2 for y^2. Thus $y^2 \notin N[Y|\Lambda]$.

Remark 7.13. Note that $h^k \cdot y$, $k = 1, \ldots, r$, are linear (value) functions. If $c(i)$ is the satisficing level for all $h^k \cdot y$, $k \neq i$, then Theorem 7.8 essentially says that $y^0 \in N[Y|\Lambda]$ iff y^0 uniquely maximizes $h^i \cdot y$ for all y which reach the satisficing levels $\{c(k)\}$, for all other $h^k \cdot y$, $k \neq i$. Furthermore, the choice of objective function $h^i \cdot y$ is arbitrary. Thus, in search of N-points, the maximization criterion and constraints are *interchangeable*. Note that Theorem 7.8 converts locating $N[Y|\Lambda]$ into a family of mathematical programming problems or optimal control problems. Recall that Y can be any arbitrary set, discrete or convex, defined by inequalities or differential equations.

7.3.4. Cone-Convexity and N-Points

In this section we shall discuss the cone-convexity concept which generalizes ordinary convexity, and then describe the necessary and sufficient conditions for $N[Y|\Lambda]$ when cone convexity is present. The concept was first introduced in Ref. 495. Throughout this subsection, all cones are assumed to be convex.

Definition 7.9. Y is Λ-convex iff $Y + \Lambda$ is a convex set.

Example 7.8. With Λ in Figure 7.4a, Y_1 in Figure 7.4b is Λ-convex, Y_2 in Figure 7.4c is not Λ-convex. Note that Y_1, although very irregular, can be cone-convex, while Y_2, although relatively more regular, may not be cone-convex when the cone is properly chosen. Note that each point of $N[Y_1|\Lambda]$ in Figure 7.4b has a linear supporting functional with respect to $Y_1 + \Lambda$, while most points of $N[Y_2|\Lambda]$ in Figure 7.4c have no linear supporting functional

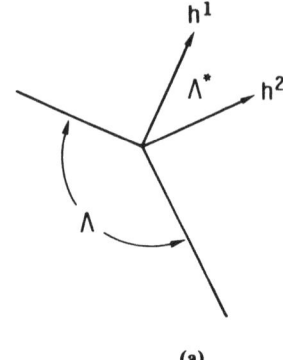

(a)

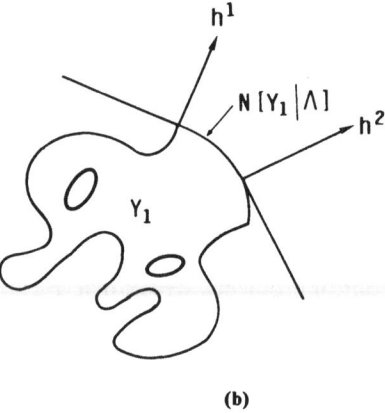

(b)

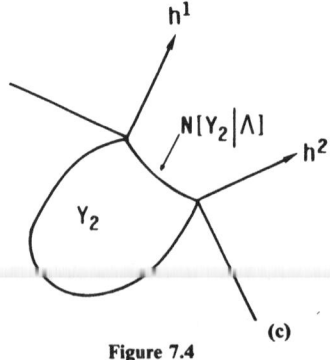

(c)

Figure 7.4

with respect to $Y_2 + \Lambda$. This example can serve to motivate our interest in the cone convexity concept.

In deriving necessary conditions for (discrete) optimal control (see Ref. 287 for instance), the concept of directional convexity plays an important role. A set Y is *directionally convex* in $u \neq 0$ iff for any y^1, y^2 of Y and $\lambda \in [0, 1]$, there is $y(\lambda) \in Y$ and $\mu \geqq 0$ such that $\lambda y^1 + (1 - \lambda)y^2 = y(\lambda) - \mu u$. It can be readily shown that Y is directionally convex in u iff Y is U-convex, where U is the negative half-line generated by u (i.e., $U = \{\lambda u | \lambda \leqq 0\}$). (See Exercise 7.17.) Also it can readily be verified that Y is convex iff Y is $\{0\}$-convex. (See Exercise 7.17.) These observations and the following Theorem warrant that cone convexity is a generalization of ordinary convexity.

Theorem 7.9. If $\Lambda_1 \subset \Lambda_2$ and Y is Λ_1-convex, then Y is also Λ_2-convex.

Proof. $Y + \Lambda_2 = Y + (\Lambda_1 + \Lambda_2) = (Y + \Lambda_1) + \Lambda_2$. As $Y + \Lambda_1$ and Λ_2 are convex, so is their sum. Thus Y is also Λ_2-convex. $\square$

Remark 7.14. From Theorem 7.9, it is seen that if Y is Λ-convex, then Y is also Cl Λ-convex. The converse is not generally true. As an example in R^2, let $Y = \{0\} \cup \{(x, y) | x + y = 1, x, y \geqq 0\}$ and $\Lambda = (\Lambda^>)'$. We see that Y is Cl Λ-convex. However, because the line segment $[(0, 0), (1, 0)]$ is not contained in $Y + \Lambda$, Y is not Λ-convex. By defining $\Lambda = \Lambda^{\geqq}$, the same example shows that Y is Λ-convex, but does not imply that Y is $(\text{Int } \Lambda)'$-convex.

Remark 7.15. If Y is convex, then Cl Y and ri Y (relative interior of Y) are also convex. (See Chapter 3 of Ref. 438.) This nice property is not preserved in cone convexity. As an example, in R^2 let

$$Y_1 = \{(x, y) | (x - 1)^2 + (y - 3)^2 < 1\},$$

$$Y_2 = \{(x, y) | (x - 3)^2 + (y - 1)^2 < 1\},$$

$$Y = \{0\} \cup Y_1 \cup Y_2.$$

Then Cl $Y = \{0\} \cup$ Cl $Y_1 \cup$ Cl Y_2 and ri $Y = Y_1 \cup Y_2$. Let $\Lambda = (\Lambda^>)'$. Then Y is Λ-convex. However, because the line segment $[(0, 0), (0, 3)]$ is not contained in Cl $Y + \Lambda$, Cl Y is not Λ-convex. It can also be checked that ri Y is not Λ-convex.

We are interested in the cone convexity of $Y = f[X]$.

Lemma 7.4. (i) $Y = f[X]$ is Λ-convex iff, for every x^1, x^2 of X (which may not be convex) and $\mu \in [0, 1]$, $\mu f(x^1) + (1 - \mu)f(x^2) \in f[X] + \Lambda$. [Equivalently, Y is Λ-convex iff, for every y^1, y^2 of Y and $\mu \in [0, 1]$, $\mu y^1 + (1 - \mu)y^2 \in Y + \Lambda$.]

(ii) $f[X]$ is $\Lambda^{\leq}$-convex iff, for every x^1, x^2 of X and $\mu \in [0, 1]$, there is $x^3 \in X$ such that $\mu f(x^1) + (1 - \mu)f(x^2) \leq f(x^3)$.

(iii) $f[X]$ is $\Lambda^{\geq}$-convex iff, for every x^1, x^2 of X and $\mu \in [0, 1]$, there is $x^3 \in X$ such that $\mu f(x^1) + (1 - \mu)f(x^2) \geq f(x^3)$.

(iv) If there is $x^0 \in X$ such that $f(x^0) \geq f(x)$ [or $f(x^0) \leq f(x)$] for all $x \in X$, then $f[X]$ is $\Lambda^{\leq}$ (or, respectively, $\Lambda^{\geq}$)-convex.

Proof. (ii)–(iv) are immediate consequences of (i). We shall prove only (i). The necessity is obvious. In order to see the sufficiency, let $y^1 = f(x^1) + h^1$, $y^2 = f(x^2) + h^2$, where $h^1, h^2 \in \Lambda$. Then, $\mu y^1 + (1 - \mu)y^2 = \mu f(x^1) + (1 - \mu)f(x^2) + [\mu h^1 + (1 - \mu)h^2] \in f[X] + \Lambda + \Lambda = f[X] + \Lambda$. Thus, $f[X] + \Lambda$ is a convex set or $f[X]$ is Λ-convex, as we wish to show. $\qquad\square$

Theorem 7.10. Let X be a convex set. Then
  i. $f[X]$ is Λ^*-convex if $\lambda \cdot f(x)$ is concave over X for each $\lambda \in \Lambda$;
  ii. $f[X]$ is $-\Lambda^*$-convex if $\lambda \cdot f(x)$ is convex over X for each $\lambda \in \Lambda$.

Proof. (i) Let x^1, $x^2 \in X$ and $\mu \in R^1$, $0 \leq \mu \leq 1$. For any $\lambda \in \Lambda$, by assumption, we have

$$\mu(\lambda \cdot f(x^1)) + (1 - \mu)[\lambda \cdot f(x^2)] \leq \lambda \cdot f(\mu x^1 + (1 - \mu)x^2).$$

Thus,

$$\lambda \cdot [\mu f(x^1) + (1 - \mu)f(x^2) - f(\mu x^1 + (1 - \mu)x^2)] \leq 0$$

for all $\lambda \in \Lambda$. That is,

$$\mu f(x^1) + (1 - \mu)f(x^2) - f(\mu x^1 + (1 - \mu)x^2) \in \Lambda^*$$

or

$$\mu f(x^1) + (1 - \mu)f(x^2) \in f(\mu x^1 + (1 - \mu)x^2) + \Lambda^* \subset f[X] + \Lambda^*.$$

By invoking Lemma 7.4(i), our assertion is clear.

(ii) By the assumptions, $-\lambda \cdot f(x)$ is concave for each $\lambda \in \Lambda$. Thus, $\lambda \cdot f(x)$ is concave for each $\lambda \in -\Lambda$. The assertion (ii) follows from (i), because $(-\Lambda)^* = -\Lambda^*$. $\qquad\square$

Recall (Lemma 7.1) that if Λ is a closed convex cone then $(\Lambda^*)^* = \Lambda$. This and Theorem 7.10 yield the following.

Theorem 7.11. Let X be a convex set and Λ be a closed convex cone. Then,
  i. $f[X]$ is Λ-convex if $\lambda \cdot f(x)$ is concave over X for each $\lambda \in \Lambda^*$;
  ii. $f[X]$ is Λ-convex if $\lambda \cdot f(x)$ is convex over X for each $\lambda \in -\Lambda^*$.

Theorem 7.12. Let X be a convex set and Λ be a polyhedral cone with a generator $\{h^j | 1 \leqq j \leqq r\}$. Then,
    i. $f[X]$ is Λ^*-convex if each $h^j \cdot f(x)$, $1 \leqq j \leqq r$, is concave;
    ii. $f[X]$ is $-\Lambda^*$-convex if each $h^j \cdot f(x)$, $1 \leqq j \leqq r$, is convex.

Proof. For each $\lambda \in \Lambda$, we can write

$$\lambda = \sum_{j=1}^{r} \mu_j h^j, \qquad \mu_j \geqq 0.$$

Thus,

$$\lambda \cdot f(x) = \sum_{j=1}^{r} \mu_j h^j \cdot f(x).$$

Since $\mu_j \geqq 0$, $\lambda \cdot f(x)$ is concave (or convex) whenever each $h^j \cdot f(x)$ is concave (or convex). The assertions follow immediately from Theorem 7.10. $\square$
Similarly, from Theorem 7.11, we have the following theorem.

Theorem 7.13. Let X be a convex set and Λ be a polyhedral cone. Let $\{h^j | 1 \leqq j \leqq r\}$ be a generator for Λ^*. Then,
    i. $f[X]$ is Λ-convex if each $h^j \cdot f(x)$, $1 \leqq j \leqq r$, is concave;
    ii. $f[X]$ is Λ-convex if each $-h^j \cdot f(x)$, $1 \leqq j \leqq r$, is convex.

Let e^j be the jth row of the $q \times q$ identity matrix. Then $\{e^j | j = 1, \ldots, q\}$ and $\{-e^j | j = 1, \ldots, q\}$ are, respectively, a generator for $\Lambda^{\geqq}$ and $\Lambda^{\leqq}$. Note that $e^j \cdot f(x) = f_j(x)$. This observation and Theorem 7.13 offer the following.

Corollary 7.3. Suppose X is a convex set. Then,
    i. $f[X]$ is $\Lambda^{\leqq}$-convex when f is concave (i.e., each f_j is concave) over X (corresponding to Theorem 3.7);
    ii. $f[X]$ is $\Lambda^{\geqq}$-convex when f is convex over X.

In view of Theorem 7.9 and Corollary 7.3, we have the following.

Corollary 7.4. Suppose that $f(x)$ is defined over a convex set X. Then, $f[X]$ is Λ-convex whenever f is concave over X and $\Lambda \supset \Lambda^{\leqq}$ or whenever f is convex over X and $\Lambda \supset \Lambda^{\geqq}$.

Remark 7.16. Suppose that Λ is an arbitrary convex cone. In order to check the Λ-convexity of $f[X]$, we could select a polyhedral cone $\Lambda_1 \subset \Lambda$. If $f[X]$ is Λ_1-convex (by Theorem 7.13, say), then, by Theorem 7.9, we know that $f[X]$ is also Λ-convex.

Example 7.9. Consider X and $f(x_1, x_2)$ defined in Example 4.3. Note that X defined by linear inequalities is convex. Because $f_1(x_1, x_2) = x_1 + x_2$ and

$f_2(x_1, x_2) = 10x_1 - x_1^2 + 4x_2 - x_2^2$, $(\lambda_1, \lambda_2) \cdot (f_1, f_2)$ is concave for all $(\lambda_1, \lambda_2) \in$ $\Lambda_1 = \{(\lambda_1, \lambda_2)|\lambda_2 \geqq 0\}$. Note that Λ_1 can be generated by $h^1 = (-1, 0)$, $h^2 = (1, 0)$ and $h^3 = (0, 1)$; while Λ_1^* is the half-line generated by $h^4 = (0, -1)$. According to Theorems 7.11, 7.12, or 7.13 we can conclude that $f[X]$ is Λ_1^*-convex; and according to Theorem 7.9, $f[X]$ is Λ-convex for any $\Lambda \supset \Lambda_1^*$. (Refer to Figures 4.3 and 4.4.)

Example 7.10. Assume we want to invest \$100,000 for one year in n possible stocks, denoted by $\{1, \ldots, n\}$. Let $x = (x_1, \ldots, x_n)$ be a portfolio of investment. Note $\sum_{i=1}^{n} x_i \leqq 100,000$. The rate of return, R_i, is a random variable. Assume we know that $ER_i = r_i$ and $V = \text{cov}(R_1, \ldots, R_n)$ (the covariance matrix) and that we are interested in

$$f_1(x) = ER(x) = \sum_{i=1}^{n} r_i x_i,$$

$$f_2(x) = \text{Var}(x) = x^T V x.$$

Note that since V is positive semidefinite, $f_2(x)$ is convex and $-f_2(x)$ is concave. It is seen that $(\lambda_1, \lambda_2) \cdot (f_1, f_2)$ is concave for all $(\lambda_1, \lambda_2) \in \Lambda_1 = \{(\lambda_1, \lambda_2)|\lambda_2 \leqq 0\}$. Note that $h^1 = (1, 0)$, $h^2 = (-1, 0)$, and $h^3 = (0, -1)$ form a generator for Λ_1 and $h^4 = (0, 1)$ is a generator for Λ_1^*. We thus conclude that $f[X]$ is Λ_1^*-convex or Λ-convex for any $\Lambda \supset \Lambda_1^*$. The shape of $f[X]$ is depicted in Figure 7.5.

Now let us address some characteristics of N-points. The results to be stated are parallel to those of Theorems 3.8–3.11. Note that throughout the remaining part of this subsection we assume that $\Lambda^\perp \neq \{0\}$. The pathological case of $\Lambda^\perp = \{0\}$ is excluded. See Remark 7.11.

Theorem 7.14. Assume that $\Lambda^\perp \neq \{0\}$ and Y is Λ-convex. Then a necessary condition for $y^0 \in N[Y|\Lambda]$ is that y^0 maximizes $\lambda \cdot y$ over Y for some $\lambda \in \Lambda^* \setminus \{0\}$.

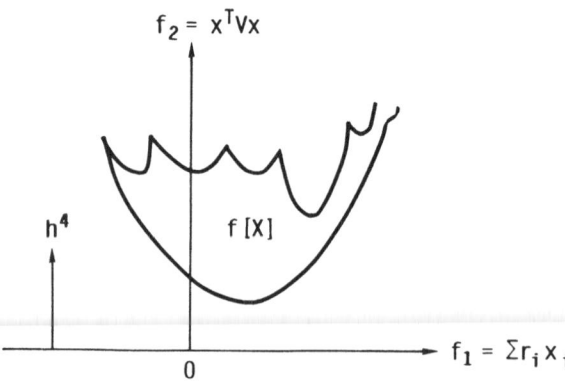

Figure 7.5

Proof. By Corollary 7.1, $y^0 \in N[Y|\Lambda]$ implies that $y^0 \in \partial(Y + \Lambda)$ where $\partial(Y + \Lambda)$ is a boundary point of $Y + \Lambda$. Since $Y + \Lambda$ is convex, there is $\lambda \neq 0$ such that $\lambda \cdot y^0 \geqq \lambda \cdot y$ for all $y \in Y + \Lambda$. Such λ must be in $\Lambda^* \backslash \{0\}$; otherwise we will have a contradiction (check it). Since $Y \subset Y + \Lambda$, $\lambda \cdot y^0 \geqq \lambda \cdot y$ must also hold for all $y \in Y$, as we needed to show. □

Remark 7.17. In the above theorem the need for cone convexity is obvious. Example 3.3 demonstrates such a need. The condition that $\Lambda^\perp \neq \{0\}$ is also needed for the theorem to be valid. As an example, consider $Y \subset R^2$ as depicted in the shaded area of Figure 7.6. Let $\Lambda = \{(d_1, d_2) | d_1 = 0\}$. Note that Λ is the vertical line passing through $\{0\}$. Then Y is Λ-convex and $N[Y|\Lambda] = \{0\}$, which does not have any supporting functional over Y.

Recall (Definition 3.3) that $Y^0(\lambda)$ is the set of all maximum points on Y with respect to $\lambda \cdot y$, and $Y^0(\Lambda^*) = \cup \{Y^0(\lambda) | \lambda \in \Lambda^*\}$.

Using Lemma 7.3 and Theorem 7.14, we have the following.

Theorem 7.15.
  i. $Y^0(\text{Int } \Lambda^*) \subset N[Y|\Lambda]$ [note, we understand that if Int $\Lambda^* = \varnothing$ then $Y^0(\text{Int } \Lambda^*) = \varnothing$].
  ii. If Y is Λ-convex and $\Lambda^\perp \neq \{0\}$, then $N[Y|\Lambda] \subset Y^0(\Lambda^* \backslash \{0\})$ and $Y^0(\text{Int } \Lambda^*) \subset N[Y|\Lambda] \subset Y^0(\Lambda^* \backslash \{0\})$.
  iii. If Λ is open and $\Lambda^\perp \neq \{0\}$, then $N[Y|\Lambda] = Y^0(\Lambda^* \backslash \{0\})$.

The above can further be strengthened as follows.

Theorem 7.16. (i) If Λ is closed and pointed and *either* Y is closed and convex, *or* $Y + \Lambda$ is convex and closed, then $Y^0(\text{Int } \Lambda^*) \subset N[Y|\Lambda] \subset$ Cl $Y^0(\text{Int } \Lambda^*)$.

(ii) If Y and Λ are both polyhedral then $N[Y|\Lambda] = Y^0(\text{Int } \Lambda^*)$.

Proof. For (i) see Ref. 195 of Hartley and for (ii) see Chapter 8 or Ref. 508 of Yu and Zeleny.

Using Theorem 7.15, we have the following.

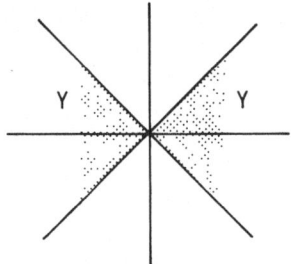

Figure 7.6

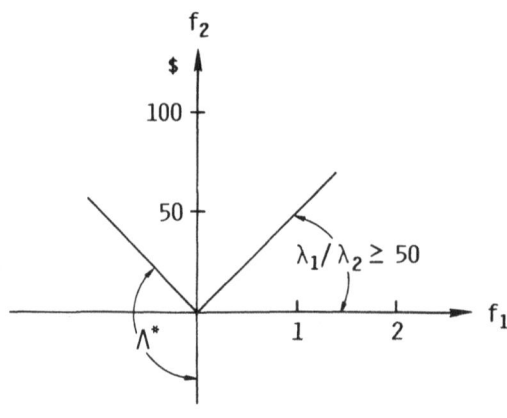

Figure 7.7

Theorem 7.17. (i) If y^0 is a maximum point over Y for some value function that is decreasing in a convex cone Λ, then $y^0 \in N[Y|\Lambda]$.

(ii) If y^0 is a maximum point over Y for some value function that is decreasing in Λ, and Y is Λ-convex then there is a $\lambda \in \Lambda^* \backslash \{0\}$ such that y^0 also maximizes $\lambda \cdot y$ over Y.

Remark 7.18. Theorem 7.17 offers a connection between N-points and maximum points of additive value functions. If we know that the decreasing directions of the preference are represented by Λ, and Y has suitable cone convexity, then an additive value function may be used to approximate the "maximum" preference. The corresponding weight is bounded by $\Lambda^* \backslash \{0\}$.

Remark 7.19. Suppose a worker reveals that he would be happy to work on Sunday if he can get paid at least \$50 an hour. Let f_1 denote the leisure time (in hours) and f_2 the monetary income. The worker reveals that in terms of $v(\lambda) = \lambda_1 f_1 + \lambda_2 f_2$, $\lambda_1/\lambda_2 \geqq 50$ is acceptable to him, or $\Lambda = \{(\lambda_1, \lambda_2)|\lambda_1/\lambda_2 \geqq 50, \lambda_1 > 0, \lambda_2 > 0\}$ are the increasing directions for his preference. (See Figure 7.7.) Thus, Λ^* is an approximation of his dominated cone. Note that Λ^* is smaller than a half space but larger than $\Lambda^{\leqq}$. Observe that unless Y is Λ^*-convex, $N[Y|\Lambda^*]$ may not be obtainable using maximization of $\lambda_1 f_1 + \lambda_2 f_2$. The final solution which is in $N[Y|\Lambda^*]$ may not be obtainable by maximizing additive weight functions.

7.3.5. N-Points in the Decision Space

In this subsection we shall discuss conditions for N-points in the decision space. As these are just "restatements" of the results in Sections 7.3.3 and

7.3.4, and similar restatements have been done in Section 3.4 for Pareto preference, we will state only a few and leave the rest to the reader as exercises.

Definition 7.10. A point x^0 in the decision space X is an $N_X[\Lambda]$-point iff $f(x^0) \in N[Y|\Lambda]$, where $Y = f[X]$. The set of all $N_X[\Lambda]$-points in X will be denoted by $N_X[\Lambda]$.

The statements below follow from Lemma 7.3 and Theorems 7.6 and 7.8. [See Exercise 7.18(a).]

Theorem 7.18. (i) $x^0 \in N_X[\Lambda]$ if x^0 maximizes $\lambda \cdot f(x)$ over X for some $\lambda \in \text{Int } \Lambda^*$ *or* uniquely maximizes $\lambda \cdot f(x)$ over X for some $\lambda \in \Lambda^* \backslash \{0\}$.

(ii) Given Assumption 7.1, a necessary condition for $x^0 \in N_X[\Lambda]$ is that for any $i \in \{1, \ldots, r\}$, $h^i \cdot f(x^0)$ uniquely maximizes $h^i \cdot f(x)$ for all $x \in X_i(x^0) = \{x \in X | h^k \cdot f(x) \geqq h^k \cdot f(x^0), \ k \neq i, i = 1, \ldots, r\}$; $x^0 \in N_X[\Lambda]$ if indeed x^0 is the unique maximum point of the above problem.

(iii) Given Assumption 7.1, a necessary condition for $x^0 \in N_X[\Lambda]$ is that for any $i \in \{1, 2, \ldots, r\}$ there are $r - 1$ constants $c(i) = \{c_k | k \neq i, k = 1, \ldots, r\}$ so that $h^i \cdot f(x^0)$ uniquely maximizes $h^i \cdot f(x)$ over $X(c(i)) = \{x \in X | h^k \cdot f(x) \geqq c_k, \ k \neq i, \ k = 1, \ldots, r\}$; $x^0 \in N_X[\Lambda]$ if indeed x^0 is the unique maximum point of the above problem.

Note that if $y = f(x)$ then there may be many y^0 which maximize $h^i \cdot y^0$ and in turn there may be many points x of X so that $f(x) = y^0$.
The result follows from Theorem 7.14. [See Exercise 7.18(b).]

Theorem 7.19. (Parallel to Theorem 3.15.) If $\Lambda^\perp \neq \{0\}$ (or Λ is not a linear space) and $f[X]$ is Λ-convex, then for $x^0 \in N_X[\Lambda]$ it is necessary that x^0 maximizes $\lambda \cdot f(x)$ over X for some $\lambda \in \Lambda^* \backslash \{0\}$.

Recall that $X = \{x | g(x) \leqq 0\}$, where $g: R^n \to R^m$ [i.e., $g = (g_1, \ldots, g_m)$]. We have the following [see Exercise 7.18(c)].

Theorem 7.20. [Parallel to Theorems 3.16 and 7.18(iii).] Assume that Assumption 7.1 holds and that $g(x)$ and $f(x)$ are differentiable over X. Then, a necessary condition for $x^0 \in N_X[\Lambda]$ is that there exist $c(i) = \{c_k | k \neq i, i = 1, \ldots, r\}$, $\mu_k \geqq 0$, $k = 1, \ldots, r$, and $\lambda_j \geqq 0$, $j = 1, \ldots, m$, where not all μ_k and λ_k are zeros, such that, with respect to

$$L = \sum_{k=1}^{r} \mu_k h^k \cdot f(x) - \sum_{j=1}^{m} \lambda_j g_j(x) - \sum_{k \neq i} \mu_k c_k,$$

the following conditions are satisfied:

$$\nabla_x L(x^0) = 0,$$

$$\mu_k(c_k - h^k \cdot f(x^0)) = 0, \qquad k = 1, \ldots, r, \qquad k \neq i,$$

$$c_k - h^k \cdot f(x^0) \leqq 0, \qquad k = 1, \ldots, r, \qquad k \neq i,$$

$$\lambda_j g_j(x^0) = 0, \qquad j = 1, \ldots, m,$$

$$g_j(x^0) \leqq 0, \qquad j = 1, \ldots, m.$$

To obtain results similar to Theorem 3.19, we first define

$$X_A^I(\Lambda) = \{x \in X | f(x) \in Y^0(\text{Int } \Lambda^*)\},$$

$$X_A(\Lambda) = \{x \in X | f(x) \in Y^0(\Lambda^* \backslash \{0\})\}.$$

Let $I(x^0) = \{i | g_i(x^0) = 0\}$, and let $\mu_{I(x^0)}$ and $g_{I(x^0)}(x^0)$ be the vectors derived from μ and $g(x^0)$ by deleting all components of μ and $g(x^0)$ which are not in $I(x^0)$. Define

$$F(x^0, \Lambda) = \{\lambda \cdot \nabla f(x^0) | \lambda \in \Lambda^*, \lambda \neq 0\},$$

$$F^I(x^0, \Lambda) = \{\lambda \cdot \nabla f(x^0) | \lambda \in \text{Int } \Lambda^*\},$$

$$G(x^0) = \{\mu_{I(x^0)} \cdot \nabla g_{I(x^0)}(x^0) | \mu_{I(x^0)} \geqq 0\}.$$

It is understood that $G(x^0) = \{0\}$ if $I(x^0) = \varnothing$.

Using necessary and sufficient conditions for maximum points and Theorem 7.15 we obtain the following theorem [see Exercise 7.18(d)].

Theorem 7.21. (A) Suppose that X is convex, $\Lambda^\perp \neq \{0\}$ and that over X, (a) $g(x)$ is quasiconvex and differentiable, (b) $\lambda \cdot f(x)$ is concave and differentiable for all $\lambda \in \Lambda^*$, and (c) the Kuhn–Tucker constraint qualification is satisfied. Then,

    i. $x^0 \in X_A(\Lambda)$ iff $x^0 \in X$ and $F(x^0, \Lambda) \cap G(x^0) \neq \varnothing$;

    ii. $x^0 \in X_A^I(\Lambda)$ iff $x^0 \in X$ and $F^I(x^0, \Lambda) \cap G(x^0) \neq \varnothing$;

    iii. $X_A^I(\Lambda) \subset N_X[\Lambda] \subset X_A(\Lambda)$

    (B) Suppose also that Λ is open. Then,

    iv. $N_X[\Lambda] = X_A(\Lambda)$.

Note that, in view of (iii), $X_A^I(\Lambda)$ and $X_A(\Lambda)$ are "inner" and "outer" approximation sets to $N_X[\Lambda]$.

Remark 7.20. To speed up the procedure of locating the entire set $N_X[\Lambda]$, one can use the decomposition theorem on the index set of constraint $\{g_i\}$, which is described in detail in Section 3.4.3 and with an example in Section 3.4.4. The decomposition theorem is still valid for general constant dominated cones when suitable conditions hold. We shall not repeat this procedure. The interested reader is referred to Ref. 495 and Section 3.4.3. (See Exercise 7.19.)

7.3.6. Existence, Properness, and Duality Questions

In this subsection we shall briefly discuss existence problems of N-points and concepts of proper efficient points. For details the reader is referred to the quoted references.

Theorem 3.3 can be readily expanded as (see Exercise 7.20):

Theorem 7.22. If Y is Λ-compact and Λ is acute then
i. $N[Y|\Lambda] \neq \varnothing$;
ii. Y is nondominance bounded. Thus, $Y \subset N[Y|\Lambda] + \Lambda$. (For Λ-compactness and nondominance boundedness the reader is referred to Definitions 3.1 and 2.7, respectively.)

Corollary 7.5. If Y is compact and Λ is acute, then $N[Y|\Lambda] \neq \varnothing$ and Y is nondominance bounded.

Proper efficient or proper N-points have drawn the attention of a number of authors. Because of the pathological cases of "unbounded" trade-off ratios (as discussed in Section 3.3.3) for improper N-points, researchers have tried to discover the conditions that separate proper from improper N-points. The conditions and definitions of improperness become a focus when more general dominated cones are studied. Using Theorem 7.5 the conditions and definition for proper N-points with respect to $\Lambda^{\leq}$ as the dominated cone can be readily extended to the case of acute polyhedral dominated cones. We shall leave these to the reader as exercises. (See Exercise 7.21.)

For dominated cones other than acute polyhedral ones, a number of scholars have proposed definitions and conditions for proper N-points. For instance, just to mention a few, Hartley (Ref. 195) uses the bound of the inner products with the vectors in polar cones, Borwein (Ref. 58) uses limits of sequences, and Benson (Ref. 40) uses the closure of the projecting cone of $Y + \Lambda$ to define the concept. For other types, the reader is referred to White (Ref. 481). Here we shall adopt Henig's definition (Ref. 205), because of its simplicity and generality and because of its important implication for applications. While the details and extensions can be found in Ref. 205, here we shall only sketch some interesting results.

Definition 7.11. (i) $y \in Y$ is a *global proper N-point*, with respect to Λ, if $y \in N[Y|\theta]$ for some convex cone θ with $'\Lambda \subset \text{Int } \theta$. The set of all global proper N-points will be denoted by $\text{GPN}[Y|\Lambda]$.

(ii) $y \in Y$ is a *local proper N-point*, with respect to Λ, if for every $\varepsilon > 0$, there exists a convex cone θ with $'\Lambda \subset \text{Int } \theta$, such that $y \in N[(Y + \Lambda) \cap (y + \varepsilon B)|\theta]$, where B is the unit ball in R^q. The set of all local proper N-points will be denoted by $\text{LPN}[Y|\Lambda]$.

Remark 7.21. According to the definition, if $'\Lambda$ is open, one can set $\theta = '\Lambda$. Then $N[Y|\Lambda] = \text{GPN}[Y|\Lambda] = \text{LPN}[Y|\Lambda]$. Thus "properness" becomes a problem only when $'\Lambda$ is not open. In applications, a slight perturbation as to make $'\Lambda$ open is not a serious problem. "Properness" is therefore an interesting mathematical problem, rather than a serious application problem. Henig showed (Ref. 205) that when Λ is closed and acute, $\text{LPN}[Y|\Lambda]$-points are equivalent to those of Borwein while $\text{GPN}[Y|\Lambda]$-points are equivalent to those of Benson.

The following are some interesting results of Ref. 205.

Theorem 7.23. Assume that Λ is acute and closed. Then
  i. $\text{GPN}[Y|\Lambda] = \text{LPN}[Y|\Lambda]$ if $\text{GPN}[Y|\Lambda] \neq \varnothing$.
  ii. $Y^0(\text{Int } \Lambda^*) \subset \text{GPN}[Y|\Lambda]$.
  iii. If, in addition, there is $A \subset \Lambda$, $0 \in A$ such that $Y + A$ is closed and convex, then $Y^0(\text{Int } \Lambda^*) = \text{GPN}[Y|\Lambda] = \text{LPN}[Y|\Lambda]$.

As $N[Y|\Lambda]$-points are generalizations of maximum points of a single criterion, the duality concept of the latter can be extended to the former. Many interesting results are reported in this area. For instance, see Tanino and Sawaragi (Ref. 445), Nakayama (Ref. 317), Bitran (Ref. 51), Isermann (Ref. 233), Kornbluth (Ref. 265), Jahn (Ref. 235), Ponstein (Ref. 358), and Nieuwenhuis (Ref. 324). In Chapter 8 we shall discuss the simplest case—duality in linear cases.

7.4. Local and Global N-Points in Domination Structures

In this section we shall discuss local N-points and global N-points with some regularity assumptions on the domination structures. Results of local maximum points implying global maximum points of mathematical programming are extended to those of N-points.

Given $\varepsilon > 0$, the ε-neighborhood of y^0 on Y is defined by

$$Y_\varepsilon(y^0) = Y \cap (y^0 + \varepsilon B), \tag{7.11}$$

where B is the unit ball of R^q.

Definition 7.12. Given $\{>\}$, $y^0 \in Y$ is an LN-point (local nondominated point) iff y^0 is an N-point over $Y_\varepsilon(y^0)$ for some $\varepsilon > 0$. The set of all LN-points will be denoted by LN, or LN $(Y, \{>\})$, LN (Y), LN $(\{>\})$ whenever the corresponding parameters (i.e., Y or $\{>\}$) are emphasized.

Note that each (global) N-point (see Definition 2.5) is, by definition, an LN-point. The converse is certainly not generally true, just as local maximum points are not necessarily global maximum points.

As Remark 7.2 pointed out, from $\{>\}$ we can always construct the corresponding domination structures. The converse is not always true. It is interesting for the reader to explore under what conditions a domination structure can recover the entire information of a preference $\{>\}$ (similar to under what conditions "partial derivatives" can allow the construction of a value (potential) function which has the particular derivatives).

Recall that LD (y), LP (y), $T(y, <)$ are local dominated cones, preferred cones, and tangent cones of $\{y<\}$ at y (Definitions 7.2, 7.4, 7.7), and $T(y, Y)$ is the tangent cone of Y at y.

Lemma 7.5. Given $\{>\}$, the following are some necessary conditions for $y^0 \in$ LN (Y):

    i. There is an $\varepsilon > 0$ such that $Y_\varepsilon(y^0) \cap [y^0 + \text{LP}(y^0)] = \{y^0\}$.

    ii. Int $T(y^0, Y) \cap \text{LP}(y^0) = \varnothing$ if for each $h \in$ Int $T(y^0, Y)$ there is an $\varepsilon > 0$ such that $y^0 + \delta h \in Y$ for all $0 \leqq \delta \leqq \varepsilon$.

    iii. $T(y^0, Y) \cap$ Int LP $(y^0) = \varnothing$, if $T(y^0, Y)$ is convex and has a nonempty interior and for each $h \in$ Int (y^0, Y), there is an $\varepsilon > 0$ so that $y^0 + \delta h \in Y$ for all $0 \leqq \delta \leqq \varepsilon$.

Proof. (i) and (ii) are obvious, otherwise we would have a contradiction.

To see (iii), observe that if $T(y^0, Y) \cap$ Int LP $(y^0) \neq 0$ then Int $T(y^0, Y) \cap$ LP $(y^0) \neq 0$ because $T(y^0, Y)$ is convex and has a nonempty interior. In order to see this point, let $h^0 \in T(y^0, Y) \cap$ Int LP (y^0). Then any neighborhood $N(h^0) \subset$ LP (y^0) of h^0 will contain some interior point of $T(y^0, Y)$. Our conclusion then follows from (ii).

Remark 7.22. The condition imposed in (ii) is usually satisfied in most mathematical or optimal control problems. It is needed to avoid pathological cases. As an example of a pathological case, let $Y = \Lambda^\geqq \backslash A$, where A is any nonzero half-line in $\Lambda^>$. Then $T(0, Y) = \Lambda^\geqq$ and $A \subset$ Int $T(0, \Lambda^\geqq)$. It is readily verified that the condition imposed in (iii) of Lemma 7.5 is not satisfied and the result is not valid when LP $(0) = A$.

Similarly the condition imposed in (iii) serves to avoid pathological cases. The following example is derived from Hazen and Morin (Ref. 199). In Figure 7.8, $T(y^0, Y)$ is convex but has no interior. Note that $y^0 \in$ LN but $h^0 \in T(y^0, Y) \cap$ Int LP (y^0).

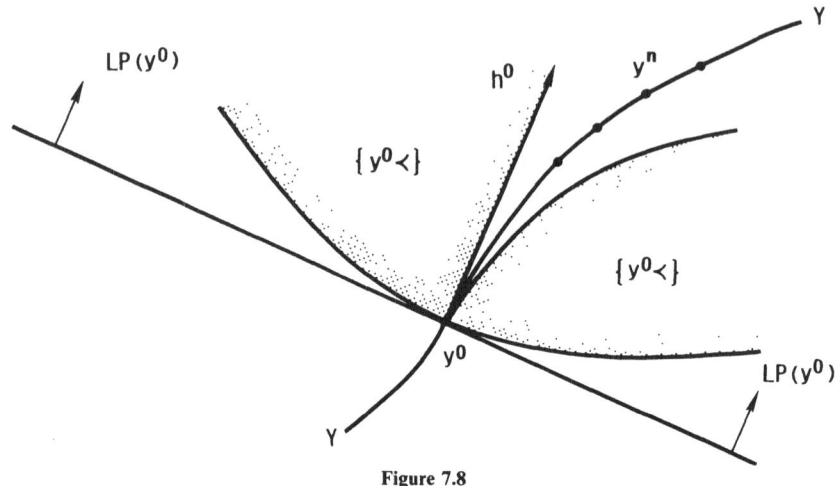

Figure 7.8

To avoid pathological cases, we introduce the following definition.

Definition 7.13. An LN-point y^0 is a *regular LN-point* if $T(y^0, Y) \cap$ Int LP$(y^0) = \varnothing$ or Int $T(y^0, Y) \cap$ LP$(y^0) = \varnothing$ holds.

Note that Lemma 7.5(ii) and (iii) give some sufficient conditions for regular LN-points.

Using a separation theorem of convex sets (for instance, see Ref. 438), and Definition 7.13 we can obtain a necessary condition for LN-points as follows:

Theorem 7.24. Suppose that $T(y^0, Y)$ and LP(y^0) are convex. Then for y^0 to be a regular LN-point it is necessary that there is a nonzero $\lambda \in -[\mathrm{LP}(y^0)]^*$ [the negative of the polar cone of LP(y^0)] such that $\lambda \cdot h \leq 0$ for all $h \in T(y^0, Y)$.

Note that $\lambda \in -[\mathrm{LP}(y^0)]^*$ implies that $\lambda \cdot h \geq 0$ for all $h \in \mathrm{LP}(y^0)$.

Remark 7.23. (i) The above theorem converts finding regular LN-points into a mathematical programming problem. [Note that 0 is the maximum point of $\lambda \cdot h$ for all $h \in T(y^0, Y)$.] We shall demonstrate this shortly.

(ii) One can also see that y^0 is a regular LN-point only when $0 \in N[T(y^0, Y)| - \mathrm{LP}(y^0)]$. This is a generalization of a necessary condition for y^0 to be a local maximum point of one objective function. Note that in the single objective case, LP(y^0) and $T(y^0, Y)$ are only one dimensional. If y^0 is a local maximum point then LP(y^0) and $T(y^0, Y)$ must be in the opposite direction of 0.

(iii) One also observes that Theorem 7.24 indicates that $\lambda \neq 0$ and $\lambda \in [-\mathrm{LP}(y^0)]^* \cap [T(y^0, Y)]^*$.

Definition 7.14. $x^0 \in X$ is an LN-point or a regular LN-point iff $f(x^0) = y^0$ is an LN-point (or a regular LN-point) in Y. The set of all LN-points in X will be denoted by LN_X or $\mathrm{LN}_X(\{>\})$.

To obtain necessary conditions for regular LN_X-points, recall that $X = \{x | g(x) \leqq 0\}$, where $g : R^n \to R^m$. Suppose that $x^0 \in X$ and both g and f are differentiable. When a constraint qualification is satisfied, the tangent cone of X at x^0 is given by

$$T(x^0, X) = \{h | \nabla g_{I(x^0)}(x^0) \cdot h \leqq 0\}, \tag{7.12}$$

where $I(x^0) = \{i | g_i(x^0) = 0\}$ and $\nabla g_{I(x^0)}$ are defined in Section 7.3.5. Note that $T(x^0, X)$ as in (7.12) is a polyhedral cone. One obtains

$$T(f(x^0), Y) \supset \{\nabla f(x^0) \cdot h | h \in T(x^0, X)\}, \tag{7.13}$$

which is another polyhedral cone.

In view of Theorem 7.24, if x^0 is a regular LN-point then there is $\lambda \in [-\mathrm{LP}(f(x^0))]^*$, $(\lambda \neq 0)$ so that

$$\lambda \cdot \nabla f(x^0) \cdot h \leqq 0$$

for all h satisfying

$$\nabla g_{I(x^0)}(x^0) \cdot h \leqq 0.$$

That is,

$$\lambda \cdot \nabla f(x^0) \cdot h > 0 \quad \text{and} \quad \nabla g_{I(x^0)}(x^0) \cdot h \leqq 0$$

has no solution. By Farkas' lemma, there is $\mu_{I(x^0)} \geqq 0$, such that

$$\lambda \cdot \nabla f(x^0) = \mu_{I(x^0)} \cdot \nabla g_{I(x^0)}(x^0). \tag{7.14}$$

Define

$$\mathrm{LF}(x^0) = \{\lambda \cdot \nabla f(x^0) | \lambda \in [-\mathrm{LP}(x^0)]^*, \lambda \neq 0\} \tag{7.15}$$

$$G(x^0) = \{\mu_{I(x^0)} \cdot \nabla g_{I(x^0)}(x^0) | \mu_{I(x^0)} \geqq 0\}, \tag{7.16}$$

with $G(x^0) = \{0\}$ if $I(x^0) = \varnothing$. Note that 0 may not be contained in $\mathrm{LF}(x^0)$. Then (7.14) implies that $\mathrm{LF}(x^0) \cap G(x^0) \neq \varnothing$.

We summarize the above into the following theorem.

Theorem 7.25. Assume that f and g are differentiable at x^0, a constraint qualification is satisfied, and that $LP(f(x^0))$ is convex. Then a necessary condition for x^0 to be a regular LN-point is that $LF(x^0) \cap G(x^0) \neq \emptyset$ where $LF(x^0)$ and $G(x^0)$ are defined in (7.15) and (7.16).

Remark 7.24. The reader may find it instructive to compare the above theorem with Theorems 3.18 and 7.21. We have established that the necessary condition for regular LN-points is similar to $N_X[\Lambda]$-points with $-LP(f(x))$ replacing Λ. One notices that $-LP(f(x))$ may not be equal to $LD(f(x))$ as pointed out in Remark 7.3.

A domination structure is *regular* at $f(x) = y$ iff $Cl\, LD(y) = -Cl\, LP(y)$. In other words, the domination structure is regular at y iff for each local preferred direction h at y, $-h$ is either a local dominated direction or a limit of local dominated directions, and vice versa at y. In most application cases the "regular" condition holds. For instance, the domination structures induced by Pareto preference, constant dominated cones, and differentiable value functions all satisfy the regularity condition. Unfortunately there are many pathological cases in which regularity does not hold. Simple examples are those points at which a value function is not differentiable. Observe that if $v(y)$ is differentiable at y^0 then $Int\, LP(y^0) = \{h | \nabla v(y^0) \cdot h > 0\} = H(y^0)$, which is uniquely determined by $\nabla v(y^0)$. In the general domination structures, the half-space $H(y^0)$ is replaced by $Int\, LP(y^0)$, which is just a cone. The regularity of domination structures is a generalization of the continuity of $H(y^0)$ or $\nabla v(y^0)$. To avoid distraction, we provide some results concerning regularity in Exercise 7.24.

In the remainder of this subsection we shall explore those conditions under which an LN-point is also an N-point. We first start with the Y-space.

Given that Y is convex, $\{>\}$ is *strictly quasi-concave* on Y if $y^1 > y^2$ implies $y^3 > y^2$ for any $y^3 \in [y^1, y^2[$ (the line interval from y^1 to y^2 including y^1 but excluding y^2) (see Exercise 2.13; this is similar to strict quasi-concave functions). We have the following.

Theorem 7.26. Suppose that Y is convex and $\{>\}$ is strictly quasi-concave on Y. Then each LN-point in Y is also a (global) N-point.

Proof. Let $y^0 \in LN$ and $y^0 \notin N$. Then there is y^1 with $y^1 > y^0$. By strict quasi-concavity $y^2 > y^0$ for any $y^2 \in]y^0, y^1]$. This leads to a contradiction that y^0 is an LN-point. $\square$

To establish that an LN_X-point is also an N_X-point in the X space we need a natural extension of the concave function for $\{>\}$ as introduced in Ref. 199.

Definition 7.15. Given $\{>\}$, a vector function $f: R^n \to R^q$ is $>$-concave over X iff for any x^1, x^2 of X, the following holds:

$$f((1 - \lambda)x^1 + \lambda x^2) > (1 - \lambda)f(x^1) + \lambda f(x^2) \qquad (7.17)$$

for all $\lambda \in]0, 1[$.

Remark 7.25. In (7.17) we use "$>$" to substitute "$>$" of the ordinary definition for strictly concave functions. The concept of $>$-concavity is an extension of strictly concave real-valued functions.

Theorem 7.27. Suppose that X is convex, $\{f(x^0) <\}$ is convex in Y, and $\{>\}$ is transitive. Then f is $>$-concave implies that $S(x^0) = \{x \in X | f(x) > f(x^0)\}$ is a convex set.

Proof. Given x^1, $x^2 \in S(x^0)$ we prove that $(1 - \alpha)x^1 + \alpha x^2 \in S(x^0)$. Note that by $>$-concavity we have $f((1 - \alpha)x^1 + \alpha x^2) > (1 - \alpha)f(x^1) + \alpha f(x^2) > f(x^0)$. The last $>$-relation is due to the fact that $\{f(x^0) <\}$ is a convex set. By transitivity, we thus have $(1 - \alpha)x^1 + \alpha x^2 \in S(x^0)$. $\qquad \square$

The following theorem offers a sufficient condition for an LN_X-point to be an N_X-point. Recall that $\{>\}$ being strictly quasi-concave implies that if $y^2 > y^1$ then $y^3 > y^1$ for all $y^3 \in]y^1, y^2]$.

Theorem 7.28. Suppose that $\{>\}$ is transitive and strictly quasi-concave. If f is $>$-concave over X which is convex then $x^0 \in \mathrm{LN}_X$ implies that $x^0 \in N_X$ (thus, $\mathrm{LN}_X = N_X$; why?).

Proof. If $x^0 \notin N_X$, then there is $x^1 \in X$ such that $f(x^0) < f(x^1)$. Thus, by strict quasi-concavity of $\{>\}$, for all $\lambda \in]0, 1[, f(x^0) < (1 - \lambda)f(x^0) + \lambda f(x^1) < f((1 - \lambda)x^0 + \lambda x^1)$. The last $<$-relation is due to the fact that f is $>$-concave. By transitivity, we have $f(x^0) < f((1 - \lambda)x^0 + \lambda x^1)$ for all $\lambda \in]0, 1[$. Let λ become sufficiently small and we will get a contradiction. $\qquad \square$

The following gives a relationship between Λ-convexity of $f[X]$ and $>$-concavity of f. Note that given a convex dominated cone Λ, we can construct the corresponding preference $\{>\}$ by $y^1 > y^2$ iff $y^2 \in y^1 + '\Lambda$, as we studied in Section 7.3. For convenience, preference so induced will be called *preference of the dominated cone* Λ, or simply *preference of* Λ.

Theorem 7.29. If f is $>$-concave over a convex set X and $\{>\}$ is the preference of Λ, then $f[X]$ is Λ-convex. The converse is not generally true.

Proof. By $>$-concavity, for any x^1, $x^2 \in X$, and $\lambda \in]0, 1[$, we have $f((1 - \lambda)x^1 + \lambda x^2) > (1 - \lambda)f(x^1) + \lambda f(x^2)$ or $(1 - \lambda)f(x^1) + \lambda f(x^2) \in f((1 - \lambda)x^1 + \lambda x^2) + '\Lambda$. Since X is convex, $(1 - \lambda)x^1 + \lambda x^2 \in X$. Thus, $f[X]$ is Λ-convex by Lemma 7.4(i).

To show that the converse is not generally true, consider an example: $f_1(x) = x$, $f_2(x) = x^3$, $X = [0, 1]$. Let $\{>\}$ be the preference of dominated cone $\Lambda^\leqq$. Then it can be verified that $f[X]$ is $\Lambda^\leqq$-convex but f is not $>$-concave.

□

As pointed out in Remark 7.25, $>$-concavity is a natural extension of concave functions; many known results for concave functions can be extended to $>$-concave functions when $\{>\}$ has suitable properties. Theorem 7.27 and the following Theorem 7.30 are just some examples of the extensions. To avoid distraction the rest will be left to the reader to explore (Exercise 7.25).

Theorem 7.30. Let $\{>\}$ be the preference of the closed and pointed convex dominated cone Λ and let f be differentiable over a convex set X. Then f is $>$-concave over X iff for each x^1, x^2 of X

$$f(x^2) - f(x^1) < \nabla f(x^1) \cdot (x^2 - x^1) \tag{7.18}$$

or

$$f(x^2) - f(x^1) - \nabla f(x^1) \cdot (x^2 - x^1) \in {}'\Lambda. \tag{7.19}$$

[Note that (7.18) is similar to the result for differentiable strict concave functions. Why?]

Proof. *For Sufficiency*: By (7.19), if $z = (1 - \lambda)x^1 + \lambda x^2$ then

$$f(x^1) - f(z) - \nabla f(z) \cdot (x^1 - z) \in {}'\Lambda, \tag{7.20}$$

$$f(x^2) - f(z) - \nabla f(z) \cdot (x^2 - z) \in {}'\Lambda. \tag{7.21}$$

Note that ${}'\Lambda$ is convex because Λ is pointed. Multiplying (7.20) and (7.21) by $(1 - \lambda)$ and λ, respectively, for any $\lambda \in {]}0, 1{[}$ and summing up, we obtain $(1 - \lambda)f(x^1) + \lambda f(x^2) - f(z) - \nabla f(z) \cdot 0 \in {}'\Lambda$ or $(1 - \lambda)f(x^1) + \lambda f(x^2) \in f(z) + {}'\Lambda$ or $(1 - \lambda)f(x^1) + \lambda f(x^2) < f((1 - \lambda)x^1 + \lambda x^2)$.

For Necessity: For any $\lambda \in {]}0, 1{[}$,

$$(1 - \lambda)f(x^1) + \lambda f(x^2) - f((1 - \lambda)x^1 + \lambda x^2) \in {}'\Lambda$$

or

$$\lambda[f(x^2) - f(x^1)] - [f((1 - \lambda)x^1 + \lambda x^2) - f(x^1)] \in {}'\Lambda.$$

Thus,

$$f(x^2) - f(x^1) - \frac{1}{\lambda}[f((1 - \lambda)x^1 + \lambda x^2) - f(x^1)] \in {}'\Lambda.$$

Since Λ is closed, when $\lambda \to 0$, we have

$$f(x^2) - f(x^1) - \nabla f(x^1) \cdot (x^2 - x^1) \in \Lambda. \qquad (7.22)$$

Note that (7.22) holds for all x^1, x^2 of X. It remains to show that

$$f(x^2) - f(x^1) - \nabla f(x^1) \cdot (x^2 - x^1) \neq 0.$$

Assume the contrary. Then

$$f(x^2) = f(x^1) + \nabla f(x^1) \cdot (x^2 - x^1).$$

From (7.17) in Definition 7.15, for $\lambda \in \,]0, 1[$,

$$f((1 - \lambda)x^1 + \lambda x^2) > (1 - \lambda)f(x^1) + \lambda f(x^2)$$

$$= (1 - \lambda)f(x^1) + \lambda[f(x^1) + \nabla f(x^1) \cdot (x^2 - x^1)]$$

$$= f(x^1) + \lambda \nabla f(x^1) \cdot (x^2 - x^1).$$

Thus

$$f(x^1) + \lambda \nabla f(x^1) \cdot (x^2 - x^1) - f((1 - \lambda)x^1 + \lambda x^2) \in \,'\Lambda$$

or

$$f((1 - \lambda)x^1 + \lambda x^2) - f(x^1) - \lambda \nabla f(x^1) \cdot (x^2 - x^1) \in -'\Lambda. \qquad (7.23)$$

Now applying (7.22) at the point $(1 - \lambda)x^1 + \lambda x^2$ (instead of x^2), we obtain

$$f((1 - \lambda)x^1 + \lambda x^2) - f(x^1) - \nabla f(x^1) \cdot [(1 - \lambda)x^1 + \lambda x^2 - x^1]$$

$$= f((1 - \lambda)x^1 + \lambda x^2) - f(x^1) - \lambda \nabla f(x^1) \cdot (x^2 - x^1) \in \Lambda,$$

which contradicts (7.23) because Λ is pointed. $\qquad\qquad \square$

7.5. Interactive Approximations for N-Points with Information from Domination Structures

For notational convenience, we shall denote $D(y)' = D(y) \cup \{0\}$ simply by $D(y)$ if no confusion can arise, while $'D(y)$ is used to emphasize the case where $\{0\}$ is not included. Throughout this subsection we shall discuss problems that satisfy the following assumption.

Assumption 7.2. The preference $\{>\}$, defined on R^q, is such that for each $y \in Y$, $\{y>\} - y = {}'D(y)$ is a convex cone.

We can readily verify the following (see Exercise 7.27).

Lemma 7.6. Under Assumption 7.2, $y^0 \in Y$ is an N-point iff there is no y in Y such that $y^0 \in y + {}'D(y)$.

Remark 7.26. Under Assumption 7.2, LD $(y) = D(y)$ for all $y \in Y$. (Check it!) Pareto preference structures and constant dominated cone structures all satisfy this assumption. Indeed we have generalized the constant dominated cone structures in two ways: (i) we let $D(y)$ vary with y, and (ii) the preferred cones $[P(y)$ and LP $(y)]$ are unspecified. Fortunately, Lemma 7.6 provides us with a unique characterization of N-points which is a straightforward extension of Section 7.3 for constant dominated cone structures. One observes that Assumption 7.2 may not always be satisfied for general domination structures. As an example, preference structures represented by convex value functions may not satisfy the assumption. (Check it!)

Let us derive a few preliminary results to facilitate our presentation of two approximation methods. Recall that we use N to denote the set of all N-points with respect to $\{>\}$ or $\{D(y)|y \in Y\}$, and $N[Y|\Lambda]$ to denote the set of all N-points with respect to a *constant* dominated cone Λ.

Given $y \in Y$, define

$$Y_y = [y + D(y)] \cap Y.$$

Thus, Y_y is the subset of Y which contains y and those points that are dominated by y.

Lemma 7.7. If each $D(y)$ is convex and pointed then
  i. given $y^0 \in Y$, then $\{y^0\} = N[Y_{y^0}|D(y^0)]$;
  ii. given $N_0 \subset N$ and $Y_{N_0} = \cup \{Y_y|y \in N_0\}$, then $N_0 \subset N[Y_{N_0}|\Lambda]$, where $\Lambda = \cap \{D(y)|y \in N_0\}$;
  iii. If Y is nondominance bounded (i.e., $Y = \cup \{Y_y|y \in N\}$), then $N \subset N[Y|\Lambda]$, where $\Lambda = \cap \{D(y)|y \in N\}$;
  iv. $N \subset N[Y|\Lambda^0]$, where $\Lambda^0 = \cap \{D(y)|y \in Y\}$.
The "pointed" assumption is not needed for (iv).

Proof. (i) Since every point of Y_{y^0} other than y^0 cannot be a point of $N[Y_{y^0}|D(y^0)]$, it suffices to show that

$$y^0 \in N[Y_{y^0}|D(y^0)]$$

Suppose that

$$y^0 \notin N[Y_{y^0}|D(y^0)].$$

Then, there is

$$y^1 = y^0 + d^1, \qquad d^1 \neq 0, \qquad d^1 \in D(y^0),$$

with

$$y^0 = y^1 + d^0, \qquad d^0 \neq 0, \qquad d^0 \in D(y^0).$$

Thus,

$$y^0 = y^0 + d^1 + d^0.$$

Since $D(y^0)$ is pointed and thus contains no subspace, $d^1 + d^0 \neq 0$, resulting in a contradiction.

(ii) Let $y^0 \in N_0 \subset Y_{N_0}$. Suppose that $y^0 \notin N[Y_{N_0}|\Lambda]$. Then, there is $y^1 \in Y_{N_0}$, $y^1 \neq y^0$, such that $y^0 \in y^1 + \Lambda$. Since $y^1 \in Y_{N_0}$, there is $y^2 \in N_0$ such that $y^1 \in y^2 + D(y^2)$. Since $y^0 \in y^1 + \Lambda$,

$$y^0 \in y^2 + D(y^2) + \Lambda = y^2 + D(y^2),$$

because $D(y^2)$ is a convex cone and $\Lambda \subset D(y^2)$. Thus, $y^0 \notin N_0$, again resulting in a contradiction. Note that $y^0 \neq y^2$ because $D(y^2)$ contains no subspace.

(iii) This part of the proof is a special case of (ii). We shall not repeat it.

(iv) Suppose that $y^0 \notin N[Y|\Lambda^0]$. Then, for some $y^1 \neq y^0$,

$$y^0 = y^1 + \Lambda \subset y^1 + D(y^1).$$

Thus, $y^0 \notin N$.   □

Remark 7.27. The assumption in (iii) of Lemma 7.7 cannot be eliminated. As an example, let $Y = Y_1 \cup Y_2$, with

$$Y_1 = \{(y_1, y_2)|y_1, y_2 \leq 0\}, \qquad Y_2 = \{(y_1, y_2)|y_1 = 1, y_2 < 1\},$$

and

$$D((y_1, y_2)) = \begin{cases} \{(d_1, d_2)|d_1, d_2 \leq 0\} & \text{if } (y_1, y_2) \in Y_1, \\ \{(d_1, d_2)|d_1 = 0, d_2 \leq 0\} & \text{if } (y_1, y_2) \in Y_2. \end{cases}$$

We see that

$$N = \{(0, 0)\},$$

$$\Lambda = \cap \{D(y)|y \in N\} = \{(d_1, d_2)|d_1, d_2 \leq 0\},$$

$$N[Y|\Lambda] = \varnothing.$$

Thus, $N[Y|\Lambda]$ does not contain N. Note that Y is not nondominance bounded.
Now, suppose that

$$\Lambda^0 = \cap \{D(y)|y \in Y\} \neq \{0\}.$$

For $n = 0, 1, 2, \ldots$, we could construct two sequences $\{Y^n\}$ and $\{\Lambda^n\}$ as follows:

$$Y^{n+1} = N[Y^n|\Lambda^n],$$

where

$$\Lambda^n = \cap \{D(y)|y \in Y^n\} \quad \text{and} \quad Y^0 = Y.$$

Since $Y^{n+1} \subset Y^n$, $\{Y^n\}$ has a limit

$$\tilde{Y} = \cap \{Y^n|0 \leqq n < \infty\}.$$

Theorem 7.31. The following results hold:
  i. for each n, $Y^n \supset N$;
  ii. $\tilde{Y} \supset N$.

Proof. We prove (i) by induction. In view of (iv) of Lemma 7.7, it suffices to show that, if $Y^n \supset N$, then $Y^{n+1} \supset N$. Suppose that

$$y^1 \in N \cap Y^n,$$

but

$$y^1 \notin Y^{n+1} = N[Y^n|\Lambda^n].$$

Then there is $y^0 \in Y^n \subset Y$ such that $y^1 \neq y^0$ and

$$y^1 \in y^0 + \Lambda^n \subset y^0 + D(y^0).$$

But this shows that $y^1 \notin N$, resulting in a contradiction.
For (ii), since $Y^n \supset Y^{n+1}$,

$$\tilde{Y} = \cap \{Y^n|0 \leqq n < \infty\}.$$

The conclusion follows immediately from (i).   □

Remark 7.28. In the above procedure, because $\Lambda^{n+1} \supset \Lambda^n$, by Lemma 7.2(iii) $N[Y|\Lambda^{n+1}] \subset N[Y|\Lambda^n]$. By induction on n, one has no difficulty in showing that $N[Y|\Lambda^n] \subset N[Y^n|\Lambda^n]$ for $n = 1, 2, \ldots$. However, it is not generally true that $N[Y|\Lambda^n] = N[Y^n|\Lambda^n]$. Consider the example given in Remark 7.27. We see that

$$\Lambda^0 = \{(d_1, d_2)|d_1 = 0, d_2 \le 0\},$$

$$Y^1 = N[Y|\Lambda^0] = \{(y_1, y_2)|y_1 \le 0, y_2 = 0\}.$$

Thus,

$$\Lambda^1 = \{(d_1, d_2)|d_1, d_2 \le 0\}, \qquad N[Y^1|\Lambda^1] = \{(0, 0)\} = N.$$

However,

$$N[Y|\Lambda^1] = \varnothing, \qquad N[Y|\Lambda^1] \ne N[Y^1|\Lambda^1].$$

Remark 7.29. The above procedure yields a sequential approximation method toward N. Although $N \subset \tilde{Y}$, it is not generally true that $N = \tilde{Y}$ even if some strong conditions are satisfied. As an example, in R^2 let

$$Y = \{(y_1, y_2)| - 1 \le y_1 \le 1, -1 \le y_2 \le 1\},$$

$$D((y_1, y_2)) = \begin{cases} \{(d_1, d_2)|d_1, d_2 \le 0\} & \text{if } y_1 \le 0, \\ \{(d_1, d_2)|d_1 \le 0, d_2 \le [y_1/(1 - y_1)]d_1\} & \text{if } 0 < y_1 < 1, \\ \{(d_1, d_2)|d_1 = 0, d_2 \le 0\} & \text{if } y_1 \ge 1. \end{cases}$$

See Figure 7.9 for $D((y_1, y_2))$, $0 < y_1 < 1$. We see that

$$\Lambda^0 = \cap \{D((y_1, y_2))|(y_1, y_2) \in Y\} = \{(d_1, d_2)|d_1 = 0, d_2 \le 0\}$$

and

$$Y^1 = N[Y|\Lambda^0] = \{(y_1, y_2)| - 1 \le y_1 \le 1, y_2 = 1\}.$$

Note that

$$\Lambda^1 = \cap \{D((y_1, y_2))|(y_1, y_2) \in Y^1\} = \Lambda^0$$

and

$$Y^2 = N[Y^1|\Lambda^1] = Y^1.$$

It is seen that

$$\tilde{Y} = Y^1 = \{(y_1, y_2)| - 1 \le y_1 \le 1, y_2 = 1\}.$$

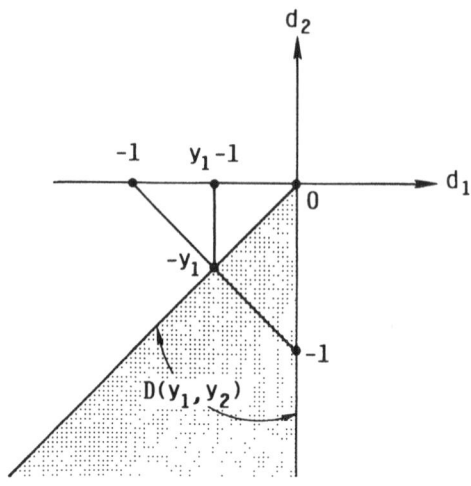

Figure 7.9

Since

$$N = \{(y_1, y_2) | 0 \leqq y_1 \leqq 1, y_2 = 1\},$$

we have

$$N \subset \tilde{Y} \quad \text{but} \quad \tilde{Y} \not\subset N.$$

Note that $D((y_1, y_2))$ is continuous over Y in the sense of the point to set mapping (see Refs. 198 and 446, for instance). The example shows that even if Y is a square and $D((y_1, y_2))$ is continuous, the limit set of our deduction procedure is not necessarily equal to the set of all nondominated solutions. Thus, when we get $\tilde{Y}$, it is still necessary to check whether $\tilde{Y} \subset N$. The definition, as well as the results in the previous sections, would be useful for the checking.

Theorem 7.31 allows us to locate the set N according to Figure 7.10 which was proposed in Ref. 494.

Figure 7.10 is self-explanatory. Although the method guarantees a convergent set containing the N-points, it may not be effective and efficient, as Remark 7.29 points out. One notices that the approximation can be more efficient if Lemma 7.7(iii) can be incorporated in Box (1). According to the lemma, if Y is nondominance bounded, to locate Λ^n we can focus on those points that are candidates for N-points. That is, we do not have to worry about $D(y)$ if we are sure that y is a dominated point. This observation and the desire to more efficiently reach a set containing good alternatives suggest the following heuristic method in Figure 7.11, which was proposed in Ref. 502.

Let us explain the method according to the flow chart.

Box 0. One first explores the relationships among the criteria and locates some plausible aspiration levels and tradeoffs among the criteria. Then one uses the results of the previous sections and chapters to locate a set of initial "good" alternatives corresponding to different aspiration levels and tradeoffs, using mathematical programming if necessary. One can also start with the points which, respectively, maximize the individual criteria. This initial set is denoted by Z^0. It need not contain too many points, but it should be fairly representative so as to avoid missing possible N-points.

Box 1. One should first estimate $D(y)$ for some representative points in Z^n and find their intersection for Λ^n. The more representative points are considered, the smaller is Λ^n and the less chance there is to miss N-points; but it may take longer to find the final solutions. In estimating $D(y)$, one can use the definition to locate it directly, or one can use the bounds of tradeoff ratios to locate it indirectly as Remark 7.19 explained.

Box 2. Here one can use the results of the previous sections to locate the entire set of Z^{n+1} or to locate a representative set for Z^{n+1}, depending on how much we want to avoid missing some N-points.

Boxes 3 and 4. Box 3 is a comparison to see if the process has reached a steady state. If not, the process will continue to box 4, which serves to eliminate dominated points in Z^{n+1}. Here $\hat{D}(Z^{n+1})$ denotes the set of estimated

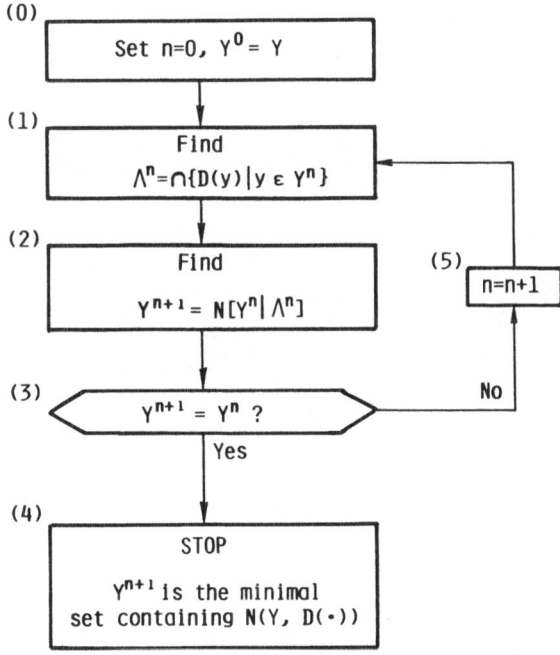

Figure 7.10

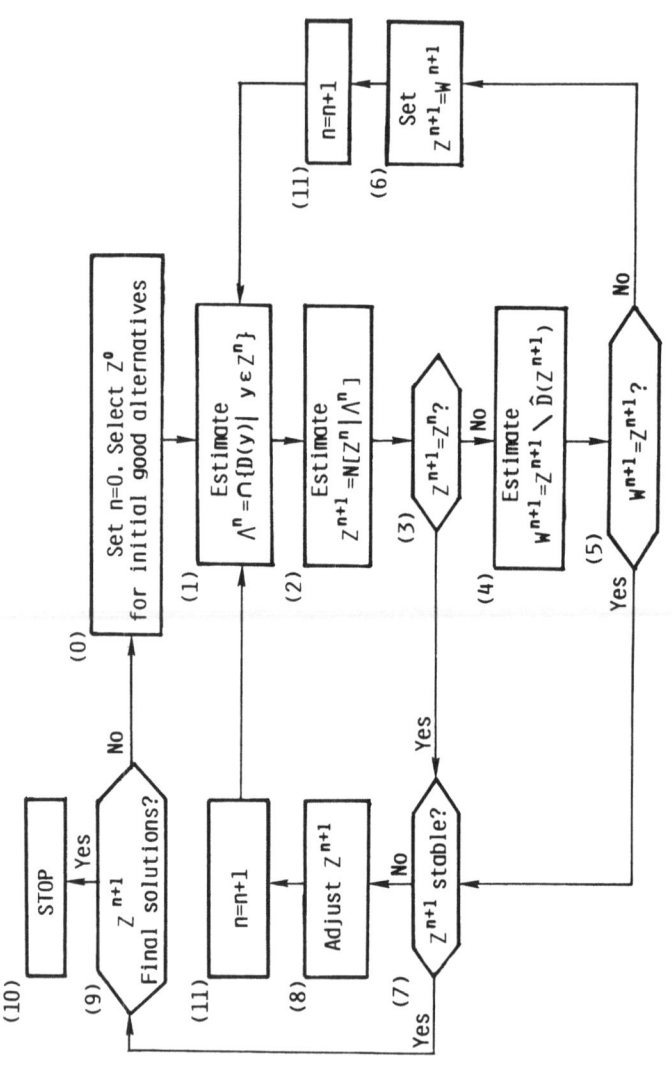

Figure 7.11

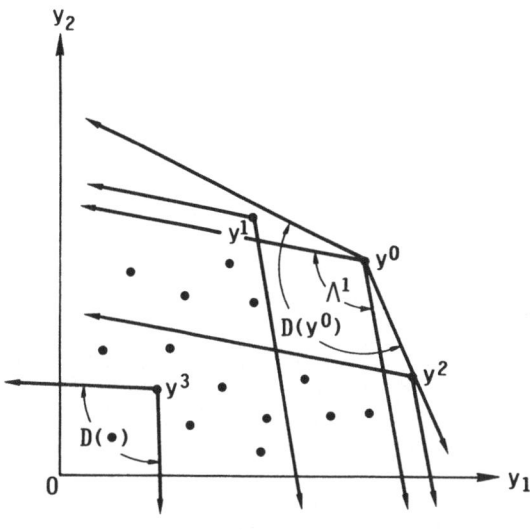

Figure 7.12

dominated points in Z^{n+1}, and W^{n+1} will be the remaining "good" alternatives after the elimination.

Boxes 5 and 6. Box 5 is a comparison to see if the elimination in box 4 is effective. If $W^{n+1} = Z^{n+1}$, then Z^{n+1} can be a set of N-points and the process can reach its steady state. Box 6 is to replace Z^{n+1} by W^{n+1} for the next operation.

Boxes 7-10. Z^{n+1} is *stable* if no element in Z^{n+1} is dominated by any other element in Z^{n+1}, and every element outside of Z^{n+1} is dominated by some element in Z^{n+1}. [This is similar to stable solutions in n-person games in characteristic form (see Ref. 301 for instance).] If this condition is "fulfilled," Z^{n+1} probably can be the set of all N-points. In box 9, nondominance is verified by the results of previous sections. If Z^{n+1} is the set of all N-points, the process is stopped at box 10 with Z^{n+1} as the set containing a final good decision. Otherwise, the process should be repeated again from box 0. If Z^{n+1} is not stable, then Z^{n+1} contains some dominated points or there are N-points not contained in Z^{n+1}. We shall accordingly either eliminate the dominated points from Z^{n+1} or add new N-points into Z^{n+1}. This adjustment on Z^{n+1} is performed at box 8.

Box 11. This step is obvious for changing the "step variable" in the process.

Example 7.11. Consider Y and $D(\cdot)$ given in Figure 7.12. Y is the set of all dotted points including $\{y^0, y^1, y^2, y^3\}$.

Using the first method (Figure 7.10), we start with $\Lambda^0 = \Lambda^\leqq$ and find $Y^1 = \{y^0, y^1, y^2\}$. Taking $\Lambda^1 = \cap \{D(y^j)|j = 1, 2, 3\}$, we have $Y^1 = N(Y^1, \Lambda^1)$. Thus, the process of Method 1 converges with $\hat{Y} = Y^1$.

Now one uses Method 2 (Figure 7.11) and starts with $Z^0 = \{y^0, y^1, y^2, y^3\}$ and $\Lambda^0 = \Lambda^\leqq$ in boxes 1 and 2, respectively, then box 2 will produce $Z^1 = \{y^0, y^1, y^2\}$ ($= Y^1$ in method 1). Note that $Z^1 \neq Z^0$. Boxes 3 and 4 will make $W^1 = \{y^0\} \neq Z^1$. The process then goes through boxes 5, 6, 11, 1, 2 with $Z^2 = \{y^0\}$. Since $Z^2 = W^2$, the process goes through boxes 3, 4, 5, and 7. At boxes 7 and 9 we verify that indeed Z^2 is stable and contains the only N-point. The process ends with $Z^2 = \{y^0\}$ as the final solution.

Observe that Method 1 and Method 2 can be used for interactive processes by involving the decision maker (DM) in each or some of the steps. The DM's inputs in estimating Λ^n, Z^n, $D(\cdot)$, and W^n can greatly simplify the process, not to mention that it is a learning process which, when properly executed, can be very interesting and convincing to both the researchers and the DM. The process will, in all practical cases, terminate in a finite number of steps: either final solutions are obtained, or a time limit is reached, or no further useful conclusion can be derived to justify continuation of the process.

7.6. Further Comments

Using domination structures we have discussed a common denominator of preferences described in the previous Chapters 2-6. Constant dominated (or preferred) cone structures are a direct extension of Pareto preference. We have been motivated by the results derived in Ref. 495 of Yu and Refs. 198 and 199 of Hazen and Morin. Many interesting problems need to be addressed. For instance, in domination structures we have $\mathcal{D}(y) = \{LP(y), P(y), LD(y), D(y), T(y, >), T(y, <)\}$. In applications, we do not need all of them. Sections 7.3 and 7.5 are just some examples. An interesting research problem is to study under what conditions of $\{>\}$ and Y, a subset of $\mathcal{D}(y)$ will be adequate for specifying $\{>\}$ without losing N-points. What are the interrelationships among those components of $\mathcal{D}(y)$? [For instance, under what conditions do we have $LP(y) = P(y)$, $LP(y) = T(y, <)$, $LP(y) = -LD(y)$?] Finally we emphasize again that domination structures $\mathcal{D}(y)$ are just *local* properties for $\{>\}$, like properties of continuity and differentiability of real-valued functions. One might be interested in conditions under which information of $\{>\}$ can be recovered by $\mathcal{D}(y)$ (like solving differential equations).

The reader who is interested in generalized constraint qualifications, necessary conditions for LN-points, and steepest descending computing methods is referred to Hazen and Morin's work (Ref. 198). Those who are interested in the sensitivity of N with respect to dominated cones are referred to Tanino and Sawaragi's work (Ref. 446) and Hazen and Morin (Ref. 199).

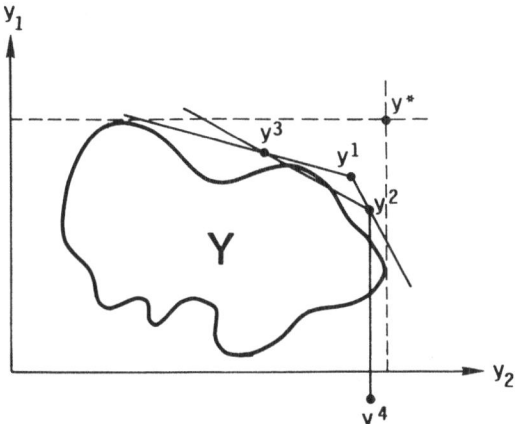

Figure 7.13

Before we close this chapter, it is worthwhile to emphasize that domination structure is another important concept to study complex preference information. The concept complements those discussed in Chapters 3–6. In application all of these concepts (Chapters 3–7) are our tools. Depending on the situation some tools may be more convenient to use than others. However, all of them combined seem to offer the most powerful set of tools. For instance, transitivity on $\{>\}$ and some preference ranking can offer much information on preference. In Figure 7.13, Y and the ideal point y^* are as depicted. If we assume transitivity on $\{>\}$ and $\{y>\} = D(y)$ to be a convex cone, and we also know (ranking information) that $y^1 > y^2 > y^3$, then we can assure that $D(y^1)$ contains the convex cone generated by $y^3 - y^1$ and $y^2 - y^1$, and $D(y^2)$ contains the convex cone generated by $y^3 - y^2$ and $y^4 - y^2$ if we know that more is better for y_1.

The process of using the ideal point y^* as the initial reference point and using pairwise comparisons to obtain ranking may offer much information on domination structures and the preference. How to extract the most preference information with a minimum of effort (comparisons and computations) is certainly an art! The more we practice, the better the result will be. We shall leave it to the reader!

7.7. Appendix: A Constructive Proof of Theorem 7.3

Lemma 7.8. Let Λ be an acute polyhedral cone in R^q with dim $\Lambda = s$. Then, for each containing open half-space H of Λ, there exist s independent vectors $U = \{u^i | i = 1, \ldots, s\}$ such that the polyhedral cone Λ_1 generated by U enjoys $\Lambda \subset \Lambda_1 \subset H \cup \{0\}$.

Proof. Let $H = \{x | c \cdot x > 0\}$, and $V = \{v^j | j = 1, \ldots, r\}$ be a generator of Λ. Let $B = \{b^k | k = 1, \ldots, q\}$ be a basis of R^q such that (i) b^1 is the projection of c into L, which is the linear space spanned by V, (ii) $\{b^k | 1 \leq k \leq s\}$ are independent vectors in L, and (iii) $\{b^k | s \leq k \leq q\}$ are independent vectors in the orthogonal space of L. Then, with respect to B, each v^j could be written as $v^j = (x_1^j, x_2^j, \ldots, x_s^j, 0, \ldots, 0)$, with $x_1^j > 0$ and $c = (1, 0, \ldots, 0, c_{s+1}, \ldots, c_q)$. Since we are dealing with cones, without loss of generality, we could assume $x_1^j = 1$.

Let us consider $U(M) = \{u^i | 1 \leq i \leq s\}$, with

$$u^1 = (1, M, 0, \ldots, 0, 0, \ldots, 0),$$

$$u^2 = (1, 0, M, \ldots, 0, 0, \ldots, 0),$$

$$\cdots$$

$$u^{s-1} = (1, 0, 0, \ldots, M, 0, \ldots, 0),$$

$$u^s = (1, -M, -M, \ldots, -M, 0, \ldots, 0).$$

Note that the jth component, u_j^i, of the ith vector, $1 \leq i \leq s - 1$, is given by

$$u_j^i = \begin{cases} 1 & \text{if } j = 1, \\ M & \text{if } j = i + 1, \\ 0 & \text{otherwise.} \end{cases}$$

Obviously, $U(M)$ is a set of s independent vectors. Observe that $U(M) \subset H$, because $c \cdot u^j = 1 > 0, j = 1, \ldots, s$. Thus, the cone generated by $U(M)$ is also contained by $H \cup \{0\}$. It suffices now to show that

$$v^j = \sum_{i=1}^{s} \lambda_i^j u^i, \qquad \lambda_i^j \in R^1, \qquad \lambda_i^j \geq 0 \qquad \text{for } j = 1, 2, \ldots, r, \qquad (7.24)$$

when M is large enough. Now, given

$$v^j = (1, x_2^j, \ldots, x_s^j, 0, \ldots, 0)$$

and $U(M)$, by treating λ_i^j as variable, (7.24) could be written as

$$\sum_{i=1}^{s} \lambda_i^j \quad 1, \qquad (7.25)$$

$$\lambda_k^j M - \lambda_s^j M = x_{k+1}^j, \qquad k = 1, 2, \ldots, s - 1. \qquad (7.26)$$

Note that (7.26) implies that

$$\lambda^j_k = \lambda^j_s + x^j_{k+1}/M, \qquad k = 1, 2, \ldots, s - 1. \tag{7.27}$$

By (7.25) and (7.27), we get

$$s\lambda^j_s + \sum_{k=2}^{s} x/M = 1 \quad \text{or} \quad \lambda^j_s = 1/s - \sum_{k=2}^{s} x^j_k/sM. \tag{7.28}$$

By (7.27) and (7.28), it is clear that, when M is large enough, we could have a nonnegative solution λ^j_i for (7.24). Since $V = \{v^j\}$ is a finite set, by selecting a large value for M, (7.24) could be satisfied for all $j = 1, 2, \ldots, r$. $\square$

Lemma 7.9. Let

$$U = \{u^i | 1 \leq i \leq r\}$$

be a set of r independent vectors in R^q and

$$\Lambda = \left\{ \sum_{i=1}^{r} \lambda_i u^i \Big| -\infty < \lambda_i < \infty, i = 1, \ldots, s; 0 \leq \lambda_i, i = s + 1, \ldots, r \right\}.$$

Then, Λ^* contains a $(q - r)$-dimensional subspace and dim $\Lambda^* = q - s$.

Proof. Select

$$\{u^k | r + 1 \leq k \leq q\},$$

so that

$$U_1 = \{u^i | 1 \leq i \leq q\}$$

is a set of q independent vectors in R^q. Let U_1 also denote the square matrix with u^i in its ith column. Since U_1 is nonsingular, $U_1^T U_1$ is positive definite and nonsingular. Let A be the inverse of $U_1^T U_1$ and set $W = U_1 A$. Then,

$$U_1^T W = U_1^T U_1 A = [U_1^T U_1][U_1^T U_1]^{-1} = I.$$

Thus, the columns of W and columns of U_1 satisfy

$$u^i \cdot w^j = \begin{cases} 1 & \text{if } i = j, \\ 0 & \text{otherwise.} \end{cases}$$

Since A is nonsingular, W is also a basis in R^q. Thus, every $x \in R^q$ can be written as

$$x = \sum_{i=1}^{q} \alpha_i w^i.$$

If $x \in \Lambda^*$ and $v \in \Lambda$, then

$$x \cdot v = \left(\sum_{i=1}^{q} \alpha_i w^i \right) \left(\sum_{i=1}^{r} \lambda_i u^i \right) = \sum_{i=1}^{r} \alpha_i \lambda_i \leqq 0.$$

Since $-\infty < \lambda_i < \infty$, $i = 1, \ldots, s$, and $\lambda_i \geqq 0$, $i = s + 1, \ldots, r$, the inequality can be held for all $v \in \Lambda$ iff $\alpha_i = 0$ for $i = 1, \ldots, s$, $\alpha_i \leqq 0$ for $i = s + 1, \ldots, r$, and $-\infty < \alpha_i < \infty$ for $i = r + 1, \ldots, q$. This shows that Λ^* contains a $(q - r)$-dimensional subspace and $\dim \Lambda^* = q - s$.   □

Corollary 7.6. Let Λ be a polyhedral cone in R^q. Then,
   i. if L is the maximal subspace contained by Λ and $\dim L = s$, then $\dim \Lambda^* = q - s$;
   ii. if Λ is acute, then $\dim \Lambda^* = q$ and Int $\Lambda^* \neq \emptyset$.

Proof. *For* (ii): Note that, by Lemma 7.8, there are r, $r \leqq q$, independent vectors which generate a polyhedral cone $\Lambda_1 \supset \Lambda$. In view of Lemma 7.9, $\dim \Lambda_1^* = q$. Since $\Lambda_1^* \subset \Lambda^*$, this shows that $\dim \Lambda^* = q$, and Int $\Lambda^* \neq \emptyset$.
   For (i): By theorem 7.1, we can write $\Lambda = L + \Lambda'$, where Λ' is an acute polyhedral cone contained by $L^\perp$, where $L^\perp$ is the orthogonal space of L. Note that, if $\dim \Lambda = r$, then $\dim \Lambda' = r - s$. In view of Lemma 7.8 we can find $r - s$ independent vectors which generate Λ_0 such that $\Lambda' \subset \Lambda_0 \subset L^\perp$. On the other hand, we could select $r - s$ independent vectors from the generators of Λ' and let Λ_2 be the cone generated by those vectors. Note that

$$\Lambda_0 \supset \Lambda' \supset \Lambda_2, \qquad L + \Lambda_0 \supset L + \Lambda' = \Lambda \supset L + \Lambda_2.$$

Observe that both $L + \Lambda_0$ and $L + \Lambda_2$ can be written in the form stated in Lemma 7.9, and

$$\dim (L + \Lambda_0)^* = \dim (L + \Lambda_2)^* = q - s.$$

Since

$$(L + \Lambda_2)^* \supset (L + \Lambda')^* = \Lambda^* \supset (L + \Lambda_0)^*,$$

we see that $\dim \Lambda^* = q - s$.   □

Proof of Theorem 7.3. (i) Suppose that Int $\Lambda^* \neq \emptyset$. Let $y^0 \in$ Int Λ^* and

$$H = \{x | y^0 \cdot x < 0\}.$$

We show that Cl $\Lambda \subset H \cup \{0\}$ or $y^0 \cdot x < 0$ for all $x \in$ Cl Λ and $x \neq 0$. Suppose that there is $x^0 \in$ Cl Λ, $x^0 \neq 0$, such that

$$y^0 \cdot x^0 \geqq 0. \tag{7.29}$$

Since $\Lambda^* = (\text{Cl } \Lambda)^*$ and $y^0 \in$ Int Λ^*, there is N_{y^0}, a neighborhood of y^0, such that, for all $y \in N_{y^0}$,

$$y \cdot x^0 \leqq 0. \tag{7.30}$$

If we treat $y \cdot x^0$ as a linear function in y, (7.29) and (7.30) show that the linear function assumes its maximum point at y^0, an interior point of N_{y^0}. This is impossible, unless $y \cdot x^0$ is constant over N_{y^0}. Obviously, the latter is also impossible, because $x^0 \neq 0$. This proves the necessity.

In order to show the sufficiency, let Cl Λ be contained by $H = \{x | a \cdot x > 0\}$, that is, Cl $\Lambda \subset H \cup \{0\}$. Let $H_1 = \{x | a \cdot x = 1\}$. We first show that Cl $\Lambda \cap H_1$ is bounded.

Suppose that Cl $\Lambda \cap H_1$ is not bounded. We could select a sequence $\{x^n\}$ from Cl $\Lambda \cap H_1$ such that $n \leqq |x^n|$. Let $y^n = x^n/|x^n|$. We see that $a \cdot y^n = a \cdot x^n/|x^n| = 1/|x^n|$. Since $\{y^n\}$ is a sequence on the compact unit sphere, we can find a subsequence $\{y^{n_i}\}$ which converges to a point y^0 in the unit sphere. Note that $a \cdot y^0 = 0$. On the other hand, since each $y^{n_i} \in$ Cl Λ and Cl Λ is closed, $y^0 \in$ Cl Λ or $a \cdot y^0 > 0$. This leads to a contradiction.

Since Cl $\Lambda \cap H_1$ is closed and bounded, we could select a polygon $P \supset$ Cl $\Lambda \cap H_1$ on H_1. The cone that is generated by the extreme points of P is an acute polyhedral cone. Recall that $S_1 \subset S_2$ implies that $S_1^* \supset S_2^*$. In view of Corollary 7.6, we see that Int $(\text{Cl } \Lambda)^* =$ Int $\Lambda^* \neq \emptyset$.

(ii) The fact that Int $\Lambda^* \subset \{y | y \cdot x < 0$, for all nonzero $x \in$ Cl $\Lambda\}$ can be proved by a contradiction similar to that for the necessity of (i). In order to show that Int $\Lambda^* \supset \{y | y \cdot x < 0$ for all nonzero $x \in$ Cl $\Lambda\}$, let y^0 be such that $y^0 \cdot x < 0$ for all nonzero $x \in$ Cl Λ. It suffices to show that there is a neighborhood N_{y^0} of y^0 such that $y \cdot x \leqq 0$ for all $x \in$ Cl Λ and $y \in N_{y^0}$. Assume the contrary. Let $\Lambda_1 = \{x | x \in$ Cl $\Lambda, |x| = 1\}$. Since a cone is uniquely determined by its unit vectors, we could find two sequences: $\{y^n\} \to y^0$ and $\{x^n\} \subset \Lambda_1$ such that $y^n x^n > 0$. Since Λ_1 is compact, there is a convergent subsequence $\{x^t\} \to x^0 \in \Lambda_1$. We see that

$$\lim_{t \to \infty} y^t \cdot x^t = y^0 \cdot x^0 \geqq 0.$$

This contradicts the statement that $y^0 \cdot x^0 < 0$ for all nonzero $x \in$ Cl Λ. $\square$

Exercises

7.1. Let $\Lambda = \{(d_1, d_2)|2d_1 + d_2 \leqq 0, 2d_1 + 3d_2 \leqq 0\}$.
    a. Sketch Λ and Λ^*.
    b. Λ can be written as $\Lambda = \{\sum a_i v^i | a_i \geqq 0, a_i \in R^1\}$, where v^i represents a generator of Λ. Write out Λ using a set of generators $V = \{v^i | i = 1, \ldots, m\}$. (Note that the generators of Λ may not be unique.)
    c. Find the generators of Λ^*.

7.2. In R^2, let $Y_1 = \{(y_1, y_2)|2y_1 + y_2 \leqq 2\}$ and $Y_2 = \{(y_1, y_2)|y_1^2 + y_2^2 \leqq 1\}$.
    a. Is $Y_1 \backslash Y_2$ $\Lambda^{\geqq}$-convex? Justify your answer.
    b. Is $Y_1 \backslash Y_2$ $\Lambda^{\leqq}$-convex? Justify your answer.
    c. Is $Y_1 \cup Y_2$ Λ_i-convex? where Λ_i, $i = 1, \ldots, 4$, defined, respectively, by

$$\Lambda_1 = \Lambda^{\leqq},$$

$$\Lambda_2 = \Lambda^{\geqq},$$

$$\Lambda_3 = \{(d_1, d_2)|d_1 \geqq 0, d_2 \leqq 0\},$$

$$\Lambda_4 = \{(d_1, d_2)|d_1 \leqq 0, d_2 \geqq 0\}.$$

    Justify your answer.

7.3. Consider the following problem:

$$f_1(x) = \quad x_1 + 2x_2 - x_1^2 + x_2^2,$$

$$f_2(x) = -x_1 + \quad x_2 - x_1^2 - x_2^2,$$

$$\text{s.t. } x_1 + x_2 \leqq 10,$$

$$2x_1 - x_2 \geqq 3,$$

$$x_1, x_2 \geqq 0.$$

    Let $Y = \{(f_1(x), f_2(x))|x \in X\}$.
    a. Specify the shape of Y. What kind of cone convexity does Y enjoy? [Hint: what combinations of (λ_1, λ_2) would make $\lambda_1 f_1 + \lambda_2 f_2$ concave?]
    b. Let $\Lambda = \{(d_1, d_2)|-d_1 + d_2 \leqq 0, -d_1 + 2d_2 \leqq 0\}$. How do you find $N[Y|\Lambda]$?
    c. Let $\Lambda = \{(d_1, d_2)|d_1 + d_2 \leqq 0, d_1 + 2d_2 \leqq 0\}$. How do you find $N[Y|\Lambda]$?

7.4. Find the domination structures, i.e., identify $LP(y)$, $GP(y)$, $LD(y)$, $GD(y)$, $T(y, >)$, $T(y, <)$ and $T(y, \sim)$ for
    a. the preference represented by an additive value function

$$v(y) = \sum_{i=1}^{q} \lambda_i y_i;$$

    b. Pareto preference;
    c. lexicographic ordering;
    d. the preference induced by a compromise solution (see Chapter 4);
    e. the preference induced by a satisficing solution;

    f. the preference represented by a differentiable concave value function;

    g. the preference represented by a differentiable convex value function.

    h. Compare the domination structures you described for (a)-(g). What assumptions are needed for the individual preferences to be valid? In applications, what precaution do we need to take in assuming the individual assumptions?

7.5. Describe the domination structures for the preferences revealed in Exercises 2.2 and 2.7, respectively. What are the implications for applicability of domination structures?

7.6. In R^2, let the preference be represented by

$$v(y, \varepsilon) = (2 + \varepsilon_1)y_1 + (5 + \varepsilon_2)y_2,$$

where ε_1 and ε_2 are random variables ranging over $]-0.2, 0.2[$ and $]-1, 1[$, respectively.

    a. Identify the convex cone, Λ, in which $v(y, \varepsilon)$ is always decreasing irrespective of the value of ε.

    b. Show that the maximum point of $v(y, \varepsilon)$ over Y, no matter what value ε is, is contained in $N[Y|\Lambda]$.

    c. Let $Y_1 = \{(y_1, y_2)|(y_1 - 2)^{1.2} + (y_2 - 2)^{1.2} \leq 2\}$. Is Y_1 Λ-convex? Find $N[Y_1|\Lambda]$ graphically.

    d. Let $Y_2 = \{(y_1, y_2)|0 \leq y_1 \leq 2, 0 \leq y_2 \leq 2\}$ and $Y = Y_1 \backslash Y_2$. Is Y Λ-convex? Can you find all $N[Y|\Lambda]$ by the additive method? Justify your answer.

    e. Suppose that the "true" value function, $u(y)$, is decreasing in Λ and can be nonlinear, instead of the representation of $v(y, \varepsilon)$. Then the maximum point of $u(y)$ over Y may not be obtained by the additive weight method when Y is not Λ-convex, but the maximum point is still contained in $N[Y|\Lambda]$. Does this imply that, in order not to omit good solutions, it is better to work with $N[Y|\Lambda]$, instead of working directly with the additive method? Justify your answer.

7.7. Suppose that $q = 2$ and it is revealed that $v(y) = w_1 y_1 + w_2 y_2$, $w_1, w_2 > 0$, with $1 \leq w_2/w_1 \leq 3$, is a representation of preference. Find a constant dominated cone structure for the preference.

7.8. Suppose that $q = 3$ and it is revealed that $v(y) = w_1 y_1 + w_2 y_2 + w_3 y_3$, $w_i > 0$, $i = 1, 2, 3$, with $1 \leq w_2/w_1 \leq 2$ and $1/2 \leq w_2/w_3 \leq 1$, is a representation of the preference. Find a constant dominated cone structure for the preference.

7.9. "Given $y^1 > y^2$, it is not necessarily true that $d = y^2 - y^1$ is a local or global dominated direction for y^1." Is the above statement true? Why or why not? Find a similar statement for the case of real-valued functions (instead of $\{>\}$). Discuss under what conditions the above statement holds.

7.10. Consider a value function

$$v = \tfrac{1}{16} y_1 y_2,$$

where

$$y_1 = f_1(x_1, x_2) = 4x_1 - 2x_2,$$

$$y_2 = f_2(x_1, x_2) = -x_1 + 5x_2,$$

and

$$X: \begin{cases} 4x_1 + 3x_2 \leqq 48, \\ -3x_1 + 2x_2 \leqq 12, \\ x_1 \leqq 10, \\ x_2 \leqq 8, \\ x_1, x_2 \geqq 0. \end{cases}$$

a. Sketch the outcome space Y and the contour of v in Y.
b. Identify the optimal solution $y^* \in Y$ that will maximize the above value function.
c. Sketch the global dominated cone of y^*, $D(y^*)$. In this problem $D(y^*) = $ LD (y^*). Why?
d. For each $y \in Y$, identify its domination structures [i.e., find LP (y), GP (y), LD (y), GD (y), $T(y, >)$, $T(y, <)$, and $T(y, \sim)$]. What are the relationships among the components of the domination structures?

7.11. Refer to Example 7.10. Let us re-index the criteria as $f_1(x) = \text{var}[R(x)]$ and $f_2(x) = E[R(x)]$ and let $Y = \{(f_1(x), f_2(x)) | x \in X\}$.
a. What kind of cone convexity does Y enjoy? Specify the shape of Y.
b. As "the more volatile portfolio requires higher expected return to justify risk," it is revealed that for each unit increase of f_1, the decision maker wants to be compensated by at least 0.05 of f_2. Identify the convex cone in Y in which the preference is reducing as revealed. Let such a convex cone be Λ.
c. Identify $N[Y|\Lambda]$.

7.12. Continuation of Exercise 3.4. Define

$$\Lambda_1 = \{(d_1, d_2) | d_1 + d_2 \leqq 0, -d_1 + d_2 \leqq 0\},$$

$$\Lambda_2 = \{(d_1, d_2) | -d_1 + d_2 \leqq 0, -d_1 - d_2 \leqq 0\}.$$

i. For $i = 1, 2$, is Y Λ_i-convex? Justify your answer.
ii. Identify $N[Y|\Lambda_i]$, $i = 1, 2$.

7.13. Continuation of Exercise 3.9. Define

$$\Lambda_1 = \{(d_1, d_2) | d_1 + 0.5d_2 \leqq 0, -d_1 + 0.5d_2 \leqq 0\},$$

$$\Lambda_2 = \{(d_1, d_2) | d_1 + d_2 \leqq 0, d_1 - 0.5d_2 \leqq 0\}.$$

i. For $i = 1, 2$, is Y Λ_i-convex? Justify your answer.
ii. Identify $N[Y|\Lambda_i]$, $i = 1, 2$.

7.14. Verify the statements of Remark 7.5(i) and (ii).

7.15. Explore under what condition the following equalities hold:
a. LP $(y) \cup$ LD $(y) \cup$ LI $(y) \cup \{0\} = R^q$,
b. $T(y, >) \cup T(y, <) \cup T(y, \sim) = R^q$.

7.16. a. Prove Theorem 7.6.
b. Prove Theorem 7.7.
c. Prove Theorem 7.8.

7.17. Verify the following statements:
a. Y is convex iff Y is $\{0\}$-convex;

    b. Y is directionally convex in u iff Y is U-convex, where U is the negative half-line generated by u.

7.18. a. Prove Theorem 7.18.
    b. Prove Theorem 7.19.
    c. Prove Theorem 7.20.
    d. Prove Theorem 7.21.

7.19. Refer to Remark 7.20. Derive decomposition theorems similar to those described in Section 3.4.3 for general constant dominated cone structures.

7.20. Prove Theorem 7.22.

7.21. Use Theorem 7.5 and Theorems 3.12 and 3.13 to derive conditions for proper $N[Y|\Lambda]$-points when Λ is an acute polyhedral dominated cone.

7.22. Suppose that $\text{Cl }\Lambda$ is not a polyhedral cone. In view of Theorem 7.2, Λ^* cannot be a polyhedral cone. In this case, we could construct two polyhedral cones Λ_1 and Λ_2 such that $\Lambda_1 \subset \Lambda \subset \Lambda_2$. By invoking (ii) of Lemma 7.2, we get $N[Y|\Lambda_2] \subset N[Y|\Lambda] \subset N[Y|\Lambda_1]$.
    Let $\{H_1^k|k = 1, \ldots, q_1\}$ and $\{H_2^k|k = 1, \ldots, q_2\}$ be the generators of Λ_1^* and Λ_2^*, respectively. For any arbitrary i, j such that $1 \leqq i \leqq q_1$ and $1 \leqq j \leqq q_2$, define $M_1^0(i) = \{y^0|H_1^i y^0 > H_1^i y$ for all $y \in Y_{i1}(y^0), y \neq y^0\}$, where $Y_{i1}(y^0) = \{y|y \in Y, H_1^k y \geqq H_1^k y^0, k = 1, \ldots, q_1, k \neq i\}$, and $M_2^0(j) = \{y^0|H_2^j y^0 > H_2^j y$ for all $y \in Y_{j2}(y^0), y \neq y^0\}$, where $Y_{j2}(y^0) = \{y|y \in Y, H_2^k y \geqq H_2^k y^0, k = 1, \ldots, q_2, k \neq j\}$. Show that $M_1^0(i) \supset N[Y|\Lambda] \supset M_2^0(j)$.

7.23. A set Y is said to be piecewise Λ-convex if there is a finite partition $\mathcal{Y} = \{Y_k|k = 1, \ldots, m\}$ of Y such that each Y_k is Λ-convex. Prove the following results:
    a. Let $\mathcal{Y} = \{Y_k|k = 1, 2, \ldots, m\}$ be a partition of Y. Then $\cup\{Y^0(\lambda)|\lambda \in \text{Int }\Lambda^*\} \subset N[Y|\Lambda] \subset \bigcup_{k=1}^{m} N[Y_k|\Lambda]$, where $Y^0(\lambda) = \{y^0 \in Y|\lambda \cdot y^0 = \sup \lambda \cdot y, y \in Y\}$.
    b. If $\Lambda^\perp \neq \{0\}$ and Y is piecewise Λ-convex with respect to $\mathcal{Y}$, then

$$\bigcup_{k=1}^{m} N[Y_k|\Lambda] \subset \bigcup_{k=1}^{m} [\cup\{Y_k^0(\lambda)|\lambda \in \Lambda^*, \lambda \neq 0\}],$$

where $Y_k^0(\lambda) = \{y^0 \in Y_k|\lambda \cdot y^0 = \sup \lambda \cdot y, y \in Y_k\}$.

7.24. a. $\{>\}$ is LP-regular at y^0 if for each $h \in \text{Int LP}(y^0)$ there is a neighborhood $M(y^0, h)$ of y^0 and $\varepsilon > 0$ such that $y + \delta h > y$ for all $\delta \in]0, \varepsilon[$ and $y \in M(y^0, h)$. Show that if $\{>\}$ is LP-regular at y^0 then $-\text{Int LP}(y^0) \subset \text{LD}(y^0)$.
    b. $\{>\}$ is LD-regular at y^0 if for each $h \in \text{Int LD}(y^0)$ there is a neighborhood $R(y^0, h)$ of y^0 and $\varepsilon > 0$ such that $y + \delta h < y$ for all $\delta \in]0, \varepsilon[$ and $y \in R(y^0, h)$. Show that if $\{>\}$ is LD-regular at y^0 then $-\text{Int LD}(y^0) \subset \text{LP}(y^0)$.
    c. $\{>\}$ is regular at y^0 if it is LP-regular and LD-regular at y^0. Prove that if $\{>\}$ is regular at y^0 then $-\text{Cl LP}(y^0) = \text{Cl LD}(y^0)$.
    d. Show that $\{>\}$ induced by a differentiable value function with nonzero gradient is regular.

7.25. Extend the concepts of pseudoconcave functions and quasi-concave functions to $>$-pseudoconcave and $>$-quasi-concave functions, and specify suitable conditions on $\{>\}$ so that known results of the former can be extended to the latter. [For instance, f is $>$-pseudo concave over X iff f is differentiable over X and $f(x) > f(x^0)$ implies that $\nabla f(x^0) \cdot (x - x^0) \in \text{Int LP}(x^0)$.] Show that if x^0 is an LN_X-point then x^0 is also an N_X-point.

7.26. Assume that $\{y<\} = P(y)$ is a convex cone for all y. Derive results and methods similar to those discussed in Section 7.5.

7.27. Prove Lemma 7.6.

Suggested Reading

The following references are particularly pertinent to this chapter: 40, 51, 58, 195, 198, 199, 205, 233, 235, 265, 287, 301, 317, 324, 358, 438, 443, 445, 446, 481, 492, 494, 495, 502, 508.

8

Linear Cases, MC- and MC²-Simplex Methods

We shall discuss some interesting properties of N-points when X is a polyhedron and the *constant dominated cone* is also polyhedral in Section 8.1. A multiple-criteria (MC) simplex method is then described in Section 8.2 to facilitate the location of N-points. Identification of optimal weights for each nondominated extreme point is also discussed. In Section 8.3 we shall discuss a method to generate all N-points using known extreme N-points. As a natural extension of MC simplex methods, a multiple-criteria and multiple-constraint level (MC²) simplex method is then described in Section 8.4. Potential solutions and duality theory of MC- and MC²-simplex are then discussed. MC- and MC²-simplex methods have been extensively studied by Gal (see Ref. 155) in the context of sensitivity analysis of linear programming problems. Here we use them as tools for locating N-points as well as formulating solution concepts. Note that throughout this chapter we focus on constant dominated cone structures for N-points, unless otherwise specified.

8.1. N-Points in the Linear Case

In order to simplify the presentation, let us assume that

$$X = \{x \in R^n \mid Ax \leq d, x \geq 0\}, \qquad A \text{ is of order } m \times n. \qquad (8.1)$$

Let $C = C_{q \times n}$ be a matrix with its kth row denoted by C^k so that $C^k \cdot x$, $k = 1, \ldots, q$, is the kth objective function. The criteria space is thus given by

$$Y = \{Cx \mid x \in X\}. \qquad (8.2)$$

Given a convex dominated cone Λ and x^1, $x^2 \in X$, x^1 is dominated by x^2 if $Cx^1 \in Cx^2 + '\Lambda$. A point $x \in X$ is a N-point if it is not dominated by any other feasible point of X; otherwise it is a D-point.

For simplicity, the sets of all N-points and all D-points will be denoted by N and D, respectively.

Lemma 8.1. Given a dominated cone Λ, suppose x^1, $x^2 \in X$ and $x^1 \in D$. Then $[x^1, x^2[\subset D$, where

$$[x^1, x^2[= \{\alpha x^1 + (1 - \alpha)x^2 | 0 < \alpha \leq 1\},$$

is the line segment bounded by x^1 and x^2 including x^1 but excluding x^2.

Proof. Since $x^1 \in D$, there are $x^3 \in X$ and $h \in '\Lambda$, so that $Cx^1 = Cx^3 + h$. Thus, for any α, $0 < \alpha \leq 1$,

$$C(\alpha x^1 + (1 - \alpha)x^2) = \alpha Cx^3 + \alpha h + (1 - \alpha)Cx^2$$

$$= C(\alpha x^3 + (1 - \alpha)x^2) + \alpha h.$$

Since

$$\alpha x^3 + (1 - \alpha)x^2 \in X, \qquad \alpha h \in '\Lambda \text{ and } h \neq 0,$$

we see that $\alpha x^1 + (1 - \alpha)x^2 \in D$ [it is dominated by $\alpha x^3 + (1 - \alpha)x^2$]. From the lemma, we obtain Theorem 8.1 immediately. $\qquad\square$

Theorem 8.1. The set D is convex.

Let K be an arbitrary convex subset of X and ri K be its relative interior. Suppose that $x^1 \in$ ri K. By the accessibility lemma (see Ref. 438, p. 90) for each $x^2 \in$ Cl K we have $[x^1, x^2) \subset$ ri K.

Theorem 8.2 (i) Suppose $x^1 \in$ ri K and $x^1 \in D$. Then ri $K \subset D$.
(ii) Suppose $x^1 \in$ ri K and $x^1 \in N$. Then Cl $K \subset N$.

Proof. (i) This follows immediately from the accessibility lemma and Lemma 8.1.

For (ii): From (i), we know that ri $K \subset N$. It suffices to show that if $x^2 \in \partial K$ (the boundary of K) then $x^2 \in N$. Suppose $x^2 \in D$. In view of Lemma 8.1, $]x^2, x^1[\subset D$. Since (the accessibility lemma) $]x^2, x^1[\subset$ ri K we thus get a contradiction of ri $K \subset N$. $\qquad\square$

Now let X_{ex} be the set of all extreme points in X and let $N_{ex} = N \cap X_{ex}$ (the set of all nondominated extreme points). We see that N_{ex} is finite.

Theorem 8.3. If X is compact, then $N \subset \mathcal{H}(N_{ex})$ (the convex hull of N_{ex}).

Proof. Suppose that x cannot be written as a convex combination of N_{ex}-points. It suffices to show that x is a D-point. Since X is compact, each point of X is a convex combination of X_{ex}. Let $X_{ex} = \{x^i | i = 1, \ldots, r\}$. By the assumption, there is at least a point $x^k \in D \cap X_{ex}$ and α_k, $1 \geq \alpha_k > 0$, $1 \leq k \leq r$, so that

$$x = \alpha_k x^k + \sum_{j \neq k} \alpha_j x^j,$$

where $\alpha_j \geq 0$, $j = 1, \ldots, r$, and $\sum_{j=1}^{r} \alpha_j = 1$. When $\alpha_k = 1$, $x = x^k$. Clearly x is a D-point. Suppose $\alpha_k < 1$. Then

$$x = \alpha_k x^k + \beta \sum_{j \neq k} \frac{\alpha_j}{\beta} x^j,$$

where $\beta = \sum_{j \neq k} \alpha_j$. Observe that $\sum_{j \neq k} (\alpha_j/\beta) x^j \in X$ and $\alpha_k + \beta = 1$. In view of Lemma 8.1, x is a D-point. $\square$

Remark 8.1. Usually $N \neq \mathcal{H}(N_{ex})$. In view of Theorem 8.3, if X is compact we could first locate the set N_{ex}, and then use N_{ex} to generate the entire set N. In Section 8.2, we shall describe a method for locating N_{ex}, and in Section 8.3 we sketch a method to generate N by N_{ex}.

Given $\lambda \in R^q$, let

$$X^0(\lambda) = \{x^0 \in X | \lambda C x^0 \geq \lambda C x, x \in X\}. \tag{8.3}$$

Thus, $X^0(\lambda)$ is the set of all maximum points of $\lambda C x$ over X. Note that $\lambda C x$ is bilinear in λ and x.

In view of Theorem 7.15 we have the following.

Theorem 8.4. Suppose the dominated cone Λ has the property that $\Lambda^{\perp} \neq \{0\}$ (i.e., Λ is not a linear space). Then

$$\bigcup \{X^0(\lambda) | \lambda \in \text{Int } \Lambda^*\} \subset N \subset \bigcup \{X^0(\lambda) | \lambda \in \Lambda^* \backslash \{0\}\}. \tag{8.4}$$

To obtain our main result (Theorem 8.5), we need the following lemma. To avoid distraction its proof is given in Appendix 8.1.

Lemma 8.2. Let Λ be a polyhedral cone and Y be a polyhedron containing the origin. Suppose for each $\alpha \in \text{ri } \Lambda^*$ there is $y \in Y$ such that $\alpha \cdot y > 0$ (i.e., there is no $\alpha \in \text{ri } \Lambda^*$ for which $y = 0$ maximizes $\alpha \cdot y$ over Y). Then $0 \in y + {}'\Lambda$ for some $y \in Y$.

Theorem 8.5. Suppose that Λ is a polyhedral cone. Then

i. $N \subset \bigcup \{X^0(\lambda) \,|\, \lambda \in \text{ri } \Lambda^*\}$,

ii. if Λ is acute, then $N = \bigcup \{X^0(\lambda) \,|\, \lambda \in \text{Int } \Lambda^*\}$.

Proof. For (i). Suppose that $x^0 \in X$ and $x^0 \notin \{X^0(\lambda) \,|\, \lambda \in \text{ri } \Lambda^*\}$. Then, for each $\lambda \in \text{ri } \Lambda^*$, there is $x \in X$ such that $\lambda Cx > \lambda Cx^0$. Let $y = Cx$ and $y^0 = Cx^0$. Then for each $\lambda \in \text{ri } \Lambda^*$ there is $y \neq y^0$, $y \in Y$ such that $\lambda \cdot y > \lambda \cdot y^0$ or $\lambda \cdot (y - y^0) > 0$. Now let $Y' = Y - \{y^0\}$. Then $0 \in Y'$ and for each $\lambda \in \text{ri } \Lambda^*$, there is $\tilde{y} \in Y'$ such that $\lambda \cdot \tilde{y} > 0$. By applying Lemma 8.2, on Y', we see that there is $y - y^0 \in Y'$, $y \in Y$, $y \neq y^0$, such that $0 \in y - y^0 + \Lambda$, or $y^0 \in y + \Lambda$. Thus, $y^0 \notin N$ and $x^0 \notin N$.

For (ii). Note, when $\text{Int } \Lambda^* \neq \varnothing$, $\text{Int } \Lambda^* = \text{ri } \Lambda^*$. Our assertion is clear from (i) and Theorem 8.4.   □

It will be shown that when Λ is a polyhedral cone, the computation of N_{ex} could be simplified a great deal. Suppose Λ is not a polyhedral cone. We may first find a polyhedral cone $\Lambda' \subset \Lambda$, and use the N-points with respect to Λ' as the first step to approximate the set N (with respect to Λ) (because each N-point with respect to Λ is also an N-point with respect to Λ' [see Lemma 7.2(ii)]. To verify whether an N-point with respect to Λ' is also an N-point with respect to Λ, we could use the results discussed in Chapter 7.

From now on we shall assume that Λ is a polyhedral cone.

Recall that, if Λ is a polyhedral cone, then Λ^* is also a polyhedral cone. Furthermore, there is a set of vectors $H = \{H^1, \ldots, H^r\}$ so that

$$\Lambda^* = \left\{ \sum_{i=1}^{r} \alpha_i H^i \,\middle|\, \alpha_i \geq 0 \right\}.$$

In matrix notation, let $\alpha = (\alpha_1, \ldots, \alpha_r)$ and let H denote the matrix with H^k as its kth row, $k = 1, \ldots, r$. Then,

$$\Lambda^* = \{\alpha H \,|\, \alpha \geq 0\} \tag{8.5}$$

and

$$\text{ri } \Lambda^* = \{\alpha H \,|\, \alpha > 0\}. \tag{8.6}$$

Now if $\lambda = \alpha H$, then $\lambda Cx = \alpha HCx$. Given α, let

$$X^0(\alpha) = \{x^0 \in X \,|\, \alpha HCx^0 \geq \alpha HCx, x \in X\}. \tag{8.7}$$

From (8.3), (8.6), and (8.7), we see that

$$\bigcup \{X^0(\lambda) \,|\, \lambda \in \text{ri } \Lambda^*\} = \bigcup \{X^0(\alpha) \,|\, \alpha > 0\}. \tag{8.8}$$

From (8.8) and Theorem 8.5, we have (compare with Theorem 7.5)

Theorem 8.6. Suppose that Λ is a polyhedral cone. Then
i. $N \subset \bigcup \{X^0(\alpha) \,|\, \alpha > 0\}$
ii. $N = \bigcup \{X^0(\alpha) \,|\, \alpha > 0\}$ if Λ is acute, where $X^0(\alpha)$ is defined in (8.7).

Remark 8.2. In view of (8.7) and Theorem 8.6, by treating HCx as a new set of objective functions, we see that in the process of finding N, each polyhedral dominated cone can be converted into the form of $\Lambda^{\leqq}$ (the dimension of $\Lambda^{\leqq}$ depends on the number of vectors in H). When Λ is acute, our conversion yields all of N. However, when Λ is not acute (i.e., Cl Λ contains a nontrivial subspace), in view of (i) of Theorem 8.6, we obtain a set containing N. To actually obtain N, some verification through the definition is needed.

In view of Remark 8.2 and Theorem 8.6 we may and will assume that $\Lambda = \{d \in R^q \,|\, d \leqq 0\} = \Lambda^{\leqq}$, to simplify the presentation.

Remark 8.3. Although each polyhedral dominated cone can be transformed into $\Lambda^{\leqq}$, from the point of view of computing all N_{ex}-points this transformation may not always be the most efficient. (See Remark 8.5.)

8.2. MC-Simplex Method and N_{ex}-Points

In this section, we shall describe an MC-simplex method which may be regarded as a natural generalization of the simplex method. The method not only identifies N_{ex}-points but also locates the set of optimal weights for each N_{ex}-point. This is discussed in Section 8.2.1. The decomposition of the weight space by N_{ex}-points is discussed in Section 8.2.2. Connectedness, adjacency of N_{ex}-points, and a method of locating N_{ex} set are described in Section 8.2.3.

8.2.1. MC-Simplex Method and Set of Optimal Weights

Recall that (for simplicity) we limit ourselves to the dominated cone $\Lambda = \Lambda^{\leqq}$ and Int $\Lambda^* = \Lambda^>$.

As $X^0(\lambda)$ is the set of the maximum solutions of λCx over X, treating λC as a row vector, we see that to find $X^0(\lambda)$ is a linear programming problem. Without loss of generality we can assume that $d \geqq 0$. For the extension to other types of d see Refs. 77 and 78, for instance. Note that d indicates the vector of right-hand side values of the linear programming problem.

From (8.1), by adding slack variables, X could be redefined as the set of all $x \in R^{m+n}$, $x \geqq 0$ and

$$(A, I_{m \times m})x = d. \tag{8.9}$$

Our new C becomes $(C, 0_{q \times m})$. The purpose of this step is to get the identity matrix in $A' = (A, I)$. If there is an identity matrix in A, this step can be skipped.

Given x, let $v = v(x) = \lambda Cx$. Thus,

$$v - \lambda Cx = 0. \tag{8.10}$$

Now, let $B = B_{m \times m}$ be a nonsingular submatrix (also called a basis) of (A, I) and B' be the remaining submatrix. Thus, we can write (renumber the indices if necessary)

$$(A, I) = (B, B'). \tag{8.11}$$

Let $(x_B, x_{B'})$ and $(\lambda C_B, \lambda C_{B'})$ be the variables and criterion coefficients associated with B and B', respectively. Then (8.9) and (8.10) together could be written as

$$\begin{pmatrix} 0 & B & B' \\ 1 & -\lambda C_B & -\lambda C_{B'} \end{pmatrix} \begin{bmatrix} v \\ x_B \\ x_{B'} \end{bmatrix} = \begin{bmatrix} d \\ 0 \end{bmatrix}. \tag{8.12} \tag{8.13}$$

which, after dropping the first column and v, can be written as

$$\begin{bmatrix} I & B^{-1}B' \\ 0 & \lambda C_B B^{-1}B' - \lambda C_{B'} \end{bmatrix} \begin{bmatrix} x_B \\ x_{B'} \end{bmatrix} = \begin{bmatrix} B^{-1}d \\ \lambda C_B B^{-1}d \end{bmatrix} \tag{8.14} \tag{8.15}$$

where $(8.14) = B^{-1} \cdot (8.12)$ [i.e., premultiply by B^{-1} on both sides of (8.12)] and $(8.15) = (8.13) + \lambda C_B \cdot (8.14)$.

We see that from (8.14) and (8.15) if $B^{-1}d \geqq 0$ then $(x_B, x_{B'}) = (B^{-1}d, 0)$ is a basic feasible solution with a value $\lambda C_B B^{-1}d$.

Dropping λ in (8.15) and the variables, we obtain from (8.14) and (8.15) the following basic format of MC-simplex method:

$$
\begin{array}{|ccc|}
\hline
I & B^{-1}B' & B^{-1}d \\
\hline
0 & C_B B^{-1}B' - C_{B'} & C_B B^{-1}d \\
\hline
\end{array} \tag{8.16}
$$

When the columns of (A, I) are not arranged according to (8.11), the general tableaus corresponding to (8.12)-(8.15) and (8.16) are given by

(dropping the first column)

$$
\begin{array}{c|cc}
A & I & d \\
\hline
-\lambda C & 0 & 0
\end{array}
\tag{8.17}
$$

$$
\begin{array}{ccc}
\hline
B^{-1}A & B^{-1} & B^{-1}d \\
\hline
\lambda C_B B^{-1}A - \lambda C & \lambda C_B B^{-1} & \lambda C_B B^{-1}d \\
\hline
\end{array}
$$

(8.18)

(8.19)

$$
\begin{array}{ccc}
\hline
B^{-1}A & B^{-1} & B^{-1}d \\
\hline
C_B B^{-1}A - C & C_B B^{-1} & C_B B^{-1}d \\
\hline
\end{array}
$$

(8.20)

(8.21)

Note that (8.18) and (8.19) together are the simplex tableau for maximizing $\lambda Cx, x \in X$; while (8.20) and (8.21) together are the MC-simplex tableau when B is the basis. Since each basis B is uniquely associated with a column index subset

$$
J = \{j_1, j_2, \ldots, j_m\} \subset \{1, 2, \ldots, m + n\},
$$

we could use J to represent B and $J' = \{1, \ldots, m + n\}\backslash J$ to represent B'. We shall also call J a basis whenever B is a basis.

Rewrite (8.20) and (8.21) as

$$
\left[\begin{array}{c|c}
Y & Y^0 \\
\hline
Z & V
\end{array}\right],
\tag{8.22}
$$

where

$$
Y = [B^{-1}A, B^{-1}], \qquad Y^0 = B^{-1}d,
$$
$$
Z = [C_B B^{-1}A - C, C_B B^{-1}],
\tag{8.23}
$$

and

$$
V = C_B B^{-1}d.
\tag{8.24}
$$

Similarly, (8.18) and (8.19) can be written as

$$
\left[\begin{array}{c|c}
Y & Y^0 \\
\hline
z(\lambda) & v(\lambda)
\end{array}\right],
\tag{8.25}
$$

where Y and Y^0 are as above, while

$$z(\lambda) = [\lambda C_B B^{-1} A - \lambda C, \lambda C_B B^{-1}], \tag{8.26}$$

$$v(\lambda) = \lambda C_B B^{-1} d. \tag{8.27}$$

Given a basis J, to emphasize J, the corresponding Z and $z(\lambda)$ etc., will be denoted by $Z(J)$ and $z(\lambda, J)$, respectively.

Comparing (8.22) with (8.25), (8.23) with (8.26), (8.24) with (8.27), we immediately obtain

$$z(\lambda, J) = \lambda Z(J), \tag{8.28}$$

$$v(\lambda, J) = \lambda V(J). \tag{8.29}$$

Theorem 8.7. (i) $x(J)$, the basic feasible solution of J, maximizes λCx over X for all

$$\lambda \in \Lambda(J) = \{\lambda \,|\, \lambda Z(J) \geqq 0\} \tag{8.30}$$

(ii) $x(J) \in N_{\text{ex}}$ iff $\Lambda^> \cap \Lambda(J) \neq \varnothing$.

Proof. (i) This follows from the known result that $x(J)$ is a maximum solution of λCx over X iff $z(\lambda, J) \geqq 0$. The assertion follows immediately from (8.28) and (8.30).

(ii) This follows immediately from (i) and Theorem 8.5 because $\text{Int}\,(\Lambda^\leqq)^* = \Lambda^>$. $\qquad\square$

To verify (ii), we can use the following.

Theorem 8.8. Given a basis J, $\Lambda(J) \cap \Lambda^> \neq \varnothing$ [or $x(J)$ is an N_{ex}-point] iff $w_{\max} = 0$, which is the solution for

$$\max w = \sum_{j=1}^{q} e_j,$$

$$\text{s.t. } Z(J)x + e = 0,$$

$$x \geqq 0, \qquad e \geqq 0,$$

where

$$e = (e_1, e_2, \ldots, e_q).$$

Proof. By Motzkins' theorem of the alternative (Ref. 307; p. 28) exactly one of the following two systems has a solution:

$$\text{(I)} \quad \lambda > 0, \qquad Z^T \lambda \geqq 0,$$

or

$$(\text{II})\quad x_1 + Zx = 0, \qquad x_1 \geq 0, \qquad x \geqq 0.$$

However, (II) is equivalent to

$$(\text{II}')\quad Zx \leq 0, \qquad x \geqq 0,$$

which has no solution iff $w_{max} = 0$. Note that (I) has a solution iff $\Lambda(J) \cap \Lambda^> \neq \varnothing$. This completes our proof. $\square$

Remark 8.4. The conditions of the above theorem are easily checked since only the submatrix Z of the original tableau is required. The related simplex tableau is

$Z(J)$	I	0
$\mathbb{1} \cdot Z(J)$	0	0

,

where $\mathbb{1} = (1, \ldots, 1)$ is a vector of ones. To facilitate testing, we append to the MC-simplex tableau (8.20) and (8.21) an extra row corresponding to the objective function $\mathbb{1} \cdot C$. This extra row will also be required for other verifications. In practice, since $Z_j(J) = 0$ for all $j \in J$, they can be dropped in the verification procedure.

Before we give an example, the following are worth mentioning: From (8.22), let $M = [{}^Y_Z]_{(m+q) \times (m+n)}$. Then M has the following characteristics [refer to (8.16) also]

    i. the submatrix $\{Y_j | j \in J\}$ (Y_j is column j of Y), when properly permutated, forms the identity matrix of order $m \times m$;

    ii. the submatrix $\{Z_j | j \in J\}$ is the zero matrix of order $q \times m$.

    For $j \in J'$, define

$$\theta_j = \begin{cases} y_{p0}/y_{pj} = \min_r \{y_{r0}/y_{rj} | y_{rj} > 0\} \\ \infty \qquad \text{if each } y_{rj} \leqq 0, \qquad r = 1, \ldots, m, \end{cases} \tag{8.31}$$

where y_{r0} is the rth component of Y^0 (the "right-hand side" of the simplex tableau) and y_{rj} is the component of Y at the rth row and the jth column.

If $\theta_j < \infty, j \in J'$, by *introducing the jth column into the basis*, we shall mean to convert M_j into E_p in the next tableau, where E_p is the pth column of the identity matrix of order $m + q$, and p, determined by (8.31), is such that (p, j) is the pivot element. With this kind of operation, at each iteration M can enjoy the above properties (i)-(ii), and Y and Z can be easily computed.

Let Z^k (or Z_j) denote the kth row (or the jth column) of Z. The following can be readily established by using known results in the ordinary simplex method and the definition of N-points. (See Exercise 8.5.) (Note that the row Z^k, $k = 1, \ldots, q$, is associated with $C^k x$ in the single-criterion linear programming problem.)

Theorem 8.9. (i) If $j \in J'$ and $\theta_j = \infty$, then for each $\lambda \in \Lambda^j_\infty = \{\lambda \,|\, \lambda Z_j < 0\}$, λCx has an unbounded solution over X.

(ii) If $j \in J'$ and $\theta_j Z_j \leq 0$ (i.e., $\theta_j > 0$ and $Z_j \leq 0$), then $x(J) \notin N_{\text{ex}}$.

(iii) If $j \in J'$ with $\theta_j < \infty$ and $\theta_j Z_j \geq 0$, then $x(J^0) \notin N_{\text{ex}}$, where J'' is the new basis by introducing j into the basis.

(iv) Let j, $k \in J'$ with θ_j, $\theta_k < \infty$ and J_j and J_k be the new bases by introducing j and k, respectively, into the basis. If $\theta_j Z_j \geq \theta_k Z_k$ then $x(J_j) \notin N_{\text{ex}}$.

(v) If $Z^i_j > 0$ for all $j \in J'$ for some i, then $x(J)$ uniquely maximizes $C^i x$ over X and $x(J) \in N_{\text{ex}}$.

Example 8.1. Let C, A, and d be as follows:

$$C = \begin{bmatrix} -2 & -1 & -3 \\ 1 & -1 & 0 \end{bmatrix},$$

$$A = \begin{bmatrix} 1 & 1 & 2 \\ 0 & 1 & -1 \\ 1 & 1 & 1 \end{bmatrix},$$

$$d = (3, 2, 2)^T.$$

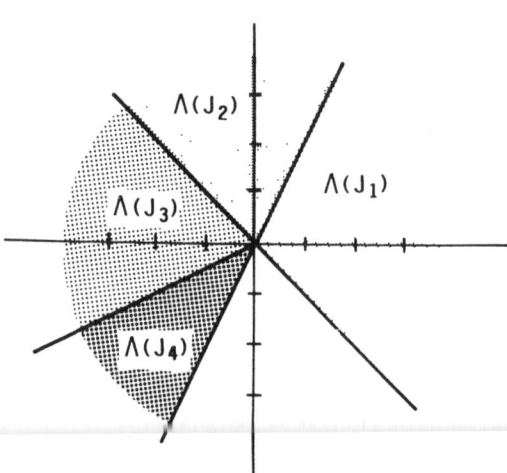

Figure 8.1

The initial MC-simplex tableau is given by Tableau 8.1. From Tableau 8.1, we obtain the basis $J_1 = \{4, 5, 6\}$, the basic feasible solution $x(J_1) = (0, 0, 0, 3, 2, 2)$, the objective values $Cx(J_1) = (0, 0)^T$. Note that $Z^1 \geq 0$ and $Z_j^1 > 0$ for all $j \in J'$. Thus,

		x_1	x_2	x_3	x_4	x_5	x_6	RHS
		1	1	2	1	0	0	3
	A	0	1	-1	0	1	0	2
Tableau 8.1. $J_1 = \{4, 5, 6\}$		①	1	1	0	0	1	2
	C	2	1	3	0	0	0	0
		-1	1	0	0	0	0	0
	$1 \cdot C$	1	2	3	0	0	0	0
		0	0	①	1	0	-1	1
		0	1	-1	0	1	0	2
		1	1	1	0	0	1	2
Tableau 8.2. From pivoting $(3, 1)$		0	-1	1	0	0	-2	-4
of Tableau 8.1, $J_2 = \{1, 4, 5\}$		0	2	1	0	0	1	2
		0	1	2	0	0	-1	-2
		0	0	1	1	0	-1	1
		0	1	0	1	1	-1	3
		1	①	0	-1	0	2	1
Tableau 8.3. From pivoting $(1, 3)$		0	-1	0	-1	0	-1	-5
of Tableau 8.2, $J_3 = \{1, 3, 5\}$		0	2	0	-1	0	2	1
		0	1	0	-2	0	1	-4
		0	0	1	1	0	-1	1
		-1	0	0	2	1	-3	2
		1	1	0	-1	0	2	1
Tableau 8.4. From pivoting $(3, 2)$		1	0	0	-2	0	1	-4
of Tableau 8.3, $J_4 = \{2, 3, 5\}$		-2	0	0	1	0	-2	-1
		-1	0	0	-1	0	-1	-5

$x(J_1)$ uniquely maximizes C^1x. Indeed, it also uniquely maximizes $C^1x + C^2x$ over X. Clearly, $x(J_1) \in N_{\text{ex}}$. (Why?) The corresponding $\Lambda(J_1)$, the set of optimal weights, is given by $\Lambda(J_1) = \{\lambda \mid \lambda[\begin{smallmatrix} 2 & 1 & 3 \\ -1 & 1 & 0 \end{smallmatrix}] \geq 0\}$. Refer to Figure 8.1.

Now let us pivot $(3, 1)$ of Tableau 8.1. We obtain Tableau 8.2. The corresponding basis $J_2 = \{1, 4, 5\}$, $x(J_2) = (2, 0, 0, 1, 2, 0)$, and $Cx(J_2) = (-4, 2)^T$. Let us use Theorem 8.8 and Remark 8.4 to verify if $x(J_2) \in N_{\text{ex}}$. [Even if we know beforehand that $x(J_2) \in N_{ex}$ because $x(J_2)$ uniquely maximizes C^2x over X. (Why?)] We construct the corresponding tableau in Tableau 8.5. Note that the columns of $j \in J_2$ are dropped. After one iteration we obtain $w_{max} = 0$. By Theorem 8.8,

Tableau 8.5

	x_2	x_3	x_6	e_1	e_2	RHS
Z	-1	1	-2	1	$\cdot 0$	0
	2	1	①	0	1	0
	1	2	-1	0	0	0
	3	3	0	1	2	0
	2	1	1	0	1	0
	3	3	0	0	1	0

$x(J_2) \in N_{ex}$. The corresponding set of optimal weights is given by $\Lambda(J_2) = \{\lambda \,|\, (\lambda_1, \lambda_2) [\begin{smallmatrix} -1 & 1 & -2 \\ 2 & 1 & 1 \end{smallmatrix}] \geqq 0\}$ as depicted in Figure 8.1.

Next, by pivoting $(1, 3)$ of Tableau 8.2 we obtain Tableau 8.3. The corresponding basis is $J_3 = \{1, 3, 5\}$, $x(J_3) = (1, 0, 1, 0, 3, 0)$, and $Cx(J_3) = (-5, 1)^T$. Since $Z_4 < 0$, Theorem 8.9(ii) implies $x(J_3) \notin N_{ex}$. The corresponding set of optimal weights is $\Lambda(J_3) = \{\lambda \,|\, (\lambda_1, \lambda_2) [\begin{smallmatrix} -1 & -1 & -1 \\ 2 & -1 & 2 \end{smallmatrix}] \geqq 0\}$ as depicted in Figure 8.1. Note that $\Lambda(J_3) \cap \Lambda^> = \varnothing$.

Finally, by pivoting $(3, 2)$ of Tableau 8.3 we obtain Tableau 8.4. The corresponding basis is $J_4 = \{2, 3, 5\}$, $x(J_4) = (0, 1, 1, 0, 2, 0)$, and $Cx(J_4) = (-4, -1)^T$. Note that $Cx(J_4) \leq Cx(J_2)$. Thus, $x(J_4) \notin N_{ex}$. This can be verified by Theorem 8.8. Tableau 8.6 is constructed for this purpose.

Tableau 8.6

x_1	x_4	x_6	e_1	e_2	RHS
1	-2	1	1	0	0
-2	1	-2	0	1	0
-1	-1	-1	0	0	0
-3	0	-3	1	2	0
-2	1	-2	0	1	0
-3	0	-3	0	1	0

In one iteration, we obtain unbounded solutions (because of the columns of x_1 or x_6). Thus, $w_{max} > 0$, and $x(J_4) \notin N_{ex}$. In Figure 8.1, we notice that $\Lambda(J_4) \cap \Lambda^> = \varnothing$.

8.2.2. Decomposition of the Weight Space

Given a basis J, the set of optimal weights $\Lambda(J)$ is defined as in (8.30). Suppose that for some $k \in J'$, $Z_k(J) \neq 0$ and there is $\lambda \in {}'\Lambda(J)$ so that $\lambda Z_k(J) = 0$. Then $Z_k(J)$ will be called *an effective constraint* of $\Lambda(J)$. Suppose that $Z_k(J) = 0$, $k \in J'$. We will call $Z_k(J)$ a *null constraint*.

Let us introduce the kth column into the basis. Suppose that (p, k) or y_{pk} is the pivot element. We will produce an adjacent basis K such that $K' = J' \cup \{j_p\}\backslash\{k\}$. Without confusion (rearrange the indices, if necessary), let $p = j_p$. Then

$$K' = J' \cup \{p\}\backslash\{k\}. \tag{8.32}$$

For simplicity let $Z = Z(J)$ and $W = Z(K)$. We want to study the relation between $\Lambda(J)$ and $\Lambda(K)$.

Suppose that $Z_k(J)$ is a null constraint. Then $W = Z$ and $\Lambda(J) = \Lambda(K)$. If $Z_k(J)$ is an effective constraint, by the Gaussian technique we obtain

$$W_j = \begin{cases} 0 & \text{if } j \in K, \\ -Z_k/y_{pk} & \text{if } j = p \in K', \\ Z_j - y_{pj}Z_k/y_{pk} & \text{if } j \in K'\backslash\{p\}. \end{cases} \tag{8.33}$$

where $\{y_{ij}\}$ are components of Y of (8.22). Since (p, k) is the pivot element, $y_{pk} > 0$.

Let

$$H_k = \{\lambda \,|\, \lambda Z_k = 0\}. \tag{8.34}$$

Since $y_{pk} > 0$, $\lambda(-Z_k/y_{pk}) \geq 0$ if and only if $\lambda Z_k \leq 0$. We see that

$$\Lambda(K) \subset \{\lambda \,|\, \lambda Z_k \leq 0\}. \tag{8.35}$$

But,

$$\Lambda(J) \subset \{\lambda \,|\, \lambda Z_k \geq 0\}. \tag{8.36}$$

We see from (8.34)–(8.36), that H_k is a hyperplane in R^q, which separates the polyhedral cones $\Lambda(K)$ and $\Lambda(J)$.

Next, since $\lambda \in H_k$ implies that $\lambda Z_k = 0$, we have

$$H_k \cap \Lambda(J) = \{\lambda \,|\, \lambda Z_k = 0, \lambda Z_j \geq 0, j \in J'\backslash\{k\}\}, \tag{8.37}$$

and from (8.33) we also have

$$H_k \cap \Lambda(K) = \{\lambda \,|\, \lambda Z_k = 0, \lambda Z_j \geq 0, j \in K'\backslash\{p\}\}. \tag{8.38}$$

However from (8.32), we have $K'\backslash\{p\} = J'\backslash\{k\}$. Thus, (8.35)–(8.38) imply that

$$H_k \cap \Lambda(J) = H_k \cap \Lambda(K) = \Lambda(J) \cap \Lambda(K). \tag{8.39}$$

We summarize the above results in the following theorem.

Theorem 8.10. Given a basis J, let $k \in J'$ and K be the new basis obtained by introducing k into the basis.
  (i) Suppose that $Z_k(J)$ is a null constraint. Then $\Lambda(J) = \Lambda(K)$.
  (ii) Suppose that $Z_k(J)$ is an effective constraint of $\Lambda(J)$. Then H_k, defined as in (8.34), separates $\Lambda(J)$ and $\Lambda(K)$ as in (8.35) and (8.36). Furthermore, the equalities of (8.39) hold.

Example 8.2. (Continuation of Example 8.1.) Refer to Tableau 8.1 and Figure 8.1. Note that $Z_1(J_1)$ is an effective constraint of $\Lambda(J_1)$. By introducing column 1 into the basis we obtain the new basis J_2. Figure 8.1 reflects the properties of Theorem 8.10 between $\Lambda(J_1)$ and $\Lambda(J_2)$. Note that $Z_3(J_1)$ is not an effective constraint of $\Lambda(J_1)$. The properties of Theorem 8.10 may not be valid for $\Lambda(J_1)$ and $\Lambda(J_5)$, where $J_5 = \{3, 5, 6\}$ which is obtained by introducing column 3 into the basis. (Check it!) The reader may find it instructive to study the separation properties of the bases J_2, J_3, and J_4. (See Exercise 8.6.)

Observe that for a given λ, $\lambda C x$ will either have an unbounded or an optimal solution over X. In either case, λ will be contained by some Λ_∞^j or $\Lambda(J_k)$ [where Λ_∞^j as specified in Theorem 8.9(i) is an open half-space], so that when $\lambda \in \Lambda_\infty^j$, $\lambda C x$ has unbounded solutions and when $\lambda \in \Lambda(J_k)$, J_k is an optimal basis [Theorem 8.7(i)]. Since we have only a finite number of bases and each basis has only a finite number of columns, we know that there is a finite number of Λ_∞^j and $\Lambda(J_k)$ which cover R^q and $\Lambda^>$, the weight space for the criteria. This observation leads to the following.

Theorem 8.11. There is a finite number of Λ_∞^j, $j = 1, \ldots, p$ and $\Lambda(J_k)$, $k = 1, \ldots, r$, such that $R^q \subset \bigcup \{\Lambda_\infty^j | j = 1, \ldots, p\} \cup \{\Lambda(J_k) | k = 1, \ldots, r\}$.

As a corollary, we have the following.

Corollary 8.1. There is a finite number of Λ_∞^j, $j = 1, \ldots, p$ and $\Lambda(J_k)$, $k = 1, \ldots, r$, such that each Λ_∞^j or $\Lambda(J_k)$ has a nonempty intersection with $\Lambda^\cong$ and
  i. $\Lambda^> \subset \bigcup \{\Lambda_\infty^j | j = 1, \ldots, p\} \cup \{\Lambda(J_k) | k = 1, \ldots, r\}$;
  ii. $\Lambda^> \cap [\bigcup \{\Lambda(J_k) | k = 1, \ldots, r\}]$ is a convex cone.

Proof. (i) is straightforward from Theorem 8.11 because $\Lambda^> \subset R^q$. In order to see (ii), observe that $\lambda C x$ cannot simultaneously have an optimal solution and an unbounded solution. Thus, $\{\Lambda_\infty^j\}$ and $\{\Lambda(J_k)\}$ are mutually disjoint, and thus $\Lambda^> \cap (\bigcup \{\Lambda(J_k) | k = 1, \ldots, r\}) = \Lambda^> \cap \text{comp}\,[\bigcup \{\Lambda_\infty^j | j = 1, \ldots, p\}] = \Lambda^> \cap [\bigcup \{\text{comp}\,\Lambda_\infty^j | j = 1, \ldots, p\}]$, where "comp" designates the complement to a set. Our conclusion is now clear because comp Λ_∞^j is a closed half-space. $\square$

Remark 8.5. Corollary 8.1 indicates that $\Lambda^>$ can be decomposed into a finite number of convex cones. Theorem 8.10 suggests that if we pivot the columns of effective constraints of $\Lambda(J)$, we can "flip over" the covering of $\Lambda^>$ when the effective constraints are properly chosen. This suggests that one may locate N_{ex} through a process of covering $\Lambda^>$ by $\{\Lambda(J_k)\}$ and $\{\Lambda_\infty^j\}$. Unfortunately, this process proves to be ineffective in locating N_{ex}. This is because (i) it may not be easy to trace the covering of $\Lambda^>$, (ii) N_{ex}-points may correspond to multiple bases which produce several $\Lambda(J_k)$, and (iii) λCx may have alternative optimal bases and the correspondence between $\{\Lambda(J_k)\}$ and N_{ex}-points may not be one-to-one. The following example is constructed (see Ref. 509) to illustrate the above difficulties (ii) and (iii). We shall leave the details for the interested reader to verify. (See Exercise 8.8.)

Example 8.3.

$$C = \begin{bmatrix} 1 & 2 & -1 & 3 & 2 & 0 & 1 \\ 0 & 1 & 1 & 2 & 3 & 1 & 0 \\ 1 & 0 & 1 & -1 & 0 & -1 & -1 \end{bmatrix},$$

$$A = \begin{bmatrix} 1 & 2 & 1 & 1 & 2 & 1 & 2 \\ -2 & -1 & 0 & 1 & 2 & 0 & 1 \\ -1 & 0 & 1 & 0 & 2 & 0 & -2 \\ 0 & 1 & 2 & -1 & 1 & -2 & -1 \end{bmatrix},$$

$$d^T = (16, 16, 16, 16) \quad \text{and} \quad x \in R^7.$$

The set of all N_{ex}-points (bases) is given by Tableau 8.7 (note that slack variables have been added).

Tableau 8.7

		Corresponding basis	Values of criterion functions			Corresponding subset of Λ
			C^1x	C^2x	C^3x	
Nondominated	x^1	$\{5, 9, 10, 11\}$	16	24	0	$\Lambda(x^1)$
extreme	x^2	$\{4, 9, 10, 11\}$	48	32	-16	$\Lambda(x^2)$
points	x^3	$\{1, 9, 10, 11\}$	16	0	6	$\Lambda(x^3)$
	x^4	$\{1, 3, 9, 10\}$	0	8	16	$\Lambda(x^4)$
	x^5	$\{3, 4, 9, 10\}$	16/3	64/3	16/3	$\Lambda(x^5)$
	x^6	$\{3, 5, 9, 10\}$	16/3	64/3	16/3	$\Lambda(x^6)$
Some other	$x^{1(3)}$	$\{1, 5, 10, 11\}$	16	24	0	$\Lambda(x^{1(3)})$
degenerate	$x^{2(1)}$	$\{1, 4, 10, 11\}$	48	32	-16	$\Lambda(x^{2(1)})$
bases	$x^{2(2)}$	$\{3, 4, 10, 11\}$	48	32	-16	$\Lambda(x^{2(2)})$
	$x^{6(1)}$	$\{1, 3, 5, 9\}$	16/3	64/3	16/3	$\Lambda(x^{6(1)})$

Here $x^1 = (0, 0, 0, 0, 8, 0, 0)$, $x^2 = (0, 0, 0, 16, 0, 0, 0)$, $x^3 = (16, 0, 0, 0, 0, 0, 0)$, $x^4 = (8, 0, 8, 0, 0, 0, 0)$, $x^5 = (0, 0, 32/3, 16/3, 0, 0, 0)$, and $x^6 = (0, 0, 16/3, 0, 16/3, 0, 0)$.

Note that for each N_{ex}-point x^j, its associated $\Lambda(x^j)$ can be obtained from the multicriteria simplex tableau. In order to give a two-dimensional graphical representation of the parametric space in R^3, we first normalize it by $\lambda_1 + \lambda_2 + \lambda_3 = 1$, which yields $\lambda_1 = 1 - \lambda_2 - \lambda_3$. By deleting the redundant constraints of each $\Lambda(x^j)$, we obtain $\{\Lambda(x^j)\}$ as follows. The graphical representation of $\{\Lambda(x^j)\}$ is given by Figure 8.2.

$$\Lambda(x^1) = \left\{\lambda \left| \frac{3\lambda_2}{2} - \lambda_3 \geqq 0; \frac{3\lambda_2}{2} + 3\lambda_3 \geqq 2; \frac{3\lambda_2}{2} + 3\lambda_3 \leqq 2 \right.\right\},$$

$$\Lambda(x^2) = \{\lambda \,|\, 4\lambda_3 \leqq 2; 3\lambda_2 + 6\lambda_3 \leqq 4; 3\lambda_2 + 6\lambda_3 \leqq 4\},$$

$$\Lambda(x^3) = \{\lambda \,|\, 3\lambda_2 + 2\lambda_3 \leqq 2; 4\lambda_3 \geqq 2; -3\lambda_2 + 2\lambda_3 \geqq 0\},$$

$$\Lambda(x^4) = \left\{\lambda \left| -\frac{3\lambda_2}{2} + 3\lambda_3 \geqq 1; -\frac{3\lambda_2}{2} + 3\lambda_3 \geqq 1; \frac{3\lambda_2}{2} + \lambda_3 \geqq 1 \right.\right\},$$

$$\Lambda(x^5) = \{\lambda \,|\, -\lambda_2 + 2\lambda_3 \leqq \tfrac{2}{3}; \lambda_2 + 2\lambda_3 \geqq \tfrac{4}{3}\},$$

$$\Lambda(x^6) = \{\lambda \,|\, -\lambda_2 + 2\lambda_3 \leqq \tfrac{2}{3}; \lambda_2 + 2\lambda_3 \geqq \tfrac{4}{3}\},$$

and

$$\Lambda(x^{1(3)}) = \left\{\lambda \left| 2\lambda_2 + \frac{8\lambda_3}{3} \leqq 2; \frac{3\lambda_2}{2} + 3\lambda_3 \geqq 2; \tfrac{1}{2}\lambda_2 - \tfrac{1}{3}\lambda_3 \geqq 0 \right.\right\},$$

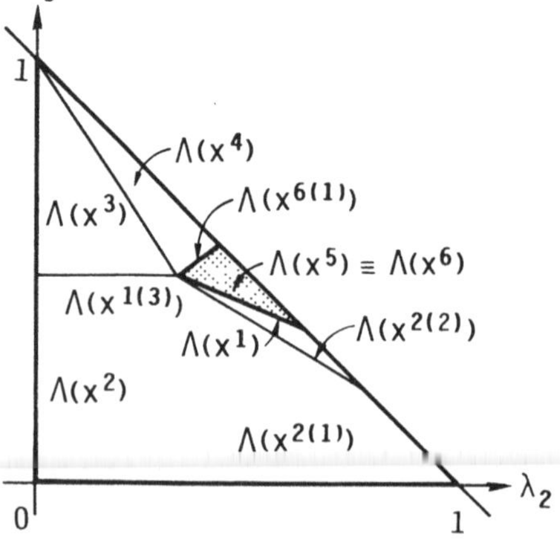

Figure 8.2

$$\Lambda(x^{2(1)}) = \{\lambda \,|\, 9\lambda_2 + 14\lambda_3 \leqq 10; 4\lambda_3 \leqq 2\},$$

$$\Lambda(x^{2(2)}) = \{\lambda \,|\, 9\lambda_2 + 14\lambda_3 \geqq 10; 3\lambda_2 + 6\lambda_3 \leqq 4; 3\lambda_2 + 6\lambda_3 \geqq 4\},$$

$$\Lambda(x^{6(1)}) = \{\lambda \,|\, -\tfrac{1}{2}\lambda_2 + \lambda_3 \geqq \tfrac{1}{3}; -\tfrac{1}{2}\lambda_2 + \lambda_3 \leqq \tfrac{1}{3}; \lambda_2 + 2\lambda_3 \geqq \tfrac{4}{3}\}.$$

8.2.3. Connectedness and Adjacency of N_{ex}-Points, and a Method for Locating the N_{ex} Set

Given $x(J) \in N_{ex}$, we know that $\Lambda(J) \cap \Lambda^> \neq \varnothing$. If $Z_k(J)$ is an effective constraint for $\Lambda(J)$ with the property that $H_k \cap \Lambda(J) \cap \Lambda^> \neq \varnothing$ [Where H_k is defined by (8.34)], then the new basis K obtained by introducing k into the basis will also be such that $H_k \cap \Lambda(J) \cap \Lambda^> \neq \varnothing$ [because of (8.39)]. Thus (by Theorem 8.5 or 8.7), $x(K) \in N_{ex}$. An effective constraint with such a property [i.e., $H_k \cap \Lambda(J) \cap \Lambda^> \neq \varnothing$] will be called an N_{ex}-*effective constraint*.

The following was derived by Ecker and Kouada (Ref. 119). However, the straightforward proof follows Seiford and Yu (Ref. 406).

Theorem 8.12. Given $x(J) \in N_{ex}$, then $Z_k(J)$ is an N_{ex}-effective or null constraint for $\Lambda(J)$ iff ther is $(v, w) \geqq 0$ such that $vZ(J) + \mathbb{1} \cdot Z(J) = w$ or

$$-vZ(J) + w = \mathbb{1} \cdot Z(J) \tag{8.40}$$

with $w_k = 0$, where $\mathbb{1} = (1, 1, \ldots, 1)$.

Proof. Since $\Lambda(J) \cap \Lambda^>$ is a convex cone, for any $\alpha \in R^1$, $\alpha > 0$, $\lambda \in \Lambda(J) \cap \Lambda^>$ iff $\alpha\lambda \in \Lambda(J) \cap \Lambda^>$. We can therefore assume that $\lambda \geqq \mathbb{1}$. Thus, $Z_k(J)$ is an N_{ex}-effective or null constraint iff $\{\lambda \,|\, \lambda \geqq \mathbb{1}, \lambda Z(J) \geqq 0, \lambda Z_k(J) = 0\} \neq \varnothing$. Let $v = \lambda - \mathbb{1}$. Then the above becomes $\{v \,|\, v \geqq 0, (v + \mathbb{1})Z(J) \geqq 0, (v + \mathbb{1})Z_k(J) = 0\} \neq \varnothing$, which yields the result of the theorem (with w as the surplus variable). $\qquad\square$

Remark 8.6. Although the conditions of Theorem 8.12 do not look seductive, the ease with which they are verified makes them positively attractive. Considerable information can be gained by simply observing the form of the corresponding tableau. No linear programming subproblems need to be solved. The theorem indeed greatly simplifies the task of determining N_{ex}-effective or null constraints. We shall provide an example later (see Example 8.4).

Let $E = \{x(i) \,|\, i = 1, \ldots, p\}$ be the set of extreme points of X. We say that E is *connected* either if it contains only one point, or if for any two points $x(j)$, $x(k)$ in E, there is a sequence $\{x(i_1), \ldots, x(i_r)\}$ in E such that $x(i_l)$, and $x(i_{l+1})$, $l = 1, \ldots, r - 1$, are adjacent and $x(i_1) = x(j)$, $x(i_r) = x(k)$. Observe that the set of all extreme points of a polyhedron is connected. In order to see this point, observe that given two extreme points of the polyhedron we can define a linear functional which has its unique maximum point at one of the two points (see Ref. 438, pp. 42–43). By treating the other point as the initial basic feasible solution, we know that by the simplex method we can generate the desired sequence of adjacent points for the connectedness. Thus, we have the following.

Lemma 8.3. (i) The set of all extreme points of a polyhedron (not necessarily bounded) is connected.

(ii) The set of all maximum (or minimum) extreme points of a linear functional over a polyhedron is connected.

Proof. (i) This has been derived above. In order to see (ii), observe that the set of all maximum (or minimum) points of a linear functional over a polyhedron is a face which again is a polyhedron (Ref. 438, pp. 42 and 43). From (i) our assertion of (ii) is clear.   □

Theorem 8.13. N_{ex} is connected.

Proof. Let $x(i)$, $x(j) \in N_{ex}$. Suppose I and J are the bases associated with $x(i)$ and $x(j)$, respectively. Then, by (ii) of Theorem 8.5 or Theorem 8.7 both $\Lambda(I) \cap \Lambda^>$ and $\Lambda(J) \cap \Lambda^>$ are not empty. Let $\lambda_i \in \Lambda(I) \cap \Lambda^>$ and $\lambda_j \in \Lambda(J) \cap \Lambda^>$. Note, that $[\lambda_i, \lambda_j] \subset \Lambda^>$. By Corollary 8.1(ii), we can find a finite sequence $\{\Lambda(J_k) | k = 1, \ldots, r\}$ such that $[\lambda_i, \lambda_j] \cap \Lambda(J_k) \neq \varnothing$ and $[\lambda_i, \lambda_j] \subset \bigcup \{\Lambda(J_k) | k = 1, \ldots, r\}$. Using $\{\Lambda(J_k) | k = 1, \ldots, r\}$ as a guide for pivoting, Lemma 8.3(ii) and Theorem 8.10 ensure a sequence of N_{ex}-points $\{x(i_1), \ldots, x(i_r)\}$ so that $x(i_k)$ is adjacent to $x(i_{k+1})$, for $k = 1, \ldots, r - 1$ and $x(i_1) = x(i)$, $x(i_r) = x(j)$. Note that Lemma 8.3(ii) is needed when there is a number of alternative optimal solutions associated with one λ (see Example 8.3).   □

The above theorems and those discussed in the previous sections can be used systematically to locate N_{ex}. A method to do so is to first find a basis J_1 for an N_{ex}-point [using $\sum_i C^i x$ (or $\mathbb{1} \cdot Cx$, the last row of MC-simplex tableau) as guide for instance]. If there is any other N_{ex}-point, Theorem 8.13 implies that we can find an N_{ex}-basis J_2 adjacent to J_1. Indeed Theorem 8.12 can help us identify N_{ex}-effective constraints or null constraints for adjacent N_{ex}-bases very efficiently. Certainly Theorem 8.9, which is closely related to Theorem 8.12 (see Exercise 8.11), can also be very useful for such an identification. If there is no such J_2, J_1 is the unique N_{ex}-point. Otherwise, we consider all adjacent, but unexplored feasible bases to $\{J_1, J_2\}$ to see if there is any other N_{ex}-basis among them. If there is none, $\{J_1, J_2\}$ represents the set N_{ex}. Otherwise, we add a new N_{ex}-basis to $\{J_1, J_2\}$ and continue with the procedure until the entire set N_{ex} is located.

An extensive computer code has been derived by Steuer (Ref. 433). Here we shall offer an example to illustrate the above concept so that the interested reader can write his own computer code.

Example 8.4. (Continuation of Example 8.2.) Refer to Tableau 8.1. We know that $x(J_1) \in N_{ex}$. We want to identify the N_{ex}-effective constraints of $\Lambda(J_1)$. Using (8.40) of Theorem 8.12, we construct Tableau 8.8 as follows:

	v_1	v_2	w_1	w_2	w_3	RHS
	-2	①	1	0	0	1
Tableau 8.8	-1	-1	0	1	0	2
	-3	0	0	0	1	3
	-2	1	1	0	0	1
Tableau 8.9	-3	0	1	1	0	3
	-3	0	0	0	1	3

By pivoting $(1, 2)$ on Tableau 8.8 we obtain Tableau 8.9, which implies a basic feasible solution $v_2 = 1$, $w_1 = v_1 = 0$, $w_2 = 3$, $w_3 = 3$. Thus the column x_1 which corresponds to $w_1 = 0$ is an N_{ex}-effective constraint. Tableau 8.9 also implies that w_2 and w_3 cannot ever be zero. Thus, the corresponding columns for x_2 and x_3 cannot be N_{ex}-effective constraints. From Figure 8.1 one can also verify the above conclusion.

To locate adjacent N_{ex}-points, we only have to introduce the column for x_1 into the basis. (Columns for x_2 and x_3 are not needed, why not?) Doing this leads us to Tableau 8.2, which yields $x(J_2) \in N_{ex}$. To identify the N_{ex}-effective constraints of $\Lambda(J_2)$, we construct Tableau 8.10 using Tableau 8.2 and (8.40) as follows:

	v_1	v_2	w_1	w_2	w_3	RHS
	1	-2	1	0	0	1
Tableau 8.10	-1	-1	0	1	0	2
	2	⦵-1	0	0	1	-1
	-3	0	1	0	-2	3
Tableau 8.11	-3	0	0	1	-1	1
	-2	1	0	0	-1	1

Note that Tableau 8.11 is obtained by dual pivoting $(3, 2)$. From Tableau 8.11 we obtain a basic feasible solution $v_1 = w_3 = 0$, $v_2 = 1$, $w_1 = 3$, and $w_2 = 1$. Thus, the column for x_6 which corresponds to w_3 is an N_{ex}-effective constraint.

From Tableau 8.11, we notice that w_1 and w_2 can never be zero. Thus, their corresponding columns cannot be N_{ex}-effective. Now if we introduce x_6 into the basis we obtain $x(J_1)$ and there is no other adjacent N_{ex}-point to $x(J_2)$. We thus obtain N_{ex} as two connected N_{ex}-points [i.e., $x(J_1)$ and $x(J_2)$]. One can verify this with Figure 8.1. The task for locating N_{ex}-points is now completed. The reader is urged to use the procedure to locate N_{ex}-points for the problem described in Example 8.3. (See Exercise 8.8.)

8.3. Generating the Set N from N_{ex}-Points

We shall briefly describe the need for the entire set N in Section 8.3.1. A decomposition theorem and necessary and sufficient conditions for a face to be nondominated are described in Section 8.3.2. A method to systematically locate nondominated faces will be discussed briefly with examples in Section 8.3.3.

8.3.1. The Need for the Entire Set N

Observe that in the complicated multicriteria decision problems we first screen out some good alternatives—the set of all nondominated solutions, for the final decision. Suppose that we are the researchers or the consultants to a decision maker. Clearly, our responsiblity is to suggest some good alternatives for the decision maker to make his final decision, rather than to make the decision for him. In this sense the concept of nondominated solutions becomes

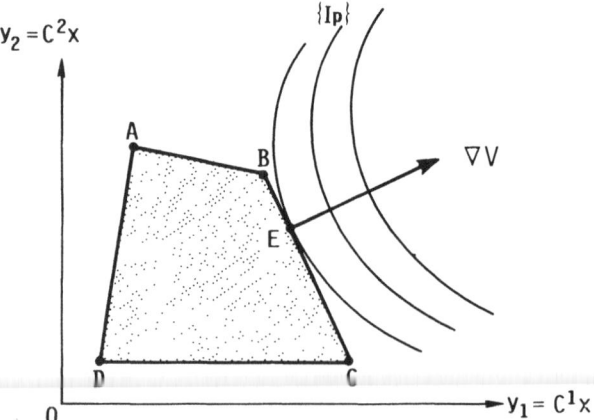

Figure 8.3

especially useful. Now suppose that our criteria space is given as is Figure 8.3. And suppose that the decision maker's value function has the isovalued curves represented by $\{I_p\}$ so that E is the final decision (recall that the value function may not be known precisely to the researchers, even not to the decision maker himself; see Chapters 5 and 9).

The following are worth mentioning:

    i. With respect to the dominated cone $\Lambda^{\leqq}$, $N_{ex} = \{A, B, C\}$. Not all convex combinations of N_{ex} can be nondominated.

    ii. The final decision can be any N-point. It is not necessarily an N_{ex}-point.

From (ii) we see that our search for good solutions may not be completed until the entire set N is located. From (i) we see that N cannot be completely described by the set N_{ex}. How to use N_{ex} and our original criteria and constraints to specify N remains to be explored.

8.3.2. Decomposition of the Set N into Nondominated Faces

In this section we shall describe a decomposition theorem of the set N into nondominated faces, and derive some necessary and sufficient conditions for a face of X to be nondominated. The decomposition theorem is similar to that described in Section 3.4.3. However, in the case of linearity, we have a special kind of result. The results will be used in the next subsection to develop a systematic method to specify N.

In order to simplify our presentation, in the remaining two subsections, we shall put the nonnegativity constraints (i.e., $x_j \geqq 0$, $j = 1, \ldots, n$) into the matrix A. Thus, from now on A has $m + n$ rows. The last n rows are the nonnegativity constraints.

Throughout Sections 8.3.2 and 8.3.3, let $M = \{1, \ldots, m + n\}$ and $\mathcal{M} = \{I \mid I \subset M\}$. (Please do not get confused with the M in the MC-simplex method of the previous section!) Given $I \subset M$, let A^I be the matrix derived from A by deleting those rows that are not in I. Similarly, d^I is derived. Define

$$F(I) = \{x \in X \mid A^I x = d^I\}. \tag{8.41}$$

Observe that if $F(I)$ is not empty then it is a face of the polyhedron X and that $F(\varnothing) = X$. Clearly from (8.41),

$$\text{if} \quad I \subset J \subset M, \quad \text{then} \quad F(I) \supset F(J), \tag{8.42}$$

$$X = \bigcup_{I \in \mathcal{M}} F(I). \tag{8.43}$$

Note that given a face of X, its representation by $F(I)$ may not be unique. In particular the linear manifold spanned by $F(I)$ may be smaller than that spanned by $\tilde{F}(I) = \{x \in R^n \,|\, A^I x = d^I\}$. However, for every face of X there is a maximum index set I such that the linear manifold spanned by $F(I)$ is equal to that spanned by $\tilde{F}(I)$ and if $F(J)$ also represents the same face then $J \subset I$ (see Ref. 438, Lemma 2.4.6 and Theorem 2.4.7). Such $F(I)$ will be called the *full face representation* of the face. On the other hand, if $F(I)$ is a full face representation of some face of X, we will simply say it is a *full face*.

Now, given I, let $[I]$ denote the number of elements in I. For $k = 0$, $1, \ldots, m + n$ define

$$\mathscr{I}^k = \{I \subset M \,|\, [I] = k\}. \tag{8.44}$$

Then

$$N = N \cap X = N \cap \left[\bigcup_{I \in \mathscr{M}} F(I) \right] = \bigcup_{I \in \mathscr{M}} [N \cap F(I)]$$

$$= \bigcup_{k=0}^{m+n} \bigcup_{I \in \mathscr{I}^k} [N \cap F(I)]. \tag{8.45}$$

[The second equality follows from (8.43); the third from the distributive law of set operations; the last from (8.44) and a rearrangement of the order of I in $\mathscr{M}$.]

Define

$$N(I) = N \cap F(I). \tag{8.46}$$

Then (8.45) and (8.46) imply the following decomposition theorem. (Compare with Theorem 3.20.)

Theorem 8.14.

$$N = \bigcup_{k=0}^{m+n} \bigcup_{I \in \mathscr{I}^k} N(I).$$

Remark 8.7. Since $x \in R^n$, except rank $(A^I, d^I) = $ rank (A^I), $F(I) = \varnothing$ if $I \in \mathscr{I}^k$ with $k > n$.

Theorem 8.14 allows us to use a systematic way to locate N. The procedure starts with the checking of $F(I)$, $I = \varnothing$, then those I of $\mathscr{I}^1$, then those I of $\mathscr{I}^2$, until all N-points are located.

Remark 8.8. Let $x \in \mathrm{ri}\, F(I)$ [the relative interior of $F(I)$]. In view of Theorem 8.2, if $x \in N$, then $F(I) \subset N$; otherwise $\mathrm{ri}\, F(I) \subset D$. If $F(I) \subset N$, we shall call it an N-face (*nondominated face*). Thus, in checking whether $F(I)$ is nondominated or not, it is sufficient to check only one point of its relative interior. In order to facilitate our checking, we shall derive some easily applied conditions. Toward this end, given $x \in X$, let

$$I(x) = \{i \,|\, A^i x = d^i\} \tag{8.47}$$

and

$$A[x] = \begin{cases} \{\mu_{I(x)} A^{I(x)} \,|\, \mu_{I(x)} \geq 0\} & \text{if } I(x) \neq \varnothing, & (8.48) \\ \{0\} & \text{otherwise.} & (8.49) \end{cases}$$

Note that $\mu_{I(x)}$ is a row vector with $[I(x)]$ components, and $A[x]$ is the nonnegative cone generated by those constraints which hold as an equality at x. Also define

$$C[\Lambda^>] = \{\lambda C \,|\, \lambda \in \Lambda^>\}. \tag{8.50}$$

Immediately from Theorem 7.21, we have the following.

Theorem 8.15. $x \in \cup \{X^0(\lambda) \,|\, \lambda \in \Lambda^>\}$ if and only if

$$C[\Lambda^>] \cap A[x] \neq \varnothing.$$

Remark 8.9. In view of Theorem 8.5, Theorem 8.15 essentially is a necessary and sufficient condition for $x \in N$. Observe that from (8.50) $C[\Lambda^>]$ is independent of x. Also, since $0 \in A[x]$ for all $x \in X$, if $0 \in C[\Lambda^>]$, then Theorem 8.15 and 8.5 yield that every x of X is an N-point, no matter whether x is in the interior of X or not.

Remark 8.10. Given a full face $F(I)$ of X, from (8.47)-(8.49), we see that $A[x]$ is identical for all $x \in \text{ri } F(I)$. More precisely, define

$$A[I] = \begin{cases} \{\mu_I A^I \,|\, \mu_I \geq 0\} & \text{if } I \neq \varnothing, & (8.51) \\ \{0\} & \text{if } I = \varnothing. & (8.52) \end{cases}$$

Then

$$A[x] = A[I] \qquad \text{whenever } x \in \text{ri } F(I). \tag{8.53}$$

Theorem 8.16. (i) A nonempty full face $F(I)$ is nondominated if and only if $C[\Lambda^>] \cap A[I] \neq \varnothing$. (ii) A nonempty face $F(I)$ is nondominated if $C[\Lambda^>] \cap A(I) \neq \varnothing$.

Proof. (i) This follows immediately from Remark 8.8, Theorems 8.15 and 8.5. (ii) This follows from (i) and from $A[I] \subset A[K]$ if $F(K)$ is the full face representation of the face which is also represented by $F(I)$. $\qquad \square$

Remark 8.11. Verifying whether or not $C[\Lambda^>] \cap A(I) \neq \varnothing$ is equivalent to checking whether or not a system of linear inequalities has a solution. Although the verification procedure of each individual face is not very complicated, checking all possible faces may be a prohibitive job (imagine that $\mathcal{M}$ has 2^{m+n} elements). The following results can help us eliminate a large number of faces from checking.

Theorem 8.17. (i) If $I \subset J$ and $F(I) \subset N$, then $F(J) \subset N$.

(ii) If $F(I) \subset N$, then each extreme point of $F(I)$ must be an N_{ex}-point.

(iii) Assume that X is compact. Let $F(I)$ be a full face and be such that $N_{ex}(I) = N_{ex} \cap F(I) \neq \varnothing$. Then $F(I) \subset N$ only if $N_{ex}(I)$ has at least $n - [I] + 1$ elements.

Proof. (i) This is obvious, because $F(J) \subset F(I)$.

(ii) This is a special case of (i).

(iii) Since $N_{ex}(I) \neq \varnothing$, $F(I) \neq \varnothing$. Since $F(I)$ is a full face, $F(I)$ has at least dimensionality $n - [I]$. Let $[N_{ex}(I)] = r$. Then $\mathcal{H}(N_{ex}(I))$ [the convex hull generated by $N_{ex}(I)$] has at most dimensionality $r - 1$.

Since $F(I) \subset N$, each extreme point of $F(I)$ is an N_{ex}-point. Since $F(I) \subset X$ is compact, $F(I)$ is the convex hull generated by its extreme points. That is, $F(I) = \mathcal{H}[N_{ex}(I)]$. Thus, we must have

$$r - 1 \geqq n - [I] \quad \text{or} \quad r \geqq n - [I] + 1. \qquad \square$$

Remark 8.12. Observe that (ii) and (iii) are two necessary conditions for a face to be nondominated. By keeping track of the dominated extreme points in our MC-simplex tableaus, (ii) is extremely valuable in verifying whether a face is dominated or not. In order to see this point, observe that at least n faces pass through each extreme point x. That is, $[I(x)] \geqq n$ [see (8.47)]. Let $\{x^1, \ldots, x^p\}$ be the known dominated extreme points. Define $\mathcal{B} = \{I(x^k) | k = 1, \ldots, p\}$. We see that every face $F(J)$ with $J \subset I \in \mathcal{B}$ contains at least a dominated extreme point. In view of (ii) of Theorem 8.17, $F(J)$ is not a nondominated face. We shall further utilize this result in the next section. For an example see Section 8.3.3.

Remark 8.13. Suppose that $F(I) \subset N$. Then any subset (or subface) of $F(I)$ is nondominated. Thus, once we locate an N-face, its subfaces can be eliminated from further testing for nondominance. Assume that X is compact. Then each $F(I)$ can be written as the convex hull of the extreme points contained in $F(I)$. Thus, if we could systematically arrange N_{ex} into a minimum number of subsets so that the convex hull of each such subset is an N-face and each N-point is contained in at least one of such faces, our job to locate all N-faces is essentially done. With this in mind suppose that $N_{ex}(J) \subset N_{ex}(I)$ and that $F(I) \subset N$. Then any face $F(K)$ such that $K \supset I$ or $K \supset J$ can be eliminated from further consideration for N-face, because

$$N_{ex}(K) \subset N_{ex}(I) \quad \text{and} \quad \mathcal{H}(N_{ex}(K)) \subset \mathcal{H}(N_{ex}(I))$$

is nondominated.

Remark 8.14. Suppose that $N_{ex}(I)$ is empty or contains only one point. Then for every $J \supset I$, $N_{ex}(J)$ will be empty or contain only one point. It follows from Theorem 8.17(ii) that, except when $F(I)$ or $F(J)$ is a single point, $F(I)$ or $F(J)$ cannot be nondominated. Thus, in checking the nondominance, we may discard this kind of I and J from further consideration.

Remark 8.15. Since each face of X has a full face representation, if we focus on those $\{F(I)\}$ that satisfy the necessary conditions for a full face we will not lose track of any N-face. In our systematic checking, this observation can be incorporated.

The results of Theorems 8.16 and 8.17 and Remarks 8.12–8.15 can be used efficiently to generate the set of all N-faces.

8.3.3. Method to Locate All N-Faces and Examples

In this section we shall utilize the results derived in the previous subsection and describe a systematic method to locate all N-faces. Throughout this subsection we shall assume that X is compact. The relaxation of this assumption is left to the interested reader. (See Exercise 8.12.)

Given $k = 0, 1, \ldots, m + n$, for $\mathcal{I}^k = \{I_k^1, \ldots, I_k^r\}$, we construct the incidence matrix between $N_{ex} = \{x^1, \ldots, x^p\}$ and $\mathcal{I}^k$, denoted by $T = \{t_{ij}\}_{p \times r}$ as follows:

$$t_{ij} = \begin{cases} 1 & \text{if } x^i \in F(I_k^j), \\ 0 & \text{otherwise.} \end{cases} \tag{8.54}$$

Note that the rows and the columns of T correspond to the elements of N_{ex} and the faces of $\mathcal{I}^k$, respectively.

Remark 8.16. The incidence matrix provides some useful information for checking the nondominance of a face in $\mathcal{I}^k$. Observe that

$$[N_{ex}(I_k^j)] = \sum_{i=1}^{p} t_{ij}. \tag{8.55}$$

This information makes it easier to apply (iii) of Theorem 8.17 and Remark 8.14. Also suppose that $T_j \geqq T_l$ (recall that T_j is the jth column of T). Then $N_{ex}(I_k^j) \supset N_{ex}(I_k^l)$. In view of Remark 8.13, if $F(I_k^l) \subset N$ then $F(I_k^l)$ could be eliminated from further consideration for N-face. This observation yields a good application for the incidence matrix and also suggests that if the incidence matrix is arranged in the way that if $[N_{ex}(I_k^j)] \geq [N_{ex}(I_k^l)]$ then $j < l$ (i.e., the column of T is arranged in descending order in terms of $[N_{ex}(I_k^j)]$), then our computation could be carried out more easily. From now on, unless otherwise specified, we shall assume that the incidence matrix is so constructed.

A method to locate N using Theorem 8.14 is as follows. Starting with $k = 0$, the "face" of no equality constraint (i.e., X), then $k = 1$, faces of one equality constraint, then $k = 2, 3, \ldots$ we locate the corresponding N-faces. Utilizing Theorem 8.17 and Remarks 8.12–8.15, we skip those faces that are obvious N-faces and D-faces, and using Theorem 8.16 we verify those faces for which this is not obvious. The process certainly will terminate in a finite number of steps because the total number of constraints is finite. The following two examples illustrate the procedure.

Example 8.5. (Continuation of Example 8.3.) Because there is an extreme point of X which is a D-point, we know immediately that it is not true that $X = N$ [by (ii) of Theorem 8.17]. We construct the incidence matrix between N_{ex} and $\mathscr{I}^1$ as in Tableau 8.12, where $A^5, \ldots, A^{11}$ are the constraints associated with $x_j \geq 0$, $j = 1, \ldots, 7$.

Tableau 8.12

	A^1	A^2	A^3	A^4	A^5	A^6	A^7	A^8	A^9	A^{10}	A^{11}
x^1	1	1	1	0	1	1	1	1	0	1	1
x^2	1	1	0	0	1	1	1	0	1	1	1
x^3	1	0	0	0	1	1	1	1	1	1	1
x^4	1	0	0	1	0	1	0	1	1	1	1
x^5	1	0	0	1	1	1	0	0	1	1	1
x^6	1	0	1	1	1	1	0	1	0	1	1

By inspection we see that N_{ex} is contained in the faces $F(\{1\})$, $F(\{6\})$, $F(\{10\})$, and $F(\{11\})$ simultaneously. Thus, $N_{ex} \subset F(\{1, 6, 10, 11\})$. To verify if $\mathscr{H}[N_{ex}] \subset N$, it is sufficient to verify whether $F(\{1, 6, 10, 11\}) \subset N$ or not.

By applying Theorem 8.16, we want to verify whether there are $(\lambda_1, \lambda_2, \lambda_3) > 0$, and $(\mu_1, \mu_2, \mu_3, \mu_4) \geq 0$ such that

$$(\lambda_1, \lambda_2, \lambda_3) \begin{bmatrix} 1 & 2 & -1 & 3 & 2 & 0 & 1 \\ 0 & 1 & 1 & 2 & 3 & 1 & 0 \\ 1 & 0 & 1 & -1 & 0 & -1 & -1 \end{bmatrix}$$

$$= (\mu_1, \ldots, \mu_4) \begin{bmatrix} 1 & 2 & 1 & 1 & 2 & 1 & 2 \\ 0 & -1 & 0 & 0 & 0 & 0 & 0 \\ 0 & 0 & 0 & 0 & 0 & -1 & 0 \\ 0 & 0 & 0 & 0 & 0 & 0 & -1 \end{bmatrix}.$$

We find that

$$(\lambda_1, \lambda_2, \lambda_3, \mu_1, \mu_2, \mu_3, \mu_4) = (\lambda_1, 2\lambda_1, 3\lambda_1, 4\lambda_1, 0, 5\lambda_1, 10\lambda_1)$$

is the solution to the above system. By setting $\lambda_1 > 0$, it follows that all $\lambda_j > 0$ and $\mu_i \geqq 0$. We see that

$$C[\Lambda^>] \cap A[\{1, 6, 10, 11\}] \neq \varnothing$$

and that

$$\mathcal{H}(N_{ex}) = F(\{1, 6, 10, 11\}) \subset N.$$

Note that $(\lambda_1, 2\lambda_1, 3\lambda_1)$, $\lambda_1 > 0$, is the optimal weight for $F(\{1, 6, 10, 11\})$ to be a maximum.

In view of Remark 8.13, we do not need any further investigation.

Example 8.6. The criteria are

$$\begin{bmatrix} 4 & 1 & 2 \\ 1 & 3 & -1 \\ -1 & 1 & 4 \end{bmatrix} \begin{bmatrix} x_1 \\ x_2 \\ x_3 \end{bmatrix}.$$

The constraints are

$$\begin{bmatrix} 1 & 1 & 1 \\ 2 & 2 & 1 \\ 1 & -1 & 0 \\ -1 & 0 & 0 \\ 0 & -1 & 0 \\ 0 & 0 & -1 \end{bmatrix} \begin{bmatrix} x_1 \\ x_2 \\ x_3 \end{bmatrix} \leqq \begin{bmatrix} 3 \\ 4 \\ 0 \\ 0 \\ 0 \\ 0 \end{bmatrix}.$$

By the method described in Section 8.2, we find

$$N_{ex} = \{x^1, \ldots, x^5\} = \{(0, 0, 3), (0, 1, 2), (\tfrac{1}{2}, \tfrac{1}{2}, 2), (0, 2, 0), (1, 1, 0)\}.$$

Observe that $(0, 0, 0)$ is a dominated extreme point of X and that $I((0, 0, 0)) = \{3, 4, 5, 6\}$. Thus, in view of Theorem 8.17, and Remark 8.12 $X \not\subset N$ and no subset of $\{3, 4, 5, 6\}$ can produce a nondominated face. For

$k = 1$, we construct the incidence matrix (8.54) of N_{ex} and $\mathscr{I}^1$ as follows:

Tableau 8.13

	A^1	A^2	A^3	A^4	A^5	A^6
x^1	1	0	1	1	1	0
x^2	1	1	0	1	0	0
x^3	1	1	1	0	0	0
x^4	0	1	0	1	0	1
x^5	0	1	1	0	0	1
$[N_{ex}(I)]$	3	4	3	3	1	2

As noted above, we need only to verify whether $F(I) \subset N$, for $I = \{1\}$ and $\{2\}$ (because the others are obviously dominated).

We first investigate $I = \{1\}$. By applying Theorem 8.16, we want to verify that there is $(\lambda_1, \lambda_2, \lambda_3) > 0$ and $\mu \geq 0$ such that

$$(\lambda_1, \lambda_2, \lambda_3) \begin{bmatrix} 4 & 1 & 2 \\ 1 & 3 & -1 \\ -1 & 1 & 4 \end{bmatrix} = \mu(1, 1, 1).$$

We find that $(\lambda_1, \lambda_2, \lambda_3, \mu) = (7, 5.5, 5, 28.5)$ satisfies the above system. Thus

$$\mathscr{H}[\{x^1, x^2, x^3\}] = F(\{1\}) \subset N.$$

Similarly, to find whether or not $F(\{2\}) \subset N$ we try to find $(\lambda_1, \lambda_2, \lambda_3) > 0$ and $\mu \geq 0$ such that

$$(\lambda_1, \lambda_2, \lambda_3) \begin{bmatrix} 4 & 1 & 2 \\ 1 & 3 & -1 \\ -1 & 1 & 4 \end{bmatrix} = \mu(2, 2, 1).$$

We find that $(\lambda_1, \lambda_2, \lambda_3, \mu) = (8, 9, 3, 19)$ satisfies the above system. Thus

$$\mathscr{H}[\{x^2, x^3, x^4, x^5\}] = F(\{2\}) \subset N.$$

Thus for $k = 1$, we produce two N-faces [i.e., $F(\{1\})$ and $F(\{2\})$]. For any $I \supset \{1\}$ or $I \supset \{2\}$, we know $F(I) \subset N$. Thus, we do not have to spend time to verify its nondominance. Note that $F(\{5\})$ contains a single point and $N_{ex}(\{6\}) \subset N_{ex}(\{2\})$, by Remarks 8.14 and 8.13, respectively, we can drop any $I \supset \{5\}$ or $I \supset \{6\}$ from further consideration for nondominance test. With the above understanding, for $k = 2$, there is only one $I = \{3, 4\} \in \mathscr{I}^2$ that needs to be checked. However, from Tableau 8.13, we notice that only one N_{ex}-point (i.e., x^1) is contained by $F(\{3,4\})$. Again, Remark 8.14 suggests that we do not have to verify its nondominance. Indeed, we have completed the task of locating the entire N set and obtained $N = F(\{1\}) \cup F(\{2\})$. From the final decision point of view constraints 1 and 2 are certainly more important than the other constraints! (Why?)

8.4. MC²-Simplex Method and Potential Solutions in Linear Systems

8.4.1. Introduction

In this section we shall extend the MC-simplex method to a MC²-problem involving both multiple criteria and multiple constraint levels (i.e., multiple and discrete right-hand sides). This type of problem actually occurs in decision modeling. For example, in the design of optimal systems one wishes to determine the initial configuration(s) of resource levels which "optimize" the objective function(s). (See Ref. 516 of Zeleny.) As a practical example, each constraint level (each column of D) may be interpreted as the resource level initially preferred by a member of a decision-making committee. Alternatively, one may view the constraint levels as occurring according to some random rule or influenced by some uncertain factor but contained within a set. Finally, recall that in converting a MC decision problem into a single-criterion mathematical programming problem, the objective function and the constraints are interchangeable. (See Remarks 3.2 and 7.13.)

Note that in algebraic form, the MC simplex method can be represented by

$$\max Cx,$$

$$\text{s.t. } Ax \leqq d, \tag{8.56}$$

$$x \geqq 0,$$

where $C = C_{q \times n}$ and $A = A_{m \times n}$ are matrices, $d \in R^m$ is the constraint level, and $x \in R^n$. In the MC² problem, (8.56) is replaced by

$$\max Cx,$$

$$\text{s.t. } Ax \leqq D, \tag{8.57}$$

$$x \geqq 0,$$

where $D = D_{m \times k}$. (Note that we replace the vector d by the matrix D.)

We may regard the constraint portion of (8.57) as giving a set of "feasible" solutions, x, whenever Ax is contained in the cone generated by the columns of D. Thus, the columns of D may be interpreted as possible initial resource levels or extreme points (rays) of the set which contains the random constraint levels. The problem "x is feasible if Ax lies in a convex set generated by D" has a similar interpretation.

In Ref. 153, Gal studies the RIM multiparametric linear programming problem which has a form similar to (8.57). The author primarily treats the problem in terms of a parameter that simultaneously affects the criteria and the constraints. His main objective is the location of optimal solutions corresponding to various values of the parameter. His method is an extension of Ref. 156. For the details we refer to his book (Ref. 155).

Instead of considering the parametric programming problem, let us consider (8.57) as a mathematical model for decision problems. We will supply a solution concept (that of a potential solution) which is a natural extension of the nondominated solution of an MC decision problem. The meaning and properties of this concept will be discussed in Section 8.4.2.

In Section 8.4.3 we shall introduce the MC^2 simplex method as a symmetric extension of the MC simplex method discussed in the previous sections. This MC^2 method will be used to find (locate) the potential solutions to be discussed in Section 8.4.2. Both the format and the pivoting rule for primal and dual potential solutions will be discussed. An efficient subroutine, which is analogous to Theorem 8.8, for checking primal and dual potentiality will be stated.

In Section 8.4.4 we shall explore the properties of separation, adjacency, and connectedness of potential solutions in such a way that the set of all potential solutions can be located according to the guidelines of a connected graph.

In Section 8.4.5 we shall explore the duality theorems for the problem described in (8.57). Several significant results will be reported. An example that illustrates the above ideas will be considered in Section 8.4.6.

8.4.2. Potential Solutions of Linear Systems

For the MC problem (8.56), the following lemma is a partial restatement of Theorem 8.5.

Lemma 8.4. x^0 is a nondominated solution iff there exists some $\lambda > 0$ such that x^0 solves

$$\max \lambda Cx,$$

$$\text{s.t. } Ax \leq d, \qquad (8.58)$$

$$x \geq 0.$$

The dual problem of (8.58) is given by

$$\min u^T d,$$

$$\text{s.t. } u^T A \geqq \lambda C, \tag{8.59}$$

$$u^T \geqq 0.$$

By dropping λ, (8.58) and (8.59) become

$$\max Cx,$$

$$\text{s.t. } Ax \leqq d, \tag{8.60}$$

$$x \geqq 0$$

and

$$\min u^T D,$$

$$\text{s.t. } u^T A \geqq C, \tag{8.61}$$

$$u^T \geqq 0.$$

We see that (8.61) is a natural dual problem of (8.60). (Further discussion of this will be given in Section 8.4.5.) Thus the solution concept of (8.61) can be derived from the solution concept of the MC problem (8.60).

Definition 8.1. A basis J is a potential basis (without confusion we also call J a potential solution) for the MC² problem (8.57) iff there exist $\lambda > 0$, $\sigma > 0$ such that J is an optimal basis for

$$\max \lambda Cx,$$

$$\text{s.t. } Ax \leqq D\sigma, \tag{8.62}$$

$$x \geqq 0.$$

Remark 8.17. If D contains a single vector d, then (8.57) reduces to (8.60) by normalization such that $|\sigma| = 1$. Thus, a basis J is a potential basis (or solution) for (8.60) iff there exists $\lambda > 0$ such that J is an optimal basis for (8.58). In view of Lemma 8.4, the potential solution of (8.60) is exactly a nondominated (or Pareto-optimal) solution of (8.60). Next, applying Definition 8.1 to problem (8.59) which has a single-criterion vector, we see that a basis J is a potential basis (or solution) for (8.61) iff there exists $\lambda > 0$ such that J is an optimal basis for (8.59).

From the above observations, it is seen that the concept of potential solutions or bases is a generalization of that of nondominated or efficient solutions discussed in Chapter 3.

Remark 8.18. For a potential basis J, let $x(J)$ be the basic solution associated with J. In contrast to the MC case, our solution is a function of σ. We will denote this solution by $x(J, \sigma)$ when it is necessary to emphasize the dependence on σ.

In order to facilitate our discussion in the subsequent sections we need the following distinction.

Definition 8.2. A basis J is a primal potential solution (or basis) for the MC^2 problem (8.57) iff J is an optimal basis for (8.62) with $\lambda = 0$ and some $\sigma > 0$.

Definition 8.3. A basis J is a dual potential solution (or basis) for the MC^2 problem (8.57) iff J is an optimal basis for (8.62) with $\sigma = 0$ and some $\lambda > 0$.

Remark 8.19. We label Definition 8.2 as a primal potential since the basic solution is primal infeasible for a negative right-hand side. A similar remark holds for Definition 8.3. (See also Remark 8.29.) Clearly, a basis J is a potential solution iff J is both a primal and a dual potential solution.

8.4.3. The MC^2-Simplex Method

Consider the problem mentioned in Definition 8.1:

$$\max \lambda Cx,$$

$$\text{s.t. } Ax \leqq D\sigma, \tag{8.63}$$

$$x \geqq 0.$$

The tableau for (8.63) can be written as

A	I	$D\sigma$
λC	0	0

Let B be the basic matrix associated with the basis J. Since each set of basic vectors, J, is uniquely associated with a column index set, as before we shall, without confusion, let J be this set of indices and J' the set of nonbasic columns. The tableau associated with J is

$B^{-1}A$	B^{-1}	$B^{-1}D\sigma$
$\lambda C_B B^{-1}A - \lambda C$	$\lambda C_B B^{-1}$	$\lambda C_B B^{-1}D\sigma$

,

where C_B is the submatrix of criteria columns associated with the basic vectors. [Compare with (8.18) and (8.19).]

Dropping σ and λ, we obtain the MC²-simplex tableau associated with basis J [compare with (8.20) and (8.21)]:

$B^{-1}A$	B^{-1}	$B^{-1}D$
$C_B B^{-1}A - C$	$C_B B^{-1}$	$C_B B^{-1}D$

,

which we write as [compare with (8.22)-(8.24)]

$$
\begin{array}{cc}
Y & W \\
\hline
Z & V
\end{array} , \qquad (8.64)
$$

where

$$Y = [B^{-1}A, B^{-1}], \qquad W = B^{-1}D,$$

$$Z = [C_B B^{-1}A - C, C_B B^{-1}]$$

and

$$V = C_B B^{-1}D.$$

Remark 8.20. It is immediately obvious that the MC² tableau is a symmetric extension of the MC tableau. In fact, for a particular value of σ, the MC² problem reduces to the MC problem.

Let $W(J)$ and $Z(J)$ be the submatrices of the tableau associated with the basis J. Define

$$\Gamma(J) = \{\sigma > 0 \,|\, W(J)\sigma \geqq 0\},$$

$$\Lambda(J) = \{\lambda > 0 \,|\, \lambda Z(J) \geqq 0\}.$$

Note that here $\Lambda(J)$ is different from the previous section. Here we already restrict $\lambda > 0$ in the definition of $\Lambda(J)$. This change is just for convenience and should cause no confusion. We clearly have the following.

Theorem 8.18.
   i. J is a primal potential solution iff $\Gamma(J) \neq \varnothing$.
   ii. J is a dual potential solution iff $\Lambda(J) \neq \varnothing$.
   iii. J is a potential solution iff $\Lambda(J) \times \Gamma(J) \neq \varnothing$.

Remark 8.21. We call $\Gamma(J)$ the *primal potential set*, $\Lambda(J)$ the *dual potential set*, and $\Lambda(J) \times \Gamma(J)$ the *potential set* of the basis J. We notice that if the kth column of $Z(J)$, $Z_k(J) \leq 0$ [thus $Z_k(J) \neq 0$] then $\Lambda(J) = \varnothing$. Also $W^i(J)$, the ith row of $W(J)$, satisfying $W^i(J) \leq 0$ implies $\Gamma(J) = \varnothing$.

Remark 8.22. Given a basis J, recall that J' represents the set of nonbasic vectors. For any element of Y, $y_{pk} \neq 0$ and $k \in J'$, we can pivot to a new tableau associated with the basis $K = J \cup \{k\} \backslash \{j_p\}$, where j_p is the basic vector associated with the pth row of the tableau. We classify such a pivot as a *primal pivot* if $y_{pk} > 0$ and a *dual pivot* if $y_{pk} < 0$. Thus, if a particular basis J is a dual potential but not a primal potential we could dual pivot to remove the primal infeasibility (if possible). More specifically, since J is a dual potential solution, our tableau is dual feasible for any $\lambda \in \Lambda(J)$. If the constraint set is consistent for σ_0 we can use the dual simplex method which pivots to remove primal infeasibility. The pivot selection rule requires $y_{pk} < 0$, hence the classification "dual pivot". Similar remarks can be made concerning primal pivots and a primal (but not dual) potential solution.

For a basis J, we could use Remark 8.21 or other similar observations to test whether J is a potential solution. Such results cannot, however, cover all possible cases. The following potential subroutine can always detect the potentiality of J in a simple way. The result can be derived similarly to that for Theorem 8.8. We shall leave it to the reader. (See Exercise 8.13.)

Theorem 8.19
   (i) $\Lambda(J) \neq \varnothing$ iff $w_{\max} = 0$ for

$$\max w = \sum e_i,$$

$$\text{s.t. } Z(J)y + e = 0,$$

$$y \geq 0, \qquad e \geq 0.$$

(ii) $\Gamma(J) \neq \varnothing$ iff $w'_{max} = 0$ for

$$\max w' = \sum e_i,$$

$$\text{s.t. } yW(J) + e = 0,$$

$$y \geqq 0, \qquad e \geqq 0.$$

(where e is defined as in Theorem 8.8).

Remark 8.23. We thus have a method of testing the dual and primal potentiality of any basis J. The conditions are easily checked since only the submatrices Z and W of the original tableau are required. To verify condition (i), for example, the related simplex tableau is

$Z(J)$	I	0
$\mathbb{1}Z(J)$	0	0

where $\mathbb{1} = (1, \ldots, 1)$ is a vector of ones. The reader may recall Example 8.1 for an illustration. To facilitate testing, we append to the simplex tableau an extra column corresponding to the constraint level $D \; \mathbb{1}^T$ and an extra row corresponding to the objective function $\mathbb{1}C$. This extra row and column will also be required for other verifications. (See Remark 8.28 and the comprehensive example of Section 8.4.6.)

8.4.4. Separation, Adjacency, and Connectedness

In the previous section a potential subroutine was derived which can determine the potentiality of a basis J. Later in this section (see Theorem 8.22), we prove the connectedness of the set of all potential solutions. Thus, one method of locating all potential solutions would be the following. Starting from an initial potential solution J, we pivot to each basis K which is adjacent to J and use the potential subroutine to determine its potentiality. For each K that is also a potential solution, we again pivot to each of its adjacent bases and determine their potentiality. Continuing in this manner, we could effectively, but perhaps not efficiently, locate all potential solutions. The inefficiency can be a result of the unnecessary pivots that would be made.

We need a method of determining, *a priori*, which of the adjacent bases are actually potential solutions and then perform only these pivots. In order to develop this idea, we must study the relationship between the potential sets of two adjacent bases.

Definition 8.4. Suppose J is a dual potential solution. If for some $k \in J'$, $Z_k(J) \neq 0$ and there exists $\lambda_0 \in \Lambda(J)$ such that $\lambda_0 Z_k(J) = 0$, we call $Z_k(J)$ an *effective constraint* of $\Lambda(J)$. If for some $k \in J'$, $Z_k(J) = 0$, we call $Z_k(J)$ a *null constraint* of $\Lambda(J)$.

Definition 8.5. Suppose J is a primal potential solution. If there exists $\sigma_0 \in \Gamma(J)$ such that $W^p(J)\sigma_0 = 0$, $W^p(J) \neq 0$ we call $W^p(J)$ an *effective constraint* of $\Gamma(J)$. If for some row p, $W^p(J) = 0$, we call $W^p(J)$ a *null constraint* of $\Gamma(J)$.

Now let $y_{pk} \neq 0$ be the pivot element and suppose that we pivot to a new basis $K = J \cup \{k\}\backslash\{j_p\}$. (See Remark 8.22.) In order to see how $\Lambda(J) \times \Gamma(J)$ is related to $\Lambda(K) \times \Gamma(K)$, observe that after pivoting we have [compare with (8.33) of Section 8.2.2]

$$Z_j(K) = 0 \qquad\qquad\qquad \text{if } j \in K,$$

$$Z_j(K) = -Z_k(J)/y_{pk} \qquad\qquad \text{if } j = j_p \in K',$$

$$Z_j(K) = Z_j(J) - Z_k(J)\frac{y_{pj}}{y_{pk}} \qquad \text{if } j \in K'\backslash\{j_p\},$$

and

$$W^i(K) = W^p(J)/y_{pk} \qquad\qquad \text{if } i = p,$$

$$W^i(K) = W^i(J) - \frac{y_{ik}}{y_{pk}} W^p(J) \quad \text{if } i \neq p.$$

Next, define

$$H_k \equiv \{\lambda \,|\, \lambda Z_k(J) = 0\},$$

$$G_p \equiv \{\sigma \,|\, W^p(J)\sigma = 0\},$$

and consider the following two cases.

Case 1. $Z_k(J)$ is an effective constraint for $\Lambda(J)$ and $y_{pk} > 0$ is the primal pivot element.

Since

$$\Lambda(J) \subseteq \{\lambda \,|\, \lambda Z_k(J) \geqq 0\}$$

and

$$\Lambda(K) \subseteq \{\lambda \,|\, \lambda Z_k(J) \leqq 0\},$$

we see that H_k is a hyperplane which separates $\Lambda(J)$ and $\Lambda(K)$ and furthermore

$$H_k \cap \Lambda(J) = H_k \cap \Lambda(K) = \Lambda(J) \cap \Lambda(K). \tag{8.65}$$

We also remark that the pivot on y_{pk} will preserve any value of $\sigma_0 \in \Gamma(J)$ that would cause the selection of y_{pk} as the pivot element. Observe that if σ_0 causes the selection of y_{pk} as the pivot element then σ_0 must lie in

$$\Gamma(K) \cap \Gamma(J) = \left\{ \sigma > 0 \mid W(J)\sigma \geqq 0 \text{ and } W^i(J)\sigma \geqq \frac{y_{ik}}{y_{pk}} W^p(J)\sigma, (\forall y_{ik} > 0) \right\}.$$
$$\tag{8.66}$$

Remark 8.24. When the above holds we say that the potential sets $\Lambda(J) \times \Gamma(J)$ and $\Lambda(K) \times \Gamma(K)$ are *primal adjacent*. Notice that the sets $\Lambda(J)$ and $\Lambda(K)$ "abut," while $\Gamma(J)$ and $\Gamma(K)$ "overlap."

Case 2. $W^p(J)$ is an effective constraint for $\Gamma(J)$ and $y_{pk} < 0$ is the dual pivot element.
Since

$$\Gamma(J) \subseteq \{\sigma \mid W^p(J)\sigma \geqq 0\}$$

and

$$\Gamma(K) \subseteq \{\sigma \mid W^p(J)\sigma \leqq 0\},$$

we see that G_p is a hyperplane which separates $\Gamma(J)$ and $\Gamma(K)$ and furthermore

$$G_p \cap \Gamma(J) = G_p \cap \Gamma(K) = \Gamma(J) \cap \Gamma(K). \tag{8.67}$$

The relation analogous to (8.66) is

$$\Lambda(K) \cap \Lambda(J) = \left\{ \lambda > 0 \mid \lambda Z(J) \geqq 0 \text{ and } \lambda Z_j(J) \leqq \lambda Z_k(J) \frac{y_{pj}}{y_{pk}}, (\forall y_{pj} < 0) \right\},$$
$$\tag{8.68}$$

which can be interpreted in the same way as (8.66).

Remark 8.25. When the above holds we say that the potential sets are *dual adjacent*. If the potential sets are either primal or dual adjacent, we say they are *adjacent*.

We summarize the above results as follows (compare with Theorem 8.10).

Theorem 8.20. Let J be a potential solution and $y_{pk} \neq 0$ be the pivot element which yields an adjacent basis K.

(i) If $y_{pk} > 0$ and $Z_k(J)$ is an effective constraint, then H_k as defined above is a hyperplane which separates $\Lambda(J)$ and $\Lambda(K)$ and (8.65) and (8.66) hold.

(ii) If $y_{pk} < 0$ and $W^p(J)$ is an effective constraint then G_p as defined above is a hyperplane which separates $\Gamma(J)$ and $\Gamma(K)$ and (8.67) and (8.68) hold.

Remark 8.26. Theorem 8.20 thus illustrates the connection between potential sets of adjacent bases. Notice that Z_k must be an effective constraint for (8.65) to hold. If Z_k is a null constraint then $\Lambda(J) = \Lambda(K)$. Similarly, if W^p is a null constraint then $\Gamma(J) = \Gamma(K)$.

We shall now prove (Theorem 8.22) that the set of potential bases is connected, i.e., given any two potential bases J and K, we can reach K from J by a sequence of pivots, each to an adjacent potential basis. We begin by establishing the following intermediate results.

Lemma 8.5. Suppose (λ_1, σ_1) and (λ_2, σ_2) are points in the potential sets of potential solutions L and J, respectively. Then there is a potential solution K whose potential set contains the point (λ_2, σ_1).

Proof. Consider the simplex tableau associated with basis L:

$Y(L)$	$W(L)\sigma_1$
$\lambda_2 Z(L)$	$\lambda_2 V(L)\sigma_1$

.

Since $W(L)\sigma_1 \geqq 0$, L is a feasible basis. Unless the solution is unbounded, we can pivot (in a finite number of steps) to an optimal basis K for which $\lambda_2 Z(K) \geqq 0$ and $W(K)\sigma_1 \geqq 0$. If the solution was unbounded, however, the constraints for the dual problem, $(u^T A \geqq \lambda_2 C, u^T \geqq 0)$, would be infeasible, contradicting the potentiality of J. Thus, the solution is bounded and there is a potential solution K, as required. $\square$

Theorem 8.21. Let (λ_1, σ_0) and (λ_2, σ_0) be points in the potential sets of potential solutions J and K, respectively. Then there is a finite sequence of potential solutions $\{J_i\}_{i=1}^m$ with $J_1 = J$ and $J_m = K$. Furthermore, J_i and J_{i+1} are adjacent potential solutions with J_{i+1} obtained by introducing either an effective or null constraint for $\Lambda(J_i)$. The $\{J_i\}$ also satisfy

  i. $\sigma_0 \in \bigcap_i \Gamma(J_i)$,
  ii. $[\lambda_1, \lambda_2] \subseteq \bigcup_i \Lambda(J_i)$,
  iii. $\Lambda(J_i) \cap [\lambda_1, \lambda_2] \neq \varnothing (\forall_i)$, where $[\lambda_1, \lambda_2]$ is the line segment connecting λ_1 and λ_2.

Proof. For $\alpha \in [0, 1]$, let $\lambda(\alpha) \equiv (1 - \alpha)\lambda_1 + \alpha\lambda_2$.

Since $\lambda(\alpha)Cx_n \to +\infty$ implies either $\lambda_1 Cx_n \to +\infty$ or $\lambda_2 Cx_n \to +\infty$, which contradicts the potentiality of J or K, we have that

$$\max \lambda(\alpha)Cx,$$

$$\text{s.t. } Ax \leqq D\sigma_0,$$

$$x \geqq 0,$$

is bounded for $\alpha \in [0, 1]$.

For a basis L, define

$$\alpha(L) = \{\alpha \in [0, 1] | \lambda(\alpha) \in \Lambda(L)\},$$

which is convex and closed.

Set $J_1 = J$ and let $\alpha_1 = \sup_\alpha \alpha(J_1)$. [$\alpha_1$ is the "distance" we can travel along the line segment $[\lambda_1, \lambda_2]$ and remain in $\Lambda(J_1)$.] If $\alpha_1 < 1$ then there exists $k \in J_1$ such that $Z_k(J_1)$ is an effective constraint for $\Lambda(J_1)$. We travel along $[\lambda_1, \lambda_2]$ until $\lambda Z_k(J_1)$ "hits" zero for some $k \in J_1$. Let J_2 be the basis obtained by introducing k into the basis. If $\alpha_2 = \sup_\alpha \alpha(J_2) < 1$, we again pivot across an effective constraint to a basis J_3. Continuing in this manner we will reach a basis J_r such that $\alpha_r = 1$.

Suppose $J_r \neq K$. Then J_r and K are alternate optimal solutions for (λ_2, σ_0). Hence, there exists a sequence of null pivots each yielding an adjacent basis, J_i, which eventually reaches K. Properties (i), (ii), and (iii) follow from the above construction and Theorem 8.20 and Remark 8.26. $\square$

Remark 8.27. Theorem 8.21 has an obvious "dual" for pivoting from (λ_0, σ_1) to (λ_0, σ_2) which we use, but do not state, in the proof of Theorem 8.22. See Exercise 8.14. We also see that in pivoting, we only need to consider effective and null constraints. By doing so, we reduce the number of unnecessary pivots.

Theorem 8.22. The set of potential solutions, P, is connected.

Proof. Let L and J be potential solutions with (λ_1, σ_1) and (λ_2, σ_2) in their respective potential sets. By Lemma 8.5, there exists a potential solution K whose potential set contains (λ_2, σ_1). By Theorem 8.21 there exists a sequence of adjacent potential solutions $\{J_i\}_{i=1}^m$, such that $J_1 = L$ and $J_m = K$. By the "dual" of Theorem 8.21 (see Remark 8.27) there exists a sequence of adjacent potential solutions $\{K_i\}_{i=1}^r$ such that $K_1 = K$ and $K_r = J$. Since L and J were arbitrary, P is connected. $\square$

The following, which is an extension of Theorem 8.12 allows one to locate the effective or null constraints without pivoting. We shall leave its derivation to the reader. (See Exercise 8.15.)

Theorem 8.23. (i) $Z_k(J)$ is an effective or null constraint for $\Lambda(J)$ iff there exists $(v, w) \geqq 0$ such that $v \cdot Z(J) + \mathbb{1} \cdot Z(J) = w$ with $w_k = 0$.

(ii) $W^p(J)$ is an effective or null constraint for $\Gamma(J)$ iff there exists $(v, w) \geqq 0$ such that $W(J) \cdot v + W(J) \cdot \mathbb{1}^T = w$ with $w_p = 0$.

Remark 8.28. Recall (Remark 8.23) that we have appended an extra row and column to the tableau. To verify (i) see Example 8.4 for an illustration. Similarly, to verify condition (ii) we use as an initial tableau

v	w	
$-W(J)$	I	$W(J) \cdot \mathbb{1}^T$

If $W(J) \cdot \mathbb{1}^T$ has negative entries, we dual pivot to a feasible tableau and then verify the condition.

Although conditions (i) and (ii) do not look seductive, the ease with which they are verified makes them positively attractive. As discussed before, considerable information can be gained by simply observing the form of the tableau. No linear programming subproblems need to be solved. Thus, Theorem 8.23 greatly simplifies the task of determining the effective or null constraints. (See the example discussed in Section 8.4.6 for further illustration.)

Suppose now that we have found a potential solution. By Remark 8.27, it is sufficient to consider only adjacent bases obtained from effective or null constraints. However, this will not eliminate all unnecessary pivots. To be more specific, let J be a potential solution and $Z_k(J)$, an effective constraint. For each $y_{pk} > 0$, there is an adjacent basis K^p, obtained by introducing the kth column into the basis and removing the basic element corresponding to the pth row. Theorem 8.20 guarantees that $\Lambda(k^p)$ will be nonempty. However, $\Gamma(K^p)$ may be empty unless y_{pk} is "selected" as the pivot element for some $\sigma \in \Gamma(J)$. [See (8.65) and (8.66).] If no $\sigma \in \Gamma(J)$ causes the selection of y_{pk} as the pivot element, we would possibly pivot to a nonpotential basis.

To eliminate all unnecessary pivots we could derive a verifiable condition using, for example, the methods of Theorem 8.23. However, the necessity of checking such a condition for each $p \in \{p \mid y_{pk} > 0\}$, and the simplicity of the potential subroutine, stop us from doing so.

Our method for locating the set of potential solutions is, therefore, the following. We start with a potential solution J and test, using the potential subroutine, all adjacent bases that are obtained from effective or null constraints. For those adjacent bases that are potential solutions, we again consider all adjacent bases obtained from effective or null constraints. We continue in this manner until the entire set of potential solutions is located. See the example of Section 8.4.6 for an illustration.

8.4.5. Duality of MC²-Programs

As was evident in the previous sections, the MC^2 problem has a duality concept analogous to that of ordinary linear programming. We exploit this fact to develop a MC^2 duality theory that maintains the following fundamental properties:

   i. The dual of the dual is the primal.

   ii. The duality inequality is always satisfied.

   iii. The duality is perfect; i.e., if one program has a finite optimal solution then both have an optimal solution and the two values are equal.

Consider the problem

$$\max Cx,$$

$$\langle P \rangle \qquad \text{s.t. } Ax \leqq D,$$

$$x \geqq 0,$$

where $C = C_{q \times n}$, $A = A_{m \times n}$, $D = D_{m \times k}$ are matrices and $x \in R^n$.

We define the dual of $\langle P \rangle$ to be

$$\min u^T D$$

$$\langle D \rangle \qquad \text{s.t. } u^T A \geqq C,$$

$$u^T \geqq 0,$$

where $u \in R^m$.

It is obvious that $\langle P \rangle$ and $\langle D \rangle$ so defined satisfy property (i).

As mentioned earlier, we regard the constraint portion of $\langle P \rangle$ as giving a set of "feasible" solutions, x, whenever Ax is contained in the cone generated by the columns of D. A similar interpretation holds for $\langle D \rangle$. We formalize this in the following.

Definition 8.6. $(x; \sigma)$ is a $\langle P \rangle$-feasible solution iff $\sigma > 0$ and x satisfies

$$Ax \leqq D\sigma,$$

$$x \geqq 0.$$

Definition 8.7. $(u; \lambda)$ is a $\langle D \rangle$-feasible solution iff $\lambda > 0$ and u satisfies

$$u^T A \geqq \lambda C,$$

$$u^T \geqq 0.$$

Definition 8.8. $(x; \sigma)$ is a nondominated solution to $\langle P \rangle$ iff x is a nondominated solution (with respect to the dominated cone $\Lambda^{\leqq}$) to

$$\max Cx,$$

$$\text{s.t. } Ax \leqq D\sigma,$$

$$x \geqq 0.$$

Definition 8.9. $(u; \lambda)$ is a nondominated solution to $\langle D \rangle$ iff u is a nondominated solution (with respect to the dominated cone $\Lambda^{\geqq}$) to

$$\min u^T D,$$

$$\text{s.t. } u^T A \geqq \lambda C,$$

$$u^T \geqq 0.$$

In Section 8.4.2 we defined potential solutions in terms of bases. We chose to work with bases since some values of σ may cause degeneracy and hence there will not be a one-to-one correspondence between bases and extreme points. The following remark shows that with each basis there are associated "solutions" for $\langle P \rangle$ and $\langle D \rangle$, with the potentiality of the basis equivalent to the feasibility of the "solutions."

Remark 8.29. Recalling Definition 8.2, we see that J is a primal potential solution iff for some $\sigma > 0$, the basic solution for J, $x(J, \sigma)$, satisfies

$$Ax \leqq D\sigma,$$

$$x \geqq 0.$$

Thus the basic solution, $x(J, \sigma) = B^{-1} D\sigma$, associated with a primal potential basis J is $\langle P \rangle$-feasible for all $\sigma \in \Gamma(J)$.

Similarly, J is a dual potential solution iff for some $\lambda > 0$, $\lambda Z(J) \geqq 0$. But $Z(J) = [C_B B^{-1} A - C, C_B B^{-1}]$. Thus for each $\lambda \in \Lambda(J)$, $u^T(J, \lambda) = \lambda C_B B^{-1}$ is $\langle D \rangle$-feasible.

Since our computation is accomplished via the tableau, we state the following theorems in terms of both bases and solutions. Since the results for solutions follow immediately from the results for bases, we only prove the latter.

We first establish the MC² duality inequality. Recall that in partitioning our tableau, we defined (8.64)

$$V(J) = C_B B^{-1} D.$$

Therefore $\lambda V(J)\sigma$ is the (functional) value of (8.62) for the basic solution $x(J)$.

Theorem 8.24. (i) If J is a primal potential basis and K is a dual potential basis then

$$\lambda V(J)\sigma \leqq \lambda V(K)\sigma \qquad \text{for all } (\lambda, \sigma) \in \Lambda(K) \times \Gamma(J).$$

(ii) If $(x; \sigma)$ and $(u; \lambda)$ are feasible solutions for $\langle P \rangle$ and $\langle D \rangle$, respectively, then $\lambda Cx \leqq u^T D\sigma$.

Proof. (i) Let

$$X_\sigma = \{x | Ax \leqq D\sigma, x \geqq 0\}$$

and

$$U_\lambda = \{u | u^T A \geqq \lambda C, u^T \geqq 0\}.$$

Then

$$\lambda V(J)\sigma \leqq \max_{x \in X_\sigma} \lambda Cx \leqq \min_{u^T \in U_\lambda} u^T D\sigma \leqq \lambda V(K)\sigma. \qquad \square$$

(Note that the second inequality follows from the duality of ordinary linear programming.)

Actually, we can prove a stronger version of Theorem 8.24. From this (Theorem 8.25), the property (iii) that the duality is perfect is extended.

Theorem 8.25. (i) Let J be a primal potential basis and K a dual potential basis. Then for each $(\lambda, \sigma) \in \Lambda(K) \times \Gamma(J)$ there is a potential basis L such that $\lambda V(J)\sigma \leqq \lambda V(L)\sigma \leqq \lambda V(K)\sigma$.

(ii) Let $(x; \sigma)$ and $(u; \lambda)$ be feasible solutions for $\langle P \rangle$ and $\langle D \rangle$, respectively. Then there exist feasible solutions $(\bar{x}; \sigma)$ and $(\bar{u}; \lambda)$ for $\langle P \rangle$ and $\langle D \rangle$, respectively, such that

$$\lambda Cx \leqq \lambda C\bar{x} = \bar{u}^T D\sigma \leqq u^T D\sigma.$$

Proof. (i) Let $(\lambda_0, \sigma_0) \in \Lambda(K) \times \Gamma(J)$. The proof of Theorem 8.24 shows that $\max_{x \in X_{\sigma_0}} \lambda_0 Cx$ is finite.

Hence, there exists an optimal basis L. [L is a potential solution since $(\lambda_0, \sigma_0) \in \Lambda(L) \times \Gamma(L)$.]

Thus

$$\lambda_0 V(J)\sigma_0 \leq \max_{x \in X_{\sigma_0}} \lambda_0 Cx = \lambda_0 V(L)\sigma_0 = \min_{u \in U_{\lambda_0}} u^T D\sigma_0 \leq \lambda_0 V(K)\sigma_0. \qquad \square$$

Corollary 8.2. (i) Suppose J is a primal potential basis and K is a dual potential basis. If, for some $(\lambda, \sigma) \in \Lambda(K) \times \Gamma(J)$,

$$\lambda V(J)\sigma = \lambda V(K)\sigma,$$

then J and K are both potential solutions.

(ii) Suppose $(x; \sigma)$ and $(u; \lambda)$ are feasible solutions for $\langle P \rangle$ and $\langle D \rangle$, respectively. If

$$\lambda Cx = u^T D\sigma,$$

then J and K are both nondominated solutions.

Proof. (i) In the proof of Theorem 8.25, the inequalities become equalities. Since J is a primal potential solution and the tableau is optimal, J is a potential basis. Similarly, K is a potential basis. $\qquad \square$

In view of Definitions 8.6 and 8.7, it is easily seen how to modify other duality characterizations. For example, complementary slackness becomes the following theorem.

Theorem 8.26. Let $(x; \sigma)$ and $(u; \lambda)$ be feasible solutions for $\langle P \rangle$ and $\langle D \rangle$, respectively. They are nondominated solutions if

$$u^T(Ax - D\sigma) = 0$$

and

$$(\lambda C - u^T A)x = 0.$$

8.4.6. An Example

Consider the problem

$$\langle P \rangle \qquad \max \begin{bmatrix} 1 & -1 & 1 \\ 2 & 1 & 2 \\ 1 & 1 & -1 \end{bmatrix} \begin{bmatrix} x_1 \\ x_2 \\ x_3 \end{bmatrix}$$

$$\text{s.t.} \begin{bmatrix} 0 & 1 & 1 \\ 2 & 3 & -1 \\ 2 & -1 & 0 \end{bmatrix} \begin{bmatrix} x_1 \\ x_2 \\ x_3 \end{bmatrix} \leqq \begin{bmatrix} 1 & -1 & 2 \\ -1 & 3 & 0 \\ 0 & 1 & -3 \end{bmatrix},$$

$$x_1, x_2, x_3 \geqq 0.$$

We form the initial MC² tableau (Tableau 8.14).

Tableau 8.14

	x_1	x_2	x_3	x_4	x_5	x_6				Σ
x_4	0	1	①	1	0	0	1	-1	2	2
x_5	2	3	-1	0	1	0	-1	3	0	2
x_6	2	-1	0	0	0	1	0	1	-3	-2
	-1	1	-1	0	0	0	0	0	0	0
	-2	-1	-2	0	0	0	0	0	0	0
	-1	-1	1	0	0	0	0	0	0	0
Σ	-4	-1	-2	0	0	0	0	0	0	0

Since $Z_1 < 0$, we immediately see that $J = \{4, 5, 6\}$ is not a dual potential solution. However, $J = \{4, 5, 6\}$ is a primal potential solution [e.g., $\sigma = (3, 3, 1)$].

Each ray of the cone, $\Gamma(\{4, 5, 6\})$ is uniquely represented by a point of the simplex

$$S = \left\{ \sigma \, \middle| \, \sum_{i=1}^{3} \sigma_i = 1, \sigma_i \geqq 0 \right\}.$$

This allows us to represent the three dimensional set $\Gamma(\{4, 5, 6\})$ by the two-dimensional graph given in Figure 8.4.

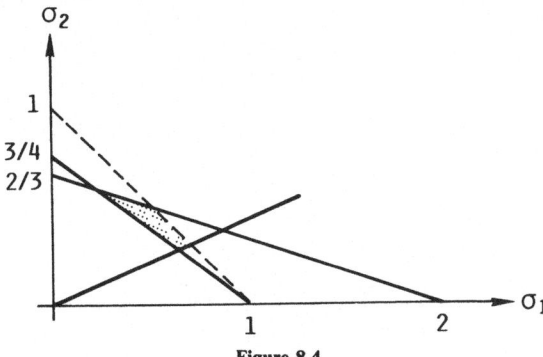

Figure 8.4

We now pivot (on the circled element in Tableau 8.14) to the basis $J = \{3, 5, 6\}$. The resulting Tableau 8.15 is as follows.

Tableau 8.15

	x_1	x_2	x_3	x_4	x_5	x_6				Σ
x_3	0	1	1	1	0	0	1	−1	2	2
x_5	2	4	0	1	1	0	0	2	2	4
x_6	②	−1	0	0	0	1	0	1	−3	−2
	−1	2	0	1	0	0	1	−1	2	2
	−2	1	0	2	0	0	2	−2	4	4
	−1	−2	0	−1	0	0	−1	1	−2	−2
Σ	−4	1	0	2	0	0	2	−2	4	4

As before, since $Z_1 < 0$, $J = (3, 5, 6)$ is not a dual potential solution. If we graph $\Gamma(\{3, 5, 6\})$ (see Figure 8.5) we notice that it contains $\Gamma(\{4, 5, 6\})$, in agreement with equation (8.66). (See also Remark 8.24.)

Pivoting again we obtain Tableau 8.16 associated with the basis $J_1 = \{1, 3, 5\}$.

Tableau 8.16

	x_1	x_2	x_3	x_4	x_5	x_6				Σ
x_3	0	1	1	1	0	0	1	−1	2	2
x_5	0	5	0	1	1	−1	0	1	5	6
x_1	1	$-\frac{1}{2}$	0	0	0	$\frac{1}{2}$	0	$\frac{1}{2}$	$-\frac{3}{2}$	−1
	0	$\frac{3}{2}$	0	1	0	$\frac{1}{2}$	1	$-\frac{1}{2}$	$\frac{1}{2}$	1
	0	0	0	2	0	1	2	−1	1	2
	0	$-\frac{5}{2}$	0	−1	0	$\frac{1}{2}$	−1	$\frac{3}{2}$	$-\frac{7}{2}$	−3
Σ	0	−1	0	2	0	2	2	0	−2	0

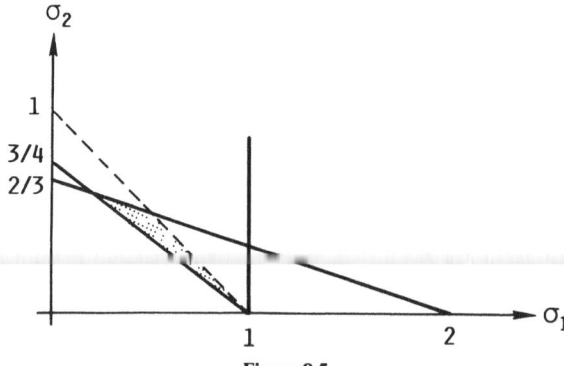

Figure 8.5

Since $Z_{1k} > 0$ for $k \in J'$, $\lambda = (1, \varepsilon, \varepsilon) \in \Gamma(J_1)$ if ε is a small positive number. Thus $J_1 = \{1, 3, 5\}$ is a dual potential solution. To check primal potentiality, we form the initial Tableau 8.17 (using Theorem 8.19) and pivot to obtain Tableau 8.18.

Tableau 8.17

	y_1	y_2	y_3	e_1	e_2	e_3	
e_1	1	0	0	1	0	0	0
e_2	-1	1	$\frac{1}{2}$	0	1	0	0
e_3	2	5	$-\frac{3}{2}$	0	0	1	0
Σ	2	6	-1	0	0	0	0

Tableau 8.18

	y_1	y_2	y_3	e_1	e_2	e_3	
e_1	1	0	0	1	0	0	0
y_3	-2	2	1	0	2	0	0
e_3	-1	8	0	0	3	1	0
Σ	0	8	0	0	2	0	0

Since the maximal value is zero, we conclude that $J_1 = \{1, 3, 5\}$ is primal potential and hence a potential solution.

We now wish to find which constraints are effective or null. Using Theorem 8.23 and Remark 8.28, we form the Tableau (8.19) for $\Gamma(J_1)$.

Tableau 8.19

	v_1	v_2	v_3	w_1	w_2	w_3	Σ
w_1	-1	1	-2	1	0	0	2
w_2	0	-1	-5	0	1	0	6
w_3	0	$-\frac{1}{2}$	$\frac{3}{2}$	0	0	1	-1

Tableau 8.20

	v_1	v_2	v_3	w_1	w_2	w_3	Σ
w_1	-1	0	1	1	0	2	0
w_2	0	0	-8	0	1	-2	8
v_2	0	1	-3	0	0	-2	2

Pivoting to a feasible Tableau 8.20 we see $w_1 = 0$ and $w_3 = 0$ (since it is nonbasic) and w_2 will always be positive. Thus, the rows corresponding to x_3 and x_1 in Tableau 8.16 are effective.

To check the effective constraints for $\Lambda(J_1)$, we form Tableau 8.21 (using Theorem 8.23) and pivot to Tableau 8.22.

Tableau 8.21

	v_1	v_2	v_3	w_1	w_2	w_3	Σ
w_1	$\left(-\frac{3}{2}\right)$	0	$\frac{5}{2}$	1	0	0	-1
w_2	-1	-2	1	0	1	0	2
w_3	$-\frac{1}{2}$	-1	$-\frac{1}{2}$	0	0	1	2

Tableau 8.22

	v_1	v_2	v_3	w_1	w_2	w_3	Σ
v_1	1	0	$-\frac{5}{3}$	$-\frac{2}{3}$	0	0	$\frac{2}{3}$
w_2	0	-2	$-\frac{2}{3}$	$-\frac{2}{3}$	1	0	$\frac{8}{3}$
w_3	0	-1	$-\frac{4}{3}$	$-\frac{1}{3}$	0	1	$\frac{7}{3}$

The only effective constraint is that corresponding to w_1 (because w_2 and w_3 are always positive). Therefore, the only effective column of Tableau 8.16 is x_2.

We now determine the adjacent bases of J_1. We need to consider only those obtained by introducing x_2 [effective constraint of $\Lambda(J_1)$] or removing either x_3 or x_1 [the effective constraints of $\Gamma(J_1)$]. To introduce x_2, we could remove x_3 or x_5 (since the pivot element must be positive). The resulting bases are $\{1, 2, 5\}$ and $\{1, 2, 3\}$. In removing x_1, since the pivot element must be negative, the only possibility for introduction into the basis is x_2, which results in $\{2, 3, 5\}$. Since $Y^1 \geq 0$ (no negative pivot elements in the first row) we cannot remove x_3. Thus the bases adjacent to $J_1 = \{1, 3, 5\}$ which must be checked are $\{1, 2, 5\}$, $\{1, 2, 3\}$, and $\{2, 3, 5\}$. Pivoting to each of these in turn and using the potential subroutine we find that they are potential solutions. Continuing in the above manner, we find the entire set of potential solutions. It consists of the nine bases: $\{1, 3, 5\}, \{1, 2, 5\}, \{1, 2, 3\}, \{2, 3, 5\}, \{1, 3, 4\}, \{1, 4, 6\}, \{1, 2, 4\},$ $\{2, 3, 4\}, \{3, 4, 6\}$.

Now let us consider the dual of problem $\langle P \rangle$,

$$\min (u_1, u_2, u_3) \begin{bmatrix} 1 & -1 & 2 \\ -1 & 3 & 0 \\ 0 & 1 & -3 \end{bmatrix}$$

$$\langle D \rangle \qquad \text{s.t.} \ (u_1, u_2, u_3) \begin{bmatrix} 0 & 1 & 1 \\ 2 & 3 & -1 \\ 2 & -1 & 0 \end{bmatrix} \geq \begin{bmatrix} 1 & -1 & 1 \\ 2 & 1 & 2 \\ 1 & 1 & -1 \end{bmatrix}$$

$$u_1, u_2, u_3 \geq 0.$$

Tableau 8.16, associated with the potential solution $J_1 = \{1, 3, 5\}$, contains the submatrices

$$B^{-1}D = \begin{bmatrix} 1 & -1 & 2 \\ 0 & 1 & 5 \\ 0 & \frac{1}{2} & -\frac{3}{2} \end{bmatrix}$$

and

$$C_B B^{-1} = \begin{bmatrix} 1 & 0 & \frac{1}{2} \\ 2 & 0 & 1 \\ -1 & 0 & \frac{1}{2} \end{bmatrix}.$$

If we choose $\sigma = (5, 5, 1) \in \Gamma(J_1)$ and $\lambda = (5, 1, 1) \in \Lambda(J_1)$, then

$$x(J_1) = B^{-1}D\sigma = (2, 10, 1)^T$$

and

$$u(J_1) = \lambda C_B B^{-1} = (6, 0, 4).$$

Thus

$$(x_1, x_2, x_3) = (1, 0, 2)$$

and

$$(u_1, u_2, u_3) = (6, 0, 4)$$

are $\langle P \rangle$ and $\langle D \rangle$ feasible for $\sigma = (5, 5, 1)$ and $\lambda = (5, 1, 1)$. Furthermore, the functional values λCx and $u^T D\sigma$ are equal. This will be true for any $(\lambda, \sigma) \in \Lambda(J_1) \times \Gamma(J_1)$ since

$$\lambda Cx = \lambda C_B x(J_1) = \lambda C_B B^{-1}D\sigma = u^T D\sigma.$$

The verification of further relationships is left to the reader.

8.5. Further Comments

As linear functions have many unique properties, linear multicriteria problems enjoy a number of unique features. To facilitate computation, we have introduced the MC and MC²-simplex methods as natural extensions of the ordinary simplex method. Our description is based on Yu and Zeleny (Ref. 508) and Seiford and Yu (Ref. 406). However, there are many interesting and related articles. Just to list a few: Koopmans (Ref. 262) discussed interesting economic applications in terms of activity analysis. Charnes and Cooper (Vol. 1, Ref. 77) talked about some extensions including functional efficiency. Evans and Steuer (Ref. 127) derived a procedure to locate N-points. Gal (Ref. 155) discussed extended simplex methods from a parametric programming point of view. Ecker, Hegner, and Kouada (Ref. 121) derived a procedure to locate N-faces from N_{ex}-points. Many more references can be found in the references quoted above.

8.6. Appendix: Proof of Lemma 8.2

We shall restate and prove the lemma after deriving two results.

Lemma 8.6. Suppose that Y is a polyhedron that contains the origin. Then the cone $\hat{Y}$, generated by Y (i.e.,

$$\hat{Y} = \{\alpha y \mid \alpha \geq 0, \, \alpha \in R^1, \, y \in Y\})$$

is a polyhedral cone.

Proof. By the finite basis theorem (Ref. 438, p. 46), there are $Y_1 = \{y^1, \ldots, y^p\}$, $Y_2 = \{y^{p+1}, \ldots, y^r\}$, $r \geq p$, such that each y of Y can be written as

$$y = \sum_{j=1}^{p} \alpha_j y^j + \sum_{j=p+1}^{r} \beta_j y^j,$$

where

$$\alpha_j, \beta_j \geq 0 \quad \text{and} \quad \sum_{j=1}^{p} \alpha_j = 1.$$

Since $0 \in Y$, we can write

(A) $$0 = \sum_{j=1}^{p} \alpha_j^0 y^j + \sum_{j=p+1}^{r} \beta_j^0 y^j,$$

where

$$\alpha_j^0, \beta_j^0 \geq 0 \quad \text{and} \quad \sum_{j=1}^{p} \alpha_j^0 = 1.$$

Suppose that

$$y = \sum_{j=p+1}^{q} \beta_j y^j, \qquad \beta_j \geqq 0.$$

Then, by (A),

$$y = y + 0 = \sum_{j=1}^{p} \alpha_j^0 y^j + \sum_{j=p+1}^{r} (\beta_j^0 + \beta_j) y^j \in Y.$$

Our proof will be completed once we have shown that

$$\hat{Y} = \Lambda \equiv \left\{ \sum_{j=1}^{r} \gamma_j y^j \,\middle|\, \gamma_j \geqq 0 \right\}.$$

Clearly $\hat{Y} \subset \Lambda$. In order to see that $\hat{Y} \supset \Lambda$, let

$$y^0 = \sum_{j=1}^{q} \gamma_j y^j, \qquad \gamma_j \geqq 0.$$

We must show that $y^0 = \alpha y$ for some $y \in Y$ and $\alpha \geqq 0$. Observe that if $\gamma_j = 0$, for all $j = 1, \ldots, p$, then $y^0 \in Y$ as established before. We have no problem. Now suppose that at least one $\gamma_j > 0$, $0 \leqq j \leqq p$. Then

$$\gamma_0 = \sum_{j=1}^{p} \gamma_j > 0.$$

It is easily verified that

$$\frac{1}{\gamma_0} y^0 = \frac{1}{\gamma_0} \sum_{j=1}^{r} \gamma_j y^j \in Y.$$

Thus $\alpha = \gamma_0$ and our proof is complete. $\square$

If $\Lambda = \{x | Ax \leqq 0\}$ is a polyhedral cone, we see that $\Lambda^* = \{yA | y \geqq 0\}$. It can be shown that (Ref. 495, Remark 5.9) the relative interior of Λ^* is given by ri $\Lambda^* = \{yA | y > 0\}$. (It is understood that x is a column vector; y a row vector.)

Lemma 8.7. Let Λ_1 and Λ_2 be two polyhedral cones in R^q. Then $\Lambda_1 \cap (-\Lambda_2) = \{0\}$ implies that ri $\Lambda_1^* \cap$ ri $\Lambda_2^* \neq \varnothing$.

Proof. Since Λ_1 and Λ_2 are polyhedral cones, we can write

$$\Lambda_1 = \{x | Ax \leqq 0\} \quad \text{and} \quad \Lambda_2 = \{x | Bx \leqq 0\},$$

where A and B are two matrices of proper orders.

Since $-\Lambda_2 = \{x | -Bx \leqq 0\}$, $\Lambda_1 \cap (-\Lambda_2) = \{0\}$ implies that

$$\Lambda_3 = \{x | (_{-B}^{A})x \leqq 0\} = \varnothing.$$

This is true because $\Lambda_3 \subset \Lambda_1 \cap (-\Lambda_2)$ and $x \in \Lambda_3$ implies $x \neq 0$. By Stiemke's alternative theorem (see Ref. 307, p. 32) there are $y_1 > 0$, $y_2 > 0$ so that $-y_1 A + y_2 B = 0$ or $y_1 A = y_2 B$. Since $y_1 > 0$, $y_2 > 0$, $y_1 A \in \text{ri } \Lambda_1^*$ and $y_2 B \in \text{ri } \Lambda_2^*$. This shows that $\text{ri } \Lambda_1^* \cap \text{ri } \Lambda_2^* \neq \varnothing$. □

Lemma 8.2. Let Λ be a polyhedral cone and Y be a polyhedron containing the origin. Suppose for each $\beta \in \text{ri } \Lambda^*$, there is $y \in Y$ such that $\beta \cdot y > 0$. Then $0 \in y + {}'\Lambda$ for some $y \in Y$.

Proof. Assume the contrary. Then $Y \cap (-\Lambda) = \{0\}$. Let

$$\hat{Y} = \{\alpha y | \alpha \geqq 0, \alpha \in R^1, y \in Y\}.$$

From Lemma 8.6, we know that $\hat{Y}$ is a polyhedral cone. We first show that $\hat{Y} \cap -\Lambda = \{0\}$. In order to see this point, suppose $y^0 \neq 0$ and $y^0 \in \hat{Y} \cap -\Lambda$. Then $y^0 = \alpha y$ for some $\alpha > 0$ and $y \in Y$, $y \neq 0$. Since $y^0 \in -\Lambda$ and $-\Lambda$ is a cone, $y \in -\Lambda$. This shows that $y \neq 0$ and $y \in Y \cap -\Lambda$, which leads to a contradiction of $Y \cap -\Lambda = \{0\}$.

Since $\hat{Y} \cap -\Lambda = \{0\}$ and both are polyhedral cones, by Lemma 8.7, $\text{ri } Y^* \cap \text{ri } \Lambda^* \neq \varnothing$. Let $\beta \in \text{ri } \hat{Y}^* \cap \text{ri } \Lambda^*$. Then $\beta \cdot y \leqq 0$ for all $y \in Y \subset \hat{Y}$. This leads to a contradiction. □

Exercises

8.1. Consider the following single-objective linear programming problem:

$$\text{maximize } z = x_1 + x_2$$

$$\text{s.t. } 3x_1 + x_2 \leqq 12,$$

$$2x_1 + x_2 \leqq 9,$$

$$x_1 + 2x_2 \leqq 12,$$

$$x_1, x_2 \geqq 0.$$

The following is one of its possible simplex tableaus:

x_1	x_2	x_3	x_4	x_5	
1	$\frac{1}{3}$	$\frac{1}{3}$	0	0	4
0	$\frac{1}{3}$	$-\frac{2}{3}$	1	0	1
0	$\frac{5}{3}$	$-\frac{1}{3}$	0	1	8
0	$-\frac{2}{3}$	$\frac{1}{3}$	0	0	4

Using the notation in (8.20) and (8.21), identify the following:
a. B^{-1}
b. $B^{-1}A$
c. $C_B B^{-1} A - C$
d. $C_B B^{-1} d$

8.2. Consider the following intermediate MC-simplex tableau for the multicriteria problem with three decision variables (x_1, x_2, and x_3) and three linear constraints (all "$\leq$" inequalities). There are two objective functions to be maximized.

x_1	x_2	x_3	x_4	x_5	x_6	RHS
2	1	-3	-1	0	0	2
-1	0	2	1	1	0	1
-1	0	-1	0	0	1	1
-2	0	1	1	0	0	5
1	0	-2	-2	0	0	3

a. Using the notation in (8.22)–(8.24), identify the following:
   i. $Z(J)$
   ii. Z^1
   iii. $Z_j^1, j \in J'$
   iv. $C_B B^{-1} d$
b. In the above tableau, $x(J) = (0, 2, 0, 0, 1, 1)$. Identify $\Lambda(J)$ and sketch it on the graph as shown in Figure 8.1. Is $\Lambda(J) \cap \Lambda^> = \emptyset$?
c. Using the nondominance test given by Theorem 8.8, find w_{max}. Is $x(J) \in N_{ex}$? Explain.

8.3. The following is an intermediate MC-simplex tableau with seven decision variables (x's) and four linear constraints (all "$\leq$"), thus there are four slack variables (y's). There are three objective functions for this problem.

x_1	x_2	x_3	x_4	x_5	x_6	x_7	y_1	y_2	y_3	y_4	RHS
$\frac{1}{2}$	1	$\frac{1}{2}$	$\frac{1}{2}$	1	$\frac{1}{2}$	1	$\frac{1}{2}$	0	0	0	8
-3	-3	-1	0	0	-1	-1	-1	1	0	0	0
-2	-2	0	-1	0	-1	-4	-1	0	1	0	0
$-\frac{1}{2}$	0	$\frac{3}{2}$	$-\frac{3}{2}$	0	$-\frac{5}{2}$	-2	$-\frac{1}{2}$	0	0	1	8
0	0	2	-2	0	1	1	1	0	0	0	16
$\frac{3}{2}$	2	$\frac{1}{2}$	$-\frac{1}{2}$	0	$\frac{1}{2}$	3	$\frac{3}{2}$	0	0	0	24
-1	0	-1	1	0	1	1	0	0	0	0	0
$\frac{1}{2}$	2	$\frac{3}{2}$	$-\frac{3}{2}$	0	$\frac{5}{2}$	5	$\frac{5}{2}$	0	0	0	40

a. Identify J, $x(J)$, and $Cx(J)$.
b. Use the nondominance test (Theorem 8.8) to see whether $x(J)$ is nondominated. What is w_{max}?
c. Is $x(J) \in N_{ex}$? Why or why not?
d. If $x(J) \in N_{ex}$, then find the optimal weight for $x(J)$.

e. By pivoting $(1, 4)$ (i.e., by entering x_4 into the basis and departing x_5 from the basis), we get the next MC-simplex tableau as follows:

x_1	x_2	x_3	x_4	x_5	x_6	x_7	y_1	y_2	y_3	y_4	RHS
1	2	1	1	2	1	2	1	0	0	0	16
-3	-3	-1	0	0	-1	-1	-1	1	0	0	0
-1	0	1	0	2	0	-2	0	0	1	0	16
1	3	3	0	3	-1	1	1	0	0	1	32
2	4	4	0	4	3	5	3	0	0	0	48
2	3	1	0	1	1	4	2	0	0	0	32
-2	-2	-2	0	-2	0	-1	-1	0	0	0	-16
2	5	3	0	3	4	8	4	0	0	0	64

    i. Specify J, $x(J)$, and $Cx(J)$.
    ii. Clearly, $x(J) \in N_{ex}$. Why?
    iii. Using the nondominance test (Theorem 8.8), verify $x(J) \in N_{ex}$.
    iv. Find the set of optimal weights $\Lambda(J)$.
  f. By pivoting $(1, 1)$, construct the next MC-simplex tableau.

8.4. Refer to Exercise 8.3.
  a. Find the N_{ex}-effective constraints of $\Lambda(J)$ where $x(J) = (0, 0, 0, 0, 8, 0, 0, 0, 8)$ in the first tableau.
  b. Identify the columns that cannot be N_{ex}-effective constraints of $\Lambda(J)$.

8.5. Prove Theorem 8.9.

8.6. Refer to Example 8.1 in Section 8.2.1.
  a. Identify the effective constraints of $\Lambda(J_1)$.
  b. Find H_k that separates $\Lambda(J)$ and $\Lambda(K)$ where $\Lambda(J) = \Lambda(J_1)$ and $\Lambda(K) = \Lambda(J_2)$.
  c. What is $\Lambda(J_2) \cap \Lambda(J_3) \cap \Lambda^>$?
  d. The separation properties given by Theorem 8.10 are not valid for $\Lambda(J_1)$ and $\Lambda(J_3)$. Why not? (See Figure 8.1.) Describe the separation properties for bases J_2, J_3, and J_4.

8.7. Consider the following linear multiobjective problem:

$$\text{maximize } y_1 = f_1(x_1, x_2) = 2x_1 + 3x_2,$$

$$\text{maximize } y_2 = f_2(x_1, x_2) = 2x_1 + x_2,$$

$$\text{subject to } x_1 + x_2 \leq 10,$$

$$x_1 \leq 6,$$

$$x_2 \leq 6,$$

$$x_1, x_2 \geq 0.$$

Find all nondominated extreme-points (N_{ex}) to the above problem and specify their corresponding weights for optimality.

8.8. Solve the problem stated in Example 8.3 using the MC-simplex method. Specify $x(J)$ and $Cx(J)$ in each iteration and identify whether $x(J)$ is an N_{ex}-point. For each N_{ex}-point specify the effective constraints for the set of optimal weights. Verify your solutions with those stated in Example 8.3.

8.9. The following tableau is an intermediate MC²-simplex tableau with three decision variables (x_1, x_2, and x_3) and three constraints (all "$\leq$", thus three slack variables x_4, x_5, and x_6).

x_1	x_2	x_3	x_4	x_5	x_6				Σ
0	−2	0	1	−2	−1	4	−1	−5	−2
1	1	0	0	1	0	−1	1	2	−2
0	2	1	0	1	1	−1	1	2	2
0	5	0	0	4	2	−4	4	8	8
0	3	0	0	3	2	−3	3	6	6
0	2	0	0	3	1	−3	3	6	6
Σ 0	10	0	0	10	5	−10	10	20	20

a. Identify the basis J.
b. J is a dual potential solution. Why? Explain.
c. Run the subroutine defined by Theorem 8.19 to check the primal potentiality of J. What is w_{max}?
d. Check the effective constraints of $\Gamma(J)$ and $\Lambda(J)$ and identify the corresponding optimal weights.
e. By pivoting $(1, 2)$ (i.e., departing x_4 from the basis and entering x_2 into the basis), construct the next tableau.

8.10. Find all potential solutions for the following linear systems and specify their corresponding weights for optimality.

$$\max Cx$$

$$\text{s.t. } Ax \leq D,$$

$$x \geq 0,$$

where

$$C = \begin{bmatrix} 1 & 0 & 1 \\ -1 & 1 & 0 \\ 0 & 1 & 1 \end{bmatrix},$$

$$D = \begin{bmatrix} 20 & 40 \\ 20 & 30 \\ 20 & 10 \end{bmatrix},$$

$$A = \begin{bmatrix} 1 & 1 & 1 \\ 1 & -1 & 0 \\ 0 & 1 & 1 \end{bmatrix}.$$

8.11. Identify the relationship between Theorem 8.9 and Theorem 8.12. How do you incorporate both of them to locate all N_{ex}-points?

8.12. Derive a method to locate all N-faces from N_{ex}-points when X may be unbounded.

8.13. Prove Theorem 8.19.

8.14. Refer to Remark 8.27. State and prove a "dual" theorem to Theorem 8.21.

8.15. Prove Theorem 8.23.

8.16. Prove Theorem 8.26.

8.17. Identify all potential solutions for the problem stated in the example of Section 8.4.6. Compare your solutions with those stated in the example.

Suggested Reading

The following references are particularly pertinent to this chapter: 77, 78, 119, 121, 127, 153, 155, 156, 262, 307, 406, 433, 438, 495, 508, 509, 516.

9

Behavioral Bases and Habitual Domains of Decision Making

9.1. Introduction

Through the last seven chapters we have studied the fundamental concepts and techniques for decision making with multiple criteria. It is time for us to pause and ask ourselves two questions: (i) Can we apply the techniques to handle our own important problems? I.e., can we use the techniques to help solve the problem of buying a good house, choosing a good job, improving our career, becoming happier and more successful in working with other people and businesses? (ii) Can we sell our techniques to help other people? (I.e., can we help solve other people's nontrivial problems—career selection, conflict resolution; can we solve "product design," distribution and marketing planning problems for a corporation?)

Most likely we will find ourselves powerless and unable to apply what we have learned to the problems mentioned above. This does not imply that what we have learned is useless; rather, it implies that what we have learned is inadequate for us to apply. Let us ask ourselves: (i) Do we really know how we, as a living system, make a decision and behave as we have behaved? and (ii) Do we actually know the people with whom we work; do we know how they reach their final decision and behave as they have manifested? If we cannot have a good understanding of ourselves and the people we work with, how can we expect to have successful sales of our techniques to ourselves and others!?

The purpose of this chapter is to fill in the gap between the technical concepts and the application arts by presenting the basic mechanism of human behavior and decision making in a larger scope than just mathematical optimization. A good digestion of the materials presented here will enable us to understand and know more about ourselves and others and consequently

271

allow us to solve our problems and the problems of others more effectively and more successfully, not to mention that it could make our lives happier and more meaningful!

Observe that human beings as living systems may be, in abstract, regarded as "supercomputers" that encode, store, and retrieve information. The computers allocate their information processing time over various jobs according to certain rules, and so does our brain. This similarity allows us to use supercomputers to conceptualize the working of human brains and behaviors. Admittedly, our brains, after millions of years of evolution and debugging, are far more complex and advanced than any supercomputer. The abstract analogy gives us a concrete conceptualization of the working of the brains for decision making. The reader is urged to use "computer systems" concepts for a better understanding of the concepts presented here. But conception of human brains and behaviors should not be limited by computer concepts.

The main idea of our model for human decision/behavior is that each human being has an endowed internal information processing capacity which is consciously allocated to various activities and events *over time* so as to achieve many-dimensional aspects of life goals and equilibrium points. The allocation activity is called *attention.* It serves to allocate this capacity according to a *least resistance principle* so as to efficiently discharge the tension (or charge) which results from the deviation of *perceived* goal states from *ideal* goal states. The whole framework utilizes eight hypotheses which are based upon the observations of the psychologists. The framework also utilizes optimization concepts of management scientists. However, the concepts used here are somewhat broader than the traditional ones.

The entire framework is given in Section 9.2, with an overview in Section 9.2.1. Section 9.2.2 is devoted to the basic working of the internal information processing center; Section 9.2.3 to goal setting, self-suggestions, and state valuation; Section 9.2.4 to hierarchical structures of charges and attention; Section 9.2.5 to discharges, problem solving, and attention outputs; Section 9.2.6 to external information inputs. In the description of Section 9.2, we borrow heavily from the observations of experimental psychologists, especially from Lindsay and Norman (Ref. 297) and Vernon (Ref. 459). A variety of other sources (Refs. 186, 201, 209, 323, 351, 370, 521) also have influenced us. The hypotheses are formed as a summary of the observations. In Sections 9.2.3–9.2.5 the reader can skip the mathematics, but not the hypotheses, without losing any understanding of the main conceptual model. The mathematics are used to make our concepts precise and for further development.

We then devote Section 9.3 to the discussion of habitual domains. Section 9.3.1 is devoted to the definition and formulation of habitual domains in terms of the hypotheses in Section 9.2; Section 9.3.2 to the expansion of habitual domains; Section 9.3.3 to the interaction of habitual domains. Again the reader may read the introduction of each section and skip the mathematics without losing the main ideas. The concepts of habitual domains play important roles in later applications.

In Section 9.4 we summarize some observations contributed by social psychologists. These observations are related to the hypotheses discussed in Section 9.2 and are important in applications.

Finally we devote Section 9.5 to applications in which theoretical observations and practical applications are integrated. Section 9.5.1 is devoted to self-awareness, happiness, and success; Section 9.5.2 to decision making; Section 9.5.3 to persuasion, negotiation, and gaming; and Section 9.5.4 to career management.

Hopefully, this chapter can help us better understand human decision/behavior so that we can better apply what we have learned. For the scientist, we hope to show how to build a conceptual model that is practically applicable. For the practitioners, we hope to provide a basic conceptual model that will improve their success and happiness and will broaden their wisdom.

9.2. Behavioral Bases for Decision Making

9.2.1. A Model for Decision/Behavior Processes—Overview

In order to capture the main ideas, and the dynamic and integrative features of human decision/behavior processes, Figure 9.1 is constructed. The main ideas of the model are worth mentioning.

(i) Each individual is endowed with an internal information-processing and problem-solving capacity, which can vary with time. *Attention (box 6) is identified as human conscious time allocation of his internal information processing and problem solving capacity over various activities and events.* The time could be measured in milliseconds as units. The allocation has a direct impact on his allocation of internal body resources and external economic resources.

(ii) A number of state variables are used to describe human physiological conditions, social situation, and self-suggested goals. Each state variable is constantly monitored and interpreted. When its current value is significantly different from its goal value (ideal state), a charge (tension) will be produced. The charges produced by the various states form a hierarchical system. Depending on the relative importance of the states and how significant the deviations of the perceived values are from the ideal values, the hierarchy is determined. The system can be reframed dynamically (boxes 1-5).

(iii) The purpose of attention is to release the charges in the most efficient way. These involve (A) actions and discharges when solutions are obtained (boxes 8 and 9), (B) acquiring external information (boxes 7, 12, and 13), or (C) self-suggestion for internal thinking, justification, and rationalization (box

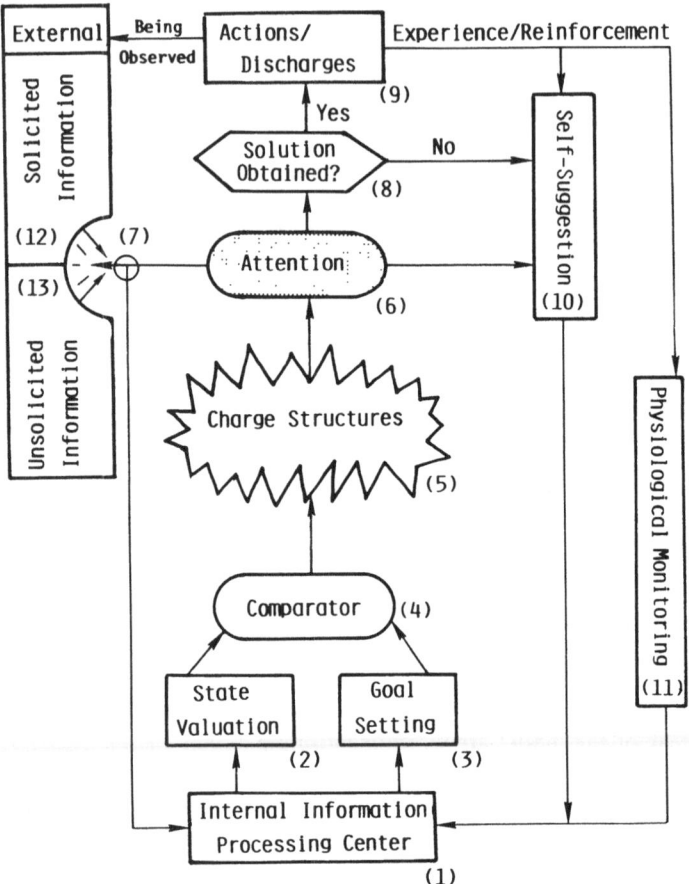

Figure 9.1. A model of decision/behavior processes.

10). All of these functions feed back to the internal information processing center.

(iv) All functions/components of the figure are interconnected. Through time they interact with each other. For instance, once an action is taken (box 9), say accepting an offer or having a good time, the event and its consequence will be observed and registered in the decision maker's memory (box 1) and most likely will be observed and interpreted by other parties (boxes 12 and 13), which may in turn react upon the original decision maker (boxes 7 and 1).

9.2.2. Internal Information Processing Center—The Brain

Although there is disagreement among psychologists in interpreting experimental results, there is no disagreement that the brain is the human internal information processing center. Furthermore, they all recognize that when external stimuli are presented to and attended by a human being, a sequence of circuit patterns of activated neural cells (neurons) appears in the brain. This sequence is regarded as the interpretation and thinking process engendered by the stimuli. Much is known and more is unknown about the human brain. (For a discussion see Refs. 201 and 297.)

The brain is a very fascinating and complex device. It performs the functions of computers such as encoding, storing, retrieving, and interpretation. Four hypotheses on this performance, central to our analysis of human behaviors/decisions, follow.

H1. Circuit Pattern Hypothesis

(i) Each unit of thought, concept or message is encoded and represented as a circuit pattern which diffuses to many sections of the brain. The encoding occurs when the attention is paid.

(ii) When the thoughts, concepts or messages are repeated, the corresponding circuit patterns will be reinforced and strengthened. Furthermore, they will be imprinted in new sections of the brain.

(iii) The stronger the circuit patterns and the more sections of the brain containing the patterns, the more easily the corresponding thoughts, concepts, or messages are retrieved and employed in the thinking and interpreting processes.

(iv) A thinking and interpreting process of an event corresponds to a *time sequence* of circuit patterns activated in the brain. When such is sufficiently strong to be unbreakable, it may be regarded as a *process* or *sequence unit.*

Remark 9.1. (i) Some interesting accounts concerning (ii) and (iii) can be found in Ref. 297, pp. 287–327.

(ii) H1 implies that new thoughts or concepts are the results of new circuit patterns. Since it always takes time to imprint new circuit patterns, no matter how small, it implies that time is required to create or accept new ideas.

(iii) H1(iv) implies that a thinking or interpreting process unit can be regarded, in computer parlance, as a (sub-) program unit. When a program unit is sufficiently strengthened by repetition, it can easily be retrieved and will appear in thinking and interpreting processes [see H1(iii)]. Note that this phenomenon can be used to interpret human conditioned behavior. (That is a fixed response pattern to a particular stimulus.) (See Hilgard and Bower, Ref. 209, for further discussion of conditioned behaviors.)

One wonders what the capacity of the brain is for encoding and storing thoughts, concepts, and messages. We adopt the following hypothesis.

H2. Unlimited Capacity Hypothesis

"Practically each normal brain has the capacity to encode and store all thoughts, concepts, and messages that one ever attends to."

Remark 9.2. (i) Theoretically the brain is a finite device. However, there are at least ten billion (10^{10}) neurons in the brain. According to H1, the brain can recognize approximately $2^{10^{10}}$ basic thoughts, concepts, or messages from the neurons at any point of time. This number is astronomical. If one represents the thoughts, concepts, and messages in terms of *sequences* of patterns over time, then the number of thoughts, concepts, and messages which can be encoded and stored in the brain is almost unlimited. (See page 289 of Ref. 297 for a further discussion.) The hypothesis is therefore not unreasonable.

(ii) H1 has an implication that the stored thoughts, concepts, and messages are never complete. They can be expanded as long as we want. Consequently, *everyone is subject to suggestions of new ideas.*

H3. Most Efficient Restructuring Hypothesis

"The encoded thoughts, concepts, and messages (H1) are organized and stored systematically as data bases for efficient retrieving. Furthermore, according to the dictation of attention, they are continuously restructured so that the relevant ones can be most efficiently retrieved to release charges."

Remark 9.3. (i) Attention plays a vital role in encoding through self-suggestion and in controlling the inputs of external information (H1) (boxes 7 and 10). It is also vital for storing and retrieving thoughts, concepts, and messages (H3). Thus, when facing uncertainty, one usually will be better off in coping with it if one prepares. Thus attention is paid and the memory structure is reorganized, so that the methods to cope with the uncertainty can be retrieved more easily.

(ii) Combining H1 and H3 we see that there are three ways that influence retrieving a concept, thought, or message: the strength of the corresponding circuit pattern, the number of sections of the brain in which the circuit pattern is encoded, and the storage structure. The attention not only affects the first two (H1), but also dynamically changes the last (H3). Thus, if we have not paid attention to a friend for a long time, we may forget his name because his name may be stored in a remote area in the brain and is difficult to retrieve.

(iii) This hypothesis is partially motivated by the findings in experimental psychology as discussed in Ref. 297, pp. 375-434.

H4. Analogy/Association Hypothesis

"The perception or conception of new events, subjects, or ideas can be learned primarily by the analogy and/or association with what is already known. Confronted with a new event, the brain first investigates its features and attributes to establish a relationship, an analogy, and/or association, of the new event to those already known. Once the "right" relationship has been established, the whole of the past knowledge (preexisting memory structures) is automatically brought to bear on the interpretation and understanding of the new event."

Remark 9.4. (i) Suppose it is known that property A implies property B. Now suppose that property C is very analogous to A. Then, according to H4, it will likely be inferred that property C will imply an analogon of property B. Thus, if we learn that a particular monkey likes bananas, then we may infer that another monkey will also like bananas.

(ii) Let A be a set of causes that is known to imply state B, and C a new set of causes with $A \cap C \neq \emptyset$. Then, if the size of $A \cap C$ relative to A and C is sufficiently large, it may be inferred that B follows from C. The actual learning process could be more complicated than H4. However, H4 does express a general tendency of learning.

(iii) H4 has an implication that new things can be more easily learned if they are similar to some things already known. The hypothesis also has a built-in *cognitive consistency* over time. Thus, if James was good at job A yesterday and job B today is similar to job A, then it is likely that James will be perceived as being good at job B today.

(iv) H4 also has important effects on labeling theory and other observations of social psychology. We shall discuss these later.

(v) See Ref. 297, pp. 403-434, for some related findings in experimental psychology.

9.2.3. Goal Setting, Self-Suggestion, and State Valuation

Through several million years of evolution and many years of living experience, men have acquired, consciously or unconsciously, a set of living goals. Each goal can be represented by a function that describes one of many dimensional life aspects. The goal functions described in this paper have been studied extensively by psychologists under the name of motivational needs. For instance, see Vernon (Ref. 459) and those quoted in his article.

Table 9.1. A Structure of Goal Functions

---

i. *Survival and security*: physiological health (right blood pressure, body temperature, and balance of biochemical states); right level and quality of air, water, food, heat, clothes, shelter, and mobility; safety and danger free; acquisition of money and other economic goods.

ii. *Perpetuation of the species*: sexual activities; giving birth to the next generation; family love, health, and welfare.

iii. *Self-importance feeling*: self-respect and self-esteem; esteem and respect from others; power and dominance; recognition and prestige; achievement; creativity; superiority; accumulation of money and wealth; giving and accepting sympathy and protectiveness.

iv. *Social approval*: esteem and respect from others; friendship; affiliation with (desired) groups; conformity with group ideology, beliefs, attitudes, and behaviors; giving and accepting sympathy and protectiveness.

v. *Sensuous gratification*: sexual; visual; auditory; smell; taste; tactile.

vi. *Cognitive consistency and curiosity*: consistency in thinking and opinions; exploring and acquiring knowledge, truth, beauty, and religion.

vii. *Self-actualization*: ability to accept and depend on the self, to cease identifying with others, to rely on one's own standard, to aspire to the "ego-ideal" and to detach oneself from social demands and customs when desirable.

There are many ways to describe the structure of goal functions such as those in Ref. 459. None can be expected to be complete and perfect all the time for all people; otherwise H1 to H4 would be contradicted. For the convenience of our later discussion, in Table 9.1 we list a number of goal functions.

Remark 9.5. Observe that the listing of Table 9.1 is neither mutually exclusive nor collectively exhaustive. On the one hand, the goal functions may not be exactly defined and each of them may be associated with the others. For instance, self-importance may depend on survival and security, social approval, cognitive consistency and curiosity, etc. On the other hand, since no life is complete (H1–H4 of the previous section), no listing, including Table 9.1, can be expected to be complete.

Remark 9.6. The headings of Table 9.1 may be replaced. A subgoal function within a heading may be used as a heading itself when it is to be emphasized. For instance, when desired and emphasized, self-esteem may be a heading that contains survival and security, perpetuation of the species, social approval, cognitive consistency and curiosity, and self-actualization as its elements. In general, when a goal function is emphasized, it can be used as a heading and all other goal functions that are associated with it can be regarded as its possible elements.

Remark 9.7. Note that each goal function in Table 9.1 can further contain or be measured by a set of subgoal functions. For instance, physiological health can contain or be measured by blood pressure, heart beats, body temperature, hormones, and other balanced biochemical states. Wealth can contain or be measured by assets, liabilities, and their potential growth paths over time. Friendship can contain or be measured by the frequency of meeting, conformity of attitudes and behaviors, degree of mutual affection, etc. In abstract, one may think of the existence of *elementary goal functions* which contain no other subgoal functions in the data base of the internal information processing center. Then each goal function is a subset of the collection of all elementary goal functions. Two goal functions are related or associated if the two corresponding subsets have a nonempty intersection. Such ideas may supply a way to study the structures of goals.

Now no matter how many goals we are aware of, we can specify each goal function by a state variable. Our remaining questions are: how is the ideal value of each state variable selected (*goal setting*) and how is the actual value of each state variable perceived (*state valuation*); what are the consequences when a discrepancy occurs between the two values? The last question will be discussed in the next subsection.

For most people, except for some physiological goal functions which are too basic for human conscious control, almost all other goal functions are directly or indirectly subject to human conscious control and self-suggestion. By *self-suggestion* we mean the thinking and interpretation process (including goal setting) initiated by the self and uninterrupted by external stimuli. The influence of self-suggestion can be very pervasive and important in human behavior and decisions. Since it has a direct access to the internal information processing center, it can exert its influence through H1–H4. Thus, self-suggestion can generate circuit patterns to create new concepts or perceptions, to produce new goal state variables, and influence goal setting and state valuation. It can also arouse attention to restructure the data bases in the internal information processing center, and so affect information processing.

In Figure 9.1, there are three forces: self-suggestion (box 10), physiological monitoring (box 11), and external information inputs (boxes 12–13) that can affect the setting of the ideal values of the goal states (*goal setting*). When physiological health is maintained, no charge will be produced by physiological monitoring, and attention will then be determined by self-suggestion and external information. Since self-suggestion has direct access to the information processing center, and external information has access only when attention is paid, it may be fair to say that self-suggestion plays a more active role in goal setting than "external information." Because of H1–H4 we shall also realize that goal setting is a dynamic and interactive process as depicted in Figure 9.1. Except for those states related to physiological health, the ideal value of each goal function can vary with time.

The perception of the actual value of each goal state (*state valuation*) is again influenced by the three forces: self-suggestion, physiological monitoring, and external information. Again when physiological health is maintained, self-suggestion may play a more active role than external information. Like goal setting, state valuation is a dynamic and interactive process.

As goal setting and state valuation are strongly influenced and/or determined by self-suggestion, wishful thinking may occur. This is particularly possible when physiological health is maintained and when external assessment information is not available.

One also notices that both goal setting and state valuation are subject to the influence of the data base (memory) in the internal information processing center. Thus, H1–H4 of the previous section exert their influence on goal setting and state valuation. When a goal state is stored in a remote area its valuation may pass unnoticed.

Let us summarize the above discussion:

H5. Goal Setting and State Valuation Hypothesis

(i) There exists a set of goal functions in the internal information processing center which are used to measure the many dimensional aspects of life. A probable set is given in Table 9.1. The goal functions can be interdependent and interrelated to each other, but they cannot be completely listed for any individual such that they are valid for him all the time.

(ii) The "goal setting" and "state valuation" of each goal function is dynamic, interactive, and subject to the influence of self-suggestion, physiological monitoring, external information, the current data base, and the information processing capacity. When physiological health is maintained and no charge is produced by physiological monitoring, self-suggestion can play a more active role in goal setting and state valuation than external information.

(iii) The influence of self-suggestion can be very pervasive and important to goal setting and state valuation, as well as the consequential behavior and decisions. Because of its direct access, self-suggestion can exert its influence on the internal information processing through H1–H4. It can create new conceptions, perceptions, and goal state variables. It can also cause restructuring of the data bases in the information processing center.

9.2.4. Charge Structures and Significance Ordering of Events

In this section we shall discuss the inputs to attention. The charge structures of goal functions and events and their ordering will be hypothesized.

When the perceived value of a goal function is significantly different from its ideal value, a charge (tension) will be produced. Some charges are very strong, demanding an immediate release. Others are very mild, demanding no such effort. The charges at time t produced by the goal functions are then formed into a dynamic hierarchical structure which will determine the attention (allocation of internal information processing capacity over activities/events) at time t.

In this section a more detailed account of the hierarchical structures and attention will be provided.

Maslow has suggested, according to Ref. 459, that human needs (goals) are organized in a hierarchy. At the bottom are the physiological needs; then safety; then love; then self-esteem and the esteem of others; and at the summit, self-actualization. He suggested that the higher needs will not appear and function, until the lower needs are reasonably satisfied. Maslow's observation is valid for a large variety of human behavior, but is by no means adequate for our discussion. A man, even in a hungry state, when sufficiently insulted, may risk his life just to defend his honor and integrity. This kind of behavior defies Maslow's construct.

There are two types of charges. One is called a *two-sided* charge: the charge is increasing in both directions, over or below, as the perceived value deviates from the ideal. (See Figure 9.2.) Thus, charges produced from the goal functions of the right amount and quality of air, water, and biochemical states belong to this class.

The other type is called a *one-sided charge*: the charge increases only in one direction. (See Figure 9.3.) When the perceived value exceeds the ideal, no charge will be produced, although it increases in the contrary case. The charges resulting from the goal functions of reputation, wealth accumulation, achievement, etc. belong to this type. For convenience, *unfavorable deviations* will mean those that produce a positive charge. Note that when the perceived value exceeds the ideal, the ideal can be reset to a "higher" level.

Different goal functions can produce different levels of charge even if their magnitude of unfavorable deviation is the same. For instance, a slight

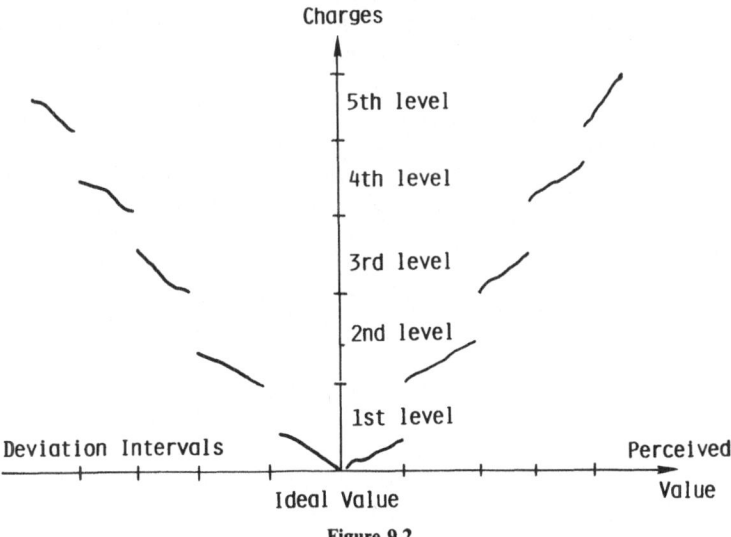

Figure 9.2

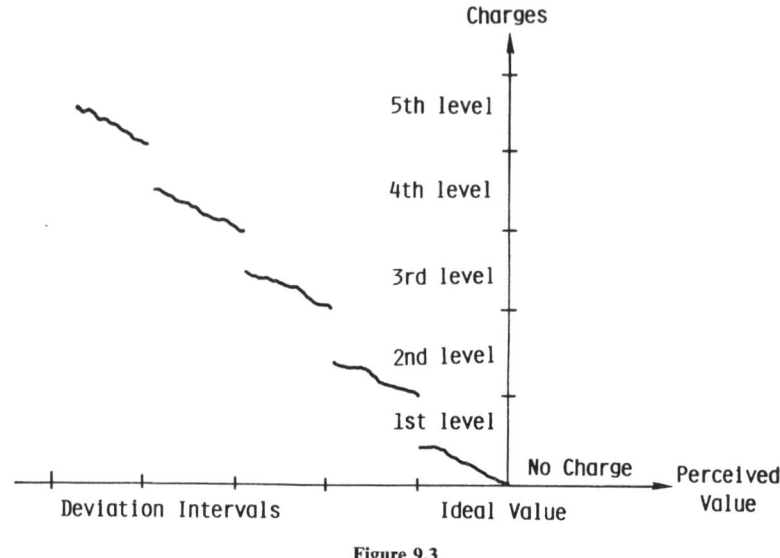

Figure 9.3

unfavorable deviation in the function of body temperature can produce an intense charge, while a large unfavorable deviation in the function of exploring and acquiring knowledge may just produce a mild charge. It must be emphasized that each individual has his unique way of generating a charge system (refer to H1–H5).

In order to facilitate our discussion, we shall use five different levels to describe the intensity of a charge as in Table 9.2. Note that when a charge is generated, an unpleasant feeling occurs. The more intense the charge, the stronger the feeling. When it is discharged, a pleasurable sensation may occur. The degree of the sensation is roughly proportional to that of the charge. In Table 9.2, *the allowable time for discharge* is the subjective perception that a charge must be released by the time specified, otherwise great danger or damage to life may ensue. The allowable time gives a measure of the intensity of the charge.

In Figures 9.2 and 9.3, the corresponding charge levels and deviations are depicted. For $j = 1, 2, 3, 4, 5$, by *the jth deviational interval* we mean that when the deviation is in the interval, the jth level of charge will be produced. When the state value must be maintained closely to the ideal, the deviational intervals are relatively very small. Attention will be very sensitive to this kind of goal deviation. In general, those goal functions related to physiological health are two-sided charges and their goal deviation can result in a high level of charge. When such a deviation occurs, attention will almost automatically and immediately allocate all body energy to reduce it, and little attention will be paid to other events/activities.

Table 9.2. Level of Charges

---

i. *Fifth level*: The charge is extremely intense; the allowable time for discharge is very short. For instance the charge produced can be at this level when a man is robbed at gun point and his life is threatened. The charge produced by the survival and security goal function (see Table 9.1) could reach this level.

ii. *Fourth level*: The charge is intense with a short allowable time for discharge. This level occurs when sickness, hunger, or thirst occurs, or when sexual desire has been sufficiently aroused.

iii. *Third level*: The charge is less intense but still strong with a little longer allowable time for discharge. Almost all goal functions can reach this level of charge, when corresponding unfavorable deviations from the ideals are created.

iv. *Second level*: The charge is mild and the allowable time for discharge is fairly long. This level again can be produced by almost all goal functions.

v. *First level*: The charge is slight with no specific discharge time. Again this level can be produced by almost all goal functions.

Note that our five levels of charges are just for convenience of discussion. In general the charge system has a finite number of levels. Each individual has his own number of levels. Sometimes, three levels—intense, mild, and slight—may be adequate to describe the charge systems.

In order to have a precise mathematical description of the charge structure and their ordering, let $i = 1, 2, 3, \ldots$ be the indices of the known goal functions and x_t^i and I_t^i be the perceived value and the ideal value of the ith goal function at time t. Then the charge of the ith goal function at time t can be represented by

$$f_t^i(x_t^i - I_t^i) = (f_{t5}^i, f_{t4}^i, f_{t3}^i, f_{t2}^i, f_{t1}^i), \tag{9.1}$$

where each $f_{tj}^i \in [0, 1]$, $j = 1, \ldots, 5$ representing the index of the jth level of charge—the larger the f_{tj}^i the larger the charge of the jth level. To reflect the "preemptiveness" of the level we require that if $f_{tj}^i \neq 0$ then $f_{tj-1}^i = 1, j = 5$, 4, 3, 2. That is, the lower levels of charge must be fully activated before a higher level can be activated.

Now given two goal functions, p and q, we say that *the charge of p is equal to that of q at time t* if $f_t^p = f_t^q$ (that is, each $f_{tj}^p = f_{tj}^q, j = 1, \ldots, 5$); and *$p$'s charge is greater than q's* iff f_t^p is lexicographically larger than f_t^q. That is, $f_{tj}^p \geq f_{tj}^q, j = 1, 2, 3, 4, 5$, and at least one $f_{tj}^p \neq f_{tj}^q$. Note that because of the preemptiveness requirement, the strict inequality will occur on the largest j such that $f_{tj}^p \neq 0$. The reader can verify that p's charge is greater than q's iff $f_t^p \geq f_t^q$. We shall later hypothesize that if the goal function p has a stronger charge than the goal function q then p has a priority over q in obtaining attention, and if p and q produce the same amount of charge, then they will have the same degree of priority in obtaining attention at time t. Self-suggestion or new information may be required to resolve the equal priority.

Observe that in our five level classification, the fifth and the fourth level do not occur very often. Thus, most of the time, f_t^i is nonzero only on the last three components. Because of the preemptiveness requirement, many f_t^i (with respect to i) may have the same intensity of charge. This is especially true when 0 or 1 (nonactivated or activated) are used to indicate the level of charge. Thus, most of the time, there may be many goal functions which simultaneously have the same priority of attention. Such equal priority for many goal functions may be broken when new information arrives or self-suggestion is activated as mentioned before.

Given at time t, the collection of

$$F_t = \{f_t^i | i = 1, 2, \ldots\}, \tag{9.2}$$

where i is the index of the goal functions, will be called *the charge structure* at time t. In order to compare the relative strength of the charge structures, we shall rearrange the index of i in F_t, so that $f_t^i \geq f_t^{i+1}$, $i = 1, 2, \ldots$ is maintained. The new set denoted by F_t' will be called the *ordered charge structure at time t*. Note that the index of the goal functions in F_t' is a function of time. Thus, goal functions can be indexed differently in F_t' over time. Note that the first element in F_t' is the charge produced by the highest charged goal function, which has the first priority for attention.

Note that, by adding zero vectors when necessary, two charge structures can be comparable as follows.

Definition 9.1. Given two charge structures F_t and G_t and their corresponding ordered structures $F_t' = \{f_t^i | i = 1, 2, \ldots\}$ and $G_t' = \{g_t^i | i = 1, 2, \ldots\}$ we say that *the charge of F_t is equal to that of G_t* iff $F_t' = G_t'$; and that *the charge of F_t is larger than G_t* iff F_t' is lexicographically larger than G_t', (that is, $F_t' \neq G_t'$ and either $f_t^i \geq g_t^i$ for all $i = 1, 2, \ldots$, or if there is some i such that g_t^i is lexicographically larger than f_t^i then there is $k < i$ so that f_t^k is lexicographically larger than g_t^k).

Example 9.1. Consider two charge structures given by Table 9.3. Note that we only list five goal functions for ease of presentation. Rearranging F

Table 9.3

Goal functions (i)	Charge structures									
	F					G				
1. Survival and security	(0,	0,	0,	0,	1)	(0,	0,	0,	0,	0.5)
2. Self-importance feeling	(0,	0,	0.3,	1,	1)	(0,	0,	0,	0.7,	1)
3. Social approval	(0,	0,	0.0,	1,	1)	(0,	0,	0,	0.8,	1)
4. Sensuous gratification	(0,	0,	0,	0.2,	1)	(0,	0,	0.7,	1,	1)
5. Self-actualization	(0,	0,	0,	1,	1)	(0,	0,	1,	1,	1)

and G, we obtain the ordered structures F' and G' as follows:

$$F' = \begin{pmatrix} 0 & 0 & 0.6 & 1 & 1 \\ 0 & 0 & 0.3 & 1 & 1 \\ 0 & 0 & 0 & 1 & 1 \\ 0 & 0 & 0 & 0.2 & 1 \\ 0 & 0 & 0 & 0 & 1 \end{pmatrix},$$

$$G' = \begin{pmatrix} 0 & 0 & 1 & 1 & 1 \\ 0 & 0 & 0.7 & 1 & 1 \\ 0 & 0 & 0 & 0.8 & 1 \\ 0 & 0 & 0 & 0.7 & 1 \\ 0 & 0 & 0 & 0 & 0.5 \end{pmatrix}.$$

Comparing F' with G' we know that the charge of G is larger than that of F.

We are now ready for discussing the charge structure and attention to *a set of events*. Because of H4 (analogy/associations), attention could be processed in terms of events. Here, "events" is used in a broad sense. It includes all incoming, ongoing, or future projects, activities, ambitions, or concerns. One notices that in reality, at any single time, there may be only a small number of events which have charges significantly high enough to call for attention.

Let $\mathscr{E} = \{E_t^k | k = 1, 2, \ldots\}$ be the collection of all possible events at time t which have the potential of being considered for attention. Clearly these events may overlap.

At time t, the charge structure is given by F_t, which encompasses all possible events and information including $\mathscr{E}$. Now let

$F_t(-E_t^k) = $ the remaining charge structure at time t if E_t^k

is ignored or resolved at that time.   (9.3)

Then the marginal contribution of E_t^k to the charge structure can be expressed by the difference between F_t and $F_t(-E_t^k)$. Since F_t is fixed for all events, the *relative significance* of event E_t^k on the charge structures is dependent on $F_t(-E_t^k)$. The more intense the charge of $F_t(-E_t^k)$, the less significant is E_t^k. That is, if the charge of $F_t(-E_t^m)$ is stronger than that of $F_t(-E_t^n)$ then E_t^n is a more significant event than E_t^m at time t on the charge structures. Thus, E_t^n will have priority over E_t^m in obtaining attention at time t, no matter how small this priority is.

Example 9.2. (Continuation of Example 9.1.) Assume that $E_t^1 = $ "taking a trip" and $E_t^2 = $ "taking part in a social event," and that $F_t(-E_t^1) = F$,

$F_t(-E_t^2) = G$, where F and G are given in Table 9.3. Since G has a charge larger than that of F, we know that E_t^1 (taking a trip) is a more significant event than E_t^2 (taking part in the social event).

Note that F_t and $F_t(-E_t^k)$ could change rapidly over time. The priority of an event at time t does not imply that the priority will be maintained for all later t. Information inputs, self-suggestion, and physiological monitoring could change the priority, perhaps rapidly.

One of the important sets of events is a collection of decision problems which involve specific objectives, uncertainty, or risk, and which must be resolved by a certain time. The attention to each problem will depend on its significance in the charge structures. It is fair to say that a decision problem will have a low significance and attention priority if it has a low stake (that is, its impact on the state valuations of the goal functions is small), and/or if the decision maker is confident obtaining a satisfactory solution within the time limit (thus the deviations of the perceived values from the ideal are small).

Now let us incorporate the above discussion into the following hypothesis.

H6. Charge Structures and Ordering Hypothesis

(i) There are several (say five) levels of charge for each goal function (Table 9.2) that are dependent on the deviation of the perceived value from the ideal. The higher level is preemptive over the lower in obtaining attention. Most physiological related goal functions have two-sided charges with respect to the *fixed* ideal values. Their deviational intervals are usually small and their potential level of charge can be very high. The rest of the goal functions may have only one-sided charges with large deviational intervals from somewhat *self-adjustable* ideal values. Usually the fifth and the fourth levels of charge do not occur. As a consequence, many goal functions may have nearly the same level of charge at almost any particular time.

(ii) The charge of each goal function at time t can be represented by f_t^i [see (9.1)]. The collection of all f_t^i over all i (goal functions) at time t, denoted by F_t, is the charge structure at time t [see (9.2)]. Both f_t^i and F_t can be changed, perhaps rapidly, over time.

(iii) The strength of charge structures can be compared according to Definition 9.1 in terms of the lexicographical ordering of the corresponding ordered charge structures.

(iv) Each event can involve many goal functions. Its significance on the charge structures at time t can be measured by the remaining structure $F_t(-E_t^k)$ when E_t^k is removed. [See (9.3).] Given a fixed set of events, the priority of attention over the events at time t is dependent upon the relative significance of the events on the charge structures at time t. The higher the remaining charge structure $F_t(-E_t^k)$ after E_t^k is removed, the less relative significance for E_t^k and the lower the priority for E_t^k to obtain attention.

(v) For decision problems involving uncertainty and risk, the smaller the stake of the problem and the more confident the decision maker is in obtaining a satisfactory solution for the problem within a prescribed time, the less the significance of the problem for the charge structures, and consequently, the lower its priority for obtaining attention.

9.2.5. Least Resistance Principle, Discharge, and Problem Solving

In this section, possible outputs of attention will be discussed. A general scheme for discharge according to the *least resistance principle* and for problem solving will be described and hypothesized.

Given the charge structures F_t at time t, let $\mathscr{A}_t = \{A_t^m | m = 1, 2, \ldots\}$ be the set of all possible available actions (alternatives). Here $\mathscr{A}_t$ contains a large number of alternatives including soliciting or emitting various information, making decisions on various problems, implementing a decision, deferring making decisions, social activities, physiological activities (resting, activating physiological states), restructuring attitude and belief systems for life, reminiscence of past events, daydreaming about future events, etc.

Now let $F_t(+A_t^m)$ be the *perceived charge structures* if the action A_t^m is taken at time t. Note that the $F_t(+A_t^m)$, $m = 1, 2, \ldots$, could contain "opportunity cost" and are comparable to the strength of the charge (H6 and Definition 9.1). We introduce the following definition.

Definition 9.2. (Least Resistance Principle.) Given $\mathscr{A}_t$, $\{F_t(+A_t^m) | m = 1, 2, \ldots\}$, the rule of selecting the action which yields the lowest remaining charge strength of $F_t(+A_t^m)$ over $\mathscr{A}_t$ for discharge is called the *least resistance principle*.

Remark 9.8. As F_t, the charge structure, can be changed rapidly, so can $F_t(+A_t^m)$. Once an action is taken or a discharge occurs, the charge structure will be changed. The original event of the top charge may be no longer at the top after the discharge. The new event of the highest charge will take priority of the input to attention. Discharge priority on various actions will then be evaluated, yielding the selection of an action according to the least resistance principle. The "least resistance" makes sense here because $F_t(+A_t^m)$ is the "remaining charge" after A_t^m is taken. The remaining charge is a measure of "resistance" to a complete release of all charges.

Example 9.3. Assume that $\mathscr{A}_t = \{A_t^1, A_t^2\}$, with A_t^1 as solving a problem actively and A_t^2 as avoiding the problem. Assume that $F_t(+A_t^1) = F$ and $F_t(+A_t^2) = G$, where F and G are as specified in Example 9.1. Since F has a lower charge strength than G, according to the least resistance principle, A_t^1 (solving the problem actively) will be taken at time t. However, this does not guarantee that A_t^1 will be always taken after time t, because the charge structure can vary with time and with the result of A_t^1.

In Figure 9.1, there are three output channels from attention (box 6) indicating the consequence of allocation of the internal information processing capacity (or resources). The first one is to boxes 7, 12, 13 for further information. This may stem from the need for understanding the surrounding environment in order to survive or achieve other goals. (See the next section for further discussion.)

The second is to *self-suggestion* (box 10) for reminiscence of past events, goal setting, cognitive extension of imagination, internalization of external worlds, thinking and inference processes, etc. When the charges from physiological needs are at the lowest level, the activities in self-suggestion may have the highest priority and become important functions in our lives.

The last output of attention is to boxes 8 and 9. This stems from the decision-making process in the usual sense. As mentioned in the previous section, because of H4 (analogy and association) information processing may be done in terms of events: When a decision-making problem has top priority for attention, feasible alternatives for solving the problem will be generated. If the problem or a similar problem has a low stake (low significance in charge structure) and has been repeated and solved satisfactorily many times before, a readily satisfactory solution will be retrieved from the memory and will be implemented immediately. Most of our daily choice problems are of this type and require but little effort to resolve. Clearly, once a problem is resolved, its priority will be lost and replaced by new ones.

When the problem is new and its stake (the significance on the charge structures) is high, usually it cannot be solved easily, especially when it entails uncertainty and high risk. Then the charge may not be released quickly, because no truly satisfactory solutions may be at hand. Many things can occur. On one hand, self-suggestion can be activated to deliberate and search out feasible solutions, their evaluation criteria, and their possible consequences (box 10). On the other hand, external information can be actively solicited in search for feasible solutions (box 12). These activities, called *active search for solutions*, usually occur when one has confidence in finding a truly satisfactory solution in due time.

When one has little or no confidence in finding a truly satisfactory solution, self-suggestion can be activated to restructure the problem. This includes distorting or degrading its importance, thereby justifying the delay for the final decision and shifting the responsibility for making decisions. These activities, called *avoidance justification*, are not very unusual in human behavior.

Note that the results of *active search for solutions* and/or *avoidance justification* will feed back to the information processing center (box 1). The new emerging charge structures may shift the problem to a lower attention priority. As a consequence, our mind can be turned off from the problem, perhaps temporarily.

One possible situation in decision-making problems is being caught by surprise. The decision maker is totally unprepared for a very high stake decision problem which must be resolved immediately. Because of time pressure, thorough deliberation or solicitation of information is impossible and the charge maintains a very high level. Under these circumstances, one may act quickly, perhaps unwisely, to release the high charge and the time pressure. Imagine what you would do if you were robbed at gun point unexpectedly.

Janis and Mann (Ref. 236) have supplied a very interesting account of human decision behaviors in terms of "vigilance," "time pressure," and "confidence in obtaining satisfactory solutions." Chan, Park, and Yu (Ref. 74) carried an empirical study on high-stake decision problems which roughly supported the above observations. Roy discussed "decision aid" in Ref. 386. In Yu (Refs. 497 and 499), a "time optimality" concept was introduced to treat "decision dynamics." The interested reader may find that the above references and the quotes therein will help understand human decision/behavior.

We summarize the above discussion as follows.

H7. Discharge Hypothesis

(i) Given the charge structures and the set of alternatives at time t, the selection of the alternatives for discharge will follow the least resistance principle.

(ii) A majority of daily decision problems are often repetitive with low stakes and truly satisfactory solutions are usually readily available for discharge.

(iii) When the decision problem is of high stakes and/or involves great uncertainty, *active search for solutions* or *avoidance justification* can be activated. This depends on whether the decision maker has confidence in finding a truly satisfactory solution in due time. Either activity can restructure the charge structures and may put off the decision problem, perhaps temporarily.

(iv) When one is caught unprepared and by surprise (a high-stake decision problem requiring immediate resolution), he may act quickly and perhaps unwisely because of time pressure and high charges.

9.2.6. External Information Inputs

In this section we shall discuss the inputs of external information into the information processing center. Sending out information is an alternative for discharge and will not be discussed here. Reception of messages, the degree of their processing, and credibility are some of the topics which are considered below.

Over several million years of evolution, man has developed a very sophisticated system of gathering information concerning his security and survival, because life is full of uncertainty and risk. Our visual, auditory, smell, taste, and tactile senses are parts of the system. It is fair to say that maintaining an effective information-gathering system is essential for achieving the goals of life, including security and survival, perpetuation of the species, self-importance feeling, social approval, etc. (See Table 9.1.) It is also fair to say that there is a continual possibility that gathering information can become the first priority for discharge. In a strict sense, gathering information is an alternative for discharge. Because of its special significance in human decision/behavior we treat it separately.

There are many ways to gather information. Information can arrive or be collected through public channels: TV programs, radios, newspapers, magazines, and public speeches. It can also arrive or be collected through private or semiprivate channels: private conversations, group discussions, telephones, telegraphs, letters, organizations' reports, etc. The messages can be communicated linguistically or nonverbally. Sometimes, creating a scene or posture can be more effective than a verbal conversation.

It is possible that an arriving message may not catch our attention. Without attention, the message cannot reach the internal information processing center and cannot be interpreted. In box 7 of Figure 9.1, attention is paid if the corresponding "extruding lines" are connected. In a crowded party, we may concentrate so much on a private conversation that we are unaware of the other people. Thus, the line of attention is not connected to the surrounding environment.

Whether an arriving message catches our attention depends on our charge structures. A sudden explosive sound or unusual squeak can activate our security or curiosity need to a higher level of charge and therefore catch our attention. A message that contains desired information can catch our attention more easily than nonrelevant messages.

Depending on the duration of the attention (in units of milliseconds) the degree of message processing may vary. If the duration is very short, we may just have a glimpse of the message and forget it quickly. If the duration is sufficiently long, the message can be encoded and stored in our memory (H1), and be interpreted according to our previous knowledge and experience (H4). The message so processed (box 1) can trigger the functions of goal setting and state valuation. Perhaps it can change the charge structures and their hierarchy. It is fair to say that the messages that are relevant to the long-lasting events of high significance in the charge structures can command the attention for a long duration. It has long been recognized that each message, to a certain degree, contains some untruthful and/or deceptive ideas. Credibility of the messages is an important judgmental problem. It depends on the source of the messages, the channels used for transmission to us, and our past knowledge, beliefs, and experience. It can also depend on our charge structures. When one is in a desperate situation (high charges), one is more likely to believe relevant messages [see H7(iv)].

In Figure 9.1, external information inputs have been classified into *solicited information* (box 12) and *unsolicited information* (box 13). The former are those actively sought by us; the latter are those arriving without our initiation. This classification makes it easier to discuss interaction of decision/behavior among people including persuasion, negotiation, and games. See Refs. 497 and 499 for a discussion.

We now summarize the above into the following.

H8. Information Inputs Hypothesis

(i) In order to achieve the goals of life, human beings continuously have the need to gather information.

(ii) Information inputs, solicited or unsolicited, will not enter the internal information processing center unless attention is allotted.

(iii) Allocation of attention to a message depends on its relevance to the charge structures. The messages which are highly related to long-lasting events which have high significance in the charge structures can command a long duration of attention. In turn, that can change the charge structures and decision/behavior.

(iv) Each message can contain untruthful and/or deceptive ideas. Depending on its contents, the source, the channels, and the charge structures, credibility of each message is judged according to previous knowledge, belief, and experience (see box 1 and H1-H4).

9.3. Habitual Domains

It has been recognized that each human being has habitual responses to stimuli. Conditioned or programmed behaviors are some of these habitual responses. We shall capture these behaviors in terms of *habitual domains*. Understanding the habitual ways of making decisions by ourselves and others is certainly important for us to make better decisions or avoid expensive mistakes. In Section 9.3.1 the definition and formation of stable habitual domains will be described. As defined, habitual domains are dynamic processes; their growth will be described in Section 9.3.2. Section 9.3.3 is devoted to a discussion of the interaction of different habitual domains among people.

Finally Section 9.3.4 offers some important implications of stable habitual domains.

9.3.1. Definition and Formation of Stable Habitual Domains

By the *habitual domain at time t*, denoted by HD_t, we mean the collection of ideas and actions that can potentially be activated at time t. In view of Figure 9.1, we see that habitual domains involve self-suggestion, external information inputs, physiological monitoring, goal setting, state valuation, charge structures, attention, and discharges. They also concern encoding, storing, retrieving, and interpretation mechanisms (H1-H4). When a particular aspect or function is emphasized, it will be designated as "habitual domain on that function." Thus, habitual domain on self-suggestion, habitual domains on charge structures, habitual domain on attention, habitual domain on making a particular decision, etc. all make sense. When the responses to a particular event are of interest, we can designate it as "habitual domains on the responses to that event," etc.

Note that conceptually habitual domains are dynamic sets which evolve with time. We shall now justify the adjective "habitual."

Recall from H1 that each idea (thought, concept, and perception) is represented by a circuit pattern or a sequence of circuit patterns; otherwise, it is not encoded and not available for retrieving. From H2, we see that the brain has an infinite capacity for storing encoded ideas. Thus, $|HD_t|$, the number of elements in the habitual domain at time t, is a monotonic nondecreasing function of time t.

Now, from H4 (analogy and association), new ideas are perceived and generated from existing ideas. The larger the number of existing ideas, the larger the probability that a new arriving idea is one of them; therefore, the smaller the probability that a new idea can be acquired. Thus, $|HD_t|$, although increasing, is increasing at a decreasing rate. If we eliminate the rare case that $|HD_t|$ can forever increase at a rate above a positive constant, we see that $|HD_t|$ will eventually level off and reach its steady state. Once $|HD_t|$ reaches its steady state, unless extraordinary events occur, habitual ways of thinking and responses to stimuli can be expected. Two mathematically precise models [of Chan and Yu (Ref. 73)] which describe conditions for stable habitual domains to exist are given in Appendix 9.1. There is a rich literature devoted to the study of formation of habits under such names as personality, human development, and the origins of intellect. Interested readers are referred to Refs. 186 and 351 and quotes therein.

Note that through self-suggestion and/or external information inputs, one idea or a set of ideas can be used to stimulate or generate other ideas. This indicates that there exists a set of *operators* defined on subsets of HD_t which generate ideas in HD_t from the subsets of HD_t. For example, suppose one is interested in investing a fixed amount of cash in stocks A and B. The concept (the operator) that any portfolio (a convex combination) of A and B would also be of interest will expand the alternative set of A and B into the set of all convex combinations of A and B. Note that the operators are also elements of HD_t.

Let $I_t \subset HD_t$ be a set of ideas in HD_t, and O_t be a set of operators which generate ideas in HD_t from subsets of HD_t. Define $R(I_t, O_t)$, called a *reachable domain*, to be the set of ideas/actions that can be *reached* (or attained) from I_t and O_t. More precisely, $R(I_t, O_t)$ is the set of ideas/actions that can be cumulatively generated by any sequence of operators from the set O_t which act on I_t and the resulting ideas/actions from the operations. We say that $\{I_t, O_t\}$ is a *generator* of HD_t iff $HD_t = R(I_t, O_t)$, and that $\{I_t, O_t\}$ is a *basis* for HD_t iff $\{I_t, O_t\}$ is a generator of HD_t and no proper subset of $\{I_t, O_t\}$ can be a generator of HD_t.

Note that HD_t is the set of ideas and actions that can be *potentially* activated, rather than *actually* activated at time t. In order to distinguish the difference, the latter will be denoted by AD_t, called the *actual domain at time t*. Clearly $AD_t \subset HD_t$. The relationship between AD_t and HD_t is similar to that of *the realized value* and the *sampling space* of a random variable. The set AD_t, varying with time, will be affected by the charge structures and attention at time t. The probability or confidence level for an idea/action to be activated will depend on how strongly the idea/action has been encoded (H1) and how easily the idea/action can be retrieved from its storage (H3). It is also closely related to $R(I_t, O_t)$ with I_t as the set of initially activated ideas and O_t as the set of active operators around time t. One can then formally introduce a probability or a confidence structure (similar to Ref. 505 of Yu and Leitmann), denoted by P_t, to indicate the probability that a set of ideas/actions in HD_t is in AD_t.

We summarize the concepts discussed above by listing the related abstract symbols as follows:

  i. HD_t (habitual domain): The collection of ideas/actions that can be *potentially* activated at time t;
  ii. AD_t (actual domain): The set of ideas/actions that are *actually* activated at time t;
  iii. P_t: The probability or confidence structure at time t which indicates the possibility of a set of ideas/actions of HD_t to be in AD_t;
  iv. $R(I_t, O_t)$ (reachable domain): The reachable (attainable) set of ideas/actions from the initial set of ideas I_t through the set of operators O_t.

In studying habitual domains, we shall be interested simultaneously in the above four concepts. In the appendix, conditions for stable HD_t and P_t are described following Chan and Yu (Ref. 73).

9.3.2. The Expansion of Habitual Domains

In this section we shall discuss the growth or expansion of habitual domains. *Singular expansion* and *jump out of habitual domain* will be our focus of discussion.

Let s, the *starting* time, and $R(I_s, O_s)$ be known. We are interested in the set of all reachable ideas/actions at time $t > s$.

To facilitate our discussion, consider our earlier simple investment problem concerning the generation of feasible investment alternatives. At time s, let $I_s = \{A, B\}$ and $O_s = \{O^1\}$ with O^1 representing the operator of "convexization" (i.e., forming portfolios by convexization). Then $R(I_s, O_s)$ can be depicted as the line segment $[A, B]$. Note that if I_s is expanded to include C in Figure 9.4a, the reachable domain will not be affected. However, if D, a new stock, is included as in Figure 9.4b, the reachable domain will be expanded. On the other hand, the operators may or may not affect the reachable domain. If we add an operator O^2: equal weight portfolio (thus in Figure 9.4a, such operator generates E from $\{A, B\}$), we see that the reachable domain is unaffected by adding O^2. However, when we add O^3—any portfolio is acceptable as long as it does not exceed the budget—then the reachable domain expands from the line segment $[A, B]$ to the triangle of $[A, B, O]$ and its interior, where O is the origin, in Figure 9.4c. These examples illustrate that the expansion of the reachable domain is dependent on the suitable expansion of the idea/action set I_s and that of the operator set O_s.

In order to formalize the above observation, let $\tilde{I}_t$ and $\tilde{O}_t$, respectively, be the set of new ideas/actions and new operators produced during the time interval $]s, t]$ (excluding s but including t). Denote the resulting reachable domain of all ideas/actions at time t by $Q_{st}(I_s, O_s; \tilde{I}_t, \tilde{O}_t)$, and call it the *reachable domain from s to t*.

Throughout this section we assume that during the time interval $[s, t]$, all activated ideas/actions and operators are readily retrievable or continuously activated. For convenience this will be referred to as the *activation continuity assumption*. Then, by definition, we have

$$Q_{st}(I_s, O_s; \tilde{I}_t, \tilde{O}_t) = R(R(I_s, O_s) \cup \tilde{I}_t, O_s \cup \tilde{O}_t) \qquad (9.4)$$

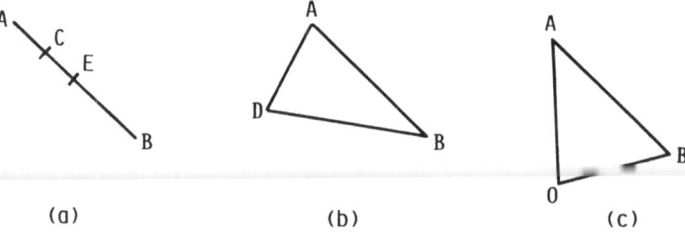

(a)   (b)   (c)

Figure 9.4

If we define $I_t = R(I_s, O_s) \cup \tilde{I}_t$ and $O_t = O_s \cup \tilde{O}_t$, we see that $Q_{st}(I_s, O_s; \tilde{I}_t, \tilde{O}_t) = R(I_t, O_t)$. Thus, Q_{st} and R are closely related.

Note that the activation continuity assumption is usually satisfied when the time span is short or when a particular project/event is emphasized and good records are kept. To better understand the reachable domain Q_{st}, we mention some properties of the operation of the reachable domain R:

(i) *Expansion Property*:

$$R(I_s, O_s) \supset I_s,$$

$$R(I_s, \varnothing) = I_s.$$

(ii) *Monotonicity Property*:

$$I_s \supset I_s^* \quad \text{implies that } R(I_s, O_s) \supset R(I_s^*, O_s),$$

$$O_s \supset O_s^* \quad \text{implies that } R(I_s, O_s) \supset R(I_s, O_s^*).$$

(iii) *Completeness Property*: For any $O_s^* \subset O_s$,

$$R(R(I_s, O_s), O_s^*) = R(I_s, O_s).$$

(iv) *Superadditivity Property*:

$$R(I_s \cup J_s, O_s) \supset R(I_s, O_s) \cup R(J_s, O_s).$$

If equality holds, we say that the *additivity property* holds. Note that the superadditivity property follows from the fact that the operators are defined on the subsets of I_s. When the number of subsets is reduced, so is the number of ideas/actions that can be produced by the operators. See Example 9.4. Note that if each operator of O_s operates only on subsets of $R(I_s, O_s)$ or $R(J_s, O_s)$ distinctively (i.e., the subsets are not crossing over), then additivity is satisfied. In particular, if each operator of O_s operates only on the *single* idea or action of I_s and J_s then the additivity is satisfied.

(v) *Supermultiplicativity Property*:

$$R(I_s, O_s \cup O_s^*) \supset R(R(I_s, O_s), O_s^*)$$

and

$$R(I_s, O_s \cup O_s^*) \supset R(R(I_s, O_s^*), O_s).$$

If equality holds for the above two relations, we say that the *multiplicativity property* holds. Note that the collection of all sequences produced by the operators of $O_s \cup O_s^*$ contains that by the operators of O_s alone or that by the operators of O_s^* alone. This observation yields the supermultiplicativity.

See Example 9.5. If the ideas/actions generated by any sequence of operators from $O_s \cup O_s^*$ can also be generated by a sequence of operators which can be divided into two parts with the first part all from O_s (or O_s^*) and the second part all from O_s^* (or O_s), then the multiplicative property is satisfied. Usually, one would expect that the multiplicativity property is satisfied.

Example 9.4. Consider an investment problem. Let a, b, c, d be four possible securities to invest in. Let O_s be the operator of convexization, $I_s = \{a, b\}$ and $J_s = \{c, d\}$. Then $R(I_s, O_s) \cup R(J_s, O_s) = \mathcal{H}(\{a, b\}) \cup \mathcal{H}(\{c, d\})$, [recall $\mathcal{H}(A)$ is the convex hull of set A], and $R(I_s \cup J_s, O_s) = \mathcal{H}(\{a, b, c, d\})$. Clearly, *strict* superadditivity holds. For instance, the portfolio of $1/4$ for each stock is not contained in $\mathcal{H}(\{a, b\})$ nor in $\mathcal{H}(\{c, d\})$.

Example 9.5. Consider a planning problem of taking a trip from city A to city B to city C. Let $I_s = (A \rightarrow B \rightarrow C)$, indicating from A to B to C. Define

$$O_s = \begin{cases} \text{using "car" if at city } A, \\ \text{using "airplane" if at city } B; \end{cases}$$

$$O_s^* = \begin{cases} \text{using "airplane" if at city } A, \\ \text{using "car" if at city } B. \end{cases}$$

Then

$$O_s \cup O_s^* = \begin{cases} \text{using "car" or "airplane" if at city } A, \\ \text{using "car" or "airplane" if at city } B. \end{cases}$$

Then

$$R(R(I_s, O_s), O_s^*) = \{A \xrightarrow{\text{car}} B \xrightarrow{\text{car}} C\} \text{ (i.e., using car from } A \text{ to } B$$
$$\text{and using car from } B \text{ to } C)$$

$$R(R(I_s, O_s^*), O_s) = \{A \xrightarrow{\text{air}} B \xrightarrow{\text{air}} C\} \text{ (note, "air" means "using airplane")}$$

$$R(I_s, O_s \cup O_s^*) = \begin{cases} A \xrightarrow{\text{car}} B \xrightarrow{\text{car}} C, \\ A \xrightarrow{\text{car}} B \xrightarrow{\text{air}} C, \\ A \xrightarrow{\text{air}} B \xrightarrow{\text{car}} C, \\ A \xrightarrow{\text{air}} B \xrightarrow{\text{air}} C. \end{cases}$$

Clearly, strict supermultiplicativity holds.

The following lemma shows some relationships between $R(I_s, O_s)$ and $Q_{st}(I_s, O_s ; \tilde{I}_t, \tilde{O}_t)$.

Lemma 9.1. (i) $R(I_s, O_s) \subset Q_{st}(I_s, O_s ; \tilde{I}_t, \tilde{O}_t)$.
(ii) $R(I_s, O_s) = Q_{st}(I_s, O_s ; \tilde{I}_t, \tilde{O}_t)$ if $\tilde{I}_t \subset R(I_s, O_s)$ and $\tilde{O}_t = \varnothing$, or $\tilde{I}_t = \varnothing$ and $R(I_s, O_s) = R(I_s, O_s \cup \tilde{O}_t)$.
(iii) Assume that the additivity and the multiplicativity property hold. Then $R(I_s, O_s) = Q_{st}(I_s, O_s ; \tilde{I}_t, \tilde{O}_t)$ if

$$R(R(I_s, O_s), \tilde{O}_t) \subset R(I_s, O_s) \qquad (9.5)$$

and one of the following holds:

$$R(\tilde{I}_t, \tilde{O}_t) \subset R(I_s, O_s), \qquad (9.6)$$

$$R(\tilde{I}_t, O_s) \subset R(I_s, O_s). \qquad (9.7)$$

Proof. *For* (i): It follows from (9.4) and the expansion property.
For (ii): It follows from (9.4) and the completeness property.
For (iii): From (i), it suffices to show that

$$Q_{st}(I_s, O_s ; \tilde{I}_t, \tilde{O}_t) \subset R(I_s, O_s).$$

From (9.4) and the additivity we have

$$Q_{st}(I_s, O_s ; \tilde{I}_t, \tilde{O}_t) = R(R(I_s, O_s) \cup \tilde{I}_t, O_s \cup \tilde{O}_t)$$

$$= R(R(I_s, O_s), O_s \cup \tilde{O}_t) \cup R(\tilde{I}_t, O_s \cup \tilde{O}_t). \qquad (9.8)$$

Assume that (9.5) and (9.6) hold. Using (9.8) and the multiplicativity we have

$$Q_{st}(I_s, O_s ; \tilde{I}_t, \tilde{O}_t) = R(R(R(I_s, O_s), \tilde{O}_t), O_s) \cup R(R(\tilde{I}_t, \tilde{O}_t), O_s)$$

$$\subset R(R(I_s, O_s), O_s) \cup R(R(I_s, O_s), O_s)$$

$$= R(I_s, O_s).$$

[Note that the inclusion follows from (9.5) and (9.6) and the monotonicity property.]
Similarly, assume (9.5) and (9.7) hold. We obtain the same result by using the other part of the multiplicativity property [i.e., in (9.8) we first use O_s and then $\tilde{O}_t$ to generate ideas/actions].

Remark 9.9. What (9.5) and (9.7) mean is that $\tilde{O}_t$ and $\tilde{I}_t$ individually cannot generate new ideas/actions and (9.6) means that jointly $\tilde{I}_t$ and $\tilde{O}_t$ cannot generate new ideas/actions. Note that (ii) and (iii) give conditions under which the reachable domain cannot be expanded during the interval $]s, t]$.

Definition 9.3. We say that during the time interval $]s, t]$,

   i. $\tilde{I}_t$ (or $\tilde{O}_t$) *triggers a singular expansion* [*of the reachable domain* $R(I_s, O_s)$] if $Q_{st}(I_s, O_s ; \tilde{I}_t, \varnothing)$ [or $Q_{st}(I_s, O_s ; \varnothing, \tilde{O}_t)$] contains $R(I_s, O_s)$ as a proper subset.

   ii. $\tilde{I}_t$ and $\tilde{O}_t$ *jointly trigger a singular expansion* [*of the reachable domain* $R(I_s, O_s)$] if $Q_{st}(I_s, O_s ; \tilde{I}_t, \tilde{O}_t)$ contains $R(I_s, O_s)$ as a proper subset.

   iii. The reachable domain $R(I_s, O_s)$ *has a singular expansion* if there exist $\tilde{I}_t$ and/or $\tilde{O}_t$ which trigger a singular expansion of the reachable domain.

Note that the negation of (ii) and (iii) of Lemma 9.1 give necessary conditions for the singular expansion of a reachable domain. We observe that a singular expansion does not necessarily imply that the resulting reachable domain is still not contained in the habitual domain HD_s.

Definition 9.4. We say that during the time interval $]s, t]$,

   i. $\tilde{I}_t$ (or $\tilde{O}_t$) *triggers* (*the reachable domain to make*) *a jump out of the habitual domain* HD_s if $Q_{st}(I_s, O_s ; \tilde{I}_t, \varnothing)$ [or $Q_{st}(I_s, O_s ; \varnothing, \tilde{O}_t)$] is *not* contained in HD_s.

   ii. $\tilde{I}_t$ and $\tilde{O}_t$ *jointly trigger* (*the reachable domain to make*) *a jump out of the habitual domain* HD_s if $Q_{st}(I_s, O_s ; \tilde{I}_t, \tilde{O}_t)$ is *not* contained in HD_s.

   iii. The reachable domain *has jumped out of the habitual domain* HD_s, if there exist $\tilde{I}_t$ and/or $\tilde{O}_t$ that trigger a jump out of HD_s.

From Definitions 9.3 and 9.4, we immediately see that triggering a jump out of HD_s implies triggering a singular expansion in the reachable domain. Also, a necessary condition for a reachable domain to have a singular expansion without jumping out of HD_s is that $HD_s \backslash R(I_s, O_s) \neq \varnothing$. Note, $HD_s \supset R(I_s, O_s)$.

Theorem 9.1. (i) A necessary and sufficient condition for $\tilde{I}_t$ to trigger a singular expansion of $R(I_s, O_s)$ is that $\tilde{I}_t \backslash R(I_s, O_s) \neq \varnothing$.

(ii) A necessary and sufficient condition for $\tilde{I}_t$ to trigger a jump out of HD_s is that $\tilde{I}_t \backslash HD_s \neq \varnothing$.

(iii) The condition that $R(R(I_s, O_s), O_t) \backslash R(I_s, O_s) \neq \varnothing$ is sufficient for $\tilde{O}_t$ to trigger a singular expansion of $R(I_s, O_s)$. It is also a necessary condition when the multiplicativity property holds.

(iv) The condition that $R(R(I_s, O_s), \tilde{O}_t)\backslash \text{HD}_s \neq \varnothing$ is sufficient for $\tilde{O}_t$ to trigger a jump out of HD_s. It is also a necessary condition when the multiplicativity property holds.

Proof. *For* (*i*) *and* (*ii*): From (9.4) we have

$$Q_{st}(I_s, O_s ; \tilde{I}_t, \varnothing) = R(R(I_s, O_s) \cup \tilde{I}_t, O_s).$$

The conclusions follow immediately from the expansion, monotonicity, and completeness properties of R and Definitions 9.3 and 9.4.

For (*iii*) *and* (*iv*):

$$Q_{st}(I_s, O_s ; \varnothing, \tilde{O}_t) = R(R(I_s, O_s), O_s \cup \tilde{O}_t)$$

$$\supset R(R(R(I_s, O_s), O_s), \tilde{O}_t)$$

$$= R(R(I_s, O_s), \tilde{O}_t). \tag{9.9}$$

From (9.9) and the assumption, the conclusions are evident. $\qquad\square$

Remark 9.10. (i) Note that (i) and (ii) of Theorem 9.1 imply that if $\tilde{I}_t$ triggers a singular expansion but not a jump out of HD_s then $\tilde{I}_t\backslash R(I_s, O_s) \neq \varnothing$ and $\tilde{I}_t \subset \text{HD}_s$. Here the new set $\tilde{I}_t$ is generated through *retrieving* from the encoded ideas/actions in the memory at time s (Refer to H1). New Information input and/or self-suggestion could help the retrieving. (Refer to Section 9.2.) However, if $\tilde{I}_t$ triggers a jump out of HD_s, $\tilde{I}_t$ is not in the memory at time s. The set needs to be *encoded and retrieved* during the time interval $]s, t]$. Thus, it is more difficult to get this kind of $\tilde{I}_t$. Again new information and/or self-suggestion may help the creation. (See H1.)

(ii) Similar to (i), from (iii) and (iv) of Theorem 9.1, one can conclude that it is more difficult to generate a new set $\tilde{O}_t$, which triggers a jump out of HD_s, than to generate $\tilde{O}_t$, which triggers a singular expansion. External information inputs and self-suggestion can help the creation of a new $\tilde{O}_t$.

Remark 9.11. From (9.4) and the above discussion, we have no difficulty extending the concepts of the expansion of habitual domains over several periods, instead of two periods as discussed here. In the extension the reader is reminded of the activation continuity assumption, which may disappear if we consider multiple periods.

9.3.3. Interaction of Different Habitual Domains

In this section we shall discuss the interaction of different habitual domains among different people. From H1–H4, we can conclude that everyone's habitual domain is surely unique. That is, there is a probability of zero that two persons' habitual domains are identical all the time. Ideally we can, in abstract, represent two habitual domains HD_s^1 and HD_s^2 for persons I and II, respectively, as in Figure 9.5. The origin is the common intersection point. Suppose that HD_s^1 and HD_s^2 are generated by $\{I_s^1, O_s\}$ and $\{I_s^2, O_s\}$, respectively, with $I_s^1 = \{A\}$ and $I_s^2 = \{B\}$ and $O_s = \{L\}$, where L is the *linear operator*. (That is, if $A \in HD_s$ then $\{\lambda A \mid -\infty < \lambda < \infty\} \subset HD_s$.) Now suppose that person I can expand his generator during the time interval $]s, t]$ to $\{I_t^1, O_t\}$ with $I_t^1 = \{A, B\}$ and $O_t = \{L, K\}$, where K is the *convexization operator*. We see that the habitual domain HD_t^1 has been expanded to the two-dimensional space containing HD_s^1 and HD_s^2 as subspaces. If HD_t^2 remains as HD_s^2, then $HD_t^2 \subset HD_t^1$. Then the ideas/actions that can be potentially activated by II are thus contained by those of I. In this situation, we may expect some dominance relationship between I and II. In real life, the above inclusion relationship rarely occurs unless a special event or problem is in focus.

The above example illustrates that in the interaction of different habitual domains the "new" idea/action set $\tilde{I}_t$ and the "new" operator set $\tilde{O}_t$ play an important role. The generation of $\tilde{I}_t$ and $\tilde{O}_t$ will depend on the individual's charge structures, attention, and information inputs, etc. as described in Figure 9.1 and H1–H8.

Note that in real life the habitual domain is not easily observed. Recall that the actual domain AD_s is a subset (perhaps very small) of HD_s. Usually only a portion of AD_s is observable, and without attention even the observable part of AD_s can be overlooked and/or misinterpreted. *Sincere appreciation and genuine interest in our own and others' abilities, skills, and well-being, open-minded discussions, the attitude that others' opinions/beliefs can be valid,* and *the willingness to think in terms of the others' interests* have been regarded as important operators that can make us aware of our own and the others' habitual domains, and accept them as a part of our own.

According to H4 (analogy/association), new ideas/actions or operators can more easily be learned if they are similar to those that are already known or activated. Thus, two habitual domains can more easily be synthesized when their difference is less dramatic.

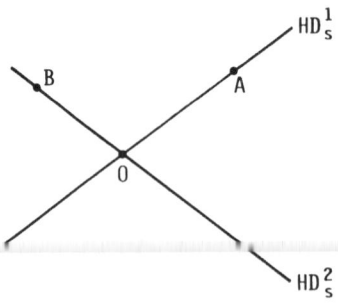

Figure 9.5

Note that the reachable domain $Q_{st}(I_s, O_s; \tilde{I}_t, \tilde{O}_t)$ can be expanded as a result of the interaction of different habitual domains. In this context, $\tilde{I}_t$ and $\tilde{O}_t$ will contain those ideas/actions and operators due to the interactions of habitual domains. Recall that $\tilde{I}_t$ and $\tilde{O}_t$ may be contained by HD_s. In this case, only retrieving is involved; otherwise both encoding and retrieving are involved.

Depending on the degree of cooperation, rivalry, and intimacy, humans consciously and/or unconsciously reveal their habitual domains to their "partners." Their revealed ideas/actions or operators may be *accepted* because they are similar to those of the partners or because the partners make a special effort to do so. The ideas/actions or operators can also be *rejected* because they are strange to the partners and/or because the partners do not care, or they activate their self-suggestion to distort and/or avoid them. The acceptance or rejection will certainly depend on the partners' charge structures and attention, etc. (See H7 and H6.) We shall not repeat it here.

In closing this section, we may summarize that it is not easy to understand our own and the other persons' habitual domains completely and precisely. However, by genuine interest in our own and others' habitual domains, we may notice their different ideas/actions and operators which can expand our own habitual domain so as to embody more of the others'. The acceptance or rejection of new ideas/actions and operators will depend on the individual's charge structures and attention as described in H6 and H7.

9.3.4. Implications of Studying Habitual Domains

We have discussed the main concepts of habitual domains, its components, growth, expansion, interaction, and the formation of stable states (see Appendix 9.1 for a mathematical proof). It may be fair to say that habitual domains are usually stable. Singular expansion and jump-outs of current habitual domains do not occur frequently. Note that in the stable states, we can expect habitual ways of thinking, response, and reaction to stimuli and events. Thus, personality, attitudes, conditioned or programmed behavior, as discussed in psychology, will be formed for each human being. Such formation has great impact on decision-making styles and optimization theories. We shall briefly sketch some important implications of the existence of stable habitual domains as follows:

(*i*) *For high-stake decision problems*: Although the four decision elements [alternatives, criteria, perceived outcomes of decisions, and preference (see Chapter 1)] can vary with time, information inputs and psychological states of the decision maker can become stabilized. In Section 10.4.1 and Ref. 74 an empirical study of this observation was demonstrated. Applications of optimization theories to high-stake decision problems become feasible. Before the stabilization, a formal analysis using optimization theory is not fruitful.

During the transition period, we might be better off letting our HD_t remain open to expansion to vigilantly search for all relevant information on the four decision elements to make sure we would not miss "good" alternatives.

(ii) *For optimal solutions*: As the decision process depends on HD_t, so does the resulting optimal solution. Since HD_t can vary with time (even though it can reach its stable states most of the time), the optimal solutions will change with time. This occurs when the set of alternatives, the set of criteria, dimension of consequences, perception of outcomes, and preference change. This suggests that in a dynamic setting, "time-optimality" is important and that an alternative that is perceived as optimal is only valid over a time horizon. See the next chapter and Refs. 497 and 499 for further details. Today's optimal solution does not imply that it will be optimal forever. As the HD_t changes, it may become an inferior solution. If we are aware of this fact we can prevent our surprise at others' (decision makers') "irrational" decisions. After all, a decision is rational if it is consistent with the decision maker's HD_t. Everyone's HD_t is unique. What we perceive as irrational may be very rational from another's viewpoint (HD_t).

(iii) *For gaming and conflict dissolution*: Each player has a unique HD_t. Understanding our own HD_t and the opponents' HD_t is essential to win competitive games or to dissolve conflicts. If we know our own HD_t but do not know the opponents' HD_t, we cannot confidently construct a winning strategy. Indeed we could lose the game entirely, like the Pearl Harbor disaster (see Ref. 236 for a detailed discussion of the mistake). If we do not know our own and the opponents' HD_t, very likely we will lose most of the games.

In partially cooperative and partially competitive games, like international trade or companies competing for a market share and a market volume for some products, it might be desirable for the players to settle in peace and to ensure that each one benefits. To maintain some stability, the settlement must allow each player to declare a victory, so the terms of agreement must be a time-optimal solution from the viewpoint of each player's HD_t. Certainly this is not an easy task. Proposing new alternatives, creating new conceptions of the criteria, and suggesting outcomes for the players to change their corresponding HD_t will become vital. Without a new set of compatible HD_t, an agreement can hardly be reached. Certainly, to successfully restructure HD_t we must first be aware of the existing HD_t of each player. We shall further discuss these as "second-order games" in the next chapter.

(iv) *For career management.* In a broader sense, each social organization (family, company, school, society, nation, etc.) can be regarded as a living entity and can have a habitual domain HD_t. The habitual domain can also stabilize. The people performing a variety of functions within an organization also have their own HD_t. The match of these habitual domains is important in considering career success and happiness. If the HDs are compatible and if they enhance each other, we may expect a fairly happy individual in the organization if the latter is prosperous; otherwise, conflict and frustration can arise and adjustment must be made in order to keep the individual happy with the organization.

If we regard individuals as "adapting living entities" to their environments, then choosing an organization for association becomes an optimal match problem between the individuals' HD_t and the organization's HD_r. Is there an *ideal* organization HD_t to which an individual can adapt? Can he change the organizational HD_t or is it easier to change his? Should he leave an organization for a different one that reveals a more compatible HD_t? These are important questions that each individual must address for career success. They deserve a careful exploration.

9.4. Some Observations in Social Psychology

The tremendous literature in social psychology has contributed to the understanding of human social behavior. References 145 and 521 are good examples. In this section, we shall list some interesting observations which will complement and strengthen our understanding of human decision/behavior processes. All observations listed appear in Ref. 145. They are also discussed in greater detail with documentation in most textbooks. We shall not repeat the documentation. A brief indication of their relevance to our model and hypotheses, however, will be given.

All the observations listed below should be carefully interpreted by tacitly adding "in general" or "there is a tendency."

9.4.1. Social Comparison Theory

"People have a drive to evaluate themselves and in the absence of objective nonsocial means, they evaluate themselves by comparison with other people."

This theory is closely related to H5 (goal setting and state valuation) of Section 9.2.3. Many goal functions (refer to Table 9.1) are difficult to evaluate by ourselves. Through comparison with other people (H4—analogy/association law) we know "better" where we stand with respect to the goals. This theory clearly complements and strengthens H8 (information inputs).

As a consequence of this theory and the goal functions of self-importance feelings, people may resent those capable of better performance than themselves and may look down on those whose performance is worse.

9.4.2. Halo Effect

"Most judgments of other people are made primarily in terms of *good* and *bad*. Thus all their other qualities are deduced from this judgment. One labeled *good* is surrounded with a positive aura and all good qualities are attributed to him. Conversely, one labeled *bad* is seen as having all bad qualities."

This observation is clearly related to H4 (analogy/association) of Section 9.2.2. As a consequence, we see that one who has a "right" posture can command favorable responses and one who has a "wrong" posture may suffer from unfavorable reactions.

9.4.3. Projection Effect (Assumed Similarity)

"There is a strong tendency for people to assume that others are similar to them."

Thus, if one likes large parties, one tends to assume that other people like large parties; if one is aggressive, he assumes others are also aggressive; and so on. This tendency is related to H4 (analogy/association) and social comparison behavior.

Note that there are two implications from this observation. First, an individual rates another more similar to himself than he actually is; he distorts the other's personality to make it more like his own (self-suggestion). Second, this distortion is usually so great that his rating of the other person corresponds more to his own personality (as he sees it) than to the other's personality (as the other sees it).

9.4.4. Proximity Theory

"People who live near each other are much more likely to be friends and like each other than those who live far apart."

When people live near each other, they have more opportunity to meet and understand each other. According to H1 (pattern circuit) and H3 (dynamic restructuring), each one will have a better image of the other than when they do not meet. Predictability, familiarity, and reinforcement will help the development of friendship. We see that the working of this theory is actually involved with all of H1–H8, but clearly there are exceptions.

9.4.5. Reciprocation Behaviors

"One tends to like (or dislike) people who one knows like (or dislike) him."

This behavior is related to rewards. People like others who reward them or who are associated with pleasant experiences. Conversely, people dislike others who punish them or who are associated with unpleasant experiences. Clearly this behavior is related with H1, H4, H6, and H7. Note that reciprocation also works for the feeling of cooperation, respect, helpfulness, hatred, etc. The reader may be interested in Ref. 410 of Shenoy and Yu. Using the simple nonzero sum game model, they described conditions under which "reciprocation strategy" is the best strategy for the players.

9.4.6. Similarity Effect

"There is a strong tendency for people to like others who are similar to them. Moreover, society generally assumes this to be true."

This may be due to the need of cognitive consistency. People want things to fit together and to be logical and harmonious. This holds for their own beliefs, cognitions, thoughts, and feelings. This need, together with H4 (analogy/association), can produce the similarity effect. Of course, the effect can also involve other goal functions and hypotheses.

9.4.7. Scapegoating Behavior (Displacement of Aggression)

"When the source of frustration or annoyance cannot be attacked, people have a tendency to express aggression against a *substitute* for the original source."

This behavior can be expressed in terms of charge structures and their releases by the least resistance principle (H5–H7).

9.4.8. Responsibility Diffusion or Deindividuation in Group Behavior

"To some extent people lose their personal sense of responsibility when they are in a group. Instead of feeling, as they usually do, that they personally are morally accountable for their actions, group members somehow share the responsibility with one another, and none of them feels it as strongly as he would if he were alone."

When people are in a group, they tend to feel a part of the group. Responsibility and consequences of their individual actions are perceived to be shared among the group members and less identifiable. As a consequence, people in a group are more likely to take high-risk activities or engage in acts they would not perform alone. The degree of deindividuation will certainly depend on the individual's charge structures and his commitment to and relationship with the group. Therefore it also involves H5–H8.

9.5. Some Applications

In this section some applications of observations discussed in the previous sections will be sketched. It is not my intent to engage in superficial musing.

However, our common wisdom, which is so powerful in daily living and is so often overlooked, deserves mention in this section. Although this wisdom may be articulated in terms of our conceptual framework, we shall leave it to the reader, because of limited space. The reader who is not interested in this kind of application may skip this section entirely. It has been recognized that the applications are an art that takes persistent practice and a conscious driving effort to master. (Refer to H1, H3, H4.) Section 9.5.1 is devoted to self-awareness, happiness and success; Section 9.5.2 to decision making; Section 9.5.3 to persuasion, negotiation and gaming; Section 9.5.4 to career management.

9.5.1. Self-Awareness, Happiness, and Success

As discussed in Section 9.3, through years of life experience, we gradually, perhaps subconsciously, reach a steady habitual domain and develop habitual responses to stimuli. Such habitual domains and responses may not be effective in coping with the dynamic changing world. They may be a major cause of our unhappiness or failure. Self-awareness is an essential step in expanding our habitual domains and improving our happiness and success. The following are just some suggestions.

(i) When we have a new idea, concept, or event, do we adequately rehearse it or make a special effort so that it can be encoded for later retrieving? (Refer to H1.)

(ii) Do we think that things cannot be changed because a decision has been made? Recall that people are subject to suggestion because of H2.

(iii) When confronting uncertainty, are we always prepared so that all relevant information, analyses, and judgment can readily be retrieved? (Refer to H3.)

(iv) In interpreting and thinking, are we too much bound by our previous thoughts and experiences? Do we pay special attention to distinguish the difference and the uniqueness among events? (Refer to H4.)

(v) Do we know the operations of our goal functions? When we are frustrated, do we know which goal functions trigger the frustration? Have these operations become so habitual that we are addicted to them? Can we exercise our self-suggestion power so as to replace them by other goal functions that we can be more positive and happier? (Refer to H5 and H6.)

(vi) Do we have so many goals simultaneously that we cannot concentrate on some particular achievable goals? Do we have clear-cut goals that can *produce charges* and fruitfully utilize our endowed information processing capacity? Do we exercise our self-suggestion power to focus on some meaningful and achievable goals? (Refer to H5 and H6.)

(vii) How often do we let the least resistance principle play tricks on us so that we are distracted from paying attention to the main projects? Can we build a barrier (increase the resistance) to the distractions and increase the charge (award) to the main projects? Without continuous attention good projects cannot be successfully completed. (Refer to H7.)

(viii) How often has our self-suggestion been exercised to an "active search for solutions" rather than an "avoidance justification" when we are confronted with difficult problems? The former is a positive way to solve the problems; the latter is a negative way which usually results in frustration and defeat. (Refer to H7.)

(ix) Are our external information inputs extensive and accurate enough for us to accomplish our goals? Do we habitually shut off information inputs which are not consistent with our wishes and charge structures? (Refer to H8.)

(x) Are we aware of our habitual domains and their working on our decision/behavior? Are our habitual domains stagnant and too closed for further growth? (Refer to Section 9.3.)

(xi) Are our habitual domains large enough to appreciate other people's habitual domains and to understand and appreciate the difficulty and complexity of the problems? (Refer to Section 9.3.)

(xii) Do our habitual domains have large enough an idea/action set and operator set to allow them to expand and jump out of the previous ones? Such ideas/actions and operators include sincere appreciation and genuine interest in others' abilities, skills, and well-being, open-minded discussion, and the attitude that others' opinions/beliefs can be valid. (Refer to Section 9.3.)

(xiii) Do we know the systems in which, over which, and under which we are operating? Each system can be regarded as a living entity. Do we know their habitual domains and how they are working? (Refer to Section 9.4, and Ref. 313 for a discussion on systems.)

When consciously followed and answered periodically (say once a week), the above 13 suggestive questions can help us expand our habitual domains and sharpen our minds and to increase the possibility of success and happiness. The self-awareness questions can be applied to daily transactions to enhance our lives when they are suitably rephrased. We shall leave this to the reader.

Before we close this section, we shall emphasize that happiness and success are relative. If we can reduce the ideal values of our goal functions (except those related to physiology), lower charges will be produced. As a consequence, we are more content. No frustration and no excitement can occur. Also, an achievement (a success) of one goal does not imply achievement of other goals. Similarly the failure of one need not imply failure of the others. Thus, *each success can contain seeds for failure; and each failure can contain seeds for success.*

A way to assess our success or failure is to periodically review our resources and powers for achieving our goals. The following is a list of resources/powers which we can periodically review so as to increase our self-awareness.

(i) *Human resources/power*: No one can attain outstanding achievements without the help of others. Almost all the goals in Table 9.1 need other people for fulfillment. The number of people and the degree to which they can trust and cooperate with us, the number of people who appreciate and value our work and friendship, and the number of people we have helped to achieve their goals are just some measurements. Genuine interest in other people and constant willingness to help other people achieve their goals are two important ways to establish good human relationships. The interested reader is referred to Ref. 68 for Carnegie's excellent description of how to win friends and influence people.

(ii) *Knowledge, skill, and technology*: No one can sell an empty box. Our knowledge, skill, and technology are essential to make contributions to our society. Without the contributions, we will have difficulty in making a good living and achieving our higher goals. In reviewing, we need to categorize this knowledge, skill, and technology and assess the progress we have made in each category.

(iii) *Information and communication power*: Our lives are filled with uncertainty. People who can supply *accurate* information or judgment are extremely in demand. Effective ways to communicate our ideas to others are essential to sell our knowledge, skills, technology, and information. In review, we need to see how far we have extended and improved our information gathering systems and their degree of accuracy, and how we have improved our communication skill and ability.

(iv) *Economic assets and liabilities*: In review, we need to pay attention to the changes in each asset/liability in terms of ownership, utilization, and control.

(v) *Job position and its implied authority, responsibility, and rewards*: This has a pervasive and important impact on other resources/powers. Since position and its rewards are usually proportional to our contributions to the jobs, it needs to be carefully reviewed periodically. Another important measurement is how many significant contributions have we made to our jobs? Are people with whom, over whom, and under whom we work, happy and satisfied with our performance?

(vi) *Physiological health and habitual domains*: Health not only enhances our internal body energy but also releases our endowed internal information processing capacity for the pursuit of other life goals (see Section 9.2). Habitual domains will affect our effectiveness in working with people and business and in achieving our goals. The importance of its expansion cannot be overstated. In review, again we need to classify the health and habitual domains and verify the change and advancement in each class.

9.5.2. Decision Making

Figure 9.1 gives a general framework for decision-making processes. The 13 suggestive questions listed in the previous section can expand our vision in the search of a good decision. In addition, the following suggestions can be valuable for important decision problems.

(i) What are the feasible alternatives for the decision problem? Can we expand the feasible set?

(ii) What are the goal functions, and to what extent are they involved in the problem? What will be suitable and effective criteria for measuring the consequences of our decision?

(iii) How do we assess the consequence of our decision in terms of our criteria? How do we reduce uncertainty and risk in decision making? Can we share the risk with others?

(iv) How do we assess the short-term and long-term impacts of our decision on our career? Can we rank the preference, even partially, of the possible consequences?

(v) Do we have contingent plans for the case when the consequences are undesirable?

(vi) Who are the people who may have an impact on the outcomes of our decision? What are their interests, their habitual domains and charge structures? Can we predict their behavior or persuade them to take an alternative action favorable to us in the short run and long run?

(vii) Do we exercise our self-suggestion to "active search for a solution" or to "avoidance justification?" Whenever possible, should we drive ourselves to the former?

(viii) What are those *reliable* external information sources? How do we obtain accurate information from them? Are we aware of deceptive information?

For some further discussion, the reader is referred to Section 10.4 and Refs. 497 and 499.

9.5.3. Persuasion, Negotiation, and Gaming

Persuasion, negotiation, and gaming may be regarded as an extension of one person's decision making. See Section 10.4 for a discussion. The 13 suggestive questions for self-awareness in Section 9.5.1 and the eight suggestive questions for decision making in Section 9.5.2 are useful for achieving our objectives of persuasion, negotiation, or gaming. However, the suggested questions must be answered from our viewpoint as well as from what we perceive all other players' viewpoint to be. The following are worth reemphasizing:

(i) Who are the players? What are their interests and their habitual domains? Can we expand our habitual domains to absorb theirs?

(ii) What are our common interests? What are the conflicting interests? What are the impacts of a decision on our and the other players' short-run and long-run careers?

(iii) Can we emphasize the common goals so as to encourage cooperation and reduce competition?

(iv) Can we trigger a high level of charge on some goal functions of the other players so that for their own interest they will take an action favorable to us?

(v) Are we aware of who else can influence the other players' decisions? Do we know their interests, charge structures, and habitual domain? How can we influence them to influence the other players' decisions?

(vi) Can we introduce new players so that the gaming situation becomes favorable to us?

(vii) Can we change the rules of games (the time and the habitual constraints) so that the outcomes can be in our favor?

(viii) Can we reframe a one-stage decision into multiple-stage adaptive decisions, and vice versa, so that the outcomes can be in our favor?

(ix) Can we expand our deals into a package (including risk sharing) so that the offer can be more acceptable to each player?

(x) Can we form a coalition with other players so that a better result can be obtained?

(xi) Could the consequence of the game be very significant and irreversible? If so, do we have contingency plans? How do we avoid being caught by surprise?

(xii) Do we have adequate and accurate information or intelligence to make a right decision? Are we aware of deceptive information? How do we improve the accuracy of information and intelligence?

(xiii) Do we communicate well with the other players? Do we give them enough time to digest our ideas?

Further discussion, references and reframing tactics for second order games can be found in Section 10.4 and Ref. 499. We shall not repeat them here.

9.5.4. Career Management

In our careers, we inevitably meet with people, deal with business, make decisions, and engage in persuasion, negotiation, and gaming. All the suggestive questions of the previous three sections can be used to enhance our success. The following are some of the suggestions reemphasized.

(i) Understand your goals precisely. Exercise your self-suggestion power so that the goals can produce high levels of charges (drive) in your daily life. You cannot achieve more than you can imagine.

(ii) Write down a concrete plan for your short-term and long-term goals. Execute the plan and review daily the progress of your achievement in comparison to your targets. Find out what can be improved and improve it.

(iii) Understand the time efficiency of your internal information processing capacity over different periods of the day. Make a conscious effort to allocate daily the time over various events and activities so that your daily performance and achievement are maximized. You cannot achieve anything without conscious effort and concentration. The sequence and the time periods of the allocation become important in reaching your career goals.

(iv) Understand as precisely as possible the systems in which, under which, and over which you are working. Regarding each system as a dynamic living entity, you must know its charge structures and habitual domains.

(v) Periodically review and answer the suggestive questions posed in Sections 9.5.1–9.5.3.

Conarroe (Ref. 96) gives 32 ground rules for business success. We copy them as follows, because they are complementary to our suggestions and the reader may benefit from them.

(1) Pick the people who can most strongly determine your success and stay in direct, personal, continuous touch with them.

(2) Never assume that the way things are today is the way they will be tomorrow—or even after lunch.

(3) No matter what your job is, think of yourself as a salesman.

(4) Never fail to consider the future significance of what you say and do.

(5) In business, as in other indoor sports, position is not everything—but almost.

(6) Know what it is you can do better than anyone else—and do it.

(7) Never say anything about anyone you would not say in exactly the same way to his face.

(8) Search for the seeds of victory in every disaster—and the seeds of disaster in every victory.

(9) Do not lie. If you cannot tell the truth, keep quiet. When you start lying, you are dead.

(10) Never expect someone to keep a secret. There are no secrets.

(11) Bet on people—but be prepared to lose.

(12) Unsolvable problems do not disrupt the routine—they are the routine.

(13) Make as few mistakes as possible. Assume that any random error could be fatal.

(14) Never fail to consider the pervasive power of personal self-interest.

(15) Everybody's motives are different. Make certain you know what motivates each person you deal with.

(16) Know exactly what your goals are.

(17) Surprise is a powerful tactic. Use it carefully. It can be disastrous.

(18) Revenge is sweet but it is God's privilege, not yours.

(19) Enemies are a fact of life, but a few are plenty.

(20) Never make a decision until you have to.

(21) Follow your own instincts. They are probably no more wrong than everyone else's carefully reasoned logic.

(22) Build a reputation as a winner by smiling when you win—and when you lose.

(23) Keep every promise you have made—or that others think you have made.

(24) Never assume that others are operating under the same rules you are.

(25) Play the business game for all you are worth—but not as if your life depended on it.

(26) Never permit a situation to continue in your company where someone can profit from your loss.

(27) Never underestimate the power of the number two man.

(28) Express your thanks, give lots of praise, but do not get left holding the bag.

(29) You can size up a man by the size of the problems he likes to solve.

(30) No matter what you do, do it as if you were competing with an equal.

(31) Success has many ingredients, but the greatest of these is confidence.

(32) Do not win too soon. You will miss half the fun of playing the business game.

Concerning career management, the reader may also find it interesting to read Hill (Ref. 211).

9.6. Further Comments

It is sincerely hoped that the model has clearly shown the basic forces in human decision/behavior and ways to happiness and success. Since every model is an abstraction of reality, it is not expected that our model can be valid universally. However, with an appropriately flexible interpretation, the model should be able to cover a fairly large scope of human activity. The description of this chapter is based on Yu (Ref. 501). Many interesting psychological results can be found in the references and those quoted therein.

Many research problems remain open. For instance, how do different habitual domains among people interact? Can we learn about it by computer simulation? What are the effective ways to expand habitual domains? How could we effectively absorb, rather than reject, other people's habitual domains? If we regard an organization or social group as a dynamic living entity, how do we assess and expand its habitual domains? This clearly is an important aspect in studying organization and leadership. In Ref. 72, Chan has applied the concept to study conflict solvability. She also supplies a framework to describe personality and indicates a way to classify habitual domains.

9.7. Appendix: Existence of Stable Habitual Domains

Two kinds of stable habitual domains are studied in this appendix. The first one is the stability of the number of elements in HD_t (Section 9.7.1); the other is the stability of the activation propensity P_t of the elements in HD_t (Section 9.7.2). The presentation follows the work of Chan and Yu (Ref. 73).

9.7.1. Stability Theories on the Number of Elements in Habitual Domains

Theoretically our mind is capable of almost unlimited expansion (H2) and with sufficient effort one can learn almost anything new over a period of time. However, the amount of knowledge or ideas that exist in one's mind may increase with time, but the rate of increment tends to decrease as time goes by. As mentioned in Section 9.3.1, this may be due to the fact that the probability of learning new ideas or actions becomes lower as a number of ideas or actions in the HD is larger. These observations enable us to show that the number of ideas in one's HD_t converges when suitable conditions are met.

First let us introduce the following notation:

(i) Let a_t be the number of *additional* new ideas or concepts acquired during the period $]t - 1, t]$. Note that the time scale can be in seconds, minutes, hours, or days, etc. Assume that $a_t \geqq 0$, and that once an idea is registered or learned, it will not be erased from the memory, no matter whether it can be retrieved easily or not. This assumption is consistent with the *law of mass action* (for instance see Ref. 297), which states that once an idea is learned it will be registered, though scattered throughout the brain, and it is almost impossible to erase the idea completely. When a particular event is emphasized, a_t designates the *additional* ideas or concepts acquired during $(t - 1, t]$ concerning that event.

(ii) For convenience denote the sequence of a_t throughout a period of time by $\{a_t\}$. Note that due to the biophysical and environmental conditions of the individuals, $\{a_t\}$ is not necessarily monotonic. It can be up or down and subject to certain fluctuation. For instance, people may function better and more effectively in the morning than at night. Consequently, the a_t in the morning will be higher than that at night. Also observe that $\{a_t\}$ may display a pattern of periodicity (day/night for instance) which is unique for each individual. The periodicity can be a result of biophysical rhythms or rhythms of the environment.

The following can readily be proved by applying the ratio test of power series.

Theorem 9.2. Suppose there exists T such that whenever $t > T$, $a_{t+1}/a_t \leqq r < 1$. Then as $t \to \infty$, $\sum_{t=0}^{\infty} a_t$ converges.

Remark 9.12. (i) Theorem 9.2 says that supposing the amount of ideas or learning in one's HD is nondecreasing at $t > T$ and the rate of increase is strictly decreasing with bounded ratio in time t, then as t gets larger the total number of ideas or knowledge will approach a stable state.

(ii) The assumption of monotonicity of a_t in Theorem 9.2 can be relaxed as follows.

Theorem 9.3. Assume that (i) there exists a time index s, periodicity constant $m > 0$, and constants D and M, such that $\sum_{n=0}^{\infty} a_{s+nm} \leq D$, where $\{a_{s+nm}\}$ is a subsequence of $\{a_t\}$ with periodicity m, and (ii) for any period n, $\sum_{i=1}^{m} a_{s+nm+i} / m a_{s+nm} \leq M$. Then $\sum_{t=0}^{\infty} a_t$ converges.

Proof. By the assumption (ii) we have

$$\sum_{i=1}^{m} a_{s+nm+i} \leq M m a_{s+nm} \tag{9.10}$$

$$\sum_{t=0}^{\infty} a_t = \sum_{t=0}^{s} a_t + \sum_{i=1}^{m} a_{s+i} + \sum_{i=1}^{m} a_{s+m+i} + \cdots + \sum_{i=1}^{m} a_{s+km+i} + \cdots$$

$$\leq \sum_{t=0}^{s} a_t + M m a_s + M m a_{s+m} + \cdots + M m a_{s+km} + \cdots$$

$$\leq \sum_{t=0}^{s} a_t + M m D < \infty \qquad \text{as desired.} \qquad \square$$

[Note, the inequalities follow from Theorem 9.2 and assumption (i).]

Note that for HD to converge, Theorem 9.3 does not require a_t to be monotonically decreasing as required in Theorem 9.2. As long as there exists a convergent subsequence, and the sum of a_t within a time period of length m is bounded, then a_t can fluctuate up and down without affecting the convergence of HD_t. Thus the assumptions in Theorem 9.3 are a step closer to reality than those in Theorem 9.2.

Remark 9.13. Theorems 9.2 and 9.3 imply that if the subsequence $\{a_{s+nm}\}$ is monotonically decreasing with a bounded ratio as $n \to \infty$, then $\sum_{t=0}^{\infty} a_t$ converges. This idea is summarized as Corollary 9.2.

Corollary 9.2. Suppose that assumption (ii) of Theorem 9.3 holds and that $a_{s+nm} / a_{s+(n-1)m} \leq \gamma < 1$. Then $\sum_{t=0}^{\infty} a_t$ converges.

Remark 9.14. The regular periodicity assumption in Theorem 9.3 can be removed and substituted by a more general assumption and result in an *imbedding theory* of Theorem 9.4.

Theorem 9.4. Assume that (i) there exists a subsequence $\{a_{s_k} | k = 1, 2, \ldots\} \subset \{a_t\}$, and constants D and M, such that $\sum_k a_{s_k} \to D$ and (ii) $\sum_{i=1}^{s_{k+1}-s_k} a_{s_k+i} \leq M a_{s_k}$. Then $\sum_{t=0}^{\infty} a_t$ converges.

Proof. Note that

$$\sum_{t=0}^{\infty} a_t = \sum_{t=0}^{s_1} a_t + \sum_{i=1}^{s_2-s_1} a_{s_1+i} + \sum_{i=1}^{s_3-s_2} a_{s_2+i} + \cdots$$

$$\leq \sum_{t=0}^{s_1} a_t + M(a_{s_1} + a_{s_2} + \cdots)$$

$$\leq \sum_{t=0}^{s_1} a_t + MD < \infty \qquad \text{as desired.} \qquad \square$$

Observe that Theorem 9.3 assumes a regular periodicity m in $\{a_t\}$, which is replaced, in Theorem 9.4, by a more general subsequence $\{a_{s_k}\}$, in which the length of periodicity $s_k - s_{k-1}$ can be varied for different k's. The HD_t still converges as $t \to \infty$ as long as the sum of subsequence $\{a_{s_k}\}$ converges and the total rate of increase between $(s_{k-1}, s_k]$ is bounded as required.

Remark 9.15. (i) By allowing $s_k - s_{k-1}$ to vary for different k's, we actually generalize the single periodicity to multiple periodicities. This generalization makes it possible to cover a variety of fluctuations of $\{a_t\}$.

(ii) From Theorems 9.2 and 9.4 we see that if the subsequence $\{a_{s_k}\}$ is strictly decreasing in ratio as $k \to \infty$, then $\sum_{t=0}^{\infty} a_t$ converges. Precisely, we have Corollary 9.2.

Corollary 9.2. Suppose that the assumptions (ii) in Theorem 9.4 holds and $a_{s_k}/a_{s_{k-1}} \leq \gamma < 1$, then $\sum_{t=0}^{\infty} a_t$ converges.

9.7.2. The Stability of Habitual Domains—In Terms of Activation Propensity

In this section the stability of the "strength" of the elements in HD_t to be activated, called *activation propensity*, is studied. Note that the activation propensity, like probability mass, is a measurement for P_t discussed in Section 9.3.1. Define $x_i(t)$, $i \in HD_t$, to be the *activation propensity* of element i at time t. For simplicity let $HD_t = \{1, 2, \ldots, n\}$ and $x = (x_1, \ldots, x_n)$. Note that n, the number of elements in HD_t, can be very large. As $x_i(t)$ is a measurement of the force for idea i to be activated, we can assume that $x_i(t) \geq 0$. Also $x_i(t) = 0$ means that idea i cannot be activated at time t, by assigning $x_i(t) = 0$ we may assume that HD_t contains all possible ideas of interest that may be acquired now and in the future.

Similar to charge structures (Section 9.2), $x_i(t)$ may be a measurement of charge or force for idea i to occupy the "attention" at time t. Note, $x_i(t)/\sum_t x_i(t)$ will be a measurement of relative strength for idea i to be activated. If all $x_i(t)$

become stable after some time, the relative strength of each i to be activated will also be stable. In this case one may think that the idea i can be activated with probability $x_i(t)/\sum_i x_i(t)$. We shall explore under what conditions all $x_i(t)$ can become stable. In Section 9.7.2.1 we shall first formulate the dynamic change of $x(t)$ in terms of a system of differential equations by utilizing the results discovered in neuropsychology and mathematical psychology. For instance, see Ref. 297, 174, and 176. In Section 9.7.2.2 we shall prove a theorem of stability of $x(t)$.

9.7.2.1. Formulation of the Dynamics of Activation Propensity

Let us reframe H1, *The Circuit Pattern Hypothesis*, as follows:

(i) Each element or idea in the HD is represented by a unique circuit pattern of neural cells. The pattern can be imprinted in a number of sections of the brain. When the circuit pattern is activated by an appropriate stimulus, the corresponding idea will emerge.

(ii) The strength or the activation propensity $x_i(t)$ can be enhanced through its repeated activations. The stronger the circuit pattern and the more sections of the brain in which the circuit pattern is imprinted, the easier the corresponding idea or element can be retrieved or activated. Thus, $x_i(t)$ is an increasing function of the strength of the pattern and the number of sections of the brain in which circuit pattern i corresponding to idea i is imprinted.

Since idea i is represented by an activated circuit pattern of neural cells, the factors that influence the activation of the neural cells will also influence the activation propensity $x(t)$. According to the finding of neural psychology (see Refs. 297, 174, and 176, for instance), there are at least three factors that may influence the neural pattern circuits and $x_i(t)$.

(i) *Spontaneous decay*: When an idea or concept is not rehearsed, its propensity to activate tends to degenerate with time because (1) the relative strength of the circuit pattern against others may be reduced, and (2) according to the most efficient restructuring hypothesis of memory (H3) the idea, if not activated, may be stored, perhaps gradually, in a relatively remote area and is relatively more difficult to be retrieved or activated.

(ii) *Internal excitation and inhibition effects*: When a circuit pattern i corresponding to element $i \in HD_t$ is activated, the circuit pattern can send out both excitation and inhibition signals. The excitation signal activates the circuit pattern i imprinted in other sections of the brain, and at the same time imprints the circuit pattern i in new sections of the brain. While the activated circuit pattern i sends out excitation signals, it also sends out inhibition signals which inhibit or suppress the excitation of the other circuit patterns.

(iii) *External influence*: External stimuli or information inputs as stimuli to the memory can affect various circuit patterns to be imprinted and stored in the brain. They have the impact on excitation or inhibition of various circuit patterns.

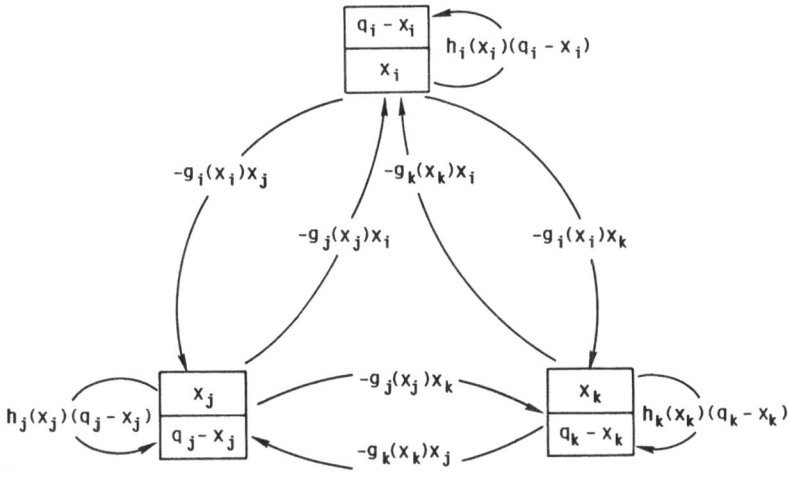

Figure 9A.1

With the above observation and the work of neural cognition (for instance, see Refs. 297, 174-176), we are ready for describing relevant assumptions and constructing the dynamic evolution of $x(t)$ as follows. Refer to Figure 9A.1 for the interaction among ideas i, j, and k.

Assumption 9.1. Given $x(t)$ and a sufficiently small time interval Δt, $x(t + \Delta t) - x(t)$ is given by

$$x_i(t + \Delta t) - x_i(t) = -\alpha_i x_i(t)\Delta t + [q_i - x_i(t)][h_i(x_i(t)) + I_i]\Delta t$$

$$-x_i(t)\left[\sum_{k \neq i} g_k(x_k(t)) + J_i\right]\Delta t, \qquad (9.11)$$

where (i) $\alpha_i > 0$ is the instantaneous decaying factor for $x_i(t)$; thus $-\alpha_i x_i(t)\,\Delta t$ is the reduction of the propensity due to natural spontaneous decay.

(ii) $q_i > 0$ is a maximum potential propensity value for idea i; thus $q_i - x_i(t)$ is a measurement of "under potential," which gives the magnitude to which $x_i(t)$ can further be increased.

(iii) $h_i(x_i(t))$ is the self-excitation function for idea i so that during the time interval $]t, t + \Delta t]$, the propensity of idea i is increased by $[q_i - x_i(t)]h(x_i(t))\,\Delta t$ due to the impact of $x_i(t)$.

(iv) $I_i \geqq 0$ is the external rate of excitation by the environment on idea i so that the propensity of idea i is increased by $[q_i - x_i(t)]I_i\,\Delta t$ during the time interval $]t, t + \Delta t]$.

(v) $g_k(x_k)$ is the inhibition function of idea k so that the propensity reduction of idea i by $x_k(t)$ during $]t, t + \Delta t]$ is given by $g_k(x_k(t))x_i(t) \Delta t$.

(vi) $J_i \geq 0$ is the rate of inhibition of the external environment acting on idea i. Thus idea i's propensity is reduced by $x_i(t)J_i \Delta t$ during the time interval $]t, t + \Delta t]$.

Remark 9.16. Assumption 9.1 is an additive model which is similar to well-known on-center off-surround models for cognition patterns. Roughly speaking, when a cognition pattern is activated, on the one hand it tends to enhance its strength for further activation, and on the other hand, it tends to reduce the strength for activation of other cognitive patterns. For a more detailed discussion see Refs. 297, 174-176. Note that the model proposed here is slightly different from that proposed in Refs. 174-176 in which it is assumed that the effective rate of excitation signals and inhibition signals are the same [i.e., $h_i(x_i) = g_i(x_i)$, for each $i = 1, \ldots, n$]. We do not make such an assumption.

Now, by taking

$$\lim_{\Delta t \to 0} \frac{x_i(t + \Delta t) - x_i(t)}{\Delta t} = \dot{x}_i(t),$$

from (9.11), one obtains

$$\dot{x}_i(t) = -\alpha_i x_i(t) + [q_i - x_i(t)][h_i(x_i(t)) + I_i]$$

$$-x_i(t)\left[\sum_{k \neq i} g_k(x_k(t)) + J_i\right], \tag{9.12}$$

which can be written as

$$\dot{x}_i(t) = x_i(t)\left\{-\alpha_i - J_i + g_i(x_i(t)) + \frac{q_i - x_i(t)}{x_i(t)}[h_i(x_i(t)) + I_i]\right.$$

$$\left. -\sum_k g_k(x_k(t))\right\}$$

$$= a_i(x(t))\{b_i(x_i(t)) - c(x(t))\}, \tag{9.13}$$

with

$$a_i(x(t)) = x_i(t), \tag{9.14}$$

$$b_i(x_i(t)) = -\alpha_i - J_i + g_i(x_i(t)) + \frac{q_i - x_i(t)}{x_i(t)}[h_i(x_i(t)) + I_i], \tag{9.15}$$

$$c(x(t)) = \sum_{k=1}^{n} g_k(x_k(t)). \tag{9.16}$$

Note that $b_i(x_i(t))$ depends on x_i only, while $c(x)$ depends on all x_i, $i = 1, \ldots, n$. Equation (9.13) has been extensively studied by Grossberg (Ref. 175) for its stability.

We summarize the above discussion in the following theorem.

Theorem 9.5. If Assumption 9.1 is satisfied, then the time derivative of $x(t)$ at time t satisfies equations (9.13)–(9.16).

9.7.2.2. Stability of Activation Propensity $x(t)$

In this subsection, conditions that guarantee the existence of $\lim_{t \to \infty} x(t)$ will be derived. Note that when the limit exists, the activation propensity $x(t)$ will reach its steady state. Toward this end, we shall first quote a known result of Grossberg (Ref. 175) concerning the stability of the solution to equation (9.13).

Theorem 9.6. With respect to equation (9.13), $\dot{x}_i = a_i(x)[b_i(x_i) - c(x)]$, assume that the following conditions hold:

(I) Smoothness:

(a) $a_i(x)$ is continuous for $x \geq 0$;

(b) $b_i(x_i)$ is either continuous with piecewise derivatives for $x_i \geq 0$, or is continuous with piecewise derivatives for $x_i > 0$ and $b_i(0) = \infty$;

(c) $c(x)$ is continuous with piecewise derivatives for $x \geq 0$.

(II) Nonnegativity:

$$a_i(x) > 0 \quad \text{if } x_i > 0 \quad \text{and} \quad x_j \geq 0, \quad j \neq i;$$

$$a_i(x) = 0 \quad \text{if } x_i = 0 \quad \text{and} \quad x_j \geq 0, \quad j \neq i.$$

Moreover, there exists a function $\bar{a}_i(x_i)$ such that, for sufficiently small $\lambda > 0$, $\bar{a}_i(x_i) \geq a_i(x)$ if $x \in [0, \lambda]^n$ and

$$\int_0^\lambda \frac{dw}{\bar{a}_i(w)} = \infty.$$

(III) Boundedness:

$$\limsup_{w \to \infty} b_i(w) < c(0, \ldots, 0, \infty, 0, \ldots, 0),$$

where "∞" occurs in the ith entry, $i = 1, 2, \ldots, n$.

(IV) Competition:

$$\frac{\partial c}{\partial x_k} \geqq 0, \qquad k = 1, 2, \ldots, n.$$

Then, given any initial point $x(0) \geqq 0$, all the limits $b_i(x_i(\infty)) = c(x(\infty))$ exist (called "weak global stability"). Furthermore, if all $b_i(x_i)$ possess finitely many local maxima within the range of x_i, then given any $x(0) \geqq 0$, all limits $x_i(\infty) = \lim_{t\to\infty} x_i(t)$ exist, $i = 1, \ldots, n$. (This is called "strong global stability".)

Theorem 9.7. Assume that (i) Assumption 9.1 is satisfied so that the evolution of $x(t)$ is described by equations (9.13)–(9.16) and that for each $i = 1, \ldots, n$ the inhibition function $g_i(w)$ and the self-activation function $h_i(w), i = 1, \ldots, n$, are bounded, nondecreasing, and continuous with piecewise derivative for $w \geqq 0$, and (ii) $g_i(0) = 0$, $h_i(0) = 0$. Then given any initial point $x(0) \geqq 0$, all the limits $b_i(x_i(\infty)) = \lim_{t\to\infty} b_i(x_i(t))$ exist and $b_i(x_i(\infty)) = c(x(\infty))$ (i.e., weak global stability is achieved). Furthermore, if all $b_i(x_i)$ defined in equation (9.15) possess finitely many local maxima within the range of x_i, then given any $x(0) \geqq 0$, all limits $x_i(\infty) = \lim_{t\to\infty} x_i(t)$ exist, $i = 1, \ldots, n$ (i.e., strong global stability achieved).

Proof. In view of Theorem 9.6, it suffices to verify that conditions (I)–(IV) are satisfied. That (I), the smoothness condition is satisfied is clear from equation (9.14)–(9.16) and the assumption that each g_i and h_i is continuous with piecewise derivatives. That (II), the nonnegativity condition is satisfied is also clear by equation (9.14) and by selecting $\bar{a}_i(x_i) = x_i = a_i(x)$. To verify that (III), the boundedness condition is satisfied, note that by equations (9.15) and (9.16)

$$\limsup_{w\to\infty} b_i(w) = -\alpha_i - J_i + g_i(\infty) - h_i(\infty) - I_i < c(0, \ldots, 0, \infty, 0, \ldots, 0)$$

$$= g_i(\infty).$$

Note that since each $g_i(w)$ and $h_i(w)$ are nondecreasing and bounded, $g_i(\infty)$ and $h_i(\infty)$ do exist. The strict inequality holds because $\alpha_i > 0$. Finally, for (IV), by equation (9.16), $\partial c/\partial x_k = dg_k(x_k)/dx_k \geqq 0$, whenever it exists, as each g_k is nondecreasing. $\square$

Remark 9.17. In the weak global stability, because $b_i(x_i(\infty)) = c(x(\infty))$, oscillations of $x_i(t)$, $i = 1, \ldots, \infty$, that might occur become arbitrarily small as $t \to \infty$. To ensure the strong global stability, we need $b_i(x_i)$ to possess finitely many local maxima within the range of x_i. This condition is usually satisfied in most applied problems. When all $g_i(x_i)$ and $h_i(x_i)$ are analytic functions, the condition will be satisfied.

Remark 9.18. The ideas of HD$_t$ discussed in Theorem 9.7 may be regarded as "elementary" ideas (like "elementary events" in a sample space in statistics). An idea can be regarded as a collection of these elementary ideas. The similarity of two ideas may be represented by the intersection of the elementary ideas contained in the two ideas (or common elementary ideas). This definition may be used to study the concept that one idea may activate other ideas through the association/analogy hypothesis [H4]. The problem is very complex and needs further exploration.

Exercises

9.1. Using behavior bases (H1–H8) explain the following human behavior: (Please take the time to do it in detail. It will help you grasp the main ideas.)
   a. Hunger and eating. (Are there physiological monitors and thresholds that trigger the action?)
   b. Thirst and drinking.
   c. Making love and sexual behavior.
   d. Aggression and submission behavior.
   e. Sleeping.
   f. Dreaming.
   g. Religious belief and worship.

9.2. Refer to the structure of goal functions in Table 9.1. Can you add new goals that are not listed? Can you think of a better way to classify them? Justify your classification.

9.3. Refer to Remark 9.7. Explore the possibility of using "elementary goal functions" to study the interrelations among goals.

9.4. The analogy/association hypothesis plays a very important role in our daily life. Our language and mathematics are just some of man's inventions based on association laws. Explore what would happen to our lives if we do not have a common language and mathematics.

9.5. Self-suggestion is a very important function in human behavior. To illustrate this, close your eyes and imagine, as vividly as you can (never mind the inconsistency with your daily belief):
   a. A mountain that stands alone in a desert and is covered with green trees. All of a sudden a giant stands on top of the mountain greeting you happily...
   b. An infant is crying and all of a sudden he becomes a handsome young man dressed in red and greets you...
   c. A tiger sits in a forest and then talks to you in a friendly way...
   d. You are a king and accept the greeting from your subordinates. Then the queen asks you to go inside...

9.6. Analyze how many times you have exercised "self-suggestion" to solve problems and to avoid problems.

9.7. Construct one or two counterexamples against the behavior bases (H1–H8). Justify your answer carefully.

9.8. The least resistance principle is the rule of selecting the action that yields the lowest charge strength of the remaining charge structures after that action is taken. Discuss the similarity and difference between this principle and compromise solutions. How do you apply the compromise solution concept discussed in Chapter 4 to the least resistance principle?

9.9. Consider the two charge structures F_t and G_t at time t as follows:

Goal function (i)	F_t					G_t				
1	(0,	0,	0,	0,	0.6)	(0,	0,	0,	0,	0.8)
2	(0,	0,	0.2,	1,	1)	(0,	0,	1,	1,	1)
3	(0,	0,	0.5,	1,	1)	(0,	0,	0,	0.4,	1)
4	(0,	0,	0,	0.4,	1)	(0,	0,	0,	0,	1)
5	(0,	0,	0,	1,	1)	(0,	0,	0,	0.7,	1)

a. Construct the ordered charge structure F'_t and G'_t.
b. Which charge structure is larger? Why?
c. Let E^1_t and E^2_t be event 1 and event 2 at time t, respectively. Assume $K_t(-E^1_t) = F_t$ and $K_t(-E^2_t) = G_t$, where $K_t(-E^i_t)$, $i = 1, 2$, is the remaining charge structure at time t if E^i_t is resolved at time t. Which event, E^1_t or E^2_t, will command the attention? Why?
d. Assume that the charge structure K_t is given as follows:

i	K_t				
1	(0,	0,	0,	0,	1)
2	(0,	0,	1,	1,	1)
3	(0,	0,	0.5,	1,	1)
4	(0,	0,	0,	0.5,	1)
5	(0,	0,	0,	1,	1)

The marginal contributions of E^i_t, $i = 1, 2$, are then given by $K_t - K_t(-E^i_t)$. Verify that the lower is $K_t(-E^i_t)$, the higher is the charge of E^i_t.

9.10. Consider a decision problem involving two alternatives A^1 and A^2 at two different times $t = 1$ and $t = 2$. Thus $\mathscr{A}_t = \{A^1_t, A^2_t\}$, $t = 1, 2$. Let $F_t(+A^k_t) = \{f^i_t(A^k_t) | i = 1, 2, 3, 4, 5\}$, $k = 1, 2$, be the remaining charge structure after A^k_t, $k = 1, 2$ being taken.

t	i	$F_t(+A^1_t)$					$F_t(+A^2_t)$				
1	1	0,	0,	0,	0.5,	1	0,	0,	1,	1,	1
	2	0,	0,	0,	1,	1	0,	0,	0,	0.6,	1
	3	0,	0.4,	1,	1,	1	·0,	0,	0.8,	1,	1
	4	0,	0,	0.6,	1,	1	0,	0,	0.2,	1,	1
	5	0,	0,	0,	0,	1	0,	0,	0,	1,	1
2	1	0,	0,	1,	1,	1	0,	0,	0.5,	1,	1
	2	0,	0,	0,	0.0,	1	0,	0,	0,	1,	1
	3	0,	0,	0.6,	1,	1	0,	0,	1,	1,	1
	4	0,	0,	0,	1,	1	0,	0,	0.8,	1,	1
	5	0,	0,	0,	0,	1	0,	0,	0,	0,	1

Which alternative, A_t^1 or A_t^2, will be taken at time $t = 1, 2$ according to the least resistance principle? Justify your answer.

9.11. Explore the similarity and difference between ordinary optimization theory and the least resistance principle. Can ordinary optimization theory fully capture the human decision mechanism? Justify your answer.

9.12. Prove Lemma 9.1(iii) when (9.5) and (9.7) hold.

9.13. Refer to Remark 9.11. Explore the expansion of habitual domains over multi-periods of time.

9.14. Refer to Example 9.4. Construct an example to show that strict superadditivity can hold for reachable domains.

9.15. Refer to Example 9.5. Construct an example to show that strict supermultiplicativity can hold for reachable domains.

9.16. Selecting a university to enroll at is an important decision. State the criteria, alternatives, perception of the alternatives, and preference when you were making the choice. During the process of making a decision, did you notice any time evolution of the above four decision elements? If you would be faced with the same choice, how would you do it? Do you notice that your HD for this problem has changed?

9.17. Suppose you are going to have two important job interviews. (The jobs are suitable and much desired by you.)
    a. How would you prepare for the interviews?
    b. Now let your creative mind expand a little bit. Do you see your HD on job interviews has been expanded?
    c. Now talk to your trusted friends or advisers. Do they suggest some new dimensions to prepare for the interview? Do you absorb or reject their suggestions? Why? Does your HD expand?
    d. Do you know the HDs of the interviewers? How do you match your own HD and the interviewers' HDs so that they will offer you the job?
    e. Do you know who are the applicants competing for the same jobs? Do you know or can you estimate their HDs? How do you prepare your interview so that you may get the job offer?
    f. Compare the HDs over different time points, after you have finished (b), (c), (d), and (e), respectively. Do you see the expansion of your HDs? Identify those $\{\tilde{I}_t, \tilde{O}_t\}$ that trigger the expansion of your HD_t.

9.18. Explain, using behavior bases (H1–H8), why the following conceptions (operators) can help us expand our habitual domains.
    a. sincere appreciation and genuine interest in our own and others' abilities, skills, and well-being;
    b. open-minded discussion;
    c. attitude that others' opinion/beliefs can be valid;
    d. willingness to think in terms of the other persons' interest.

9.19. Explore, using behavior bases (H1–H8), under what conditions and how the following social psychological observations become valid:
    a. social comparison theory;
    b. halo effect;
    c. projection effect (assumed similarity);
    d. proximity theory;
    e. reciprocation behaviors;
    f. similarity effect;

    g. scapegoating behaviors;

    h. responsibility diffusion behaviors.

9.20. Explore, using behavior bases (H1-H8), the validity and applicability of the suggestions listed in Section 9.5.1 for self-awareness, happiness, and success. Identify specifically under which circumstances the individual suggestions can be especiallly powerful or failing.

9.21. Explore, using behavior bases (H1-H8), the validity and applicability of the suggestions listed in Section 9.5.2 for reaching good decisions. Identify specifically under which circumstances the individual suggestion can be especially powerful or failing.

9.22. Explore, using behavior bases (H1-H8), the validity and applicability of the suggestions listed in Section 9.5.3 for successful persuasion, negotiation, and gaming. Identify specifically under which circumstances the individual suggestions can be especially powerful or failing.

9.23. Explore, using behavior bases (H1-H8), the validity and applicability of the suggestions listed in Section 9.5.4 for career management. Identify specifically under which circumstances the individual suggestions can be especially powerful or failing.

9.24. Explore, using behavior bases (H1-H8), the validity and applicability of the suggestions of Conarroe (listed in Section 9.5.4) for career success. Identify specifically under which circumstances the individual suggestions can be especially powerful or failing.

Suggested Reading

The following references are particularly pertinent to this chapter: 68, 72, 73, 74, 96, 145, 174, 175, 176, 186, 201, 209, 211, 236, 297, 313, 323, 351, 370, 386, 410, 459, 497, 499, 501, 505, 521.

10

Further Topics

Up to this point we have discussed the basic concepts and methods of multi-criteria decision problems. Many interesting topics remain to be explored. Being limited by space, we can only sketch them and point out relevant references so that interested readers can find the literature and results they need. In Section 10.1 we shall discuss more interactive methods assuming that a value function exists in such a way that the reader can create his own. Section 10.2 is devoted to the preference and dominance involved in uncertain outcomes of decision. In Section 10.3 we discuss multicriteria optimal control and dynamic programming problems. In Section 10.4 we sketch second-order games which are waiting for the reader to explore and make contributions.

10.1. Interactive Methods for Maximizing Preference Value Functions

In Sections 4.2.3 and 4.3.5 we discussed interactive methods using goal setting and satisficing concepts, and in Section 7.5 we described interactive methods for locating N-points for the final decision. As we noticed in interactive methods, on the one hand we identify good candidates for the final decision and on the other hand we search for further preference information to identify better candidates. This process continues until further "significant" improvement is impossible.

Interactive methods are useful because to obtain the entire set of preference information is practically impossible or painful. Regarding preference information obtaining as a task or event, for the task to command our attention and/or the attention of the decision makers it must have the strongest charge among all possible events (see Section 9.2). Usually a long duration of attention to obtain preference information is hard to achieve because other important events can occur in the meantime. The charge for searching for preference information can be dropped quickly when one realizes that one can make a fairly "good" choice even though the complete information of preference is not clearly specified.

Theoretically, one can construct as many interactive methods as one wishes by using different elicitation techniques and "optimization" methods at different stages of the interaction process. Indeed, there are many interactive methods in the literature. (For instance, see Ref. 223 of Hwang and Masud and Ref. 222 of Hwang and Yoon.) In this section we shall describe three methods modified from Ref. 164 of Geoffrion, Dyer, and Feinberg (Section 10.1.1), Ref. 182 of Hall and Haimes (Section 10.1.2), and Ref. 525 of Zionts and Wallenius (Section 10.1.3). These three methods are chosen for illustration only. There are many other interesting ones waiting for the reader to explore and create. One should keep in mind that the success of an interactive method is dependent not only on the method itself but also on the habitual domains of the applicant and the decision maker and how they communicate and become cooperative enough to solve the problem. Sometimes the salesmanship and charisma of the salesman of a method may be more important than the method itself! (By the association/analogy hypothesis (H4), if the decision maker can trust a consultant, he may accept a suggestion without carefully studying the suggestion itself!)

10.1.1. Adapted Gradient Search Method

Suppose that $v(x)$ is differentiable and concave on a compact convex set X. Then $x^0 \in X$ is a maximum point of v over X if $\nabla v(x^0) \cdot (x - x^0) \leq 0$ for all $x \in X$. (For instance, see Ref. 307.) This observation produces a number of gradient search methods. The following is a typical one.

Frank and Wolfe Gradient Method.

Step 0. Set $i = 1$. Choose initial point $x^1 = x^i \in X$.

Step 1. Find $\nabla_x v(x^i)$ and the solution z^i for the problem max $\nabla v(x^i) \cdot z$, $z \in X$. If $z^i = x^i$, stop with x^i as the solution of max $v(x)$ over X. Otherwise, go to Step 2.

Step 2. Let $h^i = z^i - x^i$ ("best" improving direction). Find t^i which solves max $v(x^i + th^i)$, $t^i \in [0, 1]$.

Step 3. Let $x^{i+1} = x^i + t^i h^i$. If $v(x^{i+1}) - v(x^i) \leq \varepsilon$, where $\varepsilon > 0$ is preassigned, then stop, with x^{i+1} as the solution to the problem of max $v(x)$ over X. Otherwise go to Step 1.

The above procedure will be terminated in a finite number of iterations (depending on ε, v, and X) and offer "approximate" optimal solutions when v is continuously differentiable and concave and X is convex and compact. Geoffrion, Dyer, and Feinberg (Ref. 164) artfully converted the above method into an "adapted gradient method" in interactive procedure to obtain a final "optimal" solution even though the value function $v(y)$ is not known *a priori*.

Basically, their method is as follows.

Adapted Gradient Search Method.

Step 0. Set $i = 1$. Select an initial point $x^1 = x^i \in X$.

Step 1. (A) Estimate $\nabla_f \hat{v}(f(x^i))$ [the gradient of v with respect to f at $f(x^i)$]. The reader is referred to Sections 6.1.1 and 6.1.2 for the details of an elicitation method.

(B) Compute

$$\nabla_x \hat{v}(f(x^i)) = \nabla_f \hat{v}(f(x^i)) \frac{\partial(f_1, \ldots, f_q)}{\partial(x_1, \ldots, x_n)} (x^i),$$

where $\nabla_f \hat{v}(f(x^i))$ is estimated as in (A), while

$$\frac{\partial(f_1, \ldots, f_q)}{\partial(x_1, \ldots, x_n)} (x^i)$$

is the Jacobian of f evaluated at x^i. The equation is suggested by the chain rule.

(C) Find the solution z^i for max $\nabla_x \hat{v}(f(x^i)) \cdot z$, $z \in X$. If $z^i = x^i$, stop with x^i as the final solution; otherwise go to Step 2.

Step 2. Let $h^i = z^i - x^i$ ("best" improving direction). Find t^i such that $x^i + t^i h^i$ is the most preferred in the segment $[x^i, z^i]$ {i.e., find t^i which solves max $\hat{v}(x^i + t^i h^i)$, $t^i \in [0, 1]$.}

As v is unknown, the interval $[0, 1]$ can be equally spaced by a net $\{0, \delta, 2\delta, 3\delta, \ldots, 1\}$. The corresponding values of $f(x^i + k\delta h^i)$, $k = 0, \ldots, 1/\delta$, can be displaced. The decision maker is then asked to choose the "best" one to decide optimal step size t^i.

Step 3. Let $x^{i+1} = x^i + t^i h^i$, and $\Delta^i = \nabla_f \hat{v}(f(x^i)) \cdot [f(x^{i+1}) - f(x^i)]$. If $\Delta^i/\Delta^{i-1} < \varepsilon$ ($\varepsilon > 0$, preassigned), or $\hat{v}(f(x^{i+1})) \leq \hat{v}(f(x^i)) + \varepsilon$ (i.e., the improvement is nominal or not significant), stop with x^{i+1} as the "approximate" optimal solution; otherwise go to step 1.

Similarly to the Frank and Wolfe gradient method, the adapted gradient search method will converge when proper conditions are met (see Exercise 10.4). The reader may be reminded that artful elicitation of the gradient $\nabla_f \hat{v}$ (step 1) and skillful determination of the optimal step size (step 2) are the keys to a successful application of this interactive method. They are by no means trivial.

10.1.2. Surrogate Worth Tradeoff Method

Refer to Figure 10.1. With Y as depicted, the nondominated set N is in the curve connecting points D, B, A, C, and E. Assuming that $\nabla v(y)$ is as depicted, we note that the normal vector of Y is not collinear with ∇v at B and C, and neither B nor C is a maximum point of v. But at point A, the

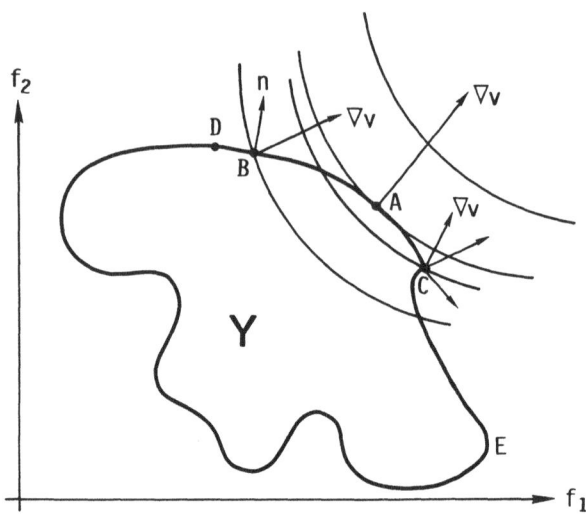

Figure 10.1

normal vector of Y and ∇v is collinear and A is the maximum point. Since
the normal vector of Y and ∇v is collinear, the *marginal rates of substitution*
(MRS) along the curve N and along the isovalued curve of v are identical.
When N is "smooth" at a point $y \in N$, the MRS along N at y can be obtained
using the Lagrangian multiplier for solving the problem specified in Theorem
3.16. This information can be presented to the decision maker (DM) to see if
he would be interested in trading with the MRS at a particular point of $y \subset N$.
The "trading" information will offer important information of the MRS at y
along the isovalued curve of v. If the DM wants to trade, then the MRS of N
and that of the isovalued curve are not the same and the current y of N will
not be a maximum point of v. A new point y' of N is then generated using
the "trading" information. This process is then repeated until a point y^0 of N
is obtained and the DM is indifferent to trade with the MRS of N at y^0.

The above is the main idea of the surrogate worth tradeoff method
suggested by Haimes and Hall (Ref. 182).

Let us make the above ideas more precise and expand a bit on the method.

Although it is not difficult to use general dominated cones, in the remaining
part of this section whenever we say N-points we mean N-points with respect
to the $\Lambda^{\leq}$-dominated cone (or Pareto preference). When the differentiability
condition holds Theorem 3.16 is satisfied. According to equation (3.10), $f(x^0)$
is an N-point only when x^0 locally maximizes $\sum_{i=1}^{q} \mu_i f_i(x)$ over X for some
$\mu = (\mu_1, \ldots, \mu_q) \geq 0$. Thus, μ will be a vector contained in $T^*(f(x^0), f[X])$
[the polar cone of the tangent cone of $f[X]$ at $f(x^0)$]. Without loss of generality
assume $\mu_1 = 1$. (Renumber the indices and normalize them if necessary.)

When N is a smooth $(q - 1)$-dimensional surface, μ is unique. Note that $\mu = (1, \mu_2, \ldots, \mu_q)$ is normal to $h^p(f(x^0)) = (1, 0, \ldots, 0, -1/\mu_p, 0, \ldots, 0)$ whenever $\mu_p > 0$ and $h^p(f(x^0))$ is a tangent vector of N at $f(x^0)$. It offers a meaning that marginally at $f(x^0)$ the substitution rate along N is one unit of f_1 for $1/\mu_p$ unit of f_p. Conversely, one unit of f_p is worth μ_p units of f_1.

When N is not smooth at $f(x^0)$ (for instance see point C of Figure 10.1), then the local weight for the optimal μ is not unique. For convenience, denote such local weights at $f(x^0)$ by $L\Lambda(x^0)$. Note that when both f and g are linear,

$$L\Lambda(x^0) = \Lambda(x^0) = \bigcup \Lambda(J), \tag{10.1}$$

where $\Lambda(J)$ can be obtained by the MC-simplex method as defined in (8.30) and the union is over all bases J such that $x^0 = x(J)$.

If $\mu \in L\Lambda(x^0)$ with $\mu = (1, \mu_2, \ldots, \mu_q)$, μ_p still offers the MRS of f_1 for each unit of f_p along the hyperplane $H(\mu) = \{h | h \cdot \mu = 0\}$. Note that if $\nabla_f v(f(x^0)) \in \text{Int } L\Lambda(x^0)$ then $f(x^0)$ is a local maximum point of v and if, in addition, Y is $\Lambda^{\leqq}$-convex then $f(x^0)$ is a global maximum point of v.

We summarize the above observation as follows.

Lemma 10.1. Assume that f and g are differentiable over X. Then we have the following.

(i) $f(x^0) \in N$ implies the set of local weights $L\Lambda(x^0) \neq \varnothing$; when both f and g are linear $L\Lambda(x^0) = \Lambda(x^0)$, which can be obtained by the MC-simplex method and (10.1).

(ii) If N is smooth at $f(x^0)$, the normalized vector (renumber the indices if necessary) $\mu = (1, \mu_2, \ldots, \mu_q)$ is unique. If $\mu_p > 0$ then along N the MRS (marginal rate of substitution) for one unit of f_p is μ_p units of f_1.

(iii) When N is not smooth at $f(x^0)$, if $\mu \in L\Lambda(x^0)$ with $\mu = (1, \mu_2, \ldots, \mu_q)$ and $\mu_p > 0$ then along the hyperplane $H(\mu)$, the MRS for one unit of f_p is μ_p units of f_1.

(iv) Let v be a differentiable function. Then a necessary condition for $f(x^0)$ to be a local maximum point of v is $\nabla_f v(f(x^0)) \in L\Lambda(x^0)$. If $f[X]$ is $\Lambda^{\leqq}$-convex and v is increasing in f and concave over $f[X] + \Lambda^{\leqq}$, then $\nabla_f v(f(x^0)) \in L\Lambda(x^0)$ ensures that $f(x^0)$ is a global maximum point of v. [A sufficient condition for this to hold is that each $f_i(x)$ is differentiable and concave over X which is convex, and v is increasing in f and concave over $f[X] + \Lambda^{\leqq}$.] (See Exercise 10.5.).

We are ready to describe a modified surrogate worth tradeoff method as follows (modified from Ref. 182).

Step 0. Identify the ideal (utopia) point $y^* = (f_1^*, \ldots, f_q^*)$, where $f_i^* = \sup \{f_i(x) | x \in X\}$ (see Section 4.3). If y^* is obtainable, stop; otherwise go to step 1.

Step 1. Present y^* and $\{y^{k^*}|k = 1, \ldots, q\}$, where $y^{k^*} = (f_1(x^{k^*}),$ $f_2(x^{k^*}), \ldots, f_q(x^{k^*}))$ and x^{k^*} maximizes f_k over X, and interact with the DM to identify a reference criterion say, f_1 (renumber if necessary) and some concession values ε_k, $k = 2, \ldots, q$, so that the DM would not mind accepting $f_k^* - \varepsilon_k$ for the kth criterion. Set $i = 1$.

Step 2. Find an N-point x^{*i} that solves the problem of max $f_1(x), f_k(x) \geq f_k^* - \varepsilon_k$, $k = 2, \ldots, q$, and $x \in X$. If there is no feasible solution then go to step 1 to readjust ε_k, $k = 2, \ldots, q$. Otherwise identify $L\Lambda(x^{*i})$. Note that $(1, \mu_2, \ldots, \mu_q) \in L\Lambda(x^{*i})$, where μ_k, $k = 2, \ldots, q$, are the Lagrangian multipliers for solving the above problem.

Step 3. (A) Select a vector $\mu = (1, \mu_2, \ldots, \mu_q)$ of $L\Lambda(x^{*i})$ and present $f(x^{*i}) = y^i$ to the DM.

(B) For $k = 2, \ldots, q$, ask the DM the question: "Given the status quo $f(x^{*i})$, for each unit of f_k you can trade μ_k units of f_1. *How many units of f_k would you like to increase or decrease in trading for f_1?*" For simplicity let $w_k \in [-10, 10]$ be the number of units the DM is willing to increase f_k by trading with f_1. The response of w_k is called the "surrogate worth function at $f(x^{*i})$" with respect to the tradeoff ratio μ_k. It reveals the following preference information:

(i) If $w_k(\mu_k) > 0$, the DM wants to increase f_k or reduce ε_k; or the tradeoff ratio μ_k is too low, the DM prefers to increase f_k.

(ii) If $w_k(\mu_k) < 0$, the DM wants to decrease f_k or increase ε_k; or the tradeoff ratio μ_k is too high, the DM prefers to increase f_1.

(iii) If $w_k(\mu_k) = 0$, the DM is indifferent to the trade. Thus, the tradeoff ratio μ_k is about right when the status quo point is $f(x^{*i})$.

Note that if a differentiable value function $v(f(x))$ exists, then, along the isovalued surface of v at $f(x)$,

$$\text{(A)} \quad w_k(\mu_k) > 0 \text{ implies that } -\frac{\partial f_1}{\partial f_k} = \frac{\partial v}{\partial f_k} \Big/ \frac{\partial v}{\partial f_1} > \mu_k,$$

$$\text{(B)} \quad w_k(\mu_k) < 0 \text{ implies that } -\frac{\partial f_1}{\partial f_k} = \frac{\partial v}{\partial f_k} \Big/ \frac{\partial v}{\partial f_1} < \mu_k,$$

and

$$\text{(C)} \quad w_k(\mu_k) = 0 \text{ implies that } -\frac{\partial f_1}{\partial f_k} = \frac{\partial v}{\partial f_k} \Big/ \frac{\partial v}{\partial f_1} = \mu_k.$$

Step 4. If all $w_k(\mu_k) = 0$, $k = 2, \ldots, q$, then x^{*i} is a candidate for the "optimal" solution and go to step 6. Otherwise, go to step 5.

Step 5. Using the information of $w_k(\mu_k)$, whenever possible, select a different $\mu^1 \in L\Lambda(x^{*i})$ which is consistent with the information $\{w_k(\mu_k)\}$ [i.e., if $w_k(\mu_k) > 0$ then select $\mu_k' > \mu_k$; if $w_k(\mu_k) < 0$ then select $\mu_k' < \mu_k$; and if $w_k(\mu_k) = 0$ then set $\mu_k' = \mu_k$] and go to step 3 with $i := i + 1$. Otherwise, adjust ε_k according to the information on $\{w_k(\mu_k)\}$ [i.e., if $w_k(\mu_k) > 0$, then decrease ε_k; if $w_k(\mu_k) < 0$ then increase ε_k; and if $w_k(\mu_k) = 0$, then leave ε_k unchanged], and go to step 2 with $i := i + 1$.

Step 6. Interact with the DM. If the optimal solution is obtained, then stop; otherwise, go to step 1.

Remark 10.1. (i) In the surrogate tradeoff worth method, we do not have to generate all N-points to begin the interaction with the DM. However, when both f and g are linear all N-points with corresponding $\Lambda(x)$ can be generated. One may want to generate a number of such points before interacting with the DM.

(ii) At each iteration, only N-points are of interest. In contrast with this, the gradient search method may not generate an N-point at each iteration.

(iii) When each f_i is concave and X is convex, $f[X]$ will be $\Lambda^{\leqq}$-convex. The additive weight method (Sections 3.3.2 and 3.4) is applicable. The interactive method can be adjusted to take advantage of this observation. We shall leave this to the reader. (See Exercise 10.6.)

10.1.3. Zionts–Wallenius Method

Zionts and Wallenius (Ref. 525) suggest an interactive method by first assuming that both f and g are linear and then extending to the case where f and g can be approximated by linear functions. With the MC-simplex program (Section 8.2) we can present a modified method as follows.

Step 0. Select a weight vector $\lambda^1 > 0$. Let $i = 1$.

Step 1. (A) Find an optimal solution of $\lambda^i Cx$ over $X = \{x | Ax \leqq d\}$. This can easily be done using the MC-simplex method with $\lambda^i C$ (instead of $1C$) at the bottom row as a guide for introducing nonbasic variables into a new basis. Note, the solution $x(J^i) = x^i$ of the above problem must be an N-point. (Why?)

(B) Determine the nonbasic columns whose introduction can lead to an adjacent N_{ex}-basis. This can be done by using Theorem 8.12 to check for *effective* constraints of $\Lambda(J^i)$ (see Remark 10.2). Denote the set of such columns by $R(J^i)$.

Step 2. Present $x(J^i)$, $Cx(J^i)$, and other relevant information to the DM and for each $j \in R(J^i)$, ask the DM "is the tradeoff vector $-Z_j$ among the objective values desirable, undesirable, or neither?" [Note, by introducing j into the basis the objective values will be increased by $-\theta_j Z_j$ (see Theorem 8.9). Thus, $-Z_j$ represents a marginal tradeoff vector among the objective values.] The answer offers the following information.

(i) If $-Z_j$ is desirable, then in the DM's mind, the optimal weight vector λ enjoys

$$-Z_j \cdot \lambda > 0$$

or

$$Z_j \cdot \lambda \leq -\varepsilon \qquad (10.2)$$

for some small $\varepsilon > 0$.

(ii) If $-Z_j$ is undesirable, then [similar to (i) but in reverse order]

$$Z_j \cdot \lambda \geq \varepsilon \qquad (10.3)$$

for some small $\varepsilon > 0$.

(iii) If the answer is neither, then

$$Z_j \cdot \lambda = 0. \qquad (10.4)$$

Step 3. Find λ^{i+1} which satisfies constraints (10.2)-(10.4) specified by step 2 for each $j \in R(J^i)$. Set $i = i + 1$ and go to step 1(A). If the solution $x^{i+1} = x^i$, stop with x^i as the "optimal" solution; otherwise repeat steps 1(B)-3.

Remark 10.2. For step 1(B), to verify if $j \in R(J^i)$, Zionts and Wallenius suggest solving for each $j \in (J^i)'$, min $w_j = Z_j \cdot \lambda$ s.t. $Z_k \cdot \lambda \geq 0$, $k \in (J^i)'$, $k \neq j$ and

$$\sum_{r=1}^{q} \lambda_r = 1, \qquad \lambda \geq 0.$$

The result is $j \in R(J^i)$ iff min $w_j < 0$. We shall leave it to the reader to compare this method with the "effective constraint" verification (Theorem 8.12). Certainly, the latter is much simpler. (See Exercise 10.10.)

Remark 10.3. Using the MC-simplex, one can first generate a candidate subset of N_{ex}-points and identify their corresponding set of optimal weights $\Lambda(x^i)$. Then the interactive process can be revised and simplified. We shall leave this to the reader. (See Exercise 10.11.)

Remark 10.4. The Zionts-Wallenius method, in spirit, is very similar to the surrogate tradeoff worth method. Both try to identify the "optimal weight vector" or local gradient of an implicit value function. However, the former takes advantage of linearity, while the latter does not. In essence, these two methods and the gradient search method are similar. All of them estimate the local gradient and use it as a guide for optimality.

Again, before closing this section of interactive methods, we emphasize that implementation or design of interactive methods is an art. Its success depends not only on the method itself but also on the trust and communication between or among the people who perform the task! Just think: can we successfully implement any method described in this section with anyone (DM) who does not understand the meaning of the marginal rate of substitution and the value function or with someone who does not trust us at all? It cannot be overemphasized that knowing our own habitual domains and the DM is very essential to successfully selling any interactive method. Understanding this point, the reader should have no difficulty in designing other interactive methods based on the problem setting and the basic concepts described in Chapters 2–9. (See Refs. 222 and 223 for some interesting combinations of the methods.)

10.2. Preference over Uncertain Outcomes

Like investments in the stock market, the decision outcomes are not always certain. Indeed many decision problems have such a feature. A large volume of literature (for instance see Refs. 217, 254, 520) has been devoted to studying these problems. In this section we shall sketch how this kind of problem has been studied and how they are related to multicriteria problems. Being limited by space we shall only sketch the main concepts and results. For more details the interested reader is referred to the quoted references.

According to Chapter 9, depending on our experience and learning, we gradually form our habitual ways of thinking and attitudes toward dealing with risk and uncertainty. Each person is unique. There are at least four basic kinds of concepts in formulating and analyzing preference for decisions with uncertain outcomes. All start with one simplifying assumption that the "uncertain outcomes" of a decision can be represented by a one-dimensional random variable x whose cumulative distribution (CDF) denoted by F_x is well defined. Thus, selection of an alternative is the selection of a random variable.

10.2.1. Stochastic Dominance (Concepts Based on CDF)

(i) The random variable x *stochastically dominates* y *in the first degree*, denoted by $x \, s_1 \, y$, iff $F_x(a) \leqq F_y(a)$ for all $a \in R^1$, and the inequality holds strictly for some a^0; (ii) x stochastically dominates y in the second degree, denoted by $x \, s_2 \, y$ iff $\int_{-\infty}^{a} F_x(t) \, dt \leqq \int_{-\infty}^{a} F_y(t) \, dt$, for all $a \in R^1$, and the inequality holds strictly for some a^0.

Note that each random variable is uniquely represented by its CDF. Regarding a in $F_x(a)$ or $\int_{-\infty}^{a} F_x(t) \, dt$ as magnitude of dimension, we see that stochastic dominance is essentially a "Pareto preference" in the infinite-dimensional space. As the dominated cone of a Pareto preference is so small in the infinite-dimensional space, the set of nondominated random variables will be relatively very large (compared to all the possible alternatives or random variables) (see Section 7.1 and Remark 7.7). That is, a large number of random variables will remain nondominated if stochastic dominance, first or second degree, is the only source of preference information (unless the problem has some special structure).

10.2.2. Mean-Variance Dominance (Concepts Based on Moments)

Assume that the moments in question, such as the mean (first moment) and variance (second moment), exist. As each random variable is uniquely associated with its moment generating function, moments play an important role in studying probability. A typical dominance concept in this category is *mean-variance* dominance. We say that the x *mean-variance dominates* y, denoted by $x \, \text{mv} \, y$, iff $Ex \geq Ey$, $\text{Var} \, x \leq \text{Var} \, y$ and at least one inequality holds strictly.

Note that in security investment, if the criterion is the rate of return on the investment, then higher is better for its expected value, and as variance is a measurement of risk, lower is better for its variance. Also note that the mean-variance dominance concept is a Pareto-preference concept after converting the random variable into two measuring criteria (mean and variance). When the random variable has a special structure (such as a normal distribution, gamma distribution, etc.) these two moments (mean and variance) can uniquely characterize the corresponding distribution. We shall explore this more later.

10.2.3. Probability Dominance (Concept Based on Outperforming Probability)

This concept is based on the following, frequently heard, rationale that A is chosen, because A is likely to outperform B or because A's prospect is likely to be better than B's. *Probability dominance* explores this rationale. We say that x dominates y with probability $\beta \geq 0.5$, denoted by $x \, \beta \, y$, iff $\Pr[x > y] \geq \beta$. Note that $\Pr[x > y]$ is the probability that x outperforms y and β is the likelihood of the outperformance. If $\beta > 0.5$, then $x \, \beta \, y$ implies that $\Pr[y > x] \leq \Pr[y \geq x] = 1 - \Pr[x > y] \leq 1 - \beta < 0.5$. Thus, $x \, \beta \, y$ means that x is likely to outperform y, and y is not likely to outperform x, where "likely" indicates a more than 50–50 chance of occurring.

Note that probability dominance utilizes only one measurement (i.e., $\Pr[x > y]$) to establish the relation. The concept is different from the previous two, which are essentially Pareto preference. For further discussion on this concept, see Ref. 489 of Wrather and Yu.

10.2.4. Utility Dominance (Concept Based on Utility Functions)

In dealing with uncertain outcomes, Von Neumann and Morgenstern (Ref. 465) suggested constructing a utility function $u : R^1 \to R^1$ such that $x > y$ iff Eu $(x) >$ Eu (y), where

$$\text{Eu } (x) = \int_{-\infty}^{\infty} u(t)dF_x(t) \tag{10.5}$$

or

$$= \sum_{t=-\infty}^{\infty} u(t)P_x(t). \tag{10.6}$$

(10.6) is valid when x is discrete and P_x is its mass function.

Much research has been devoted to studying the existence condition of such a utility function. For instance see Ref. 139. Undoubtedly the conditions must be extremely strict. To see this point, observe from (10.6) and (10.5) that a utility function essentially is a weight function defined for "infinite"-dimensional space (index by t which varies from $-\infty$ to $+\infty$) in Eu (x). For "additive weights" to exist, strong conditions such as "weak order," ">-dense," and very strong >-separability (see Sections 5.3.2 and 5.3.3) must be imposed. When x is a continuous random variable, mentally it is hard to imagine that such conditions can hold, especially when one becomes familiar with the behavior bases of Chapter 9. Nevertheless, construction of a utility function produces a focus of effort. If we regard the utility function as an approximation and a simplification, as a value function construction of Chapters 5-6, then it may be a good tool to analyze complex decision problems with uncertainty. However, one should not be overhypnotized by the power of utility functions. For further discussion on utility functions the reader is referred to Fishburn (Ref. 139), Keeney and Raiffa (Ref. 254), and those quoted therein.

Now, let u be a Von Neumann-Morgenstern utility function as discussed above. We say that x *dominates* y *through* u, *denoted by* $x \, u \, y$, iff Eu $(x) >$ Eu (y).

Let U_1 be the class of all nondecreasing utility functions. By $x \, U_1 \, y$, we mean Eu $(x) \geqq$ Eu (y) for all $u \in U_1$ and the inequality holds strictly for some $u^0 \in U_1$.

Similarly, let U_2 be the class of all nondecreasing concave utility functions. Then, *by* $x \, U_2 \, y$, we shall mean Eu $(x) \geqq$ Eu (y), for all $u \in U_2$, and the inequality holds strictly for some $u^0 \in U_2$.

10.2.5. Some Interesting Results

The above four basic concepts are interrelated. Let us sketch some of the well-known results without proof.

Theorem 10.1.
i. $x\, s_1\, y$ iff $x\, U_1\, y$;
ii. $x\, s_2\, y$ iff $x\, U_2\, y$.

Remark 10.5. Both $x\, s_i\, y$ and $x\, U_i\, y$, $i = 1, 2$, are essentially Pareto preference in the infinite-dimensional space. Theorem 10.1 shows their equivalence.

Theorem 10.2. (i) Let $F_{y|x}(t) = \Pr[y \le t|x = t]$. Then $E_x(F_{y|x}(x)) = \int_{-\infty}^{\infty} F_{y|x}(t)\, dF_x(t) \ge \beta$ is a necessary condition for $x\, \beta\, y$. It is also a sufficient condition when $F_{y|x}$ is continuous on R^1.

(ii) Let x and y be independent. Then $E_x(F_y(x)) \ge \beta$ is a necessary condition for $x\, \beta\, y$. It is also a sufficient condition when F_y is continuous on R^1.

Remark 10.6. To state x and y are independent is a reasonable assumption, since in the choice model we are going to choose only one of the random outcomes. When we have to select a combination of random outcomes, each combination may be regarded (by redefinition) as a random outcome. Note that $F_{y|x}$ and F_y are nondecreasing functions (i.e., they are two functionals in U_1). Theorem 10.2 converts probability dominance into a comparison in terms of expected values by regarding $F_{y|x}$ or F_y as the functional for expectation.

Theorem 10.3. Let x and y be independent, with F_x and F_y continuous. Then $x\, s_1\, y$ implies that $x\, \beta\, y$ for $\beta > 0.5$. [The result fails, when x and y are dependent (see Ref. 489).]

Theorem 10.4. Let x, y, and z be any normally distributed random variables. Then
i. $x\, s_2\, y$ iff $x\, \text{mv}\, y$,   iff $x\, U_2\, y$;
ii. $x\, \text{mv}\, y$ and $y\, \beta\, z$ imply that $x\, \beta\, z$.

10.3. Multicriteria Dynamic Optimization Problems

We shall discuss finite stage dynamic programming problems in Section 10.3.1 and optimal control problems in Section 10.3.2. Relevant references will be offered.

10.3.1. Finite Stage Dynamic Programs with Multicriteria

Let us consider finite stage decision problems with multicriteria as depicted in Figure 10.2. The decision variable is $x = (x_1, \ldots, x_n)$ with each $x_j \in X_j\, (s_j)$.

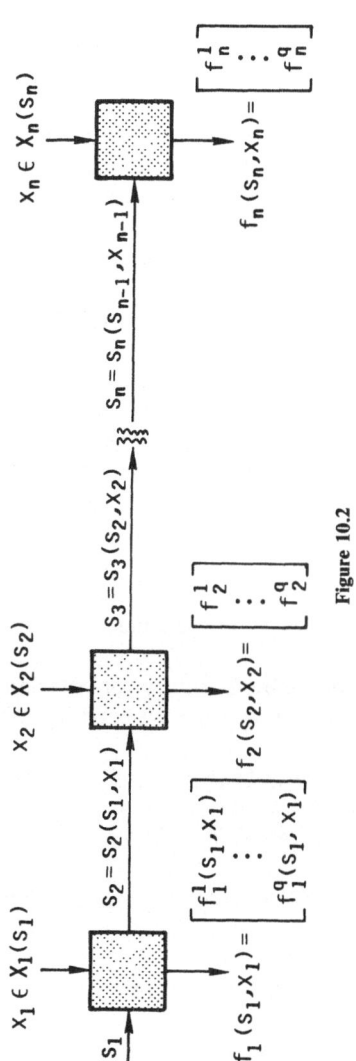

Figure 10.2

The state variables $\{s_j\}$ are generated by

$$s_{j+1} = s_{j+1}(s_j, x_j), \qquad j = 1, \ldots, n - 1. \tag{10.7}$$

Note that $X_j(s_j)$ is a set that specifies the set of alternatives when the state s_j is reached. The sequence $\{s_j\}$ generated serially by $\{x_j\}$ is a *path* in the "state space." The familiar constraints in mathematical programming such as $\sum_j x_j \geq c$, $\prod_j g_j(x_j) \geq c$ or $\max_j \{g_j(x_j)\} \geq c$ can be converted to the above serial formulation (i.e., see Chapters II and III, of Ref. 322).

The only deviation from the traditional finite stage dynamic programming is that at each stage j there are q criteria $(f_j^1, \ldots, f_j^q)$, $q \geq 1$. In a serial production process, the criteria at each stage can be *cost* and *quality*. The overall measurement in terms of criterion i is denoted by $F^i = (f_1^i(x_1), \ldots, f_n^i(x_n))$, $i = 1, \ldots, q$.

For convenience, the following notation will be used:

$$f^i = (f_1^i(s_1, x_1), \ldots, f_n^i(s_n, x_n)),$$

$$f_j = (f_j^1(s_j, x_j), \ldots, f_j^q(s_j, x_j)),$$

and

$$F = (F^1, \ldots, F^q).$$

Note that the superscript is used for the index of criteria, and the subscript is for the index of stage or decision variables and their related contributions.

Definition 10.1. (Separability.) The vector criterion F is *separable* if there exist vector functions $\{h_j | j = 1, \ldots, n - 1\}$, each $h_j: R^p \to R^p$, such that

$$F = h_1(f_1(s_1, x_1), h_2(f_2(s_2, x_2), h_3(\ldots h_{n-2}(f_{n-2}(s_{n-2}, x_{n-2}),$$

$$h_{n-1}(f_{n-1}(s_{n-1}, x_{n-1}), f_n(s_n, x_n))) \ldots))) \tag{10.8}$$

(the above should be read from the most inside term, i.e., $h_{n-1}(\cdot, \cdot)$, and gradually to h_1). When no confusion occurs, (10.8) will be written as

$$F = f_1(s_1, x_1) \circ f_2(s_2, x_2) \circ \cdots \circ f_n(s_n, x_n). \tag{10.9}$$

Observe that each "$\circ$" represents a vector operator which may contain different operations in its component.

Example 10.1. (i) Let $p = 2$ and $F^1(x_1, x_2, x_3) = \sum_{j=1}^3 f_j^1(x_j)$ and $F^2(x_1, x_2, x_3) = \max_j \{f_j^2(x_j)\}$. Then $F = (F^1, F^2)$ is separable. Note, $F^2(x_1, x_2, x_3) = \max \{f_1(x_1), \max \{f_2(x_2), f_3(x_3)\}\}$.

(ii) Let $F = (F^1, F^2)$ with $F^1 = f_1^1(x_1)f_2^1(x_2) + f_3^1(x_3)$ and $F^2 = f_1^2(x_1) + f_2^2(x_2)f_3^2(x_3)$. Then F is not separable.

Now suppose that F is separable. Let Y be the set of attainable outcomes. Recall that there are n stages, and the (input) state variable is s_n for the nth stage. We shall use $N[Y]$ to denote the set of all N-points on Y. A dynamic programming for multicriteria problem may be described as follows: Define

$$Z_n(s_n) = \{f_n(s_n, x_n) | x_n \in X_n(s_n)\}. \tag{10.10}$$

Note that $Z_n(s_n)$ is the set of attainable points from s_n. For $k = 2, \ldots, n$, the following are backwardly and recursively defined:

$$N_k(s_k) = N(Z_k(s_k)), \tag{10.11}$$

$$Z_{k-1}(s_{k-1}) = \bigcup \{f_{k-1}(s_{k-1}, x_{k-1}) \circ N_k(s_k) | x_{k-1} \in X_{k-1}(s_{k-1})\}, \tag{10.12}$$

where

$$f_{k-1}(s_{k-1}, x_{k-1}) \circ N_k(s_k) = \{f_{k-1}(s_{k-1}, x_{k-1}) \circ z_k | z_k \in N_k(s_k)\}.$$

Note that $Z_{k-1}(s_{k-1})$ is the set of attainable points from s_{k-1} when only N-points will be chosen at the immediate resulting state s_k.

Recursively, $N_1(s_1)$ can be computed. Note that the computation process (10.10)-(10.12) for $N_1(s_1)$ is similar to that of dynamic programming. For each stage, instead of maximizing or minimizing, we compute the set of N-points. To see this point, define the *attainable set* from s_k, $k = 1, \ldots, n$, recursively and backwardly as follows:

$$A(s_n) = \{f_n(s_n, x_n) | x_n \in X_n(s_n)\}, \tag{10.13}$$

for $k = n, n - 1, \ldots, 2$,

$$A(s_{k-1}) = \bigcup \{f_{k-1}(s_{k-1}, x_{k-1}) \circ A(s_k(s_{k-1}, x_{k-1}))|$$

$$x_{k-1} \in X_{k-1}(s_{k-1})\}, \tag{10.14}$$

where

$$f_{k-1}(s_{k-1}, x_{k-1}) \circ A(s_k) = \{f_{k-1}(s_{k-1}, x_{k-1})$$

$$\circ z_k | z_k \in A(s_k)\}. \tag{10.15}$$

From (10.10)-(10.15), it is seen that $Z_k(s_k) \subset A(s_k)$ for $k = 1, \ldots, n$, and $Y = A(s_1)$.

We are ready to answer the main question. Under what conditions, does $N[Y] = N_1(s_1)$? First we introduce the following definition.

Definition 10.2. (Serial-Monotonicity.) A separable multicriteria $F = f_1 \circ f_2 \circ \cdots \circ f_n$ is serial-monotonic with respect to preference iff $z_{k+1} > z'_{k+1}$ and $z_{k+1}, z'_{k+1} \in A(s_{k+1}(s_k, x_k))$ imply that $f_k(s_k, x_k) \circ z_{k+1} > f_k(s_k, x_k) \circ z'_{k+1}$.

Theorem 10.5. Suppose that F is separable (Definition 10.1) and that the serial-monotonicity condition (of Definition 10.2) is satisfied. Then $N[Y] \subset N_1(s_1)$.

Proof. Let $y \in N[Y]$ and y be the outcome of $x = (x_1, \ldots, x_n) \in X$. Thus, $y = f_1(s_1, x_1) \circ \cdots \circ f_n(s_n, x_n)$ and s_k satisfies (10.7), $k = 1, \ldots, n$. For simplicity, let $y_k = f_k(s_k, x_k)$. Note that by definition, $y_n \in Z_n(s_n) = A(s_n)$. Suppose that $y \notin N_1(s_1)$. Let $\bar{k}$ be the largest index such that $y_{\bar{k}} \circ y_{\bar{k}+1} \circ \cdots \circ y_n \in Z_{\bar{k}}(s_{\bar{k}}) \backslash N_{\bar{k}}(s_{\bar{k}})$. Note that $1 \leq \bar{k} \leq n$. Thus, there exists $z_{\bar{k}} \circ z_{\bar{k}+1} \circ \cdots \circ z_n \in Z_{\bar{k}}(s_{\bar{k}}) \subset A(s_{\bar{k}})$ and $z_{\bar{k}} \circ \cdots \circ z_n > y_{\bar{k}} \circ \cdots \circ y_n$. Then by serial-monotonicity, $(y_1 \circ \cdots \circ y_{\bar{k}-1} \circ z_{\bar{k}} \circ \cdots \circ z_n) > (y_1 \circ \cdots \circ y_{\bar{k}-1} \circ y_{\bar{k}} \circ \cdots \circ y_n) = y$, which leads to a contradiction. $\qquad\square$

Remark 10.7. Theorem 10.5 states that when the serial-monotonicity condition is satisfied, $N_1(s_1)$ contains $N[Y]$. Thus, $N[Y]$ can be approximated by $N_1(s_1)$. Further conditions are needed to ensure $N[Y] = N_1(s_1)$.

Recall that the preference over Y is *nondominance bounded* if for each $y \in Y$ either y is an N-point or it is dominated by an N-point in Y (Definition 2.7).

Theorem 10.6. Suppose that F is separable and that the serial monotonicity and the nondominance boundedness are satisfied. Then $N_1(s_1) \subset N[Y]$.

Proof. Assume the contrary. Let $y^0 \in N_1(s_1) \backslash N[Y]$. By nondominance boundedness, there exists $y' \in N[Y]$ and $y' > y^0$. However, by Theorem 10.5, $y' \in N_1(s_1) \subset Z_1(s_1)$. Since $y^0 \in N_1(s_1)$, y' cannot dominate y^0. This leads to a contradiction. $\qquad\square$

The following example shows that the nondominance boundedness condition cannot be relaxed in Theorem 10.6.

Example 10.2. In a two-stage problem (refer to Figure 10.3), let $x_1(s_1) = \{x_{11}, x_{12}\}$, with $f_1(s_1, x_{1i}) = y_{1i}$, $i = 1, 2$;

$$s_2(s_1, x_{1i}) = s_{2i}, \qquad i = 1, 2;$$

$$X_2(s_{21}) = \{x_{21}^1, x_{21}^2\} \quad \text{with } f_2(s_{21}, x_{21}^k) = y_{21}^k, \qquad k = 1, 2;$$

$$X_2(s_{22}) = \{x_{22}\} \quad \text{and} \quad f_2(s_{22}, x_{22}) = y_{22}.$$

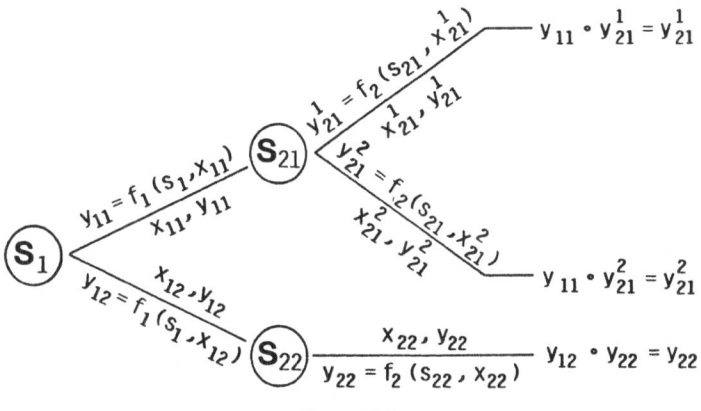

Figure 10.3

Let

$$y_{11} \circ y_{21}^k = y_{21}^k,$$

$$y_{12} \circ y_{22} = y_{22}.$$

Assume that $y_{21}^2 > y_{21}^1$, $y_{21}^1 > y_{22}$ but $y_{22} \notin \{y_{21}^2 >\}$ (i.e., y_{22} is not dominated by y_{21}^2). Then,

$$Z_2(s_{21}) = \{y_{21}^1, y_{21}^2\},$$

$$N_2(s_{21}) = \{y_{21}^2\},$$

$$Z_2(s_{22}) = \{y_{22}\} = N_2(s_{22}),$$

$$Z_1(s_1) = \{y_{21}^2, y_{22}\} = N_1(s_1).$$

But,

$$Y = \{y_{21}^1, y_{21}^2, y_{22}\} \quad \text{and} \quad N[Y] = \{y_{21}^2\}.$$

Thus,

$$N[Y] \subsetneq N_1(s_1).$$

Observe that y_{22} is not nondominance bounded. It is dominated only by y_{21}^1, which is a D-point.

Several research problems remain to be solved. For instance, in computing $N_k(s_k)$, $k = 1, \ldots, n$, it is desirable to have *cone convexity*. If each F^i is additive in its components f_j^i which is convex, and each $X_j(s_j)$ is convex, then

$Z_k(s_k)$ will have the desired cone convexity. This will simplify the computation. What conditions, $Z_k(s_k)$, $k = 1, \ldots, n$, can preserve cone convexity backwardly? Since our main interest is in $N_1(s_1)$ (to locate $N[Y]$), not all $N_k(s_k)$ ($k = 1, \ldots, n$, for all possible s_k) are needed. Is there any way to locate only those $N_k(s_k)$ that are needed? Finally, if the form of F of f_j is changed, what is the impact on $N_1(s_1)$?

There are many interesting articles related to dynamic programming. i.e., Hartley (Ref. 196), Henig (Ref. 203), Villarreal and Karwan (Ref. 460), Kim and White (Ref. 256), White (Ref. 481, Chap. 10), and those quoted therein.

10.3.2. Optimal Control with Multicriteria

In optimal control problems, state variables evolve with time and form paths. The payoff will depend on which path is chosen. When multicriteria are involved, one can still regard Y as all possible outcomes measured by the criteria. The results of Chapters 3–7 are then immediately extended to optimal control problems. In this subsection we shall only illustrate and sketch some of the extensions when constant dominated cones are involved. Necessary and sufficient conditions for N-control and cone convexity are our focus.

Consider the differential system

$$\dot{x}(t) = f(x(t), t, u(t)), \qquad t \in [a, b], \tag{10.16}$$

where $x(\cdot): [a, b] \to \mathscr{E} \subset R^n$ is absolutely continuous, where $\mathscr{E}$ is an open set, $u(\cdot): [a, b] \to \mathscr{S}^p$ is piecewise continuous, where $\mathscr{S}^p$ is a p-dimensional sphere of radius $\rho = $ const, and $f(\cdot): \mathscr{R} \to R^n$ is C^2 (i.e., having continuous second derivatives), where $\mathscr{R}$ is a region of $R^n \times R^1 \times R^p$.

A control $u(\cdot)$ is admissible provided it generates a solution $x(\cdot)$ satisfying (10.16), with $x(t) \in \mathscr{E}$ for all $t \in [a, b]$, and

$$x(a) = x^a, \qquad x(b) = x^b, \tag{10.17}$$

where x^a, x^b are given. Let Δ denote the set of admissible controls.

Suppose now that the performance vector $\mathscr{I}(u(\cdot))$ has components

$$\mathscr{I}_i(u(\cdot)) = \int_a^b L_i(x(t), t, u(t)) \, dt, \qquad i = 1, 2, \ldots, q, \tag{10.18}$$

where the $L_i(\cdot)$ are C^2 functions on $\mathscr{R}$. We shall write

$$L(x(t), t, u(t)) = (L_1(x(t), t, u(t)), \ldots, L_q(x(t), t, u(t)))^T$$

Remark 10.8. If the performance index is a scalar ($q = 1$), the problem is a fixed end-point optimal control problem. As we shall see, the problem with $q \geqq 2$ can be treated as a fixed end-point optimal control problem with isoperimetric constraints. The discussion here is based on Chapter 6 of Ref. 207 (however, the notation differs from that used in Ref. 207). Problems with other boundary conditions and other constraints can be treated in similar fashion (see Section 3.10 of Ref. 287).

As a consequence of Theorem 7.6, we have the following theorem.

Theorem 10.7. Suppose that Λ is a polyhedral cone with Λ^* generated by $\{h^1, h^2, \ldots, h^r\}$. Then we have the following:

(i) In order for $u^0(\cdot) \in \Delta$ to be a nondominated control in Δ with respect to Λ, it is necessary that there exist $j \in \{1, 2, \ldots, r\}$ and $r - 1$ real numbers $\{c_k | k \neq j, k = 1, 2, \ldots, r\}$ such that $u^0(\cdot)$ results in the maximum of

$$h^j \mathscr{I}(u(\cdot)) = \int_a^b h^j L(x(t), t, u(t)) \, dt \qquad (10.19)$$

for Problems (10.16) and (10.17) subject to the isoperimetric conditions

$$h^k \mathscr{I}(u(\cdot)) = \int_a^b h^k L(x(t), t, u(t)) \, dt \geqq c_k, \qquad k \neq j, \qquad k = 1, 2, \ldots, r. \tag{10.20}$$

(ii) If $u^0(\cdot)$ is the unique maximizing control for the problem stated in (i), then $u^0(\cdot)$ is nondominated in Δ with respect to Λ.

The following theorem follows from (i) of Theorem 10.7 above and from Theorem 2.1 of Chapter 6 of Ref. 207. Let $x^0(\cdot)$ denote the solution of (10.16) generated by $u^0(\cdot)$. Then, we have the following theorem.

Theorem 10.8. Suppose that Λ is specified as in Theorem 10.7 and $u^0(\cdot)$ is nondominated in Δ with respect to Λ. Then, there exist $j \in \{1, 2, \ldots, r\}$, $r - 1$ real numbers $\{c_k | k \neq j, k = 1, 2, \ldots, r\}$, a constant multiplier $\lambda = (\lambda_1, \lambda_2, \ldots, \lambda_r)^T$, a continuous function $p(\cdot): [a, b] \to R^n$ with $p(t) \neq 0$ on $[a, b]$, and a function

$$\mathscr{H}(\cdot): R^n \times R^1 \times R^p \times R^n \times R^r \to R^1,$$

where

$$\mathscr{H}(x, t, u, p, \lambda) = p^T f(x, t, u) + \lambda^T H L(x, t, u)$$

and H is the matrix whose jth row is h^j, such that
i. $\lambda_k \geqq 0$ for all $k \in \{1, 2, \ldots, q\}$ and $\lambda_k = 0$ if $k \neq j$ and $h^k \mathscr{I}(u^0) > c_k$;
ii. $p(\cdot)$ is a solution to

$$\dot{p}_i(t) = -\partial \mathscr{H}(x^0(t), t, u^0(t), p(t), \lambda)/\partial x_i, \qquad i = 1, 2, \ldots, n;$$

Chapter 10

iii. $\mathcal{H}(x^0(t), t, u^0(t), p(t), \lambda) \geqq \mathcal{H}(x^0(t), t, u, p(t), \lambda)$ for all u satisfying $|u| \leqq \rho$;

iv. the function $M(\cdot): [a, b] \to R^1$, where

$$M(t) = \mathcal{H}(x^0(t), t, u^0(t), p(t), \lambda),$$

is continuous on $[a, b]$ and satisfies $\dot{M}(t) = \partial\mathcal{H}(x^0(t), t, u^0(t), p(t), \lambda)/\partial t$ on every continuity interval of $u^0(\cdot)$.

Remark 10.9. Theorem 10.8 is a necessary condition for the problem in (i) of Theorem 10.8. Given an admissible control $u^0(\cdot)$, one can use Theorem 10.9 to test whether or not $u^0(\cdot)$ can be nondominated. Note that, by setting

$$c_k = h^k\mathcal{I}(u^0(\cdot)), \qquad k \neq j, \qquad k = 1, 2, \ldots, r,$$

the statement in (i) that $\lambda_k = 0$ if $k \neq j$ and $h^k\mathcal{I}(u^0(\cdot)) < c_k$ becomes superfluous. In locating candidates for nondominated control, the set $\{c_k\}$ is predetermined; for each choice of $\{c_k\}$, the theorem yields a candidate.

The following theorem follows from Theorem 3.6 and is a special case of Theorem 10.7.

Theorem 10.9. (i) In order for $u^0(\cdot)$ to be efficient (Pareto optimal) in Δ, it is necessary that there exist $j \in \{1, 2, \ldots, q\}$ and $q - 1$ real numbers $\{r_k | k \neq j, k = 1, 2, \ldots, q\}$ such that $u^0(\cdot)$ results in the maximum of

$$\mathcal{I}_j(u(\cdot)) = \int_a^b L_j(x(t), t, u(t)) \, dt$$

for Problems (10.16) and (10.17), subject to isoperimetric conditions

$$\mathcal{I}_k(u(\cdot)) = \int_a^b L_k(x(t), t, u(t)) \, dt \geqq r_k, \qquad k \neq j, \qquad k = 1, 2, \ldots, q;$$

and (ii) if $u^0(\cdot)$ is the unique maximizing control for the problem stated in (i), then $u^0(\cdot)$ is efficient (Pareto optimal) in Δ.

The following theorem is then analogous to Theorem 10.8.

Theorem 10.10. Suppose that $u^0(\cdot)$ is efficient (Pareto optimal) in Δ. Then, there exist $j \in \{1, 2, \ldots, q\}$, $q - 1$ real numbers $\{r_k | k \neq j, k = 1, 2, \ldots, q\}$, a constant multiplier $\lambda = (\lambda_1, \lambda_2, \ldots, \lambda_q)^T$, a continuous function $p(\cdot): [a, b] \to R^n$ with $p(t) \neq 0$ on $[a, b]$, and a function $\mathcal{H}(\cdot): R^n \times R^1 \times R^p \times R^n \times R^q \to R^1$, where

$$\mathcal{H}(x, t, u, p, \lambda) = p^Tf(x, t, u) + \lambda^TL(x, t, u),$$

such that (i)-(iv) of Theorem 10.8, apply, with r replaced by q, and c_k by r_k.

As a consequence of Lemma 7.3, we have the following sufficient conditions.

Theorem 10.11. The control $u^0(\cdot) \in \Delta$ is nondominated in Δ with respect to Λ if one of the following conditions is satisfied: (i) there is a $\lambda \in \text{Int } \Lambda^*$ such that $u^0(\cdot)$ yields the maximum of $\lambda^T \mathscr{I}(u(\cdot))$ for all $u(\cdot) \in \Delta$; or (ii) there is a $\lambda \in \Lambda^*$, $\lambda \neq 0$, such that $u^0(\cdot)$ is the unique control yielding the maximum of $\lambda^T \mathscr{I}(u(\cdot))$ for all $u(\cdot) \in \Delta$.

The necessary conditions embodied in the following theorem are a consequence of Theorem 7.14.

Theorem 10.12. Suppose that Λ is such that $\Lambda^\perp \neq \{0\}$ and Y is Λ-convex. If $u^0(\cdot) \in \Delta$ is nondominated in Δ with respect to Λ, then there is a $\lambda \in \Lambda^*$, $\lambda \neq 0$, such that $u^0(\cdot)$ maximizes $\lambda^T \mathscr{I}(u(\cdot))$ for all $u(\cdot) \in \Delta$.

Remark 10.10. The problems involving the maximization of $\lambda^T \mathscr{I}(u(\cdot))$ in Theorems 10.11 and 10.12 are optimal control problems. Usual necessary conditions (see, for example, Refs. 207 and 287) and sufficient conditions (see, for example, Refs. 287 and 427) for optimal control problems are therefore applicable. To illustrate the implications of cone convexity, let us state a theorem embodying the necessary conditions.

Theorem 10.13. Suppose that Λ is as specified in Theorem 10.7 and that $u^0(\cdot) \in \Delta$ is nondominated in Δ with respect to Λ. Then, there exist a nonnegative vector $\lambda = (\lambda_1, \lambda_2, \ldots, \lambda_r)^T$, a continuous function $p(\cdot): [a, b] \to R^n$ with $p(t) \neq 0$ on $[a, b]$, and a function

$$\mathscr{H}(\cdot): R^n \times R^1 \times R^p \times R^n \times R^r \to R^1,$$

where

$$\mathscr{H}(x, t, u, p, \lambda) = p^T f(x, t, u) + \lambda^T HL(x, t, u)$$

and H is the matrix whose jth row is h^j, such that (ii)-(iv) of Theorem 10.8 apply.

Remark 10.11. Note that Theorems 10.8 and 10.13 are very similar. However, as a consequence of the assumption of cone convexity, Theorem 10.13 is stronger. The condition requiring the existence of $j \in \{1, 2, \ldots, r\}$ and of $\{c_k | k \neq j, k = 1, 2, \ldots, r\}$ is dropped in Theorem 10.13, as is part of condition (i) of Theorem 10.8.

In the remaining part of this section we shall derive some sufficient conditions for Y to be Λ-convex.

Following the proof of Theorem 7.12, one can exhibit the following theorem.

Theorem 10.14. Let Δ be a convex set, and let $\mathcal{I}(\cdot): \Delta \to R^m$ be given. Suppose that $\Lambda \subset R^m$ is a polyhedral cone and that its polar cone Λ^* is generated by $\{h^j | j = 1, 2, \ldots, r\}$. If each $h^j \mathcal{I}(u(\cdot))$, $j = 1, 2, \ldots, r$, defines a concave function on Δ, then $Y = \{\mathcal{I}(u(\cdot)) | u(\cdot) \in \Delta\}$ is Λ-convex.

Let us consider the following class of control problems. The differential system is

$$\dot{x}(t) = A(t)x(t) + B(t)u(t) + v(t), \tag{10.21}$$

where $A(t)$ is an $n \times n$ matrix, $B(t)$ is an $n \times p$ matrix, $u(t)$ is a p-vector, $v(t)$ is an n-vector, and the components of $A(\cdot)$, $B(\cdot)$, and $v(\cdot)$ are integrable functions on a given interval $[a, b]$.

Let $\Omega \subset R^p$ be convex and compact, and let $C \subset R^n$ be convex.

A control $u(\cdot): [a, b] \to \Omega$ is preadmissible iff $u(\cdot)$ is measurable and $u(t) \in \Omega$ for all $t \in [a, b]$. A control $u(\cdot): [a, b] \to \Omega$ is *admissible* iff it is preadmissible and the corresponding solution $x(\cdot)$ of (10.21) satisfies $x(a) = x^a$, x^a given, and $x(b) \in C$. Let Δ denote the set of admissible controls.

Finally, let there be a criterion vector function $\mathcal{I}(\cdot)$ whose components are defined by

$$\mathcal{I}_i(u) = \int_a^b L_i(x(t), t, u(t)) \, dt, \qquad i = 1, 2, \ldots, q, \tag{10.22}$$

where the $L_i(\cdot)$ are continuous on $R^n \times [a, b] \times \Omega$.

Given a preadmissible control $u(\cdot)$, let $\phi(\cdot, u(\cdot)): [a, b] \to R^n$ be an absolutely continuous function satisfying (10.21); that is,

$$\phi(t, u(\cdot)) = x^a + \int_a^t [A(s)\phi(s, u(s)) + B(s)u(s) + v(s)] \, ds$$

for all $t \in [a, b]$.

Let $\Phi(t)$ denote the fundamental matrix of the homogeneous system

$$\dot{x}(t) = A(t)x(t).$$

Then (see Ref. 280 for a derivation)

$$\phi(t, u(\cdot)) = \Phi(t)x^a + \Phi(t) \int_a^t \Phi^{-1}(s)[B(s)u(s) + v(s)] \, ds. \tag{10.23}$$

From (10.23), we have the following lemma.

Lemma 10.2. Let $u^1(\cdot)$ and $u^2(\cdot)$ be preadmissible controls, and let $\mu \in [0, 1]$. Then,

$$\phi(t, \mu u^1(\cdot) + (1 - \mu)u^2(\cdot)) = \mu\phi(t, u^1(\cdot)) + (1 - \mu)\phi(t, u^2(\cdot))$$

for all $t \in [a, b]$.

Lemma 10.3. (i) The set of admissible controls Δ is convex; and (ii) the set $X(t) = \{\phi(t, u(\cdot)) | u(\cdot) \in \Delta\}$ is convex for all $t \in [a, b]$.

Proof. (i) follows from Lemma 10.2 and the convexity of set C; and (ii) is a result of Lemma 10.2 and (i).   □

Theorem 10.15. Let Δ and $\mathscr{I}(\cdot)$ be as specified above and Λ as in Theorem 10.14, and let $L = (L_1, L_2, \ldots, L_q)^T$. Suppose that for all $t \in [a, b]$ each $h^j L(x, t, u)$, $j = 1, 2, \ldots, r$, defines a concave function on $X(t) \times \Omega$. Then, $Y = \{\mathscr{I}(u(\cdot)) | u(\cdot) \in \Delta\}$ is Λ-convex.

Proof. In view of Theorem 10.14 and Lemma 10.3, it suffices to show that each $h^j \mathscr{I}(u(\cdot))$ defines a concave function on Δ. Given $u^1(\cdot)$, $u^2(\cdot) \in \Delta$, $\mu \in [0, 1]$, we wish to show that

$$h^j \mathscr{I}(\mu u^1(\cdot) + (1 - \mu)u^2(\cdot)) \geqq \mu h^j \mathscr{I}(u^1(\cdot)) + (1 - \mu)h^j \mathscr{I}(u^2(\cdot)).$$

Note that

$$h^j \mathscr{I}(\mu u^1(\cdot) + (1 - \mu)u^2(\cdot))$$

$$= \int_a^b h^j L(\phi(t, \mu u^1(\cdot) + (1 - \mu)u^2(\cdot)), t, \mu u^1(t) + (1 - \mu)u^2(t)) \, dt$$

$$= \int_a^b h^j L(\mu\phi(t, u^1(\cdot)) + (1 - \mu)\phi(t, u^2(\cdot)), t, \mu u^1(\cdot) + (1 - \mu)u^2(\cdot)) \, dt$$

$$\geqq \int_a^b [\mu h^j L(\phi(t, u^1(\cdot)), t, u^1(\cdot)) + (1 - \mu)h^j L(\phi(t, u^2(\cdot)), t, u^2(\cdot))] \, dt$$

$$= \mu h^j \mathscr{I}(u^1(\cdot)) + (1 - \mu)h^j \mathscr{I}(u^2(\cdot)),$$

where we have utilized Lemma 10.2 and the concavity of $h^j L(x, t, u)$. This concludes the proof.   □

Corollary 10.1. Let Δ, $\mathcal{I}(u(\cdot))$, and Y be as in Theorem 10.15. Suppose that, for all $t \in [a, b]$, each $L_i(x, t, u)$, $i = 1, 2, \ldots, q$ defines a concave function on $X(t) \times \Omega$. Then, Y is Λ-convex for every $\Lambda \supset \Lambda^{\leq}$.

Proof. The corollary follows at once from Theorem 10.15 and Corollary 7.3. $\square$

There are many interesting articles related to multicriteria optimal control problems. For instance, see Ref. 288.

10.4. Second-Order Games

The theory of games (Ref. 465) and differential games (Ref. 228) considers decision problems involving more than one person (player) in which the players' payoffs are functions of their own choices as well as the other players' choices. This consideration makes the modeling of a large class of decision-making problems much closer to real life. The impact of game theory and differential games on management science, economics, psychology, social science, biology, and engineering science is immeasurable. Not only are new concepts formed, but also new dimensions of problems are being raised and are waiting to be answered. Much interest has been aroused and many research results have been reported in thousands of scholarly written articles. Unfortunately, the applications to real life problems are still fairly limited and far from the original expectations. Besides the mathematical difficulties, the limitations may be primarily due to the simplifying assumptions underlying the theoretical development of the topics. The following are some of the simplifying assumptions which are usually invalid in real life decision problems.

(i) In both game theory and differential games it is assumed that the strategy sets for each player (decision maker) are fixed and foreknown. In reality, strategy sets evolve and vary with time and are difficult to define or predict accurately.

(ii) In both topics it is assumed that each player has only one criterion for maximization or minimization. In reality, each player is interested in several objectives, which can vary with time. They vary not only in the form of the objectives, but also in the dimensions of the objectives.

(iii) In both topics, it is assumed that the players' perceived payoffs, measured in terms of the criteria and resulting from the decisions or strategies, are preknown and deterministic. In reality, because human perception varies with time, psychological states, and the constant inputs of information, the payoffs perceived by the players will not always remain constant.

(iv) In both topics, it is implicitly assumed that the preferences of the players (over the payoffs) are stable and constant. In reality, because the human mind is involved, such an assumption cannot always be justified.

Because of the simplifying assumptions, many mathematically beautiful results have been derived. (For instance, see Refs. 228, 301, 338 and 465.) Also due to the simplifying assumptions, the results are difficult to apply to real life decision problems. Many people have made contributions to game theory by extending the existing results and by relaxing the assumptions. However, these contributions are so bound to the original assumptions and mathematical constructions that the new results are still hard to apply in most cases. In terms of "habitual domains," as described in Section 9.3, the research results are so habitually bounded that their applications are difficult. In order to really expand the horizon of knowledge, we must try to jump out of the existing habitual domain or break loose from the assumptions of the existing game theory.

In this section we intend to show how one can jump out of the existing assumptions in game theory and differential games and substitute them with more realistic conceptions and models. While the technical details can be found in the references quoted, we shall concentrate on the description of the main concepts so that the reader can grasp the main ideas without getting lost in the details.

In Section 10.4.1 we focus on decision dynamics and time-optimality concepts. We then describe in Section 10.4.2 the concepts of second-order games and time stability. In Section 10.4.3 we briefly integrate the concept of habitual domains with that of second-order games.

10.4.1. Decision Elements and Decision Dynamics

In order to have a concrete feeling, let us consider a decision process of buying a house, assuming we are financially and psychologically ready for such an attempt. (Refer to Figure 9.1.) There are four important decision elements that are involved in the process.

(i) The set of alternatives is denoted by X_t. The alternatives include those houses available or potentially available in the market. In a broad sense, an alternative is a package which consists of the house itself, financial arrangement, and risk sharing (guarantee or insurance) for a transaction. Clearly the set X_t under our consideration will evolve with time, information inputs and our own thinking processes.

(ii) The set of criteria is denoted by F_t. This set can include the appearance of the home, interior design, neighborhood, resale value, price, tax, number of bedrooms, number of bathrooms, etc. Indeed in Ref. 74, 26 criteria (attributes) which are identified by the American Homebuilder's Association are used in an experimental study of high-stake decision processes. The criteria/attributes are found to change with time and then stabilize before the final decision. (See Ref. 74 for details.)

(iii) The subjective judgment of the outcomes of each alternative in terms of the criteria is denoted by $\tilde{F}_t$. Note that the judgmental outcomes like resale value, neighborhood, etc., may not be precise. They involve confidence levels of judgment. These "confidence structures" are part of $\tilde{F}_t$ and are needed for consideration. Again, elements of $\tilde{F}_t$ probably evolve with time, information inputs, and psychological states of the decision maker.

(iv) The preference/domination structures of the decision maker over the potential outcomes of possible choice is denoted by D_t. The preference structure over the number of bedrooms, the neighborhood, interior design, resale value, etc., is very important in determining the final choice of house. As with "the number of bedrooms," it is not always more is better. As with "interior design" and "the number of bedrooms," the preference can be changed with time, information inputs, and psychological states of the decision maker.

Observe that for each of the above four elements, a subscript "t" is used to emphasize that they may vary with time. The four elements exist only as the decision maker perceives them. Their existence and variation can be strongly influenced by the decision maker's experience and psychological state.

The four decision elements can interact with one another and can be influenced by three forces:

(i) The decision maker's internal information processing. His/her thinking processes, judgment/value processing, problem-solving patterns, self-suggested goals and illusion, defense mechanisms, attention and charge structures, physiological conditions, etc., are parts of the internal information processing. All of them may have great impact on the variation of the four elements.

(ii) Solicited information inputs, denoted by I_t. These information inputs are actively sought by the decision maker. They may come from internal management information systems or accounting reports, or they may come from consultation with specialists, colleagues, friends, or relatives.

(iii) Unsolicited information inputs, denoted by $\tilde{I}_t$. These inputs are collected passively. They come to us suddenly without our actively seeking them. The sudden outbreak of a war, a sudden delivery of a threat from a rival or competitor, a sudden offer of a new job or new business venture, etc., belong in this category.

The effect that information inputs have on the four decision elements X_t, F_t, $\tilde{F}_t$, D_t, and hence, on the final decision, depends to a large extent on the credibility that the decision maker assigns to the source. Source credibility depends on the channels and personal context in which the decision maker is evaluating the information.

Note that the decision process starts with the decision maker's recognition of the need for making a decision to achieve his/her goals. Once the process starts, unless it is a trivial problem, the four decision elements will be, wittingly or unwittingly, produced and changed with the information inputs and the psychological states of the decision maker. As time passes, the four elements may be stabilized. But until the final solution (including abandoning the problem) is found, the process will continue and evolve. Also the process can be shut off because other more urgent problems appear, and it can recur when no more urgent problems need to be solved. This on/off process in decision making is not unusual when one considers the decision maker as a living system which has multiple goals and equilibrium states to achieve and maintain. (See Chapter 9 for further discussion.)

Now, let $[t_1, t_2]$ be the time interval from t_1 to t_2, inclusive. We introduce the following *time-optimality* concept of Ref. 497.

Definition 10.3. An alternative x^0 is $[t_1, t_2]$-optimal iff $x^0 \in X_t$ and x^0 is the unique nondominated alternative for each $t \in [t_1, t_2]$.

Here by "x^0 is nondominated in X_t," we mean that there is no feasible alternative in X_t which is "better" than x^0 in view of the preference/domination structure of the decision maker as discussed in Chapters 3–7.

Note that three conditions are implicitly imposed on x^0 to be $[t_1, t_2]$-optimal. First, x^0 must be the *unique nondominated solution.* Until this condition is satisfied, the decision maker will hesitate about which one to choose.

The second condition is that x^0 must yield a *satisfactory outcome.* One can easily construct a domination structure so that each unsatisfactory outcome is dominated. Thus, when x^0 is nondominated it must yield a satisfactory outcome.

The final condition is that the decision maker must be *convinced* that x^0 enjoys the above two conditions over $[t_1, t_2]$. This condition is built into the confidence structure of $\tilde{F}_t$. Until this condition is satisfied the decision maker will continue to seek additional information, advice, or suggestions in order to increase his/her confidence in his/her own judgment.

With the definition of time-optimality one can derive a technical result which generalizes "the maximum principle." The interested reader is referred to Ref. 499 and Exercises 10.22 and 10.23. The following is worth mentioning.

Suppose that at time t_1 of the decision process, the decision maker wants to reach a final decision by time $T(t_1)$. If x^0 is perceived as $[t_1, t_2]$-optimal and $[t_1, T(t_1)] \subset [t_1, t_2]$ then the decision process may terminate with x^0 as the final decision. Observe that the terminal time $T(t_1)$ may depend on t_1. Suppose that the terminal time T is fixed. As t_1 approaches T, new criteria such as *information stress* and *frustration* will, perhaps unwittingly, surface when suitable time-optimality cannot be found. These new criteria will force the decision maker to settle for a final decision which is perceived as time-optimal with respect to the new set of criteria.

On the other hand, even though a solution appears at time t_1 to be $[t_1, t_2]$-optimal, the arrival of new information during $[t_1, t_2]$ may render the solution no longer $[t_1, t_2]$-optimal. This is an important feature of decision dynamics. We must keep it in mind when second-order games are under consideration.

10.4.2. Second-Order Games

Any game that is not restricted in spirit to the assumptions imposed by the traditional game theory models (as mentioned above) will be broadly called a second-order game. Using the concepts of decision dynamics of the previous section and the appearance of the players, we can summarize the main differences between second-order games and traditional game models as in Table 10.1.

While Table 10.1 is self-explanatory, the following two examples are constructed to further illustrate the concepts of second-order games.

Example 10.3. Consider the problem of a policeman who has to guard two warehouses (denoted by 1 and 2) and a thief who tries to steal from one of the two warehouses. In traditional game models, one may define P_{ij} to be the probability of catching the thief if the policeman guards the ith warehouse and the thief operates on the jth warehouse. Here, $i, j = 1$ or 2. The policeman is then to choose a strategy to maximize P_{ij}, while the thief, to minimize P_{ij}. This formulation reduces the problem to a simple zero-sum game. In real life or second-order games, the policeman's and the thief's problems are not so

Table 10.1. The Main Differences between Second-Order Games and Traditional Game Models

Decision elements	Second-order games	Traditional game models
X_t	Varies with time, generated as needed	Fixed set
F_t	Multiple criteria, usually varies with time	Fixed single criterion
$\tilde{F}_t$	Outcomes specified with confidence structures which may vary with time	Decision outcome is usually deterministic and occasionally with known probability distributions
D_t	Preference, dominance and satisficing can all vary with time	One fixed-valued function
$I_t, \tilde{I}_t,$ and internal information processing	Vary with time, they are important parts of "strategies," and must be considered	Rarely or never considered
Players	May be hidden or change with time	Well known to all players

simple. For instance, the policeman may consider a "decoy" or "adding a mechanical aid" as part of the alternatives (X_t); his own life security, future promotion, and family life may be as important as catching the thief (F_t); the outcomes of each alternative choice may be very fuzzy to him $(\tilde{F}_t)$; and his overall preference (D_t) among the tradeoffs of his own life security, future promotion, and family life may not be very clear to himself and may change with time and experience. Similarly, the thief may consider "setting fire to another building before his operation" as an alternative (X_t); life safety, retaliation, and ego satisfaction may be part of his criteria of choice (F_t); outcomes of each choice $(\tilde{F}_t)$ and the preference over the possible outcomes (D_t) may be extremely unclear to him, not to mention that they may change with time and experience.

Example 10.4. (Adapted from a historical case in Ref. 440.) About 2,000 years ago there were two rival nations in Asia, designated for convenience by C (China—Han Dynasty) and M (the earlier tribe of Mongolia), M's king and queen commanded an overwhelming army and had C's emperor and troops surrounded in an isolated city. The emperor, his aides, and troops were desperate in the national crisis and feared being captured and killed. A wise aide, Chen Ping, finally came up with an innovative idea to dissolve the crisis.

A famous artist was asked to paint an imaginatively charming and beautiful lady. The painting was secretly sent to M's queen with the message that the charming lady was going to be offered to the king for his victory and that she was so charming and attractive that the current queen would surely be deposed.

On the same night she received the painting, the queen, beloved by the king, kept sobbing and weeping in front of the king at the bedside before bedtime. After many inquiries for the reason, the queen finally told the king that the other night she had had a very bad dream that both of them were killed in a battle with C. She then successfully persuaded the king to retreat to their own country to cherish their love the next day!

Observe that from the queen's point of view, the glory of conquering C was not as important as having the love of the king. The thought of being deposed did not appeal to her at all! From the king's point of view, it was much better to be alive as a king than to be killed in battle. The glory of conquering C could of course never make up for his own death.

The reader will notice that superstition was important in the thinking processes of the king and the queen. The interested reader may also want to reexamine how an additional person was introduced into the game so as to effectively change the four decision elements of the players in resolving the difficult problem of C.

Since each player is a decision maker, he/she will, implicitly or explicitly, have decision elements that may evolve with time, information inputs, and psychological states. The concepts of decision dynamics and time optimality become handy for a solution concept of second-order games.

In order to make our discussion more concrete, let $\{X_t^i, F_t^i, \tilde{F}_t^i, D_t^i\}$ be the ith person's elements of decision dynamics at time t. Let $x_t^i \in X_t^i$, $x_t = (x_t^1, \ldots, x_t^n)$, and $\bar{x}_t^i = \{x_t^j | j \neq i, j = 1, \ldots, n\}$. The main difference between the decision dynamics of one person and of n persons is that in the former, $\tilde{F}_t^i$ is dependent only on x_t^i and in the latter, $\tilde{F}_t^i$ is dependent not only on x_t^i but also on $\bar{x}_t^i$ (that is, $x_t^j, j \neq i, j = 1, \ldots, n$), which is not under the control of the ith person.

Observe that tremendous uncertainty is involved in n-person decision dynamics for each player. Since $\tilde{F}_t^i$ is dependent on x_t^i and $\bar{x}_t^i$, and since the latter is not under the control of the ith person, the unpredictability of $\bar{x}_t^i$ will lead to that of $\tilde{F}_t^i$. In order to make $\bar{x}_t^i$ more predictable, the ith person may want to predict $\{X_t^j, F_t^j, \tilde{F}_t^j, D_t^j\}$ for each $j \neq i, j = 1, \ldots, n$. However, such a prediction cannot always be accurate because of the gaps existing in the players' perceptions, information inputs, and judgments. The problem can be further complicated when some or all of the players are trying to influence the other players. Various information is either given or concealed concerning decision making in such a way to influence the other players to choose alternatives that are favorable for those having the information. This complication has existed daily, since the existence of man in our nontrivial decision problems.

Through the processes of deliberation and interpretation of information inputs (solicited or unsolicited), each player modifies and reframes his decision elements $\{X_t^i, F_t^i, \tilde{F}_t^i, D_t^i\}$. Our concern is when and under what conditions the players can reach a stable settlement in their conflicting environments.

Toward this end we observe that a player will constantly look for a "better" choice until he is convinced (correctly or erroneously) that "optimality" has been obtained. Since the decision elements of the players interact with one another, a game cannot reach a stable settlement until every player in the game is convinced that "optimality" for himself is obtained. This observation yields the following definition.

Definition 10.4. Let $x_0 = (x_0^1, \ldots, x_0^n)$ be such that x_0^j is an action of the jth player at t_0 (i.e., $x_0^j \in X_{t_0}^j$). We say that x_0 is a $[t_0, t_s]$-*stable solution* for the game iff for each j, x_0^j is a $[t_0, t_j]$-optimal solution for the jth player with respect to $\{X_t^j, F_t^j, \tilde{F}_t^j, D_t^j\}$ and each $t_j \geqq t_s$.

Note that the above time-stability is derived from time-optimality (Section 10.4.1). Although the condition is fairly strong, it can be achieved occasionally since the decision elements are subject to change from time to time. (Refer to Example 10.4.) On the other hand, the fact that x_0 is a $[t_0, t_s]$-stable solution does not guarantee that the game will be stable with each player choosing x_0^j throughout the time interval $[t_0, t_s]$. This is due to information inputs (solicited or unsolicited) constantly reaching each player and that the players' psychological states may change during the time interval $[t_0, t_s]$, which may upset the previous perception of optimality and break off the previously conceived stability.

Based on the time-stability concept, one can derive technical results that generalize the semipermeable condition of differential games. (See Refs. 228 and 499.) In Ref. 499, one can find a systematic description of how the four decision elements $\{X_t^i, F_t^i, \tilde{F}_t^i, D_t^i\}$ can be reframed to solve the problems involving conflict.

10.4.3. Second-Order Games and Habitual Domains

In Chapter 9, we regard human beings as living systems that try to attain a set of goals or equilibrium states. Unless extraordinary events arrive, the systems will reach their steady habitual domains and have habitual ways of conception, judgment, prediction, action, and reaction to various events. In decision dynamics, unless the four decision elements reach their steady state, a formal analysis and time-optimal solution may be very difficult to obtain. A rushed solution, especially for high-stake decision problems, without adequate cool study (i.e., without reaching the steady state and without careful study), usually cannot guarantee a satisfactory time-optimal solution.

In second-order games, concepts of decision dynamics and habitual domains become extremely important both for dissolving conflict and for self-survival. In his classic work (Ref. 441), Sun-Tzu summarized the *Principle of War* as follows:

i. Knowing yourself and knowing your enemy, you lose none in 100 battles!

ii. Knowing yourself but not your enemy or knowing your enemy but not yourself, you win 50 times in 100 battles!

iii. Not knowing yourself and not knowing your enemy, you lose 100 times in 100 battles!

The above statements may be seemingly oversimplified! If we interpret "knowing" as knowing the details of the habitual domains, their formation and expansion, and the details of the decision dynamics of $\{X_t, F_t, \tilde{F}_t, D_t, I_t, \tilde{I}_t\}$ for each player involved, then we can better appreciate the penetrating view of the statements. In war, creating and implementing a strategy that is totally outside our enemy's habitual domains is fundamentally important. The tragic 1941 Pearl Harbor event is an example. Without knowing our own and our enemy's habitual domains, such a strategy is very difficult to create and implement. The reader may find it amusing to review Example 10.4. If the wise aide, Chen Ping, had not had a good understanding of the habitual domains of the king and queen of M and of C itself, then the innovative strategy would not have been created and successfully implemented.

The following are some restated suggestive questions from Section 9.5 which can help us cope with difficulties when we are engaged in a second-order game.

(i) Who are the players? What are their interests and their habitual domains? What are their four decision elements and information inputs? Can we expand our habitual domains so as to understand and absorb theirs?

(ii) Do we understand precisely the respective systems *in which, under which*, and *over which* each player, including ourselves, is working? Each system may be regarded as a dynamic living entity. Do we know the charge structures and habitual domains of each related system?

(iii) What are our common interests? What are the conflicting interests? What are the impacts of a decision on our and other players' short-run and long-run careers?

(iv) Can we emphasize the common goals so as to encourage cooperation and reduce competition?

(v) Can we trigger a high level of "charge" on some goal functions of the other players so that for their own interest they will take an action favorable to us?

(vi) Are we aware of who can influence the other players' decisions? Do we know their interests, charge structures, and habitual domains? How can we influence them to influence the other players' decisions?

(vii) Can we introduce new players so that the gaming situation is favorable to us?

(viii) Can we change the rules of games (the time and the habitual constraints) so that the outcomes can be in our favor?

(ix) Can we reframe a one-stage decision into a multiple-stage adaptive decision, and vice versa, so that the outcomes can be in our favor?

(x) Can we expand our deals into a package (including risk sharing) so that the offer can be more acceptable to each player?

(xi) Can we form a coalition with other players so that a better result can be obtained?

(xii) Could the consequence of the game be very significant and irreversible? If so, do we have contingency plans? How do we avoid being caught by surprise?

(xiii) Do we have adequate and accurate information or intelligence to make a correct prediction and decision? Are we aware of deceptive information? How do we improve the accuracy of information and intelligence?

(xiv) Do we communicate well with the other players? Do we give them enough time to digest our ideas?

Further discussion and reframing tactics for second-order games can be found in Ref. 499. Brown (Ref. 62), Ilich (Ref. 227), Karrass (Ref. 244), and Schelling (Ref. 402) are worth reading. Indeed we shall report and describe second-order games more fully, conceptually and mathematically, in a forthcoming book.

Exercises

10.1. Consider the following multicriteria decision problem.

$$\text{maximize } f_1 = 4x_1 - x_2,$$

$$\text{maximize } f_2 = x_1 + 2x_2,$$

$$\text{subject to } -2x_1 + x_2 \leqq 0,$$

$$x_1 \leqq 4,$$

$$x_1 + x_2 \leqq 6,$$

$$x_1, x_2 \geqq 0.$$

Assume that the value function is given by $v = f_1 f_2$.
  a. Sketch the decision space (X) and the outcome space (Y) and find the maximum point of v both in X and Y.
  b. With $v = f_1 f_2$ as a guide (even if we assume v is not known beforehand) for estimating $\nabla_f \hat{v}$ and with the initial point $x^1 = (2, 1)$, find the convergent optimal solution by the adapted gradient search method (Section 10.1.1).

10.2. (Continuation of Exercise 10.1.)
  a. Find the maximum point of $2f_1 + f_2$ over X and Y, respectively. Let the solutions be x^{*1} and y^{*1}, respectively.
  b. With $v = f_1 f_2$ as a guide (even though we assume v is not known beforehand) and with x^{*1} and y^{*1} as the initial points, find the convergent optimal solution by the surrogate worth tradeoff method (Section 10.1.2).
  c. Compare your results with those of Exercise 10.1.

10.3. (Continuation of Exercise 10.1 and 10.2.)
  a. Let x^{*1} and y^{*1} be defined as in (a) of Exercise 10.2. With $v = f_1 f_2$ as a guide and with x^{*1} and y^{*1} as the initial points, find the convergent optimal solution by the Zionts–Wallenius Method (Section 10.1.3).
  b. Compare your answer with that of Exercise 10.1 and 10.2. Do you observe any difference? Why? How do you resolve the difficulty, if any?
  c. How could you use the MC-simplex and the MC^2-simplex methods (Chapter 8) to modify and improve the method?

10.4. Specify the conditions that would assure the convergence of the adapted gradient search method as described in Section 10.1.1. Justify your answer.

10.5. If $f[X]$ is $\Lambda^\leqq$-convex and v is increasing in f and concave, then $\nabla_f v(f(x^0)) \in L\Lambda(x^0)$ ensures that $f(x^0)$ is a global maximum point of v. Show that a sufficient condition for this to hold is that each $f_j(x), j = 1, 2, \ldots, q$, is differentiable and concave over the convex set X and v is increasing in f and concave over $f[X] + \Lambda^\leqq$.

10.6. When each $f_j, j = 1, 2, \ldots, q$, is concave and X is convex, then the additive weight method is applicable for generating N-points. Discuss how you can adjust the interactive method discussed in Section 10.1.2 to take advantage of the above observations (i.e., $f[X]$ is $\Lambda^\leqq$-convex).

10.7. What are the main motivations and underlying assumptions for applying interactive procedures for the multicriteria decision problem? Criticize some of the assumptions you listed.

10.8. Summarize similarities and differences of the three interactive methods discussed in Section 10.1.

10.9. Suppose that you have linear multicriteria Cx and constraints $Ax \leq d$ and $x \geq 0$. How do you use the multicriteria simplex method to improve
a. the surrogate worth method and
b. the Zionts–Wallenius method?
Construct a simple example to illustrate your method.

10.10. Both the "effective constraint" method discussed in Theorem 8.12 in Chapter 8 and the method suggested by Zionts and Wallenius in Section 10.1.3 are mathematical programming approaches of finding an entering variable that leads to an adjacent N_{ex}-point. Compare these two methods in terms of ease in computation and understanding. Can you show their equivalence?

10.11. Using MC-simplex, one can first generate a set of candidates for N_{ex}-points and identify their corresponding set of optimal weights $\Lambda(x^i)$. Discuss how to revise and simplify the Zionts–Wallenius interactive process.

10.12. Let two random variables x and y be such that $p(x = 0) = 0.2$, $p(x = 1) = 0.8$, and $p(y = 0.1) = 1$.
a. Do x and y dominate each other stochastically? Justify your answer.
b. Do x and y mean-variance dominate each other? Justify your answer.
c. Is $x \beta y$ with probability $\beta \geq 0.5$? Justify your answer.
d. Does $x U_1 y$ or $y U_1 x$ hold? Justify your answer.
e. Does $x U_2 y$ or $y U_2 x$ hold? Justify your answer.

10.13. (From Ref. 489) Define x, y, and z as follows:

$$\Pr[x = x] = \begin{cases} 1/3 & \text{if } x = 0, \\ 2/3 & \text{if } x = 3, \end{cases}$$

$$\Pr[x = y] = 1 \quad \text{if } y = 2,$$

$$\Pr[x = z] = \begin{cases} 2/3 & \text{if } z = 1, \\ 1/3 & \text{if } z = 4. \end{cases}$$

Assume x, y, z are mutually independent. Show that for $\beta = 2/3$, $x \beta y$ and $y \beta z$, but not $x \beta z$. Thus probability dominance may not be transitive. (See Ref. 489 for an illustration of more pitfalls.)

10.14. Prove Theorem 10.1.

10.15. Prove Theorem 10.2.

10.16. Prove Theorem 10.3.

10.17. Prove Theorem 10.4.

10.18. Comparison among random variables is similar to comparison in the infinite-dimensional vector space. Many more criteria can be introduced for comparison. Can you suggest more criteria beyond those discussed in Section 10.2?

10.19. Use multiple criteria dynamic programming to find all Pareto optimal solutions for the following problem:

$$\max f_1 = 2x_1 + x_2 + x_3,$$

$$\min f_2 = \max \{5 - x_1, 5 - x_2, 5 - x_3\},$$

$$\text{Subject to} \quad x_1 + x_2 + x_3 = 12,$$

$$x_i \geqq 0, \quad \text{and } x_i \text{ are integers.}$$

10.20. Find the N-controls for the following problem (see Ref. 504 for the solution):
  i. dynamics: $\dot{x}_1 = x_2, \dot{x}_2 = u, t \in [0, T]$,
     $$\varepsilon = \{(x_1, x_2) \mid |x_1| \leq 3\}; \text{ and}$$
  ii. control: $u \in [-1, 1]$;
  iii. initial condition $x_1(0) = 1, x_2(0) = 0$;
  iv. terminal condition: $x_1(T) = 0, T$ not specified;
  v. criteria: (A) $\min f_1(u(\cdot)) = T$;
                 (B) $\max f_2(u(\cdot)) = x_2(T)$.
  (Note, by setting $x_3 = t$, then $\dot{x}_3 = 1$ and $T = x_3(T) = \int_0^T dt$, $x_2(T) = \int_0^T \dot{x}_2(t)\, dt = \int_0^T u\, dt$, we can convert the problem to the format discussed in Section 10.3.2.)

10.21. Characterize the significant features of a high-stake decision problem and relate it to the behavior bases (H1–H8) as discussed in Chapter 9.

10.22. Let $\text{Dom}_t(x) = \cap \{y + D_t(y) \mid y \in F_t(x)\}$ where $D_t(y)$ is the set of dominated directions at $y \in Y$ at time t and $F_t(x)$ is the set of likely outcomes as perceived by the decision maker at time t.
  a. Show that for $x^0, x \in X_t$, x^0 dominates x at time t if $F_t(x^0) \neq F_t(x)$ and $F_t(x) \subset \text{Dom}_t(x^0)$.
  b. Show that x^0 is not dominated by x at time t iff $F_t(x^0) = F_t(x)$ or $F_t(x^0) \backslash \text{Dom}_t(x) \neq \varnothing$.
  c. Let x^0 be $[t_1, t_2]$-optimal. (See Definition 10.1.) Show that x^0 is $[t_1, t_2]$-optimal iff, for each $t \in [t_1, t_2]$ and for each $x \in X_t \backslash \{x^0\}$, the following hold:
     i. $F_t(x^0) \backslash \text{Dom}_t(x) \neq \varnothing$;
     ii. there exists $x^1 \in X_t$ so that $F_t(x) \subset \text{Dom}_t(x^1)$ and $F_t(x) \neq F_t(x^1)$.

10.23. Define the domination structure D_t to be *consistent* if $y^2 \in y^1 + D_t(y^1)$ and $y^3 \in y^2 + D_t(y^2)$ then $y^3 \in y^1 + D_t(y^1)$. That is, if y^1 dominates y^2 and y^2 dominates y^3, then y^1 dominates y^3. Define $\{X_t, F_t, \tilde{F}_t, D_t\}$ to be *nondominance bounded* iff, for each $x \in X_t$, either x is nondominated or it is dominated by $x^1 \in X_t$, $x^1 \neq x$, and x^1 is nondominated. Assume that, for each $t \in [t_1, t_2]$, D_t is consistent. Show that
  a. x^0 is $[t_1, t_2]$-optimal if, for each $t \in [t_1, t_2]$ and $x \in X_t \backslash \{x^0\}$, $F_t(x) \neq F_t(x^0)$ and $F_t(x) \subset \text{Dom}_t(x^0)$;
  b. the converse of (a) holds if in addition $\{X_t, F_t, \tilde{F}_t, D_t\}$ is nondominance bounded for all $t \in [t_1, t_2]$, where $\text{Dom}_t(x)$ is defined as in Exercise 10.22.

10.24. In a second-order game, what are good criteria for reframing the game from A (the payoff of the game) to $\tilde{A}$ so that with $\tilde{A}$ every player can claim victory. (See Ref. 276.)

10.25. The retiring chief executive officer (CEO) of a corporation is to select one from two candidates to succeed him in his position. He invites the two candidates to his ranch. One is given a black horse, the other a white horse. After marking the race course, the CEO tells the two candidates that the assignee of the horse that is the slowest in completing the course will win and succeed him. If you were one of the candidates and you want to win, what should you do? (Hint: switching.)

Suggested Reading

The following references are particularly pertinent to this chapter: 62, 74, 139, 164, 182, 196, 203, 207, 217, 222, 223, 227, 228, 244, 254, 256, 280, 287, 288, 301, 307, 322, 338, 402, 427, 440, 441, 460, 465, 481, 489, 497, 499, 504, 520, 525, 526.

Bibliography

1. ABAD, P., and SWEENEY, D. J., An interactive algorithm for optimal control of a system with multiple criteria, *Int. J. Syst. Sci.* **8**, 221-229 (1977).
2. ADDELMAN, S., Orthogonal main-effect plans for asymmetrical factorial experiments, *Technometrics* **4**, 21-46 (1962).
3. ADULBHAN, P., and TABUCANON, M. T., Bicriterion linear programming, *Comput. Operations Res.* **4**, 147-153 (1977).
4. ADAMS, E. W., and FAGOT, R., A model of riskless choice, *Behav. Sci.* **4**, 1-10 (1959).
5. ALLESIO, F. J., Multiple criteria in environmental control: use of economic maximization rules to determine relative standards, *Multiple Criteria Decision Making*, Edited by J. L. Cochrane and M. Zeleny, pp. 544-549, University of South Carolina Press, Columbia (1973).
6. ANEJA, Y. P., and NAIR, K. P. K., Bicriteria transportation problem, *Manage. Sci.* **25**, 73-78 (1979).
7. APOSTOL, T. M., *Calculus, Vol. II*: Multi-Variable Calculus and Linear Algebra with Applications to Differential Equations and Probability, Blaisdell, Waltham, Massachusetts (1969).
8. ARROW, K. J., *Social Choice and Individual Values*, Wiley, New York (1951).
9. ARROW, K. J., Rational choice functions and orderings, *Economica* **26**, 121-129 (1959).
10. ARROW, K. J., BARRANKIN, E. W., and BLACKWELL, D., Admissible points of convex sets, *Contributions to the Theory of Games*, Edited by H. W. Kuhn and A. W. Tucker, pp. 87-91, Princeton University Press, Princeton, New Jersey (1953).
11. ASHOUR, S., Measures of performance, *Sequencing Theory*, Springer-Verlag, New York (1972).
12. ASHTON, D. J., and ATKINS, D. R., Multicriteria programming for financial planning, *J. Oper. Res. Soc.* **30**, 259-270 (1979).
13. ATHANS, M., and GEERING, H. P., Necessary and sufficient conditions for differentiable non-scalar-valued functions to attain extrema, *IEEE Trans. Autom. Control* **AC-18**, 132-139 (1973).
14. AUMANN, R. J., Subjective programming, *Human Judgements and Optimality*, Edited by M. W. Shelley and G. L. Bryan, Wiley, New York (1964).
15. BACOPOULOS, A., and SINGER, I., On convex vectorial optimization in linear spaces, *J. Optim. Theory Appl.* **21**, 175-188 (1977).
16. BAMBA, E., Constrained optimization under vector-valued performance index, *Syst. Control* **16**, 405-418 (1972).
17. BAMMI, DE., and BAMMI, DA., Development of a comprehensive land use plan by means of a multiple objective mathematical programming model, *Interfaces* **9**, 50-63 (1979).

18. BANKER, R. L., and GUPTA, S. K., A process for hierarchical decision making with multiple objectives, *Omega* **8**, 137–149 (1980).

19. BAPTISTELLA, L. F. B., and OLLERO, A., Fuzzy methodologies for interactive multicriteria optimization, *IEEE Trans. Syst. Man Cybern.* **SMC-10**, 353–365 (1980).

20. BARON, D. P., Stochastic programming and risk aversion, *Multiple Criteria Decision Making*, Edited by J. L. Cochrane and M. Zeleny, pp. 124–138, University of South Carolina Press, Columbia (1973).

21. BARRETT, J. H., *Individual Goals and Organizational Objectives: A Study of Integration Mechanisms*, University of Michigan Press, Ann Arbor (1970).

22. BARRON, F. H., and PERSON, H. B., Assessment of multiplicative utility functions via holistic judgments, *Organ. Behav. Human Performance* **24**, 147–166 (1979).

23. BARTON, R. F., Models with more than one criterion—Or why not build implementation into the model, *Interfaces* **7**, 71–75 (1977).

24. BASSLER, J. H., MacCRIMMON, K. R., STANBURY, W. T., and WEHRUNG, D. A., Multiple criteria dominance models: An empirical study of investment preferences, *Multiple Criteria Problem Solving: Proceedings*, Edited by S. Zionts, pp. 494–508, Springer-Verlag, New York (1978).

25. BAUM, S., and CARLSON, R. C., Multigoal optimization in managerial science, *Omega* **2**, 607–623 (1974).

26. BAUMGARTNER, T., BURNS, T. R., DEVILLE, P. and MEEKER, L. D., A systems model of conflict and change in planning systems with multi-level, multiple-objective evaluation and decision making, *Gen. Syst. Yearbook* 167–183 (1975).

27. BECHTEL, G. G., *Multidimensional Preference Scaling*, Mouton, The Hague (1976).

28. BEDELBAEV, A. A., DUBOV, J. A., and SHMULYAN, B. L., Adaptive decision procedures in multicriterion problems, *Autom. Remote Control* **37**, 76–85 (1976).

29. BEEDLES, W. L., A micro-economic investigation of multiobjective firms, *J. Finance* **32**, 1217–1234 (1977).

30. BEISECKER, T. D., and PARSON, D. W., Editors, *The Process of Social Influence, Readings in Persuasion*, Prentice-Hall, Englewood Cliffs, New Jersey (1972).

31. BEKENBACH, E. F., and BELLMAN, R., *Inequalities*, Springer-Verlag, New York (1965).

32. BELL, D. E., Multiattribute utility functions: Decompositions using interpolations, *Manage. Sci.* **25**, 744–753 (1979).

33. BELL, D. E., KEENEY, R. L., and RAIFFA, H. (Editors), *Conflicting Objectives in Decisions*, Wiley, New York (1977).

34. BELLMAN, R. E., *Dynamic Programming*, Princeton University Press, Princeton, New Jersey (1957).

35. BELLMAN, R. E., and ZADEH, L. A., Decision-making in a fuzzy environment, *Manage. Sci.* **17**, B141–164 (1970).

36. BENAYOUN, R., DEMONTGOLFIER, J., TERGNY, J., and LARTITCHEV, O., Linear programming with multiple objective functions: Step method (STEM), *Math. Programming* **1**, 366–375 (1971).

37. BENAYOUN, R., ROY, B., and SUSSMAN, N., Manual de reference du programme electre, *Note de Synthese et Formation*, No. 25, Direction Scientifique SEMA, Paris (1966).

38. BENAYOUN, R., TERGNY, J., and KEUNEMAN, D., Mathematical programming with multi-objective function: A solution by P.O.P. (progressive orientation procedure), *METRA* **9**, 279–299 (1970).

39. BEN-ISRAEL, A., BEN-TAL, A., and CHARNES, A., Necessary and sufficient conditions for a Pareto-optimum in convex programming, *Econometrica* **45**, 811–822 (1977).

40. BENSON, H. P., An improved definition of proper efficiency for vector maximization with respect to cones, *J. Math. Anal. Appl.* **71**, 232–241 (1979).

41. BENSON, H. P., Finding an initial efficient extreme point for a linear multiple objective program, *J. Oper. Res. Soc.* **32**, 495–498 (1981).

42. BENSON, H. P., Optimization over the efficient set, *J. Math. Anal. Appl.* **98**, 562-580 (1984).
43. BENSON, H. P., and MORIN, T. L., The vector maximization problems: Proper efficiency and stability, *SIAM J. Appl. Math.* **32**, 64-72 (1977).
44. BEN-TAL, A., Characterization of Pareto and lexicographic optimal solutions, *Multiple Criteria Decision Making Theory and Application*, Edited by G. Fandel and T. Gal, pp. 1-11, Springer-Verlag, New York (1980).
45. BENEVENISTE, M., Testing for complete efficiency in a vector maximization problem, *Math. Programming* **12**, 285-288 (1977).
46. BERGSTRESSER, K., and YU, P. L., Domination structures and multicriteria problems in *N*-person games, *Int. J. Theory Decision* **8**, 5-48 (1977).
47. BERGSTRESSER, K., CHARNES, A., and YU, P. L., Generalization of domination structures and nondominated solutions in multicriteria decision making, *J. Optim. Theory Appl.* **18**, 3-13 (1976).
48. BERHOLD, M., Multiple criteria decision making in consumer behavior, *Multiple Criteria Decision Making*, Edited by J. L. Cochrane and M. Zeleny, pp. 570-576, University of South Carolina Press, Columbia (1973).
49. BITRAN, G. R., Theory and algorithms for linear multiple objective programs with zero-one variables, *Math. Programming* **17**, 362-390 (1979).
50. BITRAN, G. R., Linear multiple objective problems with interval coefficients, *Manage. Sci.* **26**, 694-706 (1980).
51. BITRAN, G. R., Duality for nonlinear multiple-criteria optimization problems, *J. Optim. Theory Appl.* **35**, 367-401 (1981).
52. BITRAN, G. R., and MAGNANTI, T., The structure of admissible points with respect to cone dominance, *J. Optim. Theory Appl.* **19**, 573-614 (1979).
53. BLACKWELL, D., An analog of the minimax theorem for vector payoffs, *Pacific J. Math.* **6**, 1-8 (1956).
54. BLACKWELL, D. and GIRSHICK, M. A., *Theory of Games and Statistical Decisions*, Wiley, New York (1954).
55. BLAIR, P. D., *Multiobjective Regional Energy Planning: Applications to the Energy Park Concept*, Martinus Nijhoff, Boston (1979).
56. BLAQUIERE, A., GERARD, F., and LEITMANN, G., *Quantitative and Qualitative Games*, Academic, New York (1969).
57. BLIN, J. M., and DODSON, J. A., A multiple criteria decision model for repeated choice situations, *Multiple Criteria Problem Solving*, Edited by S. Zionts, pp. 8-22, Springer-Verlag, New York (1978).
58. BORWEIN, J., Proper efficient points for maximizations with respect to cones, *SIAM J. Control Optim.* **15**, 57-63 (1977).
59. BRACKEN, J., and MCGILL, J. Y., Production and marketing decisions with multiple objectives in a competitive environment, *J. Optim. Theory Appl.* **24**, 449-458 (1978).
60. BRILL, E. D., The use of optimization models in public-sector planning, *Manage. Sci.* **25**, 413-422 (1979).
61. BRISKIN, L. E., A method of unifying multiple objective functions, *Manage. Sci.* **12**, B406-B416 (1966).
62. BROWN, J. A. C., *Techniques of Persuasion, from Propaganda to Brainwashing*, Penguin, Baltimore (1963).
63. BUFFA, E. S., and DYER, J. S., *Management Science/Operations Research*, Wiley, New York (1977).
64. BURNS, J. M., *Leadership*, Harper & Row, New York (1978).
65. BURNS, T., and MEEKER, L. D., A mathematical model of multi-dimensional evaluation, decision making and social interaction, *Multi-Criteria Decision Making*, Edited by J. L. Cochrane and M. Zeleny, pp. 141-163, University of South Carolina Press, Columbia (1973).

66. CAPLAN, D. A., and KORNBLUTH, J. S. H., Multiobjective investment planning under uncertainty, *Omega* **3**, 423-441 (1975).
67. CARLSON, R. C., and THORP, H. H., A multicriteria approach to strategic planning: An application in inventory control, *Advances in Operations Research*, Edited by M. Roubens, pp. 75-83, North-Holland, Amsterdam (1977).
68. CARNEGIE, D., *How to Win Friends and Influence People*, Pocket Books, New York (1940).
69. CARTWRIGHT, D., Editor, *Studies in Social Power*, University of Michigan Press, Ann Arbor (1959).
70. CENZOR, Y., Pareto-optimality in multiobjective problems, *Appl. Math. Optim.* **4**, 41-59 (1977).
71. CHALMET, L. G., FRANCIS, R. L., and LAWRENCE, J. F., On characterizing supremum and l_p-efficient facility designs, *J. Optim. Theory Appl.* **35**, 129-141 (1981).
72. CHAN, S. J., Decision dynamics, habitual domains and conflict solvability, Ph.D. dissertation, University of Kansas, School of Business, Lawrence, 1982 (to appear in *J. math. Anal. Appl.*).
73. CHAN, S. J., and YU, P. L., Stable habitual domains: Existence and implications, University of Kansas, School of Business, Working Paper, Lawrence, 1983.
74. CHAN, S. J., PARK, C. W., and YU, P. L., High-stake decision making—An empirical study based on house purchase processes, *Human Syst. Manage.* **3**, 91-106 (1982).
75. CHANKONG, V., and HAIMES, Y. Y., The interactive surrogate worth tradeoff (ISWT) method for multiobjective decision making, *Multiple Criteria Problem Solving: Proceedings*, Edited by S. Zionts, pp. 42-67, Springer-Verlag, New York (1978).
76. CHARNES, A., and COOPER, W. W., Chance-constrained programming, *Manage. Sci.* **6**, 73-80 (1959).
77. CHARNES, A., and COOPER, W. W., *Management Models and Industrial Applications of Linear Programming*, Vol. I, Wiley, New York (1961).
78. CHARNES, A., and COOPER, W. W., *Management Models and Industrial Applications of Linear Programming*, Vol. II, Wiley, New York (1961).
79. CHARNES, A., and COOPER, W. W., Deterministic equivalents for optimizing and satisficing under chance constraints, *Oper. Res.* **11**, 18-39 (1963).
80. CHARNES, A., and COOPER, W. W., Goal programming and constrained regression—A comment, *Omega* **3**, 403-409 (1975).
81. CHARNES, A., and COOPER, W. W., Goal programming and multiple objective optimization—Part I, *Eur. J. Oper. Res.* **1**, 39-54 (1977).
82. CHARNES, A., COOPER, W. W., and IJIRI, Y., Break-even budgeting and programming to goals, *J. Accounting Res.* **1**, 16-43 (1963).
83. CHARNES, A., and STERDY, A., Investigations in the theory of multiple budgeted goals, in *Management Controls* (C. P. Bonini, R. K. Jaedicke, and H. M. Wagner, eds.), McGraw-Hill, New York (1964).
84. CHARNETSKI, J. R., Multiple criteria decision making with partial information: A site selection problem, in *Space Location and Regional Development* (M. Chatterji, ed.), Pion, London (1976).
85. CHARNETSKI, J. R., Linear programming with partial information, *Eur. J. Oper. Res.* **5**, 254-261 (1980).
86. CHOO, E. U., and ATKINS, D. R., An interactive algorithm for multicriteria programming, *Comput. Oper. Res.* (Special Issue on Mathematical Programming with Multiple Objectives, Edited by M. Zeleny), **7**, 81-87 (1980).
87. CHU, A. T. W., KALABA, R. E., and SPINGARN, K., A comparison of two methods for determining the weights of belonging to fuzzy sets, *J. Opt. Theory Appl.* **27**, 531-538 (1979).
88. CHU, K. C., On the noninferior set for the systems with vector-valued objective function, *IEEE Trans. Autom. Control* **AC-15**, 591-593 (1970).
89. CHURCHMAN, C. W., and ACKOFF, R. L., An approximate measure of value, *J. Oper. Res. Soc. Am.* **2**, 172-187 (1954).

90. COCHRANE, J. L., and ZELENY, M. (Editors), *Multiple Criteria Decision Making*, University of South Carolina Press, Columbia (1973).
91. COGGER, K. O., and YU, P. L., Eigen weight vectors and least distance approximation for revealed preference in pairwise weight ratios, *J. Optim. Theory Appl.* **46**, (4) (1985).
92. COHON, J. L., Applications of multiple objectives to water resources problems, *Multiple Criteria Decision Making: Kyoto 1975*, Edited by M. Zeleny, pp. 255-270, Springer-Verlag, New York (1976).
93. COHON, J. L., *Multiobjective Programming and Planning*, Academic, New York (1978).
94. COHON, J. L., and MARKS, D. H., A review and evaluation of multiobjective programming techniques, *Water Resour. Res.* **11**, 208-220 (1975).
95. COLSON, G., and ZELENY, M., Multicriterion concept of risk under incomplete information, *Comput. Oper. Res.* (Special Issue on Mathematical Programming with Multiple Objectives, Edited by M. Zeleny), **7**, 125-141 (1980).
96. CONARROE, R. R., *Bravely, Bravely in Business*, American Management Association, New York (1972).
97. CONTINI, B., A stochastic approach to goal programming, *Oper. Res.* **16**, 576-586 (1968).
98. CONTINI, B., and ZIONTS, S., Restricted bargaining for organizations with multiple objectives, *Econometrica* **36**, 397-414 (1968).
99. COOK, W. D., and SEIFORD, L. M., Priority ranking and consensus formation, *Manage. Sci.* **24**, 1721-1732 (1978).
100. CRONKHITE, G., *Persuasions, Speech and Behavioral Change*, Bobbs-Merrill, Indianapolis, Indiana (1969).
101. DACUNHA, N. O., and POLAK, E., Constrained minimization under vector-valued criteria in finite-dimensional space, *J. Math. Anal. Appl.* **19**, 103-124 (1967).
102. DANTZIG, G. B., *Linear Programming and Extensions*, Princeton University Press, Princeton, New Jersey (1963).
103. DAVIS, O. A., DEGROOT, M. H., and HINICH, M. J., Social preference orderings and majority rule, *Econometrica* **40**, 147-157 (1972).
104. DEBREU, G., Representation of a preference ordering by a numerical function, in *Decision Processes* (R. M. Thrall, C. H. Coombs, and R. L. Davis, eds.), Wiley, New York (1954).
105. DEBREU, G., *Theory of Value*, Wiley, New York (1959).
106. DEBREU, G., Topological methods in cardinal utility theory, *Mathematical Methods in Social Sciences* (K. J. Arrow, S. Karlin, and P. Suppes, eds.), Stanford University Press, Stanford, California (1960).
107. DEBREU, G., Smooth preferences, Université Catholique de Louvain, CORE Discussion Paper No. 7203, Heverlee, Belgium, 1972.
108. DENARDO, E. V., Contraction mapping in the theory underlying dynamic programming, *SIAM Rev.* No. 9 (1967).
109. DINKELBACH, W., Multicriteria decision models with specified goal levels, *Multiple Criteria Decision Making Theory and Application*, Edited by G. Fandel and T. Gal, pp. 52-59, Springer-Verlag, New York (1980).
110. DINKELBACH, W., *Entscheidungs-Modelle*, Walter de Gruyter, Berlin (1982).
111. DINKELBACH, W., and ISERMANN, H., On decision making under multiple criteria and under incomplete information, *Multiple Criteria Decision Making*, Edited by J. L. Cochrane and M. Zeleny, pp. 302-312, University of South Carolina Press, Columbia (1973).
112. DRESHER, M., SHAPLEY, L. S., and TUCKER, A. W., *Advances in Game Theory*, Princeton University Press, Princeton, New Jersey (1964).
113. DRESHER, M., TUCKER, A. W., and WOLFE, P., *Contributions to the Theory of Games*, Vol. 3, Princeton University Press, Princeton, New Jersey (1957).
114. DYER, J. S., Interactive goal programming, *Manage. Sci.* **19**, 62-70 (1972).
115. DYER, J. S., A time-sharing computer program for the solution of the multiple criteria problem, *Manage. Sci.* **19**, 1379-1383 (1973).

116. DYER, J. S., The effect of error in the estimation of the gradient on the Frank-Wolfe algorithm, with implications for interactive programming, *Oper. Res.* **22**, 160-174 (1974).

117. DYER, J. S., and SARIN, R. K., Measurable multiattribute value function, *Oper. Res.* **27**, 810-822 (1979).

118. EASTON, A., *Complex Managerial Decisions Involving Multiple Objectives*, Wiley, New York (1973).

119. ECKER, J. G., and KOUADA, I. A., Finding all efficient extreme points for multiple objective linear programs, *Math. Program.* **14**, 249-261 (1978).

120. ECKER, J. G., and SHOEMAKER, N. E., Multiple objective linear programming and the trade off-compromise set, *Multiple Criteria Decision Making Theory and Application*, Edited by G. Fandel and T. Gal, pp. 60-73, Springer-Verlag, New York (1980).

121. ECKER, J. G., HEGNER, N. S., and KOUADA, I. A., Generating all maximal efficient faces for multiple objective linear programs, *J. Optim. Theory Appl.* **30**, 353-394 (1980).

122. EDWARDS, W., Use of multiattribute utility measurement for social decision making, *Conflicting Objectives in Decisions*, Edited by D. E. Bell, R. L. Keeney, and H. Raiffa, pp. 247-276, Wiley, New York (1977).

123. EILON, S., Goals and constraints in decision making, *Oper. Res. Q.* **23**, 3-15 (1972).

124. EINHORN, H. J., The use of nonlinear noncompensatory models in decision making, *Psychol. Bull.* **73**, 221-230 (1970).

125. EINHORN, H. J., and HOGARTH, R. M., Unit weighting schemes for decision making, *Organ. Behav. Human Performance* **13**, 171-192 (1975).

126. EVANS, J. P., and STEUER, R. E., Generating efficient extreme points in linear multiple objective programming: Two algorithms and computing experiences, *Multiple Criteria Decision Making*, Edited by J. L. Cochrane and M. Zeleny, pp. 349-365, University of South Carolina Press, Columbia (1973).

127. EVANS, J. P., and STEUER, R. E., A revised simplex method for linear multiple objective programs, *Math. Program.* **5**, 54-72 (1973).

128. FABOZZI, F. J., and BACHNER, A. W., Mathematical programming models to determine civil service salaries, *Eur. J. Oper. Res.* **3**, 190-198 (1979).

129. FANDEL, G., Public investment decision making with multiple criteria: An example of university planning, *Multiple Criteria Problem Solving: Proceedings*, Buffalo, Edited by S. Zionts, pp. 116-130, Springer-Verlag, New York (1978).

130. FANDEL, G., Perspectives of the development in multiple criteria decision making, *Multiple Criteria Decision Making Theory and Application*, Edited by G. Fandel and T. Gal, pp. ix-xvi, Springer-Verlag, New York (1980).

131. FANDEL, G., and GAL, T. (Editors), *Multiple Criteria Decision Making Theory and Application*, Springer-Verlag, New York (1980).

132. FANDEL, G., and WILHELM, J., Rational solution principles and information requirements as elements of a theory of multiple criteria decision making, *Multiple Criteria Decision Making*: Jouy-en-Josas, France, Edited by H. Thiriez and S. Zionts, pp. 215-231, Springer-Verlag, New York (1976).

133. FARQUHAR, P. H., A survey of multiattribute utility theory and applications, *Multiple Criteria Decision Making*, Edited by M. K. Starr and M. Zeleny, pp. 59-90, North-Holland, New York (1977).

134. FERGUSON, C. E., The theory of multidimensional utility analysis in relation to multiple-goal business behavior: A synthesis, *South. Econ. J.* **32**, 169-175 (1965).

135. FERGUSON, T. S., *Mathematical Statistics, A Decision Theoretic Approach*, Academic, New York (1967).

136. FICHEFET, J., GPSTEM: An interactive multiobjective optimization method, *Progress in Operations Research, Edited by A. Prekopa, pp. 317-332, North-Holland, Amsterdam (1976).*

137. FISCHER, G. W., Multidimensional utility models for risky and riskless choice, *Organ. Behav. Human Performance* **17**, 127-146 (1976).

138. FISCHER, G. W., Utility models for multiple objective decisions: Do they accurately represent human preferences? *Decision Sci.* **10**, 451-479 (1979).
139. FISHBURN, P. C., *Utility Theory for Decision Making*, Wiley, New York (1970).
140. FISHBURN, P. C., Convex stochastic dominance with continuous distribution functions, *J. Econ. Theory* **7**, 143-158 (1974).
141. FISHBURN, P. C., Lexicographic orders, utilities and decision rules: A survey, *Manage. Sci.* **20**, 1442-1471 (1974).
142. FISHBURN, P. C., Multiattribute utilities in expected utility theory, *Conflicting Objectives in Decisions*, Edited by D. E. Bell, R. L. Keeney, and H. Raiffa, pp. 172-196, Wiley, New York (1977).
143. FISHBURN, P. C., Multicriteria choice functions based on binary relations, *Oper. Res.* **25**, 989-1012 (1977).
144. FISHBURN, P. C., and KEENEY, R. L., Seven independence concepts and continuous multiattribute utility functions, *J. Math. Psychol.* **11**, 294-327 (1974).
145. FREEDMAN, J. L., CARLSMITH, J. M., and SEARS, D. O., *Social Psychology*, Prentice-Hall, Englewood Cliffs, New Jersey (1974).
146. FREIDMAN, A., *Differential Games*, Wiley, New York (1971).
147. FREIMER, M., and YU, P. L., An approach toward decision problems with multiobjectives, University of Rochester, Center for System Science, CSS 72-03, Rochester, New York, 1972.
148. FREIMER, M., and YU, P. L., The applications of compromise solutions to reporting games, *Games Theory as a Theory of Conflict Resolution*, Edited by A. Rapoport, pp. 235-260, D. Reidel, Boston (1974).
149. FREIMER, M., and YU, P. L., Some new results on compromise solutions for group decision problems, *Manage. Sci.* **22**, 688-693 (1976).
150. FREELAND, J. R., A note on goal decomposition in a decentralized organization, *Manage. Sci.* **23**, 100-102 (1976).
151. FRENCH, J. R. P., JR., and RAVEN, B., The bases of social power, *Studies in Social Power*, Edited by D. Cartwright, University of Michigan Press, Ann Arbor (1959).
152. GAL, T., Determining all efficient solutions and an enlarged efficiency theorem in linear vector optimization, Arbeitsbericht 75/20, Institut für Wirtschaftswissenschaft RWTH Aachen, West Germany, 1975.
153. GAL, T., RIM Multiparametric linear programming, *Manage. Sci.* **21**, 567-575 (1975).
154. GAL, T., A general method for determining the set of all efficient solutions to a linear vector maximum problem, *Eur. J. Oper. Res.* **1**, 307-322 (1977).
155. GAL, T., *Postoptimal Analyses, Parametric Programming and Related Topics*, McGraw-Hill, New York (1979).
156. GAL, T., and NEDOMA, J., Multiparametric linear programming, *Manage. Sci.* **18**, 406-421 (1972).
157. GEARHART, W. B., Compromise solutions and estimation of the noninferior set, *J. Optim. Theory Appl.* **28**, 29-47 (1979).
158. GEARHART, W. B., On the characterization of Pareto-optimal solutions in bicriterion optimization, *J. Optim. Theory Appl.* **27**, 301-307 (1979).
159. GEMBICKI, F. W., Performance and sensitivity optimization: A vector index approach, Ph.D. dissertation, Case Western Reserve University, Cleveland, Ohio (1974).
160. GEMBICKI, F. W., and HAIMES, Y. Y., Approach to performance and sensitivity multi-objective optimization—Goal attainment method, *IEEE Trans. Autom. Control* **20**, 769-771 (1975).
161. GEOFFRION, A. M., Solving bicriterion mathematical programs, *Oper. Res.* **15**, 39-54 (1967).
162. GEOFFRION, A. M., Strictly concave parametric programming, Parts I and II, *Manage. Sci.* **13**, 244-253, 359-370 (1967).
163. GEOFFRION, A. M., Proper efficiency and the theory of vector maximization, *J. Math. Anal. Appl.* **22**, 618-630 (1968).

164. GEOFFRION, A. M., DYER, J. S., and FEINBERG, A., An interactive approach for multi-criterion optimization with an application to operation of an academic department, *Manage. Sci.* **19**, 357-368 (1972).
165. GIESY, D. P., Calculation of Pareto-optimal solutions to multiple-objective problems using threshold-of-acceptability constraints, *IEEE Trans. Autom. Control* **23**, 1114-1115 (1978).
166. GIORDANO, J. L., and SUQUET, J. C., On multicriteria decision making: An application to a work-shop organization problem, *Advances in Operations Research*, Edited by M. Roubens, pp. 181-192, North-Holland, Amsterdam (1977).
167. GOFFIN, J. L., and HAURIE, A., Necessary conditions and sufficient conditions for Pareto optimality in a multicriterion perturbed system, *Fifth Conference on Optimization Techniques, Part I*, Edited by B. Contini and A. Ruberti, pp. 184-193, Springer-Verlag, New York (1973).
168. GOODWIN, G. C., KABAILA, P. V., and NG, T. S., On the optimization of vector-valued performance criteria, *IEEE Trans. Autom. Control* **AC-20**, 803-804 (1975).
169. GORMAN, W. M., Conditions for additive separability, *Econometrica* **36**, 605-609 (1968).
170. GORMAN, W. M., The structure of utility functions, *Rev. Econ. Stud.* **35**, 367-390 (1968).
171. GOROKHOVIK, V. V., On the problem of vector optimization, *Eng. Cybern.* **10**, 995-1002 (1972).
172. GREEN, P. E., and CARMONE, F. J., *Multidimensional Scaling: A Comparison of Approaches and Algorithms*, Holt, Rinehart and Winston, New York (1979).
173. GREEN, P. E., and WIND, Y., *Multiattribute Decisions in Marketing: A Measurement Approach*, Dryden Press, Hinsdale, Illinois (1973).
174. GROSSBERG, S., Contour enhancement, short term memory, and constancies in reverberating neural network, *Stud. Appl. Math.* **III**, 213-256 (1973).
175. GROSSBERG, S., Competition, decision, and consensus, *J. Math. Anal. Appl.* **66**, 470-493 (1978).
176. GROSSBERG, S., How does a brain build a cognitive code? *Psychol. Rev.* **87**, 1-51 (1980).
177. GUM, R. L., ROEFS, T. G., and KIMBALL, D. B., Quantifying societal goals: Development of a weighting methodology, *Water Resour. Res.* **12**, 612-622 (1976).
178. GUSEV, M. J., Vector optimization of linear systems, *Sov. Math. Dokl.* **13**, 1440-1444 (1972).
179. HABENICHT, W., Efficiency in general vector maximum problems, *Ric. Operativa* **8**, 89-101 (1978).
180. HADLEY, C., *Linear Programming*, Addison and Wesley, Reading, Massachusetts (1963).
181. HAIMES, Y. Y., The surrogate worth trade-off (SWT) method and its extensions, *Multiple Criteria Decision Making Theory and Application*, Edited by G. Fandel and T. Gal, pp. 85-108, Springer-Verlag, New York (1980).
182. HAIMES, Y. Y., and HALL, W. A., Multiobjectives in water resources systems analysis: The surrogate worth trade off method, *Water Resour. Res.* **10**, 615-623 (1974).
183. HAIMES, Y. Y., and HALL, W. A., Analysis of multiple objectives in water quality, *ASCE J. Hydraulics Div.* **101**, 387-400 (1975).
184. HAIMES, Y. Y., HALL, W. A., and FREEDMAN, H. T., *Multiobjective Optimization in Water Resources Systems, The Surrogate Worth Trade-Off Method*, Elsevier, New York (1975).
185. HAITH, D. A., and LOUCKS, D. P., Multiobjective water-resources planning, *Systems Approach to Water Management*, Edited by A. K. Biswas, McGraw-Hill, New York (1976).
186. HALL, C. S., and LINDZEY, G., *Theories of Personality*, Wiley, New York (1970).
187. HALL, W. A., and HAIMES, Y. Y., The surrogate worth trade-off method with multiple decision-makers, *Multiple Criteria Decision Making*: Kyoto, Edited by M. Zeleny, pp. 207-234, Springer-Verlag, New York (1976).
188. HAMMOND, K. R., Externalizing the parameters of quasirational thought, *Multiple Criteria Decision Making*: Kyoto, Edited by M. Zeleny, pp. 75-96, Springer-Verlag, New York (1975).
189. HARTLEY, R. L., Using duality theory for identification of primal efficient points and for sensitivity analysis in multiple objective linear programming, *J. Oper. Res. Soc.* **29**, 643-649 (1978).

190. HANNAN, E. L., Nondominance in goal programming, *INFOR* **18**, 300–309 (1980).
191. HANSSMANN, F., *Operations Research in Production and Inventory Control*, Wiley, New York (1962).
192. HARNETT, R. M., and IGNIZIO, P., A heuristic program for the covering problem with multiple objectives, *Multiple Criteria Decision Making*, Edited by J. L. Cochrane and M. Zeleny, pp. 738–740, University of South Carolina Press, Columbia (1973).
193. HARRINGTON, T. C., and FISCHER, W. A., Portfolio modeling in multiple-criteria situations under uncertainty: Comment, *Decision Sci.* **11**, 171–177 (1980).
194. HARSANYI, J. C., The tracing procedure: A Bayesian approach to defining a solution for N-person noncooperative games, *Int. J. Game Theory* **4**, 61–94 (1975).
195. HARTLEY, R., On cone-efficiency, cone-convexity and cone-compactness, *SIAM J. Appl. Math.* **34**, 211–222 (1978).
196. HARTLEY, R., Finite, disconnected, vector Markov decision processes, University of Manchester, Working Paper, Manchester, England, 1979.
197. HAURIE, A., On Pareto optimal decisions for a coalition of a subset of players, *IEEE Trans. Autom. Control* **AC-18**, 144–149 (1973).
198. HAZEN, G. B., and MORIN, T. L., Steepest ascent algorithms for nonconical multiple objective programming, Northwestern University, Department of Industrial Engineering and Management Science, Working Paper, Evanston, Illinois, 1982.
199. HAZEN, G. B., and MORIN, T. L., Optimality conditions in nonconical multiple-objective programming, *J. Optim. Theory Appl.* **40**, 25–59 (1983).
200. HEENAN, D. A., and ADDLEMAN, R. B., Quantitative techniques for today's decision makers, *Harvard Business Rev.* **54**, 32–62 (1976).
201. HELD, R., and RICHARDS, W., (Editors), *Perception: Mechanism and Models*, Reading from Scientific American, W. H. Freeman, San Francisco (1972).
202. HEMMING, T., Multiobjective decision making under certainty, Economic Research Institute, Stockholm School of Economics, Stockholm, Sweden, 1978.
203. HENIG, M. I., Multicriteria dynamic programming, Ph.D. dissertation, Yale University, New Haven, Connecticut (1978).
204. HENIG, M. I., A cone separation theorem, *J. Optim. Theory Appl.* **36**, 451–455 (1982).
205. HENIG, M. I., Proper efficiency with respect to cones, *J. Optim. Theory Appl.* **36**, 387–407 (1982).
206. HERNER, S., and SNAPPER, K. J., Application of multiple-criteria utility model to evaluation of information systems, *J. Am. Soc. Inf. Sci.* **29**, 289–296 (1978).
207. HESTENES, M., *Calculus of Variations and Optimal Control Theory*, Wiley, New York (1966).
208. HICH, J., *The Art and Skill of Successful Negotiation*, Prentice-Hall, Englewood Cliffs, New Jersey (1973).
209. HILGARD, E. R., and BOWER, G. H., *Theories of Learning*, Appleton-Century-Crofts, New York (1966).
210. HILL, M., Goals-achievement matrix for evaluating alternative plans, *J. Am. Inst. Planners* **34**, 19–28 (1968).
211. HILL, N., *Think and Grow Rich*, Fawcett, Greenwich, Connecticut (1960).
212. HO, Y. C., Final report of the First International Conference on the Theory and Applications of Differential Games, Amherst, Massachusetts, 1970.
213. HOBBS, B. F., A comparison of weighting methods in power plant siting, *Decision Sci.* **11**, 725–737 (1980).
214. HOPPER, R., *Human Message Systems*, Harper and Row, New York (1976).
215. HOUTHAKKER, H., Revealed preference and the utility function, *Economica*, **17**, 159–174 (1950).
216. HOVLAND, C. I., JANIS, I. L., and KELLEY, H. H., *Communication and Persuasion*, Yale U.P., New Haven, Connecticut (1953).
217. HOWARD, R., *Dynamic Probabilistic Systems*, Vols. I and II, Wiley, New York (1971).

218. HU, S. T., *Elements of Real Analysis*, Holden-Day, San Francisco (1967).
219. HUANG, S. C., Note on the mean-square strategy of vector valued objective functions, *J. Optim. Theory Appl.* **9**, 364-366 (1972).
220. HUBER, G. P., Methods for quantifying subjective probabilities and multiattribute utilities, *Decision Sci.* **5**, 430-458 (1974).
221. HUBER, G. P., Multi-attribute utility models: A review of field and field-like studies, *Manage. Sci.* **20**, 1393-1402 (1974).
222. HWANG, C. L., and YOON, K., *Multiple Attribute Decision Making—Methods and Applications: A State-of-the-Art Survey*, Springer-Verlag, New York (1981).
223. HWANG, C. L., and MASUD, A. S. M., (in collaboration with S. R. Paidy and K. Yoon), *Multiple Objective Decision Making—Methods and Applications: A State-of-the-Art Survey*, Springer-Verlag, New York (1979).
224. IGNIZIO, J. P., *Goal Programming and Extensions*, D. C. Heath, Lexington, Massachusetts (1976).
225. IGNIZIO, J. P., *Linear Programming in Single- and Multiple-Objective Systems*, Prentice Hall, Englewood Cliffs, New Jersey (1982).
226. IJIRI, Y., *Management Goals and Accounting for Control*, North-Holland, Amsterdam (1965).
227. ILICH, J., *The Art and Skill of Successful Negotiation*, Prentice-Hall, Englewood Cliffs, New Jersey (1973).
228. ISAACS, R., *Differential Games*, Wiley, New York (1965).
229. ISAACS, R., Differential games: Their scope, nature, and future, *J. Optim. Theory Appl.* **3**, 283-295 (1969).
230. ISERMANN, H., A note on proper efficiency and the linear vector maximum problem, *Oper. Res.* **22**, 189-199 (1974).
231. ISERMANN, H., Existence and duality in multiple objective linear programming, *Multiple Criteria Decision Making*, Edited by H. Thiriez and S. Zionts, pp. 64-75, Springer-Verlag, New York (1976).
232. ISERMANN, H., The enumeration of the set of all efficient solutions for a linear multiple objective program, *Oper. Res. Q.* **28**, 711-725 (1977).
233. ISERMANN, H., Duality in multiple objective linear programming, *Multiple Criteria Problem Solving* (S. Zionts, ed.), Springer-Verlag, New York (1978), pp. 274-285.
234. JACQUET-LAGRÉZE, E., Explicative models in multicriteria preference analysis, *Advances in Operations Research* (M. Roubens, Ed.), North-Holland, Amsterdam (1977), pp. 213-218.
235. JAHN, J., Duality theory for vector optimization problems in normed linear spaces, Reprint No. 534, Fachbereich Mathematik, Technische Hochschule, Darmstadt, West Germany, 1980.
236. JANIS, I. L., and MANN, L., *Decision Making: A Psychological Analysis of Conflict, Choice and Commitment*, The Free Press, New York (1977).
237. JOHNSEN, E., Experiences in multiobjective management processes, *Multiple Criteria Decision Making*, Edited by M. Zeleny, pp. 135-152, Springer-Verlag, New York (1976).
238. JOHNSEN, R. L., *Studies in Multiobjective Decision Models*, Monograph No. 1, Economic Research Center in Lund, Sweden, 1968.
239. JOHNSON, E. M., and HUBER, G. P., The technology of utility assessment, *IEEE Trans. Syst. Man. Cybern.* **SMC-7**, 311-325 (1977).
240. JURKIEWICZ, E., Stability of compromise solution in multicriteria decision-making problems, *J. Optim. Theory Appl.* **40**, 77-83 (1983).
241. KANTARIYA, G. V., Optimal choice of strategy based on compromise agreement among alternative selection criteria, *Eng. Cybern.* **12**, 39-42 (1974).
242. KARLIN, S., Mathematical methods and theory in games, *Programming and Economics*, Vol. I, pp. 210-217, Addison-Wesley, Reading, Massachusetts (1959).
243. KARLINS, M., and ABELSON, H. I., *Persuasion*, Springer-Verlag, New York (1970).
244. KARRASS, C. L., *Give and Take: The Complete Guide to Negotiating Strategies and Tactics*, Thomas Y. Crowell, New York (1974).

245. KARWAN, M. H., and VILLARREAL, B., Dynamic programming approaches for multicriterion integer programming, State University of New York, Department of Industrial Engineering, Technical Report No. 78-4, Buffalo, New York, 1978.

246. KEEFER, D. L., Allocation planning for R and D with uncertainty and multiple objectives, *IEEE Trans. Eng. Manage.* **25**, 8-14 (1978).

247. KEEN, P. G. W., The evolving concept of optimality, multiple criteria decision making, *TIMS Studies in the Management Sciences*, Vol. 6, Edited by M. K. Starr and M. Zeleny, pp. 31-58, North-Holland, Amsterdam (1977).

248. KEENEY, R. L., Utility independence and preferences for multiattributed consequences, *Oper. Res.* **19**, 875-893 (1971).

249. KEENEY, R. L., Utility functions for multiattributed consequences, *Manage. Sci.* **18**, 276-287 (1972).

250. KEENEY, R. L., A decision analysis with multiple objectives: The Mexico City Airport, *Bell J. Econ. Manage.* **4**, 101-117 (1973).

251. KEENEY, R. L., Risk, independence and multiattributed utility functions, *Econometrica* **41**, 27-39 (1973).

252. KEENEY, R. L., Multiplicative utility functions, *Oper. Res.* **22**, 22-34 (1974).

253. KEENEY, R. L., The art of assessing multiattribute utility functions, *Organ. Behav. Human Performance* **19**, 267-310 (1977).

254. KEENEY, R. L., and RAIFFA, H., *Decisions with Multiple Objectives: Preferences and Value Tradeoffs*, Wiley, New York (1976).

255. KHAIRULLAH, Z. Y., and ZIONTS, S., An experiment with some algorithms for multiple criteria decision making, *Multiple Criteria Decision Making Theory and Application*, Edited by G. Fandel and T. Gal, pp. 178-188, Springer-Verlag, New York (1980).

256. KIM, K. W., and WHITE, C. C., Solution procedures for vector criterion Markov decision processes, *Large Scale Syst.* **1**, 129-140 (1980).

257. KIRKWOOD, C. W., Parametrically dependent preferences for multiattributed consequences, *Oper. Res.* **24**, 92-103 (1976).

258. KLAHR, C. N., Multiple objectives in mathematical programming, *Oper. Res.* **6**, 849-855 (1958).

259. KNOLL, A. L., and ENGELBERG, A., Weighting multiple objectives—The Churchman-Ackoff technique revisited, *Comput. Oper. Res.* **5**, 165-177 (1978).

260. KOJIMA, M., Duality between objectives and constraints in vector maximum problems, *J. Oper. Res. Soc. Jpn*, **15**, 53-62 (1972).

261. KOOPMAN, B. O., Fallacies in operations research, *Oper. Res.* **4**, 422-426 (1956).

262. KOOPMANS, T. C., Analysis of production as an efficient combination of activities, in *Activity Analysis of Production and Allocation* (T. C. Koopmans, ed.), pp. 33-97, Wiley, New York (1951).

263. KOOPMANS, T. C., Objectives, constraints, and outcomes in optimal growth models, *Econometrica* **35**, 1-15 (1967).

264. KORHONEN, P., WALLENIUS, J., and ZIONTS, S., A bargaining model for solving multiple criteria problem, *Multiple Criteria Decision Making Theory and Application*, Edited by G. Fandel and T. Gal, pp. 178-188, Springer-Verlag, New York (1980).

265. KORNBLUTH, J. S. H., Duality, indifference and sensitivity analysis in multiple objective linear programming, *Oper. Res. Q.* **25**, 599-614 (1974).

266. KORNBLUTH, J. S. H., The fuzzy dual: Information for the multiple objective decision maker, *Comput. Oper. Res.* **4**, 65-72 (1977).

267. KORNBLUTH, J. S. H., Using duality theory for identification of primal efficient points and for sensitivity analysis in MOLP: A comment, *J. Oper. Res. Soc.* **30**, 285-287 (1979).

268. KRANTZ, D. H., LUCE, R. D., SUPPES, P., and TVERSKY, A., *Foundations of Measurement* Vol. I, Academic Press, New York (1971).

269. KRASNENKAR, A. S., Method for local improvements in vector-optimization problem, *Autom. Remote Control* **36**, 419-422 (1975).

270. KRUEGER, R. J., and DAUER, J. P., Multiobjective optimization model, *SIAM Rev.* **20**, 629 (1978).

271. KUHN, H. W., and TUCKER, A. W., *Contributions to the Theory of Games*, Vol. 1, Princeton University Press, Princeton, New Jersey (1950).

272. KUHN, H. W., and TUCKER, A. W., *Nonlinear Programming*, Proceedings of the Second Berkeley Symposium on Mathematical Statistics and Probability, Edited by J. Neyman, pp. 481-491, University of California Press, Berkeley (1951).

273. KUHN, H. W., and TUCKER, A. W., *Contributions to the Theory of Games*, Vol. 2, Princeton University Press, Princeton, New Jersey (1953).

274. KUMAR, P. C., and PHILIPPATOS, G. C., Conflict resolution in investment decisions: Implementation of goal programming methodology for dual-purpose funds, *Decision Sci.* **10**, 562-576 (1979).

275. KUZIMIN, I. V., DEDIKOV, E. O., and KUKHAREV, B. Y., Choice of global solution criterion in problems with several objective functions, *Sov. Autom. Control* **7**, 59-62 (1974).

276. KWON, Y. K., and YU, P. L., Conflict dissolution by reframing game payoffs using linear perturbations, *J. Optim. Theory Appl.* **39**, 187-214 (1983).

277. LADANY, S. P., and AHARONI, M., Maintenance policy of aircraft according to multiple criteria, *Int. J. Syst. Sci.* **6**, 1093-1101 (1975).

278. LARICHEV, O. I., Man-machine procedures for decision making (Review), *Autom. Remote Control* **32**, 1973-1983 (1971).

279. LAWRENCE, K. D., and BURBRIDGE, J. J., A multiple goal linear programming model for coordinated production and logistics planning, *Int. J. Production Res.* **14**, 215-222 (1976).

280. LEE, E. B., and MARKUS, L., *Foundations of Optimal Control Theory*, Wiley, New York (1967).

281. LEE, S. M., *Goal Programming for Decision Analysis*, Auerbach, Philadelphia, Pennsylvania (1972).

282. LEE, S. M., and LERRO, A. J., Capital budgeting for multiple objectives, *Financial Manage* **3**, 58-66 (1974).

283. LEE, S. M., and MOORE, L. J., Multi-criteria school busing models, *Manage. Sci.* **23**, 703-715 (1977).

284. LEE, S. M., and NICELY, R., Goal programming for marketing decisions: A case study, *J. Market.* **38**, 24-32 (1974).

285. LEGASTO, A. A., A multiple-objective policy model: Results of an application to a developing country, *Manage. Sci.* **24**, 498-509 (1978).

286. LEHMANN, R., and OETTLI, W., The theorem of the alternative, the key-theorem, and the vector-maximum problem, *Math. Program.* **8**(3), 332-344 (1975).

287. LEITMANN, G., *An Introduction to Optimal Control*, McGraw-Hill, New York (1966).

288. LEITMANN, G. (Editor), *Multicriteria Decision Making and Differential Games*, Plenum Press, New York (1976).

289. LEITMANN, G., Some problems of scalar and vector-valued optimization in linear visco-elasticity, *J. Optim. Theory Appl.* **23**, 93-99 (1977).

290. LEITMANN, G., and MARZOLLO, A. (Editors), *Multicriteria Decision Making*, Springer-Verlag, New York (1975).

291. LEITMANN, G., ROCKLIN, S., and VINCENT, T. L., A note on control space properties of cooperative games, *J. Optim. Theory Appl.* **9**, 379-390 (1972).

292. LEONTIEF, W., Introduction to a theory of the internal structure of functional relationships, *Econometrica* **15**, 361-373 (1947).

293. LEONTIEF, W., A note on the interrelation of subsets of independent variables of a continuous function with continuous first derivatives, *Bull. Am. Math. Soc.* **53**, 343-350 (1947).

294. LIN, J. G., Maximal vectors and multi-objective optimization, *J. Optim. Theory Appl.* **18**, 41-64 (1976).

295. LIN, W. T., An accounting control system structured on multiple objective planning models, *Omega* **8**, 375-382 (1980).

296. LIN, W. T., Multiple objective budgeting models: A simulation, *Account. Rev.* **53**, 61-76 (1978).

297. LINDSAY, P. H., and NORMAN, D. A., *Human Information Processing, An Introduction to Psychology*, Academic, New York (1972).

298. LOUCKS, D. P., An application of interactive multiobjective water resources planning, *Interfaces* **9**, 70-75 (1977).

299. LUCAS, H. C., and MOORE, J. R., A multiple-criterion scoring approach to information system project selection, *INFOR* **14**, 1-12 (1976).

300. LUCAS, W. F., Some recent developments in *N* person game theory, *SIAM Rev.* **13**, 491-523 (1971).

301. LUCE, R. D., and RAIFFA, H., *Games and Decisions*, Wiley, New York (1967).

302. LUCE, R. D., and TUKEY, J. W., Simultaneous conjoint measurement: A new type of fundamental measurement, *J. Math. Psychol.* **1**, 1-27 (1964).

303. MacCRIMMON, K. R., Decision making among multiple-attribute alternatives: A survey and consolidated approach, The Rand Corporation, Memorandum No. RM-4823-ARPA, 1968.

304. MacCRIMMON, K. R., Decision making among multiple-attribute alternatives: A survey and consolidated approach, RAND Memorandum, RM-5877-00T, 1969.

305. MacCRIMMON, K. R., An overview of multiple objective decision making, *Multiple Criteria Decision Making*, Edited by J. L. Cochrane and M. Zeleny, pp. 18-44, University of South Carolina Press, Columbia (1973).

306. MAJOR, D. C., Multiobjective water resource planning, *Water Resources Monograph* 4, American Geophysical Union, Washington, D.C. (1977).

307. MANGASARIAN, O. L., *Nonlinear Programming*, McGraw-Hill, New York (1969).

308. MANGASARIAN, O. L., Optimal simplex tableau characterization of unique and bounded solutions of linear programs, *J. Optim. Theory Appl.* **35**, 123-128 (1981).

309. MARTIN, W. S., and BARCUS, A., A multiattribute model for evaluating industrial customer's potential, *Interfaces* **10**, 40-44 (1980).

310. MARZOLLO, A., and UKOVICH, W., On some broad classes of vector optimal decisions and their characterization, *Multicriteria Decision Making*, Edited by G. Leitmann and A. Marzollo, pp. 281-324, Springer-Verlag, New York (1975).

311. McGREW, D. R., and HAIMES, Y. Y., Parametric solution to the joint system identification and optimization problem, *J. Optim. Theory Appl.* **13**, 582-605 (1974).

312. MEHRABIAN, A., *Tactics of Social Influence*, Prentice-Hall, Englewood Cliffs, New Jersey (1970).

313. MILLER, J. G., *Living Systems*, McGraw-Hill, New York (1978).

314. MILLER, J. R. III., *Professional Decision Making: A Procedure for Evaluating Complex Alternatives*, Praeger, New York (1970).

315. MITTEN, L. G., Preference order dynamic programming, *Manage. Sci.* **21**, 43-46 (1974).

316. NACCACHE, P. H., Connectedness of the set of non-dominated outcomes in multicriteria optimization, *J. Optim. Theory Appl.* **25**, 459-467 (1978).

317. NAKAYAMA, H., A geometric consideration on duality in vector optimization, *J. Optim. Theory Appl.* **44**, 625-655 (1984).

318. NAKAYAMA, H., TANINO, T., and SAWARAGI, Y., An interactive optimization method in multicriteria decision making, *IEEE Trans. Syst. Man Cybern.* **SMC-10**, 163-169 (1980).

319. NARISIMHAN, R., Goal programming in a fuzzy environment, *Decision Sci.* **11**, 325-336 (1980).

320. NASH, J. F., The bargaining problem, *Econometrica* **18**, 155-162 (1950).

321. NEGOITA, C. V., and SULARIA, M., A selection method of nondominated points in multi-criteria decision problems, *Econ. Comput. Econ. Cybern. Stud. Res.* **12**, 19-23 (1978).

322. NEMHAUSER, G. L., *Introduction to Dynamic Programming*, Wiley, New York (1966).

323. NEWELL, A., and SIMON, H. A., *Human Problem Solving*, Prentice-Hall, Englewood Cliffs, New Jersey (1972).

324. NIEUWENHUIS, J. W., Some results about nondominated solutions, *J. Optim. Theory Appl.* **36**, 289-301 (1982).
325. NIJKAMP, P., *Multidimensional Spatial Data and Decision Analysis*, Wiley, New York (1979).
326. NIJKAMP, P., and RIETVELD, P., *Conflicting Social Priorities and Compromise Social Decisions*, Analysis and Decision in Regional Policy, Pion, London (1979).
327. NIJKAMP, P., and SPRONK, J. (Editors), *Multiple Criteria Analysis: Operational Methods*, Gower Press, London (1981).
328. NIJKAMP, P., and VAN DELFT, A., *Multi-Criteria Analysis and Regional Decision-Making*, Martinus Nijhoff Social Sciences Division, Leiden (1977).
329. NUTT, P. C., Comparing methods for weighting decision criteria, *Omega* **8**, 163-172 (1980).
330. ODOM, P. R., SHANNON, R. E., and BUCKLES, B. P., Multi-goal subset selection problems under uncertainty, *AIIE Trans.* **11**, 61-69 (1979).
331. ÖLANDER, F., Search behavior in non-simultaneous choice situations: Satisficing or maximizing?, *Utility, Probability, and Human Decision Making*, Edited by D. Wendt and C. Vlek, pp. 297-320, D. Reidel, Boston (1975).
332. OLECH, C., Existence theorems for optimal problems with vector-valued cost function, *Trans. Am. Math. Soc.* **136**, 159-180 (1969).
333. OLENIK, S. C., and HAIMES, Y. Y., A hierarchical-multiobjective method for water resources planning, *IEEE Trans. Syst. Man Cybern.* Special Issue on Public Systems Methodology, 1979.
334. OLMSTED, J. M. H., *Advanced Calculus*, Appleton-Century-Crofts, New York (1956).
335. OLSON, M., JR., *The Logic of Collective Action—Public Goods and the Theory of Groups*, Harvard U. P., Cambridge, Massachusetts (1965).
336. OPPENHEIMER, K. R., A proxy approach to multi-attribute decision making, *Manage. Sci.* **24**, 675-689 (1978).
337. OSTERYOUNG, J. S., Multiple goals in the capital budgeting decision, *Multiple Criteria Decision Making*, Edited by J. L. Cochrane and M. Zeleny, pp. 447-457, University of South Carolina Press, Columbia (1973).
338. OWEN, G., *Game Theory*, Saunders Company, Philadelphia (1968).
339. OZERNOI, V. M., Using preference information in multistep methods for solving multiple criteria decision problems, *Multiple Criteria Decision Making Theory and Application*, Edited by G. Fandel and T. Gal, pp. 314-328, Springer-Verlag, New York (1980).
340. PARETO, V., *Sociological Writings*, Selected and Introduced by S. E. Finer, Translated by D. Mirfin, Praeger, New York (1966).
341. PARETO, V., *Manuale di Economia Politica*, Societá Editrice Libraria, Milano, Italy, 1906; Piccola Biblioteca Scientifica No. 13, Societá Editrice Libraria, Milano, Italy, 1919. Translated into English by A. S. Schwier, as *Manual of Political Economy*, MacMillan, New York (1971).
342. PASCOLETTI, A., and SERAFINI, P., Comment on cooperative games and vector-valued criteria problems, by W. E. Schmitendorf, *IEEE Trans. Autom. Control* **AC-21**(5), 806-808 (1976).
343. PASCOLETTI, A., and SERAFINI, P., Scalarizing vector optimization problems, *J. Optim. Theory Appl.* **42**, 499-524 (1984).
344. PASCUAL, L. D., and BEN-ISRAEL, A., Vector-valued criteria in geometric programming, *Oper. Res.* **19**, 98-104 (1971).
345. PASSY, U., and LEVANON, Y., Manpower allocation with multiple objectives—The min max approach, *Multiple Criteria Decision Making Theory and Application*, Edited by G. Fandel and T. Gal, pp. 329-343, Springer-Verlag, New York (1980).
346. PAU, L. F., Two-level planning with conflicting goals, *Multiple Criteria Decision Making*, Edited by H. Thiriez and S. Zionts, pp. 263-273, Springer-Verlag, New York (1976).
347. PERLMAN, M. D., Jensen's inequality for a convex vector-valued function on an infinite-dimensional space, *J. Multivariate Anal.* **4**, 52-65 (1974).
348. PESCHEL, M., and RIEDEL, C., Use of vector optimization in multiobjective decision making, *Conflicting Objectives in Decisions*, Edited by D. E. Bell, R. L. Keeney, and H. Raiffa, pp. 97-122, Wiley, New York (1977).

349. PHILIP, J., Algorithms for the vector maximization problem, *Math. Program.* **2**, 207-229 (1972).

350. PHILIPPATOS, G. C., On the specification of viable financial goals, *Manage. Plan.* **20**, 11-16 (1971).

351. PHILLIPS, J. L. JR., *The Origins of Intellect—Piaget's Theory*, W. H. Freeman, San Francisco (1969).

352. PICHLER, J. A., Power, influence, and authority, *Contemporary Management—Issues and Viewpoints*, Edited by J. W. McGuire, Prentice-Hall, Englewood Cliffs, New Jersey (1974).

353. PITKANEN, E., Goal programming and operational objectives in public administration, *Swedish J. Econ.* **72**, 207-214 (1970).

354. PODREBARAC, M. L., and SENGUPTA, S. S., Parametric linear programming: Some extensions, *INFOR* **9**, 305-319 (1971).

355. POLAK, E., On the approximation of solutions to multiple criteria decision making problems, *Multiple Criteria Decision Making*, Edited by M. Zeleny, pp. 271-282, Springer-Verlag, New York (1976).

356. POLAK, E., and PAYNE, A. N., On multicriteria optimization, *Directions in Large-Scale Systems*, Edited by Y. C. Ho and S. K. Mitter, pp. 77-94, Plenum Press, New York (1976).

357. PONSTEIN, J., On the use of purely finitely additive multipliers in mathematical programming, *J. Optim. Theory Appl.* **33**, 37-56 (1981).

358. PONSTEIN, J., On the dualization of multiobjective optimization problems, University of Groningen, Econometric Institute, Working Paper, Groningen, The Netherlands, 1982.

359. POWELL, J., and VERGIN, R., A heuristic model for planning corporate financing, *Financial Manage.* **4**, 13-20 (1975).

360. PRICE, W. L., Goal programming and a manpower problem, *Mathematical Programming in Theory and Practice*, Edited by P. L. Hammer and G. Zoutendijk, pp. 395-416, North-Holland, New York (1974).

361. PUN, L., Multicriteria decision-aid-making in production-management problems, *Multiple Criteria Decision Making Theory and Application*, Edited by G. Fandel and T. Gal, pp. 344-373, Springer-Verlag, New York (1980).

362. RADNER, R., *Satisficing, Optimization Techniques: IFIP Technical Conference*, Edited by G. Marchuk, pp. 252-263, Springer-Verlag, New York (1975).

363. RAIFFA, H., *Decision Analysis*, Addison-Wesley, Reading, Massachusetts (1968).

364. RAIFFA, H., *Preferences for multi-attributed alternatives*, The RAND Corporation, Memorandum No. RM-5868-DOT/RC, 1969.

365. RAO, C. R., *Linear Statistical Inference and Its Applications*, Wiley, New York, (1973).

366. RAPOPORT, A., *N-Person Game Theory—Concepts and Applications*, The University of Michigan Press, Ann Arbor (1970).

367. RAPOPORT, A., Interpersonal comparison of utilities, *Multiple Criteria Decision Making: Kyoto 1975*, Edited by M. Zeleny, pp. 17-43, Springer-Verlag, New York (1976).

368. RASMUSEN, H. J., Multilevel planning with conflicting objectives, *Swedish J. Econ.* **76**, 155-170 (1974).

369. REEVES, G. R., A note on quadratic preferences and goal programming, *Decision Sci.* **9**, 532-534 (1978).

370. REGUSH, N., and REGUSH, J., *Mind-Search*, Berkeley, New York (1977).

371. REID, R. W., and CITRON, S. J., On noninferior performance index vectors, *J. Optim. Theory Appl.* **7**, 11-28 (1971).

372. RIETVELD, P., *Multiple Objective Decision Methods and Regional Planning*, North-Holland, Amsterdam (1980).

373. RITZMAN, L. P., BRADFORD, J., and JACOBS, R., A multiple objective approach to space planning for academic facilities, *Manage. Sci.* **25**, 895-906 (1979).

374. RITZMAN, L. P., and KRAJEWSKI, L. J., Multiple objectives in linear programming—An example in scheduling postal resources, *Decision Sci.* **4**, 364-378 (1973).

375. RIVETT, B. H. P., Indifference mapping for multiple criteria decisions, *Omega* **8**, 81-94 (1980).

376. ROCKAFELLAR, R. T., *Convex Analysis*, Princeton University Press, Princeton, New Jersey (1972).

377. RÖDDER, W., A duality theory for linear vector optimum problems, *Advances in Operations Research*, Edited by M. Roubens, pp. 405-407, North-Holland, Amsterdam (1977).

378. ROM, W. O., and HUNG, M. S., Application of primitive sets to multicriteria optimization problems, *J. Math. Econ.* **7**, 77-90 (1980).

379. ROSENBLATT, M. J., The facilities layout problem: A multi-goal approach, *Int. J. Production Res.* **17**, 323-332 (1979).

380. ROSINGER, E. E., Duality and alternative in multiobjective optimization, *Proc. Am. Math. Soc.* **64**, 307-313 (1977).

381. ROSINGER, E. E., Interactive algorithm for multiobjective optimization, *J. Optim. Theory Appl.* **35**, 339-365 (1981).

382. ROSS, G. T., and SOLAND, R. M., A multicriteria approach to location of public facilities, *Eur. J. Oper. Res.* **4**, 307-321 (1980).

383. ROY, B., Problems and methods with multiple objective function, *Math. Program.* **1**, 239-266 (1971).

384. ROY, B., How outranking relations helps multiple criteria decision making, *Multiple Criteria Decision Making*, Edited by J. L. Cochrane and M. Zeleny, pp. 179-201, University of South Carolina Press, Columbia (1973).

385. ROY, B., From optimization to multi-criteria decision aid: Three main operational attitudes, *Multiple Criteria Decison Making: Jouy-en-Josas*, France, Edited by H. Thiriez and S. Zionts, pp. 1-34, Springer-Verlag, New York (1976).

386. ROY, B., A conceptual framework for a prescriptive theory of decision-aid, *TIMS Studies in Management Sciences*, No. 6, North-Holland, Amsterdam (1977).

387. ROY, G. G., A man-machine approach to multicriteria decision making, *Int. J. Man-Machine Stud.* **12**, 203-215 (1980).

388. RUBIN, J. Z., and BROWN, B. R., *The Social Psychology of Bargaining and Negotiation*, Academic, New York (1975).

389. SAATY, T. L., A scaling method for priorities in hierarchical structures, *J. Math. Psychol.* **15**, 234-281 (1977).

390. SAATY, T. L., Exploring the interface between hierarchies, multiple objectives and fuzzy sets, *Fuzzy Sets Syst.* **1**, 57-68 (1978).

391. SAATY, T. L., *The Analytic Hierarchy Process*, McGraw-Hill, New York, (1980).

392. SAKAWA, M., An approximate solution to linear multicriteria control problems through the multicriteria simplex method, *J. Optim. Theory Appl.* **22**, 417-427 (1977).

393. SAKAWA, M., Multiobjective optimization by the surrogate worth trade-off method, *J. Oper. Res. Soc.* **31**, 153-158 (1980).

394. SALAMA, A. I. A., and GOURISHANKAR, V., Optimal control of systems with a single control and several cost functionals, *Int. J. Control* **14**, 705-725 (1971).

395. SALUKVADZE, M. E., Optimization of vector functionals, I. The programming of optimal trajectories, *Autom. Remote Control* **32**, 1169-1178 (1971).

396. SALUKVADZE, M. E., Optimization of vector functionals, II. The analytic construction of optimal controls, *Autom. Remote Control* **32**, 1347-1357 (1971).

397. SALUKVADZE, M. E., On the existence of solutions in problems of optimization under vector-valued criteria, *J. Optim. Theory Appl.* **13**, 203-217 (1974).

398. SARIN, R. K., Interactive evaluation and bounded procedure for selecting multi-attributed alternatives, multiple criteria decision making, *TIMS Studies in the Management Sciences*, Vol. 6, Edited by M. K. Starr and M. Zeleny, pp. 211-224, North-Holland, Amsterdam (1977).

399. SAWARAGI, Y., INOUE, K., and NAKAYAMA, H., Multiobjective decision making with applications to environmental and urban design, *Conflicting Objectives in Decisions*, Edited by D. E. Bell, R. L. Keeney, and H. Raiffa, pp. 358-366, Wiley, New York (1977).

400. SAYEKI, Y., and VESPERS, K. H., Allocation of importance in a hierarchical goal structure, *Manage. Sci.* **19**, 667-675 (1973).

401. SCHAIBLE, S., Quasiconvex, pseudoconvex, and strictly pseudoconvex quadratic functions, *J. Optim. Theory Appl.* **35**, 303-338 (1981).
402. SCHELLING, T. C., *The Strategy of Conflict*, Oxford U. P., London (1960).
403. SCHROEDER, R. G., Resource planning in university management by goal programming, *Oper. Res.* **22**, 700-710 (1974).
404. SCHUBIK, M., *Readings in Game Theory and Political Behavior*, Doubleday, Garden City, New York (1954).
405. SCHWARTZ, S. L., and VERTINSKY, I., Multi-attribute investment decisions: A study of R & D project selection, *Manage. Sci.* **24**, 285-301 (1977).
406. SEIFORD, L., and YU, P. L., Potential solutions of linear systems: The multi-criteria multiple constraint levels program, *J. Math. Anal. Appl.* **69**, 283-303 (1979).
407. SENGUPTA, S. S., PODREBARAC, M. L., and FERNANDO, T. D. H., Probabilities of optima in multi-objective linear programs, *Multiple Criteria Decision Making*, Edited by J. L. Cochrane and M. Zeleny, pp. 217-235, University of South Carolina Press, Columbia (1973).
408. SHAPLEY, L. S., A value for *N*-person games, contributions to the theory of games, II, *Annals of Mathematical Studies 28*, Edited by H. W. Kuhn and A. W. Tucker, pp. 307-317, Princeton Press, Princeton, New Jersey (1953).
409. SHARPE, W., *Portfolio Theory and Capital Markets*, McGraw-Hill, New York (1970).
410. SHENOY, P., and YU, P. L., Inducing cooperation by reciprocative strategy in non-zero-sum games, *J. Math. Anal. Appl.* **80**, 67-77 (1981).
411. SHERALI, H. D., and SOYSTER, A. L., Preemptive and nonpreemptive multiobjective programming: Relationships and counterexamples, *J. Optim. Theory Appl.* **39**, 173-186 (1983).
412. SHIM, J. K., and SIEGEL, J., Quadratic preferences and goal programming, *Decision Sci.* **6**, 662-669 (1975).
413. SIMON, H. A., A behavioral model of rational choice, *Q. J. Econ.* **69**, 99-118 (1955).
414. SLOVIC, P., and LICHTENSTEIN, S., Comparison of Bayesian and regression approaches to the study of information processing judgment, *Organ. Behav. Human Performance* **6**, 649-774 (1971).
415. SMITH, R. D., and GREENLAW, P. S., Simulation of a psychological decision process in personnel selection, *Manage. Sci.* **13**, B409-B419 (1967).
416. SOBEL, M. J., Ordinal dynamic programming, *Manage. Sci.* **21**, 967-975 (1975).
417. SOLAND, R. M., Multicriteria optimization: A general characterization of efficient solutions, *Decision Sci.* **10**, 26-38 (1979).
418. SOYSTER, A. L., LEV, B., and TOOF, D. I., Conservative linear programming with mixed multiple objectives, *Omega* **5**, 193-205 (1977).
419. SPRONK, J., Capital budgeting and financial planning with multiple goals, *Multiple Criteria Analysis*, Edited by P. Nijkamp and J. Spronk, Gower Press, London (1981).
420. SRINIVASAN, V., and THOMSON, G. L., Alternate formulations for static multi-attribute assignment models, *Manage. Sci.* **20**, 154-158 (1973).
421. SRINIVASAN, V., and SHOCKER, A. D., Estimating the weights for multiple attributes in a composite criterion using pairwise judgements, *Psychometrika* **38**, 473-493 (1973).
422. SRINIVASAN, V., and SHOCKER, A. D., Linear programming techniques for multidimensional analysis of preference, *Psychometrika* **38**, 337-369 (1973).
423. STADLER, W., Preference optimality and applications of Pareto optimality, *Multicriteria Decision Making*, Edited by G. Leitmann and A. Marzollo, pp. 125-226, Springer-Verlag, New York (1975).
424. STADLER, W., Sufficient conditions for preference optimality, *Multicriteria Decision Making and Differential Games*, Edited by G. Leitmann, pp. 129-148, Plenum Press, New York (1976).
425. STADLER, W., A survey of multicriteria optimization or the vector maximum problem, Part I: 1776-1960, *J. Optim. Theory Appl.* **29**, 1-52 (1979).
426. STADLER, W., A comprehensive bibliography on multicriteria decision making and related areas, University of California, Working Paper, Berkeley, California, 1981.

427. STALFORD, H., Sufficient conditions for optimal control with state and control constraints *J. Optim. Theory Appl.* **7**, 118-135 (1971).
428. STANCH-MINASIAN, I. M., Stochastic programming with multiple objective functions, *Econ. Comput. Econ. Cybern. Stud. Res.* **1**, 49-67 (1974).
429. STARR, M. K., and GREENWOOD, L., Normative generation of alternatives with multiple criteria evaluation, multiple criteria decision making, *TIMS Studies in the Management Sciences*, Vol. 6, Edited by M. K. Starr and M. Zeleny, pp. 111-127, North-Holland, Amsterdam (1977).
430. STARR, M. K., and ZELENY, M. (Editors), Multiple criteria decision making, *TIMS Studies in the Management Sciences*, Vol. 6, North-Holland, Amsterdam (1977).
431. STEUER, R. E., ADBASE: An adjacent efficient basis algorithm for vector-maximum and interval weighted-sums linear programming problems, *J. Market. Res.* **12**, 454-455 (1975).
432. STEUER, R. E., Multiple objective linear programming with interval criterion weights, *Manage. Sci.* **23**, 305-316 (1976).
433. STEUER, R. E., ADBASE/FILTER: Computer package for solving multiple objective linear programming problems, University of Kentucky, College of Business and Economics, Lexington, Kentucky, 1977.
434. STEUER, R. E., An interactive multiple objective linear programming procedure, *TIMS Studies in Management Sciences*, Vol. 6, Edited by M. K. Starr and M. Zeleny, pp. 225-239, North-Holland, Amsterdam (1977).
435. STEUER, R. E., *Multiple Criteria Optimization*, Wiley, New York (1985).
436. STEUER, R. E., and SCHULER, A. T., An interactive multiple objective linear programming approach to a problem in forest management, *Oper. Res.* **26**, 254-269 (1978).
437. STEWART, T. J., A descriptive approach to multiple-criteria decision making, *J. Oper. Res. Soc.* **32**, 45-53 (1981).
438. STOER, J., and WITZGALL, C., *Convexity and Optimization in Finite Dimensions I*, Springer-Verlag, New York (1970).
439. STONE, J. J., *Strategic Persuasion, Arms Limitations Through Dialogue*, Columbia University Press, New York (1967).
440. SU, M. C., *Historical Records* (Shih-Chi), Vol. 56, No. 26, Han Dynasty, (Explained by Fei Yin, Song Dynasty) (in Chinese).
441. SUN, TZU., *Principle of War.* (In Chinese: many publishers with many explanations.)
442. TAKEDA, E., and NISHIDA, T., Multiple criteria decision problems with fuzzy domination structures, *Fuzzy Sets Syst.* **3**, 123-136 (1980).
443. TAMURA, K., A method for constructing the polar cone of a polyhedral cone, with applications to linear multicriteria decision problems, *J. Optim. Theory Appl.* **19**, 547-564 (1976).
444. TAMURA, K., and MIURA, S., Necessary and sufficient conditions for local and global nondominated solutions in decision problems with multi-objectives, *J. Optim. Theory Appl.* **28**, 501-523 (1979).
445. TANINO, T., and SAWARAGI, Y., Duality theory in multiobjective programming, *J. Optim. Theory Appl.* **27**, 509-529 (1979).
446. TANINO, T., and SAWARAGI, Y., Stability of nondominated solutions in multicriteria decision making, *J. Optim. Theory Appl.* **30**, 229-253 (1980).
447. TAYLOR, B. W., and KEOWN, A. J., A goal programming application of capital project selection in the production area, *AIIE Trans.* **10**, 52-57 (1978).
448. TAYLOR, B. W., DAVIS, K. R., and NORTH, R. M., Approaches to multiobjective planning in water resources projects, *Water Resour. Bull.* **11**, 999-1008 (1975).
449. TELL, B., A comparative study of some multiple-criteria methods, Stockholm School of Economics, Economics Research Institute, Stockholm, Sweden, 1976.
450. TELL, B., An approach to solving multi-person multiple-criteria decision-making problems, *Multiple Criteria Problem Solving: Proceedings*, Buffalo, New York, Edited by S. Zionts, pp. 482-493, Springer-Verlag, New York (1978).

451. TERRY, H., Comparative evaluation of performance using multiple criteria, *Manage. Sci.* **9**, 431-442 (1963).
452. TERSINE, R. J., Organizational objectives and goal programming: A convergence, *Manage. Plann.* **25**, 27-40 (1976).
453. THIRIEZ, H., and ZIONTS, S. (Editors), *Multiple Criteria Decision Making*: Jouy-en-Josas, France, Springer-Verlag, New York (1976).
454. TUCKER, A. W., and LUCE, R. D., *Contributions to the Theory of Games*, Vol. 4, Princeton University Press, Princeton, New Jersey (1959).
455. VAN WASSENHOVE, L. N., and GELDERS, L. F., Solving a bicriterion scheduling problem, *Eur. J. Oper. Res.* **4**, 42-48 (1980).
456. VEDDER, J., Multiattribute decision making under uncertainty using bounded intervals, *Multiple Criteria Decision Making*, Edited by J. L. Cochrane and M. Zeleny, pp. 93-107, University of South Carolina Press, Columbia (1973).
457. VELICHENKO, V. V., Sufficient conditions for absolute minimum of the maximal functional in the multi-criteria problem of optimal control, *Optimization Techniques: IFIP Technical Conference*, Edited by G. Marchuk, pp. 220-225, Springer-Verlag, New York (1975).
458. VEMURI, V., Multiple objective optimization in water resource systems, *Water Resour. Res.* **10**, 44-48 (1974).
459. VERNON, M. D., *Human Motivation*, Cambridge U. P., Cambridge, England (1969).
460. VILLARREAL, B., and KARWAN, M. H., Multicriteria dynamic programming with an application to the integer case, *J. Optim. Theory Appl.* **38**, 43-69 (1982).
461. VINCENT, T. L., and LEITMANN, G., Control-space properties of cooperative games, *J. Optim. Theory Appl.* **6**, 91-113 (1970).
462. VINCKE, P., A new approach to multiple criteria decision making, *Multiple Criteria Decision Making*, Edited by H. Thiriez and S. Zionts, pp. 341-350, Springer-Verlag, New York (1976).
463. VINOGRADSKAYA, T. M., and GAFT, M. G., An exact upper bound for the number of nonsubordinate solutions in multicriterion problems, *Autom. Remote Control* **35**, 1474-1481 (1974).
464. VISWANATHAN, B., AGGARWAL, V. V., and NAIR, K. P. K., Multiple criteria Markov decision processes, in *Multiple Criteria Decision Making*, (M. K. Starr and M. Zeleny eds.), pp. 263-272, North-Holland, Amsterdam (1977).
465. VON NEUMANN, J., and MORGENSTERN, O., *Theory of Games and Economic Behavior*, Princeton University Press, Princeton, New Jersey (1944).
466. VON WINTERFELDT, D., and FISCHER, G. W., Multiattribute utility theory: Models and assessment procedures, *Utility, Probability, and Human Decision Making*, Edited by D. Wendt and C. Vlek, pp. 47-85, D. Reidel, Boston (1975).
467. WALLENIUS, J., Comparative evaluation of some interactive approaches to multicriterion optimization, *Manage. Sci.* **21**, 1387-1396 (1975).
468. WALLENIUS, J., Interactive multiple criteria decision methods: An investigation and approach, The Helsinki School of Economics, Helsinki, Finland, 1975.
469. WALLENIUS, J., and ZIONTS, S., Some tests of an interactive programming method for multicriterion optimization and attempt at implementation, *Multiple Criteria Decision Making*, Edited by H. Thiriez and S. Zionts, Springer-Verlag, New York (1976).
470. WALLENIUS, J., and ZIONTS, S., A research project on multicriterion decision making, *Conflicting Objectives in Decisions*, Edited by D. E. Bell, R. L. Keeney, and H. Raiffa, pp. 76-96, Wiley, New York (1977).
471. WALTERS, A., MANGOLD, J., and HARAN, E., A comprehensive planning model for long-range academic strategies, *Manage. Sci.* **22**, 727-738 (1976).
472. WENDELL, R. E., Multiple objective mathematical programming with respect to multiple decision-makers, *Oper. Res.* **28**, 1100-1111 (1980).
473. WENDT, D., and VLEK, C., (Editors), *Utility, Probability, and Human Decision Making*, D. Reidel, Boston (1975).

474. WEHRUNG, D. A., Multidimensional line search using a binary preference relation, *Oper. Res.* **27**, 356-363 (1979).
475. WHITE, D. J., Duality, indifference and sensitivity analysis in multiple objective linear programming, *Oper. Res. Q.* **26**, 660-661 (1974).
476. WHITE, D. J., Duality and vector optima for polyhedral sets, *J. Oper. Res. Soc.* **30**, 81-83 (1979).
477. WHITE, D. J., Generalized efficient solutions for sums of sets, *Oper. Res.* **28**, 844-846 (1980).
478. WHITE, D. J., Multi-objective interactive programming, *J. Oper. Res. Soc.* **31**, 517-523 (1980).
479. WHITE, D. J., Optimality and efficiency I, *Eur. J. Oper. Res.* **4**, 346-355 (1980).
480. WHITE, D. J., Optimality and efficiency II, *Eur. J. Oper. Res.* **4**, 426-427 (1980).
481. WHITE, D. J., *Optimality and Efficiency*, Wiley, New York (1982).
482. WHITE, D. J., Multiple Objective Programming and Penalty Functions, *J. Optim. Theory and Appl.* **43**, 583-599 (1984).
483. WIEDEMANN, P., Planning with multiple objectives, *Omega* **6**, 427-432 (1978).
484. WILCOX, J. W., *A Method for Measuring Decision Assumptions*, MIT, Cambridge, Massachusetts (1972).
485. WILHELM, J., *Objectives and Multi-Objective Decision Making Under Uncertainty*, Springer-Verlag, New York (1975).
486. WILHELM, J., Generalized solution principles and out-ranking relations in multiple-criteria decision-making, *Eur. J. Oper. Res.* **1**, 376-385 (1977).
487. WILHELM, J., and FANDEL, G., Two algorithms for solving vector-optimization problems, *Autom. Remote Control* **37**, 1721-1727 (1976).
488. WOLFE, P., *Convergence Theory in Nonlinear Programming, Integer and Nonlinear Programming*, Edited by J. Abadie, North-Holland, Amsterdam (1970).
489. WRATHER, C., and YU, P. L., Probability dominance in random outcomes, *J. Optim. Theory Appl.* **36**, 315-334 (1982).
490. YAGER, R. R., Multiple objective decision making using fuzzy sets, *Int. J. Man-Machine Stud.* **9**, 375-382 (1977).
491. YU, P. L., The set of all nondominated solutions in decision problems with multiobjectives, University of Rochester, Systems Analysis Program, Working Paper Series, No. F-71-32, Rochester, New York, 1971.
492. YU, P. L., Nondominated investment policies in stock market, Systems Analysis Program, The University of Rochester, The Graduate School of Management, Rochester, New York, 1972.
493. YU, P. L., A class of solutions for group decision problems, *Manage. Sci.* **19**, 936-946 (1973).
494. YU, P. L., Introduction to domination structures in multicriteria decision problems, in *Multicriteria Decision Making*, J. L. Cochrane and M. Zeleny (eds.), University of South Carolina Press, Columbia (1973) pp. 249-261.
495. YU, P. L., Cone convexity, cone extreme points and nondominated solutions in decision problems with multiobjectives, *J. Optim. Theory Appl.* **14**, 319-377 (1974).
496. YU, P. L., Domination structures and nondominated solutions, *Multicriteria Decision Making*, Edited by G. Leitmann and A. Marzollo, pp. 227-280, Springer-Verlag, New York (1975).
497. YU, P. L., Decision dynamics with an application to persuasion and negotiation, *TIMS Studies in the Management Sciences*, Vol. 6, (M. K. Starr and M. Zeleny eds.), pp. 159-177, North-Holland, Amsterdam (1977).
498. YU, P. L., Toward second order game problems: Decision dynamics in gaming phenomena, *Multiple Criteria Problem Solving*: Proceedings, Edited by S. Zionts, pp. 509-528, Springer-Verlag, New York (1978).
499. YU, P. L., Second-order game problem: Decision dynamics in gaming phenomena, *J. Optim. Theory Appl.* **27**, 147-166 (1979).
500. YU, P. L., Behavior bases and habitual domains of human decision/behavior-concepts and applications, in *Multiple Criteria Decision Making Theory and Application*, G. Fandel and T. Gal (eds.), Springer-Verlag, New York (1980). pp. 511-539.

501. YU, P. L., Behavior bases and habitual domains of human decisions/Behavior: An integration of psychology, optimization theory, and common wisdom, *Int. J. Syst. Measurement Decisions* **1**, 39-62 (1981).

502. YU, P. L., Dissolution of fuzziness for better decisions—Perspective and techniques, *TIMS Studies in Management Sciences, Vol. 20*, M. J. Zimmerman, L. A. Zadeh and B. R. Gains (eds.), pp. 171-207, North-Holland, New York (1984).

503. YU, P. L., and LEITMANN, G., Nondominated decisions and cone convexity in dynamic multicriteria decision problems, *J. Optim. Theory Appl.* **14**, 573-584 (1974).

504. YU, P. L., and LEITMANN, G., Compromise solutions, domination structures, and Salukvadze's solution, *J. Optim. Theory Appl.* **13**, 362-378 (1974).

505. YU, P. L. and LEITMANN, G., Confidence structures in decision making, *J. Optim. Theory Appl.* **22**, 265-285 (1977).

506. YU, P. L., and SEIFORD, L., Multistage decision problems with multicriteria, *Multiple Criteria Analysis: Operational Methods*, Edited by P. Nijkamp and J. Spronk, Gower, London (1981).

507. YU, P. L., and ZELENY, M., On some linear multi-parametric programs, The University of Rochester, Center for Systems Science, CSS 73-05, Rochester, New York, 1973.

508. YU, P. L., and ZELENY, M., The set of all nondominated solutions in the linear case and a multicriteria simplex method, *J. Math. Anal. Appl.* **49**, 430-468 (1974).

509. YU, P. L., and ZELENY, M., Linear multiparametric programming by multicriteria simplex method, *Manage. Sci.* **23**, 159-170 (1976).

510. ZADEH, L. A., Optimality and non-scalar-valued performance criteria, *IEEE Trans. Autom. Control* **AC-8**, 59-60 (1963).

511. ZADEH, L. A., Fuzzy Sets, *Inform. Control* **8**, 338-353 (1965).

512. ZANGWILL, W. I., An algorithm for the Chebyshev problem—With an application to concave programming, *Manage. Sci.* **14**, 58-78 (1967).

513. ZELENY, M., A concept of compromise solutions and the method of the displaced ideal, *Comput. Oper. Res.* **1**, 479-496 (1974).

514. ZELENY, M., *Linear Multiobjective Programming*, Springer-Verlag, New York (1974).

515. ZELENY, M., The theory of the displaced ideal, in *Multiple Criteria Decision Making: Kyoto 1975*, M. Zeleny (ed.), Springer-Verlag, New York (1975). pp. 151-205.

516. ZELENY, M., Multiobjective Design of High-Productivity Systems, in *Proceedings of the Joint Automatic Control Conference*, ASME, New York, New York (1976).

517. ZELENY, M. (Editor), *Multiple Criteria Decision Making: Kyoto 1975*, Springer-Verlag, New York, New York (1976).

518. ZELENY, M., Satisficing, optimization, and risk in portfolio selection, *Readings in Strategies for Corporate Investment*, Edited by F. Derkinderen and R. Crum, Pitman, Boston (1981).

519. ZELENY, M., *Multiple Criteria Decision Making*, McGraw-Hill, New York (1982).

520. ZIEMBA, W. T., and VICKSON, R. G., (Editors), *Stochastic Optimization Models in Finance*, Academic, New York (1975).

521. ZIMBARDO, P. G. and RUCH, F. L., *Psychology and Life*, Scott, Foresman and Company, Glenview, Illinois (1975).

522. ZIMMERMAN, H. J., Fuzzy programming and linear programming with several objective functions, *Fuzzy Sets and Systems* **1**, 45-56 (1978).

523. ZIONTS, S. (Editor), *Multiple Criteria Problem Solving: Proceedings*, Buffalo, New York, 1977, Springer-Verlag, New York (1978).

524. ZIONTS, S., A multiple criteria method for choosing among discrete alternatives, *Eur. J. Oper. Res.* **7**, 143-147 (1981).

525. ZIONTS, S., and WALLENIUS J., An interactive programming method for solving the multiple criteria problem, *Manage. Sci.* **22**, 652-663 (1976).

526. ZIONTS, S., and WALLENIUS, J., Identifying efficient vectors: Some theory and computational results, *Oper. Res.* **28**, 785-793 (1980).

Index